Bloomsbury

POCKET THESAURUS

Titles available from Bloomsbury Publishing Plc in the *Bloomsbury Keys* series

Adjectives ISBN: 0 7475 1882 3
Dictionary ISBN: 0 7475 2235 9
Differences ISBN: 0 7475 1885 8
Good English ISBN: 0 7475 1777 0
Grammar ISBN: 0 7475 1775 4
Medicines ISBN: 0 7475 1883 1
Phrases ISBN: 0 7475 2058 5
Quotations ISBN: 0 7475 1884 X
Spelling ISBN: 0 7475 1776 2
Thesaurus ISBN: 0 7475 1774 6
Word Power ISBN: 0 7475 2213 8

Bloomsbury

POCKET THESAURUS

BLOOMSBURY

This edition published in 1995 by Bloomsbury Publishing Plc, 2 Soho Square, London, W1V 6HB.

This book has been derived from the *Bloomsbury Thesaurus* (ISBN 0 7475 1226 4)

A copy of the CIP entry for this book is available from the British Library

ISBN 0 7475 2234 0

10 9 8 7 6 5 4 3 2 1

Compiled and prepared for typesetting by
Market House Books Ltd, Aylesbury
Designed by Geoff Green
Typeset by Aitch Em, Aylesbury
Printed by Clays Ltd, St Ives plc

Introduction

The word 'thesaurus' comes from the Greek word for treasure; the original meaning was a place where treasure is stored. As with many words, the sense later changed and a thesaurus became a book that served as a source or repository of information – a 'treasury of information'. Thesauruses are often contrasted with dictionaries. The user of a dictionary is looking for information about a particular word, usually its meaning – the idea that the word stands for. In a thesaurus, on the other hand, the writer starts with an idea and is looking for a word to express it, or the best word to use in a particular context. The words found in a thesaurus are not necessarily synonyms of the original word. A thesaurus is also useful for providing words that are connected with other words – for instance, types of computer or examples of administrative areas or connotations or allusions.

In this book we have arranged words under main thematic categories, which are listed in alphabetical order. A selection of quotations has been included and an index is provided to assist in finding the correct category. We hope that the reader will find the book useful and informative.

How to Use this Book

The Thesaurus

The main category themes in the book are numbered and arranged in alphabetical order. Each main category is divided into parts of speech (nouns, verbs, and adjectives). The words under a category are further subdivided into numbered subsections. For example, the main category **Accord** is split into **accord, alliance, arrangement, harmony, conformity**, etc.

The Index

This contains words that occur under main categories. An index entry in bold with a capital letter and a single number indicates a main category in the text, for example,

Accord 1

shows that there is a main category for 'Accord'.

Other words are indexed to their category in the main text and their subsection number. For example,

arrangement Accord 4.3

indicates that the word 'arrangement' appears under the main category **4 Accord** and is in subsection 3.

THESAURUS

1 Absence

•*Absence makes the heart grow fonder, / Isle of Beauty, Fare thee well!* Thomas Haynes Bayly.

NOUNS 1 absence, nonpresence, nonentity, nonbeing, unbeing, inexistence, nonexistence, unreality, nonoccurrence, nullity **2 disappearance**, dematerialization, vanishment, departure, loss, lack, want, deficiency, shortage, scarcity, dearth, insufficiency, paucity **3 emptiness**, voidness, vacancy, vacuity, bareness, blankness, hollowness, barrenness, nothingness, void, gap, vacuum **4 absenteeism**, absentation, nonappearance, nonattendance, truantism, truancy, desertion, defection **5 absentee**, nonperson, missing person, defector, deserter

ADJECTIVES 6 absent, not present, nonattendant, unavailable, nonexistent, inexistent, unreal, nonoccurrent, null **7 away**, out, gone, departed, dematerialized, missing, lost, disappeared, vanished, absconded, flown **8 truant**, absentee, defected **9 missing**, lacking, wanting, wanted, deficient, minus, short, taken away, deleted, subtracted, omitted, mislaid, excluded, left out **10 vacant**, vacuous, void, devoid, empty **11 unoccupied**, empty, vacant, available, unfilled, unlived-in

VERBS 12 be absent, keep away, stay away **13 absent oneself**, leave, take leave, withdraw, retire, retreat, depart, exit, bow out, vacate

2 Accompaniment

NOUNS 1 accompaniment, concomitance, coexistence, symbiosis, cohabitation, combination, conjunction, association, union, coagency **2 synchronism**, simultaneity, contemporaneity, coincidence **3 companionship**, company, togetherness, fellowship, friendship, partnership, consortship, cohabitation, marriage, society **4 accompanier**, accompanist **5 follower**, shadow, tail, satellite, dependant, hanger-on, parasite, sycophant **6 companion**, colleague, partner, associate, co-worker, fellow, classmate, flatmate, comrade, friend, best friend, travelling companion **7 partner**, constant companion, escort, date, girlfriend, boyfriend, lover, consort, cohabitant, cohabitee, live-in lover, common-law spouse, spouse, husband

ADJECTIVES 8 accompanying, concomitant, attending, attendant, belonging, complementary, accessory, collateral, incidental, background **9 concurrent**, concurring, coincident, coinciding, simultaneous, contemporary, contemporaneous, parallel, correlative, coexistent, coexisting, symbiotic **10 associated**, partnered, coupled, paired, wedded, married, combined, joined, inseparable **11 accompanied**, attended, escorted, chaperoned

VERBS 12 accompany, go together, go with, belong with, complement, come with, concur, coincide **13 keep company with**, travel with, run with, work with, partner, escort, consort with, associate with, frequent, befriend, socialize, club together, team up, gang up, pair up, couple, live together, live with **14 escort**, squire, chaperone, protect, guard, safeguard, guide **15 attend**, wait on, follow, tag along, shadow

3 Accord

NOUNS 1 accord, accordance, unanimity, unity, agreement, consensus, concurrence, concord, concordance, one voice, vox populi, like-mindedness, one mind, mutual understanding, sympathy, acceptance, acquiescence, accedence, accommodation, concession, compromise, compliance **2 alliance**, league, union, federation, affiliation, guild, coalition, collusion, conspiracy, collaboration, synergy, partnership **3 arrangement**, settlement, compact, pact, treaty, covenant, contract, convention, bargain, deal, bond, transaction, pledge **4 harmony**, harmonization, coordination, synchronization, synchronism, coincidence, concomitance, conjunction, symmetry, balance, equilibrium, regularity, consonance, resonance **5 conformity**, conformance, uniformity, constancy, continuity, consistency, coherence, homogeneity, homology, sameness, oneness, synonymity, equivalence, interchangeability, congruence, correlation, likeness **6 consent**, assent, affirmation, approval, agreement, authorization, ratification, endorsement

ADJECTIVES 7 in accord, accordant, unanimous, united, agreeing, agreed, in rapport, consenting, consentient, in concert, concurrent, concordant, at one, sympathetic, like-minded, understanding, empathizing, amicable, congenial, compatible, conciliatory, complying, compliant, conceding, compromising, accepting, accommodating **8 allied**, corporate, affiliated, associated, bonded, joint, conjoint, combined, combining, connected, linked, merged, contributing, coactive, synergic, colluding, conspiring, conspiratorial, collaborating, collaborative, fraternal **9 arranged**, settled, negotiated, negotiating, covenanted, contractual, bargaining, pledged **10 harmonious**, coordinated, synchronized, synchronous, coincident, coinciding, conjoint, concomitant, symmetrical, balanced, in equilibrium, regulated, attuned, symphonious, symphonic, unisonous, blended, merged, modulated, in concert, choral, melodic, harmonic, echoing, resounding, resonant **11 conforming**, conformable, uniform, homogenous, homologous, identical, same, consistent, even, equivalent, interchangeable, synonymous, congruent, correlated, resembling, like, similar, analogous, matching, paired, twinned **12 fitting**, befitting, belonging, pertaining, pertinent, apposite, expedient **13 consenting**, consentient, assentient, affirming, confirming, approving, recognized, agreed, ratified, authorized, accredited, backed **14 agreeable**, acceptable

VERBS 15 be in accord, accord, concord, concur, agree, empathize, identify with, comply, accede, concede **16 form an alliance**, ally, affiliate, unite, collude, conspire, collaborate, pull together, associate with, side with, partner, fraternize, combine with **17 arrange**, settle, make terms, bargain, deal, negotiate, compromise, contract, transact, covenant, pledge **18 harmonize**, coordinate, synchronize, coincide, conjoin, symmetrize, balance, regulate, equilibrate, blend, merge, symphonize, modulate, counterpoise, attune, adjust, resolve, rhyme, resonate, chime **19 conform**, be uniform, match, mirror, tally, square with, be like, resemble, look like, sound like, reflect, interrelate, correlate, correspond, complement, be consistent, hold together, be conventional, follow, line up **20 make uniform**, standardize, order, equalize, level, homogenize, align, liken **21 fit**, serve, suit, belong, pertain **22 consent**, assent, affirm, agree, approve, authorize, ratify, confirm, certify, vouchsafe, endorse, accredit, validate, authenticate, recognize, attest, underwrite, back

4 Accounts

NOUNS 1 accounts, accountancy, accounting, cost accounting, bookkeeping, commercial arithmetic, item, entry, double entry, single entry, credit, debit, account, balance sheet, current account, cash account, deposit account, savings account **2 budgeting**, budget, cash budget **3 accounting**, reckoning, calculation, computation, enumeration, score, tally **4 statement**, bank statement, invoice **5 account book**, bankbook, passbook, cheque book, cash book, petty-cash book, daybook, journal, ledger, register, books **6 accountant**, cost accountant, book-keeper, store-keeper, cashier, paymaster, bursar, purser, treasurer, auditor

VERBS 7 account, keep accounts, balance accounts, book, enter, carry over, carry forward, debit, credit, record, register, cost, value, estimate, budget, defraud **8 audit**, inspect accounts, take stock, inventory, catalogue **9 settle accounts**, square accounts, pay up, finalize accounts, invoice

ADJECTIVES 10 accounting, bookkeeping, reckoning, computing, calculating, accountable, fiscal, financial, economic, commercial, statistical, actuarial, bursarial, budgetary, inventorial **11 accounted**, audited, balanced, tallied, registered, recorded, credited, debited, deposited, saved, received, spent, invoiced, billed, costed

5 Accuracy

NOUNS 1 accuracy, precision, exactness, meticulousness, fastidiousness, scrupulousness, refinement, strictness, rigidity, pedantry, rigorousness, acuity, perfect pitch **2 correctness**, truth, literalness, the letter, faithfulness **3 accurate thing**, precise measurement, precision instrument, fine adjustment, deadcentre, micrometer, metronome, atomic clock, fine detail, quibble, fine line

ADJECTIVES 4 accurate, precise, exact, perfect, pinpoint, detailed, meticulous, scrupulous, rigorous, pedantic **5 correct**, factual, truthful, literal, true-to-the-letter, word-perfect, true-to-life, unerring, verbatim, faithful

VERBS 6 be accurate, particularize

6 Accusation

NOUNS 1 accusation, complaint, accusing, charge, countercharge, reproach, denunciation, allegation, imputation, plaint, suit, lawsuit, action, litigation, citation, summons, arrest, prosecution, impeachment, indictment, incrimination, count, case **2 false accusation**, false charge, false evidence, fake confession, perjury, libel, slander, calumny, scandal, defamation, misrepresentation **3 accuser**, denouncer, petitioner, plaintiff, complainant, claimant, litigant, appellant, hostile witness, indicter, prosecutor, impeacher, false witness, perjurer, libeller **4 accused person**, the accused, defendant, respondent, correspondent, culprit, suspect

VERBS 5 accuse, complain, charge, countercharge, blame, insinuate, impute, reproach, denounce, allegate, sue, litigate, summon, cite, prosecute, impeach, indict, incriminate, arrest, arraign, book, try **6 accuse falsely**, commit perjury, libel, slander, defame

ADJECTIVES 7 accusatory, accusing, accused, imputative, charged, countercharged, blamed, denounced, alleged, under suspicion, cited, summoned, arrested, booked, prosecuted, impeached, indicted **8 perjurious**, perjured, libellous, slanderous, defamatory

7 Action

• *Suit the action to the word, the word to the action; with this special observance, that you o'erstep not the modesty of nature.* William Shakespeare.

NOUNS 1 action, doing, happening, performance, move, enactment, policy, accomplishment, achievement, process, procedure, practice, behaviour, movement, motion, operation, agency, force, pressure, effect, power, work, labour, exertion, endeavour, battle, war, activity, drama, occupation, implementation, administration, direction **2 deed**, act, action, exploit, feat, achievement, accomplishment, gesture, good deed, bad deed, wrongdoing, criminal act, crime, foul play, posture, step, move, tactics, stroke, blow, coup, overthrow, job, task, work, undertaking, transaction, deal, handicraft, skill, masterpiece **3 doer**, activist, lobbyist, campaigner, achiever, hero, heroine, expert, performer, artist, offender, criminal, motivator, agent, entrepreneur, manager, director, worker, operative

VERBS 4 act, do, happen, perform, carry out, execute, take action, take steps, enact, legislate, accomplish, achieve, carry through, take effect, operate, function, act upon, manipulate, motivate, manoeuvre, proceed, get going, move, do something, try, attempt, take on, undertake, perpetrate, implement, make history, become famous, practise, prosecute, pursue, ply, occupy oneself, transact, deal, officiate, direct, administrate, manage, control, work, labour, sweat, campaign, use, exploit, intervene, work for, help, aid, participate, interfere, meddle, indulge in, fool around, show off

ADJECTIVES 5 acting, doing, happening, performing, working, in action, in operation, in harness, operative, industrious, busy, active, creative, artistic, dramatic, militant, brave **6 effective**, forceful, powerful, productive, useful, functional, operational, procedural, professional

8 Activity

NOUNS 1 activity, action, activeness, movement, motion, stir, agitation, excitation, stimulation, ado, drama, commotion, disturbance, row, quarrel, fray, tumult, frenzy, maelstrom **2 social activity**, group activity, interaction, participation, sociability, mixing, active interest, hobby, pastime, occupation **3 nimbleness**, briskness, alacrity, readiness, quickness, speed, velocity, haste, dispatch, expedition, scramble, race, rat race, dash, burst, spurt, fit, spasm, hurry, flurry, hustle, bustle, fuss, bother **4 energy**, ceaseless energy, dynamism, vigour, vitality, vivacity, liveliness, animation, high spirits, pep, eagerness, enthusiasm, ardour, fervour, strong feeling, activation, motive, cause, enterprise, initiative, drive, push **5 activism**, political activism, militancy, mass movement, popular movement, uprising **6 business**, industry, busyness, hive, beehive, marketplace, workshop, press, crush, seething mob **7 restlessness**, aimlessness, desultoriness, inattention, pottering, fiddling, fidgetiness, unrest, unease, unquietness, jumpiness, nervousness, agitation, excitability, fever, fret, sleeplessness **8 assiduity**, application, concentration, intentness, attention, diligence, industriousness, hard work, drudgery, labour, determination, resolution, earnestness, tirelessness, indefatigability, perseverance, perfectionism, devotedness **9 overactivity**, hyperactivity, overextension, overambition, excess, Parkinson's law, futile activity, wasted effort, overexertion, red tape, officiousness, meddlesomeness, interference, meddling, interfering, tampering, intrigue **10 busy person**, active person, socialite, jet-setter, bustler, hustler, wheeler dealer, fidget, activist, militant, doer, participator, careerist, yuppie, enthusiast, zealot, fanatic, slogger, tireless worker, workaholic, worker, handyman **11 meddler**, busybody, interferer, dabbler, troublemaker, inquisitive person, intriguer

VERBS 12 be active, act, do, wake up, rise, move, stir, agitate, run riot, rampage, roar, rage, bluster, blow, explode, flow, surge, rush, dash, race, fly, run, hasten, hurry, scurry, scramble, hustle, bustle, fuss, bother, fret **13 be busy**, busy oneself, keep busy, thrive, hum, progress, keep moving **14 push**, shove, thrust, drive, impel, assert oneself, profit by, protest, demonstrate, defy, react, show willingness **15 try**, attempt, try hard, take pains, exert oneself, concentrate, buckle down, persist, persevere, beaver away, work, slave **16 be sociable**, interact, mingle, circulate, mix, join in **17 meddle**, intermeddle, intervene, interfere, be officious, pry, spy, butt in, interrupt, pester, dun, harass, boss, persecute, oppress

ADJECTIVES 18 active, interactive, sociable, activated, moving, going, running, working, operative, in action, incessant, unceasing, expeditious, able, strong, quick, fast, speedy, brisk, spry, nimble, agile, smart, keen, vigorous, strenuous, energetic, forceful, dynamic, thrusting, pushing, enterprising, lively, sprightly, frisky, dashing, spirited, alive, animated, vivacious **19 busy**, active, bustling, hustling, humming, hectic, lively, eventful, pottering, astir, employed, in harness, engaged, occupied, slogging **20 industrious**, sedulous, diligent, assiduous, studious, persevering, hardworking, workaholic, plodding, slogging, laborious, unflagging, tireless, indefatigable, energetic, efficient, workmanlike, businesslike **21 meddling**, officious, interfering, meddlesome, intrusive, nosy, prying, irritating, troublesome, dabbling

9 Addition

NOUNS 1 addition, adding, joining, annexation, extra load, encumbrance, burden, imposition, interposition, insertion, inclusion, attachment, supplementation, augmentation, accession, accrual, increase, increment, supplement, complement, enlargement, extension, addendum, accessory, appendage, reinforcement **2 mathematical addition**, arithmetic, adding-up, summation, computation, calculation, totalling, total, toll **3 additional item**, addition, adjunct, augmentation **4 extra**, byproduct, interest, gain, benefit, bonus, plus, tip, gratuity, free gift, windfall, find, serendipity, supernumerary, surplus, extras, sundries, spares, provisions, auxiliaries, reinforcements

VERBS 5 add, add up, count, count up, calculate, total, total up, sum, sum up, compute, carry, carry over, add to, append, annex, attach, pin to, staple to, clip to, glue onto, tag, tack on, join, tie to, unite to, conjoin, glue together, preface, prefix, affix, suffix, infix, interpolate, insert, stick in, introduce, interject, interpose, contribute to, swell, augment, expand, extend, supplement, load, saddle with, burden with, heap on, pile on, superimpose, overlay, paint over, coat, plaster, decorate, ornament, embellish, garnish, season, mix with, encompass, absorb, include, add value, accrue **6 support**, combine with, mix with

ADJECTIVES 7 additional, added, included, interpolated, annexed, loaded, reinforced, additive, adjunctive, adjunct, attached, adjoined, inserted, prefixed, adventitious, supplementary, complementary, subsidiary, incremental, auxiliary, collateral, contributory, another, further **8 extra**, new, fresh, surplus, spare, superfluous, decorative

10 Address

NOUNS 1 address, allocution, apostrophe, lecture, discourse, reading, talk, presentation, speech, oration, prepared speech, disquisition, declamation, tirade, invective, harangue, screed, sermon **2 salutation**, greeting, salaam, hail, valediction, pep talk, exhortation, peroration, appeal, invocation, advances, suit **3 place of residence**, residence, domicile, habitation, abode, home, house, habitat, location, whereabouts, house number, road name, street name, district, postcode **4 public speaker**, speechmaker, spokesperson, lecturer, reader, orator, declaimer, ranter, tub-thumper, rhetorician, rabble-rouser, demagogue, pulpiteer, preacher, sermonizer

VERBS 5 address, lecture, apostrophize, discourse, speechify, hold forth, declaim, orate, harangue, perorate, pontificate, rant, tub-thump, rabble-rouse, sermonize **6**

appeal to, invoke, entreat **7 approach**, accost, buttonhole, call to, salute, hail **8 send**, direct, address, consign, transmit, dispatch, post, mail, send on, forward, redirect **9 title**, entitle, style, term, call sir **10 address oneself to**, take up
ADJECTIVES **11 oratorical**, rhetorical, declamatory, demagogic **12 vocative**, invocatory
INTERJECTIONS **13 hail!**, greetings!

11 Adhesion

NOUNS **1 adhesion**, adhesiveness, holding together, cohesion, attachment, bonding, connection, linkage, coherence, stickiness, cementation, agglutination, soldering, welding, agglomeration, conglomeration, consolidation, congealment, inseparability **2 tenacity**, tenaciousness, pertinacious, perseverance, persistence, determination, endurance, stubbornness, obstinacy, headstrongness, bullheadedness, holding on, attachment, adherence, loyalty **3 adhesive**, glue, superglue, gum, paste, size, cement, putty, mortar, plaster, grout, sealing wax, solder, flypaper, sticky tape, Blu-tack, sticking plaster **4 adherent**, sticky label, stamp, barnacle, limpet, leech, parasite, bur, bramble, clinging vine, gum, toffee **5 follower**, disciple, apostle, adherent, supporter, suitor, fan
VERBS **6 adhere**, cohere, hang together, hold together, hold fast, bunch together, close ranks, stick, stick together, grip, clasp, grasp, hug, embrace, cling to, twine around, close with, clinch, stick onto, cleave to, coagulate, agglomerate **7 cause to adhere**, stick, stick to, affix to, stick together, hold together, gum, glue, paste, cement, weld, solder, unite **8 be tenacious**, persevere, adhere, hold on, hang on
ADJECTIVES **9 adhesive**, adherent, cohesive, connective, sticky, gummy, tacky, gluey, viscous, colloidal, congealed, coagulated, concrete, inextricable, linked, bonded, cemented, close, side-by-side, shoulder-to-shoulder, cheek-by-jowl, close-fitting, close-packed, tight, clinging, figure-hugging, moulding **10 tenacious**, pertinacious, persevering, persistent, determined, enduring, stubborn, obstinate, bull-headed, attached

12 Administrative Area

NOUNS **1 administrative area**, state, enclave, county, metropolitan county, province, region, division, district, urban district, rural district, borough, constituency, area, township, community **2 former British divisions**, hundred, riding, tithing, wapentake, soke **3 other divisions**, department, eparchy **4 community**, municipality, city, metropolis, borough, town, township, village, hamlet, quarter **5 administrative headquarters**, headquarters, administrative centre, station, capital, national capital, state capital, provincial capital
ADJECTIVES **6 administrative**, divisional, governmental, departmental, congressional, constituent, metropolitan, municipal, provincial, rural
VERBS **7 administer**, govern, have jurisdiction

13 Admittance

NOUNS **1 admittance**, admission, taking in, reception, acceptance, importation, insertion, interjection, invitation **2 receptivity**, receptiveness, openness, hospitality, welcome, refuge, sanctuary, asylum, shelter, open door, access **3 introduction**, initiation, baptism, enrolment, investiture, ordination, induction, registration, enlistment, installation, inauguration, admissibility **4 intake**, engulfment, ingestion, consumption, eating, drinking, engorgement, swallow, gulp, sucking, breathing in, inspiration, inhalation **5 absorption**, adsorption, sorption, resorption, engrossment, assimilation, incorporation, absorbency, resorbence, blotting **6 sponge**, blotter, blotting paper, chromatography paper

VERBS 7 admit, receive, take in, include, let in, allow in, allow access, import **8 show in**, usher in **9 welcome**, embrace, accept, invite, call in, grant asylum, naturalize, shelter, accommodate, protect **10 introduce**, bring in, initiate, baptize, enlist, take on, install, inaugurate, enrol, invest **11 ingest**, eat, drink, engulf, engorge, ingurgitate, swallow **12 draw in**, suck, suckle, aspirate, inhale, inspire, smell **13 absorb**, adsorb, incorporate, assimilate, take up, blot

ADJECTIVES 14 admissive, admissible, acceptable, suitable, receivable **15 receptive**, recipient, open, accessible, welcoming, hospitable **16 introductory**, introductive, initiatory **17 absorbent**, absorptive, adsorbent, sorbent, assimilative, ingestive, imbibitory

14 Adversity

NOUNS 1 adversity, difficulty, opposition, struggle, hardship, decline, troubles, predicament, misadventure, mishap, accident, misfortune, affliction, misery, pressure, suffering, distress, worry, gathering clouds, downfall, defeat, unrequited love, setback, illness, pain, bitter pill, burden, darkness, blight, scourge, disaster, desolation, destitution, calamity, catastrophe **2 economic adversity**, financial setback, negative equity, cash-flow problems, need, poverty, bankruptcy, slump, recession **3 bad fortune**, misfortune, bad luck, malign influence, evil star **4 time of adversity**, bad times, hard times, lean period, rough patch, bad patch

ADJECTIVES 5 adverse, contrary, conflicting, opposing, hostile, antagonistic, troublesome, difficult, hard, bleak, dreadful, dire, ominous, bad, sinister, disastrous, destructive, ruinous, doomed, miserable, in trouble **6 unprosperous**, badly off, poor, poverty-stricken, penniless, bankrupt, homeless **7 unlucky**, luckless, hapless, accident-prone, unfortunate, ill-fated

VERBS 8 be in trouble, have trouble, meet adversity, have difficulties, fail, lose, suffer misfortune, sink, founder, decline, go downhill, slip, grieve, suffer humiliation, suffer **9 need money**, want, be overdrawn, go bankrupt **10 cause adversity**, cause grief, cause trouble, create problems, defeat, injure, oppress, humiliate, overburden

15 Advice

• *Advice is seldom welcome; and those who want it the most always like it the least.* Earl of Chesterfield.

NOUNS 1 advice, counsel, tip, hint, wisdom, counselling, guidance, moralizing, prescription, caution, warning, recommendation, proposition, submission, opinion, view, criticism, constructive criticism, information, communication, intelligence, news, encouragement **2 consultation**, taking counsel, seeking advice, deliberation, discussion, heads together, tête-à-tête, parley, negotiations, conference **3 precept**, maxim, principle, moral, rule, guideline, commandment, law, custom, convention, practice, norm, advice, admonition, warning, direction, instruction, example, text, injunction, charge, command, mandate, order, writ, warrant, judgment, prescription, remedy, regulation, form, formula, statute, act, code, legislation, tenet

VERBS 4 advise, give advice, offer advice, counsel, guide, criticise, moralize, enjoin, prescribe, advocate, recommend, suggest, propose, move, put to, submit, press, urge, encourage, exhort, incite, dissuade, admonish, warn, caution, prompt, hint, teach, brief, instruct, tell **5 consult**, seek advice, seek opinion, refer to, call in, call on, confide in, take advice, follow advice, listen to, learn from, deliberate, discuss

ADJECTIVES 6 advising, advisory, counselling, consultative, deliberative, monitory, therapeutic, instructive, informative, moral, persuasive, encouraging, dissuasive, admonitory **7 advisable**, recommendable, prudent, wise, judicious, politic, sensible

16 Affectation

NOUNS 1 affectedness, pretentiousness, artifice, histrionics, theatricality, showmanship, euphemism, sanctimoniousness, irony, speciosity, deceptiveness, exhibition, pretension, falsity, posture **2 pretender**, actor, bluffer, deceiver, poseur, charlatan, attitudinizer

ADJECTIVES 3 affected, precious, pretentious, mannered, self-conscious, conceited, artificial, unnatural, stilted, sanctimonious, euphemistic, showy, meretricious, theatrical, histrionic, puffed up, boastful

VERBS 4 be affected, affect, attitudinize, pose, pretend, assume, posture, bluff, show off

17 Affirmation

NOUNS 1 affirmation, assertion, attestation, declaration, averment, asseveration, allegation, swearing, vouching **2 statement**, pronouncement, profession, utterance, word, say, dictum, proposition, maxim, positive declaration, proclamation, enunciation, announcement, stand, stance, manifesto, creed, submission, prepared text, thesis, supposition **3 vow**, oath, word, pledge, promise, guarantee, solemn word, sworn statement, deposition, affidavit, sworn testimony, assurance, commitment, swearing in, charging, Bible oath **4 confirmation**, corroboration, substantiation, ratification, authentication, proof, establishment, assurance, endorsement, support, written statement, backing, attestation, validation, verification, certification **5 admission**, avowal, disclosure, deposition **6 assertiveness**, self-assertion, assurance, forcefulness, decisiveness, incisiveness, outspokenness, bluntness, plainness, thrust, drive, push, insistence, peremptoriness, vigour **7 emphasis**, stress **8 definiteness**, absoluteness, categoricalness, unequivocalness, unquestionability, undisputedness, indubitability **9 affirmer**, affirmant, asserter, witness, testifier, attestant, proclaimer, enunciator, announcer, submitter, confessor, oath-taker, guarantor, backer, corroborator, advocate, assurer, supporter, sponsor, seconder, promoter, patron, ally, helpmate

ADJECTIVES 10 affirmative, affirming, affirmatory, assertive, supportive, declarative, annunciative, validatory, predicative **11 stated**, declared, asserted, pronounced, professed, uttered, proclaimed, affirmed, attested, alleged, announced, released, read, submitted, admitted, confessed, avowed **12 vowed**, pledged, promised, assured, guaranteed, committed, vouched, sworn, on oath, depositional **13 supported**, confirmed, corroborated, substantiated, ratified, authenticated, attested, validated, verified, certified, established, assured, endorsed, supported, backed **14 assertive**, self-assertive, assertory, assured, confident, forceful, decisive, decided, incisive, outspoken, blunt, plain, thrustful, driven, insistent, dogmatic, peremptory, pontifical, vehement, emphatic, vigorous **15 emphasized**, stressed, strongly worded, pointed **16 definite**, absolute, categorical, unequivocal, unquestionable, undisputed

VERBS 17 affirm, assert, attest, declare, state, pronounce, aver, asseverate, profess, utter, propose, proclaim, announce, submit, put forward, predicate, certify, allege, swear **18 vow**, pledge, promise, guarantee, commit oneself, vouch for, swear in, charge, adjure, testify, bear witness, assure **19 confirm**, corroborate, substantiate, ratify, authenticate, prove, establish, assure, endorse, support, back, attest, validate, verify, certify **20 admit**, avow, disclose, depose, confess **21 be assertive**, assert, assure, act forcefully, act decisively, thrust, drive, push **22 emphasize**, stress

18 Age

- *Being now come to the years of discretion.* The Book of Common Prayer.
- *Youth is a blunder; manhood a struggle; old age a regret.* Benjamin Disraeli.

NOUNS 1 age, timespan, lifetime **2 adulthood**, adultness, maturity, maturation, manhood **3 maturity**, matureness **4 middle age**, middle life, middle years **5 old age**, elderliness, senescence, longevity, seniority, retirement age, pensionable age, golden years, third age, advanced years, dotage **6 older person**, adult, grown-up, elder, senior, doyen, retired person, pensioner, old person, senior citizen, veteran, geriatric, greybeard, Methuselah, old fogy **7 the old**, the elderly

ADJECTIVES 8 adult, mature, senior, experienced, prepared **9 ageing**, growing old, senescent, greying, getting crow's-feet, declining, weakening, waning, sinking **10 middle-aged**, mature, fatherly, motherly, matronly, menopausal, climacteric **11 aged**, old, grown old, elderly, venerable, patriarchal, matriarchal, geriatric, well-preserved

19 Aggravation

NOUNS 1 aggravation, exacerbation, worsening, deterioration, intensification, heightening, deepening, magnification, augmentation, enhancement **2 annoyance**, exasperation, irritation, vexation, provocation **3 nuisance**, bother, trouble, victimization

ADJECTIVES 4 aggravated, worsened, not improved, exacerbated, intensified, heightened, deepened, increased, magnified, enhanced **5 aggravating**, annoying, irritating, exasperating, provoking

VERBS 6 aggravate, make worse, worsen, exacerbate, inflame, intensify, heighten, deepen, increase, augment, magnify, enhance **7 annoy**, irritate, exasperate, goad, provoke, antagonize, anger, vex

20 Agitation

NOUNS 1 agitation, perturbation, mental agitation, embarrassment, discomposure, disquiet, disquietude, inquietude, unease, nervousness, jerkiness, jumpiness, edginess **2 tumult**, turmoil, commotion, racket, din, confusion, stir, bustle, moil, tumultation, disturbance, hubbub, hurly-burly, rout, rush, furore **3 turbulence**, turbidity, ferment, fermentation, effervescence, seethe **4 fuss**, bother, fluster, bluster, flap, flurry, flutteration, bustle **5 restlessness**, unrest, fever, feverishness, the fidgets, fidgetiness, hopping, twitchiness **6 shaking**, vibrating, quaking, quivering, quavering, shivering, shuddering, juddering, tremulousness, vibration **7 shake**, tremor, quiver, wriggle, squirm, wag, waggle, wiggle, shudder, judder, falter, throb, the shakes, shivers **8 spasm**, orgasm, ejaculation, climax, cramp, convulsion, paroxysm, fit, seizure, throes, twitch, tic, nervous tic, rictus **9 jolt**, jar, knock, tremor, shock, throb, jerk, jump, sudden motion, start, judder, bump, nudge, dig, jog, joggle, jostle, jounce, bounce, bob, bobbing **10 flicker**, flutter, twinkle, flash, flit, waver, quiver **11 agitator**, shaker

ADJECTIVES 12 agitated, perturbed, troubled, disturbed, discomposed, embarrassed, nervous, nervy, edgy, uneasy, jittery, upset, unsteady, confused, ruffled, flurried, flustered, shaken, shaken up, shocked, stirred up **13 restless**, feverish, fevered, fidgety, itchy, unquiet, unpeaceful, twitchy, excited, flustered, fussing, fluttering **14 turbulent**, choppy, rough, bumpy, bouncy, pitching, rolling, stormy, tempestuous, boiling, seething, fuming **15 shaky**, shaking, quaky, quaking, quivery, quivering, quavery, quavering, unsteady, doddering, shivery, shivering, aguey, shuddering, juddering, wobbly, succussive, succussatory, vibratory, vibrating, pulsating **16 convulsive**, jerky, jolting, jarring, jolty, twitchy, twitchety, jumping, jumpy, palsied, fitful, spasmodic, paroxysmic, eclamptic, spastic, vellicative, orgasmic, saltatory, choreic, choreal, epileptic **17 flickering**, flickery, sputtering, spluttering, guttering

VERBS 18 be agitated, fuss, flap, flutter, twitter, dither, bustle, rush, mill around, jerk, jump, jump about, hop about, bounce, dance, ripple, effervesce, bubble, ferment, spit tacks, seethe, simmer

19 agitate, shake, wag, waggle, wave, flourish, brandish, flutter, fluster, perturb, disturb, perturbate, discompose, upset, untidy, disquiet, worry, stir, ruffle, rumple, move, trouble, swirl, churn, whip, whisk, beat, paddle, mix, stir up, rile, work up, roil **20 jolt**, judder, shudder, shock, jar, jerk, twitch, bump, jog, joggle, jostle, jounce, bounce, bob, hustle **21 shake**, vibrate, quake, quiver, quaver, shiver, falter, shudder, judder, throb, drum, beat, pulse, thrill, pulsate, palpitate, tremble, go pitapat, twitter, didder, fidget, twitch, jerk, jiggle **22 flicker**, flutter, twinkle, flash, splutter, sputter, spatter, spit, flick, gutter, bicker, wave

21 Agreement

•*Ah! don't say you agree with me. When people agree with me I always feel that I must be wrong.* Oscar Wilde.

NOUNS 1 agreement, concord, concordance, accord, accordance, concurrence, approval, thumbs up, assent, consent, affirmation, affirmative, confirmation, blessing, approbation, permission, willingness, consensus, cooperation, working together, comity, acquiescence, acceptance, toleration, compliance, unity, unanimity, unison, understanding, mutual support, attunement, congeniality, harmony, harmonization, sympathy, empathy, reciprocity, reconciliation, detente, coexistence, goodwill, peace **2 contract**, pact, compact, covenant, settlement, gentleman's agreement, undertaking, transaction, bargain, obligation, promise, pledge, IOU, bond, sanction, international agreement, concordat, treaty, entente cordiale, ratification, endorsement, authentication **3 compatibility**, conformation, conformity, correspondence, congruity, consistency, uniformity, synchronization, timeliness, equality, parallelism, similarity, coinciding, good fit **4 suitability**, fitness, aptness, relevance, relevancy **5 assenter**, cooperator, surrenderer, conformist, follower, yes man, sycophant, traditionalist, authenticator, endorser, ratifier, covenanter

VERBS 6 agree with, agree, concur, approve, assent, consent, respond favourably, affirm, confirm, bless, comply with, not oppose, not mind, accept, tolerate, concede, acquiesce, subscribe to, welcome, unite, understand, support, echo, ditto, harmonize, sympathize, empathize, cooperate, reciprocate, act friendly, work together, pull together, coexist **7 contract**, covenant, make terms, settle, undertake, transact, bargain, obligate, promise, pledge, sanction, ratify, endorse, second, attest, authenticate, seal, mark, stamp **8 be compatible**, be uniform, conform, match, tally, correspond, synchronize, coincide, equal **9 be suitable**, fit well, fit perfectly

ADJECTIVES 10 agreeing, agreed, agreeable, concordant, accordant, concurrent, concurring, approving, approved, voted in, carried, consenting, affirmative, confirmative, blessed, willing, acquiescent, acquiescing, accepting, compliant, united, unanimous, in unison, in chorus, attuned, in tune, congenial, harmonious, in step, sympathetic, empathetic, reciprocal, cooperative, cordial, coexisting, friendly, like-minded, reconciliatory, peaceful **11 contractual**, contracting, contracted, obligatory, promised, pledged, ratified, endorsed, authentic, signed, sealed **12 compatible**, conforming, corresponding, coinciding, congruent, congruous, consistent, matching, equal, uniform, synchronized, parallel **13 suitable**, fit, fitting, apt, appropriate

22 Agriculture

NOUNS 1 agriculture, farming, husbandry, intensive farming, factory farming, extensive farming, subsistence farming, mixed farming, share farming, sharecropping, arable farming, livestock farming, organic farming, ecofarming, biodynamic farming, agroecology, agro-ecosystem, agricultural science, agroscience, agronomy, agrology, agrobiology, agrogeology, agroforestry, geoponics, agronomics, rural economics, agrarianism, estate management **2 cultivation**, culture, tillage, tilth, ploughing, harrowing, sowing, planting, hedge-laying, hedging, pleaching, plashing, heathering, ethering, irrigation, fertilizing, muck-spreading, muck-raking, dunging, weeding, crop-spraying, harvesting, hay-making **3 farm**, collective farm, kolkhov, kibbutz, ranch, plantation, estate, holding, smallholding, croft, farmstead, homestead, steading, demesne, home farm, farmtoun **4 animal feedstuff**, feed, ration, fodder, roughage, hay, haylage, silage **5 agriculturist**, agriculturalist, agronomist, agrologist, agrobiologist, agrogeologist, agroecologist, rural economist, farmer, yeoman, granger, husbandman, tiller, gentleman farmer, tenant farmer, peasant farmer, hill farmer, crofter

VERBS 6 farm, cultivate, grow, sharecrop, till, plough, rotavate, dig, delve, spade, harrow, rake, plant, sow, drill, direct drill, scatter seed, broadcast, topdress, fertilize, muck, manure, dung, mulch, irrigate, spray, weed, hoe, mow, cut, harvest, reap, glean, gather, swathe, turn

ADJECTIVES 7 agricultural, agrarian, agronomic, agrological, agroecological, agrobiological, geoponic, farm, farming, farmhouse, rustic, rural, pastoral, peasant, bucolic, agrestic **8 farmable**, arable, cultivable, ploughable, tillable, fertile, productive, fruitful, farmed, cropped, ploughed, broken down, tilled, grazed

23 Air

NOUNS 1 air, ether, atmosphere, oxygen, gas, thin air, rarity **2 aerosphere**, ecosphere, biosphere **3 atmospheric layers**, troposphere, substratosphere, tropopause, stratosphere, strato-isothermal region, isothermal layer, ionosphere, exosphere, D region, E region, Appleton layer, F region, photosphere, chemosphere, stratum, layer **4 air flow**, wind, breeze, blast, gust, air current, updraught, downdraught **5 open air**, fresh air, out-of-doors, exposure **6 ventilation**, airing, fanning, aeration, aerage, air conditioning, air cooling, refrigeration, oxygenation **7 ventilator**, aerator, fan, blower, air conditioner, air filter, air cooler, ventilating system **8 airiness**, lightness, weightlessness, buoyancy **9 air bub-

ble, froth, foam, fluff, sponge, lather, suds, spray, spume, spindrift, air pocket, soufflé, balloon, air balloon **10 aeration**, fermentation, leavening, raising agent, yeast

ADJECTIVES **11 airy**, aery, aerial, aeriform, aeriferous, airlike, ethereal, insubstantial, lighter-than-air, weightless, light, exposed, roomy, rare, rarified **12 atmospheric**, stratospheric **13 aerial**, buoyant, inflated, blown-up, flatulent **14 breezy**, windy, blowy, fresh **15 open-air**, outdoor, out-of-door **16 ventilated**, well-ventilated, fresh, fanned, air-conditioned, cooled **17 bubbly**, foamy, frothy, fizzy, effervescent

VERBS **18 aerate**, aerify, oxygenate, air, ventilate, air-condition, air-cool, expose, freshen, deodorize **19 blow**, blast, gust, huff, puff **20 aerate**, whip, beat **21 bubble**, froth, foam, fizz, effervesce, sparkle, gurgle

24 Allocation

NOUNS **1 allocation**, alloting, allotment, assignment, appointment, job-sharing, apportionment, apportioning, appropriation, earmarking, tagging, setting aside, division, subdivision, partition, sharing, sharing out, distribution, parcelling out, doling out, dealing out, dispensing, delimitation **2 portion**, share, dividend, allocation, allotment, lot, plot, proportion, ratio, quota, dole, pittance, allowance, ration, dose, dosage, measure, dollop, helping **3 allotted task**, assigned task, assigned job, chore, stint, shift, stretch

VERBS **4 allot**, allocate, apportion, appropriate, earmark, tag, demarcate, delimit, limit, divide, prorate, subdivide, carve up, bisect, split, cut, share, share out, distribute, spread around, dispense, deal out, deal, portion out, dole out, parcel out, mete out, measure, ration **5 assign**, detail

ADJECTIVES **6 allocated**, allotted, assigned, apportioned, divided, shared out, distributed

25 Anarchy

NOUNS **1 anarchy**, lawlessness, disorder, interregnum, power vacuum, powerlessness, impotence, disorganization, misgovernment, misrule, unrestraint, unruliness, disruption, irresponsibility, indiscipline, disobedience, insubordination, arrogation, chaos, turmoil, mob rule, mob law, lynch law, sedition, subversion, fifth column, revolution, rebellion, guerrilla tactics, the underground, usurpation, abdication, forced resignation, overthrow, coup d'état, coup, dethronement **2 anarchism**, nihilism, antinomianism, syndicalism, anarcho-syndicalism, ochlocracy **3 anarchist**, revolutionary, subversive, seditionary, rebel, mutineer, fifth columnist, terrorist, guerrilla, assassin, arrogator, antinomian, nihilist, syndicalist

VERBS **4 be anarchic**, cause anarchy, cause disorder, defy authority, usurp, undermine, subvert, arrogate, resist control, disobey, practise subversion, go underground, disrupt, revolt, rebel, mutiny, overthrow, depose, unseat **5 misgovern**, misrule

ADJECTIVES **6 anarchic**, anarchical, disorganized, ungoverned, lawless, unofficial, wildcat, disobedient, insubordinate, seditious, disorderly, rampant, unruly, wild, riotous, chaotic, rebellious, revolutionary, mutinous **7 anarchistic**, nihilistic, antinomian, syndicalistic

26 Angle

NOUNS 1 angle, bend, fork, corner, sharp corner, intersection, junction, zigzag, perpendicular, chevron, hairpin bend, dog-leg, angle iron, elbow-joint, knee-joint, gonion **2 obliquity**, skewness, bias slope, bevel, cant, bezel, edge, wedge, slant, ramp, hill, slope, tilt, declivity, steepness, escarpment, scarp **3 angled figure**, triangle, quadrangle, quadrilateral, square, rectangle, parallelogram, tetragon, rhombus, lozenge, rhomboid, pentagon, pentangle, hexagon, polyhedron, prism, pyramid **4 angular measurement**, trigonometry, goniometry, geometry, goniometer, protractor, sextant, sundial, bevel square, set square, T-square, theodolite, quadrant, astrological angle, sextile, square, quintile, trine, quincunx **5 viewpoint**, aspect, standpoint, stand, view, impression, slant, bias

ADJECTIVES 6 angular, cornered, pointed, bent, hooked, jointed, forked, bifurcate, L-shaped, V-shaped, A-framed, dog-legged **7 oblique**, skew, skewed, sloping, bevelled, slanting, sloped, inclined, tilted, steep, tangential, diagonal, transverse **8 angled**, scalene, triangular, square, right-angled, perpendicular, rectangular, quadrilateral, quadrangular, polygonal, pentagonal, rhomboidal, hexagonal, trilateral, cuneate, cuneiform, polyhedral, prismatic, pyramidal, faceted **9 biased**, slanted

VERBS 10 angle, fork, intersect, zigzag, bend, hook over, tip, tilt, slope, lean, cant, bevel, bank, mitre, incline, careen, twist

27 Animal Cry

NOUNS 1 animal cry, warning cry, mating call, animal call, barking, baying, howling, belling, wailing, yowling, yawling, bleating, bellowing, roaring, ululation, bark, yelp, yap, snap, snarl, growl, woof, hiss, meow, mew, purr, baa, moo, neigh, whinny **2 bird song**, bird call, note, chirping, chirruping, chattering, twittering, warble, squeak, cheep, twitter, tweet-tweet, cuckoo, hoot, tu-whit tu-whoo, whoop, cock-a-doodle-doo, croak, caw, coo, hiss, quack, cluck, squawk **3 insect noise**, buzzing, humming, droning

ADJECTIVES 4 ululant, howling, yowling, wailing, wailful, bellowing, full-throated **5 singing**, warbling, carolling, tweeting, twittering, twittery **6 humming**, buzzing

28 Animals

NOUNS 1 animals, animal life, animal kingdom, Animalia, fauna, the bird?, beast?, and fish, wildlife, endangered species, game, big game **2 animal**, creature, beast, brute, dumb animal, dumb friend, furry friend, four-legged friend **3 domesticated animal**, pack animal, draught animal, farm animal, livestock, stock, circus animal, experimental animal, laboratory animal, tame animal, pet animal, pet **4 type of animal**, invertebrate, animalcule, zooid, protist, protozoan, worm, mollusc, gastropod, arthropod, insect, chordate, vertebrate, fish, amphibian, reptile, bird, mammal, biped, quadruped, herbivore, browser, grazer, filter-feeder, scavenger, omnivore, carnivore, flesh-eater, meat-eater, insectivore, predator, prey, parasite, bloodsucker, ectoparasite, endoparasite, host, intermediate host, vector, symbiont **5 aquatic animal**, marine animal, marine mammal, cetacean, whale, dolphin, seal, fish, starfish, echinoderm, cuttlefish, cephalopod, octopus, shellfish, bivalve, jellyfish, coelenterate, coral, sponge, plankton, zooplankton, nekton, benthos, fry, krill **6 flying animal**, flier, bird, flying insect, fly, butterfly, flying fish, flying mammal, flying fox **7 legendary beast**, unicorn, Pegasus, Cerberus, dragon, firedrake, griffin, chimaera, banshee, siren, lamia, harpy, manticore, behemoth, centaur, minotaur, cyclops, elf, gnome, goblin, orc, troll, jinn, hippogriff, wyvern, cockatrice, basilisk, phoenix, roc, snark, kraken, Sasquatch, Bigfoot, Yeti, Abominable Snowman, zoomorphism, therianthropism **8 animal science(s)**, zoology, animal taxonomy, systematic zoology, zoography, zoometry, animal anatomy, comparative anatomy, zootomy, animal physiology, zoonomy, embryology, animal biochemistry, zoochemistry, animal ecology, parasitology, marine biology, animal behaviour, animal psychology, ethology, sociobiology, zoogeography, animal pathology, zoopathology, palaeozoology, palaeontology, vertebrate zoology, mammology, ornithology, herpetology, ichthyology, invertebrate zoology, entomology, malacology, helminthology **9 zoologist**, animal taxonomist, systematic zoologist, zoographer, zoometrist, comparative anatomist, zootomist, animal physiologist, zoonomist, embryologist, zoochemist, animal ecologist, paransitologist, marine biologist, ethologist, behaviourist, zoographer, zoopathologist, palaeozoologist, vertebrate zoologist, mammologist, ornithologist, herpetologist, ichthyologist, invertebrate zoologist, entomologist, malacologist, helminthologist **10 zoophilism**, zoophilia, bestiality, animality **11 fear of animals**, zoophobia

ADJECTIVES 12 animalian, animal, animalic, animalistic, zoic, brutish, subhuman, dumb, brutal, bestial, beastly, beastlike, animal-like, zoomorphic, therianthropic **13 of animals**, invertebrate, animalcular, zooidal, chordate, vertebrate, bipedal, quadrupedal, domesticated, tamed, feral, wild, solitary, social, colonial, terrestrial, arboreal, aquatic, marine, planktonic, benthic, pelagic, littoral, diurnal, nocturnal, carnivorous, herbivorous, omnivorous, insectivorous, predacious, parasitic, bloodsucking, ectoparasitic, endoparasitic, symbiotic **14 zoological**, zoochemical, embryological, ethological, zoopathological **15 animal-loving**, zoophilic **16 animal-fearing**, zoophobic

29 Answer

NOUNS 1 answer, reply, response, rejoinder, responsion, respondence, replication, retort, riposte, comeback, repartee, back talk, backchat **2 acknowledgment**, answer, return correspondence, written reply, official reply, rescript, receipt, confirmation **3 question and answer**, dialogue, interchange, interlocution, interview, exchange **4 reaction**, answer, retroaction, recoil, reflex, return, reflux, rebuff, repercussion, reverberation, echo, response, responsory **5 counterstatement**, answer, countercharge, counterblast, retaliation, defence, plea, argument, refutation, rebuttal, contradiction, objection, vindication, last word, parting shot **6 solution**, answer, result, issue, outcome, upshot, denouement, resolution, conclusion, discovery, resolving, working out, unscrambling, clearing up, sorting out, decoding, interpretation, explanation, reason, resource, contrivance, measure, plan, remedy **7 numerical result**, answer, solution, product, sum, total, difference, equation, remainder, score **8 correspondence**, answerableness **9 answerability**, responsibility, liability, accountability, obligation

ADJECTIVES 10 answering, replying, responsive, responding, respondent, acknowledged, confirmed, returned, retorted, backchatting **11 reactive**, interlocutory, interactive, retroactive, recoiling, reflexive, returning, refluent, rebuffed, recalcitrant, repercussive, reverberatory **12 retaliatory**, counterstated, countercharged, counterblasted, argumentative, refutative, refutatory, rebutted **13 solved**, soluble, resultant, issuing, resolved, concluded, discovered, worked out, unscrambled, cleared up, sorted out, decoded, interpreted, interpretational, explanatory, explained, reasoned, contrived, measured, planned, remedial **14 correspondent**, corresponding, correlative **15 answerable**, responsible, liable, accountable, required, obliged, obligatory, under obligation, duty bound

VERBS 16 answer, reply, respond, rejoin, riposte, retort, return, acknowledge **17 answer back**, talk back, contradict, confute, counterstate, countercharge, counterblast, refute, rebut, defend, vindicate, plead, argue, object **18 react**, exchange, interact, converse, interview, interlocute, interchange, retroact, recoil, return, rebuff, kick back, recalcitrate, bounce back, reverberate **19 solve**, sum, score, equate, total, resolve, conclude, discover, work out, unscramble, clear up, sort out, decode, interpret, explain, reason, contrive, measure, plan **20 answer to**, correspond, correlate, parallel **21 be the answer**, pertain, fit, suit **22 answer for**, be responsible, represent, speak for, appear for, replace

30 Anthropology

NOUNS 1 anthropology, human studies, anthropogeny, anthropography, ethnology, ethnography, ethnogeny, ethnobotany, ethnomusicology, social anthropology, cultural anthropology, ethnoscientific studies, human geography, anthropogeography, demography, human ecology, behavioural science, anthropometry, craniometry **2 palaeoanthropology**, prehistoric anthropology, archaeological anthropology, Assyriology, Egyptology, Sumerology **3 measurement**, anthrometry, anthroscopy, biometrics, craniometry, osteology, growth study, constitutional anthropology, height-weight ratio, Sheldon scale, skinfold **4 race**, ethnic origin, colour, Caucasoid race, Caucasian, White, Nordic type, Alpine type, Aryan, Latino, Negroid race, Negro, Negrito, Negrillo, Nilotic type, Afro-Caribbean, African-American, Afro-American, Anglo-American, Anglo-African, Melanesian, Polynesian, Australasian, Mongoloid race, Oriental, Asian, Anglo-Indian, mixed race, mulatto, quadroon, octaroon, indigenous race, native people, native, aborigine, Indian, Amerindian **5 tradition**, custom, habit, praxis, ritual, rite, symbol, taboo, ancient wisdom, common law, immemorial wisdom, myth, archetypal myth, mythology, legend, lore, folklore, folk tale, folk motif, folk art, folksong, folk history, oral tradition, archetype, racial memory

ADJECTIVES 6 anthropological, anthropographical, ethnological, ethnographic, ethnogenic, anthropogenic, ethnoscientific, anthropogeographic, demographic, palaeoanthropological, epigraphic, sociological, anatomical, anthropometric, anthropometrical, anthroposcopic, craniometric, craniometrical, craniological **7 racial**, ethnic, Caucasian, Caucasoid, White, Nordic, Alpine, Aryan, albinic, albinistic, albinotic, Negroid, Black, Nilotic, Afro-Caribbean, Afro-American, Anglo-African, Melanesian, Polynesian, Australasian, Mongoloid, Oriental, Asian, Anglo-Indian, mixed, mulatto, octaroon, quadroon, indigenous, native, aboriginal, Indian **8 societal**, communal, national, tribal, racial, ethnic, cultural, folk, traditional, customary, received, handed down, mythological, legendary

31 Appearance

• *Alas, after a certain age every man is responsible for his face.* Albert Camus.

NOUNS 1 appearance, appearing, materialization, manifestation, embodiment, incarnation, realization, birth, coming, advent, arrival, debut, entrance, introduction **2 being in view**, visibility, presence, attendance, existence, being, being there, occurrence, happening, phenomenon **3 external appearance**, look, outward form, superficies, surface, form, shape, format, dimensions, outline, contour, silhouette, relief, elevation, section, aspect, outside, exterior, externals, front, façade, veneer, dress, style, demeanour, manner, mien, bearing, feature, figure, body, face, features, profile, expression, body language, skin, looks, beauty, ugliness **4 something that appears**, spectacle, sight, revelation, miracle, marvel, prodigy, apparition, ghost, emanation, hallucination, vision, mirage, hologram, seeming **5 impression**, effect, impact, visual appeal, face value, public image, reflection, similarity **6 reappearance**, return, reissue, republication, second showing, repeat

ADJECTIVES 7 appearing, apparent, material, embodied, incarnate, realized, there, present, evident, patent, manifest, showing, visible, in sight, on show, on view, exposed, displayed, revealed, epiphanic, theophanic, prominent, spectacular, beginning, coming, arriving, entering, emergent, arising, developing, unfolding, waxing, recurring **8 outer**, outward, superficial, surface, external, exterior, visual, reflected **9 ostensible**, seeming, deceptive, specious, illusory, visionary, dreamlike, chimerical, imaginary **10 aspectual**, beautiful, attractive, sightly, decorative, well-dressed, fashionable, ugly, unattractive, homely, unsightly, plain

VERBS 11 appear, show, show up, be present, attend, be at, be there, be, look, seem, appear like, imitate **12 become visible**, materialize, appear, begin, dawn, come forth, come forward, come out, emerge, surface, show, show up, show oneself, turn up, come, loom, wax **13 occur**, happen, perform, play, act, star in, be published, come out, become available, recur **14 present**, put forward, make apparent, realize, show, show up, reveal, disclose, expose, display, exhibit, expose oneself, publish, issue, launch, release, screen, point out, point up, highlight, silhouette, outline

32 Approval

NOUNS 1 approval, approbation, satisfaction, acceptance, adoption, sanction, countenance, blessing, agreement, formal agreement, permission, authorization, assent, consent, acquiescence, vote, imprimatur, endorsement, mandate, support, backing, advocacy, championship, patronage, recommendation, licence, rubber stamp, nod **2 admiration**, respect, regard, esteem, credit, acknowledgment, recognition, appreciation, gratitude, honour, favour, good opinion, good books, good graces, popularity, prestige, liking, affection **3 praise**, honour, laud, glory, extolment, exaltation, flattery, compliments, adulation, idolatry, deification, apotheosis, lionization **4 compliment**, praise, congratulation, felicitation, good word, commendation, citation, honourable mention, accolade, kudos, glowing terms, eulogy, encomium, panegyric, tribute **5 acclaim**, acclamation, plaudit, applause, clap, big hand, ovation, cheering, whistling, stamping, curtain call **6 recommendation**, testimonial, reference **7 advocate**, champion, supporter, backer, patron, sponsor **8 admirer**, supporter, follower, fan

VERBS 9 approve, approve of, hold with, like, admire, respect, regard highly, esteem, value **10 accept**, pass, adopt, sanction, countenance, agree, grant permission, authorize, ratify, assent, consent, acquiesce, condone, endorse, license, rubber-stamp, nod **11 support**, back, uphold, advocate, champion, recommend, favour **12 praise**, laud, glorify, honour, exalt, extol, magnify, flatter, compliment, adulate, idolize, deify, apotheosize, lionize **13 compliment**, praise, congratulate, commend, eulogize, panegyrize, wax lyrical, trumpet, boost, puff up **14 acclaim**, hail, applaud, clap, cheer, whistle, stamp, encore, shout bravo **15 meet with approval**, win praise, find favour, gain credit, satisfy

ADJECTIVES 16 approving, satisfied, content, appreciative, grateful, approbatory, respectful, well-inclined, favourable, complimentary, commendatory, laudatory, admiring, eulogistic, encomiastic, panegyric, acclamatory, fulsome, flattering, adulatory, idolatrous, lionizing **17 supporting**, supportive, backing, advocating, championing, recommending, in favour, for **18 acclamatory**, applauding, clapping **19 praiseworthy**, laudable, commendable, worthy, estimable, creditable, admirable, unimpeachable, meritorious **20 approvable**, satisfactory, acceptable, passable, permissible **21 approved**, passed, tested, accepted, supported, backed, endorsed, favoured **22 admired**, respected

33 Architecture

• *No person who is not a great sculptor or painter can be an architect. If he is not a sculptor or painter, he can only be a builder.* John Ruskin.

NOUNS 1 architecture, architectonics, tectonics, building design, architectural engineering, domestic architecture, civil architecture, governmental architecture, civic architecture, religious architecture, military architecture, industrial architecture, recreational architecture, landscape architecture **2 architect**, civil architect, domestic architect, designer, architectural engineer, military architect, industrial architect, landscape architect, master builder **3 arch**, rounded arch, lancet arch, parabolic arch, segmental arch, false arch, Norman arch, semicircular arch, ogee arch, Tudor arch, basket arch, horseshoe arch, catenary arch, elliptical arch, corbel arch, depressed arch, lancet arch, keel arch, raking arch, rampant arch, rowlack arch, shouldered arch, skew arch, stilted arch, strainer arch **4 roof**, flat roof, pitched roof, hipped roof, gambrel roof, imbricated roof, mansard roof, dome, saucer dome, pendentive dome **5 vault**, vaulting, barrel vault, rib vault, groin vault, fan vault, lierne vault, parabolic vault, segmental vault, quadripartite vault, intersecting vault, domical vault, voussoir **6 column**, support, pillar, post, pier, pilaster, buttress, flying buttress, abutment, monolithic column, engaged column, Salomonic column, coupled column, demicolumn, columniation, intercolumniation, colonnade, stylobate, diastyle, hexastyle, peristyle, pedestal, shaft, drum, fluting, flute, entasis, capital, chapiter, cap, entablature, impost, Doric order, Tuscan order, Ionic order, Corinthian order **7 other architectural features**, abacus, ambulatory, ancon, anta, arcade, articulation, ashlar, astylar, attic, balcony, base, beak, bolster, bow, cantilever, case, casement, cella, centering, coin, concha, corbel, cordon, cupola, dado, die, drip, dripstone, extrados, fantail, fascia, fenestella, fenestra, filler, frieze, frustrum, gable, gable end, groin, haunch, headstone, hip, imperia, impost, intrados, invert, lantern, lintel, loggia, louvre, module, naos, neck, pace, pier, podium, portico, propylaeum, prostyle, re-entrant corner, respond, reveal, rib, rotunda, rustication, shafting, spandrel, springer, squint, squinch, string, stringer, table, tailpiece, tail beam, tambour, trumeau, truss, verge, vestibule, voussoir, wall, load-bearing wall, lunette **8 church architecture**, cuniform church, crossing, conch, ambulatory, apse, transept, chancel, westwork, vestibule, narthex,

dome, flèche, spirelet, chevet, triforium, clerestory, blindstorey, basilica, tribune gallery
ADJECTIVES 9 architectural, edificial, architectonic, tectonic **10 structural**, erected, listed, designed, detached, semidetached, terraced, single storey, multistorey, highrise **11 arched**, arcuated, arcuate, rounded, lancet, parabolic **12 roofed**, pitched, hipped, imbricate, domed **13 vaulted**, ribbed **14 columned**, columnated, columnar, supported, pilastered, buttressed, fluted, Doric, Tuscan
VERBS 15 be an architect, design, draw blueprints, build, construct, structure, erect **16 decorate**, ornament, dome, arch, vault, rib, abut, buttress, coffer, articulate, flute, mould, boss

34 Argument

NOUNS 1 argument, disagreement, dispute, quarrel, controversy, discord, misunderstanding, incompatibility, diversity, difference, altercation, wrangle, squabble, bickering, tiff, spat, row, conflict, feud, fight, fray, fracas, scrimmage, donnybrook **2 logical argument**, debate, discussion, disputation, dialogue, dialectic, eristic, polemic, maieutic, hermeneutic, heuristic, elenchus, logic, sophistry, argumentation, discourse, reasoning, ratiocination, deliberation, deduction, induction, consideration, reflection, thought, challenge, questioning, inquiry **3 line of argument**, reasoning, rationale, contention, topic, issue, thesis, hypothesis, postulate, proposition, premise, pretext, point, case, claim, assertion, statement, affirmation, attestation, testimony, position, opinion, stance, grounds **4 plea**, pleading, argument, request, entreaty, cry, suit, consideration, excuse, answer, apology, defence, claim, justification, explanation, rationalization
ADJECTIVES 5 arguing, quibbling, quarrelling, wrangling, squabbling, bickering, at odds, dissenting, rowing, scuffling, clashing **6 argumentative**, quarrelsome, disagreeable, disputatious, litigious, dissentious, factious, querulous, peevish, irritable, contrary, testy, petulant, fractious, choleric, cross, irascible **7 hostile**, antagonistic, provocative, polemical, eristic, inimical, pugnacious, belligerent, bellicose, warlike, brawling, conflicting, feuding **8 arguable**, debatable, disputable, contentious, topical, controversial, questionable, doubtful, dubious, challenging, problematic, refutable, in question, moot, unsettled, undecided **9 logical**, elenctic, sophistic, heuristic, hypothetical, propositional, proposed, postulated, claimed, asserted, stated
VERBS 10 argue, disagree, bicker, wrangle, quarrel, quibble, squabble, remonstrate, altercate, gainsay, contradict, polemicize, oppose, dissent, differ, dispute, contest, spar, scuffle, clash, conflict, brawl, feud **11 discuss**, debate, exchange opinions, reason, ratiocinate, logicize, logomachize, deliberate, consider, weigh up, reflect, doubt, question, inquire, challenge, moot, deduce, induce, chop logic **12 state**, argue, maintain, say, affirm, attest, hold, claim, hypothesize, propose, postulate, suggest, imply, denote, show, establish, evince **13 plead**, argue, re-

quest, entreat, prevail upon, persuade, canvass, apologize, defend, claim, answer, justify, explain

35 Aristocrat

NOUNS 1 nobleman, noblewoman, noble, lord, lady, duke, duchess, marquis, marquess, marquise, marchioness, margrave, margravine, count, countess, earl, viscount, viscountess, baron, baronet, knight, gentleman, gentlewoman, grand duke, peer, life peer, titled person, blueblood, optimate **2 aristocracy**, nobility, lordship, *ancien régime*, peerage, gentry, landed gentry, ruling class, upper classe, gentlefolk, élite, high society **3 nobleness**, nobility, kingliness, quality, virtue, distinction, lineage, pedigree, gentility, noble family, dynasty, good breeding

ADJECTIVES 4 aristocratic, noble, blue blooded, thoroughbred, ennobled, titled, high-class, upper-class, gentlemanly, ladylike, well-bred, ducal, lordly, princely, well-born, high-born, patrician, baronial

VERBS 5 make noble, ennoble

36 Arrangement

NOUNS 1 arrangement, order, ordering, arranging, arraying, marshalling, disposition, placement, location, structuring, composition, grouping, alignment **2 array**, assemblage, arrangement, display, pattern, style, layout, structure **3 organization**, method, system, planning, charting **4 rearrangement**, reordering, reorganization, restructuring, realignment **5 categorization**, classification, codification, taxonomy, grouping, placing, placement, pigeonholing, compartmentalization, grading, ranking, rating, hierarchy, stratification, graduation, sorting, analysis, tabulation, alphabetization, cataloguing, listing, indexing **6 category**, subcategory, class, group, order, division, family, set, heading, department, section, grade, rank, level, position, place, status, slot, niche, pigeonhole **7 catalogue**, directory, gazetteer, register, digest, compendium, index, list, inventory, record, file **8 chart**, diagram, table, graph, flow chart, scatter diagram, flow sheet, spreadsheet, Venn diagram, plan, scheme, schema, schedule **9 arrangements**, plans

VERBS 10 arrange, order, structure, range, array, marshal, dispose, place, position, locate, set, set out, lay out, display, align, line up, compose, group, space, space out, distribute, allocate **11 organize**, methodize, systematize, rationalize, standardize, coordinate, plan **12 rearrange**, reorder, reorganize, restructure, shake up, realign **13 categorize**, classify, codify, program, group, pigeonhole, compartmentalize, place, grade, rank, rate, seed, sort, sift, sieve, screen, select, analyse, process, tabulate, alphabetize, catalogue, index, list, inventory, record, register **14 come to an arrangement**, compromise, agree **15 make arrangements**, arrange for, prearrange, prepare, plan, schedule, organize, manage, contrive **16 tidy**, tidy up, neaten, rearrange, straighten, clear up, untangle, disentangle, unravel, unsnarl, iron out

ADJECTIVES 17 arranged, ordered, orderly, structured, ranged, arrayed, marshalled, disposed, placed, aligned **18 organized**, methodized, systematized, rationalized, planned **19 organizational**, methodical, systematic, schematic, rational **20 rearranged**, reordered, reorganized, restructured, realigned **21 categorized**, classified, codified, grouped, pigeonholed, compartmentalized, placed, graded, ranked, rated, seeded, stratified, sorted, sifted, screened, selected, analysed, processed, tabulated, alphabetized, catalogued, indexed, listed, filed **22 categorical**, classificatory **23 diagrammatic**, graphic, tabular, schematic **24 tidied**, tidy, neat, straightened out, cleared up, untangled, disentangled

37 Arrival

VERBS 1 arrive, appear, come, be present, be found **2 reach**, get there, get to, come to, make it, come upon, light upon **3 approach**, draw up **4 land**, make port, dock, beach, berth, moor, tie up, drop anchor, step ashore, disembark, debark, alight, touch down, get off, detrain, debus, dismount, get down **5 get in**, come in, enter, burst upon, check in, clock in, punch in

NOUNS 6 arrival, coming, advent, approach, onset, advance, appearance, entrance, emergence **7 landing**, landfall, docking, touchdown, mooring, disembarkation, debarkation, coming ashore, tying up **8 reception**, hospitality, welcome, greeting, handshake, aloha **9 return**, homecoming, coming back, recursion, re-entrance, reentry **10 destination**, goal, objective, terra firma, harbour, haven, home, end, stop, last stop, terminal point, journey's end, terminus, stopping place, finish, port, aerodrome, airport, heliport, air terminal, depot

ADJECTIVES 11 arriving, incoming, immigrant, entering, emerging **12 approaching**, impending, imminent, oncoming, advancing, coming, incoming, inbound, inwardbound, homeward, homeward-bound, nearing **13 welcoming**, inviting

38 Ascent

NOUNS 1 ascent, ascension, rise, levitation, assumption, uprise, upward motion, uphill, upslope, upgo, upcoming, upping, gaining height, defying gravity, surfacing, breaking surface **2 upturn**, upsurge, surge, spurt, gush, jet, spout, fountain, uptrend, upswing, upsweep, upgrowth, upgrade, updraught, increase, spiral, uplift, elevation, rising air, rising current, upthrow, rising ground **3 taking off**, leaving ground, takeoff, liftoff, departure, soaring, gaining altitude, rocketing up **4 jump**, vault, leap, bound, spring, saltation, bounce, hop, skip, high jump, pole-vault, recoil, hurdle, hurdling, steeplechase **5 mounting**, mount, climbing, clamber, ladder-climbing, hill-climbing, mountaineering, alpinism **6 means of ascent**, stairs, steps, companion way, perron, fire escape **7 lift**, escalator, elevator, ski-lift, chair lift, cable car, springboard, vault **8 ladder**, stepladder **9 step**, stair, rest, footrest, rung, rundle, round, spoke, stave, scale, doorstep, tread, riser, bridgeboard, string, stepstool, kickstool **10 ascender**, rocket, skylark, skyrocket, lark, eagle, soarer, climber, mountaineer, alpinist, rock

climber, cragsman, excelsior figure, steeplejack
VERBS 11 ascend, climb, lift, rise, mount, levitate, soar, spiral, spire, curl upwards, upwind, upspin, upgo, go up, upsurge, upstream, upheave, swarm up, sweep up **12 climb**, mount, walk up, struggle up, shin up, shinny up, monkey up, scale, escalade, top, breast, clear, hurdle, clamber up, scramble, scrabble up, ramp, climb over, surmount **13 mount**, get on, climb on, back, bestride, board, hop in, pile in, jump in **14 stand up**, get up, rear, rear up **15 spring up**, surface, float up, break water, shoot up, jump up, leap up, vault up, start up, fly up, pop up, bob up, upshoot, upspring, upstart, upleap, spurt, gush, jet, spout **16 jump**, spring, leap, vault, hurdle, bound, bounce, hop **17 take off**, lift off, rocket, skyrocket, launch, gain altitude, gain height, claw skyward, become airborne, soar, zoom, fly, plane, kite, fly aloft, spire **18 upturn**, turn up, improve, get better, trend upwards, slope up, upcast, upsweep, upbend
ADJECTIVES 19 ascending, upward, uphill, climbing, scansorial, scandent, steep, uparching, upturned, upcast, uplifted, turned-up **20 rising**, mounting, buoyant, rampant, rearing, bullish, escalating, uprising, upgoing, upcoming, ascendant, ascensional, anabatic, soaring, zooming, rocketing, lifting, gaining height, light, floating **21 leaping**, springing, vaulting, jumping, hopping, saltatory, saltant, saltatorial, skipping, prancing, bounding, bouncing, spiralling **22 ladder-like**, scalar, scalariform, scalable

39 Assembly

NOUNS 1 assembly, assemblage, bringing together, coming together, convergence, confluence, collection, collecting, gathering, ingathering, forgathering, grouping, congregation, mobilization, muster, rally, call-up, combination, joining together, junction, collocation **2 herding**, whipping in, round-up, shepherding, driving, corralling **3 meeting**, assembly, gathering, meet **4 rally**, mass meeting, demonstration, protest meeting **5 conference**, symposium, convention, convocation, congregation, congress, caucus, synod, diet, council, legislature **6 committee**, commission, panel, board, council, cabinet **7 group**, grouping, party, company, body, band, gang, pack, ring, circle, posse **8 team**, squad, crew, outfit, complement, corps, troupe, cast, company, orchestra **9 party**, faction, movement, wing, junta **10 crowd**, mob, mass, throng, multitude, horde, host, swarm, ruck, rabble **11 flock**, herd, pack, kennel, drove, drive, stable, string, colony, set, host, troop, army, swarm, school **12 assemblage**, collection, set, batch, group, accumulation, congeries, agglomeration, conglomeration, aggregation, hoard, store **13 mass**, heap, pile, stack, mound **14 bundle**, wad, batch, clump, cluster, bunch, knot, parcel, package, bale, truss, haystack, roll, bolt, quiver, sheaf, skein, hank, tussock, hassock **15 cluster**, galaxy, constellation, nebula **16 bunch**, bouquet, posy, nosegay **17 compilation**, collection, corpus, compendium, anthology **18 miscellany**, miscellanea, collectanea, medley, assortment, mixture, potpourri, smorgasbord, jumble, hotchpotch, sundries **19 putting together**, assembly, assemblage, collage, montage, construction, erection, connection

VERBS **20 assemble**, collect, gather, bring together, group, accumulate, agglomerate, aggregate, mass, amass, hoard, store, stockpile, heap, pile, stack, build up, mound **21 group**, batch, clump, cluster, bunch, bundle, parcel, package, wrap, bale, truss **22 come together**, forgather, meet, rendezvous, congregate, group, gather round, rally round, huddle, cluster **23 crowd**, mass, throng, pack, cram, mill, seethe, teem, crawl, swarm, horde, troop, flood, stream, pour, surge, sweep, flow **24 band together**, get together, join forces, unite, team up, join up, link up, gang up **25 call together**, convene, convoke, summon, muster, marshal, rally, mobilize **26 herd**, shepherd, round up, corral, drive, whip in **27 put together**, compose, compile, colligate, connect, join, unite, combine, fit together, construct, erect

ADJECTIVES **28 assembled**, gathered, congregate, congregated, convened, summoned, mobilized, called up, herded, mustered, shepherded **29 collected**, amassed, accumulated, hoarded, stockpiled, heaped, piled, stacked **30 cumulate**, glomerate, conglomerate, agglomerate, aggregate, convergent, confluent, collective **31 grouped**, clumped, clustered, bunched, bundled, packaged, parcelled, baled, trussed, wrapped, fascicled, congressional, congregational, factional **32 crowded**, packed, crammed, congested, dense, close, serried, seething, teeming, swarming, bristling

40 Assent

NOUNS **1 assent**, corroboration, confirmation, affirmation, consent, agreement, acquiescence, compliance, acceptance, approval, approbation, admission, acknowledgment, recognition, confession, sanction, permission, concordance, harmony, accord, concurrence, consensus, unanimity, single voice **2 yes**, affirmative, ratification, validation, certification, endorsement, aye

VERBS **3 assent**, agree, concur, welcome, echo, corroborate, confirm, affirm, approve, say yes, nod, consent to, sanction, authorize, permit, allow, concede, give in, grant, admit, acknowledge, recognize, confess, support, subscribe to, second, vote for, endorse, authenticate, ratify, validate, countersign **4 assent to**, acquiesce, accede, comply, accept, tolerate, bear, submit, yield

ADJECTIVES **5 assenting**, in agreement, concurring, concordant, unanimous, solid, like-minded, confirmative, affirmative, approving, consenting, supportive, sympathetic, cooperative, collaborating, willing, acquiescent **6 agreed**, carried, signed, sealed, ratified, validated

41 Astronomy

NOUNS **1 astronomy**, star gazing, star watching, optical astronomy, observational astronomy, radio astronomy, infrared astronomy, X-ray astronomy, ultraviolet astronomy, gamma-ray astronomy, radar astronomy, astrophysics, cosmology, cosmogeny, uranography, astrometry, celestial mechanics, astrodynamics, stellar statistics, astrochemistry, cosmochemistry, astrobiology, exobiology, astrobotany, astrogeology **2 astronomer**, observer, astrophysicist, cosmologist, cosmogenist, uranographer, cosmochemist, astronomer royal **3 galaxy**, island universe, galactic nebula, anagalactic nebula, elliptical galaxy, spiral galaxy, irregular galaxy, lenticular galaxy, Hubble classification, supergiant elliptical, giant elliptical, giant spiral, dwarf elliptical, cluster, Local Group, supercluster, active galaxy, quasar, radio galaxy, Seyfert galaxy, starburst galaxy, filament, void, galactic centre, nucleus, disc, arm, halo, gravitational redshift **4 constellation**, zodiac, stellar cluster, globular cluster, open cluster, stellar group, stellar association, stellar population, double star, optical double, binary star, visual binary, eclipsing binary, spectroscopic binary, close binary, X-ray binary **5 star**, luminary, orb, sphere, heavenly body, celestial body, fixed star, evening star, Hesperus, Vesper, morning star, Lucifer, circumpolar star, nebulous star, variable star, nova, supernova, white dwarf, red giant, neutron star, pulsar, quasar, black hole **6 sun**, daystar, Sol, Helios, Hyperion, sunlight, sunshine, midnight sun, solar eclipse, corona, chromosphere, photosphere, solar activity, active sun, quiet sun, solar cycle, sunspot cycle, 11-year cycle, butterfly diagram, solar flare, prominence, sunspot, facula, filament, granule, solar spectrum **7 planet**, Mercury, Venus, Earth, Mars, Jupiter, Saturn, Uranus, Neptune, Pluto, giant planet, Jovian planet, terrestrial planet, inferior planet, superior planet, wandering star, minor planet, asteroid, planetoid **8 moon**, moonlight, phase, new moon, full moon, harvest moon, hunter's moon, crescent moon, horned moon, first quarter, last quarter, half-moon, gibbous moon, waxing moon, waning moon, terminator, libration, lunar month, lunar eclipse, Sister Moon, Selene, Diana, Cynthia **9 meteor**, shooting star, falling star, fireball, bolide, meteor shower, meteor swarm, radiant, meteorite, meteorite crater, meteoroid, micrometeorite **10 astronomical unit**, light-year, parsec **11 observatory**, astronomical observatory, ground-based observatory, optical observatory, infrared observatory, radio observatory, planetarium, planisphere, astrolable **12 telescope**, astronomical telescope, optical telescope, reflector, refractor, infrared telescope, solar telescope, heliostat, radio telescope, radio dish, antenna, receiver, array, radio interferometer, X-ray telescope **13 astronautics**, cosmonautics, space engineering, space research, space navigation, space exploration, space medicine **14 spacecraft**, space capsule, space probe, module, lunar module, space station, Mir, Salyut, Skylab, space shuttle, shuttle, Columbia, Challenger, Discovery, Atlantis, space laboratory, spacelab, space platform **15 space travel**, manned flight, spaceflight, space age, astronaut, cosmonaut, spaceman, spacewoman, weightlessness, free fall, microgravity, spacesuit, space helmet, spacewalk, space port, lunar base **16 satellite**, artificial satellite, earth satellite, unmanned satellite, sputnik, research satellite, space observatory, orbiting observatory, geophysical satellite, communications satellite, Telstar, geostationary orbit, geosynchronous orbit, weather satellite, navigational satellite, spy satellite, solar panel, telemetry **17 rocketry**, rocket propulsion, engine, booster, propellant, liquid fuel, solid fuel, burn, thrust, launch vehicle, launcher, multistage rocket, payload, retrorocket, escape velocity, orbit, perigee, apogee, parking orbit, transfer orbit, insertion, injection, trajectory, flyby, rendezvous, docking, re-entry, splashdown

ADJECTIVES 18 astronomical, astrophysical, cosmological, cosmic, celestial, heavenly, universal, galactic, intergalactic, extragalactic, interstellar, stellar, sidereal, starry, astral, star-studded, solar, heliacal, interplanetary, planetary, Mercurian, Venusian, Martian, Jovian, Saturnian, Neptunian, Uraniun, Plutonian, extraterrestrial, extramundane, terrestrial, telluric, tellurian, synodic, lunar, asteroidal, cometary, meteoric, heliocentric, geocentric, telescopic

VERBS 19 observe, orbit, revolve, rotate, eclipse, transit, radiate, shine, twinkle, emit **20 launch**, enter orbit

42 Atonement

NOUNS 1 atonement, making amends, satisfaction, expiation, reparation, rectification, redress, compensation, payment, indemnity, reimbursement, restitution, requital, recompense, redemption, making right, making good, quittance, squaring, blood money, wergild, propitiation, appeasement, conciliation, reconciliation **2 apology**, regrets, excuse, acknowledgment, repentance, remorse, confession, penitence, penance, contrition, breast-beating, offering, oblation, sacrifice, piaculum, mortification, flagellation, purification, purgation

ADJECTIVES 3 atoning, making amends, expiatory, reparatory, rectifying, redressing, compensatory, repaying, indemnificatory, restitutive, recompensing, righting, squaring, propitiatory, appeasing, satisfying, conciliatory, reconciliatory, pacifying, apologetic, sorry, regretting, penitent, repentant, contrite, lustral, purgative, cleansing, purifying, piacular, offering

VERBS 4 atone, satisfy, expiate, propitiate, appease, conciliate, reconcile, pacify, repair, rectify, redress, compensate, pay back, repay, indemnify, reimburse, requite, redeem, make right, make good **5 apologize**, express regret, beg pardon, beg forgiveness, confess, repent, pray, offer, sacrifice to, do penance, mortify oneself, flagellate oneself, purify oneself, fast **6 be punished**, receive absolution

43 Attack

VERBS 1 attack, engage, strike first, advance, march against, ride against, drive against, sail against, fly against, charge, rush, run at, dash at, gallop at, tilt at, go for, drive, thrust, push, raid, foray, strike, pound, assault, blitz, bombard, assail, harry, hunt, ram, collide with, ambush **2 fire**, level, aim, pop at, snipe at, pick off, shoot, let fly, volley, rattle, blast, bring down, torpedo, strafe, cannonade, shell, fusillade, pepper, rake, straddle **3 bomb**, blitz **4 besiege**, starve out, surround, enclose, encircle, encroach, infringe, blockade, hem in, beset, beleaguer **5 strike**, hit, go for, set on, pounce upon, fall upon, pitch into, sail into, lay into, tear into, lace into, round on, strike at, grapple with, close with, flail, hammer, punch, butt, push, kick, knock down, bring down, lay low, beat up, mug, go berserk, run amok, savage **6 stab**, lunge, thrust, pierce, cut, slash, knife, spear, lance, bayonet, impale, run through **7 stone**, lapidate, sling, pelt, shy, throw at **8 criticize**, censure, inveigh against, disparage, denigrate, malign, decry, denounce, condemn, slander, defame, libel, berate, vituperate, abuse, vilify, revile

NOUNS 9 attack, assault, aggression, aggressiveness, pugnacity, hostility, intimidation, harassment, belligerence, combativeness **10 military attack**, hostile attack, offensive, strike, onslaught, onset, charge, drive, push, thrust, rush, run, dead set, shock, surprise attack, raid, forray, find-and-destroy mission, shock tactics, blitzkrieg, pincer movement, enfilade, boarding, camisado, blitz, bombardment, barrage **11 air attack**, air strike, air raid, aerial bombardment, bombing, dive-bombing, missile strike, laser targeting, anti-aircraft fire, triple-A, ack-ack, tracer flare **12 siege**, blockade, encirclement, encroachment, infringement, inroad, investment, counterattack, counteroffensive, retaliation, rebellion, sally, sortie, break-out, breakthrough, storm, escalade, irruption, overstepping, overrunning, ingress, invasion, incursion, occupation, subjection, dragonnade, bloodbath, slaughter, devastation, laying waste, pillage, rape **13 firing**, shooting, musketry, gunnery, gunfire, broadside, volley, salvo, burst, spray, machine-gun fire, strafe, fusillade, sharpshooting **14 terrorist attack**, terror tactics, hostage taking, kidnapping, assassination, bombing, letter bombing, car bombing, guerrilla attack **15 personal attack**, physical violence, mugging, armed robbery, rape, indecent assault, foul play, injustice, verbal attack, criticism, censure, aspersion, disparagement, denigration, decrial, denunciation, slander, defamation, libel, calumny, abuse, vilification, revilement, slur **16 hit**, blow, punch, knock, swipe, kick, stab, jab, cut, thrust, lunge, foin, pass, passado, knifing, bayonetting, impalement, goring, stoning **17 bout**, spell, spasm, fit, seizure, paroxysm, match, contest

ADJECTIVES 18 aggressive, antagonistic, unfriendly, hostile, inimical, pugnacious, truculent, threatening, provocative, quarrelsome, contentious, disputatious **19 militant**, militaristic, martial, belligerent, combative, hawkish, warlike, sabre-rattling **20 attacking**, assaulting, invading, storming, charging, boarding, fighting, striking, harrying, kicking, punching, flailing, cutting, slashing, destructive, violent, bloodthirsty, savage, brutal, cruel, barbarous, bloody, uncontrollable, overpowering, overwhelming, frenzied, raging **21 critical**, censorious, disparaging, denigrating, maligning, decrying, denunciatory, defamatory, slanderous, libellous

44 Attempt

VERBS 1 attempt, try, essay, seek, aim, bid **2 try hard**, endeavour, struggle, strive, exert oneself, work, labour, pull hard, push hard, strain **3 tackle**, take on, undertake, tempt providence, tempt fate, venture **4 test**, experiment

NOUNS 5 attempt, try, essay, bid, move, step, gambit, endeavour, effort, struggle, strain, tackle, dead set, half-hearted attempt **6 venture**, adventure, quest, speculation, experiment, operation, exercise, undertaking, seeking, aim, goal, objective

ADJECTIVES 7 attempting, trying, essaying, seeking, striving, game, nothing daunted, daring, venturesome, ambitious **8 tentative**, experimental, trial, pilot, testing, searching, inquiring

45 Attention

NOUNS 1 attention, attentiveness, notice, regard, concern, consideration **2 close attention**, undivided attention, close observance, examination, watchfulness, alertness **3 carefulness**, meticulousness, fastidiousness, sedulousness, circumspection, scrutiny, surveillance, vigilance, wariness, heed, concentration, application **4 diligence**, studiousness, single-mindedness, fixation, pedantry, purism, obsession, preoccupation **5 solicitude**, care, consideration, protection, indulgence, attendance, courtesy

ADJECTIVES 6 watchful, alert, attentive, observant, sharp-eyed, vigilant, on guard, careful, wary, circumspect, scrutinizing, surveying, heedful **7 diligent**, studious, painstaking, meticulous, fastidious, sedulous, assiduous, undistracted, single-minded, rapt, engrossed, obsessed, fixated, pedantic, preoccupied **8 solicitous**, caring, concerned, protective, considerate, mindful, indulgent, attentive

VERBS 9 be attentive, regard, consider, notice, note, hover over, attend **10 take note of**, register, mark, watch, observe, examine, miss nothing, stay alert **11 scrutinize**, survey, heed, study **12 attract attention** be visible **13 be solicitous**, indulge, court, spoil, flirt, grovel, toady

46 Attraction

NOUNS 1 attraction, attractiveness, pull, draw, drag, tug, itch, desire, affinity **2 pulling power**, magnetism, gravity, centripetal force, capillarity, adhesion, cohesion, adduction, inducement, hypnotism **3 magnet**, electromagnet, solenoid, paramagnet, magnetic needle, lodestone, lodestar, polestar, magnetite **4 allurement**, allure, fascination, charm, charisma, seduction, seductiveness, temptation, appeal, enticement **5 lure**, bait, decoy, charm, siren **6 charmer**, temptress, seductress, seducer, enchantress, enchanter, vamp, ladies' man, Don Juan, Casanova, favourite, siren, sex symbol **7 centre of attraction**, focal point, cynosure

ADJECTIVES 8 attracting, pulling, drawing, dragging, tugging, adductive, associative **9 attractive**, seductive, enticing, tempting, charming, fascinating, captivating, charismatic, irresistable, alluring, fetching, appealing
VERBS 10 attract, pull, draw, adduct, drag, tug, draw towards, influence, persuade, magnetize, appeal, charm, move **11 lure**, allure, draw in, coax, bait, ensnare, seduce, decoy, lead on, tempt, entice, tantalize, fascinate, captivate, enthral

47 Authority

NOUNS 1 authority, power, control, command, leadership, direction, governance, domination, predominance, overbearance, dominance, ascendancy, hegemony, mastery, magistrality, superiority, supremacy, seniority, might, strength, potency, absolutism, legitimacy, legality, law, right, divine right, prerogative, regality, royalty, nobility, financial control, purse strings, hidden power, stringpulling, manipulation, influence, pressure **2 authoritativeness**, powerfulness, greatness, mightiness, masterfulness, lordliness, peremptoriness, imperativeness, imperiousness, majesty, self-assertion, confidence **3 permission**, authorization, sanction, justification, testimonial, declaration, evidence, permit, warrant, licence, visa, credential, reference **4 person of authority**, authority, leader, director, executive, manager, superior, head, chief, top man, patrician, ruler, autocrat, tyrant, dictator, despot, sovereign, monarch, king, queen
ADJECTIVES 5 authoritative, official, definitive, ex officio, powerful, empowered, regal, royal, noble, leading, ruling, reigning, authoritarian, dominant, predominant, overbearing, high-handed, masterful, domineering, condescending, patronizing, imperative, imperious, arrogant, coercive, lordly, superior, supreme, senior, mighty, strong, potent, legitimate, legal, lawful, rightful, influential, pre-eminent, peremptory, overruling, confident, self-assertive **6 elected**, selected, chosen, delegated, appointed, authorized **7 authorized**, sanctioned, accredited, approved, allowed, permitted, licenced, warranted, chartered **8 expert**, masterly, skilled, accomplished, professional
VERBS 9 have authority, control, command, lead, direct, rule, govern, preside over, legislate, administer, manage, hold sway, reign, predominate, keep order, police, pull strings, manipulate, influence **10 be authoritarian**, dominate, domineer, discipline, drill, subjugate, dictate to, tyrannize, oppress, play god **11 grant authority**, empower, elect, select, delegate, deputize, appoint, authorize, legitimatize, coronate, anoint, consecrate, allow, permit, approve, grant, sanction, declare, accredit, license, charter **12 be an authority on**, specialize in

48 Average

ADJECTIVES 1 average, usual, normal, par, typical, general, common, prevailing, current, popular, prevalent, predominant, sweeping, universal, generic, representative, characteristic, ordinary, everyday, familiar, household, routine, habitual, customary, accustomed, wonted, traditional, accepted, conventional, middlebrow, standard, stock, set, established, regular, classic, orthodox, normative **2 medium**, median, mesial, mean, average, middle, mid-, midmost, midway, intermediate, intermediary, balanced, halfway, fifty-fifty, central, middle-of-the-road **3 mediocre**, average, passable, fair, moderate, tolerable, adequate, not bad, alright, indifferent, lukewarm, unremarkable, undistinguished, unexceptional, unnoteworthy, unspectacular, commonplace, pedestrian, prosaic, second-class, second-best, second-division, second-rate, inferior, downmarket, banal, grey

NOUNS 4 average, norm, standard, par, rule, measure, criterion, yardstick, model, type, class, category, run, averageness, generality, commonness, prevalence, popularity, predominance, universality, ordinariness, familiarity, normality, conventionality, conformity, standardness, regularity, the usual **5 medium**, happy medium, average, mean, balance, middle, midpoint, median, halfway house, centre, midsection, middle ground, midterm, middle course, *via media*, moderation **6 mediocrity**, mediocreness, averageness, fairishness, passableness, tolerableness, adequacy, mixed blessing, half-measure, indifference, unremarkableness, second best, second division, beta minus, C grade, inferiority

VERBS 7 be average, prevail, predominate, suffice, be enough, get by, make do, be moderate, conform, go unnoticed **8 make average**, average out, normalize, generalize, conventionalize, standardize, equalize, equate, balance, symmetrize, regularize, proportion, smooth out, share out, distribute, allocate, divide, halve, bisect, go shares, go fifty-fifty

49 Aviation

NOUNS 1 aviation, flying, flight, gliding, piloting, pilotage, aerial reconnaissance, air transport, air travel, scheduled flight, air route, air corridor, air freight, air cargo, airlift, airdrop, paradrop, flying doctor, flying circus, aerobatics, crop dusting, skywriting, skyjack **2 aeronautics**, aeronautical engineering, avionics, aerothermodynamics, aeroballistics, aero-optics **3 aircraft personnel**, aviator, flyer, pilot, glider pilot, test pilot, aircrew, copilot, flight engineer, navigator, observer, pathfinder, steward, stewardess, air hostess, flight attendant, groundcrew, aircraftsman, ground engineer, air-traffic controller **4 airport**, airfield, airbase, air station, aerodrome, airstrip, landing strip, landing field, terminal, apron, hard standing, hangar, control tower, taxiway, runway, clearway, flight line, airside **5 flight**, takeoff, climb, flight level, flight formation, airspeed, groundspeed, heading, headwind, tailwind, terminal velocity, ceiling, aeropause, descent, approach, flare, glide path, landing, touchdown, belly landing, pancake landing, three-point landing, ground run, overflight, overshoot, undershoot, crash landing, manoeuvre, banking, barrel roll, buffeting, bunting, chandelle, crab, dive, crash-dive, flat spin, flutter, hunting, hedgehopping, low-level flying, Immelann turn, nose dive, pitching, rolling, stalling, shock stall, sideslip, skidding, snap roll, soaring, spin, spiral, turn, roll, vectoring, victory roll, wingover, whipstall, yawing **6 flight control**, ground control, air-traffic control, fly-by-light, fly-by-wire, landing beam, loran, navar, radar beacon, shortan, talk down, traffic pattern **7 aircraft**, heavier-than-air craft, airplane, aeroplane, airliner, glider, hang glider, rogallo, helicopter, lighter-than-air craft, balloon, hot-air balloon, helium balloon, dirigible

50 Avoidance

VERBS 1 avoid, bypass, circumvent, steer clear, keep clear, stand clear, stand back, hold off, shun, eschew, leave, let alone, stand aloof, stand apart, turn away, turn aside, ignore, cold-shoulder **2 avert**, prevent, foil, obstruct **3 abstain**, forswear, deny oneself, do without, pass up, refrain, forbear, spare, hold back, temper **4 shy**, shrink, flinch, blink, blench, fight shy, balk at, start aside, jib, refuse, back away, back off, draw back, retreat, hang back **5 shirk**, make excuses **6 evade**, dodge, duck, deflect, ward off, parry, escape, elude, skulk, cower, hide **7 be evasive**, sidestep, skirt round, talk round, equivocate, hedge, fence, fudge, prevaricate, procrastinate, delay, postpone, deny, disown, repress, suppress, ban **8 run away**, escape, desert, play truant, jump bail, abscond, elope, absent oneself, decamp, depart, leave, go, quit, withdraw, retire, retreat, make tracks, flee, fly, be off, make off, bolt, scoot, part company, break away, steal away **9 play truant**, truant

NOUNS 10 avoidance, bypassing, circumvention, averting, prevention, obstruction, hindrance, distance, wide berth, shunning, aloofness, cold shoulder **11 abstinence**, abstention, forswearing, self-denial, refraining, forbearance, temperance **12 shyness**, shrinking, unwillingness, reluctance, flinching, blinking, blenching, jibbing, refusal, revulsion, recoil, retreat, withdrawal, retirement, neutrality, noninvolvement, nonintervention, isolationism **13 shirking**, inaction, apathy, inactivity **14 evasion**, evasive action, dodge, duck, deflection, parry, defence mechanism, defensive reaction, escape, elusiveness, skulking, cowering, hide-and-seek **15 evasiveness**, sidestep, equivocation, prevarication, procrastination, delaying action, noncooperation, denial, repression **16 desertion**, truancy, French leave, elopement, absence

ADJECTIVES 17 avoiding, evasive, equivocal, elusive, slippery, untamed, wild, shy, flinching, blinking, blenching, shrinking, backward, reluctant, unwilling, noncooperative, noncommittal, unforthcoming, taciturn, passive, inert, inactive, not involved, apathetic, uncommitted, neutral, centrifugal, fugitive, escaped, runaway, hunted, hiding, skulking, cowering, hidden, latent, repressive, suppressive, preventive, censorial **18 abstaining**, abstinent, ascetic, dry, shunning, temperate **19 avoidable**, avertable, preventable, escapable, unsought, unattempted

51 Backward Motion

VERBS 1 go backward(s), regress, return, revert, relapse, backslide, slip back, lose ground, lapse, fall off, decline, recidivate, retrogress, retrograde, retroflex **2 retreat**, withdraw, retire, pull back, pull out, disengage, fall back, fall behind, draw back, back out, back down, give way, give ground, run away **3 reverse**, back, turn, backtrack, back up, back off, back pedal, back away, backtrail, countermarch, double back, ebb **4 slip back**, ebb, fall, drop **5 turn back**, double back, return, go back **6 shrink back**, avoid, shy away, shrink **7 recoil**, bounce back **8 look back**, hark back **9 turn round**, face about, about-turn, *volte-face*, turn tail, double, wheel, veer around, swivel

NOUNS 10 backward motion, going back, regression, regress, recession, reverse direction, backward step, retroflexion, retrocession, retrogression, retrogradation **11 retreat**, recess, withdrawal, retirement, fallback, pullout, pullback, disengagement **12 reversal**, reversing, inversion, backing, backing up, backup, regurgitation, voidance, re-entrance, reflux, refluence **13 about-turn**, U-turn, turnaround, swingaround **14 decline**, fall-off, ebb, falling away, drop, fall, slump, downturn, downward trend **15 looking back**, reminiscing, harking-back, reminiscence **16 countermotion**, countermovement **17 resilience**, reflex, elasticity, recoil **18 setback**, backset, throwback **19 backsliding**, lapse, relapse **20 return**, home-coming

ADJECTIVES 21 backward, retrograde, retrogressive **22 receding**, recessive, retreating, retractile, regressive, declining, ebbing, refluent, backsliding, lapsing **23 retroactive**, nostalgic, reactionary, backward-looking **24 reversed**, reverse, reversible, reflex, turned around, wrong-way round, counter, recoiling **25 resilient**, elastic **26 returning**, homing

52 Base

NOUNS 1 base, bottom, fundus, fundament, foundation, support, basis, root, footing, ground, earth, sea level, lowest point, lowest level, nadir, floor, bedrock, hardpan, rock bottom, river-bed, sea-bed, ocean-floor, substratum, underlayer, deck, paving, concrete

ADJECTIVES 2 base, ground, ground-level, supporting, underlying, basal, basilar, bottom, rock-bottom, bottommost, undermost, nethermost, lowest, basic, fundamental, essential, inherent, radical

VERBS 3 base, found, build, establish, anchor, fix, root, ground, underlie

53 Beautification

NOUNS 1 transfiguration, transformation, improvement, refurbishment, restoration **2 plastic surgery**, cosmetic surgery **3 beauty treatment**, facial, face pack, toilet, toilette, manicure **4 cosmetics**, make-up, paint, greasepaint, rouge, powder, eye make-up, blusher, lipstick, kohl, mascara, eye-liner, eye-shadow, nail polish **5 make-up box**, paint box, toilet bag, wash bag **6 toiletries**, perfume, scent, toilet water **7 hairdressing**, trichology, hair cutting, hair styling, hair colour, hair dyeing **8 hair cut**, coiffure, trim, style, hairstyle, crop, hair-do, perm, beehive, Eton crop, bob, ponytail, plait, braids, fringe, chignon, dread locks, frizz, Afro, wet-look, curls, quiff **9 shave**, depilation **10 wig**, false hair, toupé **11 hairdressing salon**, hairdressers **12 beauty parlour**, beauty shop **13 beautician**, beauty specialist, make-up artist, cosmetician, hairdresser, barber, trichologist, hairstylist, coiffeur, coiffeuse, manicurist

ADJECTIVES 14 beautified, decorated, adorned, embellished, embroidered, trimmed, tricked out, decked out

VERBS 15 beautify, prettily, glamorize, smarten up, spruce up, primp, prink **16 make up**, paint **17 crimp**, coif

54 Beauty

- *Exuberance is Beauty.* William Blake.
- *Beauty in distress is much the most affecting beauty.* Edmund Burke.
- *Beauty is altogether in the eye of the beholder.* Margaret Wolfe Hungerford.
- *A thing of beauty is a joy for ever* John Keats.
- *'Beauty is truth, truth beauty,' – that is all/ Ye know on earth, and all ye need to know.* John Keats.

NOUNS 1 gorgeousness, brightness, brilliance, beauteousness, pulchritude, radiance, magnificence, fairness, loveliness, comeliness, prettiness, attractiveness, beauty, pulchritude, agreeableness, good looks, handsomenesss, shapeliness, grace, gracefulness, refinement, elegance, chic, splendour, exquisiteness, nobility, appeal, charm, glamour, delicacy, harmony **2 beautiful thing**, ornament, adornment, decoration, masterpiece, *chef d'oeuvre*, cynosure

ADJECTIVES 3 beautiful, lovely, gorgeous, handsome, pretty, fine, good looking, attractive, fair, bright, comely, shapely, bonny, cute, sweet, winsome, exquisite, glamorous, pulchritudinous, gracile, well-built, manly, statuesque, Junoesque, aesthetically pleasing, tasteful, picturesque, scenic **4 personable**, appealing, enchanting, agreeable, charming, becoming presentable, trim, attractive, peachy, blooming, rosy

VERBS 5 be beautiful, shine, dazzle, glow **6 beautify**, adorn, prettify, decorate, bejewel, transform, transfigure

55 Beginning

- *The distance doesn't matter; it is only the first step that is difficult.* Marquise du Deffand.

NOUNS 1 beginning, start, commencement, opening, launch, onset, outset, outbreak, day one **2 creation**, genesis, origin, emergence, appearance, arrival, first beginnings, dawn, daybreak **3 source**, origin, provenance, fountainhead, wellspring, root, seed, bud, germ, embryo, egg, nucleus, primordial soup, protoplasm, nest, womb **4 conception**, pregnancy, birth, nativity, delivery, parturition **5 invention**, discovery, formation, creation, origin, conception, innovation **6 inauguration**, inception, inchoation, incipience, foundation, institution, establishment, setting up, installation, instigation, launch **7 rudiments**, basics, elements, first principles, preparation **8 enrolment**, investiture, induction, ordination, installation, initiation, christening **9 premiere**, first night, debut, coming out, curtain raiser, maiden speech, inaugural address, presentation, launch, flotation, opening ceremony, unveiling **10 introduction**, opening gambit, lead-in, prelude, preamble, exordium, preface, foreword, front matter, preliminaries, prelims, title page **11 starting point**, starting post, starting block, starting pistol, zero hour, blast-off, opening, initiative, kick-off, bully-off, jump-off **12 first move**, commencing move, first step, first base, first lap, first leg, first innings **13 new beginnings**, fresh start, new departure, new tack, fresh fields, pastures new, new leaf

VERBS 14 begin, start, commence, open, originate, initiate **15 make a beginning**, debut, embark on, go ahead, tackle, broach, face, kick off, bully off, tee off **16 start off**, start out, set off, sally forth, get moving, get underway, set sail **17 activate**, start up, turn on, switch on, prompt, provoke, spark off, trigger off, launch, kick-start **18 pioneer**, explore, guide, pilot, spearhead **19 invent**, discover, innovate, form, create, dream up, originate, generate, conceive, think of **20 inaugurate**, initiate, establish, found, institute, set up, start up, install, induct, instigate, cause, commission, launch, float **21 open**, unveil **22 enrol**, invest, crown, induct, ordain, install, institute, initiate, blood **23 produce**, give birth, bear, mother, father, sire, engender, pullulate, breed, teem, bud **24 emerge**, appear, arrive, originate, arise, issue forth, burst forth, erupt, spring, crop up, sprout, be born **25 begin again**, recommence

ADJECTIVES 26 beginning, starting, commencing, opening, first, primary, initial, initiatory, maiden, early **27 front**, frontal, leading, foremost **28 prime**, primal, primordial, primeval, primitive, aboriginal, earliest, original **29 embryonic**, budding, nascent, germinal, inchoate, developing, fetal, pregnant, gestatory, parturient, dawning, emergent, new, fresh, raw, newborn, baby, infant, unfledged **30 inventive**, innovative, creative, original **31 inaugural**, inauguratory, incipient, inchoative, foundational, institutionary, establishing **32 rudimentary**, rudimental, basic

56 Belief

NOUNS 1 belief, opinion, angle, viewpoint, standpoint, position, attitude, stance, impression, feeling, sentiment, intuition, thought, idea, notion, premise, principle, proposition, theory, hypothesis, judgment, conjecture, supposition, surmise, speculation, persuasion, conviction, certainty **2 religious belief**, religion, faith, persuasion, creed, credo, dogma, canon, principle, tenet, catechism, manifesto, doctrine, school, cult, philosophy, ideology, superstition, folklore, obi, obeah, pishogue, voodoo **3 believing**, faith, trust, confidence, assurance, reliance, dependence, credence, gullibility, blind faith, expectation, hope, acceptance **4 believability**, credibility, plausibility

VERBS 5 believe, credit, accept, trust, confide in, rely on, count on, bank on, swear by, know, maintain, hold, declare, affirm **6 be of the**

opinion, opine, presume, suppose, think, suspect, understand, imagine, fancy, deem **7 make someone believe**, assure, convince, persuade, influence, convert, win over, evangelize, proselytize, propagandize, indoctrinate, brainwash, deceive **8 be believed**, gain acceptance

ADJECTIVES 9 believing, assured, confident, convinced, sure, certain, positive, opinionated, dogmatic, trusting, unhesitating, unquestioning, undoubting, unsuspecting, faithful, conformist, orthodox, converted **10 gullible**, credulous, innocent, naive **11 believable**, credible, creditable, tenable, plausible, reasonable, realistic, possible, probable, likely, convincing, persuasive, impressive, commanding, reliable **12 believed**, undisputed, authoritative, accredited, doctrinal, creedal, received, accepted, putative, supposed

57 Benevolence

NOUNS 1 benevolence, kindness, kind-heartedness, goodness, niceness, goodwill, benignity, cordiality, geniality, affability, helpfulness, kindly disposition, openheartedness, amiability, good-naturedness, love, grace, forgiveness, compassion, tolerance, consideration, courteousness, attentiveness **2 charity**, hospitality, philanthropy, good works, generosity, bountifulness, liberality, patronage, magnanimity, altruism, unselfishness, big-heartedness **3 welfare**, welfare state, social services, social work, community service, health care, unemployment benefits **4 benevolent act**, kindness, good deed, favour, courtesy, service, benefit, charitable act, rescue, relief, loan

ADJECTIVES 5 benevolent, kind-hearted, warm-hearted, good, nice, benign, helpful, amiable, sociable, friendly, affectionate, loving, considerate, decent, thoughtful, attentive, solicitous, courteous, mindful, condolent, sympathetic, empathetic, good-natured, cordial, genial, affable, well-meaning, tolerant, compassionate, open-hearted, humane, forgiving, indulgent, soft-hearted, lax, lenient, obliging, accommodating, neighbourly, paternal **6 charitable**, beneficent, hospitable, philanthropic, Christian, generous, bountiful, magnanimous, altruistic, unselfish, big-hearted, open-handed, liberal

VERBS 7 be benevolent, be kind, treat well, love, show consideration, remember, understand, sympathize, empathize, comfort, relieve, mother, nurse, accommodate, indulge, tolerate, show mercy, forgive, reform, oblige, respect, wish well, support **8 be charitable**, give freely, aid, practise philanthropy

58 Birds

NOUNS 1 birds, birdlife, avifauna, wildfowl **2 flightless bird**, ratite, ostrich, rhea, cassowary, emu, kiwi, takahe **3 water bird**, seabird, gull, seagull, shag, tern, skua, puffin, auk, albatross, petrel, fulmar, shearwater, frigate bird, gannet, cormorant, pelican, kingfisher, diver, loon, grebe, wader, mud hen, plover, sandpiper, lapwing, curlew, snipe, avocet, oystercatcher, crane, rail, crake, coot, heron, bittern, stork, flamingo, spoonbill, ibis, waterfowl, duck, swan **4 table bird**, gamebird, game fowl, pheasant, partridge, grouse, quail, snipe, woodcock, guinea fowl, pigeon, turkey, chicken, capon **5 bird of prey**, raptor, falcon, hawk, eagle, osprey, kestrel, harrier, kite, vulture, condor, buzzard **6 songbird**, lark, wren, warbler, flycatcher, thrush, tit, shrike, wagtail, pipit, bunting, finch, weaverbird, sparrow, starling, oriole, crow, magpie, jackdaw, rook, raven **7 cagebird**, canary, songster, parrot, parakeet, budgerigar, mynah bird **8 extinct bird**, Archaeopteryx, Aepyornis, elephant bird, moa, dodo, great auk **9 fabulous bird**, phoenix, roc, garuda, senmurv, simurg, cockatrice, griffin, harpy **10 male bird**, cock, cockerel, chanticleer, rooster, tom turkey, peacock, drake, gander **11 female bird**, hen, pen, goose **12 young bird**, chick, poult, pullet, eaglet, owlet, cygnet, duckling, gosling, eyas, squab, nestling, fledgling, clutch, hatch **13 assemblage of birds**, flock, flight, gaggle [geese], skein [geese], covey [grouse, partridge], covert [coots], wing, charm

ADJECTIVES 14 avian, birdlike, birdy, struthious, goosy, anserine, anseriform, gallinaceous, rasorial, columbine, psittacine, hawkish, aquiline, vulturine, owlish, hirundine, passerine, oscine, fringilline, turdine **15 ornithological**, avicultural

VERBS 16 nest, nidify, brood, hatch, perch, peck **17 sing**, warble, chirp, chirrup, cheep, peep, tweet

59 Blackness

ADJECTIVES 1 black, sable, raven, ebon, ebony, jet, jet-black, pitch-black, inky, sooty, fuliginous, coal-black, sloe-black, blackish, nigrescent, blue-black, grey-black **2 dark**, deep, achromatic, dim, dingy, murky, smudgy, smoky, dusky, swarthy, pigmented, melanistic, dark-complexioned, Black, Negro **3 blackened**, singed, charred, tanned, suntanned **4 black-haired**, raven-haired, dark-haired, brunette, black-eyed **5 black-hearted**, evil, wicked, nefarious, heinous

NOUNS 6 blackness, inkiness, nigrescence, darkness, dark, night, dark colour, pigmentation, colour, depth, chiaroscuro, chequer, blackening, darkening, obscuration, Negroism, melanism

VERBS 7 blacken, black, blacklead, japan, niello, ink in, dirty, blot, smudge, smirch, sully, darken, deepen, singe, char, burn, tan, suntan, blackball

60 Blemish

NOUNS 1 spot, mark, scar, pockmark, welt, weal, flaw, defect, blot, imperfection, disfigurement, distortion, defect, stigma, smudge, smear, stain, blotch, tarnish **2 pimple**, spot, pustule, boil, swelling, carbuncle, bubo, blackhead, whitehead **3 blot on the landscape**, eyesore

ADJECTIVES 4 blemished, flawed, masked, defective, deformed, defaced, disfigured, imperfect, spoiled, soiled, shop-soiled, damaged, polluted **5 marked**, scarred, spotted, pitted, pock-marked, scabrous **6 seedy**, shabby, tatty, tacky, down-at-heel

VERBS 7 blemish, flaw, crack, disfigure, deface, distort, deform, spot, smudge, smear, stain, soil, impair, spoil, mutilate, pustulate, misshape

61 Blight

NOUNS 1 affliction, evil, harm, curse, plague, infestation, pestilence, distress, pest, scourge, ruin, malady, disease, visitation **2 adversity**, woe, grief, misery, sorrow, trouble, cross, trial, bugbear, bugaboo **3 burden**, imposition, charge, duty, white elephant **4 strain**, stress, fear, pressure, worry, anxiety, angst, torment, bitterness, sourness, acid, gall **5 pain**, hurt, agony, ache, pang, twinge, soreness **6 source of trouble**, Pandora's box, hornet's nest, pitfall, trap, bite, sting, serpent's tooth, thorn, briar, bur, barb, nettle **7 poisoning**, poisonousness, toxicity, venomousness, blood poisoning, toxaemia, salmonella, listeria, botulism, infection, contagion, virulence, germ, bacterium **8 poison**, toxin, venom, carcinogen, hemlock, arsenic, prussic acid, cyanide, strychnine, rat poison, ratsbane, warfarin, insecticide, rotenone, weedkiller, carbon monoxide **9 pollution**, pollutant, smoke, tar, smog, effluvium, mephitis, passive smoking, acid rain, sulphur dioxide, leaching, heavy-metal poisoning, greenhouse effect, carbon dioxide, ozone depletion, halon, contamination, dioxin, oxygen depletion **10 warfare**, chemical warfare, asphyxiant, tear gas, chlorine, lewisite, mustard gas, phosgene, nerve gas, germ warfare, anthrax, defoliant, Agent Orange, nuclear weapon, fallout, radioactivity, strontium-90 **11 intoxicant**, drug, narcotic, cannabis, marijuana, hashish, cocaine, heroin, opium, valium, tranquillizer, sleeping pill, sedative, nicotine, alcohol, caffeine, lethal dose

VERBS 12 afflict, harm, curse, strike down, plague, infest, visit, blight, blast, wither, shrivel, decay, rot, mildew, mould, rust, mar, burden, strain, worry, pressurize, torment, bite **13 poison**, intoxicate, drug, pollute, taint, contaminate, adulterate, infect, spoil

ADJECTIVES 14 blighting, rotting, decaying, mildewed, mouldy, baneful, pestilent, noisome, noxious, harmful, virulent, poisonous, venomous, toxic, malevolent

62 Blindness

• *Ask for this great deliverer now, and find him/ Eyeless in Gaza at the mill with slaves.* John Milton.

NOUNS 1 blindness, sightlessness, eyelessness, amaurosis, ablepsia, glaucoma, river blindness, onchocerciasis, trachoma, cataract, snow blindness **2 poor sight**, visual handicap, impaired vision, day blindness, hemeralopia, night blindness, nyctalopia, colour-blindness, daltonism, deuteranopia, tritanopia, amblyopia, sand-blindness, purblindness, long sight, hypermetropia, presbyopia, short sight, myopia, astigmatism, tunnel vision, detached retina, squint, strabismus, heterotropia, wandering eye, cast, walleye, exotropia, cross-eye, esotropia, nystigmus, winking, blinking, nictitation, eyestrain, double vision, diplopia, blurred vision, bleariness, bloodshot eyes, ophthalmia, retinopathy, conjunctivitis **3 aid for poor sight**, eye hospital, ophthalmology, eyewash, eye drops, optometry, optician, large-print book, spectacles, glasses, Braille, talking book, guide dog, white stick **4 visual distortion**, prism, refraction, reflection, optical illusion **5 blinder**, blindfold, blinkers, eyepatch, cover, cloak, screen, smokescreen, curtain, blind, eclipse

ADJECTIVES 6 blind, sightless, unseeing, eyeless, amaurotic, glaucomatous, registered blind, visionless, stone-blind **7 weak-sighted**, visually handicapped, visually impaired, partially sighted, one-eyed, day-blind, night-blind, colour-blind, red-blind, sand-blind, long-sighted, hypermetropic, presbyopic, short-sighted, myopic, astigmatic, squinting, strabismic, walleyed, cross-eyed, blinking, winking, nystigmatic, bleary, bleary-eyed, bloodshot, blurry, watery-eyed, red-eyed **8 blinded**, snow-blind, dazzled **9 blinding**, dazzling, stunning, darkening, obscuring, hiding, masking, deceptive **10 blind to**, imperceptive, unconcerned, thoughtless, inconsiderate, unobservant, unmindful, ignorant, unenlightened, blinkered, undiscerning **11 hidden**, dark, obscure, indistinct, camouflaged

VERBS 12 be blind, not see, go blind, black out, grope, squint, blink, wink **13 blind**, darken, obscure, blur, eclipse, dazzle, blindfold, blinker, camouflage, mask, screen, deceive **14 be blind to**, ignore, disregard, overlook

63 Blueness

ADJECTIVES 1 blue, sky blue, pale blue, powder blue, Cambridge blue, Wedgwood blue, grey-blue, saxe blue, slate blue, green-blue, duck-egg blue, eggshell blue, aquamarine, turquoise, peacock blue, kingfisher blue, cobalt blue, cyan, cerulean, sapphire, air-force blue, electric blue, ultramarine, royal blue, Oxford blue, midnight blue, navy blue, navy, French navy, perse, azure, indigo **2 bluish**, black-and-blue, livid, bruised, cyanotic, caesious **3 depressed**, dejected, downcast, despondent, blue, unhappy, sad, melancholy, glum **4 indecent**, smutty, risqué, bawdy, blue

NOUNS 5 blueness, azure, cyan, indigo, woad, bice, Prussian blue, Saxon blue, French blue, ultramarine, cobalt blue, cerulean blue, Antwerp blue, smalt

64 Bluntness

ADJECTIVES 1 blunt, blunted, unsharp, unwhetted, dull, worn, smooth, faired, stubby, snub, blunt-nosed, rounded, square, curving, flat, edgeless, unpointed, dull-edged **2 outspoken**, straightforward, frank, direct, plain-spoken, candid, curt, bluff **3 dull**, obtuse, insensitive, unperceptive, hebetudinous, dense, slow, numb **4 toothless**, edentate

NOUNS 5 bluntness, unsharpness, dullness, smoothness, flatness, stubbiness **6 outspokenness**, straightforwardness, frankness, directness, plain-spokenness, candidness, curtness, bluffness **7 dullness**, obtuseness, insensitivity, hebetude, impercipience **8 toothlessness**, toothless tiger

VERBS 9 blunt, dull, obtund, flatten, round

65 Boredom

• *Is not life a hundred times too short for*

us to bore ourselves? Friedrich Wilhelm Nietzsche.

NOUNS 1 boredom, tedium, tiresomeness, ennui, dullness, dreariness, weariness, fatigue, irksomeness, slowness, inactivity, languor, longueur, thumb-twiddling, devil's tattoo, dissatisfaction, dislike, flatness, tastelessness, insipidity, monotony, sameness, plainness, uniformity, humdrum, staleness, dryness, aridity, repetition, long-windedness, drawing out, prolixity, stodginess, stuffiness, heaviness, ponderousness, satiety, banality, triteness, prosaicness, prosiness, commonplaceness, indifference, sullenness, melancholy

ADJECTIVES 2 boring, tedious, tiresome, tiring, uninteresting, dull, dreary, drab, wearisome, wearing, irksome, slow, inactive, languorous, time-killing, thumb-twiddling, disliked, unenjoyable, repeated, repetitious, plain, flat, tasteless, insipid, cloying, satiating, too much, monotonous, uniform, unvarying, invariable, humdrum, pedestrian, suburban, prosaic, prosy, commonplace, stale, unfunny, humourless, soporific, sleep-inducing, unreadable, arid, dry, dry-as-dust, long-winded, drawn out, prolix, dragging, stodgy, banal, indifferent **3 bored**, tired, fatigued, drowsy, dreary, weary, world-weary, jaded, sated, satiated, dissatisfied

VERBS 4 be boring, be tedious, bore, pall, tire, dull, weary, fatigue, irk, dissatisfy, repeat, lack variation, drone on, never end, harp on, dwell upon, repeat oneself, drag, sate, satiate, jade, cloy

66 Borrowing

• *Neither a borrower nor a lender be;/ For loan oft loses both itself and friend,/ And borrowing dulls the edge of husbandry./* William Shakespeare.

NOUNS 1 borrowing, money-raising, fund-raising, advance, loan application, financing, mortgaging, pledging, pawning **2 adoption**, appropriation **3 illegal borrowing**, plagiarism, bootlegging, parodying, copying, piracy, imitating, fake, pastiche, stealing **4 credit**, credit card, charge card, phonecard, instalment **5 loan**, mortgage, overdraft, debt

VERBS 6 borrow, raise money, request credit, provide collateral, pledge, pawn, beg, scrounge, cadge **7 adopt**, appropriate, take on **8 borrow illegally**, plagiarize, bootleg, parody, sample, copy, imitate **9 buy on credit**, incur liabilities

ADJECTIVES 10 borrowed, loaned, mortgaged, secured, money-raising, repayable, outstanding, credit-card, instalment, pawned, adopted, appropriated, infringed, plagiarized, copied, pirated, imitated, fake, ersatz **11 adoptive**, appropriating

67 Breadth

ADJECTIVES 1 broad, wide, wide-set, splayed, patulous, transverse, extensive, expansive, roomy, ample, deep, widespread, wide-ranging, spread-out, beamy, broadcast, open, wide-open, full, wide-cut, flared, bell-bottomed, baggy, wide-angle, wide-screen, broad-gauge **2 broad-shaped**, broad-bottomed, broad-based, wide-bottomed, broad-beamed, wide-hipped, broad-tailed, wide-bodied, broad-brimmed, broad-leaved, broad-billed, wide-billed, broad-toothed, wide-mouthed, wide-eyed, broad-nosed, broad-backed, broad-shouldered, broad-chested **3 broad-minded**, open-minded, liberal, open, unprejudiced, unbiased, impartial, disinterested, unbigoted, free-thinking, free, direct, frank

NOUNS 4 breadth, broadness, width, wideness, span, wingspan, gauge, radius, diameter, bore, calibre, handbreadth, range, scope, beam, latitude, extent, catholicity, expanse, spaciousness, roominess, amplitude, bagginess, fullness, flare, splay, openness **5 broad-mindedness**, open-mindedness, liberality, openness, impartiality, free-thinker

68 Brittleness

ADJECTIVES 1 brittle, fragile, frangible, delicate, papery, wafer-thin, flimsy, frail, unsturdy, unsteady, insubstantial, shoddy, gimcrack, jerry-built, dilapidated, tumble-down, weak, vulnerable, breakable, bursting, explosive, crackable, chipping, shatterable, splitting, splintery, scissile, tearable, crushable, crumbly, short, friable, fissile, flaky, powdery, crispy, inelastic

NOUNS 2 brittleness, fragility, frangibility, delicacy, flimsiness, frailty, unsturdiness, weakness, vulnerability, breakableness, cracking, splitting, splintering, scission, crushability, crumbliness, deterioration, friability, fissility, flakiness, crispness

VERBS 3 be brittle, be fragile, deteriorate, wear thin, crash, give way, fall in, tumble, break, disintegrate, burst, explode, crack, fracture, shatter, snap off, split, splinter, chip, crush, crumble, flake

69 Brownness

ADJECTIVES 1 brown, oatmeal, beige, buff, fawn, biscuit, mushroom, café-au-lait, ecru, snuff-coloured, dun, khaki, hazel, walnut, amber, bronze, tawny, fulvous, sorrel, nutbrown, tan, foxy, bay, roan, chestnut, auburn, mahogany, copper, russet, rust-coloured, rubiginous, ferruginous, liver-coloured, maroon, puce, peat-brown, mocha, chocolate, coffee **2 browned**, bronzed, dark, brunette, tanned, suntanned, sunburnt, toasted, grilled

NOUNS 3 brownness, melanin, mole, freckle, suntan, sunburn, brunette, dark skin **4 brown pigment**, bistre, ochre, sepia, raw sienna, burnt sienna, raw umber, burnt umber, Vandyke brown

VERBS 5 brown, embrown, tan, suntan, bronze, sunburn, burn, singe, char

70 Burial

NOUNS 1 burial, interment, inhumation, entombment, sepulture, cremation, incineration, embalming, mummification, mummy-case, sarcophagus, pyre, funeral pile, crematorium, mortuary, morgue **2 funeral**, burial service, memorial service, requiem, obsequies, exequies, obituary, crematorium, mourning, keen, lamentation, wake, Irish wake, lying-in-state, cortege, dead march, knell, passing bell, muffled drum, last post, taps, eulogy, elegy, dirge **3 funeral director**, undertaker, pallbearer, gravedigger, sexton, priest, minister, mourner, weeper, keener, mute, embalmer, monument mason, eulogist, elegist, epitaphist, obituary writer **4 cemetery**, graveyard, churchyard, burial ground, plot, God's acre, catacomb, columbarium, cinerarium, necropolis **5 grave**, plague pit, tomb, mausoleum, vault, crypt, burial chamber, sepulchre, mummy chamber, pyramid, mastaba, pantheon, dakhma, fogou, narrow house, long home, barrow, mound, tumulus, earthwork, cromlech, dolmen, menhir, cairn, shrine, memorial **6 inquest**, autopsy, necropsy, post-mortem examination

VERBS 7 bury, inter, inhume, lay out, embalm, mummify, coffin, encoffin, entomb, ensepulchre, urn, cremate, incinerate, mourn, keen **8 exhume**, disinter, dig up, unearth

ADJECTIVES 9 buried, interred, inhumed, entombed, coffined, urned, cremated, embalmed, mummified **10 funeral**, burial, funerary, funebrial, funereal, sombre, black, dark, sad, mournful, lamenting, dirgelike, mortuary, cinerary, crematory, sepulchral, memorial, obsequial, eulogistic, elegiac, obituary, necrological, lapidary, epitaphic

71 Calculation

NOUNS 1 calculation, computation, numeration, enumeration, reckoning, figuring, determining, estimation, assessment, sums, addition, subtraction, multiplication, division, algebra, geometry, trigonometry, calculus, differentiation, integration, analysis, reduction, inversion, involution, evolution, convolution, approximation, interpolation, extrapolation, permutation, transformation, equation, algorithm **2 statistics**, figures, vital statistics, indexes, tables, averages **3 count**, tally, census, poll, head count, inventory, stocktaking, numbering, counting, accounting, telling, tallying, calculating, ciphering, reckoning, adding, totalling **4 computing**, computation, computer technology, information processing **5 computer**, calculator, pocket calculator, adding machine, cash register, till, abacus, ready reckoner, multiplication table, log table, ruler, slide rule, Napier's bones, tabulator, tape measure, yardstick, gauge, suan pan **6 calculator**, computer, counter, teller, enumerator, census-taker, pollster, reckoner, estimator, abacist, computer operator, computer programmer

VERBS 7 calculate, compute, work out, solve, cipher, reckon, figure, determine, estimate, tally, notch up, score **8 add**, add up, sum up, tot up, totalize, subtract, take away, deduct, multiply, divide, square, cube, extract roots, integrate, differentiate, extrapolate **9 total**, aggregate, amount to, come to, make **10 number**, numerate, enumerate, count, tell, tally, poll, count heads, take stock, inventory, list, quantify, quantize, measure **11 check**, verify

ADJECTIVES 12 calculative, computative, numerative, enumerative, estimative, calculating, computing, numerical, quantifying, statistical, actuarial **13 calculable**, computable, reckonable, estimable, countable, numerable, measurable, mensurable **14 mathematical**, arithmetical, logarithmic, algorithmic, trigonometrical, differential

72 Caprice

ADJECTIVES 1 capricious, arbitrary, erratic, fitful, uncertain, unpredictable, idiosyncratic, unexpected, volatile, mercurial, inconsistent, inconstant, variable, changeable, unstable, unreliable, fickle, feckless, irresponsible, flighty, flirtatious, coquettish, frivolous, skittish, giddy, featherbrained, light-minded, whimsical, fanciful, fantastic, eccentric, offbeat, freakish, quirky, humoursome, temperamental, moody, crotchety, irascible, fretful, weird, crazy, mischievous, prankish, wanton, motiveless, wayward, perverse, contrary, undisciplined, refractory, wilful, particular, faddy

NOUNS 2 caprice, capriciousness, arbitrariness, fitfulness, flightiness, uncertainty, unpredictability, inconsistency, inconstancy, changeableness, variability, instability, unreliability, fickleness, fecklessness, irresponsibility, coquettishness, flirtatiousness, frivolousness, giddiness, levity, light-mindedness, whimsicality, eccentricity, crankiness, freakishness, quirkiness, fretfulness, pettishness, irascibility, playfulness, mischief, waywardness, motivelessness, purposelessness **3 whim**, whimsy, idea, notion, passing fancy, impulse, flip-flop, vagary, outlandish notion, crotchet, maggot, humour, mood, temperament, fit, peculiarity, idiosyncrasy, quirk, kink, fad, craze, freak, escapade, boutade, wild-goose chase

VERBS 4 be capricious, flip-flop, vary, change, vacillate, fluctuate, trifle with, tease

73 Carefulness

NOUNS 1 carefulness, care, caution, attentiveness, attention, mindfulness, diligence, heed, assiduity, thoroughness, exactness, precision **2 consideration**, solicitude, compassion, mindfulness **3 circumspection**, watchfulness, alertness, vigilance, readiness, preparation, prudence **4 fastidiousness**, particularity, exactitude, perfectionism, orderliness, tidiness, neatness, perfection, niceness, pedantry, pernicketiness **5 watchfulness**, surveillance, vigilance, wariness, guarding, watching, watch, lookout, inspection, invigilation

ADJECTIVES 6 careful, attentive, mindful, diligent, heedful, assiduous, thorough, meticulous, circumspect, watchful, wide-awake, alert, vigilant, observant, guarding, watching, on-guard, ready, prepared, prudent, scrupulous, precise, painstaking, pedantic, perfectionist, fastidious, pernickety, faddy, particular, exact, orderly

VERBS 7 be careful, mind, heed, watch, prepare, be vigilant, be cautious, tread carefully **8 care for**, safeguard, survey, check, inspect, invigilate, watch over, attend to, chaperone

74 Cause

NOUNS 1 cause, causation, motivation, initiation, instigation, determinant, creation, authorship, attribution, origination, occasion, invention, derivation, production, propagation, cultivation, generation, evocation, provocation, compulsion, temptation, impulsion, stimulation, inspiration, fomentation, encouragement, force, spark, etiology **2 source**, spring, wellspring, mainspring, wellhead, fountainhead, fountain, fount, mine, quarry, home, birthplace, breeding ground, womb, fertile soil, hotbed, incubator, hatchery, cradle **3 rudiment**, principle, element, first step, hypothesis, raw material, germ, spore, seed, sperm, egg, embryo, larva, bud, stem, rootstock, root, radical, radix, etymon, base, foundation, bedrock, fundamentals, basics, building blocks, beginnings **4 contributing factor**, agent, leaven, stimulus, hidden cause, influence, astrological influence, destiny **5 reason**, idea behind, key, explanation, answer, basis, grounds, rationale, idea, occasion, motive, object, purpose, aim, opportunity, excuse **6 undertaking**, enterprise, attempt, action, case, subject, matter, topic, purpose, principle

VERBS 7 be the cause of, cause, create, originate, author, beget, propagate, father, make, produce, invent, derive, cultivate, generate, make happen, effect, lead to **8 awaken**, stimulate, tempt, excite, kindle, inspire, encourage, motivate, influence, impel, compel, force, make, foment, provoke, incite, set off, trigger off, spark off, evoke, bring out, draw out, induce, precipitate, hasten, elicit, plan, contrive, procure, engineer **9 inaugurate**, initiate, start, begin, launch, instigate, institute, found, erect, establish, open, broach **10 determine**, decide, contribute to, promote, advance

ADJECTIVES 11 causal, causative, etiological, explanatory, creative, inventive, original, aboriginal, primary, primal, primordial, primitive, basic, fundamental, intrinsic, foundational, elemental, ultimate, radical, effectual, pivotal, determinant, decisive, crucial, central, significant, productive, genetic, generative, germinal, seminal, embryonic, inceptive, rudimentary, formative, initiatory, suggestive, inspiring, influential, impelling, compelling, responsible

75 Caution

NOUNS 1 caution, cautiousness, carefulness, wariness, chariness, watchfulness, vigilance, alertness, heedfulness, heed, wisdom, prudence, circumspection, judiciousness, guardedness, scepticism, discretion, reticence, tentativeness, reluctance, slowness, hesitance, deliberation, careful consideration, second thoughts, doubt, suspicion, self-preservation, protection, providence, foresight **2 insurance**, insurance policy, nest egg, savings, warning

ADJECTIVES 3 cautious, careful, wary, chary, watchful, vigilant, alert, heedful, mindful, prudent, circumspect, sceptic, suspicious, doubtful, tentative, reluctant, slow, hesitant, nervous, experimental, gingerly, anticipatory, provident, thrifty, economical, frugal, canny, guarded, secretive, conservative, discreet, reticent, politic, judicious

VERBS 4 be cautious, take care, hold back, hang back, tread warily, hedge, play safe, take pains, make sure, look twice, beware, look out, anticipate, take precautions, cover oneself, hesitate, doubt **5 caution**, warn

76 Celebration

NOUNS 1 celebration, observance, festivities, fête, fiesta, festa, function, picnic, party, feast, banquet, beanfeast, rejoicing, revel, carousal, orgy, debauch, drinking bout, dithramb, *Oktoberfest*, Mardi Gras, saturnalia, performance, occasion, jubilation, jubilee, merrymaking, gaiety, jollity, conviviality, Whoopee, skylarking, jamboree, high jinks **2 commemoration**, memorialization, honouring, remembrance, observance, ceremonial, solemnization, jubilee, holiday, memorial service **3 ceremony**, function, ritual, service, office, solemn observance, rite, liturgy, ovation, coronation, triumph, barmitzvah, convocation, graduation, inauguration, initiation **4 reception**, hero's welcome, red-carpet treatment, reception committee **5 anniversary**, special day, great day, flag day, feast day, field day, saint's day, high day, Armistice Day, Remembrance Sunday, poppy day, D-Day, Thanksgiving, Independence Day, Republic Day, Bastille Day, VE Day, birthday, wedding anniversary, centenary **6 tribute**, testimonial, toast, health **7 thanksgiving**, harvest home, Te Deum, hosannah **8 salute**, salvo, fanfare, triumph, fly-past, march-past, drum roll, tattoo, flags, banners, tickertape, decorations, illuminations **9 rejoicing**, cheering, applause, ovation

ADJECTIVES 10 celebrative, celebratory, festive, merry, gay, convivial **11 commemorative**, ceremonial, solemn, memorial **12 ceremonial**, ritual, solemn, triumphal **13 congratulatory**, welcoming, complimentary **14 centennial**, bicentennial

VERBS 15 celebrate, rejoice, revel, merrymake, fête, party, junket, felicitate **16 commemorate**, honour, keep, mark, remember, memorialize, solemnize, observe, jubilate, hallow, perform **17 congratulate**, toast, drink to **18 salute**, welcome, cheer, applaud, fête, chair, lionize, garland **19 install**, enthrone, crown, inaugurate, launch, induct, initiate, instate, present **20 come out**, pass out

77 Celibacy

NOUNS 1 celibacy, unmarried condition, single state, bachelorhood, spinsterhood, independence, misogamy, misogyny **2 virginity**, chastity, continence, abstinence, self-denial, maidenhood **3 monasticism**, holy orders, reclusive life, solitary state, Encratism

ADJECTIVES 4 celibate, unmarried, single, spouseless, unpartnered, mateless, spinsterly, old-maidish, bachelorly, unwooed, unasked, unconsummated, independent, unattached, free, fancy-free, misogamic, misogynous **5 virginal**, continent, abstinent, chaste, pure, innocent, maidenly **6 monastic**, monachal, monkish, nunnish

VERBS 7 be celibate, practise celibacy, remain unmarried, stay single **8 be continent**, be chaste, abstain

78 Ceramics

NOUNS 1 ceramics, ceramic ware, sgraffito, pottery, whiteware, redware, stoneware, black stoneware, lustreware, agateware, basaltware, slipware, refractory ware, crackle, glazed ware, earthenware, ironstone, coarse pottery, ovenware, terracotta, clayware, faience, spongeware, crouch ware, porcelain, biscuit ware, enamelware, tin-enamelled ware, stanniferous ware, china, chinaware, crockery, bone china, glassware, Tiffany glass, bottle glass, lead crystal **2 raw material**, clay, argil, potter's earth, adobe, marl, kaolin, china clay, slip, engobe **3 glaze**, eggshell glaze, smear glaze, soft glaze, matt glaze, underglaze, overglaze, crackle, crazing, slip **4 ceramic object**, urn, vase, bowl, jar, amphora, jug, mug, vessel, ampulla, pipkin, cruse, crock, pot, pitcher, ewer, plate, cup, saucer, figurine, clock case, tile, mosaic **5 industrial ceramics**, porcelain insulation, electrical porcelain, brick, adobe, firebrick, cement, concrete, terracotta, quarry tile, roofing tile, floor tile, chemical porcelain, crystallized glass, devitrified glass, plate glass, safety glass, laminated glass, optical glass, photosensitive glass

ADJECTIVES 6 ceramic, enamelled, stanniferous, glazed, underglazed, overglazed, fired, encaustic, hand-painted, gilded, blunged, hand-turned, wedged, thrown, down-drawn

79 Certainty

ADJECTIVES 1 certain, known, factual, actual, historical, real, true, veracious, definite, sure, secure, absolute, given, verifiable, demonstrable, well-grounded, proved, documented, certified, ascertained, demonstrated, established, safe, self-evident, unmistakeable, ostensible, obvious, necessary, realistic, accurate **2 convinced**, certain, sure, positive, believing, accepting, trusting, unquestioning, undoubting, unswerving, unhesitating, undeviating, assured, satisfied, persuaded, confident, self-assured, self-confident, opinionated, cocksure, assertive, overconfident, doctrinaire, dogmatic, orthodox, narrow-minded, obstinate, stubborn, bigoted, biased, partisan **3 decided**, settled, fixed, established, undisputed, unrefuted, irrefutable, undeniable, uncontestable, unchallengeable, incontrovertible, indubitable, unimpeachable, unambiguous **4 guaranteed**, assured, insured, warranted, pledged **5 inevitable**, destined, predestined, determined, predetermined, fixed, set, fated, unstoppable, ineluctable, necessary, inescapable, unavoidable, inevasible, unpreventable, relentless, inflexible, inexorable, unyielding, directed **6 infallible**, reliable, dependable, trustworthy, predictable, regular, stable, solid, secure, unshakeable, unwavering, unchanging, undeviating, steady, steadfast, firm, sound, staunch, faithful, loyal **7 particular**, specific, definite, determined, stipulated, indicated, named, fixed, pinned down, distinct, singular, single **8 unspecified**, indeterminate, indefinite, unnamed, unmentioned, several

NOUNS 9 certainty, surety, knowledge, factuality, reality, actuality, historicity, truth, verity, veracity, absoluteness, definiteness, authoritativeness, indubitability, indisputability, validity, accuracy, evidence, proof, obviousness **10 conviction**, certainty, belief, acceptance, credence, trust, faith, assurance, sureness, positiveness, confidence, self-assurance, self-confidence, cocksureness, assertiveness, overconfidence, dogmatism, positivism, orthodoxy, narrow-mindedness, obstinacy, stubbornness, bigotry, bias, partisanship, fanaticism **11 something certain**, fact, foregone conclusion, winner, safe bet **12 confirmation**, assurance, verification, affirmation, demonstration, proof, ascertainment, establishment, evidence, grounds, facts **13 guarantee**, assurance, insurance, warrant, warranty, pledge **14 inevitability**, certainty, fate, destiny, fatefulness, predestination, determination, predetermination, ineluctability, necessity, unavoidability, inescapableness, inevasibleness, unpreventability, irrevocability, relentlessness, inexorability **15 infallibility**, reliability, dependability, trustworthiness, predictability, regularity, stability, solidity, security, steadiness, steadfastness, firmness, soundness, staunchness, fidelity, loyalty **16 particularity**, specification, definiteness, determination, stipulation, indication, fixing, pinning down, distinctness, singularity, the specific, the particular, quantity **17 indeterminacy**, inexactness, imprecision

VERBS 18 be certain, know, feel sure, believe, be convinced, accept, credit, rely on, depend on, assert oneself, pontificate **19 make certain**, make sure, ensure, confirm, verify, affirm, demonstrate, prove, ascertain, establish, determine, find out, settle, fix, pin down, clear up, check, decide, convince, evince, ground, guarantee, warrant, pledge, promise, authenticate, certify, endorse, substantiate, secure, stabilize, steady **20 specify**, particularize, define, determine, stipulate, indicate

80 Cessation

NOUNS 1 cessation, termination, ceasing, stopping, closing, desistance, discontinuance, relinquishment, withdrawal, abandonment, breakoff **2 stop**, dead stop, halt, holdup, standstill, deadlock, stalemate, draw, checkmate, defeat, failure, breakdown, closedown, stoppage, blockage, interruption, stay, check, hitch, hindrance, work stoppage, retirement, dismissal, strike, industrial action, walkout, lockout, permanent stoppage, end, finish, conclusion, hanging up, ringing off, breaking off, closure **3 pause**, break, lull, letup, respite, rest, sleep, nap, interruption, lacuna, gap, breathing space, interim, cooling-off period, interlude, interval, fermata, caesura, time off, day off, holiday, leisure, close season, delay, truce, moratorium, suspension, ceasefire **4 stopping place**, stop, bus stop, railway station, taxi rank, halt, petrol station, lay-by, harbour, terminal, terminus, airport **5 resting place**, bed, bedroom couch, hospital, nursing home, lodging, hotel, motel, billet

VERBS 6 cease, stop, halt, stop dead, stop short, brake, pull up, draw up, stall, stick, jam, discontinue, break down, quit, hold up, refrain from, desist, relinquish, give in, admit defeat, leave off, disappear, fade away, blow over, run down, peter out, let up, slacken off, tail off, die away, end, finish, conclude, terminate, break off, hang up, ring off, be quiet **7 stop working**, retire, resign, stand down, strike, walk out, close down, shut down, cease trading, wind up **8 cause to cease**, stay, freeze, cancel, call off, cut short, interrupt, catch, hinder, thwart, block, check, stem, arrest, restrain, hold up, stalemate, defeat, shut down, quieten down, close down, lock out, dismiss, lay off, make redundant, exhaust, use up, end, disconnect, break off **9 pause**, relax, rest, fall asleep, interrupt, suspend, stay, adjourn, recess, break, vacation, let up, cool off, hold up, hold back, hang fire, suspend hostilities

ADJECTIVES 10 finished, ended, stopped, over, complete, closed, in recess, adjourned, interrupted, pending, on hold

81 Chance

NOUNS 1 chance, randomness, unpredictability, fortuitousness, indeterminacy, uncertainty, unaccountability, inexplicability, casualness, coincidence, accident, contingency, hazard, risk, gamble **2 luck**, fortune, providence, lady luck, destiny, fate, lot, good fortune, ill fortune, fluke, lucky shot, chance hit, chance meeting **3 equal chance**, even chance, fifty-fifty, odds-on, toss-up, random sample, gambling, gaming, lottery, raffle, draw, bingo, lucky dip, tombola, sweepstake **4 fair chance**, sporting chance **5 good chance**, opportunity, occasion, good odds, long odds, odds on, probability, likelihood, small risk, safe bet, sure thing **6 poor chance**, long shot

ADJECTIVES 7 chance, random, unpredictable, unforeseeable, fortuitous, indeterminable, incalculable, uncertain, stochastic, aleatoric, haphazard, hit-or-miss, sink-or-swim, casual, aleatory, serendipitous, accidental, adventitious, contingent, unexpected, unforeseen, noncausal, epiphenomenal, incidental, coincidental, lucky, fortunate, unlucky, unfortunate **8 causeless**, groundless, unmotivated, undesigned, unplanned, unpremeditated, unmeant, unintended, unintentional, inadvertant

VERBS 9 chance, happen, occur, turn up, pop up, crop up, befall **10 chance upon**, encounter unexpectedly, run into, run across, come upon, light upon, hit upon, stumble upon **11 take a chance**, chance it, hazard, venture, gamble, speculate, bet, wager

82 Change

NOUNS 1 change, variation, mutability, alteration, difference, diversity, fluctuation, vicissitude, inconsistency, modification, adjustment, qualification, variegation, process, activation, fermentation, leavening, modulation, inflection, declension, deviation, diversion, detour, turn, U-turn, reversal, shift, eversion, inversion, relocation, passage, transference, transition, translation, interpretation, adaptation, transcription, sea change, revolution, revolt, coup, subversion, reformation, break, invention, innovation, diversification, modernization, renewal, redecoration, rearrangement, reorganization, restructuring, reordering, remoulding, reshaping, restyling, remodeling, revision, emendation, amendment, improvement, betterment, restoration, revival, repairing, amelioration, adulteration, dilution, distortion, deterioration, degeneration **2 change of mind**, conversion, tergiversation, desultoriness, vacillation, fickleness, capriciousness, whimsicality **3 transformation**, mutation, transmutation, transfiguration, transubstantiation, metamorphosis, transmogrification, metempsychosis, metabolism **4 exchange**, interchange, trade, substitution, commutability, permutation, transposition, alternation, replacement, barter

VERBS 5 be changed, become different, reform, adapt, vary, alter, modify, reorganize, modernize, diversify, adjust, fluctuate, turn, shift, divert, deviate, detour, relocate, turn back, reverse, revert, revolt, deteriorate, degenerate, improve, get better, better oneself, be converted, vacillate, tergiversate **6 cause change**, make different, convert, influence, cause, affect, alter, divert, diversify, reform, innovate, invent, modify, activate, ferment, qualify, modulate, commute, modernize, renew, remodel, reorganize, restructure, redecorate, rearrange, reorder, remould **7 transform**, transmute, transfigure, transubstantiate, transmogrify, mutate, metamorphose **8 exchange**, interchange, trade, substitute, commute, transpose, permute, alternate, replace, exchange goods, barter

ADJECTIVES 9 changeable, mutable, variable, alterable, different, diverse, fluctuating, vacillating, wavering, inconsistent, inconstant, shifty, shifting, kaleidoscopic, deviatory, turning, reverse, transitional, transitory, transient, revolutionary, subversive, reformative, inventive, innovative, ameliorative, better, worse, perverse, desultory, indecisive, fickle, capricious, whimsical, ever-changing **10 changed**, varied, altered, modified, qualified, diversified, modernized, renewed, redecorated, rearranged, reorganized, restructured, reordered, restyled, remodeled, reshaped, revised, emended, amended, improved, repaired, restored, revived, deteriorated **11 transformative**, mutative, transmutative, transubstantial, metamorphic, metamorphous, metabolic **12 exchangeable**, interchangeable, tradeable, substitutable, commutable, permutable

83 Changeableness

NOUNS 1 changeableness, mutability, mobility, flexibility, versatility, variety, iridescence, inconsistency, inconstancy, variability, irregularity, imbalance, disequilibrium, plasticity, pliancy, softness, suppleness, fluidity, flux, fluctuation, alternation, turning, veering, oscillation, uncertainty, unreliability, unpredictability, vicissitude, unsteadiness, instability, impermanence, transience **2 irresolution**, vacillation, uncertainty, tergiversation, wavering, hesitation, procrastination, fickleness, whim, whimsicality, moodiness, capriciousness, caprice, desultoriness, flightiness, light-mindedness, volatility, erraticism, restlessness, agitation, fitfulness, disquiet, inquietude, fidgeting, darting, shiftiness, equivocation, slipperiness, disloyalty, infidelity **3 changeable thing**, chameleon, kaleidoscope, shifting sands, mercury, quicksilver, weathercock, luck, chance, variable, random number, April shower

VERBS 4 be changeable, metamorphose, vary, fluctuate, alternate, oscillate, show variety, show phases, flash, flicker, twinkle, gutter, wave, flutter, whiffle, flap, falter, stagger, teeter, totter, sway, reel, rock, tremble, vibrate, shake, wobble, swing, shuttle, pitch, roll, yaw, tack, turn, veer **5 be irresolute**, tergiversate, vacillate, seesaw, waver, hesitate, hover, drift, float, dodge about, dart, flit

ADJECTIVES 6 changeable, mutable, alterable, mobile, versatile, varied, variegated, protean, kaleidoscopic, iridescent, inconsistent, inconstant, variable, irregular, imbalanced, plastic, pliant, soft, supple, flowing, melting, fluid, fluctuating, ever-changing, alternating, tidal, vibrating, oscillating, uncertain, unreliable, unpredictable, unstable, unsteady, floating, loose, unattached, labile, wobbly, rocky, shaky, swaying, tottering, teetering, unsettled, impermanent, transient, rootless, homeless, rambling, precarious, fitful, shifting, ephemeral, spasmodic, flickering **7 irresolute**, hesitating, vacillating, seesawing, fickle, whimsical, moody, wayward, capricious, desultory, malleable, impressionable, yielding, flighty, dizzy, giddy, scatterbrained, lightheaded, light-minded, volatile, mercurial, restless, fidgety, shifty, disloyal

84 Cheapness

NOUNS 1 cheapness, inexpensiveness, reasonableness, affordability, good value, easy terms, sale price, discount, cut price, rock-bottom price, peppercorn rent **2 declining prices**, price fall, bear market, bearishness, buyers' market, deflation, slump, plunge, recession, depression, devaluation, depreciation, Dutch auction, superfluity, redundance **3 shoddiness**, cheapness, gaudiness, second-ratedness, inferiority, baseness, lowness, poorness, shabbiness, scruffiness, pettiness, paltriness, pokiness, meanness, commonness, vulgarity **4 bargain**, good buy, special offer, loss leader, sale merchandise, seconds, rejects, second-class fare, off-peak fare, season ticket, bus pass **5 cheap item**, trifle, gewgaw, gimcrack, frippery, bauble, trinket, gaud, curio, knickknack, kickshaw, bagatelle, brummagem, toy, plaything, novelty, bric-a-brac, tat, junk, jumble **6 absence of charge**, free gift, freesheet, gratuitousness, gratuity, free board, grace-and-favour flat, free drink, free lunch, free postage, free admission, free seat, complimentary ticket, pass, free port, free delivery, voluntary work

ADJECTIVES 7 cheap, inexpensive, unexpensive, uncostly, reasonable, sensible, manageable, affordable, modest, moderate, down-market, bargain-basement, twopenny-halfpenny, good-value, low, underpriced, catchpenny, brummagem, going cheap, off-season, off-peak, excursion, economy-class, tourist-class, second-class, bucket-shop, concessional, nominal, budget, economy-size, bargain, discount, half-price, cut-price, markdown, knockdown, reduced, slashed, sacrificial, rock-bottom, giveaway, declining, falling, slumping, bearish, devalued, depreciated, superfluous **8 shoddy**, shabby, scruffy, base, low, mean, poor, paltry, poky, mangy, scummy, tacky, gaudy, tawdry, tatty, trashy, twopenny, second-rate, inferior, low quality, useless, unsaleable, unmarketable, valueless, worthless **9 free of charge**, free, scot-free, for free, for nothing, without charge, gratis, given free, giveaway, complimentary, courtesy, gratuitous, honorary, grace-and-favour, voluntary, unsalaried, unpaid, charity, eleemosynary, tax-free, zero-rated

VERBS 10 be cheap, go dirt-cheap, depreciate, decline, sag, fall, drift, slump, plunge **11 make cheap**, cheapen, devalue, trim, cut, mark down, slash, discount, sacrifice, undercut, undersell **12 buy cheaply**, economize, shop around, find bargains, buy wholesale, travel second-class

85 Cheerfulness

ADJECTIVES 1 cheerful, cheery, happy, glad, joyful, radiant, sunny, smiling, grinning, beaming, laughing, genial, good-natured, good-humoured, optimistic, sociable, light-hearted, exhilarated, merry, jolly, jovial, convivial, genial, gay, funny, buoyant, carefree, vivacious, lively, sparkling, high-spirited, bouncy, chirpy **2 cheering**, encouraging, heart-warming, reviving, uplifting, amusing

NOUNS 3 cheerfulness, cheeriness, happiness, joy, good spirits, sunniness, geniality, good humour, sociability, light-heartedness, exhilaration, optimism, jollity, joviality, conviviality, geniality, gaiety, levity, mirth, vivacity, jauntiness, liveliness, animation, high spirits, laughter, merriment

VERBS 4 bring cheer, gladden, cheer up, brighten, lighten, hearten, enliven, uplift, animate **5 be cheerful**, have fun, enjoy, smile, grin, beam, laugh **6 cheer**, whoop, shout, yell, applaud, clap, hurrah

86 Chemistry

NOUNS 1 chemistry, organic chemistry, inorganic chemistry, physical chemistry, theoretical chemistry, quantum chemistry, thermochemistry, analytical chemistry, analysis, synthesis, crystallography, photochemistry, radiochemistry, geochemistry, astrochemistry, polymer chemistry, metallurgy, industrial chemistry, chemical engineering, nuclear chemistry, zymurgy, zoochemy, chemurgy, iatrochemistry **2 crystal**, glass, microcrystal, crystallite, crystallization, crystal system, lattice, cubic crystal, tetragonal crystal, rhombic crystal, hexagonal crystal, crystallography **3 process**, precipitation, crystallization, filtration, separation, distillation, refluxing, chromatography, saponification, absorption **4 chemical element**, element, metal, heavy metal, nonmetal, semimetal, metalloid, noble gas, inert gas, rare gas, alkali metal, alkaline-earth element, chalconide, halogen, transition element, rare-earth element, lanthanoid, actinoid, transuranic element, superheavy element, coinage metal, platinum metal **5 chemical compound**, compound, organic compound, inorganic compound, organometallic compound, alloy, amalgam, ceramic, refractory, heterocyclic, homocyclic, aromatic, aliphatic, alicyclic, complex, coordination complex, ammine, chelate **6 acid**, mineral acid, organic acid, carboxylic acid, protonic acid, Lewis acid, sulphuric acid, hydrochloric acid **7 base**, alkali, Lewis base, caustic soda, caustic potash, ammonia **8 salt**, acid salt, basic salt, double salt, alum, hydrate, monohydrate, anhydride **9 chemical bond**, valence, valency, valence bond, ionic bond, electrovalent bond, covalent bond, coordinate bond, ligand, dative bond, donor, acceptor **10 structure**, formula, stereochemistry, isomerism, isomer, epimerism, epimer, anomerism, anomer, chirality, optical activity **11 chemical reaction**, process, reactant, product, reagent, equilibrium, fission reaction, heterolysis, ionization, homolysis, addition, condensation, substitution, elimination, displacement, disproportionation, rearrangement, cyclization, aromatization, polymerization, pyrolysis, neutralization, catalytic reaction, catalysis **12 polymer**, polymerization, macromolecule, polythene, polypropylene, polyester, nylon, polycarbonate, polyurethane, epoxide resin, polystyrene, expanded polystyrene, polymethylmethacrylate, vulcanite, isoprene rubber, chloroprene rubber, resin, plasticizer, stabilizer, plastic

VERBS 13 solidify, liquefy, vaporize, condense, melt, freeze, evaporate, concentrate, dilute, dissolve, saturate, supersaturate, precipitate, disperse, stabilize, destabilize, flocculate, gel, emulsify, separate, filter, distil, fractionate, refine, crystallize **14 react**, bond, ionize, heterolyse, neutralize, acifify, cyclize, pyrolyse, irradiate, polymerize, racemize, invert, catalyse, activate, acetylate, acylate, benzoylate, brominate, calcine, calcify, carbonate, carburize, chlorinate, deuterate, diazotize, esterify, ferment, fluormate, fluoridate, halogenate, hydrate, hydrogenate, hydrolyse, nitrate, oxidize, ozonize, reduce, saponify, solvate, sulphonate

ADJECTIVES 15 chemical, physiochemical, organic, inorganic, synthetic, crystallographic, catalytic, photochemical, radiochemical, biochemical, astrochemical, metallurgical **16 crystalline**, microcrystalline, crystallized, crystalloid, noncrystalline, amorphous **17 elemental**, metallic, metalloid, inert, transuranic **18 structural**, steric, isomeric, stereoisomeric, epimeric, anomeric, asymmetric, chiral **19 reactive**, unreactive, inactive, deactivated, passive, homolytic, heterolytic, additive, substitutional, cyclic, electrophilic, nucleophilic, polymeric, catalytic, synthetic, analytic

87 Circularity

NOUNS 1 circularity, roundness, orbicularity, sphericalness, curvedness, rotundity **2 circle**, full circle, circumference, ambit, curve, orb, sphere, cycle, orbit, epicycle, annulus, semicircle, oval, zodiac, mandala, circular path, circuit, annulation, loop, ring, roundabout, roundabout way, circuitous route, racecourse, detour, bypass, arc, round trip **3 circular thing**, headband, hairband, crown, coronet, collar, necklace, choker, belt, cummerbund, sash, girdle, bracelet, anklet, discus, plate, saucer, disc, ring, hoop, band, wheel, noose, wreath, equator, halo **4 parts of a circle**, centre, circumference, radius, diameter, quadrant, sextant, sector, segment, chord, crescent **5 circuit**, round, revolution, lap, beat, turn, tour, full circle, ring, ellipse, oval, circumference, cycle, orbit, ambit, round trip, roundabout, circling, wheeling, whirling, spinning, reeling **6 detour**, diversion, bypass, loop line, ring road, roundabout way, circuitous route, circumlocution, circumbendibus, digression, periphrasis, deviation, excursion, divagation, circumnavigation, circumambience, circummigration

ADJECTIVES 7 circular, annular, discoid, spherical, orbital, orbicular, spheric, spherelike, spheroidal, rounded, round, ring-shaped, semicircular, cyclic, elliptic, ovate, oval, ovoid, egg-shaped, rotund, circulatory **8 circular**, round, wheel-shaped, O-shaped, oval, egg-shaped, ovate, elliptical, orbital, rotary, spiral, helical, circulatory, circumambulatory, circumfluent **9 circuitous**, roundabout, deviating, digressive, periphrastic, discursive, excursive, indirect, circumlocutory, long-winded, devious, diffuse, oblique

VERBS 10 circle, encircle, surround, go round, circulate, circumambulate, circumnavigate, lap, orbit, revolve, rotate, detour, bypass **11 make circular**, circularize, make round, girdle, encompass, round **12 circuit**, circle, lap, loop, ring, edge round, circulate, go round, orbit, revolve, circumvent, circumambulate, circummigrate, circumnavigate, cycle **13 detour**, diverge, deviate, digress, bypass, avoid, short-circuit, divagate **14 encircle**, encompass, surround, skirt, flank

88 Circumstances

NOUNS 1 circumstances, conditions, situation, environment, surroundings, setting, milieu, background, the times, context, status quo, status, position, means, resources, state, posture, attitude, terms, footing, standing, contingency **2 occurrence**, event, episode, incident, case, happening, occasion, instance, juncture, stage, point, milestone, moment, opportunity **3 critical moment**, crossroads, turning point, match point **4 difficult circumstances**, awkward situation, trouble, catch-22, plight, dilemma, predicament, crisis, emergency, exigency, quandary, pretty pass, pinch, corner **5 comfortable circumstances**, comfort, ease, security, well-being, prosperity, success, luck, good fortune, halcyon days **6 aspect**, element, factor, fact, facet, datum, detail, minutia, incidental, item, particular

ADJECTIVES 7 circumstantial, relative, given, contingent, conditional, indirect, inferential, hearsay, conjectural, presumed, implied, provisional, adventitious, situational, surrounding, environmental, background, situated, placed, contextual, changeful, variable, transient, incidental, eventual **8 difficult**, awkward, critical, crucial, pivotal, decisive, troublesome **9 comfortable**, easy, secure, well, prosperous, lucky, opportune, suitable, auspicious **10 detailed**, meticulous, elaborate, minute, incidental, particular, full, precise, exact, specific, special, fussy

VERBS **11 circumstantiate**, itemize, specify, particularize, substantiate, detail, cite, instance, adduce, document, spell out

89 Cities and Towns

NOUNS **1 city**, municipality, metropolis, metropolitan area, megalopolis, conurbation, urban complex, urban spread, capital, town, community, village, hamlet, urbanization, gentrification, suburbanization **2 city district**, district, quarter, precinct, shopping precinct, ward, central city, city centre, inner city, high street, block, square, marketplace, market square, forum, plaza, shopping centre, shopping mall, business district, residential area, housing estate, ghetto, slum, no-go area **3 suburb**, suburbia, subtopia, outskirts, built-up area, green belt, dormitory suburb **4 town**, township, country town, market town, new town, county town, boom town **5 village**, rural village

ADJECTIVES **6 urban**, interurban, metropolitan, civic, municipal, citified, suburbanized, gentrified, no-go, red-light, suburban, subtopian, oppidan, parochial, countrified

VERBS **7 urbanize**, citify

90 Clarity

NOUNS **1 clarity**, clearness, lucidity, pellucidity, perspicuity, transparency, purity, limpidity, coherence, intelligibility, comprehensibility, plainness, simplicity, austerity, starkness, straightforwardness, directness, unambiguousness, explicitness, definition, definiteness, distinctness, obviousness

VERBS **2 clarify**, make clear, disambiguate, define, demonstrate, explicate, interpret, decipher, elucidate, illuminate

ADJECTIVES **3 clear**, lucid, pellucid, perspicuous, limpid, transparent, pure, coherent, intelligible, comprehensible, apodictic, plain, unadorned, simple, austere, stark, straightforward, direct, unambiguous, explicit, clear-cut, definite, distinct, obvious, exact

91 Class

• *The history of all hitherto existing society is the history of class struggles.* Karl Marx.

NOUNS **1 classification**, categorization, grouping, ranking, grading, ordering, hierarchy **2 class**, subclass, category, division, bracket, set, slot, niche, pigeonhole, compartment, pocket, section, group, grouping, head, heading, list, listing, order, branch **3 kingdom**, phylum, branch, class, order, family, genus, species, variety, sex **4 type**, sort, kind, genre, variety, version, style, ilk, strain, species, genus, league, realm, domain, sphere, brand, make, mark, marque, label, shape, cast, form, mould, frame, stripe, feather, line, grain, kidney, stamp, colour, complexion, hue, character, nature, manner **5 social class**, social status, standing, station, position, grade, rating, pecking order, rank, tier, level, stratum, band, league, order, sphere, caste, group, set, clique **6 distinc-**

tion, prestige, merit, excellence, presence, bearing, breeding

ADJECTIVES 7 classificatory, categorical, hierarchical, indexical **8 typical**, characteristic, representative, generic, stereotypical, special, specific, particular, peculiar, distinctive, defining **9 classed**, classified, categorized, grouped, ranked, graded, rated, sorted, ordered

VERBS 10 class, classify, categorize, group, type, place, pigeonhole, catalogue, designate, fix, assign, dispose, distribute, label **11 sort**, organize, assort, arrange, order, grade, rank, rate, divide, subdivide, analyse, tabulate, index **12 be in a class of one's own**, stand out

92 Cleanness

NOUNS 1 cleanness, immaculateness, spotlessness, freshness, dewiness, purity, whiteness, shine, polish, daintiness **2 cleaning**, spring-cleaning, clearing up, tidying, washing-up, wiping up, mopping up, scrubbing, dusting, sweeping, vacuuming, hoovering, polishing, washing, laundry, dry-cleaning, washing out, dialysis, cleansing, purification, purging, defecation, laxative, aperient, enema, freshening, ventilation, airing, deodorization, fumigation, desalination, decontamination, disinfestation, delousing, disinfection, sterilization, antisepsis, pasteurization, refining, distillation, clarification, filtration, hygiene, sanitation **3 religious cleansing**, purification, baptism, Asperges, lustration, purgation **4 censorship**, expurgation, bowdlerization, blue-pencilling, editing **5 ablutions**, washing, toilet, hygiene, lavage, bathing, dipping, rinsing, soaking, soaping, lathering **6 bath**, sauna, blanket bath, foot bath, shower, douche, hipbath, bidet, washbasin, washstand, bathroom, public baths, Turkish baths, thermae, sudatorium **7 washer**, washing machine, twin-tub, washer-drier, washtub, washboard, copper, boiler, launderette, dishwasher **8 laundry**, washing, dirty clothes, dirty dishes **9 cleaning agent**, purifier, antiseptic, disinfectant, carbolic acid, phenol, bleach

VERBS 10 clean, freshen up, disinfect, phenolate, carbolize, spring-clean, clear up, spruce up, groom, valet, neaten, tidy, trim, shave, wash, wipe, sponge, mop, swab, scrub, scour, dust, whisk, sweep, beat, vacuum, hoover, brush, comb, polish, shine, buff, black lead, whiten, bleach, launder, starch, iron, dry-clean, erase, strip, rake out, muck out, flush out, sandblast, holystone, scrape **11 bathe**, dip, dunk, rinse, soak, steep, soap, lather, shampoo, shower, douche, sluice **12 purify**, purge, censor, expurgate, bowdlerize, blue-pencil, edit out, sublimate, elevate, cleanse, wash, lustrate, freshen, ventilate, air, fan, deodorize, fumigate, edulcorate, desalt, decontaminate, disinfect, sterilize, antisepticize, chlorinate, pasteurize, sanitize, refine, distil, clarify, rack, skim, scum, despumate, decarbonize, elutriate, decant, strain, filter, percolate, lixivate, leach, sift, sieve, weed out, flush out

ADJECTIVES 13 clean, unsoiled, unsullied, undefiled, virginal, untainted, unmuddied, untarnished, unstained, immaculate, spotless, stainless, blank, perfect, dainty, nice, fastidious, fresh, dewy, pure, unmixed, unadulterated, unpolluted, uncontaminated, hygienic, sanitary, sterile, aseptic, antiseptic, salubrious, spruce, dapper, well-groomed, neat, tidy, spick-and-span, orderly, bright, shining, white, snowy, kosher, ritually clean **14 cleaned**, freshened, disinfected, trimmed, shaven, washed, scrubbed, scoured, swept, brushed, polished, whitened, bleached, laundered, starched, ironed, cleansed, purified, purged, expurgated, decontaminated, sterilized, pasteurized, refined, distilled **15 cleansing**, lustral, purificatory, disinfectant, hygienic, sanitary, purgative, purgatory, cleaning, detergent, abstergent

93 Closure

NOUNS 1 closure, shutdown, finish, cessation, discontinuance, stop, conclusion, resolution, fulfillment, completion, termination, end, foreclosure, imperviousness, impermeability, impenetrability, impassability, obstruction, occlusion, contraction, constriction, congestion, strangulation, blockage, blockade, bar, hindrance, let, impasse **2 stopper**, stop, cap, lid, top, cork, covering, cover, seal, plug, bandage, tourniquet, bung, peg, pin, spigot, valve, tap, faucet, wadding, stuffing, tampion, wedge, blood clot, tampon, damper, choke, trip switch **3 restrainer**, lock, padlock, latch, bolt, bar, clamp, clasp, hasp, catch, straitjacket, handcuffs, chain, rope, leash, lead **4 closed place**, dead end, cul-de-sac, blind alley, road block, enclosure, courtyard, quadrangle, reserve, sanctuary, zoo, walled garden, pen, hutch, cage, kennel, coop, pigsty, corral, paddock, fold, ghetto, grave, tomb, sepulchre, trap, prison, jail, dungeon, cell, oubliette

VERBS 5 close, shut, seal, fasten, secure, lock, bolt, bar, latch, padlock, do up, button, zip up, seal off, cover **6 stop**, plug, cap, top, cork, dam, staunch, bandage, bar, stay, block up, clog, bung, obstruct, occlude, constipate, contract, constrict, congest, strangle, throttle, choke, blockade **7 close down**, shut down, finish, cease, discontinue, terminate, end, foreclose, conclude, resolve, fulfill, complete **8 enclose**, confine, keep in, lock up, shut up, imprison, jail, cage, impound, pen, corral, intern, immure, incarcerate, bury **9 restrain**, handcuff, chain, shackle, rope, bind, tie, leash

ADJECTIVES 10 closed, unopened, shut, locked, bolted, barred, latched, padlocked, burglar-proof, fastened, secured, buttoned up, zipped up, sealed, hermetically sealed, vacuum-packed, airtight, watertight, waterproof, lightproof, nonporous, impermeable **11 stopped**, plugged, capped, corked, dammed, staunched, bandaged, blocked, obstructed, occluded, blocked up, clogged, clogged up, impenetrable, impassable, bunged up, stuffed up, constipated, costive, constricted, congested, choked up, full, stuffed, packed **12 closed down**, shut down, wound up, finished, resolved, completed **13 enclosed**, closed in, shut up

94 Cold

NOUNS 1 coldness, chill, coolness, low temperature, freshness **2 freez-**

ing, frost, freezing cold, iciness, frigidity, gelidity, algidity, sub-zero temperature **3 chill**, common cold, pneumonia, coryza, hypothermia, exposure, chilblain **4 cooler**, chiller, air-conditioning, ventilator, fan, punkah, cooling tower, refrigerator, fridge, cool box, ice bucket, ice pack, chilled counter, chill cupboard, freezer, deep-freeze, fridge-freezer, refrigerant, coolant, liquid oxygen, lox, cryogenics, cryonics, cryostat **5 ice**, ice cube, cracked ice, frosting, glaze, dry ice, glacier, pack ice, ice cap, ice floe, frost, rime, freeze-up, Jack Frost, black ice, icicle, sleet, snow, blizzard, snowflake, slush, snowball, snowdrift, avalanche, hailstone, snowman **6 Arctic**, North Pole, Antarctic, South Pole, Siberia, Arctic Circle, permafrost, snowline, snow house, igloo, Eskimo, iceberg, frigidarium **7 cold weather**, nippiness, inclemency, wind-chill factor, North Wind, Boreas, ice age

ADJECTIVES 8 cold, fresh, bracing, nippy, sharp, inclement, parky, breezy, invigorating, raw, chill, cool, shivery, pinched, biting, bitter, bleak, wintry, severe, snowy, sleety, frosty, icy, snow-bound, iced up, perishing, ice-cold, algid, glacial, frigid, freezing, frozen, gelid, polar, Arctic, Siberian, frostbitten, frozen solid, frosted, hoar, frappé, iced, glazed **9 heat-resistant**, heat-proof, insulated, air-conditioned, air-cooled, water-cooled, cooling, chilling, refrigerant, frigorific, freezable, freezing, refrigerated, unmelted, quick-frozen

VERBS 10 be cold, shiver, tremble, shudder, perish, quiver, freeze, have gooseflesh **11 become cold**, cool down, lose heat, freeze, congeal, ice up **12 make cold**, chill, freshen, sharpen, air-condition, ventilate, fan, benumb, freeze, refrigerate

95 Combatant

NOUNS 1 combatant, fighter, battler, struggler, contender, adversary, opponent, agonist, aggressor, assailant, assaulter, attacker, besieger, stormer, escalader, soldier, belligerent, militarist, man-at-arms, storm trooper, warrior, brave, dueller, swordsman, knight, paladin, gunman, strong-arm man, assassin, bully, skinhead, thug, rough, tough, bravo, phansigar **2 militarist**, warmonger, militant, hardliner, jingoist, chauvinist, imperialist, expansionist, crusader, conqueror, conquistador, samurai, mercenary, condottiere, privateer, pirate, buccaneer, freebooter, marauder, raider

ADJECTIVES 3 combative, aggressive, hostile, adversarial, opposing, inimical, agonistic, antagonistic, bellicose, belligerent, pugnacious, militant, militaristic, warlike, expansionistic, imperialistic, jingoistic, chauvinistic, hardline, crusading, buccaneering, piratical, bloodthirsty, rowdy, rough, tough **4 argumentative**, quarrelsome, litigious, controversial, trouble-making **5 martial**, naval, gladiatorial, pugilistic, mercenary, auxiliary, soldierly, brave, heroic, armed, enlisted, drafted

VERBS 6 combat, make trouble, rabble-rouse, warmonger, crusade, declare war, attack, assault, assail, storm **7 fight**, shoot, fire, gun down, bomb, blast, plant mines, charge, strike, spear, lance, joust, tilt, fence, spar, box, punch, hit, wrestle **8 conquer**, win, subdue, quell, overcome, storm, take over, invade, maraud, raid, plunder, rob, kill, assassinate, massacre **9 defend**, protect, police, guard, resist, oppose, picket **10 argue**, contend, dispute, debate, disagree

96 Combination

NOUNS 1 combination, joining together, symphysis, symbiosis, composition, synthesis, fusion, coalescence, conflation, blending, mingling, mixing, syncretism, amalgamation, merger, unification, assimilation, absorption, digestion, integration, embodiment, incorporation, centralization, coincidence, concurrence, conjunction **2 cooperation**, collaboration, concurrence, conjunction, synchronization, coagency, union, alliance, league, marriage, federation, confederation, association, plot, conspiracy, cabal, agreement, unity, concord, harmony, chord, counterpoint, orchestration, jigsaw, mosaic, tessellation, collage **3 assembly**, collection, set, compendium, anthology, aggregation, agglomeration, conglomeration, combine, syndicate, consortium, bloc, corporation, company, society, association, club, party, force, army, regiment, squadron, wing, flotilla, fleet, team, group, grouping, pressure group, rock group, band, orchestra, duo, duet, trio, string quartet, chorus, choir, congregation **4 compound**, mixture, suspension, solution, blend, alloy, amalgam, composite, make-up, hybrid

VERBS 5 combine, join together, unite, assemble, make up, compose, synthesize, integrate, fuse, merge, coalesce, consolidate, converge, blend, mingle, mix, syncretize, dilute, hydrate, interweave, intertwine, network, connect, conjoin, link, conjugate, yoke, centralize, unify, incorporate, embody, impregnate, imbue, infuse, instil, inoculate, inculcate, absorb, digest, assimilate, soak up, amalgamate, pool, collect, aggregate, congregate, compound, lump together **6 come together**, brigade, associate, partner, federate, confederate, join hands, cooperate, agree, concur, ally, collaborate, harmonize, synchronize, fraternize, bond, marry, mate, couple, copulate

ADJECTIVES 7 combined, integrated, fused, composed, blended, mingled, mixed, syncretic, harmonized, interwoven, intertwined, networked, connected, joined, conjugate, yoked, linked, united, unified, centralized, incorporated, embodied, inbred, ingrained, impregnated, absorbed, digested, coalescent **8 cooperative**, symbiotic, in agreement, in harmony, associated, orchestrated, leagued, in league, conspiratorial, cabbalistic, allied, federated, confederate, coagent, concurrent, synchronized, coincident **9 assembled**, collected, heaped up, congregated, aggregated, amalgamated, merged, collective, conglomerate

97 Command

NOUNS 1 command, order, instruction, direction, ruling, rule, regulation, directive, word, sign, signal, law, act, enactment, legislation, manifesto, prescription, precept, charge, behest, dictate, ordinance, edict, fiat, canon, bull, encyclical, decree, ukase, prescript, marching orders, statement, pronouncement, proclamation, declaration, dictum, invitation, royal command, prohibition, proscription, countermand, counterorder, interdict, veto, ban **2 demand**, claim, requisition, final warning, ultimatum, legal order, tax demand, levy, warrant, mittimus, writ, process, summons, subpoena, citation, habeas corpus, injunction, interdict, bidding, threat, extortion **3 authority**, rule, control, government, power, sway, mastery, sovereignty, suzerainty, dominion **4 authorization**, commission, charge, written authority, permit, letters patent, patronage, appointment, mandate **5 self-assurance**, self-confidence, presence **6 overview**, survey, ball-park view **7 vantage point**, observation post, watchtower, crow's nest

VERBS 8 command, order, direct, instruct, rule, regulate, signal, enact, legislate, make law, promulgate, prescribe, charge, call upon, dictate, decree, pronounce, pontificate, proclaim, declare, say so, invite, prohibit, proscribe, countermand, counterorder, interdict, veto, ban **9 demand**, ask for, call for, insist on, lay upon, require, impose, make obligatory, claim, requisition, order up, indent, levy, exact, warrant, subpoena, interdict, threaten, extort **10 have authority over**, rule, control, compel, impose, govern, dominate, dictate to **11 authorize**, commission, charge, permit

ADJECTIVES 12 commanding, ordering, imperative, directive, compelling, ruling, regulatory, enacted, legislative, prescriptive, encyclical, papal, pontifical, authoritative, governmental, mandatory, obligatory, compulsory, dictatorial, prohibitive, proscriptive, injunctive, countermanded, interdicted, vetoed, banned **13 self-assured**, self-confident, controlling, domineering, superior, lordly, powerful, autocratic, imperious, high-handed, authorized, commissioned

98 Commission

NOUNS 1 commision, delegation, devolution, decentralization, representation, deputation, empowerment, federation, power, entrustment, responsibility, assignment, appointment, patronage, accreditation, nomination, election, voting, ordination, installation, instatement, induction, inauguration, investiture, enthronement **2 engagement**, employment, enlistment, enrollment, conscription, recruitment, mission, errand, task, duty, job, office, activity, exercise, undertaking, function **3 authority**, authorization, permission, warranty, warrant, charge, mandate, trust, permit, charter, writ, licence, brevet, diploma, proxy **4 council**, board, deputation, party, group, delegation, committee, crew, establishment, agency, trusteeship, executorship, bureaucracy, public service, civil service, mission, embassy, legation, envoy, governorship

VERBS 5 commission, delegate, devolve, decentralize, name, assign, accredit, deputize, empower, entrust, patronize, consign, give responsibility, give to, nominate, elect, vote, ordain, install, instate, induct, inaugurate, invest, enthrone, crown **6 engage**, employ, hire, enlist, enrol, conscript, recruit, post, quest after **7 authorize**, permit, warrant, charge, mandate, charter

ADJECTIVES 8 commissioned, delegating, devolutionary, decentralized, representational, deputized, empowered, inaugural, responsible, assigned, appointed, accredited, nominated, authorized, vicarious, warranted, mandated, plenipotentiary, bureaucratic, ambassadorial, legationary, gubernatorial, offical **9 engaged**, employed, functional

99 Commoner

NOUNS 1 plebeian, man-in-the-street, regular guy, prole, proletarian, everyman, underling, Mr Nobody, common man, little man, bourgeois, yokel, peasant, rustic, country bumpkin, country cousin, hillbilly, serf, villein, husband man **2 the common people**, the commons, commonathy, the people, the masses, proletariat, plebeians, plebs, hoi-polloi, grassroots, lower orders, second-class citizens, working-classes, bourgeoisie, vulgar herd

ADJECTIVES 3 common, plebeian, provincial, titleless, low-down, second-class, low-born, low-caste **4 common**, parvenu, vulgar, uncultured, primitive, wild

100 Communications

NOUNS 1 communications, speech, talking, writing, correspondence, telecommunications, signalling, broadcasting, mass communication, mass media, radio, television **2 postal communication**, postal service, post office, sorting office, dead-letter office, returned-letter office, letter post, inland post, international mail, overseas mail, air mail, surface mail, special delivery, sea mail, parcel post, registered mail, recorded delivery, express delivery, metered mail, forwarded mail **3 correspondence**, mail, post, letter, aerogram **4 correspondent**, letter writer **5 telecommunication**, transmission, propagation, telephony, radiotelephony, computer networking, telegraphy, radiotelegraphy, teleinformatics, communications system, network, communications channel, transmission line, cable, coaxial cable, multiwire cable, fibre cable, fibre-optic cable, satellite communication, communications satellite **6 data transmission**, telegraph, radiotelegraph, Morse code, heliograph, telegram, cablegram, cable, wire, telex, telex machine, teleprinter, facsimile transmission, fax, fax machine, electronic mail, email **7 telephone**, phone, intercom, answering machine, radiophone, videophone, cellular phone, public telephone, payphone **8 telephone call**, phone call **9 public telephone system**, public telephone, telephoneline, telephone wire, telephone pole, telegraph pole, telephone exchange, trunk exchange, automatic exchange **10 radio transmission**, radio wave, microwaves, frequency band, waveband, radio signal, pulsed signal, radio link, microwave link, radio channel, modulation, carrier, demodulation, sideband **11 transmitter**, radio transmitter, radio microphone, radio phone, mobile phone, car phone, cellular phone **12 radio**, receiver, amplifier, booster, loudspeaker, speaker, tuner, wireless, radio set, crystal set, cat's whisker, walkie-talkie, radiopager, pager, bleep, transistor radio **13 television** (TV), black-and-white television, monochrome television, colour television, small screen, cable television, pay television, satellite television, television tube, tube, cathode-ray tube, video signal, audio signal, sequential scanning, interlaced scanning, line, field, frame, frame frequency **14 television set**, receiver, screen **15 broadcast material**, transmission, telecast, simulcast, relay, recording, repeat, rerun, audience participation, phone-in, news, live coverage, commercial break, commercial, teletext **16 recording**, audio cassette, tape, video, video cassette, video tape **17 signalling**, signal, semaphore, flag signals, Morse code, railway signals, smoke signals, radio signalling, radio navigation, radiobeacon, navigational beacon, radio marker, radio compass, radiogoniometer, radio bearing **18 radar**, pulse radar, radar station, radar beacon, racon, radar antenna, radar dish, radar beam, target, return signal, echo, radarscope, weather radar, radar navigation, radar guidance, radar tracking

VERBS 19 communicate, make contact, signal, transmit, link up, relay, propagate, amplify, radio, page, bleep, broadcast, announce, inform, televise, telecast, advertise, receive, tune in, listen in, watch, record, tape **20 correspond**, exchange letters, answer, acknowledge, mail, post, airmail, forward, dispatch, telegraph, cable, wire, telex **21 telephone**, phone

ADJECTIVES 22 communicational, transmissional, oral, verbal, epistolary, postal, telecommunicational, telephonic, telegraphic, transmitted, relayed, propagated, amplified, modulated, demodulated, broadcast, announced, advertised, radioed, televised, repeated, received, read, seen, heard, transcribed, recorded

101 Compensation

NOUNS 1 compensation, recompense, amends, amendment, reparation, indemnity, distraint, damages, replevin, reimbursement, refund, repayment, reward, remuneration, remittance, costs, money back, pay-off, golden handshake, golden parachute, redundancy money, settlement, redemption, requital, replacement, restoration, restitution, recoupment, redeemability, recovery, retrieval, rectification, redress, remedy, satisfaction, propitiation, expiation, atonement, penance, penalty, ransom **2 counterbalance**, compensation, setoff, offset, balance, counterweight, ballast, counterpoise, equilibrium, equalization, equiponderance, correction, attunement, adjustment, readjustment, allowance, countermeasure, contraposition, counteraction, neutralization, cancellation, nullification, deactivation, antidote, reprisal, atonement, retaliation, revenge **3 compensator**, amender, indemnifier, remitter, rewarder, requiter, restorer, satisfier

VERBS 4 compensate, recompense, make amends, indemnify, replevy, reimburse, refund, repay, pay off, reward, remunerate, remit, settle, distrain, redeem, requite, replace, restore, restitute, rectify, redress, remedy, mend, satisfy, propitiate, expiate, atone, do penance, overcompensate, make good, put straight **5 counterbalance**, compensate, offset, balance, counterweigh, countervail, counterpoise, equilibrate, equalize, equiponderate, level, even up, correct, square, adjust, readjust, attune, counteract, countermeasure, cancel out, write off, nullify, neutralize, deactivate, counterblast, retaliate, avenge **6 be compensated**, recover, retrieve, regain, repossess, recoup, reclaim, retake, redeem

ADJECTIVES 7 compensated, recompensed, indemnified, reimbursed, refunded, repaid, paid off, rewarded, remunerated, remitted, requited, satisfied, propitiated, overcompensated, avenged, revenged, replaced, restored, restituted, recouped, recovered, rectified, redressed, remedied, expiated, redeemed **8 compensable**, amendable, rectifiable, recoupable, reclaimable, replevisable, redeemable, remittable, requitable, restorable, recoverable, satisfiable, propitiable **9 compensatory**, reparatory, restitutory, restorative, indemnificatory, amendatory, retributive, redemptory, remedial, expiatory, propitiative, piacular **10 counterbalancing**, balancing, compensating, counterpoised, equipoised, in equilibrium, equiponderant, equalized, countervailing, levelled, evened up, offsetting, corrected, attuned, adjusted, return, counter, counterposed, counteracted, retroactive, neutralized, cancelled out, written off, nullified, deactivated, antidotal

102 Completeness

NOUNS 1 completeness, finished state, sufficiency, entirety, totality, wholeness, unity, integrality, universality, comprehensiveness, solidarity, solidity, balance, harmony, concord, fulfilment, consummation, finishing touch, the end, the limit, the utmost, summit, peak, zenith, culmination, ideal **2 fullness**, plenitude, pregnancy, capacity, maximum, saturation, satiety, repletion, filling, replenishment, brimming, full complement, requisite number, quorum, quota, full house, full load, bumper, brimmer, bellyful **3 completion**, end, finish, finalization, close, conclusion, termination, expiration, culmination, attainment, accomplishment, achievement, fulfilment, consummation, realization

VERBS 4 complete, integrate, unite, join, make whole, complement, fill in, fill out, build up, make up, construct, piece together, compose, do, perform, execute, discharge, fulfil, achieve, accomplish, crown, cap, finalize, perfect, finish, conclude **5 be complete**, have everything, reach perfection, climax, culminate, end, finish, close, terminate, want nothing, reach maturity, be full **6 fill**, refill, replenish, fill up, top up, satisfy, sate, saturate, cram, jam, stuff, bloat, pack in, ram in, squeeze in, load, stock, supply, cover, occupy

ADJECTIVES 7 complete, entire, integral, intact, unbroken, unimpaired, undivided, self-contained, self-sufficient, united, whole, plenary, quorate, sufficient, adequate, all there, unexpurgated, unabridged, uncut, unabbreviated, all-in, comprehensive, absolute, utter, total, exhaustive, full-scale, detailed, thorough, wholesale, unqualified, pure, out-and-out, consummate, full-blown, full-grown, full-fledged, mature, perfect, faultless, finished, accomplished, achieved, finalized, concluded, closed, terminated, over **8 full**, replenished, replete, satisfied, well-stocked, level with, flush, saturated, stuffed, gorged, sated, chock-a-block, crowded, crammed, jam-packed

103 Completion

NOUNS 1 completion, completeness, wholeness, entirety, totality, unity, fullness, fulfilment, exhaustiveness, thoroughness, fruition, ripeness, maturity, realization, achievement, summit, success, attainment, accomplishment, work done, performance, readiness, carrying through, culmination, consummation **2 conclusion**, finish, termination, arrival, end, wind-up, climax, payoff, close, finality, finis, finale, epilogue, final story, last words, final chapter, last act, swan song, death, resolution, solution, denouement, upshot, result **3 elaboration**, finishing touch, capstone, finisher, limit, last straw, breaking point, boiling point, finishing off

VERBS 4 complete, consummate, fulfil, follow through, carry through, follow up, drive home, clear up, tie up, peak, implement, carry out, execute, effect, enact, do, dispatch, realize, bring about, accomplish, achieve, compass **5 conclude**, culminate, terminate, arrive, end, finish, switch off, wind up, close, settle, climax, dispose of **6 elaborate**, perfect, crown

ADJECTIVES 7 completed, whole, entire, total, exhaustive, thorough, utter, perfect, well done, consummate, fulfilled, fully realized, thoroughgoing, comprehensive, unabridged, intact, unbroken, full-blown, blooming, ripe, full-grown, matured, polished, secured, accomplished, achieved, compassed, attained, effected, implemented, executed, realized, discharged, disposed of, cleaned up, wrapped up **8 concluded**, finished, terminated, ended, finalized, wound up, done, crowned, last, final

104 Component

NOUNS 1 component, content, constituent, part, integrant, ingredient, element, aspect, feature, facet, detail, particular, factor, item **2 piece**, bit, portion, part, fragment, fraction, segment, section, sector, division, category, faction, class, branch, department **3 unit**, module, building block, building brick, cell, particle, molecule, atom **4 components**, works, workings, mechanism, machinery, engine

ADJECTIVES 5 component, constituent, integral, ingredient, elemental, formative, fractional, segmental, departmental **6 modular**, cellular, molecular, atomic, integral, joined, linked, fitted **7 belonging**, appurtenant, part of, one of, essential, fundamental, intrinsic, inherent, integral **8 composing**, constituting, comprising, including, inclusive of, containing

VERBS 9 compose, constitute, comprise, make up, combine in, merge in, amalgamate, participate in, join **10 consist of**, comprise, contain, include, embrace, encompass, subsume, embody, incorporate, involve **11 be one of**, belong to, inhere, reside in **12 make**, construct, build, erect, structure, assemble, put together, fit together, set up, compound, fabricate, fashion, form

105 Compromise

NOUNS 1 compromise, adaptation, accommodation, sharing, cooperation, agreement, arrangement, practical compromise, modus vivendi, understanding, concession, give-and-take, adjustment, settlement, negotiation, arbitration, middle way, halfway, happy medium, balance, central position, meeting halfway, equal swap, trade-off **2 half-measure**, stopgap measure, temporary substitute **3 irresolution**, hesitation, lukewarmness, neutrality

VERBS 4 compromise, meet halfway, adapt, accommodate, cooperate, adjust, readjust, negotiate, arbitrate, concede, cede, average out **5 be irresolute**, lack conviction

ADJECTIVES 6 compromising, accommodating, adjusted, negotiable, adaptable, averaging out, agreeing, arranged, conceding, give-and-take, settled, halfway **7 half-measure**, stopgap, temporary **8 irresolute**, noncommital, lukewarm, neutral, evasive, discredited

106 Compulsion

NOUNS 1 compulsion, compulsiveness, irresistibility, obsessiveness, preoccupation, need, urge, drive, essential, necessity, obligation, requirement, prerequisite, zero options, no choice **2 coercion**, pressure, order, command, mandate, force, enforcement, duress, restraint, constraint, intimidation, bullying, browbeating, threat, violence **3 coercive methods**, blackmail, extortion, bribery, big stick, bludgeon, strong-arm tactics, arm-twisting, force-feeding, kidnapping, forced labour, slavery, impressment, press gang, sanctions, conscription, call-up, penalty clause, fine

VERBS 4 compel, coerce, urge, oblige, make, insist on, emphasize, pressure, press, squeeze, impel, drive, pin down, bind, constrain, restrain, hold back, oppress, necessitate, require, command, demand, dictate, mandate, order, regiment, discipline, impose **5 force**, intimidate, threaten, force-feed, foist on, take, requisition, commandeer, constrain, extort, blackmail, kidnap, exact, wring from, drag from, conscript, call up, impress, dragoon, inflict, bully, browbeat, steamroller, bludgeon, pressgang, use violence **6 be compelled**, be coerced, must

ADJECTIVES 7 compelling, compulsive, coercive, irresistible, hypnotic, mesmeric, cogent, convincing, inspiring, influential, persuasive, involuntary, unavoidable, inevitable, necessary, commanding, imperative, urgent, overriding, pressing, driving, high-pressure, oppressive, dictatorial, enforcing, binding, restraining, constraining, steamroller, forceful, violent **8 compulsory**, mandatory, necessary, unavoidable, ineluctable, obligatory, required

107 Computers

NOUNS 1 computing, computer science, systems analysis, programming, data entry, cybernetics **2 operator**, programmer, DP manager, systems analyst, hacker **3 computer**, digital computer, hybrid computer, supercomputer, parallel computer, mainframe, minicomputer, mini, microcomputer, micro, home computer, games computer, lap-top computer, personal organizer, calculator, programmable calculator, electronic computer, electronic brain, adding machine **4 processor**, central processor, microprocessor **5 memory**, store, storage, main memory, primary memory, register, cache, semiconductor memory, core store, solid-state memory, cryogenic memory, backing store, auxiliary memory, bulk memory, bubble memory, buffer, scratchpad, volatile memory, nonvolatile memory **6 peripheral**, backing store, disk, disk pack, disk reader, hard disk, Winchester, floppy disk, floppy, diskette, microfloppy, microdiskette, minifloppy, minidiskette, optical disk, CD-rom, tape streamer, cartridge, cassette, flat screen, keyboard, console, terminal, monitor, card punch, punched card, tape punch, paper tape, reader, input-output device, I/O device, port, printer, band printer, belt printer, barrel printer, drum printer, chain printer, letter-quality printer, daisywheel printer, dot-matrix printer, electrophotographic printer, electrostatic printer, golfball printer, impact printer, ink-jet printer, bubble-jet printer, serial printer, ionographic printer, laserprinter, line printer, matrix printer, colour printer, plotter, flat-bed plotter, x-y plotter, printout, pretty printing, scanner, wand, bar-code reader, light pen, digitizer, data tablet, joystick, mouse, tailless mouse, modem, acoustic coupler **7 application**, text editor, spelling checker, dictionary, thesaurus, database, spreadsheet, window **8 artificial intelligence** (AI), game-playing, perceptual computing, natural-language understanding, theorem proving, means-ends analysis, semantic net, game theory, expert system, cybernetics, robotics, neurocomputer, neural computer **9 computer game**, video game

VERBS 10 abort, access, address, archive, backup, bootstrap, boot, branch, compile, copy, crash, debug, decode, decompile, delete, downgrade, download, dump, emulate, erase, format, hardwire, input, interface, load, login, logon, logoff, logout, loop, output, patch, read, scroll, spool

ADJECTIVES 11 on-line, off-line, user-friendly, erasable, rewritable

108 Concavity

NOUNS 1 concavity, hollowness, sinking, incurvation, indentation, indention, depression **2 concave land**, hollow, cove, dip, hole, pothole, borehole, foxhole, crater, valley, vale, dell, glen, dingle, col, combe, gap, pass, ravine, gorge, abyss, crevasse, canyon, gully, den, burrow, warren, cave, cavern, trough, sap, tunnel, tube, trench, fosse, moat, grave, quarry, pit, mine, cutting, excavation, canal, inlet **3 cavity**, dent, nook, cranny, niche, recess, alcove, basin, trough, bowl, cup, sump, socket, footprint, dimple **ADJECTIVES 4 concave**, hollow, incurvate, depressed, sunken, cavernous, indented, cup-shaped, bowl-shaped, dented, dimpled, pockmarked, pitted **VERBS 5 be concave**, curve inwards, sink, cave in, collapse **6 make concave**, hollow, press inwards, impress, imprint, indent, punch in, depress, dent, stamp, stave in, excavate, delve into, tunnel, burrow, bore, dig out, scoop out, gouge out, hollow out, dig, spade, mine

109 Concealment

NOUNS 1 concealment, invisibility, disappearance, eclipse, occultation, hiding, secretion **2 hiding place**, mother's skirt, foxhole, dugout, bolt hole, bomb shelter, refuge, shelter, sanctuary, asylum, safe house, hidden cave, nook, cranny, niche, hide-out, cubbyhole, hidy-hole, cache, stash, closet, attic, cellar, mattress, secret compartment, hollow tree, safe **3 covering up**, purdah, masking, screening, veiling, anonymity, disguise, mask, masked ball, camouflage, smoke screen, ambush **4 silence**, reticence, taciturnity, reserve, closeness, discretion, confidentiality, privacy, suppression, censorship, clampdown, national security, classified information **5 evasion**, equivocation, prevarication, vagueness, obscurity, mystification, obfuscation, deception, misinformation, disinformation, untruth, lie, cover-up, Watergate, Irangate, Chernobyl, dishonesty, false evidence, perjury, deceitfulness, dissimulation, duplicity, trickery **6 privacy**, seclusion, retreat, sanctum, monastery, convent, nunnery, closed order, lair, den, study, library, boudoir, desert island, lighthouse **VERBS 7 conceal**, hide, secrete, bury, inter, confine, seclude, ensconce, stow away, lock up, seal up, wall up, bottle up, store, cover up, wrap up, paper over, whitewash, varnish, gloss over, overlay, paint over, smother, stifle, suppress, censor, screen, cloak, shroud, curtain, blanket, veil, muffle **8 disguise**, camouflage, encode, obscure, eclipse, darken, fog, cloud, muddle, obfuscate **9 deceive**, dissemble, masquerade, blindfold, mislead **10 conceal oneself**, evade, shun, hide from, dodge, avoid, take cover, go underground, lie low, hide out, disappear **11 be silent**, look blank, look natural, keep mum **12 equivocate**, prevaricate, evade, hedge **ADJECTIVES 13 concealed**, hidden, unseen, secluded, sequestered, reclusive, incommunicado, out-of-touch, private, screened, hooded, masked, recondite, veiled, covered, overprinted, eclipsed, obscured, blotted out, under wraps, smothered, stifled, suppressed **14 disguised**, distorted, camouflaged, unrecognized, incognito, anonymous, cryptic, secret, covert, occult, latent, coded, cryptographic **15 silent**, taciturn, reticent, reserved, aloof, unsociable **16 noncommittal**, uncommunicative, uninformative, clamlike, tight-lipped, poker-faced, vague, evasive, close

110 Conciseness

NOUNS 1 conciseness, brevity, briefness, shortness, succinctness, pithiness, crispness, compactness, terseness, curtness, brusqueness, monosyllabism, laconism, briskness, exactness, incisiveness, pointedness, nutshell, witticism, brachylogy, concise style, few words, clipped speech, portmanteau word, compression, telegraphese, ellipsis, elision, syncope, apocope, abbreviation, contraction, truncation, shortening, compendiousness, sententiousness **2 outline**, summary, synopsis, précis, résumé, brief sketch, compendium, condensation, monostich, haiku, epitome, maxim, aphorism

ADJECTIVES 3 concise, brief, short, succinct, pithy, crisp, compact, terse, curt, brusque, taciturn, monosyllabic, laconic, brisk, exact, incisive, trenchant, pointed, brachylogous, tight-knit, portmanteau, compressed, telegraphic, elliptic, syncopal, clipped, abbreviated, contracted, truncated, shortened, compendious, epitomical, aphoristic, epigrammatic, sententious, outlined, summarized, condensed

VERBS 4 be concise, express pithily, telescope, compress, compact, condense, abridge, cut, abbreviate, truncate, clip, shorten, contract, outline, sketch, epitomize, abstract, précis

111 Conduct

NOUNS 1 conduct, behaviour, deportment, bearing, comportment, carriage, posture, port, demeanour, mien, attitude, aspect, outlook, mood, opinion, feeling, look, appearance, tone, delivery, motion, action, gesture, manner, style, fashion, guise, air, pose, affectation, role model, example, track record, deserts, dueness, intentions, policy, course, vocation, career, observance **2 good conduct**, goodness, virtue, breeding, poise, dignity, presence, savoir-faire, etiquette, protocol, good manners, graciousness, courtesy, politeness **3 bad conduct**, misconduct, misbehaviour, mischief, naughtiness, badness, vice, wickedness, ill-breeding, bad manners, ungraciousness, boorishness, rudeness, discourtesy, selfishness **4 way of life**, lifestyle, ethos, morals, principles, ideals, customs, traditions, conventions, mores, praxis, *modus vivendi*, manners **5 way**, method, tried-and-true method, practice, routine, procedure **6 treatment**, handling, control, regulation, direction, management, administration, organization, orchestration, leadership, command, guidance, supervision, dealings, actions, transactions, affairs, deeds, tact, diplomacy, leniency, kid gloves, velvet glove, severity **7 tactics**, strategy, campaign, plan, logistics, programme, policy, line, politics, opportunism, diplomacy, statesmanship, governance, cunning, brinkmanship, skill, manoeuvres, outflanking, advantage, delay, manoeuvre, move, gambit, deed, game, tactic, stratagem, trick

VERBS 8 conduct oneself, behave, carry oneself, bear oneself, deport oneself, comport oneself, acquit oneself, act, do, gesture, posture, pose, affect, indulge in, participate, pursue, steer for, busy oneself, employ tactics, manoeuvre **9 behave well**, behave oneself **10 behave badly**, misbehave **11 behave**

towards, treat, deal with, handle, do, see to, conduct, operate, carry on, run, direct, manage, cope with, manipulate, control, organize, orchestrate, mastermind, lead, act, execute, dispatch, carry out, initiate, plan, work out, programme **12 conduct**, guide, lead, direct, navigate, steer, pilot, escort, usher, carry

ADJECTIVES 13 behaving, ethological, tactical, strategical, political, statesmanlike, governmental **14 well-behaved**, well-bred, gentlemanly, ladylike, dignified, well-mannered, gracious, courteous, polite, good, ethical, virtuous **15 badly behaved**, ill-bred, mischievous, naughty, bad, wicked, ill-mannered, ungracious, boorish, rude, discourteous, impolite, selfish

112 Conformity

NOUNS 1 conformity, accord, agreement, harmony, compatibility, consistency, uniformity, congruity, correspondence, concurrence, line, keeping, similarity, likeness, imitation, emulation **2 compliance**, obedience, observance, respect, abidance, acquiescence, submission **3 pliancy**, flexibility, malleability, plasticity, softness, adaptability, accommodation, adjustment, assimilation, naturalization, acclimatization **4 conventionalism**, conservatism, conformism, orthodoxy, traditionalism, Babbittry, bourgeois ethic, etiquette, formality, strictness, severity, primness **5 convention**, practice, form, done thing, received idea, party line, policy, rule, tradition, custom, fashion, trend

VERBS 6 conform, accord, agree, concur, correspond, match, tally, square with, harmonize, suit, fit **7 comply**, adapt, adjust, accommodate oneself, fit in, submit, yield, acquiesce, accede, consent, agree, go by, abide by, follow, observe, respect, obey, follow suit, imitate, emulate **8 make conform**, accommodate, adjust, straighten, align, fit in, trim, form, shape, mould, press, standardize **9 assimilate**, naturalize, acclimatize, rehabilitate, reeducate, indoctrinate, brainwash, imbue, instil, implant, drill, school, teach, train, coach, instruct

ADJECTIVES 10 conformable, adaptable, adjustable, flexible, pliant, malleable, soft **11 conforming**, accordant, concordant, harmonious, compatible, consistent, consonant, congruous, corresponding, agreeing, in accord, in keeping, in line **12 compliant**, willing, obedient, acquiescent, submissive, yielding, sheep-like, lemming-like, tractable, complaisant, accommodating, agreeable **13 conformist**, orthodox, kosher, conservative, law-abiding, conventional, traditional, bourgeois, provincial, correct, proper, pedantic, formal, old-fashioned, staid, strait-laced, prim **14 everyday**, quotidian, ordinary, unexceptional, common, commonplace, familiar, household, typical, stock, standard, general, usual, identikit, stereotyped, average, median, middling

113 Connection

NOUNS 1 connection, union, merger, conjunction, interconnection, attachment, graft, linking, joining, coupling, fastening, meeting, cohesion, adhesion, involvement **2**

association, relationship, liaison, nexus, network, intercourse, commerce, communication network, intercommunication **3 associate**, contact, ally, friend, kith, relation, relative, kin, kinsman, clan **4 means of connection**, bond, chain, fetter, shackle, tie, band, hoop, yoke, link, junction, arch, joint, hinge, branch, nexus, connective, bonding agent, intermedium, beam, girder, stretcher, stay, strut, interconnection, stairs, ladder, stepping stone, canal, isthmus, neck, col, ridge, copula, punctuation mark, hyphen, dash, slash, solidus, parenthesis, bracket, brace, zeugma **5 road**, A-road, motorway, toll bridge, bridge, span, causeway, exit, interchange, spaghetti junction, flyover, underpass, bypass, street, lane, path **6 line**, cable, hawser, cord, rope, guy, towrope, lifeline, umbilical cord, communication cord, ripcord, string, wire, tape, twine, binder, ligature, ligament, tendon, raffia, lashing, binding, thread, band, ribband, bandage, tourniquet, braid, plait, thong, drawstring, shoelace, tag, tie, cravat, stock, knot **7 tackle**, chain, rope, cordage, rig, sheets, ratline, shroud, clew line, stay, guy, garnet, halyard, bowline, harness **8 fastening**, fastener, button, buttonhole, eyelet, loop, toggle, stud, stitch, cufflink, tiepin, suspender, braces, brooch, clasp, clip, hairgrip, hairpin, hatpin, skewer, safety pin, cotter pin, linchpin, kingpin, peg, dowel, nail, brad, holdfast, staple, brace, nut, bolt, rivet, screw, buckle, hasp, hinge, catch, latch, lock, manacles, handcuffs, ring **9 yoke**, coupling, traces, drawbar, hook, claw, grapple, anchor, harness, reins, ribbons, halter, collar, lead, leash, tether, lasso, noose **10 band**, girdle, belt, strap, waistband, cummerbund, sash, bandoleer, collar, neckband, headband

VERBS 11 connect, link, join, unite, merge, couple, fasten, attach, interconnect, interweave, entwine, entangle, lace, braid, plait, knot, lash, bind, ligate, bandage, tie, stitch, sew, tack, buckle, hook, pin, nail, staple, peg, rivet, screw, skewer, bolt, stick, bond, glue, tape, bracket, bridge **12 bind**, tie, chain, fetter, shackle, yoke, harness, leash, tether, lasso, manacle, handcuff, secure, lock, bolt, latch, padlock, batten, clamp, clasp, grip, moor **13 intercommunicate**, contact, meet, liaise, network, interface, associate, relate, cohere, adhere, involve, entangle

ADJECTIVES 14 connective, conjunctive, cohesive, adhesive, sticky, interconnective, communicative, liaising, associated, related, joint **15 connected**, tied, linked, joined, united, merged, coupled, interfaced, fastened, attached, interconnected, interwoven, entangled, laced, braided, plaited, knotted, lashed, bound, stitched, sewn, tacked, buckled, hooked, pinned, nailed, stapled, pegged, riveted, screwed, hinged, stuck, bonded, glued, bracketed, hyphenated **16 bound**, tied, chained, fettered, shackled, yoked, harnessed, leashed, tethered, lassoed, manacled, handcuffed, secured, locked, bolted, latched, padlocked, battened, clamped

114 Consecutiveness

NOUNS 1 consecutiveness, successiveness, progression, queue, line-up **2 consecution**, sequence, series, nexus, run, course, turn, order, catenation, concatenation, chain, train, file, line, queue, string, thread, ladder, stairs, steps, colonnade, scale, arpeggio, gamut, spectrum **3 line**, lineage, bloodline, descent, pedigree, dynasty, family tree **4 repercussion**, result, consequence, effect, causality, domino theory, knock-on effect, snowball effect, chain reaction, aftermath, backlash **5 continuity**, uninterruption, unbrokenness, uniformity, sameness, undifferentiation, monotony, endlessness, ceaselessness, incessancy, constancy **6 continuum**, continuous motion, cycle, circle, round, endless round, rotation, periodicity, recurrence, assembly line, conveyor belt, treadmill, vicious circle, endless band, Möbius strip **7 stability**, steadiness, steady state, equilibrium, balance, routine, rut, flow **8 procession**, parade, pageant, promenade, march past, cortège, funeral procession, cavalcade, motorcade, caravan, train, line, column, file, crocodile, stream, queue, traffic jam

ADJECTIVES 9 consecutive, successive, following, serial, seriate, sequential, in order, running, ongoing, progressive, chronological, catenary, ordinal **10 repercussive**, causal, resultant, knock-on, consequential **11 continuous**, constant, incessant, perpetual, nonstop, endless, unending, never-ending, ceaseless, unremitting, interminable, unrelieved, unbroken, solid, smooth, serried, seamless, uninterrupted, uniform, undifferentiated, featureless **12 cyclical**, periodic, rhythmic

VERBS 13 be consecutive, succeed, come after, follow on, run on **14 continue**, not stop, extend, run **15 concatenate**, catenate, connect, join, link, string, thread **16 arrange consecutively**, array, range, rank, line, align **17 line up**, fall in, queue, parade, promenade, march past, file

115 Container

NOUNS 1 container, receptacle, holder, frame, vessel, repository, depository, reservoir **2 compartment**, cell, cage, cubicle, booth, stall, box, pew, niche, recess, nook, inglenook, cranny, bay, alcove, cubbyhole **3 cabinet**, cupboard, tallboy, whatnot, chest, commode, drawer, shelf, bookcase, unit, dresser, drinks cabinet, sideboard, bureau, davenport, escritoire, secretaire, desk, filing cabinet, freezer, refrigerator **4 rack**, shelf, shelving, layer, level, storey, floor **5 packet**, pack, packaging, cover, wrapper, sheath, envelope, jacket, document, wallet, file, folder, parcel **6 box**, chest, coffer, casket, caddy, case, locker, canister, tin, can, carton, punnet, moneybox, safe, matchbox, tinderbox, file, boxfile, crate, tea chest, coffin **7 basket**, hamper, wicker basket, wire basket, wastepaper basket, pannier, punnet, Moses basket, bassinet, creel, skep **8 bag**, sack, carryall, holdall, grip, pouch, diplomatic pouch, purse, handbag, satchel, kitbag, bundle, saddlebag **9 baggage**, luggage, suitcase, grip, holdall, carryall, Gladstone bag, Boston bag, portmanteau, valise, trunk, backpack, knapsack, rucksack, haversack, briefcase, attaché case, portfolio, wallet **10 cart**, pushcart, handcart, trolley **11 vessel**, urn, jar, tea caddy, vase, ewer, pitcher, jug, amphora, cask, vat, barrel, keg, drum, pipe, puncheon, hogshead, firkin, tun, tank, cistern, bucket, pail, watering can, dustbin, coal scuttle, silo **12 bath**, bathtub, footbath, eyebath, sitzbath, jacuzzi, bidet, tub, sink, basin, bowl, vat **13 drinking vessel**, cup, teacup, coffeecup, eggcup, mug, beaker, glass, tumbler, tankard, Toby-jug, drinking horn, cannikin, pannikin, noggin, chalice, goblet, wineglass, champagne flute, schooner, rummer, brandy balloon, brandy snifter, jigger **14 bottle**, flask, flagon, vial, phial, decanter, carafe, demijohn, magnum, jeroboam, rehoboam, methuselah, balthazar, gourd, calabash, wineskin **15 pot**, pan, cauldron, saucepan, wok, frying pan, skillet, steamer, fish kettle, roasting tin, double boiler, bain-marie, casserole, roaster, cake tin, boiler, brazier, kettle, coffeepot, coffee urn, percolator, teapot, tea urn, jamjar, honeypot, warming pan **16 crockery**, china, dishware, pottery, teaset, dinner service, glassware, utensils, bowl, porringer, tureen, ramekin, terrine, jelly mould, gravy boat, plate, platter, dish, saucer, charger

ADJECTIVES 17 containing, holding, enclosing, covering, enveloping, wrapping, sheathed, surrounded, cocooning, stabling, sheltering, storing, storage, reserved, packing, bundled, boxed, caged, canning, tinning, potting, bottling, ladled, scooped, spooned, shovelled, binned, shelved, garaged, bagged

VERBS 18 put (*or* **place**) **in a container**, store, reserve, containerize, crate up, bundle, can, tin, pot, box up, pour in, bottle, cover, wrap, pack, package, sheath, cocoon, envelope, enclose, cage, surround, shelter, stable

116 Contention

NOUNS 1 contention, conflict, struggle, fight, clash, tussle, strife, combat, war, battle, skirmish, engagement, encounter, debate, dispute, dissent, polemics, ink-slinging, mud-slinging, argument, quarrel, squabble, spat, wrangle, altercation, cold war, competition, rivalry, emulation, jealousy **2 contest**, tug-of-war, struggle, effort, essay, exertion, needle match, grudge match, revenge match, competition, free-for-all, knockout competition, tournament, match, test match, run-off, heat, athletics meeting, sports day, field day **3 race**, speed contest, foot race, flat race, road race, marathon, fun run, orienteering, obstacle race, horse racing, the turf, steeplechase, greyhound racing, dog racing, the dogs, motor racing, motor rally, drag racing, stockcar racing, speedway, dirt-track racing, autocross, rallycross, motocross, cycle racing, cyclocross, boat racing **4 fight**, showdown, roughhouse, horseplay, scuffle, brawl, broil, row, rumpus, ruction, brouhaha, affray, set-to, scrap, brush, scrum, scrummage, scrimmage, scramble, dogfight, melee, fracas, riot, gang warfare, street fight, fisticuffs, blows, hard knocks, running fight, close fighting, hand-to-hand fighting, close grips, close quarters, infighting, hostilities, belligerency, blow-up, war, warfare, fray, collision, military conflict, armed conflict, military encounter, military action, battle royal, pitched battle, stand-up fight, firefight, shoot-out, campaign, death struggle, final battle, Armageddon, theomachy, gigantomachy, psychomachia, psychic combat, battlefield, battleground **5 duel**, seconds out, single combat, gladiatorial combat, head-to-head contest, hand-to-hand fight, nose-to-nose confrontation, joust, tilt, tournament, tourney, fencing, swordplay, singlestick, quarterstaff, kendo, bullfight, tauromachy

VERBS 6 contend, combat, battle, tussle, wrestle, tackle, attempt, try, venture, essay, strive, struggle, oppose, resist, withstand, argue for, contest, compete, enter, challenge, take on, stake, wager, bet, play against, race, vie with, emulate, rival, tilt with **7 fight**, scuffle, row, scrimmage, scrap, set to, pitch into, go for, take on, engage, wade in, assail, attack, open fire, strike at, box, spar, meet, encounter, skirmish, exchange shots, give battle, grapple, duel, fence, measure swords, declare war, campaign, wage war **8 conflict**, differ, disagree, dissent, dispute, debate, quarrel, row

ADJECTIVES 9 contending, battling, fighting, grappling, struggling, competing, contesting, challenging, racing, rival, vying, outdoing, surpassing, agonistic, athletic, sporting, starting **10 contentious**, argumentative, quarrelsome, irritable, irascible, aggressive, combative, fight-hungry, pugilistic, gladiatorial, pugnacious, bellicose, warmongering, warlike, hawkish, at loggerheads, at odds, at war, belligerent, warring, head-to-head **11 competitive**, keen, cutthroat, dog-eat-dog, keenly contested, ding-dong, close-run

117 Contents

NOUNS 1 contents, ingredients, components, constituents, constitution, composition, makeup, structure, embodiment, parts, elements, factors, features, substance, stuff, material, matter, spirit, essence, quintessence, gist, meat **2 load**, lading, cargo, payload, freight, burden, charge, shipment, stowage **3 insides**, guts, pith, marrow, heart, core, kernel, entrails, bowels **4 stuffing**, filling, wadding, padding, packing **5 divisions**, sections, chapters, themes, topics, items, index, inventory, code, table, list, checklist, tally, chart, catalogue, glossary

VERBS 6 contain, hold, enclose, conceal, package, parcel, box up, containerize, load, lade **7 stuff**, fill, pad, pack, pack in, cram, jam, squeeze in, insert, pour in, make full, fill up **8 embody**, subsume, include, compose, constitute, make up **9 itemize**, index, list, enumerate, tabulate, catalogue, classify, divide, subdivide, section, register, file, tally, schedule

ADJECTIVES 10 containing, component, constituent, composed, made up, embodying, subsuming, including, inclusive, structured, featuring, elemental, substantial, material, essential **11 loaded**, laden, holding, containing, charged, burdened, burdensome, stuffed, full, lined, padded, packed, crammed, squeezed **12 itemized**, indexed, listed, coded, tabled, tabular, charted, catalogued, registered, scheduled, programmed, sectioned, divided, thematic

118 Continuity

NOUNS 1 continuity, continuation, constancy, progression, progress, succession, sequence, supplement, sequel, follow-up, postscript, repetition, recurrence, flow, run, uninterrupted course, connectedness, interrelatedness, cohesion, preservation **2 protraction**, prolongation, long duration, extension, addition, furtherance, perpetuation, endurance, persistence, perseverance

VERBS 3 continue, proceed, advance, progress, succeed, recur, repeat, connect, interrelate, add, supplement, cohere, flow, run on, go on, follow through, maintain, sustain, support, uphold, preserve, harp on **4 protract**, prolong, further, extend, maintain, perpetuate, persist, persevere, pursue, resume, follow up, endure

ADJECTIVES 5 continual, continuous, in progress, ongoing, constant, steady, incessant, progressive, sequent, additional, repetitive, recurrent, unbroken, uninterrupted, interconnected, interrelated, cohesive **6 protracted**, prolonged, extended, lengthened, drawn-out, interminable, unceasing, unremitting, unrelenting, persistent, unfailing, inexhaustible, without respite, nonstop, endless, enduring

119 Contract

NOUNS 1 contract, undertaking, assignment, engagement, obligation, commitment, promise, compact, arrangement, understanding, cooperation, accord, agreement, deal, pledge, marriage contract, alliance, partnership, covenant, pact, negotiation, bargaining, bartering, settlement, ratification, assent, seal, signature, security **2 purchase contract**, lease, insurance policy, promissory note, IOU, debenture **3 alliance**, league, cartel, consortium, trust, international agreement, trade agreement, convention, treaty

VERBS 4 contract, indent, commit oneself, wed, countersign, seal, subscribe to, underwrite, endorse, ratify, attest, confirm, covenant, league with, bargain, settle, negotiate

ADJECTIVES 5 contractual, covenanted, agreed to, promised, sworn, consensual, assenting, negotiated, ratified, assigned, arranged, matrimonial, allied

120 Contraction

NOUNS 1 contraction, systole, syneresis, synizesis, shrinking, constringency, astringency, compression, compaction, condensation, concentration, minaturization, scaling-down, squeeze, tightening, pressure, crush, pinching, clenching, clamping, cramping, constriction, coarctation, limitation, strangulation, stenosis, deflation, flattening, implosion, collapse, cave-in, shortening, abbreviation, elision, curtailment, abridgement, pruning, trimming, narrowing, drawing in, closing up, gathering, puckering, pursing, shrivelling, tabescence, atrophy, marasmus, emaciation, thinning, slimming, decrease, reduction, lessening, diminuendo **2 contractibility**, shrinkability, compressibility, compactability, condensability, crushability, limitability, circumscribability, deflatability **3 contracted thing**, epitome, compendium, digest, bottleneck, neck, isthmus, hourglass, hourglass figure **4 contractor**, astringent, styptic, compressor, compacter, condenser, tourniquet, squeezer, press, crusher, foller, mangle, clamp, vice, corset, straitjacket, constrictor

VERBS 5 make smaller, contract, shrink, compress, compact, condense, concentrate, boil down, miniaturize, scale down, squeeze, tighten, press, crush, pinch, cram, jam, roll up, clench, clamp, cramp, constrict, limit, restrict, circumscribe, strangle, deflate, flatten, implode, collapse, telescope, shorten, abbreviate, curtail, abridge, stunt, prune, trim, clip, shear, shave, whittle away, file, grind, narrow, draw in, close up, take in, gather, smock, tuck, pucker, pucker up, purse, knit, wrinkle, shrivel, sear, waste, emaciate, thin, slim, decrease

ADJECTIVES 6 smaller, contracted, shrunk, compressed, compact, condensed, concentrated, boiled-down, miniaturized, scaled-down, squeezed, tightened, pressed, crushed, pinched, rolled-up, curled-up, huddled, clenched, cramped, constricted, coarctate, limited, restricted, circumscribed, strangled, deflated, flat, collapsed, telescoped, shortened, abbreviated, curtailed, abridged, stunted, pruned, trimmed, clipped, shorn, narrowed, drawn-in, closed-up, gathered, smocked, tucked, puckered, puckered up, pursed, knitted, wrinkled, shrivelled, shrivelled-up, withered, wizened, seared, wasted, consumptive, emaciated, thin, slim, decreased **7 contracting**, shrinking, constringent, astringent, styptic, compressive, tightening, crushing, pinching, cramping, constricting, limiting, restricting, circumscriptive, strangling, deflationary, implosive, collapsing, shortening, stunting, narrowing, gathering, puckering, pursing, shrivelling, searing, wasting, tabescent, emaciating, thinning, slimming, decreasing, reducing

121 Convenience

ADJECTIVES 1 convenient, handy, helpful, practical, pragmatic, practicable, usable, workable, effective, adapted to, applicable, suitable, commodious, appropriate, fit, seemly, proper, expedient, advantageous, beneficial, useful, commendable, desirable, worthwhile, acceptable, timely, well-timed, auspicious, opportune **2 nearby**, next door, accessible, available, ready, close, adjacent, neighbouring

NOUNS 3 convenience, handiness, helpfulness, practicality, pragmatism, usability, workability, qualification, adaptation, application, suitability, fitness, propriety, expedience, contrivance, utilitarianism, opportunism, timeserving, profit, advantage, benefit, usefulness, utility, prudence, advisability, timeliness, auspiciousness **4 nearness**, proximity, closeness, juxtaposition, adjacency, accessi-

bility **5 convenience**, facilities, means
VERBS 6 be convenient, fit, suit, help, aid, promote, advance, produce results, do, serve, succeed, qualify for, accord, profit, benefit

122 Convergence

NOUNS 1 convergence, confluence, conflux, concurrence, concourse, collision, mutual approach, concentration, meeting **2 approach**, advance, confrontation, collision course **3 convergent view**, perspective **4 meeting place**, congress, congregation, assembly, union, junction **5 focus**, centre, hub, pivot, centring, concentralization, focalization, asymptote, converging line **6 narrowing**, tapering
ADJECTIVES 7 convergent, confluent, uniting, concurrent, meeting, focal, focusing, confocal, centrolineal, centripetal, radial, radiating, tangential, centring, pointed, tapering, narrowing, conical, pyramidal **8 advancing**, oncoming
VERBS 9 converge, close in, approach, draw near, intersect, close with, close, funnel, taper, pinch **10 come together**, assemble, congregate, concentrate, gather, cluster, run together, meet, unite, get together, roll up, roll in **11 focus**, centre, home in, zero in, centralize, taper, concentralize

123 Conversation

NOUNS 1 conversation, talk, chat, dialogue, duologue, two-hander, interlocution, colloquy, converse, discourse, intercourse, communication **2 chat**, natter, small talk, heart-to-heart, causerie, idle talk, prattle, tittle-tattle, gossip, chit-chat, repartee
VERBS 3 converse, discourse, talk, speak, parley, communicate, confabulate, exchange pleasantries **4 chat**, natter, chatter, prattle, prate, gossip, *tête-à-tête*, whisper together **5 confer**, parley, pow-wow, talk over, thrash out, debate, discuss, exchange views, deliberate over, analyse, canvass, consult, refer to, negotiate
ADJECTIVES 6 conversing, talking, chatting, interlocutory, confabulatory, talkative, loquacious, communicative **7 discussing**, conferring, in conference, in committee, consultatory **8 conversational**, colloquial, informal, chatty, gossipy, newsy

124 Conversion

NOUNS 1 conversion, converting, change, transition, transposition, movement, shift, transference, translation, interpretation, misinterpretation, alteration, modification, reorganization, transformation, metamorphosis, mutation, processing, chemical change, reduction, resolution, fermentation, leaven, dehydration, crystallization, melting, physical change, transmutation, transfiguration, magic, bewitchment **2 evolution**, growth, life cycle, development, progress, revolution, reformation, re-education, rebirth, regeneration, rehabilitation, improvement, naturalization, assimilation, degeneration, perversion, denaturalization **3 persuasion**, indoctrination, brainwashing, proselytizing, evangelism, revivalism **4 convert**, changed person, proselyte, catechumen, neophyte, new man, apostate, tergiversator, backslider, renegade

VERBS 5 convert into, metamorphose, mutate, transpose, move, shift, transfer, translate, alter, transform, process, reduce, resolve, ferment, leaven, dehydrate, crystallize, melt, transmute, transfigure, change into, develop into, evolve into, mature into, melt into, merge into, dissolve into **6 be transformed**, be changed, evolve, develop, mature, mellow, age, progress, improve, denaturalize, deteriorate, degenerate, reform **7 transform**, transfigure, make into, turn into, metamorphose, transmute, alchemize, mould, shape, rehabilitate, paint over, translate, modify, decorate, reshape, remodel, reform, reorganize, restructure, reeducate, rationalize, deform, distort, twist **8 be converted**, be saved, turn against, renege, apostatize, desert **9 persuade**, influence, indoctrinate, brainwash, win over, proselytize, evangelize, preach, convert

ADJECTIVES 10 converted, changed, transformed, transposed, transfigured, metamorphosed, transmuted, mutated, translated, bewitched, enchanted, brainwashed, proselytized, assimilated, naturalized, improved, regenerated **11 converting**, changing, becoming, growing, developing, maturing, altering, transforming, mutating, processing, fermenting, leavening, crystallizing, melting, transmuting, transfiguring, evolving, progressing, regenerating, improving **12 influenced**, persuaded, brainwashed, converted, saved, revived, reborn, proselytized **13 naturalized**, internationalized, assimilated, orientalized, westernized, Americanized, Anglicized, Frenchified, Germanized

125 Convexity

NOUNS 1 convexity, bulbousness, bulginess, swelling, gibbousness, billowing, distention, protrusion, protuberance, prominence, excrescence, tumescence, meniscus **2 bulge**, hump, lens, arc, bubble, knob, button, boss, bud, nose, bump, wart, knot, oedema, swelling, erection, bubo, boil, corn, tumour, cyst, pregnancy, beergut, biceps, pectoral, nipple, breast, bust **3 dome**, cupola, vault, arc, arch, beehive, barrow, mound

ADJECTIVES 4 convex, bulbous, bulging, swelling, gibbous, billowing, protruding, distended, humped, prominent, excrescent, tumescent, swollen, meniscoid, arcuated, bowed out, arched

VERBS 5 be convex, arcuate, arch, camber, bow, protrude, bulge, stick out, swell, hump, balloon out, round out

126 Convolution

NOUNS 1 convolution, involution, circumvolution, intricacy, sinuousness, undulation, twistedness **2 coil**, turn, twist, twirl, intricacy, spiral, turbination, screwthread, corkscrew, spring, whorl, curl, curlicue, ringlet, loop, meandering, squiggle, kink, corrugation, squirm, shimmy **3 convoluted thing**, snailshell, ammonite, nautilus, scallop shell, snake, whirlpool, vortex, tornado, labyrinth, maze, braid

ADJECTIVES 4 convolutional, winding, twisted, involutional, circumlocutory, sinuous, undulatory, intricate, braided, wavy, twirled, entwined, corrugated, tortuous, meandering, labyrinthine, serpentine, vermiform, wriggling, squirming, squiggly, coiled, spiral, helical, cochleate, whorled **5 ambiguous**, equivocal, involved, complicated

VERBS 6 convolute, wind together, weave together, enlace, twine, coil, roll, braid, corkscrew, spiral, twirl, curl, wave, undulate, corrugate, scallop, distort, meander, loop, snake, twist, turn, wriggle, writhe, squirm, squiggle **7 be ambiguous**, equivocate

127 Cookery

NOUNS 1 cookery, cooking, microwave cooking, pressure cooking, baking, food preparation, food processing, home economics, domestic science, gastronomy, cuisine, haute cuisine, nouvelle cuisine, lean cuisine, catering, provisioning, recipe **2 cook**, chef, sous chef, commis chef, apprentice chef, cuisinier, fast-food chef, baker, caterer, barbecue cook **3 kitchen**, cookhouse, bakehouse, bakery **4 cooker**, stove, hob, hotplate, grill, griddle, kitchen range, fan oven, kettle, toaster, sandwich-maker, barbecue, spit, microwave, Dutch oven **5 cooking technique**, boiling, parboiling, simmering, poaching, steaming, bain marie, coddling, scrambling, casseroling, baking, roasting, oven-roasting, spit-roasting, pot-roasting, broiling, charbroiling, grilling, barbecuing, toasting, sautéeing, frying, deep frying, stir-frying, curing, smoking **6 dish**, course, hors d'oeuvres, savouries, starter, soup, fish course, entrée, remove, main course, side-dish, salad, entremets, dessert, sweet, pudding, speciality **7 sandwich**, club sandwich, double-decker, finger sandwich, open sandwich, hamburger, cheeseburger, quarter-pounder, hot dog **8 hors d'oeuvre**, appetizer, starter, antipasto, smorgasbord, prawn cocktail, cold cuts, pâté, taramasalata, hummus, raita, mezze, vol-au-vent, canapé, blini, samosa **9 soup**, cream soup, clear soup, broth, Scotch broth, consommé, stock, bouillon, julienne, bisque, purée, vichysoisse, cock-a-leekie, mulligatawny, minestrone, borscht, gazpacho **10 salad**, side salad, tossed salad, green salad, mixed salad, Russian salad, Caesar salad, salad niçoise, coleslaw **11 sauce**, tomato sauce, tomato ketchup, catsup, brown sauce, Worcester sauce, soy sauce, Tabasco sauce, tartare sauce, cranberry sauce, apple sauce, mint sauce, horseradish sauce, mayonnaise, salad cream, salad dressing, French dressing, aïoli, vinaigrette, dip, fondue, bolognese sauce, milanese sauce, barbecue sauce, béarnaise sauce, bordelaise sauce, bourguignonne, sauce espagnole, sauce suprême, hollandaise sauce, béchamel sauce, white sauce, cheese sauce, onion sauce, bread sauce, roux, velouté, demi-glace, chaudfroid **12 fish dish**, fishcake, fish finger, fish pie, fish ball, fish stick, quenelle, gefilte fish, kedgeree, soft roe, hard roe, caviar, Beluga caviar, black caviar, red caviar, lumpfish caviar, taramasalata, jellied eel, smoked haddock, finnan haddock, smoked mackerel, smoked salmon, smoked trout, kippered herring, kipper, smoky, Arbroath smokey, bloater, cured fish, lox, gravadlax, pickled herring, rollmop, Bombay duck **13 meat**, flesh, red meat, white meat, beef, pork, mutton, lamb, veal, goat, poultry, chicken, turkey, goose, duck, game, rabbit, hare, venison, pheasant, grouse, partridge, pigeon, squab, woodcock, snipe, plover, quail, minced meat, mince, ground meat, meatballs, faggots, rissoles, hamburger **14 meat substitute**, soya, tofu, bean curd **15 beef (British)**: neck, chuck, blade, fore rib, thick rib, thin rib, rolled ribs, T-bone, sirloin, rump, silverside, topside, leg, flank, brisket, shin, filet steak **16 beef (US)**: chuck, rib, back rib, short loin, Porterhouse steak, tenderloin, sirloin, round, round steak, hind shank, short plate, brisket **17 pork (British)**: spare rib, blade, loin, leg fillet, hock, belly, hand **18 pork (US)**: blade shoulder, loin, tenderloin, leg, side, spare rib, shoulder **19 lamb (British)**: scrag end, middle neck, shoulder, loin, chump, chump chops, leg **20 lamb (US)**: shoulder, neck slice, rib, loin, loin chop, leg, hind shank, breast, riblets **21 poultry**, white meat, dark meat, breast, leg, drumstick, wing, parson's nose **22 sausage**, sausagemeat, pork sausage, beef sausage, chipolata, cocktail sausage, saveloy, Cumberland sausage, herb sausage, frankfurter, Vienna sausage, liver sausage, garlic sausage, salami, bologna sausage, polony, boloney, black pudding, blood sausage, blood pudding, haggis **23 bacon**, smoked bacon, unsmoked bacon, green bacon, streaky bacon, back bacon, middle cut, belly pork, rasher, flitch, bacon joint, gammon, salt pork, Danish bacon, Canadian bacon, ham **24 offal**, variety meat, liver, kidney, heart, tongue, ox cheek, pig's head, Bath chap, calf's head, brains, brawn, chitterlings, pig's fry, sweatbread, melts, stomach sweatbread, neck sweatbread, pig's feet, pig's knuckles, trotters, cowheel, tripe, thick seam, cow's udder **25 meat dish**, roast, potroast, grill, mixed grill, pie, pasty, hash, fricassée, rissole, casserole, stew, goulash **26 vegetarian dish**, vegetable curry, vegetable chilli, vegetable casserole, vegetable flan, nut cutlet, nut roast, cauliflower cheese, macaroni cheese, omelette, aubergine roll, stuffed marrow, fondue, pease pudding, chilladas **27 dessert**, sweet, pudding, cake, pie, jelly, blancmange, custard, ice cream, sorbet, granita, water ice, knickerbocker glory, marquise, crême caramel, yoghurt, fool, mousse, soufflé, sundae, banana split, peach melba, trifle, rice pudding, semolina, tapioca, bread-and-butter pudding, steamed pudding, suet pudding, Christmas pudding, plum pudding, summer pudding, roly-poly, spotted dick, pavlova, fruit flan, crumble, charlotte, charlotte russe, stewed fruit, compote, fruit salad, fresh fruit **28 cake**, gateau, birthday cake, wedding cake, Christmas cake, yule log, chocolate cake, chocolate gateau, coffee cake, fudge cake, angel cake, sponge cake, madeleine, Swiss roll, carrot cake, fruitcake, spice cake, seed cake, lardy cake, Dundee cake, gingerbread, parkin, Madeira cake, cheesecake, torte, apple pie, Bakewell tart, turnover, flan, tart, jam tart, mince pie, eclair, macaroon, fritter, apple fritter, Danish pastry, Danish, Eccles cake, Chelsea bun, Bath bun, doughnut **29 pastry**, shortcrust pastry, flaky pastry, puff pastry, choux pastry, fleur pastry, Genoese pastry, cheese pastry **30 bread**, dough, crust, crumb, sliced bread, white bread, enriched bread, soda bread, brown bread, wholemeal bread, malt bread, granary bread, black bread, rye bread, pumpernickel, fried bread, beer bread, banana-nut bread, nut bread, raisin bread, pitta bread, poppadom, puri, nan, chapatti, toast, cinnamon toast, Melba toast, French toast, rusk **31 loaf**, pan loaf, pan, cottage loaf, cob, tin, split tin, farmhouse, bloomer, plait, French bread, baguette, French stick, bread stick, roll, breakfast roll, bridge roll, bap, barm cake, pikelet, bagel, croissant, brioche, bun, currant bun, teacake, crumpet, muffin, scone, drop scone, pancake, crêpe, waffle, wafer, biscuit, digestive biscuit, shortbread, flapjack, cracker, creamcracker, crispbread, water biscuit **32 breakfast cereal**, cornflakes, bran flakes, bran, wheat germ, muesli, oatmeal, porridge, gruel, skilly **33 sweet**, sweetmeat, bonbon, comfit, confectionary, toffee, taffy, boiled sweet, barley sugar, butterscotch, caramel, chocolate, chocolate bar, fondant, fudge, gobstopper, gum, gumdrop, jelly bean, jujube, liquorice, liquorice allsort, lollipop, marshmallow, marzipan, peppermint, praline, crystallized fruit **34 preserve**, jam, jelly, marmalade, conserve, bottled fruit, pickle, chutney, dried fruit, currant, raisin

VERBS 35 cook, bake, microwave, pressure-cook, heat up, warm through, reheat, roast, spit-roast, pot-roast, brown, toast, grill, charcoal-grill, barbecue, spatchcock, griddle, devil, curry, fry, deep-fry, shallow-fry, sauté, stir-fry, double-fry, scramble, coddle, boil, parboil, blanch, scald, seethe, simmer, steam, poach, casserole, stew, braise, baste, lard, bard, flip, whip, whisk, beat, blend, knead, mix, fold in, liquidize, stir, draw, gut, bone, fillet, stuff, dress, garnish, cut, chop, dice, shred, grind, mince, grate, sauce, flavour

ADJECTIVES 36 culinary, gastronomic, epicurean, mensal, prandial, preprandial, post-prandial, dressed, oven-ready, prepared, ready-to-cook, made-up, ready-to-serve, cooked, done, well-done, overcooked, burnt, al dente, underdone, undercooked, red, rare, raw, roasted, browned, toasted, grilled, barbecued, devilled, curried, fried, deep-fried, sautéed, stir-fried, scrambled, coddled, boiled, steamed, poached, stewed, braised, beaten, stuffed, chopped, ground, minced, au gratin

128 Cooperation

NOUNS 1 cooperation, collaboration, coaction, concurrence, synergy, assistance, support, backup **2 fellowship**, comradeship, friendship, sodality, solidarity, togetherness, sympathy, fraternalism, sorority, clanship, freemasonry, community spirit, morale, concord, harmony, accord, consensus, concurrence, agreement **3 mutual relationship**, correlation, interaction, symbiosis, sharing, participation, mutualism, reciprocity, interplay, coadjuvancy, networking, compromise, concession **4 joint operation**, common endeavour, joint effort, pulling together, teamwork, working together, concerted action, mass action, united front, cooperative, collective, community **5 joint control**, coagency, coadministration, comanagement, cochairmanship, partnership, coownership, collegialism, federalism **6 movement**, communalism, collectivism, socialism, communism **7 association**, alliance, alignment, affiliation, combination, cartel, consortium, union, unification, coalition, fusion, merger, coalescence, coadunation, amalgamation, consolidation, incorporation **8 conferring**, conference, teleconferencing, consultation, connivance, collusion

VERBS 9 cooperate, collaborate, concur, coact, help, assist **10 reciprocate**, respond, interrelate, interact, interplay, requite, repay **11 work together**, pitch in, rally round, show willing, pull together, hang together, contribute, join in, participate **12 join with**, band together, club together, pool resources **13 concur**, harmonize, concert, collude, connive **14 join**, associate, ally, affiliate, combine, amalgamate, unite, fuse, merge, coalesce, consolidate

ADJECTIVES 15 cooperative, collaborative, coactive, concurrent, coadjutant, coadjuvant, helpful, obliging, willing, accommodating, supportive, contributory **16 joint**, shared, combined, collective, concerted, united, common, communal, pooled, mutual, reciprocal, correlational, interrelating, interactive, communist **17 associating**, allied, affiliated, comradely, fraternal, friendly, concordant, harmonious, concurring, commensal, conniving

129 Counteraction

NOUNS 1 counteraction, polarization, opposition, prevention, remedy, compensation, contravention, reaction, counter, retroaction, repercussion, kickback, boomerang effect, backlash, backfire, recoil, kick, recalcitrance, conflict, hostility, resistance, countermove, deterrent, defence, inhibitor, preventive, friction, hindrance, obstruction, obstacle, interference, counterpressure, repression, suppression, moderation, deregulation, deactivation, invalidation, negation, veto, counterbalance, offset **2 counteracting thing**, headwind, crosscurrent, crossfire, antidote, antitoxin, antivenin, antivenom, cure, remedy, prophylactic

VERBS 3 counteract, counter, obviate, contravene, oppose, polarize, react against, work against, cross, traverse, thwart, hinder, inhibit, prevent, prohibit, drag, block, check, obstruct, frustrate, interfere with, repress, persecute, suppress, restrain, resist, fight against, withstand, conflict with, antagonize, clash, react, recoil, backfire, boomerang, countervail, counterbalance, counterpoise, compensate for, kick back, cancel out, annul, undo, invalidate, negate, veto, abrogate, decontrol, derestrict, deregulate, decriminalize, deactivate, demagnetize, degauss, neutralize

ADJECTIVES 4 counteracting, opposing, contravening, polarized, contrary, conflicting, clashing, antipathetic, antagonistic, inimical, hostile, resistant, recalcitrant, intractable, reactionary, retroactive, reactive, frictional, restraining, frustrating, interfering, repressive, suppressive, intolerant, obstructive, preventive, antidotal, contraceptive, remedial, corrective, balancing, offsetting, moderating, neutralizing, invalidating

130 Counterevidence

NOUNS 1 counterevidence, answer, defence, apology, appeal, retort, rebuttal, rejoinder, retaliation, contradiction, confutation, refutation, denial, demurrer, comeback, contraindication, countercharge, counterblast, counteraccusation, counterclaim, countermand, equivocation, annulment, nullification, negation, invalidation, opposition, protest **2 reversal**, tergiversation, turnaround, aboutface, U-turn, second thoughts, backtracking, back-pedalling, repentance, recantation, disavowal, denial, reneging, repudiation, retraction, palinody, disclamation, disownment, abjuration, abnegation, abrogation, cassation, revocation, renunciation, forswearing, apostasy, treason, self-contradiction, hypocrisy **3 counterclaimant**, rebutter, refuter, denier **4 tergiversator**, tergiversant, traitor, equivocator, deserter, apostate, recusant, renegade

ADJECTIVES 5 countering, answering, defensive, apologetic, retaliatory, confutative, refutative, contrary, counteractive, rebutting, denying, contradictory, oppositional, apostatic, hypocritical **6 countered**, repudiated, retracted, disclaimed, disowned, abjured, abnegated, abrogated, revoked, renounced, denied, disavowed, reneged, retorted, refuted, confuted, negated

VERBS 7 counter, answer, apologize, appeal, retort, rebut, rejoin, retaliate, contradict, confute, refute, deny, demur, contraindicate, countercharge, counterblast, counterclaim, countermand, counterorder, annul, nullify, negate, invalidate, protest, oppose **8 reverse**, tergiversate, turn around, waver, vacillate, equivocate, think again, back track, backpedal, recant, repent, disavow, renege, unsay, repudiate, retract, disclaim, disown, abjure, abnegate, abrogate, revoke, renounce, forswear, apostasize, desert, betray

131 Countries

NOUNS 1 country, nation, state, land, body politic, sovereign state, sovereignty, self-governing state, independent state, free country, self-determination, democracy, parliamentary democracy, dictatorship, oligarchy, monarchy, republic, people's republic, capitalist country, socialist country, communist country, power, superpower, Western nation, third-world country, nonaligned country, neutral nation **2 union of nations**, federation, confederation, commonwealth, commonweal, British Commonwealth, Western bloc, Eastern bloc **3 dominion**, domain, realm, kingdom, principality, principate, duchy, dukedom, grand duchy, archduchy, archdukedom, earldom, palatinate, sultanate, chieftaincy, toparchy, empire, province, territory, occupied country, colony, settlement, protectorate, mandate, mandated territory, mandatory, captive nation, buffer state, ally, satellite nation, puppet regime, imperialism **4 nationalism**, ultranationalism, patriotism, chauvinism, jingoism, isolationism, protectionism, xenophobia **5 internationalism**, global outlook, universalism **6 native land**, native soil, mother country, motherland, fatherland, birthplace, cradle, home

ADJECTIVES 7 national, federal, self-governing, independent, self-determining, democratic, republican, socialist, communist, nonaligned, international, imperialistic, colonial, mandated, nationalistic, ultranationalistic

VERBS 8 become a nation, become independent, declare independence, become self-governing, democratize, socialize **9 exert sovereignty**, rule, occupy, colonize

132 Courage

NOUNS 1 courage, bravery, valour, courageousness, braveness, mettle, pluck, nerve, daring, audacity, boldness, hardiness, fearlessness, dauntlessness, spirit, vim, stoutheartedness, lion-heartedness, doughtiness, fighting spirit, backbone, grit, toughness **2 heroism**, chivalry, knightliness, gallantry, prowess, manliness, virility, aggressiveness **3 steadfastness**, confidence, self-reliance, fortitude, perseverance, endurance, tenacity, determination, resoluteness **4 adventurousness**, gameness, foolhardiness **5 bold front**, brave face, bravado **6 encouragement**, heartening, assurance, reassurance, incitement, exhortation **7 courageous act**, feat, exploit, deed, chivalry, prowess, derring-do, adventure

ADJECTIVES 8 courageous, brave, heroic, gallant, valiant, mettlesome, plucky, daring, audacious, bold, hardy, fearless, dauntless, undaunted, spirited, stout-hearted, lion-hearted, unflinching, unshrinking, unshakeable, unbowed, undismayed, indomitable, doughty **9 chivalrous**, knightly, heroic, gallant, manly **10 militant**, aggressive, bellicose, martial **11 self-reliant**, confident, unafraid, unfearing, steadfast, persevering, tenacious, dogged, determined, resolute **12 adventurous**, venturesome, game, foolhardy, rash **13 encouraging**, heartening

VERBS 14 be courageous, dare, venture, brave, face, confront, beard, defy, outface, brazen out, court disaster **15 take courage**, take heart, dare, steel oneself, endure **16 give courage**, encourage, hearten, assure, reassure, embolden, inspirit, inspire, incite

133 Courtesy

NOUNS 1 courtesy, politeness, civility, kindness, amiability, sweetness, niceness, amenity, agreeableness, affability, comity, graciousness, humility, consideration, thoughtfulness, solicitousness, decency, tact, discretion, charity, friendliness, sociability, gallantry, chivalry, courtliness, comity, noblesse oblige, gracefulness, suavity, smoothness, flattery, sweet talking, good humour, gentleness, mildness **2 good manners**, mannerliness, etiquette, breeding, refinement, polish, culture, gentility, sophistication, elegance, urbanity, savoir-vivre, savoir-faire, gentlemanliness, ladylikeness, formality, correctness, convention, protocol, custom **3 courtesies**, civilities, urbanities, amenities, graces, gentilities, pleasantries, compliments, regards, elegances, dignities, respect, formalities, rites, ceremonies, invitation, presentation, welcome, introduction, reception, acknowledgment, compliment, toast, recognition, valediction **4 deference**, obeisance, compliance, complaisance, condescension, oiliness, unctuousness, glibness, fulsomeness, sycophancy, ingratiation, bowing, nodding

ADJECTIVES 5 courteous, polite, civil, urbane, agreeable, affable, genial, amiable, gracious, humble, fair, considerate, thoughtful, solicitous, decent, tactful, discreet, generous, benevolent, charitable, accommodating, lenient, even-tempered, gentle, mild, good-humoured, obliging, amenable, sociable, friendly, kind, sweet, nice, welcoming, gallant, chivalrous, courtly, graceful, old-fashioned **6 good-mannered**, well-behaved, well-bred, well-spoken, refined, cultured, cultivated, genteel, gentlemanly, ladylike, correct, urbane, polished, elegant, conventional, suave, bland, smooth, flattering, sweet-talking, formal, de rigueur, ceremonious, diplomatic **7 deferential**, obeisant, compliant, condescending, complaisant, glib, fulsome, sycophantic, ingratiating, bowing, nodding, kowtowing, smug

VERBS 8 be courteous, show kindness, give consideration, care, use tact, oblige, invite, receive, welcome, be polite, introduce, acknowledge, compliment, recognize, toast, drink to, express regrets, love **9 have good manners**, behave well, observe etiquette, show refinement, observe protocol, follow custom **10 greet**, welcome, salute, hail, wave, smile, hug, squeeze, embrace, kiss, say hello, shake hands, honour, parade, present arms, turn out, crown, wreathe, garland, fete **11 defer to**, pay respects, pay homage, make obeisance, comply, condescend, ingratiate oneself, bow, curtsy, bob, nod, duck, kneel, kowtow, salaam, prostrate oneself

134 Covering

NOUNS 1 covering, overarching, spanning, overlaying, stratification, superimposition, overlapping, imbrication, coating, topping, paving, blanketing, cloaking, enclosement, walling in, envelopment, enfoldment, wrapping, casing, screening, shielding, overshadowing, eclipsing, blotting out, flooding over, obscuring **2 cover**, top, lid, cap, cork, plug, stopper, bung, crust, flap, shutter, gravestone, shroud, pall, topsoil, mulch, cloud **3 coating**, coat, layer, film, icing, frosting, glaze, varnish, veneer, enamel, lacquer, japan, stain, paint, wax, furniture polish **4 wrapping**, tissue paper, packaging, box, envelope, involucre, shroud, sheath, dust jacket, binding, binder, foil, cellophane, polythene

VERBS 5 cover, lay on, superimpose, lay over, top, crown, cap, cork, plug, bung, stopper **6 coat**, spread, overlay, carpet, blanket, tile, parquet, upholster, layer, daub, plaster, top, ice, frost, glaze, varnish, veneer, enamel, stain, paint, wax, polish, plate **7 wrap**, surround, envelop, enfold, shroud, package, box, pack, enclose, encase, crate, sheathe, bandage, bind, swathe **8 overlie**, overlap, lap, imbricate, jut, shingle, span, bridge, overarch, overhang **9 roof**, roof in, dome, tile, thatch, plaster, ceil **10 face**, front, revet, render, clad, brick, mortar, grout, pebble-dash, panel, plank, paint, plaster, size, stucco, parget, wallpaper, curtain, drape, mould **11 surface**, pave, concrete, cement, tar, tarmac, macadamize, gravel **12 protect**, shield, screen, shade, insulate, lag, house, guard, defend, armour, watch over, hide out **13 hide**, conceal, cover up, mask, veil, cloak, cowl, shroud, hood, disguise, camouflage, masquerade, cloud, obscure, blot out **14 include**, embody, incorporate, contain, comprise **15 cover for**, substitute for, replace, alternate, surrogate, foster, fill in, stand in, back up, relieve, understudy

ADJECTIVES 16 covered, topped, capped, corked, glazed, varnished, stained, painted, whitewashed, copperplated, roofed, tiled, thatched, faced, bricked, panelled, papered, wallpapered **17 protected**, shielded, enclosed, wrapped, packaged, boxed, crated, encased, bound, sheathed, swathed, bandaged, hidden, concealed, screened, masked, veiled, shrouded, cloaked, robed, hooded, camouflaged, disguised **18 covering**, overlaying, overlying, spanning, superimposed, epidermal, cuticular **19 inclusive**, embodied, incorporated, comprehensive **20 substitutive**, substitutable, alternative, surrogate, foster, stand-in, backup, relief

135 Cowardice

NOUNS 1 cowardice, timidity, pusillanimity, chicken-heartedness, faint-heartedness, dastardliness, cravenness, poltroonery, timorousness, fearfulness, defeatism, desertion, cowering, overcaution **2 coward**, dastard, craven, poltroon

ADJECTIVES 3 cowardly, dastardly, craven, pusillanimous, timid, shy, spineless, soft, namby-pamby, chicken-hearted, lily-livered, faint-hearted, weak-kneed, timorous, wet, fearful, afraid, scared, frightened, rattled, daunted, cowed, panicky, unheroic

VERBS 4 be a coward, lack courage, back out, cower, quail, cringe, shrink, recoil, skulk, sneak, retreat, desert, run away, turn tail

136 Credit

NOUNS 1 credit, creditworthiness, sound proposition, borrowing capacity, liquidity ratio, overdraft, the red, loan, mortgage, debt, account, deferred payment, score, tally, bill **2 credit card**, plastic money, plastic, phonecard **3 deposit**, credit account, deposit account, the black, credits, balances, right-hand entry **4 bank**, finance company, building society, friendly society, credit union, pawn shop **5 lender**, loan-maker, mortgagee, pledgee, pawnbroker, usurer, extortionist, debt collector **6 depositor**, investor **7 repute**, standing, prestige, trust, confidence

VERBS 8 credit, lend, loan, grant, seek payment **9 acquire credit**, charge, defer payment, borrow, mortgage

ADJECTIVES 12 charged, deferred **13 in credit**, creditworthy

137 Cunning

NOUNS 1 cunning, slyness, wiliness, foxiness, artfulness, craftiness, art, skill, lore, knowledge, resourcefulness, inventiveness, ingenuity, imagination, knack, guile, cleverness, smartness, sharpness, acuity, shrewdness, sophistication, intelligence, stealthiness, subtlety, latency, concealment, caution, wariness, suppleness, slipperiness, shiftiness, knavery, chicanery, trickery, imposture, foul play, finesse, jugglery, sleight, cheating, circumvention, deception, duplicity, sophistry, double-dealing, double-crossing, beguilement, disguise, insincerity, hypocrisy, manoeuvring, evasion, temporizing, tactics, diplomacy, Machiavellianism, realpolitik, jobbery, gerrymandering, improbity, sharp practice, under-the-table deal, under-the-counter purchase, gentleman's club, intrigue, plot **2 stratagem**, ruse, wile, art, artifice, device, resource, resort, ploy, shift, dodge, contrivance, expedient, machination, game, plot, subterfuge, evasion, excuse, pretext, white lie, cheat, deception, sham, swindle, fraud, confidence trick, feint, catch, net, web, ambush, Trojan horse, stalking-horse, trial balloon, trap, ditch, pitfall, Parthian shot, blind, smoke screen, red herring, manoeuvre

ADJECTIVES 3 cunning, sly, wily, foxy, artful, crafty, clever, skilful, knowledgeable, resourceful, inventive, ingenious, guileful, imaginative, disingenuous, subtle, serpentine, vulpine, feline, tricky, tricksy, devious, secret, stealthy, clandestine, underhand, scheming, contriving, practising, plotting, planning, intriguing, conspiring, calculating, Machiavellian, arch, knowing, intelligent, smart, sharp, astute, shrewd, wise, acute, sophisticated, urbane, canny, experienced, reticent, reserved, cautious, wary, tactical, strategical, well-laid, insidious, perfidious, shifty, slippery, timeserving, temporizing, equivocal, sophistical, flattering, beguiling, hypocritical, insincere, deceitful, rascally

VERBS 4 be cunning, finesse, shift, dodge, manoeuvre, jockey, twist, turn, wriggle, hide, lie low, skulk, lurk, scheme, intrigue, conspire, plot, plan, devise, contrive, wangle, confuse, tinker, circumvent, gerrymander, overreach, outsmart, outwit, outdo, trick, cheat, swindle, defraud, double-cross, deceive, betray, coax, flatter, beguile, cajole, wheedle, blarney, temporize, juggle, ambush

138 Curiosity

NOUNS 1 curiosity, inquisitiveness, questioning, interest, inquisition, inquiry **2 prying**, nosiness, snooping, meddling, officiousness, gossip, tittle-tattle, morbid curiosity, prurience **3 meddler**, gossip, gossipmonger, scandalmonger, stirrer, prier, spy, tittle-tattler, eavesdropper, voyeur

ADJECTIVES 4 curious, inquisitive, inquiring, inquisitorial, questioning, interested, keen, adventurous **5 prying**, officious, meddlesome, meddling

VERBS 6 be curious, inquire, inquire after, question, quiz, interrogate, search for, show interest, seek out, gossip, tittle-tattle, sightsee, eavesdrop

139 Curse

NOUNS 1 curse, oath, profanity, obscenity, bad language, vulgarity, scurrility, imprecation, dysphemism, swearword, four-letter word, expletive, invective, ribaldry, bawdy verse, dirty joke, filth, cursing, swearing, foul mouth, billingsgate, scatology, blasphemy, sacrilege **2 vilification**, vituperation, denunciation, fulmination, execration, revilement, scurrility, verbal abuse, thundering, reproach, opprobrium, slander, libel, defamation, calumny, obloquy, threat, evil speaking, onslaught, attack **3 malediction**, ill wishes, spell, voodoo spell, curse, charm, jinx, imprecation, damnation, ban, excommunication, anathema

VERBS 4 curse, use profanity, swear, talk dirty, use expletives, use billingsgate, scatologize, dysphemize **5 vilify**, revile, denunciate, execrate, condemn, fulminate, rebuke, scold, chide, tongue-lash, abuse, blackguard, accuse, reproach, vituperate, rail against, inveigh against, thunder, reproach, slander, libel, defame, call names, disgrace, threaten, attack **6 wish ill**, charm, damn, imprecate, anathematize, ban

ADJECTIVES 7 cursing, swearing, profane, obscene, vulgar, scurrilous, naughty, offensive, indelicate, blue, four-letter, Anglo-Saxon, invective, dirty, filthy, vile, indecent, ribald, bawdy, Rabelaisian, risque, foul, foul-mouthed, dysphemistic, blasphemous **8 vituperative**, abusive, vitriolic, vilifying, reviling, denunciatory, blasting, reproachful, ignominious, opprobrious, slanderous, libellous, defamatory, calumnious, attacking **9 maledictive**, imprecatory, damning, cursed, accursed, damned, hexed, jinxed, bewitched, unblest, execrative, banned, excommunicated

140 Curve

NOUNS 1 curvature, concavity, convexity, bending, arching, circularity, curliness, curvilinearity **2 bend**, camber, turn, U-turn, S-curve, detour, curl, arc, arch, crescent, coil, loop, spiral, circuit, circle, oval, rondure, semicircle, meniscus, parabola, hyperbola, roundness, wave **3 curved things**, horseshoe, dome, half-moon, archer's bow, rainbow, horizon

ADJECTIVES 4 curved, cambered, curviform, curvilinear, bent, concave, convex, turning, sloping, stooped, bowed, vaulted, arciform, arched, spiraled, curled, coiled, looped, round, oval, semicircular, circular, crescentic, lunar, meniscal, parabolic, hyperbolic, domical **5 well-rounded**, curvy, wavy, undulatory, pear-shaped

VERBS 6 curve, bend, loop, arc, arch, turn, detour, curl, coil, spiral, bow, circle, twine, entwine

141 Dancing

NOUNS 1 dance, ball, masquerade, tea dance, ceilidh, barn dance **2 dance**, ballroom dance, shuffle, soft-shoe shuffle, cakewalk, Castle walk, solo dance, pas seul, clog dance, step dance, tap dance, toe dance, sand dance, fan dance, hula-hula, hula, high kicks, cancan, belly dance, polka, waltz, last waltz, Viennese waltz, hesitation waltz, St Bernard, valeta, Lancers, excuse-me, Paul Jones, snowball, foxtrot, slow foxtrot, fast foxtrot, turkey trot, quickstep, Charleston, black bottom, blues, English waltz, military two-step, paso doble, tango, rumba, samba, mambo, bossanova, habanera, beguine, conga, bunny hop, cha-cha-cha, boomps-a-daisy, hokey cokey, Lambeth Walk, Palais Glide, stomp, bop, bebop, shimmy, jive, jitterbug **3 dancer**, tap dancer, clog dancer, classical dancer, high-kicker, cancan dancer, go-go dancer, entertainer, waltzer, fox-trotter, shuffler, jiver, jitterbug, bebopper, disco dancer **4 ballet steps**, attitude, chassé, glissade, bourrée, arabesque, arabesque penchée, pirouette, petit allegro, soubresauté, changement, brisé volé, batterie, cabriole, entrechat, jeté, deboulé, ballong **5 positions at the barre**, plié, tendus, glissées, battement, fondus, développés

VERBS 6 dance, go dancing, choreograph, tap-dance, waltz, foxtrot, quickstep, Charleston, tango, rumba, jive, jitterbug, stomp, bop, twist, rock, disco-dance, break-dance, bodypop, whirl, rotate, cavort, gambol, frolic, prance, caper, jig, jig about, shuffle, trip, skip

142 Danger

ADJECTIVES 1 dangerous, perilous, treacherous, hazardous, risky, unknown, uncertain, unlit, venturous, difficult, chancy, tricky, critical, serious, nasty, ugly, menacing, threatening, ominous, foreboding, alarming, frightening, at stake, in question, inflammable, explosive, radioactive, toxic, deadly, life-threatening, harmful, unhealthy **2 unsafe**, treacherous, untrustworthy, unreliable, doubtful, shaky, slippery, insecure, unsound, precarious, unbalanced, unsteady, unstable, tottering, top-heavy, tumbledown, ramshackle, dilapidated, rickety, frail, crumbling, condemned, jerry-built, shoddy, gimcrack, crazy, weak, leaky, waterlogged, critical, delicate, ticklish, risky, heart-stopping, nerve-racking, last-second, last-minute **3 vulnerable**, unprotected, undefended, liable, susceptible, open to, exposed, naked, bare, uncovered, unarmoured, unfortified, expugnable, pregnable, helpless, defenceless, unarmed, isolated, deserted, abandoned, stranded, unsupported, unshielded, unattended, unguarded, unaware, naive, unprepared **4 endangered**, in peril, at risk, in jeopardy, slipping, drifting, surrounded, trapped, at bay, cornered, under siege

NOUNS 5 danger, peril, jeopardy, risk, hazard, perilousness, riskiness, hazardousness, treacherousness, lion's mouth, dragon's lair, dire straits, predicament, emergency, urgency, crisis, insecurity, unsoundness, ticklishness, precariousness, shakiness, unsteadiness, uncertainty, razor's edge, black spot, snag, pitfall, trap, ambush, venturesomeness, daring, rashness, gambling, venture, slippery slope, impending disaster, menace, threat, apprehension, anxiety, nervousness, fear, narrow escape **6 danger signal**, strange noise, gunshot, scream, ticking parcel **7 vulnerability**, liability, susceptibility, nonimmunity, openness, exposure, nakedness, pregnability, helplessness, defencelessness, naivety, innocence, instability, insecurity, easy target, Achilles' heel, weakness, tender spot, unsoundness, failing, flaw, defect, imperfection

VERBS 8 be in danger, totter, slip, slide, tumble, fall **9 face danger**, expose oneself, risk, defy, tempt fate, court disaster, venture, dare, hazard **10 endanger**, jeopardize, imperil, compromise, hazard, risk, stake, gamble, venture, drive headlong, loom, forebode, bode ill, menace

143 Darkness

NOUNS 1 darkness, sunlessness, dimness, shadow, shade, gloom, murk, lividness, leadenness, sombreness, drabness, obscurity, bad light, twilight, blindness, blackout, eclipse, blackness, pitch-darkness, Stygian gloom, night-blindness **2 darkening**, dimming, extinguishment, obscuration, obfuscation, occultation, underexposure, blackening, blackout, eclipse, fadeout, lights out, power cut **3 dark colour**, brunette, swarthiness, blackness, dirt, grime

ADJECTIVES 4 dark, unlit, unilluminated, dim, ill-lit, underexposed, lightproof, lightless, sunless, moonless, starless, pitch-dark, shady, umbrageous, overcast, thundery, louring, dusky, gloomy, dingy, murky, tenebrous, black, Stygian, Cimmerian **5 darkening**, extinguishing, shading, shadowing, screening, obscuring, dimming, dipping **6 dark-coloured**, dark, brunette, swarthy, dusky, darkling, black, pitch-black, jet-black, inky, ebony, melanic, sable, livid, leaden, grimy, dirty, stained, drab **7 benighted**, dismal, gloomy, cheerless, depressed, dejected, mournful, clouded, murky, wicked, evil, ominous, menacing, threatening, sinister, shadowy, shady, sombre, grim, forbidding, unenlightened, ignorant, blind, oblivious, obfuscated, obscure, cryptic, mysterious, enigmatic, mystic, inscrutable, secret, arcane, hidden

VERBS 8 be dark, lack light **9 become dark**, darken, deepen, blacken, grow dark, cloud over, lour, dim **10 make dark**, darken, obscure, obfuscate, extinguish, douse, quench, snuff, dim, dip, shade, shadow, adumbrate, occult, eclipse, shutter, black out, underexpose, blindfold, hood, veil, shroud, silhouette, shade in, hatch, cross-hatch, deject

144 Daytime

NOUNS 1 morning, forenoon, dawn, waking time, daybreak, sunrise, sunup, morning light, first light, daylight, matins, prime, terce, cockcrow, dawn chorus, rosy-fingered dawn, Aurora **2 morning thing**, morning star, Venus, morning-glory, morning sickness, crowing cock, early bird, breakfast, rush hour **3 noon**, 12 o'clock, 1200 hours, noontide, midday **4 afternoon**, siesta

ADJECTIVES 5 morning, matin, matutinal, forenoon, dawn, early, fresh, dewy **6 noon**, midday **7 afternoon**, postmeridian

145 Deafness

NOUNS 1 deafness, hearing loss, deaf-mutism, unmusicalness, inattention, daydreaming, indifference,

heedlessness, oblivion, insensitivity, lip-reading, sign language, signing, dactylology, finger alphabet, deaf aid **2 inaudibility**, faintness, earplug, silencer, damper, mute, sordino, soft pedal, soundproofing, baffle, ultrasound, poor reception, interference
ADJECTIVES 3 deaf, unhearing, hearing-impaired, stone deaf, deaf-mute, tone deaf, unmusical **4 unhearing**, unaware, oblivious, deaf to, unheeding, unconcerned, indifferent, insensitive **5 deafening**, ear-splitting, piercing **6 unheard**, inaudible, toneless, faint, muted, soundproof, ultrasonic
VERBS 7 be deaf, miss, ignore, not listen, tune out **8 deafen**, make deaf **9 muffle**, mute, baffle, deaden, silence, soundproof, insulate, jam **10 be unheard**

146 Dearness

NOUNS 1 high price, dearness, expensiveness, costliness **2 unfair price**, overcharging, overpricing, surcharge, exorbitance **3 inflationary price**, mounting costs, inflation, bullish tendency, bull market **4 extortion**, usury, profiteering **5 value**, worth, valuableness, invaluableness, pricelessness, preciousness, rarity
ADJECTIVES 6 dear, expensive, costly, high-priced, extravagant, fancy, luxury, up-market, exorbitant, excessive, overcharging, unreasonable, prohibitive, extortionate, inflationary, rising, climbing, soaring, spiralling, mounting, rocketing, high-cost, sky-high, bullish, usurious **7 valuable**, invaluable, priceless, inestimable, precious, exclusive, rare
VERBS 8 be dear, appreciate, escalate, soar, mount, rocket **9 overcharge**, overprice, surcharge, sell dear, oversell, rack-rent, profiteer, mark up, inflate, extort, fleece **10 overpay**, overspend

147 Death

• *And I looked, and behold a pale horse: and his name that sat on him was Death, and Hell followed with him.* Bible: Revelations.
• *Alack he's gone the way of all flesh.* William Congreve.

NOUNS 1 death, clinical death, brain death, dying, expiry, decease, demise, mortality, extinction, stillbirth, exit, departure, passing, perishability, putrefaction, mortification, necrosis, decay, cadaverousness, ephemerality, transience, the beyond, eternal rest **2 death personified**, Azrael **3 symbol of death**, death's-head **4 death sentence**, death-knell, martyrdom, quietus, execution, capital punishment, legalized killing, hanging, electric chair, gas chamber, lethal injection, guillotine, firing squad **5 killing**, murder, poisoning, stabbing **6 dying day**, last hour, deathbed, deathwatch, deathbed confession, final words, last words, death scene, last breath, last gasp, death rattle, death throes, extreme unction, passing bell, last rites, funeral rites **7 dead person**, fatality, casualty, victim, stillbirth, the deceased, body, corpse, cadaver, carcass, mummy, skeleton, fossil, remains, relics, ashes **8 the dead**, ancestors, forefathers, precursors, loved ones **9 the spiritual world**, next world, future state, afterlife, hereafter, the shades, saints, souls, spirits, ghosts, phantoms, underworld, Sheol, Styx, Stygian shore,

Hades, hell, Elysian fields, Abraham's bosom
VERBS 10 die, succumb, expire, perish, decease, pass away, be taken, drop off, fall asleep, predecease, become extinct **11 meet one's fate**, die young, fall, get killed, founder, hang **12 bury**, entomb, embalm, mourn, grieve, lament, bemoan
ADJECTIVES 13 dying, expiring, deathly, deathlike, cadaverous, skeletal, terminally ill, hopeless, moribund, half-dead, slipping away, sinking fast, fading **14 dead**, deceased, defunct, demised, lifeless, breathless, still, inanimate, exanimate, no more, passed away, released, departed, gone, stillborn, extinct, finished, in Paradise, late, lamented, regretted, killed **15 deadly**, mortal, fatal, terminal, lethal, murderous, perishable, ephemeral **16 deathly**, cadaverous, ghastly, livid, pale, pallid, wan, ashen, ghostly, haggard **17 post-mortem**, post-obit, posthumous, funereal, embalmed

148 Debt

NOUNS 1 debt, indebtedness, owing, liability, obligation, commitment, encumbrance, accountability, responsibility, something owing, debts, bills, debit, charge, overdraft, the red, charge card **2 national debt**, national credit, trading deficit **3 loan**, capital gearage, leverage, mortgage, guaranty, collateral security, sum entrusted, lending **4 interest**, premium, bank rate **5 amount owing**, deficit, bill, account, tally, score, overdraft, receivables, overdue payment, arrears, back pay, foreclosure, repossession, defaulting, write-off **6 debtor**, cardholder, borrower, loanee, guarantor, co-signer, obligor, drawee, mortgagor, pledgor, defaulter, nonpayer, bilker
VERBS 7 be in debt, owe, borrow money, overspend, overdraw, pay interest, get credit **8 not pay**, default, bilk
ADJECTIVES 9 in debt, pledged, bound, obliged, committed, encumbered, mortgaged, liable, responsible, accountable, answerable, beholden, borrowing, owing, unpaid, due, overdrawn **10 unable to pay**, insolvent, nonpaying, defaulting

149 Deception

• *Beware of false prophets, which come to you in sheep's clothing, but inwardly they are ravening wolves.* Bible: Matthew.

NOUNS 1 deception, deceit, lying, falsehood, dishonesty, duplicity, double-dealing, circumvention, fraudulence, craftiness, artfulness, guile, cunning, craft, insidiousness, underhandedness, sneakiness, deviousness, shiftiness, furtiveness, surreptitiousness, indirection **2 self-deception**, wishful thinking, delusion **3 hypocrisy**, falseness, insincerity, mealy-mouthedness, lip service, empty gesture, veneer, hollowness, bubble, sham, pretence, Tartuffery, Pecksniffery, Pharisaism, artificiality, false face, outward show **4 false-heartedness**, duplicity, hypocrisy, treachery, treason, betrayal, perfidy **5 falseness**, deceit, trickiness, imposture, fallaciousness, misleading, misguidance, misdirection, misinformation, misconception, mockery, insubstantiality, hallucination, illusion, phantasm, mirage **6 imitation**, rubbish, tinsel, paste, ormolu, fool's gold, cultured pearl **7 tricking**, fooling, outsmarting, outmanoeuvring, mockery, ridicule, spoofing, bluffing, shamming, circumvention, outwitting, ensnarement, entrapment, entanglement, enmeshment, whitewashing, dupery, hoodwinking, manipulation, quackery, chicanery, sharp practice, dodgery, artifice, machination, sorcery, witchcraft, connivance, collusion **8 trick**, ploy, gambit, ruse, stratagem, contrivance, catch, artifice, device, scheme, design, blind, wile, shift, dodge, sleight, fetch, feint, pass, bluff, gimmick **9 fraud**, racket, dodge, swindle, cheat, dishonesty, legal chicanery, insider dealing, counterfeiting, forgery, ballot rigging, gerrymandering **10 hoax**, deception, sham, spoof, game, bluff, sport, joke **11 deceiver**, hypocrite, liar, deluder, duper, misleader, beguiler, hoaxer, spoofer, cheat, imposter, fake, charlatan, impersonator, pretender, sham, fraud, mountebank, poser, malingerer, hypochondriac, masquerader, guiser, phoney **12 liar**, fibber, perjurer, false witness, mythomaniac, pseudologue, prevaricator, fabricator, equivocator, fabulist, falsifier **13 cheat**, swindler, defrauder, confidence man, trickster, cozener, gyp, bilker, crook, short-changer, counterfeiter, horsetrader, cardsharp, pettifogger, shark, land-grabber **14 decoy,** lure, trap **15 hypocrite**, phoney, sham, fair-weather friend, whited sepulchre, canter, snuffler **16 traitor**, treasonist, quisling, betrayer, serpent, double-crosser, double-dealer, double agent, turncoat, informer **17 dupe**, victim, fool, April fool, laughing stock, fair game, greenhorn, innocent, beginner, trusting soul, puppet, cat's paw, toy

VERBS 18 deceive, be dishonest, sneak, double-cross, double-deal **19 be deceived**, fall for **20 deceive oneself**, delude oneself **21 be a hypocrite**, pretend, belie **22 be false**, betray, trick, deceive, delude, beguile, mock, misinform, mislead, misguide **23 trick**, fool, mock, ridicule, outsmart, outmanoeuvre, spoof, bluff, sham, circumvent, contrive, catch, devise, scheme, design, shift, dodge, fetch, feint, pass, fudge, divert, outwit, dupe, swindle, hoodwink, manipulate, chicane, machinate, connive, collude **24 be fraudulent**, dodge, swindle, fleece, bilk, cheat, counterfeit **25 hoax**, deceive **26 disguise**, conceal, camouflage, mask, veil, cloak, masquerade, varnish, paint, whitewash **27 snare**, trap, gin, catch, ambush, waylay, kidnap, hijack, decoy, lure, divert

ADJECTIVES 28 deceiving, misleading, double-dealing, conniving, contriving, covering up, whitewashing, colluding, dodging, feinting, designing, scheming, cheating, calculating, cunning, sharp, artful, guileful, wily, crafty, tricky, shifty, devious, dishonest, sneaky, furtive, surreptitious, indirect, smooth **29 deceptive**, false, fallacious, duplicitous, dishonest, conspiratorial, fraudulent, sorcerous, insidious, illicit, underhand, gerrymandered, contrived, gimmicky, misleading **30 deceived**, duped, tricked, hoaxed, fooled, outsmarted, hookwinked, victimized, outmanoeuvred, bluffed, cheated, outwitted, ensnared, entangled, manipulated, misled, misguided, misdirected, misinformed, mocked, ridiculed **31 hypocritical**, false, insincere, phoney, sanctimonious, mealy-mouthed, hollow, pretending **32 treacherous**, false-hearted, duplicitous, faithless, inconstant, double-dealing, betraying, treasonous, perfidious **33 imitative**, artificial, phoney, synthetic, simulated, substituted, cultured, unnatural, unoriginal, copied, plastic, man-made, fake, bogus, sham, mock, quack, counterfeit, forged, shoddy **34 disguised**, concealed, hidden, camouflaged, incognito, masquerading, masked, veiled, cloaked, varnished, painted, whitewashed **35 trapped**, snared, ginned, ambushed, mined, kidnapped, hijacked, baited, trawled, hooked, netted

150 Decoration

NOUNS 1 adornment, garnish, ornamentation, ornateness, richness, enhancement, enrichment **2 pattern**, design, fancywork, detail, flourish, illustration, etching, tattooing, pokerwork, pyrography, filigree, gilding, gold leaf, scrollwork, illumination, lettering, moulding, beading, breadwork, fluting, ormolu, mosaic, needlework, embroidery, tapestry, patchwork, crochet, lacework, smocking **3 honour**, decoration, medal, honours, title, spurs, badge, pips, stripes, star, garter, order **4 decorating**, housepainting, wallpapering **5 decorative articles**, trinkets, spangles, sparklers, gandery, frippery, flounce, ruffle, frill, furbelow, fringe, ribbon, braid **6 jewellery**, baubles, necklace, bracelet, bangle, ear ring, ring, tiara, torque, badge, pin, brooch, tie-pin, hat-pin, anklet, medallion, nose-ring

ADJECTIVES 7 decorated, ornamented, garnished, ornate, embellished, enriched, enhanced, bejewelled, gilt, gilded, embroidered, trimmed, worked, inlaid, enamelled, patterned, ornamental, fancy, non-functional, scenic, picturesque, baroque **8 decorated**, knighted

VERBS 9 decorate, embellish, adorn, enhance, ornament, bejewel, bedeck, bedizen, array, garland, crown, illuminate, illustrate, emblazon, colour, embroider, chase, tool, engrave, festoon, emboss, trace, wreathe, paint, etch **10 paint and decorate**, wallpaper, refurbish, spruce up **11 honour**, decorate

151 Decrease

NOUNS 1 decrease, deduction, subtraction, lessening, decrement, regression, de-escalation, abatement, slackening, moderation, growing soft, diminuendo, decrescendo, dimming, fading, evanescence, waning, shrinking, contraction, detumescence, dwindling, ebb, drain, degeneration, atrophy, failure, subsidence, depreciation, enfeeblement, weakening, impoverishment, shortage, slowdown, deceleration, retardation, reduction, disappearance, erosion, attrition, wear, decay, dilapidation, damage, wastage, leakage, loss, extinction, consumption, limitation, restriction, curtailment, squeeze, compression, retrenchment, rationalization, cutback, economization, shortening, abbreviation, abridgment, precis, belittlement **2 decline**, downturn,

fall, drop, sinking, plunge, collapse, slump, deflation, depression
VERBS 3 decrease, lessen, de-escalate, ease, abate, slacken, moderate, fade, evanesce, wane, wither, shrink, contract, shrivel, diminish, dwindle, ebb, drain, corrode, fail, degenerate, atrophy, die away, peter out, decline, subside, sink, plunge, collapse, slump, depreciate, level off, slow down, decelerate, lose, shed, cast off, disappear, melt away, become scarce, thin, detumesce, die out **4 make smaller**, decrease, whittle, pare down, scrape, shave, trim, prune, dock, clip, slash, reduce, cut, thin out, limit, restrict, curtail, scale down, squeeze, compress, contract, retrench, economize, shorten, abbreviate, abridge, condense, precis, decelerate, retard, depress, lower, weaken, enfeeble, debilitate, dilute, alleviate, belittle, minimize, undervalue, underestimate, degrade
ADJECTIVES 5 decreasing, declining, falling, dwindling, waning, fading, evanescent, abating, softening, diminuendo, decrescendo, sinking, subsiding, detumescent, ebbing, decaying **6 decrescent**, declinate, reductive, depressive, debilitative, deflationary, depreciatory, loss-making, regressive, corrosive, deliquescent, decompressive, decadent, decayable

152 Defiance

NOUNS 1 defiance, audacity, nerve, impertinence, pertness, impudence, insolence, belligerence, courage, boldness, bravura, bravado, daringness, presumption, temerity, self-assertion, assurance, arrogance, bluster, bumptiousness, shamelessness, contrariness, cockiness, brashness, brassiness, brazenness, rashness, effrontery, provocativeness, sauce **2 disobedience**, insubordination, resistance, opposition, dissent, disagreement, confrontation, challenge, rebelliousness, refusal, contumacy, contemptuousness, derision, disdain **3 act of defiance**, challenge, dare, threat, taunt, insult, contumely, demonstration, sit-in, march, treason, insurrection
VERBS 4 defy, challenge, oppose, protest, flout, dare, brave, withstand, outstare, presume **5 be insubordinate**, scorn, spurn, slight, disregard, ignore, resist, refuse, confront, disobey, disagree, threaten, challenge, oppose, dissent, dare, taunt, act insolent, insult, answer back
ADJECTIVES 6 defiant, outspoken, assertive, emphatic, assured, unabashed, audacious, bold, arrogant, presumptuous, stubborn, obstinate, stiff-necked, bumptious, offensive, impudent, impertinent, pert, insolent, insulting, contemptuous, disdainful, derisive, shameless, brash, brassy, brazen, courageous, daring, reckless, saucy, cocky **7 defying**, challenging, disagreeing, disobedient, recalcitrant, refractory, obstinate, antagonistic, belligerent, provocative, aggressive, rebellious

153 Degree

NOUNS 1 degree, extent, measure, amount, frequency, intensity, rate, amplitude, magnitude, value, calibre, quantity, depth, height, altitude, size, breadth, speed, gradualism, slowness, scope, range, duration, reach, compass, limitation, stint, scale, pitch, tenor, register **2 rank**, level, hierarchy, grading, echelon, precedence, order, place, position, station, circumstance, footing, standing, status, class, caste **3 gradation**, measurement, calibration, valuation, differentiation, differential, classification, rating, ranking, remove, relativeness, comparison, ratio, proportion, ration, standard, grading, shading, notation, bar, line, mark, notch, peg **4 interval**, period, time, stint, shift, portion, part, shade, shadow, nuance, point, place, step, rung, stair, stage, plane, plateau, steppingstone, turning point

VERBS 5 measure, classify, evaluate, rate, rank, order, class, grade, sort, mark, peg, score, scale, shade, graduate, place, position, estimate, quantify, calibrate, calculate, compare, differentiate, precede **6 change gradually**, lower, taper off, shade off, cut back, trim, pare, whittle down, abate, die away, fade, diminish, decrease, wane, dissolve, evolve, melt into, increase, augment, build up, expand, inflate, swell

ADJECTIVES 7 gradational, graded, measured, rated, scaled, calibrated, classified, valued, sized, sorted, differentiated, differential, relative, comparative, proportional, portioned, standard, encompassing, limited, majority, minority, level, regular, frequent, extensive, progressive, gradual, slow-ranging, slow-changing, growing, increasing, waxing, waning, tapering, fading **8 ranked**, hierarchic, leading, preceding

154 Delegate

NOUNS 1 delegate, nominee, appointee, envoy, emissary, representative, Parliamentarian, minister, cabinet member, diplomat, ambassador, legate, commissioner, chargé d'affaires, consul, negotiator, messenger, agent, middleman, intermediary, clerk, councillor, deputy **2 delegation**, authorization, appointment, nomination, assignment, election, decentralization, devolution, devolvement, job sharing

VERBS 3 delegate, depute, assign, consign, appoint, nominate, elect, authorize, commission, empower, entrust, job-share, devolve, decentralize **4 represent**, act for, stand for

ADJECTIVES 5 delegated, elected, nominated, appointed, representative, Parliamentary, ministerial, diplomatic, ambassadorial, legatine, legationary, consular, intermediary **6 decentralized**, devolved, shared, deputized

155 Deliverance

VERBS 1 deliver, save, rescue, extricate, unravel, extract, untie, unbind, unfetter, unburden, disencumber, relieve, release, emancipate, liberate, free, unlock, let out, reprieve, acquit, exempt, excuse, spare, redeem, ransom, bail out, buy off, purchase, salvage, retrieve

NOUNS 2 deliverance, saving, rescue, extrication, unravelling, untangling, extraction, disencumberment, riddance, relief, release, emancipation, freedom, liberation, let-off, amnesty, discharge, reprieve, acquittal, dispensation, excuse, exemption, escape, letout, way out, salvation, redemp-

tion, ransom, bail, buying off, purchase, salvage, retrieval, recovery, restoration, respite, delay, truce
ADJECTIVES 3 deliverable, saveable, salvable, rescuable, extricable, redeemable, salvageable, saved, rescued, liberated
INTERJECTIONS 4 to the rescue!, man overboard!

156 Demonstration

NOUNS 1 demonstration, display, manifestation, showing, exhibition, exposition, presentation, disclosure, revelation, presentment, publication, performance **2 demonstrativeness**, openness, frankness, candour, emotionality, affection, effusiveness, expansiveness, ostentation, showiness, flashiness, flamboyance, exhibitionism, dramatics, theatrics, staginess, emotionalism **3 explanation**, demonstration, clarification, elucidation, exposition, indication, illustration, description, depiction, delineation, illumination, exemplification, expounding, exegesis, briefing, instructions, lecture, discourse, example, model **4 proof**, demonstration, evidence, substantiation, confirmation, verification, determination, ascertainment, settlement, ratification, corroboration, justification, affirmation, attestation **5 demonstrability**, demonstrableness, provability, verifiability, confirmability, accountability, certainty, likelihood **6 mass demonstration**, parade, pageant, spectacle, march, rally, protest, picket, strike, boycott
ADJECTIVES 7 demonstrated, obvious, manifest, plain, clear, express, explicit, displayed, exhibited, disclosed, exposed, revealed, published, publicized, expository, exhibitional, revelatory **8 demonstrative**, open, unrestrained, frank, candid, warm, affectionate, effusive, expansive, ostentatious, showy, flashy, flamboyant, dramatic, stagy, theatrical, exhibitionist, emotional, exhibitionistic **9 explanatory**, explicatory, illustrative, indicative, descriptive, representative, exemplificatory, illuminating, exegetic, explained, clarified, cleared up, elucidated, illustrated, described, depicted, delineated, illuminated, exemplified **10 demonstrable**, provable, confirmable, attestable, verifiable, evident, self-evident, obvious, undeniable, apparent, perspicuous, distinct, indisputable, unquestionable, positive, certain, conclusive **11 proven**, shown, substantiated, confirmed, verified, determined, ascertained, settled, ratified, corroborated, borne out, justified, affirmed, attested, evidential, probative, probatory, corroborative **12 demonstrating**, protesting, objecting, opposing, dissenting, agitating, rallying, marching, parading, striking
VERBS 13 demonstrate, show, display, exhibit, manifest, disclose, expose, point out, reveal, put forward, publish, perform, flaunt, brandish **14 explain**, expound, elucidate, express, indicate, unfold, clarify, illuminate, exemplify, illustrate, quote, cite, itemize, particularize, delineate, depict, describe, brief, instruct **15 prove**, evince, substantiate, establish, evidence, validate, ratify, verify, corroborate, support, circumstantiate, justify, determine, ascertain, fix, settle, confirm, affirm **16 appear**, materialize,

speak out, assert oneself, perform, show off, dramatize **17 protest**, dissent, object, oppose, agitate, demonstrate, rally, march, strike, picket, boycott

157 Density

NOUNS 1 density, solidity, bulk, mass, thickness, compactness, concreteness, toughness, hardness, closeness, cohesion, coalescence, consistency, impenetrability, impermeability, imperviousness, coherence **2 concentration**, consolidation, condensation, coagulation, constriction, haemostasis, concretion, solidification, congealment **3 relative density**, specific gravity, densimeter, hydrometer **4 solid body**, mass, aggregate, conglomerate, hard core, nucleus, precipitate, deposit, sediment, coagulum, curd, clot, concretion, block, rock, stone, lump, chunk, clod, clump, cake, nugget, bone, obstacle

ADJECTIVES 5 dense, thick, compact, cohesive, close-packed, firm, incompressible, full, assembled, serried, massed, heavy, weighty, monolithic, solid, concrete, rigid, constrictive, strong, unbreakable, infrangible, indivisible, inseparable, consistent, impenetrable, thickset, impermeable **6 condensed**, consolidated, concentrated, solidified, binding, congealed, coagulated, constipated, costive, curdled, clotted, jelled, set, frozen, indissoluble, infusible, crystalline, caked, matted, knotted

VERBS 7 be dense, thicken, cohere, solidify, harden, cement, set, gelatinize, jell, congeal, coagulate, clot, curdle, cake, crust, consolidate, constipate, conglomerate, contract, nucleate, crystallize, fossilize, petrify, ossify, freeze **8 make dense**, bind, crowd, mass, pack, squeeze, cram, tamp, ram down, compact

158 Departure

VERBS 1 depart, leave, go, go away, get away, get along, make tracks, toddle along, trot along, slink off, slope off, flounce off, fling off, stamp off **2 withdraw**, retreat, turn back, pull out, exit, bow out, clock out, cease work, retire, resign, sign off, check out, vacate, evacuate, abandon, relinquish **3 quit**, emigrate, expatriate, move house, remove, relocate, leave home, disappear, vanish, take wing, slip away, elope, escape, abscond, absent oneself, march out, debouch, decamp **4 hurry off**, take off, make off, run off, flee, bolt, take flight, absquatulate, rush off, scamper away, skip off, dash off, nip off, whip off **5 set out**, set forth, be off, emerge, sally forth, issue forth, start out, strike out, get off, move off, march off, embark, board, jump on, hop on, mount, set sail, weigh anchor, cast off **6 part**, separate

NOUNS 7 departure, leaving, going, going away, exit, egress, exodus, emigration, migration, Hegira, flight, escape, getaway, flit, elopement, decampment, abandonment, withdrawal, retreat, retirement **8 start**, outset, embarkation, boarding, entrainment, enplanement, emplanement, takeoff, ascent, liftoff, blastoff **9 parting**, separation, leavetaking, congé, farewell, goodbye, goodnight, adieu, parting shot, valediction,

last words, obituary, epitaph, last post, golden handshake
ADJECTIVES 10 departing, leaving, farewell, valedictory, parting, leave-taking, last **11 departed**, gone, gone away, gone off **12 outgoing**, outward-bound

159 Depth

NOUNS 1 depth, deepness, drop, fall, bottomlessness, fathomlessness, cavernousness, lowering, sinking, submersion, immersion, excavation, spelunking, potholing, digging, burial, interment, mining, drilling, tunnelling **2 intensity**, strength, extent, measure **3 profundity**, understanding, wisdom, sagacity, insight, perspicacity, penetration, acuity
ADJECTIVES 4 deep, bottomless, unfathomable, fathomless, unsounded, unplumbed, abysmal, abyssal, plunging, cavernous, yawning, gaping, ankle-deep, knee-deep, deep-down, deep-set, sunken, engraved **5 deep-seated**, intense, extreme, sincere, profound, serious, heartfelt **6 wise**, profound, deep, understanding, knowledgeable, perspicacious, acute, astute **7 under**, underground, subterranean, hypogeal, buried, sunk, submerged, immersed, underwater, subaqua, undersea, submarine, suboceanic, deep-sea, deep-water, bathyal, bathypelagic **8 bathymetric**, bathometric, oceanographic, sounding, depth-sounding
VERBS 9 deepen, lower, drop, fall, sink, founder, descend, dive, plunge, yawn, gape, submerge, immerse, excavate, dig, bury, inter, mine, drill, tunnel, fathom, take soundings, probe **10 be profound**, understand

160 Deputy

NOUNS 1 deputy, assistant, right-hand man, second-in-command, number two, aide, lieutenant, viceregent, nuncio, vice president, vice chairman, viceroy, proconsul, propraetor, vicar-general, helper, secretary, girl Friday, auxiliary, relief worker, spokesperson **2 alternative**, surrogate, proxy, substitute, sub, replacement, reserve, understudy, double, stand-in, backup, stunt man, twelfth man, ghostwriter **3 agent**, go-between, representative, delegate, intermediary, middleman, trustee, broker, literary agent, contact, negotiator, arbitrator, mediator, lawyer, solicitor, attorney, diplomat, emissary, envoy, minister, ambassador, commissioner, legate, attaché, consul, matchmaker
VERBS 4 substitute for, act for, appear for, negotiate for, replace, understudy, double for, back up **5 represent**, negotiate, arbitrate, mediate, assist, help, aid **6 deputize**, commission, delegate, authorize, entrust, empower, charge, designate
ADJECTIVES 7 deputizing, representing, acting, standing in, substituting, diplomatic, ambassadorial, plenipotentiary, consular, proconsular, ministerial, deputy, intermediary, provisional, temporary, imitative

161 Derision

NOUNS 1 mockery, derisiveness, banter, badinage **2 act of derision**, satire, parody, caricature, cartoon, burlesque, lampoon, joke, denunciation **3 derider**, satirist, lam-

pooner, joker, mimic, caricaturist **4 laughing stock**, butt
ADJECTIVES 5 derisive, ridiculing, satirical, sarcastic
VERBS 6 deride, laugh at, snigger about, send up, mock, scoff at, jeer at, put down, mock, pillary, satirize, lampoon, caricature, guy, denounce

162 Descent

NOUNS 1 descent, going down, lowering, declension, decline, comedown, way down, down, downturn, downdraught, downthrow, demotion **2 sinkage**, decline, decrease, lowering, downward trend, depression, subsidence, droop, sag, catenary, slump, immersion, drowning, submergence, lapse, decurrence, cadence, gravitation **3 downflow**, downrush, downpour, shower, rain, cascade, nappe, waterfall, rapids, cataract, chute, precipice, defluxion, landslide, subsidence, avalanche **4 fall**, dropping, plummeting, plunging, swooping, dipping, tumble, overturning, stumble, titubation, trip, sprawl, crash, flop, spill, header, downfall, collapse, debâcle, failure, comedown, demotion, humiliation, ruin, end, nightfall **5 dive**, duck, stoop, dip, plunge, swoop, pounce, header, belly-flop, nose-dive, power-dive, drop, fall, landing, touchdown **6 slide**, slip, slither, glide, coast, glissade, inclination, declivity, slope, tilt, dip, acclivity **7 tunnelling**, boring, mining, burrowing, caving, speleology, digging, excavation, potholing **8 descender**, faller, free-faller, parachutist, aeronaut, sky-diver, hang-glider, diver, frogman, submariner, diving-bell
VERBS 9 descend, come down, lose height, gravitate, lower, get lower, decrease, decline, abate, ebb, fall off, drop off, go downhill, sink, seep, soak in, subside, settle, submerge, go under, drown, founder, dive, alight, abseil, rappel **10 droop**, sag, slouch, swag, slump, sit down, flop, plump, plop, hang down, prolapse, collapse, cave in, crash **11 trip**, fall, fall over, slip, totter, career, pitch, topple, overbalance, overturn, capsize, tumble, stumble, stagger, lurch, sprawl, spread-eagle, fall headlong **12 drop**, fall, plummet, plunge, swoop, dip, bow down, titubate, flutter down, spiral down, dive, parachute, skydive, bellyflop, nosedive, powerdive, prang, land, light upon, descend on, touch down, crashland **13 drip**, drizzle, patter, shower, cascade, flow down, pour down **14 slide**, slip, slither, skid, glide, skim, coast, glissade, toboggan, incline, slope, dip **15 tunnel**, bore, mine, burrow, excavate, go underground, dig down
ADJECTIVES 16 descending, down, downward, decurrent, declivitous, deciduous, downflowing, downrushing, pouring, downturning, sinking, declining, bearish, decreasing, lowering, subsiding, slumping, drowning, foundering, tottering, tumbling, crashing **17 drooping**, sagging, depressed, downcast **18 falling**, tumbling, stumbling, titubant, tripping, sprawling, flopping, spilling, lurching, plunging, plummeting, diving, dipping, nose-diving, dropping, falling, swooping, stooping, ducking, sliding, slipping, slithering, skidding

163 Description

NOUNS 1 description, account, statement, details, particulars, specification, report, record, delineation, depiction, picture, portrayal, characterization, profile, character sketch, case history, version **2 brief description**, caption, legend, indication, heading, subtitle, word portrait, thumbnail sketch, summary, outline, cameo, vignette **3 narration**, account, essay, story, plot, scenario, tale, yarn, fairy tale, folk tale, myth, legend, saga, epic, serial, fable, cautionary tale, parable, allegory, metaphor, simile, ballad, anecdote, reminiscence, chronicle, annals, history, record, journal, diary, drama, documentary, docudrama, faction, reportage, travelogue, fiction **4 factual account**, nonfiction, documentary, report, journalism, biography, autobiography, hagiography, obituary, personal account, confessions, memoirs, diary, journal **5 sort**, kind, type, genre, variety, breed, species, ilk **6 nomenclature**, naming, addressing, calling, roll call, appellation, denomination, terminology, taxonomy, classification, designation, description, identification, indication, antonomasia, christening, baptism, nicknaming, eponymy, onomastics, orismology, toponymy, misnaming **7 name**, nomen, noun, appellation, forename, praenomen, Christian name, agnomen, surname, patronymic, matronymic, cognomen, maiden name, diminutive, pen name, alias, pseudonym, allonym, sobriquet, nickname, tautonym, namesake, epithet, title, autograph, signature, label, tag, term, password, eponym, toponym, trademark, tradename **8 representation**, imitation, likeness, impression, picture, portrait, sketch, drawing, duplicate, double, spitting image, facsimile, tracing

ADJECTIVES 9 descriptive, representational, graphic, vivid, detailed, full, informative, illustrative, explicatory, explanatory, elucidatory, illuminating, expository, interpretive, amplifying, well-drawn, true-to-life, realistic, naturalistic, photographic, eidetic, convincing, picturesque, expressive, impressionistic, evocative, moving, poignant, thrilling, exciting, striking, highly coloured **10 narrative**, fictional, imaginative, kitchen-sink, factual, documentary, biographical, autobiographical, factional, mythological, epic, heroic, romantic **11 representing**, iconic, pictorial, emblematic, symbolic, figurative, diagrammatic, representational, realistic, true-to-life, photographic, artistic, primitive, naive, impressionistic

VERBS 12 describe, delineate, draw, sketch, picture, depict, portray, limn, paint, represent, illustrate, characterize, form, shape, fashion, design, draft, sketch out, adumbrate, rough out, outline, doodle **13 recount**, relate, tell, narrate, reminisce, evoke, characterize, detail, recapitulate, review, record, chronicle, repeat, recite, rehearse, communicate, report, cover, testify, correspond, fictionalize, dramatize, romanticize, mythologize **14 define**, specify, name, mention, detail, particularize, itemize, inventorize, explain **15 describe a circle**, circumscribe

164 Desire

• *Desire is the very essence of man.* Benedict Spinoza.

NOUNS 1 desire, wish, want, longing, craving, need, requirement, demand, will, urge, impulse, itch, eagerness, avidity, willingness, zeal, passion, ardour, aspiration, ambition, hope, covetousness, cupidity, greed, voracity, fascination, curiosity, inclination, penchant, predilection, preference, taste, appetancy, partiality, liking, fancy, fondness, love, lust, appetite, yearning, pining, hankering, wistfulness, nostalgia **2 desirability**, expedience, suitability, advisability, meritoriousness **3 appetite**, hunger, starvation, famine **4 sexual desire**, concupiscence, lust, lechery, libido, libidinousness, passion, concuspience, ardour, sexuality, carnality, nymphomania **5 object of desire**, desideratum, requirement, request, objective, goal, catch, prize, trophy, lure, draw, attraction

ADJECTIVES 6 desired, wished for, wanted, needed, necessary, required, requested, longed for, yearned for, coveted, envied, in demand, popular **7 desirable**, acceptable, welcome, pleasurable, pleasant, attractive, likeable, appealing, inviting, tempting, appetizing, mouth-watering, admirable, creditable, laudable, praiseworthy, meritorious, deserving, worthwhile, good, beneficial, advantageous, profitable, expedient, convenient, suitable, fitting, apt **8 desirous**, wishful, wanting, needing, demanding, longing for, coveting, craving, itching for, dying for, ardent, passionate, avid, eager, keen, partial to, fond, covetous, envious, gluttonous, voracious, greedy, acquisitive, possessive, insatiable, hoping, aspiring, yearning, pining, wistful, nostalgic **9 hungry**, starving, famished, ravenous, empty, half-starved, peckish, thirsty, dry, parched **10 lustful**, libidinous, lecherous, lascivious, concupiscent, randy, hot for, sexy, seductive

VERBS 11 desire, wish for, want, need, require, demand, ask for, request, call, summon, welcome, long for, pray for, covet, envy, dream of, hope for, aspire to, aim for, crave, itch for, hanker after, yearn for, pine for, hunger for, pant for, lust after, favour, like **12 like**, love, want, desire, woo, court, chase, run after, pursue **13 be hungry**, hunger, starve, raven, thirst **14 cause desire**, tempt, tantalize, attract, allure, excite, titillate, stimulate **15 be desirable**, suit

165 Destruction

NOUNS 1 destruction, undoing, nullification, annihilation, obliteration, deletion, erasure, liquidation, elimination, extermination, extinction, abolition, repression, suppression, silencing, stifling, smothering, suffocation, threatening, insidiousness, subversion, overturning **2 destroying**, demolition, flattening, razing, knocking down, decomposition, dissolution, breaking up, disruption, shattering, crushing, grinding, pulverization, disintegration, shredding, incineration, defoliation, eradication, uprooting, deracination, extirpation, decimation, slaughter, massacre, genocide, mass murder, mass destruction **3 destructiveness**, vandalism, sabotage, arson, fire-raising **4 ruin**, downfall, crushing blow, ruination, perdition, disaster, calamity, catastrophe, collapse, débâcle, upheaval, cataclysm, breakdown, crack-up, failure, meltdown, China syndrome, break-up, crash, smash, write-off, wreck, ruins, dilapidation, total loss, Waterloo, bankruptcy, insolvency, slippery slope, apocalypse, doom **5 havoc**, damage, turmoil, confusion, mayhem, chaos, devastation, laying waste, raiding, despoiling, pillage, looting, rape, depredation, explosion, blitz, nuclear blast, desolation, disaster area, wasteland, desert, scorched earth, shambles, carnage, slaughterhouse, holocaust **6 destroyer**, wrecker, spoiler, raider, ravager, pillager, looter, arsonist, pyromaniac, demolisher, leveller, Luddite, iconoclast, nihilist, anarchist, revolutionary, saboteur, vandal, defacer, eraser, liquidator, exterminator, killer, murderer, assassin, executioner, barbarian, Hun

VERBS 7 destroy, unmake, undo, bankrupt, annihilate, liquidate, terminate, end, exterminate, put down, dispose of, dispatch, decimate, massacre, slaughter, kill, murder, extinguish, snuff out, extirpate, eradicate, deracinate, uproot, invalidate, tear up, obliterate, efface, expunge, wipe out, erase, rub out, blot out, strike out, nullify, annul, quash, suppress, silence, muzzle, stifle, smother, suffocate, strangle, drown, overthrow, scatter, disperse, dispel, vaporize, sacrifice, counteract **8 demolish**, dismantle, take apart, rend asunder, pull apart, break, blow down, knock down, fell, tear down, bulldoze, steamroller, flatten, mow down, butcher, slaughter, topple, overthrow, mine, blast, explode, dynamite, blow up, bombard, bomb, blitz, shatter, smash, wreck, pulp, crush, pulverize, trample underfoot, atomize **9 lay waste**, devastate, desolate, defoliate, deforest, denude, strip, gut, damage, vandalize, run amok, wreak havoc, despoil, depopulate, raid, sack, ransack, pillage, rape, ravage, violate, loot **10 ruin**, spoil, mar, bedevil, sink, scupper, mutilate, deface, knock flat, floor, flatten, trounce, hamstring **11 consume**, eat up, gobble up, devour, engulf, envelop, drown, swamp, overwhelm, burn, incinerate, waste **12 be destroyed**, self-destruct, perish, go down, go under, plunge, disappear, fail, founder, disintegrate, split

ADJECTIVES 13 destructive, devastating, ruinous, internecine, cutthroat, annihilating, consuming, raging, rampaging, suicidal, deadly, lethal, fatal, disastrous, catastrophic, apocalyptic, cataclysmic, overwhelming, subversive, revolutionary, anarchistic, incendiary, insidious, pernicious, noxious, harmful, injurious **14 destroyed**, wiped out, ruined, devastated, crushed, ground, pulverized, pulped, shredded, broken up, disintegrated, shattered, wrecked, torpedoed, sunk, done for, dished, in tatters, in ruins, crumbling, falling apart, doomed, bankrupt, bust

166 Deterioration

VERBS 1 deteriorate, worsen, slip, slide, go downhill, lose ground, fall off, slump, decline, wane, ebb, sink, fail, totter, droop, stoop, slip back, retrograde, regress, revert, lapse, relapse, tergiversate, degenerate, self-destruct, crumble, collapse, break down, wear out, age, grow old, depreciate, fade, wither, wilt, wrinkle, fray, weaken **2 decay**, decompose, rot, putrefy, moulder, rust, corrode, spoil, go bad, go off, grow stale, corrupt, rankle, fester, suppurate, go septic, gangrene, smell **3 make worse**, aggravate, exacerbate, irritate, embitter, adulterate, corrupt, sophisticate, alloy, debase, denature, infect, contaminate, taint, poison, envenom, ulcerate, canker, pollute, foul, dirty, defile, desecrate **4 impair**, damage, deactivate, dismantle, spoil, mar, maul, ruin, destroy, mess up, bungle, botch, tinker, tamper, trifle with, meddle, wreck, vandalize, ravage, rape, plunder, lay waste, scorch, overthrow, crush, crumble **5 hurt**, harm, injure, wound, weaken, damnify, mutilate, maim, lame, cripple, hamstring, disable, hamper, hinder, castrate, undermine, sap, demoralize, shake, fret, bore, gnaw, eat away, erode, corrode, rust, rot, decay, blast, plague, overrun, invade, blacken, soil, stain, deface, disfigure, scar, dilapidate, fray, drain, deplete, exhaust, consume, make small, shorten, truncate, dock, curtail, expurgate, eviscerate, bowdlerize **6 pervert**, deform, warp, twist, distort, abuse, misuse, prostitute, deprave, debauch, ruin, vitiate, corrupt, subvert, lower, degrade, debase, abase, brutalize, dehumanize, barbarize, denature, brainwash, vulgarize, coarsen

NOUNS 7 deterioration, worsening, losing ground, retrogradation, regression, slipping back, backsliding, recidivism, lapse, relapse, tergiversation, setback, descent, downward course, primrose path, falling off, slump, downturn, decline, depreciation, impoverishment, Malthusianism, slowing down, wane, ebb, fading **8 perversion**, deformation, distortion, abuse, misuse, prostitution, depravation, immorality, degeneration, addiction, indulgence, intoxication, promiscuity, impureness, decadence, ruin, vitiation, corruption, subversion, degradation, debasement, abasement, brutalization, dehumanization, barbarism, vulgarization, coarsening, devaluation **9 dilapidation**, collapse, disintegration, breakdown, ruination, destruction, disrepair, neglect, shabbiness, slum, urban blight, inner-city ghetto, physical wreck, corrosion, rust, rot, decay, decomposition, putrefaction, corruption, mouldiness, blight, canker, cancer, discoloration, weathering, patina, verdigris, decrepitude, senility, marasmus, atrophy **10 impairment**, detriment, damage, spoiling, waste, loss, ruination, devastation, havoc, demolition, destruction, attack, assault, insult, outrage, sabotage, terrorism, disorganization, derangement, adulteration, debasement, watering down, infection, contagion, contamination, poisoning, intoxication, autotoxaemia, ulceration, pollution, dirtiness **11 hurt**, harm, mischief, injuriousness, pain, sprain, strain, dislocation, wound, mutilation, lameness, crippling, hobbling, dis-

abling, weakening, demoralization, draining
ADJECTIVES 12 deteriorated, worse, exacerbated, aggravated, worsening, failing, going downhill, decreasing, in decline, falling off, in recession, impoverished, falling, slipping, sliding, tottering, senile, spoilt, gone bad, off, rotten, corked, stale, flat, bland, tasteless, impaired, damaged, effete, worn out, exhausted, drained, rundown, useless, weakened, undermined, sapped, faded, decaying, withered, wasting away, ebbing, retrogressive, regressive, retrograde, outdated, recidivist, tergiversating, degenerate, depraved **13 dilapidated**, in disrepair, falling apart, in ruins, in shreds, beyond repair, cracked, broken, leaking, battered, weather-beaten, decrepit, rickety, tottery, shaky, unsteady, ramshackle, derelict, tumbledown, run-down, exhausted, weakened, ruined, slummy, worn, shopsoiled, frayed, shabby, tatty, unkempt, dingy, holey, in tatters, in rags, seedy, down-at-heel, down-and-out, rusty, mouldering, moth-eaten

167 Deviation

VERBS 1 deviate, diverge, divert, divaricate, vary, digress, branch, tralineate, detour, sheer, curve, heel, trend, bear off, filter, swerve, change direction, tack, yaw **2 divert**, change course, pull aside, slice, pull, hook, glance **3 go astray**, get lost, drift, get sidetracked, err, ramble, wander, rove, straggle, excurse, pererrate **4 lose track of**, blunder, be inattentive **5 twist**, turn, bend, meander, wind, weave, twine, snake, curve, zigzag, hairpin, pull, crook **6 distort**, warp, bias, twist, skew **7 misdirect**, divert, avert, mislead **8 sidestep**, sidle, avoid, turn away, shy, jib, avert, avoid, gee, haw **9 shove aside**, sidetrack, shunt, switch **10 slide**, sideslip, skid, swing, wobble **11 turn round**, wheel, face about, reverse, return, revert **12 deflect**, diffract, bend, diverge, scatter, disperse
NOUNS 13 deviation, disorientation, misdirection, aberration, nonconformism, eccentricity, exorbitation, wrong course, digression, excursion, departure, declension, tangent, diversion, deflection, divergence, divarication, branching off, divagation, declination, variation, indirection, obliqueness, skew, slant **14 deviating course**, curve, turn, flexure, double, declension, bend, corner, dogleg, zigzag, slope, slant, sheer, sweep, pitch, tack, detour, diversion, bypass **15 deviating motion**, swerve, skid, sideslip, sidestep, crabwalk, shift, drift, leeway, roll, pitch, yaw, swing, break **16 wandering**, drifting, circuitousness, circumlocution, circumbendibus, rambling, digression, discursion, excursus, straying, errantry, pererration, vagrancy, lapse, error **17 torsion**, twisting, torque, distortion **18 diffraction**, scatter, refraction, reflection, diffusion, dispersion
ADJECTIVES 19 deviant, misdirected, nonconformist, aberrant, eccentric, off-centre **20 indirect**, turning, curving, roundabout, winding, bending, meandering, snaking, serpentine, labyrinthine, mazy, shifting, swerving, deflected, twisting, veering, zigzag, crooked, out-of-the-way, off-

course, off target, wide, lost **21 undirected**, unguided **22 oblique**, skewed, biased, slanted, distorted **23 diverging**, divaricating, branching **24 wandering**, drifting, digressive, circuitous, devious, divagatory, rambling, digressing, discursive, straying, errant, erratic, desultory, abstracted, inattentive **25 diffractive**, refractive, refrangible, scattered, reflected

168 Difficulty

NOUNS 1 difficulty, hardness, complexity, complication, intricacy, knottiness, technicality, abstruseness, convolution, reconditeness, obscurity, unintelligibility, effort, arduousness, laboriousness, strenuousness, strain, severity, toughness **2 awkwardness**, clumsiness **3 difficult task**, hard work, labour, toil, struggle, trial, tribulation, tough assignment, tall order, big undertaking, hard graft, hard going, rough going, uphill struggle **4 problem**, worry, anxiety, quandary, dilemma, conundrum, brainteaser, brain-twister, poser, nonplus, nodus, crux, maze, puzzle, perplexity, imbroglio, Gordian knot **5 predicament**, plight, situation, tangle, mess, muddle, tricky spot, hot water, cleft stick, difficult position, fine mess, sorry plight, pretty pass, pretty pickle **6 critical situation**, tight corner, tight spot, tight squeeze, desperate straits, emergency, exigency, hardship, adversity, danger, slippery slope, quicksand, swamp **7 awkward situation**, diplomatic incident, embarrassing position, financial embarrassment, bother, bad patch, hard times, dispute **8 snag**, hitch, catch, drawback, pitfall, teething troubles, complication, aggravation, annoyance, inconvenience, obstacle, hurdle, obstruction, hindrance, impasse, stalemate, deadlock, halt, stop, cul-de-sac, blind alley, dead end

ADJECTIVES 9 difficult, hard, arduous, strenuous, laborious, toilsome, demanding, exacting, challenging, tough, heavy, onerous, burdensome, effortful, physically demanding, wearisome, backbreaking, gruelling, punishing, exhausting, fatiguing, uphill, oppressive, formidable, superhuman **10 rough**, rugged, craggy, heavy-going, impenetrable, impassable **11 problematic**, puzzling, baffling, confusing, perplexing, troubling, obfuscating, demanding, exacting, challenging, tough, complex, complicated, intricate, delicate, convoluted, involved, confused, labyrinthine, skilled, specialized, technical, abstruse, recondite, esoteric, impenetrable, obscure, unclear, unintelligible, illegible **12 inconvenient**, awkward, troublesome, bothersome, irksome, vexatious, annoying, aggravating, exasperating, tedious, tiresome, boring, trying, worrying **13 troublesome**, demanding, contrary, perverse, wayward, unmanageable, beyond control, stubborn, obstinate, obdurate, headstrong, intractable, refractory, badly behaved, naughty, disobedient, disruptive, obstreperous, critical, fault-finding, censorious, disapproving, grudging, discontented, fussy, fastidious, finicky, particular **14 clumsy**, cumbersome, unwieldy, awkward, ungainly, hulking, ponderous, bulky **15 troubled**, beset, worried, anxious, per-

turbed, bothered, vexed, annoyed, puzzled, confused, baffled, perplexed, bewildered, mystified, nonplussed, inconvenienced, put out, harassed, plagued, distressed, embarrassed, deadlocked
VERBS 16 be difficult, pose problems **17 find difficult**, struggle with **18 have difficulty**, struggle, flounder, come unstuck **19 be in difficulty**, face difficulties, tread carefully, go under **20 get into trouble**, reach a crisis **21 cause trouble**, irk, annoy, aggravate, exasperate, bedevil **22 cause difficulties**, trouble, criticize, carp, disrupt, put out, disturb, worry, bother, perturb, baffle, perplex, nonplus, puzzle, mystify, confuse, bewilder, inconvenience, discommode, obstruct, hamper, hinder, embarrass, corner, box in, trap **23 create difficulties**, criticize

169 Diffuseness

NOUNS 1 diffuseness, profuseness, copiousness, abundance, amplitude, elaboration, expansion, extension, protraction, enlargement, expatiation, filler, expletive, padding, extra, circumstantiality, minuteness, detail, blow-by-blow account, superfluity, repetitiveness, reiteration, tautology, pleonasm, excess, richness, fertility, output, productivity, vein, flow, exuberance, gush, effusiveness, verboseness, loquacity, talkativeness, verbiage, long-windedness, waffle, prolixity, rigmarole, empty talk, rhetoric, oration, tirade, disquisition, dissertation **2 circumlocution**, periphrasis, digression, deviation, discursion, excursion, rambling, wandering, indirectness, irrelevance, pointlessness, aimlessness, sidetrack
ADJECTIVES 3 diffuse, profuse, prolific, copious, abundant, detailed, minute, amplified, expanded, extended, protracted, drawn out, padded, long, loose-knit, lengthy, never-ending, nonstop, epic, repetitive, reiterative, tautologous, pleonastic, superfluous, excessive, talkative, verbose, loquacious, fluent, gushing, effuse, inspired, exuberant, rich, fertile, flowing, polysyllabic, sesquipedalian, wordy, waffling, prosy, prolix, long-winded, fustian, flatulent, pretentious, empty, incoherent, ornate, rhetorical, magniloquent, bombastic, turgid, voluminous, tedious **4 circumlocutory**, circuitous, periphrastic, roundabout, deviating, digressive, discursive, excursive, rambling, wandering, oblique, indirect, irrelevant, pointless
VERBS 5 be diffuse, amplify, enlarge upon, expatiate, dilate, expand, extend, lengthen, protract, draw out, spin out, pad out, repeat, reiterate, tautologize, gush, flow, pour out, wax eloquent, elaborate, particularize, detail, never end, waffle, orate, harangue, bore, ramble on **6 be circuitous**, digress, diverge, deviate, ramble, maunder

170 Dimness

NOUNS 1 dimness, faintness, paleness, semi-darkness, twilight, gloaming, dusk, first light, partial eclipse, penumbra, bad light, shadiness **2 murk**, fog, peasouper, smog, mist, haar, fret, vapour, condensation, steam, miasma, smoke, cloudiness, haze, poor visibility, obscurity, vagueness, indistinctness, blur, fuzziness, bleariness, cataract, dullness, tarnish, greyness, dinginess, drabness, opaqueness, semitransparency **3 dimming**, clouding over, shading, shadowing **4 stupidity**, dimness, thickness, denseness

ADJECTIVES 5 dim, half-lit, semidark, twilit, crepuscular, waning, ill-lit, dark, darkish, sombre, livid, leaden, dusky, grey, dull, overcast, cloudy, louring, stormy, sunless, shady, shadowy **6 murky**, foggy, smoggy, dusty, smoky, misty, steamy, miasmal, cloudy, nebulous, hazy, distant, remote, vague, indistinct, unclear, low-definition, soft-focus, blurred, fuzzy, bleary, muzzy, opaque, smoked, frosted, milky, veiled, filmy, obscured, shadowy, ill-defined, indistinguishable **7 dimmed**, clouded, dull, faded, drab, dingy, gloomy, lacklustre, matt, unpolished, tarnished, rusty, dusty **8 stupid**, dim, dull, dense, thick, unintelligent, obtuse

VERBS 9 be dim, darken, cloud over, film over, glaze over, mist over, steam up, lour, become grey, pale, wane, fade **10 make dim**, bedim, fade, cloud, fog, blur, blear, mist, film, smear, glaze, darken, dip, shade, shadow, obscure, obfuscate, veil **11 tarnish**, rust, dull, deaden, tone down, dirty

171 Direction

NOUNS 1 direction, location, situation, position, set, quarter, aim, goal, target, objective, steering, navigation, piloting **2 bearing**, heading, trend, tendency, run, set, inclination, bent, tenor, drift, thrust, course, route, line, track, path, way, lay, lie, short cut, beeline, compass bearing, tack **3 orientation**, bearings, collimation, adaptation, adjustment, alignment, accommodation, compass, signpost, map, tracking device, rangefinder, gauge, degrees, compass rose, lubber line **4 compass point**, cardinal point, half-point, magnetic north, northward, nor', southward, eastward, the Orient, sunrise, westward, the Occident, sunset, southeast, southwest, northeast, northwest, easting, westing, northing **5 directions**, guiding, leading, instruction, education

VERBS 6 direct, indicate, guide, signpost, steer, point, aim, determine, set, fix, present, point to, lead, conduct, set straight **7 take a direction**, bear, aim, navigate, collimate, fix on, train upon, sight on, aim at, point, turn, head, lead, go, incline, tend, trend, set, dispose, verge, head for, make for, sail for, dash for, run for **8 orient** (*or* **orientate**), adapt

172 Dirtiness

NOUNS 1 dirtiness, soiling, defilement, muckiness, grubbiness, griminess, filthiness, duskness, pollution, foulness, squalidity, sleaziness, slumminess, untidiness, slovenliness, sluttishness, blackness, dinginess, messiness, muddiness, sliminess, miriness, encrustation, turbidity, cloudiness, mustiness **2 uncleanness**, unholiness, profanity, corruption, impurity, coarseness, sepsis, infection, contamination, foulness, abomination, stink, stench, fetor, scruffiness, shabbiness, pediculosis, phthiriasis, rot, decomposition, putrefaction **3 obscenity**, rudeness, indecency, ribaldry, smuttiness, scatology, pornography, dirty joke, salaciousness, prurience, lewdness, lasciviousness **4 dirt**, muck, grime, filth, stain, mark, patch, spot, blot, smudge, smear, mud, mire, bog, soil, dung, manure, night soil, droppings, guano, mucus, snot, pus, matter, dust, mote, smut, soot, smoke, grounds, dregs, lees, sweepings, shavings, sediment, deposit, sludge, slime, ooze, goo, fur, scum, froth, dross, scoria, ash, cinder, clinker, slag, castoff, exuviae, slough, dandruff, scurf, tartar, plaque, feculence, litter, rubbish, refuse, rot, rust, mildew, mould, vermin **5 swill**, slops, hogwash, bilge, dishwater, ditchwater, sewage, drainage, wallow

ADJECTIVES 6 dirty, unclean, soiled, defiled, mucky, grubby, grimy, filthy, dusty, sooty, smoky, polluted, unwashed, unswept, littered, foul, squalid, sleazy, slummy, untidy, unkempt, bedraggled, frowzy, slatternly, slovenly, sluttish, black, dingy, unpolished, unburnished, tarnished, stained, spotted, smudged, besmirched, messy, greasy, oily, muddy, slimy, miry, clotted, caked, matted, encrusted, murky, furred up, clogged, scummy, musty, mouldy, fusty **7 unclean**, unhallowed, unholy, profane, corrupt, impure, coarse, unrefined, unpurified, septic, festering, poisonous, toxic, unsterilized, insanitary, unhygienic, infectious, contaminated, insalubrious, unhealthy, offensive, foul, nasty, abominable, disgusting, repulsive, nauseating, malodorous, stinking, fetid, sordid, squalid, scruffy, shabby, scurfy, leprous, scabby, mangy, pediculous, crawling, faecal, dungy, stercoraceous, excremental, carious, rotting, tainted, flyblown **8 obscene**, dirty, filthy, rude, indecent, risque, ribald, smutty, scatological, pornographic, blue, adult, salacious, prurient, lewd, lascivious

VERBS 9 be dirty, foul up, clog, rust, mildew, moulder, fester, gangrene, mortify, putrefy, decay, rot, go bad, go off, addle, grow rank, smell, stink **10 dirty**, soil, defile, foul, grime, stain, spot, patch, blot, sully, tarnish, blacken, untidy, mess up, daub, smear, smirch, smudge, blur, streak, grease, cake, clot, clog, muddy, roil, rile, draggle, drabble, spatter, splash, slobber, slaver, poison, taint, corrupt, pollute, contaminate, infect, profane

173 Disagreement

NOUNS 1 disagreement, difference, argument, altercation, contention, dissension, dissidence, criticism, disaccord, discordance, disharmony, friction, noncooperation, hatred, unpleasantness, controversy, confrontation, difficulty, misunderstanding, disunity, estrangement, division, polarization, incompatibility, irreconcilability, enmity, irascibility, provocativeness, cantankerousness, prickliness, quarrelsomeness, bickering, wrangling, hostility, bellicosity, aggressiveness, strife, fighting, clashing, sore point **2 argument**, debate, polemic, quarrel, row, dispute, spat, tiff, fuss, slanging match, discord, split, rift, breach, cleft, rupture, schism, struggle, scrimmage, squabble, wrangle, rumpus, tussle, scrap, brawl, fisticuffs, donnybrook, fracas, clash, conflict, feud, fight **3 difference**, dissimilarity, nonconformity, deviation, divergence, variance, disparity, discord, discrepancy, incompatibility, incongruity, inequality, ambiguity, ambivalence, inconsistency, credibility gap, misfitting, mismatching, misaligning **4 dissenter**, protester, objector, critic, quarreller, troublemaker, intruder, gatecrasher, outsider, misfit, eccentric, crank, freak, laughing stock

VERBS 5 disagree, differ, argue, altercate, contend, dissent, object to, confront, quarrel, criticize, bicker, wrangle, misunderstand, divide, polarize, sever relations, provoke, fight **6 argue**, debate, quarrel, row, dispute, tiff, fuss, squabble, wrangle, tussle, lock horns, scrap, brawl, clash, conflict, feud **7 be different**, vary, deviate, diverge, mismatch

ADJECTIVES 8 disagreeing, differing, argumentative, contentious, dissenting, dissident, discordant, disharmonious, noncooperative, hating, unpleasant, controversial, confrontational, disputing, quarrelsome, criticizing, bickering, wrangling, divisive, polarizing, schismatic, incompatible, irreconcilable, irascible, provocative, cantankerous, prickly, hostile, inimical, aggressive, antagonistic, belligerent, fighting, squabbling, brawling, warring **9 different**, dissimilar, deviating, divergent, variant, odd, alien, unsuitable, discordant, discrepant, incompatible, incongruous, unequal, ambiguous, ambivalent, inconsistent, misfit, mismatched

174 Disappearance

VERBS 1 disappear, cease, end, become extinct, die out, expire, perish, pass, wane, ebb, recede, vanish, dematerialize, evanesce, evaporate, dissolve, melt, fade, dwindle, peter out, disguise oneself, hide, lie low **2 depart**, decamp, go, escape, run, flee, fly, withdraw, retire, retreat, melt away, absent oneself, go AWOL, play truant **3 cause to disappear**, vaporize, liquidate, disembody, destroy, annihilate, waste, disperse, dissipate, dispel, scatter, dismiss, send away, expel, hide, conceal, obscure, bury, disguise, camouflage, erase, blot out, obliterate, rub, wipe, scrub, cancel, eliminate, remove, take away

NOUNS 4 disappearance, cessation, end, extinction, dying out, death, dying, passing, wane, ebb, vanishing, dematerialization, disembodiment, vaporization, evaporation, evanescence, dissolution, melting, fading, dwindling, erosion, wearing away, dispersal, dissipation, scattering, departure, exit, going, escape, running away, flight, withdrawal, retreat, desertion, truancy, absence, nonexistence, invisibility, vanishing trick, escapology, escapee, missing person, runaway, truant, blackout **5 disguise**, camouflage, blacking up, occultation, eclipse, obscuring, hiding, concealment, burial, erasure, obliteration, cancellation, elimination, annihilation

ADJECTIVES 6 disappearing, vanishing, evanescent, fugitive, going, departing, escaping, transient, fleeting, passing, fading, waning, dying, dissolving, evaporating, hiding **7 disappeared**, vanished, absent, gone, missing, lost, dead, extinct, obsolete, past, nonexistent, invisible, eclipsed, occulted, hidden, concealed, buried, disguised, camouflaged, dispersed, dissipated

175 Disappointment

• *The best laid schemes o' mice an' men/ Gang aft a-gley,/ An' lea'e us nought but grief an' pain/ For promis'd joy.* Robert Burns.

NOUNS 1 disappointment, discouragement, mortification, chagrin, regret, frustration, noncompletion, nonfulfilment, tantalization, tease, false hopes, hopelessness, despair, bafflement, false expectation, overestimation, miscalculation **2 bad outcome**, bad news, disenchantment, disillusionment, discontent, dissatisfaction, shock, blow, setback, balk, hitch, impediment, obstacle, bad luck, misfortune, anticlimax, damp squib, comedown, letdown, humiliation, humbling, failure, defeat, disaster **3 mirage**, false dawn

VERBS 4 be disappointed, fail, fall short, miscalculate, misjudge, expect better, expect otherwise, regret **5 be crestfallen**, look blue, look blank **6 disappoint**, fall short, go wrong, turn sour, disenchant, disillusion, fail, let down, tantalize, tease, dissatisfy, dishearten, sadden, upset, dumbfound, surprise **7 thwart**, frustrate, balk, bilk, foil, baffle, confound, hinder, hamper, refuse, deny, stonewall, turn away, reject, jilt, befool, humble, humiliate, disconcert, discontent **8 be dishonest**, betray, cheat, deceive, mislead, delude, dupe, trick

ADJECTIVES 9 disappointed, disenchanted, disillusioned, expecting more, let down, frustrated, thwarted, balked, bilked, foiled, baffled, confounded, confused, hindered, hampered, denied, refused, stonewalled, rejected, jilted, defeated, disconcerted, crestfallen, dejected, depressed, disheartened, discouraged, mortified, chagrined, humiliated, humbled, disgruntled, soured, dissatisfied, discontented, sad, upset, hopeless, heartbroken, crushed **10 deceived**, misled, deluded, duped, betrayed, tricked, cheated **11 disappointing**, frustrating, unfulfilling, unsatisfying, insufficient, inadequate, falling short, second-best, second-rate, poor, inferior, abortive **12 deceptive**, misleading, deceiving, dishonest

176 Disapproval

NOUNS 1 disapproval, disapprobation, dissatisfaction, discontent, unhappiness, displeasure, disfavour, disgruntlement, indignation, distaste, dislike **2 disrespect**, disesteem, disrepute, contempt, despite, low esteem **3 nonacceptance**, rejection, refusal, ostracism, cold shoulder, blackballing, ban, bar, boycott **4 disagreement**, dissension, opposition, hostility, objection, complaint, exception, contradiction **5 criticism**, bad press, dispraise, brickbat **6 faultfinding**, carping, cavilling, pettifoggery, captiousness, hairsplitting, niggling, quibbling, fastidiousness, fussing, pestering, nagging, henpecking, overcriticalness, hypercriticism **7 blame**, censure, reprobation, recrimination, complaint, charge, accusation, condemnation, denunciation, impeachment, castigation, chastisement, reproof, reprehension, reprimand, rebuke, reproach, stricture, upbraiding, scolding, chiding, admonishment, warning, lesson, lecture, home truths **8 berating**, railing, abuse, tirade, diatribe, onslaught, attack, tongue-lashing, laying into, lambasting, vituperation, execration, revilement **9 show of disapproval**, slow handclap, hiss, boo, catcall, raspberry, taunt, jeer, sneer, derision, ridicule, protest, clamour **10 disapproving look**, black look, raised eyebrow, glare, silent reproach, frown **11 critic**, fault-finder, pettifogger **12 pessimist**, misery, killjoy

VERBS 13 disapprove, disfavour, dislike, discountenance **14 withhold approval**, reject, refuse, exclude, ostracize, cold shoulder, blacklist, blackball, ban, bar, boycott, veto, disallow **15 disagree**, oppose, object to, remonstrate, complain **16 criticize**, fault, deplore, deprecate, depreciate, decry, denigrate, disparage, dispraise, belittle, run down, tear apart, snipe at **17 find fault**, carp, cavil, derogate, split hairs, niggle, quibble, pick holes, pester, nag **18 blame**, accuse, charge, reprobate, recriminate, condemn, denunciate, denounce, impeach **19 censure**, castigate, chastise, reprove, reprehend, reprimand, rebuke, reproach, upbraid, scold, chide, admonish, warn **20 berate**, rail, assail, attack, abuse, tongue-lash, lay into, pitch into **21 vituperate**, execrate, revile, pour vitriol, curse, vilify, blacken **22 show disapproval**, tut-tut, frown, scowl, hiss, boo, catcall, jeer, heckle, shout down, throw stones, deride, ridicule, mob

ADJECTIVES 24 disapproving, disapprobatory, dissatisfied, discontented, unhappy, disappointed, displeased, disgruntled, indignant **25 disagreeing**, dissenting, opposing, hostile, contradicting, against, agin, objecting **26 critical**, dispraising, abusive, execratory, vituperative, disparaging, deprecatory, damaging, defamatory, unfavourable, poor **27 fault-finding**, captious, carping, cavilling, pettifogging, hairsplitting, nagging, niggling, quibbling, fastidious **28 blaming**, accusatory, judgmental, condemning, damning, denunciatory **29 censuring**, castigatory, chastising, reprimanding, rebuking, reproaching, upbraiding, chiding, scolding, admonitory **30 disapproved**, rejected, refused, opposed, excluded, ostracized, blacklisted, banned, barred, boycotted **31 unsatisfactory**, unacceptable, unpraiseworthy, uncommendable, inadequate **32 criticized**, dispraised, uncommended **33 censured**, castigated, chastised, reprimanded, rebuked, reproached, upbraided, scolded, admonished, lambasted, berated, assailed, attacked **34 hissed**, booed, taunted, jeered, sneered at, derided **35 blameworthy**, responsible, culpable, criminal, guilty, reprehensible

177 Disbelief

NOUNS 1 disbelief, doubt, dubiousness, uncertainty, hesitancy, distrust, mistrust, misgiving, qualm, scruple, reservation, scepticism, scorn, suspiciousness, disagreement, dissent **2 unbelievability**, incredibility, impossibility, improbability, implausibility **3 incredulity**, amazement, bewilderment, bafflement, perplexity, nonbelief, discredit, rejection **4 unbelief**, infidelity, paganism, heathenism, misbelief, heresy, agnosticism, atheism **5 disbeliever**, heretic, pagan, heathen, infidel, agnostic, atheist, doubter, doubting Thomas, apostate, dissenter, dissident, nonconformist, sceptic, mocker, detractor, secularist, rationalist

ADJECTIVES 6 disbelieving, incredulous, sceptical, scornful, doubtful, dubious, uncertain, hesitant, distrustful, mistrustful, suspicious, dissenting, heretical, atheistic, agnostic, pagan, heathen, faithless **7 disbelieved**, discredited, exploded, unbelievable, incredible, impossible, improbable, implausible, untenable, far-fetched, unreliable, suspect, suspicious, so-called, self-styled

VERBS 8 disbelieve, discredit, dissent, disagree, scorn, ridicule, mock, scoff at, deny, negate, challenge, dispute, question, doubt, hesitate, waver, half-believe, have reservations, distrust, mistrust, suspect, apostatize **9 cause disbelief**, cast doubt, discredit, raise suspicions

178 Disclosure

NOUNS 1 disclosure, exposure, uncovering, unveiling, revelation, manifestation, epiphany, anagnorisis, discovery, diagnosis, denouement, resolution, explanation, showdown, catastrophe **2 divulgence** (*or* **divulgement**), communication, broadcast, announcement, declaration, publication, exposé, betrayal, leak, hint, telltale sign, giveaway, queen's evidence, tergiversation, admission, acknowledgment, avowal, affirmation **3 openness**, plain speaking, downrightness, candour, frankness, truth, honesty, unreservedness

VERBS 4 disclose, reveal, expose, show, make known, discover, diagnose, let out, bare, denude, unfold, unroll, unfurl, unpack, unwrap, uncover, unveil, open, open up, dig up, disinter, manifest, go public **5 divulge**, declare, broadcast, announce, communicate, inform, educate, publicize, publish, vent, air, speak out, tell all, talk, speak, utter, breathe, hint, confide, leak, let drop **6 betray**, give away, inform on, accuse **7 admit**, allow, acknowledge, concede, grant, assent, affirm, avow, confess, own up, plead guilty, come clean **8 be disclosed**, appear, emerge, transpire, come out, break, leak out

ADJECTIVES 9 disclosed, revealed, shown, visible, clear, obvious, transparent, open, exposed, leaked, confessed, admitted, avowed, acknowledged, uncovered, unearthed **10 disclosing**, revealing, divulging, maieutic, open, candid, frank, downright, unreserved, outspoken, forthcoming, informative, communicative, talkative, garrulous, loquacious, indiscreet, imprudent, chatty **11 revelatory**, expository, explicatory, explanatory, interpretive, apocalyptic

179 Discontinuity

NOUNS 1 discontinuity, disconnectedness, disjunction, disjointedness, irregularity, intermittence, brokenness, fitfulness, spasmodicalness, sporadicalness, disorder, incoherence, confusion, nonuniformity, unevenness, roughness, jerkiness, bumpiness, joltiness **2 cessation**, end, stop, halt, termination **3 interval**, interim, intermission, lull, pause, break, rest,

stopover **4 interruption**, break, suspension, gap, breach, fissure, crevasse, fault, split, crack, fracture, cut **5 caesura**, hiatus, lacuna, diaeresis, ellipsis, pause, rest **6 intervention**, interruption, interjection, interpolation
ADJECTIVES 7 discontinuous, unsuccessive, disconnected, disjointed, disunited, discrete, fragmented, broken, unjoined, unconnected, irregular, intermittent, fitful, spasmodic, sporadic, erratic, random, desultory, episodic, periodic, alternate, stop-go, on-off, nonuniform, uneven, rough, choppy, snatchy, jerky, bumpy, jolty, scrappy, bitty, patchy, spotty **8 discontinued**, nonrecurrent, unrepeated, ended, ceased, stopped, halted, terminated **9 interrupted**, disturbed, disrupted, broken off **10 digressive**, parenthetic, nonserial
VERBS 11 discontinue, end, cease, stop, halt, terminate, finish, quit, give up, suspend, break off, cut off, cut short, leave off, refrain from **12 pause**, rest, stop over **13 disconnect**, disjoin, disunite, separate, sever **14 lose one's train of thought**, digress, ramble **15 interrupt**, disturb, disrupt, intervene, interject, interpolate

180 Discount

NOUNS 1 discount, reduction, cut, decrease, decrement, concession, allowance, margin, rebate, refund, drawback, tare, deduction, deferment, contango, backwardation, commission, percentage, poundage, agio, brokerage **2 bargain**, special offer, incentive, cut price, dumping
VERBS 3 discount, reduce, lower, mark down, cut, slash, rebate, refund, tare, deduct, subtract, take off, knock off, depreciate
ADJECTIVES 4 discounted, marked down, cut-price, cut-rate, bargain, cheap

181 Discourtesy

NOUNS 1 discourtesy, impoliteness, incivility, inurbanity, disagreeableness, ungraciousness, ungallantness, uncourtliness, ungentlemanliness, thoughtlessness, shortness, inconsiderateness, unsolicitousness, tactlessness, insensitivity, inattention, sullenness, bluntness, acerbity, sharpness, tartness, asperity, gruffness, bluffness, roughness, harshness, severity, brusqueness, unpleasantness, surliness, crustiness, nastiness, anger, ridicule, derision, mockery, raillery, scoffing **2 bad manners**, rudeness, insolence, impudence, truculence, churlishness, impatience, interruption, vulgarity, offensiveness, coarseness, boorishness, caddishness, grossness, crudeness, loutishness, ill-breeding, misconduct **3 act of discourtesy**, rebuff, insult, jeer, snub, abuse, rude gesture, V-sign, black look, scowl, frown
ADJECTIVES 4 discourteous, impolite, uncivil, disagreeable, inurbane, ungracious, ungallant, uncourtly, ungentlemanly, unladylike, unpleasant, surly, sullen, crusty, nasty, unkind, thoughtless, offhanded, inconsiderate, unsolicitous, tactless, insensitive, inattentive, cavalier, abusive, vituperative, unsmiling, grim, unsociable, unfriendly, uncomplimentary, unflattering, disrespectful, familiar, gruff, blunt, harsh, severe, rough, rugged, brutal, brusque,

curt, short, abrupt, impatient, discontented, peevish, testy, acerbic, sharp, tart, snappy, biting, growling, bearish, acrimonious **5 bad-mannered**, unchivalrous, badly behaved, rude, insolent, impudent, impertinent, saucy, churlish, truculent, abusive, cursing, obstreperous, forward, irascible, difficult, vulgar, offensive, injurious, coarse, boorish, caddish, gross, crude, loutish, ill-bred, unrefined, uncouth, uncultured, barbarian, savage, foul-mouthed, growling

VERBS 6 be discourteous, not respect, abuse, affront, outrage, take liberties, make bold, treat rudely, flout etiquette, cause offence, insult, stare, ogle, gaze, ignore, interrupt, cut, snub **7 get angry**, pout, glower, lour, frown, scowl, growl, curse, swear

182 Discovery

VERBS 1 discover, find, locate, place, come across, happen upon, encounter, meet with, see, spy, spot, descry, perceive, sight, glimpse, notice, observe, watch, recognize **2 detect**, ferret out, track down, hunt, seek, sniff out, ensnare, catch, catch red-handed, acquire, unearth, disinter, uncover, expose, lay bare, unveil, unmask, disclose, reveal, divulge, betray **3 find out**, learn, ascertain, determine, realize **4 invent**, design, devise, contrive, originate, pioneer, herald, explore **5 be discovered**, appear

NOUNS 6 discovery, finding, location, serendipity, encounter, meeting, spotting, perception, sight, glimpse, observation, recognition **7 detection**, search, hunt, pursuit, catching, acquisition, excavation, uncovering, exposure, unveiling, unmasking, disclosure, leak, manifestation, revelation, divulgence **8 finding out**, learning, ascertaining, realization, understanding, enlightenment **9 invention**, design, device, contrivance, idea, inspiration, origination, pioneering, exploration **10 find**, discovery, treasure-trove **11 detector**, divining rod, sonar, radar, probe **12 discoverer**, finder, spotter, scout, spy, observer, dowser, water diviner, prospector, archaeologist, detective, inventor, author, founder, parent, motivator, originator, forerunner, herald, pioneer

ADJECTIVES 13 discovering, finding, warm, revelatory, inventive, pioneering, exploratory **14 discovered**, found, located, seen, spotted, unearthed, uncovered, exposed, unmasked **15 discoverable**, findable, recognizable, identifiable, perceptible

183 Discrimination

NOUNS 1 discrimination, selection, distinction, differentiation, appraisal, sorting, graduation, separation, demarcation, division, segregation, diagnosis **2 judiciousness**, judgment, discrimination, discretion, taste, sensitivity, sensibility, discernment, criticism, appreciation, feel, perception, insight, acumen, flair, connoisseurship, dilettantism, palate, refinement, delicacy, finesse, fastidiousness **3 prejudice**, discrimination, bias, bigotry, narrow-mindedness, pettiness, intolerance, insularism, parochialism, one-sidedness, partisanship, jaundice, prejudgment, inequity **4 social discrimination**, sexism, misogyny, misandry, homophobia, racism, anti-semitism, apartheid, ghettoization, xenophobia, ethnocentricity, ethnic cleansing, pogrom, McCarthyism, elitism, class prejudice, fascism, Nazism, Aryanism, jingoism, chauvinism, religious persecution, fundamentalism, fanaticism, witch-hunting **5 favouritism**, nepotism, partisanship

ADJECTIVES 6 discriminating, judicious, selective, tasteful, sensitive, differential, separating, discerning, divisional, critical, diagnostic, interpretational, appreciative, epicurean, perceptive, insightful, refined, delicate, fastidious, meticulous, perfectionist, pedantic **7 discriminatory**, prejudicial, one-sided, partisan, jaundiced, inequitable, unfair, partial, preferential, nepotistic, prejudiced, biased, bigoted, narrow-minded, blinkered, small-minded, petty, intolerant, dogmatic, insular, parochial, elitist, classist, ageist, sexist, misogynous, misandrous, homophobic, racist, anti-semitic, xenophobic, jingoistic, ethnocentric, fascist, Nazi, fundamentalist **8 judged**, selected, distinct, discrete, diagnosed, interpreted, differentiated, sorted, graded, demarcated, divided, segregated, persecuted

VERBS 9 discriminate, select, choose, favour, prefer, judge, distinguish, differentiate, discern, pick out, sort, analyse, grade, graduate, separate, demarcate, divide, segregate, diagnose, interpret **10 prejudge**, forejudge, precondemn, bias, prejudice, warp **11 discriminate against**, criticize, persecute, harass, oppress

184 Disintegration

NOUNS 1 disintegration, breakup, disorder, chaos, disturbance, derangement, explosion, collapse, wear, erosion, death, decomposition, corruption, corrosion, rust, decay, mould, rot, putrefaction, mortification **2 deconstruction**, demolition, destruction, breakdown, dismantling, decentralization, devolution, delegation, demerging, regionalization, compartmentation, division, partition, disunion, separation, dispersal, scattering, dissolution, melting, liquefaction, deliquescence, reduction, simplification, resolution, analysis, parsing, syllabification, dissection, dismemberment, anatomization, electrolysis, catabolism, fission

VERBS 3 disintegrate, break up, collapse, fall apart, explode, blow up, shatter, splinter, crumble, decompose, corrupt, corrode, rust, perish, decay, moulder, rot, putrefy, mortify **4 deconstruct**, demolish, wreck, smash, destroy, disorder, dismantle, disband, decentralize, devolve, delegate, demerge, regionalize, compartmentalize, partition, divide, disperse, scatter, dissolve, melt, liquefy, simplify, separate, analyse, parse, syllabify, dissect, dismember, electrolyse, hydrolyse, catalyse, split

ADJECTIVES 5 disintegrated, smashed, shattered, destroyed, demolished, broken down, dissolved, melted, liquefied, separated, decomposed, deconstructed, rotted, putrid, corrupted, decayed, rusty, corroded, dilapidated **6 disintegrating**, crumbling

185 Disinterestedness

NOUNS 1 disinterestedness, indifference, detachment, ataraxy, impartiality, objectivity, equitableness, fairness, fair-mindedness, justice, neutrality, nonalignment, noninvolvement, self-control, self-restraint, dispassion **2 unselfishness**, selflessness, altruism, consideration, kindness, compassion, sympathy, pity, humility, modesty, self-denial, self-effacement, self-abnegation, martyrdom, idealism, high-mindedness, honesty, magnanimity, nobleness, munificence, benevolence, charity, generosity

ADJECTIVES 3 disinterested, indifferent, detached, impersonal, impartial, unbiased, unprejudiced, objective, equitable, non-partisan, fair, fair-minded, open, just, neutral, nonaligned, uninvolved, self-controlled, dispassionate **4 unselfish**, selfless, altruistic, considerate, kind, compassionate, sympathetic, humble, modest, self-denying, self-effacing, self-abnegating, self-sacrificing, idealistic, high-minded, honest, noble, munificent, benevolent, charitable, generous

VERBS 5 be disinterested, lack bias, lack prejudice **6 be unselfish**, sacrifice oneself

186 Dislike

NOUNS 1 dislike, disapproval, disfavour, disaffection, aversion, prejudice, bias, ill feeling, distaste, disrelish, dissatisfaction, discontent, displeasure, avoidance, rejection, disinclination, reluctance, ill will, resentment, disagreement, dissent, antipathy, antagonism, enmity, animosity, abhorrence, detestation, abomination, hatred, loathing, hostility, repugnance, repulsion, disgust, horror, fear, phobia, bitterness **2 disliked thing**, pet aversion, pet hate, failure, defeat **3 sign of dislike**, drawing back, frown, scowl, shuddering, nausea, queasiness, vomiting

VERBS 4 dislike, disapprove, reject, object to, disfavour, disrelish, mind, resent, disagree, dissent, antagonize, loathe, abhor, detest, despise, abominate, hate **5 react against**, avoid, recoil, shun, shrink from, look askance, sniff at, sneer at, grimace, shudder, fight **6 cause dislike**, repel, disgust, disincline, deter, annoy, antagonize, enrage, set against, disagree, upset, revolt, repel, offend, grate, jar, displease, torment, disgust, nauseate, sicken

ADJECTIVES 7 disliking, displeased, discontented, dissatisfied, disenchanted, disillusioned, loveless, undesirous, disinclined, loath, unwilling, reluctant, averse, disaffected, squeamish, queasy, dissenting, averse, resentful, fearful, hostile, antipathetic, antagonistic, bitter, inimical, repelled, disapproving, disgusted, despising, abhorring, loathing, detesting, hating, sickened, sated **8 disliked**, unlikeable, unpopular, unappreciated, disapproved, disfavoured, unwanted, avoided, undesired, unprepossessing, unloved, rejected, jilted, spurned, thrown over, unchosen, unwelcome, unrelished, distasteful, disagreeable, insufferable, intolerable, despised, loathsome, fearsome, abhorrent, disgusting, repulsive, repugnant, rebarbative, abominable, revolting

187 Disobedience

NOUNS 1 disobedience, noncompliance, noncooperation, nonconformity, nonobservance, undutifulness, unwillingness, opposition, recalcitrance, refractoriness, obstinacy, stubbornness, intractability, hindrance, obstruction, obstreperousness, indiscipline, restlessness, unruliness, dissension, defiance, disloyalty, perfidiousness, unfaithfulness, defection, desertion, tergiversation, insubordination, strike, mutiny, resistance, immorality, wickedness, sin, misbehaviour **2 violation of the law**, infraction, infringement, transgression, felony, trespass, extortion, civil disturbance, disorder, riot, street fight, turmoil, lawlessness, crime, vandalism, robbery **3 subversion**, sedition, conspiracy, intrigue, plot, cabal, faction, agitprop, infiltration, spying, espionage, fifth columnism, agitation, sabotage, terrorism, anarchy, treason **4 revolution**, rebellion, revolt, sans-culottism, uprising, mutiny, coup d'état, putsch, breakaway, schism, secession, sedition, insurrection, insurgence, resistance, terrorism **5 troublemaker**, mischief-maker, scamp, pest, nuisance, rascal, scallywag, imp **6 nonconformist**, protestant, deviationist, radical, Jacobin, maverick, opponent, malcontent **7 protester**, suffragist, suffragette, demonstrator, marcher, dissident, recusant, recalcitrant **8 agitator**, ringleader, rabble-rouser, demagogue **9 criminal**, law-breaker, robber, bandit, thief, burglar, murderer, assassin, extortionist, killer, rapist, gangster, Mafioso, brawler, rowdy **10 seditionist**, subversive, conspirator, Guy Fawkes, traitor, collaborator, quisling, tergiversator, extremist, insurrectionist, insurgent, infiltrator, fifth columnist, anarchist, rioter, terrorist, guerrilla, saboteur **11 rebel**, secessionist, revolutionary **12 reactionary**, counter-revolutionary, conservative, monarchist, White Russian, counterterrorist, nonstriker, strike-breaker

ADJECTIVES 13 disobedient, noncompliant, noncooperative, nonobservant, undutiful, unwilling, opposing, recalcitrant, obstinate, stubborn, intractable, obstructive, insubordinate, obstreperous, undisciplined, transgressing, restless, wild, unmanageable, misbehaved, mischief-making, naughty, delinquent, disorderly, riotous, tumultuous, unruly, dissenting, defiant, recusant, disloyal, perfidious, tergiversatory, criminal, immoral, wicked **14 subversive**, seditious, conspiratorial, factional, anarchic, treasonable, revolutionary, rebellious, mutinous, breakaway, schismatic

VERBS 15 be disobedient, not heed, not cooperate, oppose, hinder, obstruct, misbehave, make mischief, dissent, flout authority, defy, defect, desert, tergiversate, strike, infringe, transgress, trespass, riot, vandalize, rob, murder **16 be subversive**, conspire, plot, betray, infiltrate, spy, agitate, sabotage, terrorize, uprise, mutiny, secede, revolt, rebel

188 Disorder

NOUNS 1 disorderliness, disorganization, disarrangement, disarray, derangement, disjunction, disharmony, discord, disruption, disturbance, upset, discomposure, discomfiture, disconcertedness, disintegration, incoherence, unintelligibility **2 irregular order**, randomness, haphazardness, nonuniformity, nonsymmetry, disproportion, misshapenness **3 untidiness**, dirtiness, uncleanness, grubbiness, messiness, unkemptness, dishevelment, scruffiness, shabbiness, neglect, carelessness, slipshodness, shoddiness, sloppiness, sluttishness, slovenliness, slatternliness, sordidness **4 litter**, rubbish, garbage, trash, mess, clutter, muddle, jumble, lumber, hodgepodge, hash, mishmash, pickle, topsy-turviness, shambles, rat's nest, pigsty, midden, dump, tip **5 confusion**, chaos, bedlam, pandemonium, hell, madhouse, beargarden, tumult, turmoil, turbulence **6 mix-up**, snarl-up, foul-up **7 tangle**, snarl, labyrinth, maze, web **8 lawlessness**, anarchy, chaos, disorder, disobedience, unruliness, boisterousness, nihilism, amorality, rebelliousness, revolution, uprising, upheaval, vandalism **9 disorder**, disturbance, commotion, pother, stir, fuss, bother, trouble, to-do, hurly-burly, fight, row, rumpus, mêlée, free-for-all, donnybrook

ADJECTIVES 10 disordered, in disarray, disarranged, deranged, disrupted, disorganized, muddled, jumbled, shuffled, displaced, misplaced, disjointed **11 unordered**, unorganized, ungraded, unsorted **12 irregular**, random, haphazard, erratic, hit-or-miss, sporadic, spasmodic, desultory, shapeless **13 untidy**, dirty, filthy, unclean, grubby, messy, scruffy, shabby, ragged, unsightly, unkempt, dishevelled, bedraggled, tousled, ruffled, crumpled, sluttish, slovenly, slatternly, careless, slipshod, shoddy **14 confused**, incoherent, convoluted, disorganized, muddleheaded, scatterbrained, featherbrained, unsystematic **15 discomposed**, discomfited, disconcerted, unsettled, disturbed, perturbed, upset, deranged **16 muddled**, jumbled, scrambled, confused, chaotic, tangled, labyrinthine, awry, askew, amiss, topsy-turvy **17 disorderly**, chaotic, lawless, unruly, undisciplined, uncontrolled, unmanageable, boisterous, disruptive, rowdy, hell-raising, harum-scarum, wild, turbulent, rampageous, riotous, rebellious, insubordinate, contumacious, mutinous, obstreperous, disobedient

VERBS 18 disorder, disorganize, disarrange, derange, muddle, jumble, shuffle, mix up, scramble, disperse, scatter, break up, disrupt **19 discompose**, disconcert, disturb, perturb, upset, pester, unsettle, disorient, addle, befuddle **20 confuse**, botch, bungle, mix up, snarl up **21 make disordered**, untidy, dishevel, tousle, ruffle, rumple, crumple, crease, turn upside-down, tangle **22 be disordered**, degenerate, disintegrate, come apart **23 be disorderly**, make trouble, run wild, run amok, riot, rampage, roister

189 Disparagement

NOUNS 1 disparagement, deprecation, depreciation, decrial, detraction, derogation, denigration, belittlement, slighting, underestimation, understatement, faint praise **2 criticism**, bad review **3 defamation**, obloquy, character assassination, slander, libel, traducement, calumny, obloquy, smear campaign, muckraking, mudslinging, scandal, gossip **4 aspersion**, insinuation, innuendo, slur, smear, defamatory remark **5**

scorn, contempt, disdain, derision, revilement, vilification, abuse, insult, degradation, debasement, scurrility, defilement, blackening **6 ridicule**, lampoon, satire, pasquinade, burlesque, skit

VERBS 7 disparage, deprecate, depreciate, decry, detract, derogate, denigrate, belittle, slight, cry down, minimize, play down, underrate **8 criticize**, find fault **9 defame**, slander, libel, traduce, calumniate, malign, damage, compromise, discredit, dishonour, blacken, tarnish, sully, soil, smear, besmirch, sling mud, muckrake **10 vilify**, revile, abuse, degrade, debase, defile, asperse, insinuate, slur, whisper **11 ridicule**, lampoon, satirize, caricature, mock, guy, scoff, sneer

ADJECTIVES 12 disparaging, deprecatory, depreciatory, decrying, detractory, derogatory, pejorative, denigratory, belittling, slighting, minimizing **13 defamatory**, slanderous, libellous, calumnious, scandalous, scurrilous, abusive, insulting, aspersive, insinuating, gossiping, whispering, mud-slinging, smearing, besmirching, blackening, tarnishing, damaging, injurious, destructive, venomous, caustic, bitter, back-biting **14 scornful**, contemptuous, contumelious, sarcastic, ridiculing, mocking, scoffing

190 Disparity

NOUNS 1 disparity, dissimilarity, difference, contrast, unrelatedness, diversity, divergence, variance, discrepancy, nonuniformity, inconsonance, incongruence, incommensurability, heterogeneity, disproportionateness, asymmetry, irregularity, inconsistency, gap, ambiguity, ambivalence, equivocality **2 contradiction**, contrariety, oppositeness, negation, jarring, grating, false note, paradox, antinomy, oxymoron, mismatch, misalliance, maladjustment **3 nonconformity**, unconventionality, individuality, distinctness, uniqueness, idiosyncrasy, singularity, peculiarity, eccentricity, freakishness, unorthodoxy, heterodoxy **4 disagreement**, discordance, disaccord, disharmony, controversy, argument, challenge, dissent, samizdat, dissonance, disunity, incompatibility, uncongeniality, irreconcilability, wrangling, confrontation, opposition, defiance, antagonism, enmity, hostility, bickering, squabbling, quarrelling, conflict, clashing **5 unfitness**, unsuitability, inappropriateness, wrongness, inappositeness, inaptitude, inapplicability, inadmissibility, irrelevance, incapacity, incompetence, unskilfulness, inexpedience, undecorousness, inelegance, infelicity, impropriety, untimeliness **6 misfit**, outsider, stranger, alien, foreigner, eccentric, individualist, loner, maverick, bohemian, beatnik, nonconformist, dissident, anarchist, dissenter, rebel, heretic, pretender, hypocrite

ADJECTIVES 7 disparate, dissimilar, different, contrasting, unrelated, unlikely, unusual, strange, foreign, alien, exotic, diverse, variant, discrepant, nonuniform, inconsonant, incongruent, immiscible, incommensurate, heterogeneous, disproportionate, irregular, odd, inconsistent, ambiguous, ambivalent, equivocal **8 contradictory**, jarring, grating, paradoxical, absurd, oxymoronic, antinomic, contrary, opposite, mismatched, misallied, ill-chosen, maladjusted, unnatural, abnormal, mutant, distorted, anomalous, odd **9 nonconforming**, unconventional, individual, distinct, unique, singular, peculiar, idiosyncratic, eccentric, maverick, outlandish, weird, bizarre, odd, freakish, unorthodox, heterodox **10 disagreeing**, moot, discordant, disharmonious, controversial, incompatible, uncongenial, irreconcilable, at cross-purposes, differing, dissenting, dissident, dissonant, at odds, confrontational, challenging, disparaging, opposite, defiant, antagonistic, argumentative, hostile, inimical, at loggerheads, wrangling, quarrelling, clashing, conflicting, fighting **11 unfit**, unsuitable, incompatible, wrong, malapropos, inapposite, inapt, ill-adapted, incapable, ineligible, unqualified, incompetent, inept, unskilful, untimely, inapplicable, inadmissible, inexpedient, inappropriate, inelegant, unbecoming, unseemly, improper, infelicitous, intrusive, outside, alien

VERBS 12 be disparate, contrast, diversify, diverge, vary, differ, mutate, deviate, distort, misfit, mismatch, mistime, interrupt, fake, equivocate, jar, grate **13 not conform**, individualize **14 disagree**, differ, contradict, confront, challenge, counter, dissent, demur, object, oppose, defy, dispute, argue, antagonize, wrangle, bicker, squabble, clash, quarrel, cross swords

191 Dispersion

NOUNS 1 dispersion, dispersal, diffusion, distribution, dissemination, sowing, strewing, casting, seeding, scattering, scatterment, circulation, publication, broadcast, spread, deployment, propagation, issuance **2 disbandment**, dissolution, demobilization, deactivation, dismissal **3 dilution**, watering down, attenuation, liquefaction, deliquescence, evaporation, vaporization **4 sprinkling**, spraying, spattering, splattering, smattering, dusting, powdering, peppering, circumfusion, studding, spotting, dotting, speckling **5 divergence**, radiation, branching out, ramification, fanning out, splaying, deflection, diffraction, disintegration, fragmentation, decomposition **6 decentralization**, deconcentration, regionalization, localization, federalization **7 driftwood**

VERBS 8 be dispersed, disperse, scatter, separate, part, break up, split up, part company, drift apart, stray, straggle, spread **9 diverge**, fork, branch out, ramify, radiate, fan out **10 explode**, burst, fly apart, break up, disintegrate, fragment, decompose, evaporate **11 disperse**, scatter, diffract, diffuse, dispel, divide, sunder, hive off **12 dismiss**, send away, disband, dissolve, demobilize, deactivate, discharge **13 dilute**, water down, dissolve, thin, attenuate, liquefy, evaporate, boil away, vaporize, volatilize **14 distribute**, disseminate, circulate, publish, broadcast, spread, deploy, propagate, issue, dispense, deal **15 sow**, seed, strew, cast, fling **16 sprinkle**, spray, splash, shower, spatter, splatter, smatter, dust, powder, flour, dredge, pepper, stud, spot, dot, speckle

ADJECTIVES 17 dispersed, scattered,

diffuse, widespread, sparse, infrequent, sporadic **18 separated**, discrete, disintegrated, fragmented, decomposed, broken-up **19 disbanded**, dissolved, dismissed, demobilized **20 distributed**, disseminated, diffused, broadcast, spread, deployed, strewn, sown, propagated, circulated, published, issued **21 divergent**, forking, radiating, branching, ramiform, dendriform **22 sprawled**, straggling, drifting, astray, wandering **23 decentralized**, deconcentrated, regionalized, localized **24 dilute**, watered down, liquefied, evaporated, boiled away, vaporized **25 dispersive**, scattering, spreading, diffractive, diffusive, distributive

192 Displacement

NOUNS 1 displacement, dislocation, dislodgment, disturbance, disarrangement, derangement, derailment, shift, shunt, removal, relocation, translocation, transference, transshipment, switch, swerve, veer, deflection, aberration **2 removal**, extraction, extrication, uprooting, ripping out, pulling up **3 replacement**, substitution, supplantation, overthrow, coup, deposition, unseating, takeover, evacuation, ejection, banishment, expulsion, eviction, deportation **4 relegation**, demotion, downgrading, dismissal, discharge, lay-off, redundancy, marching orders **5 disconnection**, separation, detachment, unhinging, disjointedness, dislocation, disarticulation, disengagement, luxation **6 misplacement**, mislaying, mislocation, misputting

ADJECTIVES 7 displaced, dislocated, dislodged, disturbed, disarranged, deranged, derailed, shifted, shunted, moved, relocated, transferred, switched, swerved, veered **8 removed**, extracted, extricated, uprooted, ripped, torn, wrested, pulled, drawn **9 replaced**, overthrown, deposed, supplanted, transferred, removed, banished, expelled, deported, exiled, ostracized, evicted, evacuated, unhoused, homeless **10 relegated**, demoted, downgraded, dismissed, discharged, laid off **11 disconnected**, disjointed, disarticulated, dislocated, unhinged, disengaged, dismembered, detached **12 misplaced**, mislaid, misput, mislocated, lost

VERBS 13 displace, dislodge, dislocate, unseat, upset, disturb, disarrange, disorder, disorganize, disrupt, derail, switch, swerve, veer, deflect, shift, move, shunt, transfer, transport **14 remove**, extract, extricate, draw out, pull out, root out, rip out, tear out **15 replace**, substitute, supplant, overthrow, dethrone, unseat, depose, oust, usurp, take over, banish, expel, exile, ostracize, deport, cast out, turn out, evict **16 relegate**, demote, downgrade, discharge, dismiss, let go, make redundant, lay off, sack **17 disconnect**, unhinge, disjoint, disarticulate, dislocate, luxate, dismember, separate **18 misplace**, mislay

193 Display

VERBS 1 display, show, exhibit, manifest, present, expose, disclose, set out, feature, spotlight, illuminate, headline, emphasize, point out, indicate, teach, instruct, explain, flourish, brandish, wave, dangle, flaunt, vaunt, show off, parade, air, sport, model, demonstrate, perform, act, dramatize, stage, release **2 reveal**, manifest, divulge, disclose, uncover, unearth, illuminate, point up, indicate, accentuate, enhance, emphasize, highlight, spotlight, proclaim, publicize, promote, advertise, publish, bring forth, expose, open up, lay bare, unmask, unveil, draw out, express, trot out, evidence, show, evince, betray, unfurl, unfold, spread out, solve **3 be visible**, attract attention, stand out, loom large

NOUNS 4 display, show, exhibition, exposition, expo, demonstration, presentation, spectacle, showing, viewing, collection, retrospective, fair, market, parade **5 showpiece**, exhibit, pride, collectable, curio, antique, museum piece, specimen, example **6 production**, performance, presentation, enactment, show, spectacle, play, musical, concert, ballet, film **7 manifestation**, revelation, disclosure, exposure, unfolding, discovery, uncovering, visibility, publicity, promotion, conspicuousness, ostentation, showing off, emphasis, spotlight, ceremony, pageant, projection, representation, symbolization, typification, personification, indication, sign, token, signal, omen, proclamation, publication, appearance, materialization, epiphany, incarnation, theophany, avatar, seance **8 openness**, obviousness, plainness, candour, glasnost, plain speech

ADJECTIVES 9 displayed, exhibited, presented, shown, on view, made public, manifested, apodictic, featured, visible, apparent, produced, cited, quoted, confronted, worn, sported, paraded, flaunted, brandished, flourished, advertised, publicized, promoted **10 manifest**, revealed, disclosed, divulged, exposed, uncovered, declared, overt, public, noticeable, conspicuous, notable, apparent, visible, obvious, ostensible, open-and-shut, appearing, token, symbolic, representative, definite, recognizable, unmistakable, incontestable, pronounced, prominent, marked, striking, salient, highlighted, accentuated, patent, evident, obtrusive, flagrant, blatant, arrant, glaring, ostentatious, eye-catching, well-known, notorious, famous, infamous, showy **11 open**, candid, frank, explicit, plain-speaking, clear, crystal-clear, truthful, honest, veracious, free, unreserved, forthright, straightforward, blunt, outspoken, emphatic, bold, no-nonsense, daring, brazen, immodest, shameless, impudent, defiant

194 Disposal

NOUNS 1 disposal, discarding, alienation, transfer, substitution, nonretention, releasing, dismissal, firing, sacking, freeing, liberation, unfreezing, decontrol, dispensation, dissolution, divorce, cession, abandonment, removal, ejection, riddance, dumping, scrapping, renunciation, relinquishment, forgoing, forswearing, cancellation, abrogation, disuse, desuetude, outflow, incontinence **2 disposal of property**, sale, selling off, closing-down sale, jumble sale, bazaar, fair, auction **3 disposable things**, junk, jumble, white elephant, castoff, flotsam

VERBS 4 dispose of, dispense with,

spare, give up, release, waive, abandon, cede, yield, surrender, relinquish, marry off, discard, eject, jettison, leak, emit, cast away, scrap, dump, destroy, derestrict, decontrol, deregulate, replace, supersede, open, dissolve, divorce, impoverish, disown, maroon, renounce, abjure, forswear, disclaim, recant, cancel, revoke, abrogate **5 dismiss**, discharge, lay off, make redundant, fire, sack, edge out, elbow out **6 dispose of property**, sell, vend, peddle, hawk

ADJECTIVES 7 disposed (of), dispensed with, relinquished, released, discarded, freed, liberated, abandoned, divorced, disowned, disinherited, forgone **8 dismissed**, discharged, fired, sacked **9 for sale**, available, transferable **10 unclaimed**, remaining, unappropriated, unowned

195 Disrepute

NOUNS 1 disrespect, bad name, notoriety, infamy, ill-repute, disreputability, hatefulness, obnoxiousness, loathesomeness, unseemliness, disfavour, discredit, dishonour, slur, ignominy, degradation, disgrace, shame **2 disreputable character**, rogue, blackguard, undesirable, ugly customer, scoundrel, bad lot, bad egg, bad influence, black sheep, ne'er-do-well, cad **3 disreputable action**, foul play, dirty trick, skullduggery, fraud

ADJECTIVES 4 disreputable, ignominious, degrading, notorious, infamous, nefarious, shady, questionable, scandalous, dishonourable, shameless, immoral, underhand, fraudulent

VERBS 5 bring into disrepute, shame, disgrace oneself, lower oneself, demeen oneself, degrade oneself, humiliate oneself, desecrate, defile

196 Disrespect

NOUNS 1 disrespect, rudeness, discourtesy, impoliteness, unmannerliness, incivility, impertinence, impudence, insolence, irreverence, blasphemy, scurrility, defamation, obloquy **2 disesteem**, undervaluation, underestimation, disregard, neglect, dishonour, disrepute, disfavour, disapprobation **3 contempt**, scorn, disdain, superciliousness, superiority, loftiness, contumely, despite, low opinion **4 ridicule**, mockery, derision, sarcasm, irony, satire, imitation, impersonation, burlesque, caricature, lampoon **5 insult**, aspersion, affront, snub, slight, rebuff, repulse, spurn, cold shoulder, backhanded compliment, cutting remark **6 taunt**, jeer, mock, scoff, jibe, dig, barb, sneer, snort, sniff, hiss, boo, catcall, hoot, raspberry, brickbat, banter, chaff **7 indignity**, humiliation, degradation, mortification, chagrin **8 butt**, dupe, target, victim, fair game, easy mark, Aunt Sally, fall guy, fool, joke

ADJECTIVES 9 disrespectful, irreverent, blasphemous, scurrilous, rude, discourteous, impolite, unmannered, uncivil, impertinent, cheeky, saucy, pert, impudent, insolent, insubordinate, brazen, bold, audacious, forward **10 insulting**, abusive, offensive, pejorative, defamatory, opprobrious, contumacious, outrageous, snubbing, slighting, rebuffing, repulsing, spurning **11 disregardful**, neglectful, dishonourable, disreputable, contemptible, despicable, worthless, shameful, base **12 contemptuous**, scornful, disdainful, pejorative, supercilious, lofty, haughty, arrogant, snobbish, snooty **13 ridiculing**, mocking, derisive, sarcastic, ironic, satirical, imitating, burlesque, caricatural **14 taunting**, jeering, mocking, flouting, scoffing, scorning, jibing, sneering, hissing, booing, catcalling, hooting, bantering, chaffing **15 humiliating**, degrading, mortifying **16 unrespected**, unrevered, unvenerated **17 undervalued**, underestimated, underrated, disparaged, belittled, denigrated, ignored

VERBS 18 disrespect, hold cheap, underrate, underestimate, undervalue, perjorate **19 scorn**, disdain, despise, asperse, disparage, belittle, trivialize, denigrate, depreciate, run down **20 disregard**, ignore, neglect, dishonour, disgrace **21 show disrespect**, be rude **22 insult**, offend, affront, snub, slight, rebuff, repulse, spurn, cold shoulder, cut dead **23 ridicule**, mock, deride, satirize, imitate, humiliate, caricature **24 taunt**, jeer, scoff, jibe at, dig at, sneer, snort, sniff, hiss, boo, catcall, hoot, heckle, rail at, laugh at, call names

197 Dissatisfaction

NOUNS 1 dissatisfaction, displeasure, disgruntlement, discontent, disappointment, disillusionment, consternation, disapprobation, disapproval, rejection, reprobation, censure, dislike, derision, deprecation, disgust, contempt **2 expression of dissatisfaction**, complaint, criticism, boo, hiss, whistle, snub, reprimand, remonstration

ADJECTIVES 3 dissatisfied, displeased, disgruntled, discontented, malcontented, sulking, brooding, disaffected, complaining, whingeing, disappointed, disillusioned, disapproving, unimpressed, critical of, perjorative, disgusted, contemptuous, scornful **4 unsatisfactory**, dissatisfactory, disappointing, disapproved of, unapproved, unpopular

VERBS 5 dissatisfy, displease, disappoint, disillusion, disgust, revolt **6 be dissatisfied**, disapprove, dislike, resent, disfavour, criticize, tut-tut at, object to, cavil, grumble, grouse, carp, complain, whine, moan, sulk, brood, run down, belittle, deride, deprecate, deplore, reprove, rebuke, condemn, perjorate, reject, abhor, scorn, defame, revile, boo

198 Dissent

NOUNS 1 dissent, variance, conflict, friction, disagreement, dispute, controversy, quarrel, feud, war, strife, clash, squabble, spat, tiff, scrap, fracas, brawl, fisticuffs, altercation **2 disapproval**, disapprobation, rejection, refusal, denial, negation, thumbs down, objection, demur, protest, complaint **3 dissentience**, dissidence, discordance, disharmony, disunion, intolerance, quarrelsomeness, recrimination, unpleasantness, disobedience, noncooperation, opposition, rebellion, sedition, strike, nonconformity, unorthodoxy, counterculture, sectarianism, separatism, factionalism, disaffection, secession **4 faction**, split, schism, separation, rift, breach, rupture **5 dissenter**, dissident, dissentient, nonconformist, protestant, sectarian, partisan, separatist, schismatic, factionalist, malcontent, protester, recusant, caviller, critic, detractor, opponent, rebel, revolutionary, tergiversator, disputer, aggressor, agitator, troublemaker, mischief maker, heckler, scold, shrew, unconventionalist, bohemian

ADJECTIVES 6 dissenting, differing, at odds, opposing, conflicting, heterodox, unorthodox, heretical, sceptical, unconvinced, dissatisfied, protesting, unwilling, resistant, intolerant, dissident, seditious, divisive, separatist, schismatic, party-minded, partisan, clannish, sectarian, nonconformist, protestant, schismatical, secessionist, breakaway, rebel, recusant, rebellious, quarrelling, arguing, cantankerous, irascible, bellicose, warlike

VERBS 7 dissent, disagree, differ, take issue, quarrel, clash, conflict, dispute, confute, argue with, schismatize, separate, divide, secede, rebel, strike **8 refuse**, say no, disapprove, object, demur, protest, complain, oppose, contradict, negate

199 Dissertation

NOUNS 1 dissertation, discourse, disquisition, treatise, tract, tractate, exposition, summary, theme, argument, descant, thesis, essay, composition, study, lucubration, examination, survey, inquiry, discussion, symposium, paper, monograph, memoir, screed, harangue, homily, sermon, oration, peroration, tirade, lecture, lesson, prolegomenon, exegesis, interpretation, explanation, gloss, annotation **2 article**, leader, editorial, column, news item, review, notice, critique

VERBS 3 dissertate, discourse, descant, speak about, write about, argue, go into, inquire into, survey, discuss, comment on, criticize, commentate, gloss, annotate, interpret, explain, elucidate, define, expound, proselytize, harangue, orate, perorate, sermonize

ADJECTIVES 4 expository, discursive, disquisitional, critical, interpretive, interpretative, exegetical, illuminating, editorial

200 Dissimilarity

NOUNS 1 dissimilarity, difference, disparity, diversity, discrepancy, divergence, extraneousness, nonuniformity, differentiation, variation, multiformity, discrimination, distinction, variance, contrast **2 unlikeness**, unrelatedness, incongruity, incompatibility, contrast, asymmetry, incommensurability, no comparison, no match **3 disguise**, camouflage, caricature, bad likeness, concealment, misrepresentation, poor imitation, copy, counterfeit

ADJECTIVES 4 dissimilar, different, disparate, divergent, diverse, various, multiform, unequal, asymmetrical, nonuniform, unresembling, unlike, incongruous, incompatible, contrasting, poles apart, unrealistic, scarcely like, discrepant, distinctive, peculiar, original, singular, unrelated, new, unique, peerless, matchless, nonpareil, untypical, unprecedented, incomparable

VERBS 5 be dissimilar, differ, diverge, deviate, depart from, contrast **6 differentiate**, distinguish, discriminate, split hairs, innovate, vary, modify, change, convert, distort, caricature, misrepresent, dissemble, disguise, deceive

201 Dissonance

NOUNS 1 dissonance, discord, disharmony, harshness, jarring, jangling, clashing, stridency **2 dissonant noise**, cacophony, Babel, cat's concert, caterwauling, yowling, row, din, clamour, uproar, racket, hullabaloo, hubbub, pandemonium, bedlam, tumult **3 musical dissonance**, tunelessness, unmelodiousness, flatness, sharpness **4 atonality**, twelve-note composition, note row, series, serialism, dodecaphony **5 atmospheric dissonance**, static, wow, flutter, hiss, white noise **6 disagreement**, disaccord, discord, dissension, difference, conflict, clash

ADJECTIVES 7 dissonant, discordant, inharmonious, jangling, jarring, clashing, grating, scraping, rasping, harsh, raucous, cacophonous, strident **8 disagreeing**, conflicting, at variance, contrary **9 unmelodious**, unmusical, tuneless, droning, singsong, untuned, cracked, off-pitch, off-key, off, sharp, flat, toneless

VERBS 10 lack harmony, jangle, jar, grate, clash, crash, saw, scrape, rasp, drone, whine, thrum, play sharp **11 disagree**, differ, conflict, clash, argue

202 Dissuasion

VERBS 1 dissuade, discourage, caution, warn, advise against, persuade against, put off, argue against, confute, castigate, reprove, expostulate, remonstrate **2 deter**, frighten off, unnerve, rattle, shake, stagger, daunt, cow, intimidate, threaten **3 deflect**, head off, disaccustom, hold back, restrain, crush, stop **4 put off**, disincline, disaffect, indispose, set against, turn against, repel, disgust **5 discourage**, dishearten, dispirit, depress, disillusion, disenchant, dampen, extinguish, quench, squelch, cool, chill, blunt

NOUNS 6 dissuasion, discouragement, contrary advice, caution, warning, reproof, admonition, expostulation, remonstrance, objection, protest, resistance, opposition, hindrance **7 deterrence**, disincentive, intimidation, terrorism, deflection, restraint, disinclination, disaffection, disheartenment, disenchantment

ADJECTIVES 8 dissuasive, discouraging, contrary, contradictory, cautionary, warning, monitory, expostulatory, chilling, damping, disheartening **9 dissuaded**, discouraged, disenchanted, disillusioned, disheartened, dampened

203 Distance

NOUNS 1 distance, farness, remoteness, inaccessibility, aloofness, removal, separation, divergence, deviation, dispersion, perspective, long range, deep space, light years **2 great distance**, step, long way, fair way, day's march, marathon **3 distant place**, background, periphery, circumference, horizon, skyline, offing, vanishing point, godforsaken place, outback, outskirts, outpost, antipodes, pole, Timbuktu, Outer Mongolia, Darkest Africa, Siberia, world's end, outer space **4 reserve**, aloofness, standoffishness, shyness

VERBS 5 be distant, outlie, outrange **6 keep away**, stand off, stand aloof,

stand back, distance oneself, separate **7 reach**, stretch, extend, go, carry, outreach
ADJECTIVES 8 distant, far, far off, far away, far-flung, remote, yonder, ulterior, farther, further, outlying, offshore, inaccessible, out-of-the-way, godforsaken, exotic, antipodean, hyperborean, overseas, transcontinental, transpolar, distal, peripheral, long-distance, long-range, farthermost, furthermost **9 reserved**, aloof, standoffish, unapproachable, untouchable, shy

204 Distortion

NOUNS 1 distortion, asymmetry, disproportion, lopsidedness, imbalance, difference, irregularity, crookedness, warp, strain, stress, contortion, bias, skewness, twist **2 facial distortion**, contortion, grimace, scowl, frown, snarl, sneer, leer, pout, rictus, tic **3 deformity**, malformation, hunchback, clubfoot, cleft palate, mutation, misshapenness, ugliness, hideousness, disfigurement, grotesquerie, defacement, imperfection, scar, cicatrix, spot, stain, mark, welt, weal, pockmark, blemish **4 distortion of the truth**, exaggeration, misrepresentation, perversion, misconstruction, false reading, fiction, deception, fabrication, falsity, spuriousness, perfidy, mendacity, deceitfulness, misinformation, disinformation, brainwashing, whitewashing, untruthfulness, lie, falsehood, travesty, burlesque, parody
ADJECTIVES 5 distorted, asymmetric, unsymmetrical, unbalanced, misshapen, irregular, lopsided, crooked, askew, disproportionate, unequal, off-target **6 deformed**, malformed, hunchbacked, clubfooted, disfigured, imperfect, ugly, hideous, grotesque, defaced, scarred, marked, pockmarked, spotty, pitted, blemished **7 exaggerated**, false, perfidious, evasive, fake, misrepresented, perverted, fictitious, deceptive, fabricated, spurious, misinformed, misguided, misleading, untruthful, deceitful
VERBS 8 distort, warp, twist, strain, stress, contort, bias, disproportion, imbalance **9 make faces**, grimace, leer, scowl, frown, snarl, sneer, pout **10 deform**, malform, disfigure, deface, damage, impair, stain, spot, mark, welt, weal, pit, pockmark, warp, cicatrize **11 distort the truth**, exaggerate, reshape, deform, misrepresent, pervert, misconceive, misconstrue, twist words, falsify, fabricate, dissemble, embroider, fake, deceive, dress up, forge, concoct, rig, misinform, mislead, misguide, be false, lie, brainwash

205 Disturbance

NOUNS 1 disturbance, perturbation, agitation, convulsion, upheaval, upset, disconcertedness, disquiet, discomfiture, discomposure, worry, anxiety, annoyance, bother **2 disarrangement**, derangement, disorder, disorganization, muddle **3 dispersion**, displacement, dislodgment, dislocation, disorientation **4 disruption**, disturbance, interruption, intrusion, interference, intervention, molestation, perversion, sabotage, hindrance, obstruction, inconvenience, untimeliness **5 commotion**, disturbance, disorder, tumult, turmoil, ferment, furore, outcry, outburst, clamour, uproar, fuss, rumpus, bedlam, hubbub, hurly-burly, hullabaloo, brouhaha, to-do, ado, racket, din, noise, bother, trouble, scuffle, fracas, fray **6 derangement**, insanity

VERBS 7 disturb, perturb, agitate, stir, convulse, upset, distress, unsettle, disconcert, disquiet, discomfit, discompose, fluster, ruffle, shake, rattle, alarm, concern, worry, trouble, bother, pester, harass, annoy, irritate, vex **8 disarrange**, derange, disorder, disorganize, muddle **9 disperse**, displace, dislodge, dislocate, disorient **10 disrupt**, interrupt, intrude, interfere, intervene, molest, pervert, tamper with, sabotage, hinder, obstruct, inconvenience, put out, distract **11 derange**, unhinge, unbalance, drive insane

ADJECTIVES 12 disturbed, perturbed, agitated, convulsed, upset, distressed, unsettled, disconcerted, disquieted, discomfited, discomposed, uncomfortable, uneasy, confused, flustered, ruffled, shaken, rattled, alarmed, concerned, worried, anxious, troubled, bothered, annoyed, irritated **13 disarranged**, deranged, disordered, disorganized, muddled, confused **14 dispersed**, displaced, dislodged, dislocated, disorientated **15 disrupted**, interrupted, interfered with, molested, sabotaged, hindered, obstructed, inconvenienced **16 deranged**, disordered, unhinged, unbalanced, maladjusted, disturbed, demented, neurotic, psychotic, unstable, mad **17 disturbing**, upsetting, distressing, unsettling, disconcerting, alarming, worrying, bothersome, annoying, vexatious, muddling

206 Divergence

NOUNS 1 divergence, divarication, aberration, declination, deviation, difference, contradiction **2 parting**, moving apart, drifting apart, spread, splaying, fanning, deployment, separation, centrifugence, division **3 radiation**, ray, radius, spoke, radiance, scattering, diffusion, dispersion **4 branching**, ramification, arborescence, forking, bifurcation, intersection, crossroads **5 fork**, prong, trident, branch, offshoot, fan, delta, groin

ADJECTIVES 6 divergent, divaricate, separated, aberrant, different, contradictory, centrifugal **7 radiating**, radial, rayed **8 fanlike**, splayed **9 branched**, arborescent, treelike, dendriform, branchlike, ramose, Y-shaped, V-shaped, forked, furcate

VERBS 10 diverge, divaricate, aberrate **11 move apart**, part, spread, fan out, deploy **12 separate**, divide, splay, split **13 radiate**, ray, diffuse, emanate, disperse **14 branch**, stem, ramify, branch off, spread-eagle, straddle, step wide, fork **15 change direction**, switch

207 Diversity

NOUNS 1 diversity, difference, variety, multiplicity, heterogeneity, miscellany, versatility, dissimilarity, contrast, deviation, variousness, divergence, variegation, incongruity, nonconformity, exception, nonuniformity, inconsistency, inequality, discontinuity, unevenness, irregularity, changeability, haphazardness, modifiability, alterability, abnormality **2 assortment**, mixture, medley, miscellany, hotchpotch, motley, multiplicity, omnifariousness, allotropy, heteromorphism **3 diverse thing**, motley collection, miscellanea, ragbag, lucky dip, mosaic, stained-glass window, patchwork quilt, rainbow **4 dissension**, disagreement, controversy

ADJECTIVES 5 diverse, varied, nonuniform, heterogeneous, dissimilar, contrasting, deviant, diverging, different, manifold, incongruous, variegated, chequered, abnormal, freakish, unique, inconsistent, changeable, unstable, spasmodic, sporadic, erratic, haphazard, fitful **6 assorted**, mixed, chequered, miscellaneous, motley, dapple, omnifarious, multifarious, allotropic, kaleidoscopic, sundry, various, multipurpose, multifaceted, multiform, diversiform, polymorphous, heteromorphous **7 dissenting**, disagreeing

VERBS 8 be diverse, diverge, branch out, differ, variegate, deviate, mutate, differentiate, vary, contrast, chequer, mix, stir, jumble, shake up, intermix, intersperse **9 dissent**, disagree

208 Divinity

- *For the Kingdom of God is not in word, but in power.* Bible: I Corinthians.
- *God moves in a mysterious way/ His wonders to perform.* William Cowper.

NOUNS 1 divinity, divineness, godhood, godhead, deity, godship, godliness **2 God**, Lord, the Lord, Providence, Jehovah, Yahweh, Allah, Almighty God, the Almighty, the Eternal, the Maker, the Creator, the Father, Everlasting Father, First Cause, Prime Mover, Buddha, Bodhisattva, the Trinity, Holy Trinity, Father **3 God the Son**, Jesus Christ, Christ, Jesus, Lord Jesus, Messiah, Emmanuel, the Saviour, the Redeemer **4 deity**, divinity, god, goddess, deva **5 angel**, angelhood, archangel, archangelship, guardian angel, seraph, cherub, celestial, heavenly being, heavenly host **6 devil**, demon, demonkind, evil spirit, incubus, succubus, afreet, fiend, imp, lost soul, fallen angel, rebel angel, the Devil, Satan, Lucifer, the Enemy, Archfiend, Antichrist, The Tempter, Belial, Beelzebub, Mephisto **7 deification**, apotheosis, divinization, immortalization, idolization, fetishization, canonization, beatification, sainting, santification, angelization, consecration, enshrinement, exaltation, adulation, glorification, elevation, assumption, dedication, dignification, ennoblement, magnification **8 deified person**, saint, martyr, patron saint, beatified soul, canonized person, redeemed soul, Madonna, Our Lady, Holy Mary **9 heaven**, sky, firmament, empyrean, welkin, Kingdom come, paradise, nirvana, Elysium, Elysian fields, Avalon **10 hell**, limbo, purgatory, lower world, underworld, nether world, Hades, inferno, abyss, bottomless pit

ADJECTIVES 11 divine, godly, godlike, deistic, theistic, Yahwistic, Elohistic, Christlike, Christly, messianic, incarnate, theomorphic, epiphanic, numinous, holy, hallowed, sacred, sacrosanct, transcendent, transcendental, enlightened, blessed, sublime, perfect, supreme, sovereign, majestic, theocratic, providential, omnipresent, ubiquitous, all-seeing, all-knowing, prescient, omniscient, all-powerful, omnipotent, almighty, absolute, immortal, eternal, infinite, immeasurable, ineffable, mystical, oracular, supernatural, supramundane, extramundane **12 heavenly**, celestial, empyrean, empyreal, on high, Elysian, paradisiac, paradisical, paradisial, Olympian, supernal, ethereal, angelic, angelical, archangelic, seraphic, cherubic **13 deified**, divinized, immortalized, canonized, beatified, sanctified, angelized, haloed, glorified, saved, redeemed, martyred, consecrated, enshrined, elevated, dedicated, dignified, ennobled, magnified, exalted, adulated **14 devilish**, devil-like, evil, satanic, diabolic, diabolical, demonic, demoniac, demon-like, Mephistophelean, fiendish, fiendlike, fallen, damned, hell-born, hellish, infernal, sulphurous, chthonian, chthonic, subterranean, pandemonic, Plutonian, Avernal, Tartarean

VERBS 15 deify, apotheosize, divinize, immortalize, canonize, bless, beatify, sanctify, angelize, consecrate, hallow, enshrine, elevate, dedicate, dignify, ennoble, magnify, exalt, adulate, glorify, idolize, ascend, transcend, sublimate **16 devilize**, diabolize, demonize, bedevil, possess, damn

209 Divorce

NOUNS 1 divorce, decree nisi, decree absolute, annulment, broken marriage, broken home, break-up **2 separation**, estrangement, living apart **3 divorce court**, co-respondent, incompatibility, cruelty, adultery, maintenance, alimony **4 widowhood**, widowerhood

VERBS 5 divorce, separate, live apart, part, break up, split up **6 desert**, abandon, leave **7 widow**, bereave

ADJECTIVES 9 divorced, dissolved, separated, legally separated, split, estranged, living apart, deserted **10 widowed**, husbandless, widowered, wifeless

210 Dress

NOUNS 1 dress, clothing, clothes, wear, apparel, accoutrement, garment, garb, frock, creation, linen, habiliments, attire, kit, rig, outfit, wardrobe, tailor-made clothes, bespoke clothes, ready-to-wear clothes, off-the-peg clothes, wash-and-wear clothes, unisex clothes, men's clothing, menswear, women's clothing, womenswear, trousseau, wedding clothes, bridal outfit, maternity wear, work clothes, formal clothes, best clothes, Sunday best, finery, regalia, caparison, panoply, array, frippery, ostrich feathers, informal clothes, sportswear, old clothes, worn clothes, cast-offs, second-hand clothes, tatters, slops, seconds **2 dressing**, covering, vestiture, investiture, investment, toilet, wardrobe, turnout, dressing up, overdressing, foppishness, underdressing, casualness, fashion, high fashion, couture **3 garment making**, tailoring, dressmaking, habilimentation, millinery, hosiery, hatmaking **4 skirt**, maxiskirt, midiskirt, miniskirt, microskirt, pleated skirt, full skirt, flared skirt, kilt, culottes, sarong, tight skirt, hobble skirt, sports skirt, riding habit, tennis skirt, ballet skirt, tutu, overskirt, hoop skirt, crinoline **5 frock**, dress, cocktail dress, dinner dress, gown, ballgown, dinner gown, tea gown, evening gown, overdress, shirtdress, mantua, cheongsam, muumuu, Mother Hubbard, maxidress, minidress, pinafore dress, tube dress, sheath dress, sack, shirtwaister, gymslip, sundress, backless dress, strapless dress, topless dress, maternity dress **6 shirt**, dress shirt, evening shirt, blouse, middy blouse, overblouse, top, tank top, halter, bustier, smock, polo shirt, T-shirt **7 trousers**, pants, long trousers, cords, flannels, pinstripes, hipsters, bell-bottoms, slacks, Oxford bags, knickerbockers, plus fours, galligaskins, breeches, knee breeches, riding breeches, overalls, jodhpurs, pedal pushers, dungarees, denims, jeans, bluejeans, lederhosen, bloomers, pantaloons, ski pants, shorts, Bermuda shorts **8 suit**, outfit, costume, ensemble, coordinates, separates, dress suit, lounge suit, pinstripe suit, tweed suit, tweeds, trouser suit, catsuit, jump suit, leotard, coveralls, boiler suit, tracksuit **9 jacket**, morning coat, midicoat, sports jacket, blazer, Eton jacket, lumber jacket, bomber jacket, parka, anorak, cagoule, reefer, windcheater, hunting jacket, shooting jacket, Norfolk jacket, donkey jacket, jerkin, spencer, bolero, tunic, tabard **10 coat**, overcoat, topcoat, surcoat, greatcoat, frock coat, raglan, ulster, duffel coat, pea jacket, fearnought, dreadnought, duster, raincoat, waterproof, mackintosh, gaberdine coat, trench coat, oilskins **11 sweater**, jersey, cardigan, pullover, slipover, woolly, cashmere sweater, knitted sweater, knit, hand-knit sweater, jumper, V-neck, polo-neck, ski sweater, turtleneck, crew-neck, Guernsey, Aran sweater, fisherman's jersey, Fair Isle **12 neckwear**, scarf, muffler, comforter, fichu, stock, neckpiece, neckerchief, bandanna, kerchief, shawl, tallith, stole, fur, boa, tippet, jabot, tucker, chemisette, cravat, neckcloth, ascot, tie, bow tie, dicky bow, Windsor tie, necklace, neckband, band, collar, choker **13 headgear**, headdress, millinery, hat, chapeau, top hat, high hat, silk hat, stovepipe hat, bowler, felt hat, homburg, fedora, trilby, pork-pie hat, deerstalker, Tyrolean hat, straw hat, boater, panama, cowboy hat, stetson, ten-gallon hat, sombrero, slouch hat, beaver, beaverskin, coonskin hat, busby, cocked hat, tricorn, mortarboard, bonnet, Easter bonnet, poke bonnet, sunbonnet, sunhat, picture hat, pillbox, toque, cloche, rain hat, southwester, clerical hat, biretta, shovel hat, woolly hat, bobble hat, helmet, pith helmet, topee, cap, cloth cap, baseball cap, beret, tam-o'shanter, glengarry, balmoral, kepi, shako, fez, balaclava helmet, crown, coronet, tiara, net, snood, headscarf, headband, ribbon, fillet, sweatband, turban, hood, cowl, wimple, veil, yashmak **14 robe**, bathrobe, lounging robe, gown, dressing gown, *robe-de-chambre*, peignoir, negligée, housecoat, wrapper, bed jacket, boudoir dress, tunic, sari, kimono, caftan, jubbah, burka, kanga, chiton, himation, toga, toga virilis, pallium, clerical robe **15 underwear**, undergarments, underclothes, underthings, scanties, lingerie, unmentionables, combinations, pants, drawers, shorts, boxer shorts, trunks, briefs, Y-fronts, panties, pantalets, bloomers, knickers, French knickers, camiknickers, vest, singlet, camisole, chemise, shift, step-ins, slip, half-slip, underskirt, petticoat, crinoline, Balmoral, teddy, crop top, body stocking, body, foundation garment, corset, stays, girdle, panty girdle, roll-on, supporter, brassiere, bra **16 footwear**, footgear, shoes, lace-ups, Oxfords, pumps, court shoes, winkle-pickers, plimsolls, trainers, sneakers, casuals, brogues, moccasins, slippers, mules, slip-ons, sandals, buskins, chappals, flip-flops, clogs, sabots, boots, waders, Wellington boots, hobnail boots, jackboots, overshoes, galoshes **17 legwear**, hosiery, hose, stockings, socks, nylons, tights, fishnet tights, fleshings, half-hose, socks, argyles, crew socks, knee-length socks, bobby socks, galligaskins, leggings **18 beachwear**, swimsuit, swimming costume, bathing suit, bikini, tanga, one-piece swimsuit **19 nightwear**, sleepwear, nightclothes, nightdress, nightshirt, bedgown, negligée, pyjamas, dressing gown, bed jacket, nightcap **20 children's clothes**, infants' wear, baby clothes, layette, rompers, matinee coat, coatee, playsuit, sunsuit, bootees, bib **21 fashion designer**, couturier, costumier, costume designer, dressmaker, tailor, garmentmaker, clothier, outfitter, milliner, modiste, hatter, hosier, glover, furrier

ADJECTIVES 22 dressed, clothed, clad, attired, garbed, apparelled, bedecked, arrayed, vested, invested, habited, habilimented, wrapped, draped, robed, frocked, mantled, cloaked, gowned, hatted, capped, bonneted, hooded, bewigged, gloved, shod, shoed, booted, decked out, turned out, rigged, kitted out, costumed, uniformed **23 dressed up**, smart, clothes-conscious, fashionable, stylish, modish, chic, dapper, spruced up, spruce, well-dressed, groomed **24 styled**, tailored, sartorial, tailor-made, bespoke, made-to-measure, designer

VERBS 25 dress, clothe, clad, garment, apparel, accoutre, attire, robe, enrobe, gown, drape, cloak, mantle, garb, enfold, envelop, wrap, swaddle, swathe, shroud, sheathe, cover, vest, invest, cap, hood, glove, shoe, uniform **26 dress up**, deck out, turn out, rig out, spruce up, titivate, bedeck, array, beautify, primp, prink **27 wear**, dress in, have on, don, clothe oneself **28 make clothing**, outfit, tailor, tailor-make, custom-make, accoutre, costume, rig out, fit out

211 Drinking

NOUNS 1 drinking, imbibing, imbibition, fluid intake, potation, sucking, lapping, sipping, tasting, nipping, supping, gulping, swallowing, swilling, swigging, quaffing, toping, soaking, pulling, wine-tasting, wine-bibbing, drunkenness, alcoholism **2 drink**, beverage, potation, libation, oblation, toast, health, mixed drink, concoction, cocktail, potion, decoction, infusion, bumper, stiff one, two fingers, short drink **3 drinker**, light drinker, social drinker, sipper, wine-taster, heavy drinker, hard drinker, guzzler, bibber, swiller, quaffer

VERBS 4 drink, imbibe, potate, suck, lap, sip, taste, nip, drink up, quaff, sup, swallow, gulp, gulp down, down, drain, knock back, put away, lap up, soak up, sponge up, wash down, swill, swig, tipple, tope **5 drink to**, pledge, toast **6 provide drink**, water, wine, suckle

ADJECTIVES 7 drinking, nursed, suckled, breast-fed, imbibing, swilling, tippling, bibulous, vinous, drunken **8 drinkable**, potable, milky, lactic, white, diluted, weak, strong, undiluted, black, nonalcoholic, soft, fizzy, alcoholic, fermented, distilled, spiritous, hard, vinous, sparkling, still, sweet, dry, light

INTERJECTIONS 9 cheers!, here's health!, to us!, bottoms up!, slainte!, *prosit!, skol!*

212 Drug-taking

NOUNS 1 drug-taking, drug addiction, drug abuse, drug dependence, habit, smoking, sniffing, gluesniffing **2 drug pushing**, drug peddling **3 drug taker**, drug user **4 drug pusher**, pusher, drug peddler, drug dealer **5 drug**, drugs, dope, narcotic, narcotics, fix, hard drug, soft drug, designer drug, ecstasy, cannabis, marijuana, hashish, cocaine, heroin, methadone, barbiturate, morphine, opium, amphetamine, stimulant, excitant, hallucinogen

ADJECTIVES 6 drugged, doped, incapacitated **7 addicted**, drug-dependent **8 addictive**, narcotic

VERBS 9 drug oneself, take drugs, smoke

213 Drunkenness

- *For when the wine is in, the wit is out.* Thomas Becon.
- *Wine is a mocker, strong drink is raging: and whosoever is deceived thereby is not wise.* Bible: Proverbs.

ADJECTIVES 1 drunk, inebriated, intoxicated **2 slightly drunk**, tipsy, maudlin, tearful, muzzy, glazed, glassy-eyed, pie-eyed, seeing double, woozy, reeling **3 dead drunk**, stupefied **4 crapulous**, hung over, dizzy, giddy **5 drunken**, inebriate, intemperate, alcoholic, sottish, sodden, gin-sodden, beery, vinous, bibulous, tippling, swilling, swigging, guzzling, hard-drinking, carousing, wassailing, red-nosed, bloodshot, gouty **6 intoxicating**, inebriating, temulent, stimulant, exhilarating, heady, winy, vinous, beery, spiritous, alcoholic, hard, potent, strong, proof, neat

VERBS 7 be drunk, hiccup, stutter, stammer, see double, lurch, stagger, reel, succumb **8 get drunk**, drink hard, tipple, tope, guzzle, swig, swill, quaff, carouse **9 be intoxicating**, inebriate, stupefy, stimulate, exhilarate

NOUNS 10 drunkenness, inebriation, intoxication, insobriety, ebriety, tipsiness, drunken stupor, stimulation, exhilaration, Dutch courage, hiccup, slurred speech, seeing double, wooziness, dizziness, staggering, reeling **11 drinking**, getting drunk, intemperance, bibulousness, tippling, swilling, sottishness, beeriness **12 alcohol**, drink, liquor, hard drink, strong drink, grog, wine, beer, spirits, John Barleycorn, cocktail **13 drink**, beverage, potation, compotation, libation, flowing bowl, tipple, nip, dram, drop, finger, snort **14 drinking bout**, binge, spree, bacchanalia **15 crapulence**, hangover, thick head, fuzzy tongue, dizziness, giddiness **16 alcoholism**, dipsomania, drink problem, tremors, delirium tremens **17 drunkard**, drunk, inebriate, sot, alcoholic, dipsomaniac, hard drinker, bibber, tippler, swiller, bacchant, maenad, Silenus

214 Dryness

ADJECTIVES 1 dry, arid, waterless, moistureless, unirrigated, unmoistened, undamped, anhydrous **2 thirsty**, dry **3 dried-up**, dried, dehydrated, desiccated, exsiccated, withered, shrivelled, faded, wizened, parchment-like, mummified, corky **4 dried-out**, drained, evaporated, squeezed dry **5 rainless**, fair, hot, sunny, fine **6 desert**, arid, Saharan, dusty, powdery, sandy, barren, bare, brown **7 adapted to drought**, xerophilous, xerophytic **8 baked**, parched, sun-dried, sun-baked, burnt, scorched **9 drying**, desiccative, dehydrating, exsiccative **10 waterproof**, rainproof, stormproof, flood proof, showerproof, dampproof, watertight

NOUNS 11 dryness, aridness, siccity, parchedness **12 thirst**, dryness, dehydration **13 drying**, desiccation, exsiccation, dehydration, airing, anhydration, dehumidification, withering, fading, bleaching, searing, mummification **14 desert**, sand dune, badlands, dust bowl, salt flat, wasteland **15 dryer**, blotting paper, mop, sponge, swab, towel, desiccator, siccative, exsiccative, dehydrator

VERBS 16 dry, dehydrate, anhydrate, drain, evaporate, vaporize, desiccate, exsiccate, freeze-dry, dehumidify **17 bake**, sun, insolate, toast, roast, scorch, bleach, apricate **18 absorb**, soak up, blot, mop up, swab **19 dry up**, parch, wither, shrivel, wilt, wizen, weazen, mummify **20 drip-dry**, spin-dry, tumble-dry, wring, mangle, peg out

215 Duration

NOUNS 1 duration, period **2 time**, time flies **3 continuity**, continuation, progress **4 long-lastingness**, endurance, permanence, fixity, constancy, durableness, stability, staying power **5 long duration**, ages, aeons, generations, a lifetime, an eternity, days

VERBS 6 last, endure, stay, stand, abide, remain, last out, hold out, survive, outlive, outlast **7 go on**, move on, continue, progress, proceed, run

ADJECTIVES 8 lasting, durable, enduring, long-lasting, long-lived, abiding, continuing, continuous, continual, longstanding, evergreen, long-term **9 permanent**, unceasing, incessant, everlasting, eternal, perpetual, perennial

216 Duty

• *England expects every man will do his duty.* Lord Nelson.

NOUNS 1 duty, bounden duty, obligation, imposition, onus, burden, charge, assignment, responsibility, liability, accountability **2 task**, function, work, service, office, station, profession, business, place, calling, engagement, commission, mission, assignment, fatigue, shift **3 allegiance**, loyalty, fealty, homage, devotion, dedication, deference, respect, reverence, obedience, compliance, comity, submission **4 sense of duty**, dutifulness, duteousness, moral obligation, moral imperative, inner voice **5 discharge of duty**, performance, acquittal **6 ethics**, rules, regula-

tions, maxim, precept, morals, professional code **7 commitment**, promise, pledge, vow, oath, word, contract, engagement, obligation, tie, bond, covenant, assurance
ADJECTIVES 8 dutiful, duteous, conscientious, scrupulous, punctilious, ethical, moral, principled, virtuous, honourable, decent **9 loyal**, devoted, dedicated, deferential, respectful, reverential, obedient, compliant, submissive, docile, tractable, amenable **10 liable**, accountable, answerable **11 duty-bound**, bound, obliged, obligated, beholden, tied, committed, engaged, pledged, sworn **12 obligatory**, mandatory, compulsory, binding, incumbent on, inescapable, unavoidable, unconditional, categorical, peremptory **13 on duty**, on call
VERBS 14 be the duty of, fall to, rest with, devolve upon, belong to, pertain to, behove, become, befit, must, should, ought to **15 be liable**, answer for, account for, commit oneself, engage oneself **16 do one's duty**, obey **17 impose a duty**, oblige, obligate, bind, saddle with, make incumbent, tie, commit, engage, pledge, require, order, command, decree, call upon, enjoin, expect, look to

217 Earliness

NOUNS 1 earliness, promptness, punctuality, immediacy, dispatch, expedition, head start, readiness, alacrity, quickness, hastiness **2 early hour**, unearthly hour, sunrise, dawn **3 early stage**, first step, early warning, primitiveness, beginning, creation **4 early comer**, first arrival, premature baby, early riser, precursor, predecessor, ancestor, forefather, prophet, primitive, aborigine, settler, colonist, scout, explorer **5 prematurity**, precipitance, prevenience, preparation, foresight, anticipation, expectation, impetuosity, haste
VERBS 6 be early, pre-empt, anticipate **7 precede**, predate, go before, colonize, settle, scout ahead, explore **8 prepare**, precipitate, reserve, order, book, engage, anticipate, expect, foresee, pre-empt, forestall **9 hasten**, make haste **10 get ahead**, advance
ADJECTIVES 11 early, first, earliest, prompt, punctual, immediate, expeditious, ready, advanced, alacritous, quick, hurried, hasty **12 imminent**, forthcoming, impending, looming, expected soon **13 primeval**, primitive **14 precursory**, precursive, preceding, ancestral, aboriginal, indigenous, colonial **15 premature**, precipitate, precocious, forward, beforehand, prevenient, preparatory, prophetic, foresighted, anticipatory, expectative, impetuous, hasty, overhasty

218 Earth Science

NOUNS 1 earth science, geoscience, geology, mineralogy, petrology, hydrology, geochemistry, marine geology, glaciology, geomorphology, physiography, pedology, geodesy, stratigraphy, palaeogeography, palaeoclimatology, geochronology, geopolitics, planetology, astrogeology, geography, human geography **2 geophysics**, geomagnetics, gravity geophysics, gravimetry, solid-earth geophysics, seismology, seismography, volcanology, plate tectonics, physical oceanography, climatology **3 geologist**, mineralogist, petrologist, hydrologist, geochemist, glaciologist, geomorphologist, physiographer, pedologist, geodesist, stratigrapher, palaeogeographer, palaeoclimatologist, palaeontologist, geochronologist **4 geophysicist**, geomagnetist, seismologist, volcanologist, oceanographer, climatologist **5 earth**, planet earth, the world, the globe, atmosphere, hydrosphere, geosphere, biosphere, ecosphere, geoid, mother earth **6 continent**, subcontinent, continental shelf, continental margin, continental drift, land, mainland, land mass, dry land, ground, topography, relief, elevation, terrain **7 landform**, basin, plain, shield, valley, rift valley, V-shaped valley, U-shaped valley, glacial valley, fjord, hanging valley, cirque, cwm, canyon, gorge, ravine, hill, plateau, scarp, mountain **8 earth's crust**, mantle, core, bedding-plane, discontinuity, Mohorovičić discontinuity, lithosphere, asthenosphere, isostacy, isostatic equilibrium, sial **9 seismic activity**, earthquake, quake, microseism, earth tremor, shock, foreshock, main shock, aftershock, focus, epicentre, Richter scale **10 volcanic activity**, volcanism, volcano, active volcano, inactive volcano, shield volcano, volcanic cone, composite volcano, crater, caldera, vent, fissure, magma chamber, magma, melt, eruption, lava, ejecta, tephra, pyroclastic material, ash, pumice, volcanic gas, lava flow, aa, pahoehoe, fumurole, gas vent, geyser, hot spring **11 mass movement**, landslide, slide, glide, slump, mudflow, debris flow, earthflow, plastic flow, lahar, creep, rock fall **12 sediment**, mud, deposit, ooze, alluvial deposit, delta, rock, boulder, stone, gravel, granules, pebbles, shingle, chesil, sand, silt, clay, loess **13 rock**, stone, igneous rock, sedimentary rock, metamorphic rock, rock formation, texture, cleavage, fabric, facies, rock-forming mineral, xenolith, batholith, laccolith, lopolith, igneous rock, sedimentary rock **14 mineral**, silicate, feldspar, chromite, magmatite, pegmatite, mica, orthoclase, oligoclase, plagioclase, olivine, chrysolite, pyroxene, amphibole, spinel **15 soil**, earth, topsoil, subsoil, regolith, soil profile, soil horizon, gravel, sand, loam, silt, clay, alluvium, pedalfer, podzol, pedocal, lateritic soil **16 fossil**, fossil record, ammonite, trilobite, graptolite, coprolite, petrified wood, coal, cast, mould, fossil track, fossil footprint, fossilization

ADJECTIVES 17 geological, mineralogical, petrological, hydrological, geochemical, glaciological, geomorphological, pedological, geodetic, stratigraphical, palaeontological, geochronological **18 geophysical**, geomagnetic, gravimetric, seismological, volcanological, oceanographic, bathymetric, hydrographic, climatological **19 terrestrial**, global, atmospheric, hydrospheric, geospheric, continental, subterranean **20 volcanic**, eruptive, seismic, pyroclastic, molten **21 petrographic**, petrographical, petrological, petrogenic, lithic, igneous, magmatic, volcanic, plutonic, pyroclastic, intrusive, extrusive, sedimentary, stratified, clastic, detrital, metamorphic **22 earthy**, rocky, stony,

gravelly, pebbly, sandy, loamy **23 fossilized**, petrified
VERBS 24 lithify, crystallize, recrystallize, mineralize, fossilize, petrify, consolidate **25 fold**, fracture, strain, cleave, subside, quake, tremble **26 map**, chart, plan, survey, explore

219 Ease

NOUNS 1 ease, relaxation, repose, rest, inactivity, idleness, stillness, restfulness, comfort, well-being, content, contentment, eudemonia, tranquillity, serenity, sweet dreams, refreshment, tea break, pause, respite, lull, recess, interval, interim, leave, holiday, vacation, leisure, free time, bank holiday
VERBS 2 take it easy, relax, repose, rest, sit back, recline, loll, lounge, laze, sleep, doze, drowse, nap, unwind, let up **3 ease**, loosen, slacken, moderate, reduce, relieve
ADJECTIVES 4 at ease, easeful, relaxed, resting, casual, carefree, laid-back, content, eudemonic, comfortable, peaceful, quiet, tranquil, leisured, idle, lazy, leisurely, unhurried, sabbatical, postprandial **5 labour-saving**, back-saving, time-saving, restful, reposeful

220 Easiness

NOUNS 1 easiness, facility, effortlessness, comfort, proficiency, competence, dexterity, fluency, ability, capability, talent, aptitude, skill, speed, efficiency **2 simplicity**, plainness, uncomplicatedness, unambiguousness, preciseness, comprehensibility, understandability, clarity, intelligibility, lucidity, facileness, glibness **3 wieldiness**, manageability, handiness, manoeuvrability, convenience, practicality, feasibility, workability, flexibility, pliability, pliancy **4 ease of manner**, poise, nonchalance, polish, insouciance, sangfroid, calmness **5 smoothness**, freedom, help **6 easy thing**, soft option, sinecure, plain sailing, clear road, soft touch, sitting duck, no trouble **7 easing**, facilitation, smoothing, expediting, hastening, speeding, quickening, streamlining, simplifying **8 disentanglement**, disembarrassment, disinvolvement, extrication, disengagement, freeing, clearing, disencumberment, uncluttering, disburdenment
ADJECTIVES 9 easy, facile, undemanding, effortless, painless, unburdensome, smooth, uncomplicated, simple, uninvolved, straightforward, plain, clear, intelligible, elementary, glib, superficial **10 feasible**, practicable, workable, possible, useful **11 made easy**, facilitated, simplified, user-friendly, accessible **12 wieldy**, manageable, manoeuvrable, tractable, flexible, pliable, malleable, ductile, yielding, handy, convenient, foolproof, untroublesome, practical, adaptable, smooth-running **13 easygoing**, undemanding, lenient, tolerant, permissive, indulgent, tractable, docile, relaxed, calm, serene, acquiescent, compliant, submissive **14 relaxed**, comfortable, painfree, carefree, troublefree, leisurely
VERBS 15 be easy, be painless **16 make easy**, facilitate, ease, assist, aid, help, smooth, grease, oil, lubricate, iron out, clear, unclog, free, promote, advance, hasten, speed, give scope, clarify, simplify **17 do easily**, freewheel, coast **18 disentangle**, disembarrass, disinvolve,

extricate, disengage, free, clear, disencumber, lighten, unload, unclutter, disburden, alleviate, obviate, untie, unravel, liberate, unscramble **19 go easily**, run smoothly, work well, flow, glide, coast

221 Eating

NOUNS 1 eating, consumption, feeding, ingestion, ingurgitation, chewing, mastication, munching, manducation, biting, gnashing, champing, chomping, swallowing, deglutition, downing, gulping, slurping, digestion **2 appetite**, hunger, craving, voraciousness, wolfishness, gluttony, greed, gourmandism, devouring, engorgement, gobbling, bolting, guzzling, overeating, overindulgence, feasting, gorging, binge, stuffing oneself, compulsive eating, bulimia nervosa **3 delicate eating**, relishing, savouring, palate-tickling, refined palate, epicurism, dainty palate, nibbling, dieting, pathological dieting, anorexia nervosa **4 eating meals**, dining, lunching, breakfasting, supping, having tea, snacking, grazing, eating out, dining out, messing, feasting, banqueting, regalement, hospitality, entertainment **5 eating habit**, carnivorousness, omophagy, creophagy, ichthyophagy, insectivorousness, anthropophagy, cannibalism, vegetarianism, veganism, herbivorousness, rumination, grazing, graminivorousness, frugivorousness **6 nutrition**, diet, dietetics, slimming, dieting, weight-watching, losing weight, dietary plan, diet sheet **7 plenty**, food mountain, cornucopia, festive board **8 scarcity**, bread-and-water diet, malnutrition, starvation **9 meal**, refreshment, refection, repast, collation, buffet, snack, potluck, square meal, three-course meal, breakfast, brunch, elevenses, lunch, luncheon, tiffin, high tea, cream tea, evening meal, dinner **10 feast**, banquet, harvest home, reception, wedding breakfast, dinner dance, Christmas dinner, party, tea party, picnic, barbecue, spread, junket, orgy **11 mouthful**, bite, nibble, morsel, bolus, gobbet, slice, sliver, titbit, helping, serving **12 eating place**, dining room, dinette, dining hall, banqueting hall, refectory, canteen, mess room, Naafi, restaurant, café, cafeteria, crêperie, trattoria, pizzeria, bistro, brasserie, steakhouse, chophouse, rotisserie, carvery, coffee bar, milk bar, ice-cream parlour, snack bar, teashop, take-away **13 food shop**, supermarket, hypermarket, fishmonger, bakery, delicatessen, health-food shop, food hall, market, sweet shop

VERBS 14 eat, subsist, consume, feed, ingest, ingurgitate, engulf, graze, browse, pasture, crop, chew, masticate, manducate, munch, chomp, gnaw, bite, nibble, peck, tear, rend, ruminate, swallow, gulp down, slurp, suck, devour, digest **15 eat well**, drool, salivate, devour, gobble, bolt, overeat, overindulge, gorge oneself, binge, guzzle, gormandize, gluttonize **16 taste**, relish, savour, lick, sample, peck at, pick at, sniff at **17 have a meal**, board, mess, partake, break bread, breakfast, lunch, dine, sup, snack, graze, dine out, regale, feast **18 provide food**, nourish, nurture, sustain, aliment, provision, cater, purvey,

nurse, breast-feed, suckle, force-feed
ADJECTIVES 19 eating, feeding, dining, grazing, carnivorous, creophagous, cannibalistic, omophagic, insectivorous, herbivorous, graminivorous, frugivorous, vegetarian, vegan, omnivorous, greedy, gluttonous, hungry, ravenous, voracious, well-fed **20 edible**, consumable, esculent, comestible, digestible, nutritious, alimental, alimentary, palatable, palate-tickling, mouth-watering, tasty, calorific, fattening, succulent

222 Economics

NOUNS 1 economics, economic policy, fiscal policy, monetary policy, welfare economics, economic theory, microeconomics, macroeconomics, Keynesian economics, private enterprise, privatization, denationalization, public enterprise, nationalization, public ownership, state-owned industry **2 economy**, free-market economy, private sector, personal sector, corporate sector, public sector, marketing, trading, exporting, importing, purchasing power, price controls, goods, capital goods, consumer goods, economic upturn, boom, boom/bust cycle, economic downturn, recession, depression, slump, stagflation, inflation, deflation, disinflation, stagnation, deficit financing, deficit spending, black market **3 economic statistics**, econometrics, regression analysis, price index, economic productivity, economic analysis, supply-side economics, national debt, budget deficit **4 economic development**, economic growth, industrialization, natural resources, labour force, capital accumulation, capital investment, improved technology, improved productivity, demographic transition **5 economic factors**, capital, market, bear market, bull market, competition, monopoly, cartel, co-operative, revenue, pricing, profit, profit motive, profit margin, commodity, productivity, production costs, production efficiency, rationalization, distribution, fiscal policy, taxation, taxable income, tax evasion, excise duty, import duty, protectionism, embargo, economic sanction, tariff, trade barrier, intervention, free port, public expenditure, services, employment, unemployment, wages, real wages, pay increases, business cycle, inflation, inflationary spiral, price-wage spiral, deflation, money supply, exchange rate, price support, subsidy, capitalism, private enterprise, mercantile system, physiocratic school **6 economist**, businessman, profiteer, trader, importer, exporter, employer, liveryman, trade unionist, spender, consumer
VERBS 7 trade with, export, import, market, encash, commercialize, monopolize, nationalize **8 deal**, take over
ADJECTIVES 9 economic, fiscal, monetary, pecuniary, financial, budgetary, inflationary, deflationary, mercantile, commercial, marketable, profitable, taxable

223 Edge

NOUNS 1 edge, border, rim, brim, margin, limit, periphery, lip, skirt, fringe, brink, verge, extremity, bounds, confines, limits, frontier, boundary, shoreline, coast, tideline, bank, verge, hard shoulder, sideline **2 edging**, hem, border, selvage, fringe, piping, trimming, valance, furbelow, gimp **3 cutting edge**, blade, sharpness **4 advantage**, upper hand

VERBS 5 border, verge, rim, skirt, verge on, bind **6 edge**, border, hem, fringe, pipe, trim, furbelow, decorate, crenellate **7 have an advantage**, outwit, outthink, outmanoeuvre

ADJECTIVES 8 edging, bordered, marginal, extreme, seaside, waterfront, coastal, littoral, beach, riverside, waterside, roadside, wayside, sideline **9 skirting**, skirted, edged, fringed **10 advantaged**, ahead, keen, sharp, acute, biting, pungent, effective, forceful

224 Education

- *Education is simply the soul of a society as it passes from one generation to another.* G. K. Chesterton.
- *And seek for truth in the groves of Academe.* Horace.

NOUNS 1 education, teaching, schooling, pedagogy, tuition, coaching, guidance, catechization, tutoring, tutelage, training, instruction, drilling, indoctrination, guidance, preparation, advice, illumination, enlightenment, edification, acculturation, cultivation, rearing, raising, upbringing **2 educational system**, nursery education, pre-school education, primary education, Froebel system, Montessori system, secondary education, tertiary education, higher education, adult education, remedial education, vocational training, job training, employment training, on-the-job training, in-service training, sandwich course, self-education, home learning, correspondence course, distance learning, autodidactics, recreational education, Open University **3 educator**, teacher, head teacher, headmaster, headmistress, principal, chancellor, dean, don, professor, doctor, lecturer, fellow, intern, reader, academic, preceptor, preceptress, tutor, instructor, governess, duenna, school teacher, schoolmistress, schoolmaster, form teacher, student teacher, supply teacher, home tutor, private tutor, crammer, pedagogue, coach, trainer, mentor, adviser, expert, guru, mullah **4 educationalist**, educationist, educational psychologist, truancy officer, governor, governing body **5 instructorship**, schoolmastery, tutorship, chair, professorship, readership, lectureship **6 learner**, student, pupil, trainee, apprentice, novice, tiro, beginner, recruit, initiate, neophyte, abecedarian, schoolboy, schoolgirl, classmate, undergraduate, scholar, researcher **7 learning**, study, scholarship, contemplation, perusal **8 educatability**, aptitude, intelligence, brightness, motivation, receptivity, curiosity, inquisitiveness, susceptibility **9 university**, polytechnic, college, sixth-form college **10 schoolroom**, classroom, formroom, staffroom, hall, assembly hall, library, laboratory, language laboratory, workshop, music room, art room, dining room, common room, playground, gymnasium, sports field, playing field, sick room, sanatorium, dormitory

ADJECTIVES 11 educational, instructive, informative, illuminating, enlightening, edifying, remedial, progressive, communicative, helpful, authoritative, academic, scholastic, pedagogical, preachy **12 educatable**, teachable, trainable, bright, autodidactic, self-taught, apt, willing, motivated, ready, receptive, curious, inquisitive, susceptible, impressionable **13 curricular**, intramural, extramural, extracurricular, doctoral, collegiate, varsity, canonical

VERBS 14 educate, teach, tutor, train, instruct, school, coach, drill, discipline, indoctrinate, instill, inculcate, prepare, equip, brief, prime, ground, verse, acquaint, inform, tell, apprise, impart, disclose, divulge, reveal, communicate, tip off, guide, advise, illuminate, enlighten, improve, cultivate, civilize, refine, advance, encourage, mould, shape, form, foster, nurture, rear, raise **15 learn**, study, train, discover, research, contemplate, peruse

225 Effect

NOUNS 1 effect, outcome, counteraction, reaction, action, event, happening, achievement, issue, end, denouement, result, upshot, termination, completion, conclusion, aftermath, aftereffect, culmination, consequence, impact, product, repercussion, spin-off, sequel, corollary, inference, derivation, precipitate, remainder **2 visible effect**, handiwork, print, imprint, impress, mark, trace, side effect, footprint, fingerprint, backwash, wake, legacy, inheritance, belongings **3 growth**, development, expansion, increase, swelling, outgrowth, bud, blossom, flower, fruit, harvest, produce, gain, profit, lump, carcinoma **4 significance**, import, meaning, purport, sense, tendency

VERBS 5 show an effect, affect, have consequence, impact upon, counteract, react, act, happen, achieve, accomplish, issue, end in, result in, eventuate in, terminate, complete, conclude, culminate, produce, precipitate, spin off **6 have a visible effect**, print, imprint, impress upon, mark **7 follow from**, ensure, supervene, borrow from, derive from, inherit, descend from, originate in, emanate from, emerge, proceed from, issue from, begin from, arise from, spring from, flow from, unfold, evolve **8 grow**, accrue, develop, expand, increase, swell, sprout, germinate, bud, blossom, flower, bear fruit, harvest, produce, gain **9 take effect**, become law, come about, transpire, arise, happen, occur, take place, end up, turn out

ADJECTIVES 10 caused, effected by, reacting to, resulting from, ensuing, following from, coming from, due to, owing to, developing from, deriving from, evolving from, arising from, descending from, inheriting from, hereditary, genetic, dependent, attributed to, consequent upon, contingent upon, subject to, subsequent, sequential, secondary, unoriginal, emergent, eventual, born of, out of **11 growing**, developing, expanding, increasing, swelling, budding, blossoming

226 Elasticity

NOUNS 1 elasticity, stretchability, suppleness, plasticity, rubberiness, extensibility, distension, flexibility, pliancy, tensibility, strain, ductility, tonicity, springiness, resilience, give, snap, recoil, rebound **2 adaptability**, resilience, buoyance, flexibility, adjustability, responsiveness, liveliness, compliance, accommodation **3 elastic thing**, whalebone, baleen, rubber band, rubber ball, stretch fabric, spandex, gum, chewing gum, spring, springboard, diving board, trampoline, pogo stick, bungee rope, catapult **4 rubber**, elastomer, latex, caoutchouc, gutta-percha, vulcanite, ebonite **5 spring**, mainspring, hairspring

ADJECTIVES 6 elastic, rubbery, stretchable, supple, plastic, extensible, distensible, flexible, pliant, tensile, ductile, tonic, springy, well-sprung, coiling, resilient, giving, yielding, snapping, recoiling, rebounding **7 adaptive**, adaptable, resilient, buoyant, flexible, adjustable, responsive, lively, compliant

VERBS 8 be elastic, stretch, extend, expand, distend, flex, show resilience, give, spring, snap, snap back, recoil, rebound **9 make elastic**, elasticize, rubberize, vulcanize **10 be adaptable**, adapt, have resilience, have buoyancy, stay flexible, adjust, respond quickly, comply, accommodate

227 Electricity

NOUNS 1 electricity, current electricity, static electricity, conduction, conductor, liquid conductor **2 electronics**, microelectronics, computer electronics, optoelectronics, telecommunications, electronics engineering, electrical engineering, electrotechnology **3 electronics engineer**, electrical engineer, electrotechnician **4 electrical property**, voltage, current, resistance, impedance, reactance, capacity, capacitance **5 circuitry**, circuit, component, terminal, anode, cathode, battery, cell, accumulator, conductor, insulator, resistor, theostat, capacitor, condenser, inductor, choke, valve, tube, semiconductor, transistor, diode, integrated circuit, chip **6 electrical instrument**, ammeter, galvanometer, voltmeter, potentiometer, electrometer, wattmeter **7 plug**, socket, power point, fuse, circuit breaker, switch, trip switch, dimmer, dimming switch, termination **8 power distribution**, power station, network, national grid, power line, transmission line, overhead wire, underground cable, feeder, pylon **9 power supply**, mains supply, power conversion, power regulation, voltage regulator, transformer, rectifier, filter, converter, inverter, power pack, electric meter, domestic wiring, ring main

VERBS 10 conduct, insulate, earth, ground, charge, discharge, amplify, oscillate, connect, disconnect, switch on, plug in, wire, fuse, electrocute

ADJECTIVES 11 electronic, electric, electrical, photoelectric, thermoelectric, piezoelectric, hydroelectric, electrodynamic, electrolytic, electromagnetic, electromechanical, electromotive, electrostatic, negative, positive, neutral, live, resistive, capacitive

228 Elegance

NOUNS 1 elegance, style, grace, delicacy, harmony, euphony, taste, propriety, beauty, politeness, gentility, refinement, sophistication, suavity, culture, purity, perspicuity, clarity, plainness, simplicity, restraint, dignity, distinction, grandeur, naturalness, classicism, Atticism, proportion, symmetry, balance, rhythm, ease, flow, smoothness, fluency, aptness, fittingness, felicity, polish, finish, neatness, well-turned phrase, elaboration, ornament **2 stylist**, euphuist, classical author, classic

ADJECTIVES 3 elegant, stylish, smart, graceful, delicate, harmonious, euphonious, tasteful, fine, beautiful, majestic, stately, exquisite, polite, courtly, refined, sophisticated, suave, cultivated, perspicacious, plain, simple, restrained, dignified, distinguished, distinctive, natural, idiomatic, correct, expressive, classic, well-proportioned, symmetrical, gracile, rhythmic, fluid, smooth, flawless, mellifluous, fluent, apt, fitting, felicitous, polished, manicured, soigné, well-groomed, finished, well-turned, artistic, elaborate, ornamented, classical, Attic

VERBS 4 be elegant, be stylish, write well, have taste, perfect, polish, refine, edit, elaborate

229 Emphasis

NOUNS 1 emphasis, stress, accent, underlining, underscoring, italics, vehemence, insistence, urgency, priority, iteration, reiteration, repetition, enthusiasm, fervour, passion, feeling, ardour, fire, inspiration, vigour, vim, gusto, zest, verve, boldness, dash, raciness, panache, vitality, vivacity, vividness, positive outlook, piquancy, poignancy, bite, pungency, penetration, asperity, acuity, intensity, incisiveness, keenness, trenchancy, strength, power, force, energy, drive **2 seriousness**, solemnity, gravity, weight, importance, significance, attention, prominence, impressiveness, loftiness, elevation, sublimity

ADJECTIVES 3 emphatic, vehement, earnest, insistent, urgent, firm, uncompromising, dogmatic, iterative, reiterative, repetitive, enthusiastic, fervent, passionate, impassioned, ardent, fiery, spirited, inspired, vigorous, zestful, bold, vivacious, positive, affirmative, categorical, unequivocal, definite, sure, certain, incisive, penetrating, keen, trenchant, pointed, sententious, pithy, meaty, thought-provoking, pungent, sharp, mordant, piquant, poignant, vivid, graphic, strong, eloquent, compelling, convincing, effective, cogent, forceful, powerful, strenuous, energetic **4 emphasized**, stressed, accentuated, highlighted, enhanced, underlined, in italics, pointed out, pointed up, marked **5 serious**, solemn, grave, weighty, important, significant, heavy, intense, solid, impressive, lofty, elevated, sublime

VERBS 6 emphasize, stress, accentuate, highlight, enhance, spotlight, feature, underline, underscore, italicize, point out, point up, insist, urge, reaffirm, reassert, reiterate, repeat, dwell on, plug, glow, dash, sparkle, provoke thought, convince, impress on, press home

230 Enclosure

NOUNS 1 enclosure (*or* **inclosure**), circumvallation, circumscription, envelopment **2 enclosed place**, enclosure, confine, precinct

VERBS 3 enclose, surround, fence in,

wall in, rail, pale, moat, dyke, shut in, hem in, pen, paddock, reserve, cloister, confine **4 wrap**, bandage, bind, sheath, net, contain, envelop, enfold, encompass

ADJECTIVES 5 enclosed, fenced-in, walled-in, shut-in, hemmed-in, built-in, penned, pent-up, indoor, cloistered, monastic, conventual, intramural, confined

231 End

NOUNS 1 end, conclusion, finish, close, finis, finale **2 cessation**, ceasing, expiry, termination, stop, halt, abrogation, cancellation **3 death**, demise, decease, expiration, passing, departure, exit, release, quietus, last gasp, last words **4 annihilation**, destruction, extermination, extinction, elimination, dissolution, liquidation **5 fate**, destiny, doomsday, eschatology, apocalypse **6 end point**, terminus, last stop, journey's end **7 limit**, boundary, frontier, border, edge, fringe, verge, extent, extreme, pole, point, tip, peak, cusp, summit, zenith **8 tail**, butt, fag end, bin end, bitter end, last penny, last cent, bottom dollar **9 close**, final stage, last lap, home stretch, last round, last innings, last ball, last over, evening, dusk, twilight **10 ending**, finale, finish, last act, climax, culmination, crowning glory, denouement, catastrophe, final curtain, epilogue, envoy, coda, end matter, back matter, appendix, suffix, last word, last laugh, punch line, parting shot **11 finality**, deadline **12 end result**, effect, consequence, issue, outcome **13 aim**, intention, aspiration, goal, target, objective, purpose

VERBS 14 end, conclude, finish, close, complete, achieve, finalize, resolve, decide, settle, finish off, round off, culminate, consummate, crown **15 cease**, stop, halt, terminate, discontinue, scotch, close down, finish off, kill off, polish off, dispose of, abort, annul, cancel **16 kill**, extinguish, annihilate, destroy, exterminate, eliminate, dissolve, liquidate, wipe out, knock out **17 come to an end**, be over, fade away, peter out, fizzle out, tail off **18 expire**, pass away, die

ADJECTIVES 19 ending, last, final, ultimate, terminal, concluding, conclusive, completing, closing, finishing, definitive, culminating, consummative, crowning, capping, apocalyptic, catastrophic **20 ended**, finished, complete, finalized, terminated, concluded, decided, settled, done, through **21 cancelled**, off, played out, called off **22 annihilated**, destroyed, exterminated, eliminated, dissolved, liquidated, ruined, doomed, fated **23 limiting**, bordering, fringing, extreme, polar, eventual **24 hindmost**, rear

232 Endearment

NOUNS 1 endearment, affection, fondness, attachment, love, compliments, blandishments, flattery, sweet nothings, soft words, pet name, kissing, osculation, lovebite, embrace, caress, hug, cuddle, squeeze, fondling **2 courtship**, amorous pursuit, dating, wooing, love-play, love suit, gallantry, addresses, advances, pass, dalliance, familiarity, going out, amourette, laying siege, favours, flirtation, coquetry, philandering, ogle, languishing look, sheep's eyes, proposal **3 love token**, ring, love letter, valentine, billet-doux, love poem, flowers, red roses, chocolates, candy **4 terms of endearment**, darling, dear, love, sweetheart, pet, poppet, precious, cherub, angel, petal, chickabiddy **5 object of endearment**, lover, teacher's pet

VERBS 6 show endearment for, cherish, love, treasure, mother, smother, spoil, spoon-feed, flatter, pamper, cosset, coddle, hug, embrace, cling, kiss, osculate, pat, caress, squeeze, goose, fondle, stroke **7 court**, woo, pursue, chase, run after, ogle, leer, eye, make overtures, make advances, flirt, trifle, dally, toy, vamp, philander, get fresh, proposition, date, hold hands, make love

ADJECTIVES 8 endearing, affectionate, demonstrative, sentimental, fond, loving, amorous, courting, wooing, pursuing, dating, familiar, flirtatious, coy, coquettish, toying, clinging, caressing, fondling, philandering

233 Engineering

NOUNS 1 engineering, civil engineering, naval engineering, agricultural engineering, electrical engineering, electronics engineering, chemical engineering, mining engineering, metallurgical engineering, nuclear engineering, production engineering, environmental engineering, engineering geology, engineering design, engineering drawing, management engineering **2 engineer**, mechanical engineer, civil engineer, electrical engineer **3 mechanical engineering**, machine-design engineering, industrial engineering, automotive engineering, aeronautical engineering **4 mechanical engineer**, mechanic, technician **5 machine element**, wheel, gear, gearwheel, pulley, shaft, crank, rod, axle, hub, cam, belt, coupling, bearing, ball bearing, roller bearing, journal, bush **6 machine tool**, drill, boring machine, lathe, milling machine, broaching machine, grinder, planer, shaper, saw, single-point tool, multipoint tool, speed, feed, cutting fluid, coolant **7 engine**, internal-combustion engine, Wankel engine, external-combustion engine, reciprocating engine, steam engine, petrol engine, car engine, diesel engine, jet engine, rocket engine, Stirling engine, piston, cylinder, crankshaft, prime mover **8 civil engineering**, structural engineering, transportation engineering, highway engineering, railway engineering, airport engineering, traffic engineering, river engineering, coastal engineering, water-supply engineering, geotechnical engineering, rock mechanics, soil mechanics, construction, architectural engineering, urban planning, photogrammetry, surveying, theodolite, level, clinometer, alidade, topographic surveying, mapping **9 civil engineer**, structural engineer, surveyor **10 structure**, construction, building, bridge, tunnel, dam, embankment, bulkhead, road, railway

VERBS 11 engineer, construct, build, erect, plan, design, survey, map, excavate, dig, dredge

ADJECTIVES 12 structural, constructional, edificial, architectural, architectonic, superstructural, substructural, foundational, mechanical, fabricated

234 Enmity

NOUNS 1 enmity, hostility, aggression, unfriendliness, inimicality, uncordiality, coolness, iciness, coldness, chilliness, frostiness, unamiability, ungeniality, disaffinity, antipathy, animosity, abhorrence, animus, opposition, incompatibility, aggression, bellicosity, antagonism, repugnance, conflict, contention, collision, clash, friction, quarrelling, dissension, belligerence, hate, dislike, loathing, malice, malevolence, spite, virulence, venom, vitriol, intolerance, bigotry, prejudice, persecution, racism, apartheid **2 personal conflict**, strain, tension, envy, jealousy, estrangement, alienation, separation, disloyalty, unfaithfulness, breach **3 ill feeling**, ill will, acrimony, bitterness, rancour, sourness, soreness, resentment, hard feelings, bad blood, grudge, peevishness, aversion, abomination, odium, detestation **4 act of hostility**, war, conflict, hostilities, vendetta **5 enemy**, archenemy, foe, adversary, opponent, rival, competitor, antagonist, traitor, combatant, aggressor, invader, public enemy, Trojan horse, xenophobe

ADJECTIVES 6 hostile, unfriendly, inimical, uncordial, cool, icy, cold, aloof, inhospitable, antisocial, unsympathetic, unamiable, strained, tense, unharmonious, ill-disposed, acrimonious, antipathetic, bitter, rancorous, sour, sore, resentful, envious, jealous, malevolent, malicious, spiteful, virulent **7 intolerant**, persecuting, oppressive, racist, prejudiced, bigotted **8 estranged**, alienated, separated, irreconcilable, distant, disloyal, unfaithful, disaffected, at variance, divided **9 aggressive**, antagonistic, repugnant, conflicting, contentious, clashing, opposing, quarrelsome, dissenting, belligerent, bellicose, militant, at loggerheads **10 hated**, disliked, loathed, scorned, abominated, detested

VERBS 11 be hostile, bear malice, resent, take offence, take umbrage, hate, detest, loathe, scorn, abhor, execrate **12 oppose**, oppress, persecute, hound, hunt down, clash, collide, conflict, quarrel, dissent, differ, fall out, fight **13 antagonize**, set against, provoke, estrange, cause offence, irritate, infuriate, madden, divide, disunite, alienate

235 Entitlement

NOUNS 1 entitlement, dueness, merit, deservingness **2 due**, merits, deserts, deservings, reward, credit, acknowledgment, recognition, cognizance, tribute, thanks, compensation, punishment **3 prerogative**, right, privilege, power, authority, title, claim, demand, birthright, human rights, animal rights, Constitution **4 duty**, responsibility, obligation **5 dues**, fees, payment, levy **6 bond**, security, title deed, patent, copyright, contract, covenant, guarantee, warranty, licence, permit, charter, franchise, grant, qualification **7 beneficiary**, heir, heiress, heir apparent, inheritor

ADJECTIVES 8 entitled, warranted, justified, qualified, worthy, just, rightful, legitimate, lawful, legal, licit, inviolable, inalienable, admitted, permitted, allowed **9 meritorious**, meriting, deserving **10 due**, deserved, merited **11 entitled to**, due **12 owed**, unpaid, unsettled, in ar-

rears, outstanding, payable, chargeable, redeemable **13 fit**, right, proper
VERBS 14 be entitled, warrant, justify **15 merit**, deserve, rate **16 entitle**, allow, permit, patent, copyright, enable, empower, enfranchise, license, warrant, authorize **17 credit**, acknowledge, recognize **18 be due**, mature **19 pay**, discharge

236 Entry

NOUNS 1 entry, entrance, ingress, intergression, access, incoming, import, input, admission, reception, enrolment, enlistment, induction, initiation, introduction, debut, appearance **2 influx**, inflow, inflooding, stream, indraught, inhalation, indrawing, intake, inrush, inrun, afflux **3 inroad**, encroachment, insertion, penetration, interpenetration, insinuation, infiltration, percolation, seepage, leakage, intrusion, invasion, raid, irruption, incursion, attack, illegal entry, trespassing, housebreaking **4 right of entry**, admission, access, permission, permit, ticket, pass, passport, visa, immigration, importation, trade, free trade, open-door policy, free market **5 entrance**, way in, entry, access, inlet, ingress, approach, adit, mouth, opening, orifice, conduit, channel **6 means of entry** (*or* **access**), porch, propylaeum, portico, portal, portecochere, doorway, threshold, door, postern, trapdoor, hatch, scuttle, gate, lychgate, archway, tollgate, turnstile, turnpike, stile, lobby
VERBS 7 enter, go in, gain admittance, arrive, visit, call in, look in, pop in, board, embark **8 invade**, irrupt, raid, attack, storm, escalade, encroach, trespass, gatecrash, barge in, rush in, burst in, storm in, butt in, interrupt, muscle in, horn in, break in **9 infiltrate**, permeate, percolate, filter in, soak in, leak in, seep, drip, insinuate, creep in, slip in, sneak in, slink in, penetrate, break through, bore in, pierce, puncture, insert **10 flood in**, flow in, rush in, pour in, swarm in, pack in, crowd in, throng in, press in, cram in, squeeze in, wedge in, jam in **11 fall into**, drop into, plunge into, dive into **12 enrol**, join, admit, enlist, inscribe, sign on, enter for, contend, induct, initiate, introduce, immigrate
ADJECTIVES 13 entering, ingressive, inward, incoming, ingoing, inbound, immigrant, imported, allowed in **14 invasive**, incursive, intrusive, trespassing, attacking, penetrating, irruptive, ingrowing, inflowing, inflooding

237 Envy

NOUNS 1 envy, covetousness, jealousy, desire, resentment, grudgingness
ADJECTIVES 2 envious, jealous, covetous, green-eyed, jaundiced, desirous, longing, resentful
VERBS 3 be envious of, envy, covet, desire, long for, hanker after, lust after, crave, resent

238 Equality

• *All animals are equal but some animals are more equal than others.* George Orwell (Animal Farm).
NOUNS 1 equality, equivalence, sameness, equal footing, correspondence, parallelism, coequality, sharing, going halves, likeness, equiponderance, egalitarianism, fairness, democracy, equal rights,

justice, evenness, levelness, parity, par **2 equilibrium**, balance, poise, counterpoise, equipoise, evennesss, steadiness, stable state, homeostasis, symmetry, proportion, stability, status quo, stop, stasis, stalemate, deadlock, hung parliament, tie, drawn game, dead heat, photo finish **3 equalization**, equation, equilibration, balancing, weighing, adjustment, levelling up, evening up, rounding up, compensation, positive discrimination, affirmative action, counteraction, offset, exchange, interchange, equipollence, isotropy, synonymity, reciprocation, fair exchange, barter **4 equalizer**, counterweight, ballast, makeweight, stopgap, counterpoise, stabilizer, rudder, fin, aileron **5 equal**, peer, twin, match, mate, fellow, counterpart, opposite number, coequal, compeer, comrade, companion, brother

ADJECTIVES 6 equal, same, similar, parallel, convertible, identical, equivalent, corresponding, egalitarian, democratic, equitable, just, fair, impartial, sharing, homologous, congruent, coextensive, equilateral, equidistant, coordinate, coincident, symmetrical, equable, stable, static, homeostatic, self-regulating, steady, balanced, fixed, rounded, squared, flush, even-sided, regular, well-ordered, commensurate, tantamount, equipollent, correspondent, proportionate **7 dividing line**, radius, diameter, coordinate, equator, bisector, longitudinal line **8 on equal terms**, even, level, one-to-one, half-and-half, neck-and-neck, ding-dong, drawn, tied, parallel **9 adequate**, capable, fit, able, competent, suitable, apt

VERBS 10 be equal, correspond to, accord with, agree with, coincide with, tie, draw, parallel, break even, cope with, go shares **11 equalize**, synchronize, even, balance, tally, make good, accommodate, adjust, even up, level up, round up, equate, counterpoise, countervail, offset, cancel out, coordinate, integrate, proportion

239 Equivocation

VERBS 1 be equivocal, be ambiguous, pun, double-talk, dissemble, deceive, mislead, fudge, hedge, quibble, avoid, evade, dodge, sidestep, trim **2 equivocate**, tergiversate, think again, vacillate, shuffle, be two-faced, wheel about, withdraw, resign **3 apostatize**, change sides, turn renegade, turn traitor, switch, desert, defect, blackleg, collaborate, betray **4 recant**, unsay, withdraw, retract, apologize, crawl, cringe, back down, backpedal, renege, disavow, disclaim, repudiate, refute, deny, negate, renounce, abjure, forswear, recall, revoke

NOUNS 5 equivocalness, ambiguity, ambivalence, indefiniteness, vagueness, uncertainty, mental reservation, concealment, prevarication, evasion, balancing act, white lie, untruth, quibble, sophistry, two voices, contrariety, double meaning, amphibology, pun, paronomasia, calembour, equivoque, newspeak, double talk, circumlocution, conundrum, riddle, oracle **6 equivocation**, tergiversation, irresolution, vacillation, inconsistency, second thoughts, deviation, versatility, reversal, back-pedalling, about-turn, U-turn, volte-face, withdrawal, temperament, whim **7 apostasy**, conversion, turning traitor, going over, recreancy, desertion, defection, collaboration, betrayal, treachery, perfidy, unreliableness, untrustworthiness **8 recantation**, withdrawal, retraction, apology, disavowal, disclaimer, repudiation, denial, negation, renunciation, abjuration, forswearing, revocation, recall **9 equivocator**, tergiversator, opportunist, toady, timeserver, double-dealer, weasel, recreant, apostate, turncoat, reneger, traitor, Judas, betrayer, quisling, fifth columnist, collaborator, defector, quitter, runaway, informer, telltale, tattler, strike-breaker, blackleg, deviationist, secessionist, recidivist

ADJECTIVES 10 equivocal, ambiguous, ambivalent, epicene, double-tongued, two-edged, prevaricating, vague, evasive, misleading, roundabout, circumlocutory, oracular, amphibolous, homonymous **11 equivocating**, tergiversating, shuffling, slippery, perfidious, double-dealing, hypocritical, two-faced, false, unfaithful, disloyal, traitorous, treacherous, apostate, recanting, renegade, recidivist, back-pedalling, vacillating, irresolute, fickle, whimsical, capricious

240 Error

NOUNS 1 mistake, error, fault, miscalculation, misconstruction, misconception, misinterpretation, misjudgment, misapprehension, misunderstanding, false conclusion, wrong turning **2 inaccuracy**, imprecision, inexactness, looseness, laxity, sloppiness, carelessness, negligence, approximation, guesswork, speculation, generalization **3 erroneousness**, wrongness, untruth, falsity, incorrectness **4 faulty reasoning**, fallacy, sophistry, flawed logic, circular argument, inconsistency, self-contradiction, sloppy thinking **5 misrepresentation**, distortion, falsification, misquotation, misstatement, travesty, parody **6 fallibility**, human error, subjectivity, prejudice, bias, self-deception, wishful thinking, delusion, illusion, hallucination, false impression, popular misconception **7 errancy**, wrongdoing, culpability, guiltiness, aberrancy, deviancy, perversion, heresy, heterodoxy **8 moral error**, transgression, misdeed, sin, offence **9 trivial error**, slip-up, lapse, oversight **10 blunder**, bungle, gaffe **11 grammatical error**, solecism, misspelling, mispronunciation, misusage, cacology, barbarism, spoonerism, malapropism, Goldwynism, bull, ambiguity, tautology, double negative, split infinitive **12 typing error**, literal, misprint, erratum **13 sporting error**, miss, mishit, miscue, no-ball, own goal, wide, dropped catch **14 computer error**, bug

ADJECTIVES 15 erroneous, wrong, untrue, incorrect, false, fallacious, illogical, faulty, flawed, falsified, inaccurate, inexact, loose, inconsistent, self-contradictory **16 errant**, erring, fallible, culpable, guilty, sinful, aberrant, deviant, perverse, perverted, heretical **17 mistaken**, wrong, self-contradicting, prejudiced

VERBS 18 be in error, misunderstand **19 make a mistake**, err, miscalculate, misconstrue, misinterpret, misjudge, misrepresent, distort, parody, caricature, falsify, misstate, misquote, overlook, omit, misspell, mispronounce, misprint, mishit, slip up, lapse, bungle **20 transgress**, err, sin, deviate

241 Escape

NOUNS 1 escape, breakout, getaway, jailbreak, freedom, decampment, flight, departure, withdrawal, retreat, disappearance, vanishing, French leave, truancy, elopement, elusion, evasion, avoidance, nonpayment, tax haven, black economy, moonlighting, near miss, reprieve, acquittal, release, liberation, immunity, impunity, exemption, escapology, rescue, deliverance, riddance **2 leak**, leakage, loss, emission, issue, seepage

VERBS 3 escape, break out, get out, decamp, flee, fly, bolt, run away, abscond, depart, find freedom, retreat, disappear, sneak off, steal away, play truant, jump bail, elope, scrape through, receive immunity, secure exemption, go scot-free **4 elude**, evade, avoid, dodge, miss, hide, lie low, stay underground, escape detection, shake off, escape notice, avoid taxes **5 leak**, flow out, emerge, issue, seep out

ADJECTIVES 6 escaping, evasive, elusive, fugitive, runaway, truant, escaped, loose, free, scot-free, reprieved, acquitted, immune, exempt, relieved, emancipated, liberated, untied

242 Essence

NOUNS 1 essence, quiddity, quid, subject, substance, structure, stuff, material, matter, fabric, medium **2 essential content**, basis, core, kernel, gist, meat, heart, backbone, nub, nucleus, marrow, pith, sap, lifeblood, crux, principle, issue, gravamen, highlight, centre, focus, pivot, keystone, cornerstone, landmark, benchmark **3 quintessence**, embodiment, incarnation, personification, epitome, archetype, soul, spirit, entelechy, flower, elixir, extract, concentrate **4 nature**, character, suchness, makeup, constitution, composition, complexion, temperament, disposition, mould, pattern, stamp, type, breed, strain, stripe, humour, mood, trait, hue, quality

ADJECTIVES 5 essential, crucial, vital, necessary, paramount, indispensable, requisite, obligatory, mandatory, compulsory, imperative, inalienable, uninfringeable **6 intrinsic**, inherent, basic, primary, fundamental, immanent, innate, inborn, inbred, deep-seated, deep-rooted, ingrained **7 integral**, inseparable, ineradicable, built-in, component, constituent, indivisible **8 quintessential**, constitutional, structural, organic, peerless, singular, unique, consummate **9 characteristic**, distinctive, distinguishing, typical, specific, particular, peculiar, defining

VERBS 10 be essential, be vital **11 characterize**, stamp, inform, mark, identify, depict, portray, represent, delineate, designate, distinguish, differentiate **12 embody**, incarnate, personify, epitomize, constitute, comprise, incorporate, assimilate, include

243 Eternity

NOUNS 1 eternity, endlessness, infinity, everlastingness, timelessness, perpetuity, permanence, continuity, incorruptibility **2 a long time**, age, aeon, olam **3 life without end**, life everlasting, deathlessness, immortality, heaven, paradise, the hereafter, the afterlife **4 eternalization**, perpetuation

VERBS 5 be eternal, last forever, outlast, outlive, endure forever, never cease **6 make eternal**, perpetuate, immortalize, memorialize **7 make permanent**, establish

ADJECTIVES 8 eternal, everlasting, neverending, unending, infinite, perpetual, timeless, sempiternal, permanent, enduring, durable, incorruptible, imperishable, immortal, undying, deathless, unchanging, immutable **9 agelong**, aeonian, millennial **10 continuing forever**, ceaseless, unceasing, continuous, constant, unending, nonstop

244 Evidence

NOUNS 1 evidence, grounds, reasons, premises, data, information, facts, record, reference, report **2 proof**, verification, demonstration, corroboration, substantiation, confirmation **3 evidentness**, manifestation, obviousness, appearance, self-evidence, visibility **4 indication**, pointer, tell-tale sign, token, symptom, clue, remains, mark, track, trail, footprint, wake, vapour trail, spoor **5 legal evidence**, prima-facie evidence, testimony, statement, declaration, admission, deposition, exhibit, confession, affidavit **6 documentation**, authority, papers, case history, record, testimonial, recommendation, reference, credential, CV, warrant, warranty, ticket, chit, receipt, voucher, passport, identity card, i.d., visa

ADJECTIVES 7 evidential, prima facie, significant, factual, relevant, informed, witnessed, attested, circumstantial, direct, documented, recorded, reported, documentary, corroborative, probative, constructive, indicative, pointing, demonstrative, tell-tale, authentic, empirical, verified, confirmed, proved **8 evident**, apparent, manifest, obvious, self-evident, visible

VERBS 9 make evident, show, represent, suggest, indicate **10 give evidence**, witness, testify, swear, attest, affirm, assert, declare, state **11 prove**, verify, validate, corroborate, support, sustain, back up, circumstantiate, authenticate, confirm, certify, countersign **12 turn Queen's evidence**, inform

245 Evil

NOUNS 1 evil, evilness, badness, wickedness, meanness, wrongness, sin, improbity, malevolence, maleficence, malignity, malice, viciousness, hatefulness, injustice, untruthfulness, unkindness, ill will, vindictiveness, revengefulness, mischievousness, devilry, obnoxiousness, offensiveness, iniquity, vice, immorality, corruption, defilement, depravity, foulness, vileness, nastiness, noxiousness, wretchedness, rottenness, worthlessness, terribleness, atrociousness **2 affliction**, adversity, plague, blight, ruin, destruction, unease, annoyance, angst, depression, suffering, distress, misery, grief, sorrow, woe, harmfulness, abuse, hurtfulness, discomfort, malaise, painfulness, sickness, illness, unhealthiness, sore, malignancy, malignity, casualty, accident, damage, injury, tragedy, calamity, disaster, catastrophe, fiasco, fatality, mortal blow **3 bad luck**, misfortune, adversity, inauspiciousness, ominousness, unfavourableness, ill wind **4 evil power**, malign influence, evil spell, malediction, curse, jinx, voodoo **5 evil thing**, bane, poison, pollution, crime, murder

ADJECTIVES 6 evil, bad, wicked, mean, wrong, sinful, sinister, nefarious, malevolent, maleficent, malignant, malicious, vicious, ungodly, hateful, unkind, untruthful, prejudicial, vindictive, revengeful, mischievous, obnoxious, offensive, odious, iniquitous, immoral, corrupt, defiled, blighted, depraved, foul, vile, nasty, wretched, deplorable, rotten, worthless, terrible, dreadful, horrible, awful, atrocious, despicable, detestable, contemptible, reprehensible **7 afflicted**, troubled, plagued, depressed, distressed, miserable, grievous, grief-stricken, sorrowful, woeful, sad, hurt, in pain, sick, ill, unhealthy, sore, damaged, injured, wounded **8 detrimental**, damaging, destructive, deleterious, harmful, injurious, hurtful, distressing, troublous, baleful, baneful, pernicious, noxious, toxic, corruptive, corrosive, malignant, catastrophic, dire, mortal **9 inauspicious**, unfavourable, unfortunate, unlucky, adverse, ominous

VERBS 10 be evil, do wrong, wrong, do ill, trouble, distress, aggrieve, afflict, plague, harass, persecute, threaten, menace, mistreat, maltreat, abuse, molest, defile, violate, despoil, befoul, torment, condemn, hurt, harm, corrupt, pervert, damage, impair, blight, pollute, poison, injure, wound, destroy, doom, kill

246 Exaggeration

NOUNS 1 exaggeration, overemphasis, overstatement, excessiveness, intensification, overenthusiasm, overstress, overexposure, extremism, exacerbation, exorbitance, inordinacy, overkill, aggravation, hyperbolism, superlative, sensationalism, overselling, embellishment, embroidery, touching up, varnish, overcolouring, prodigality, overreaction, fuss, pother, stretching, straining, labouring, overestimation, overvaluation, overcompensation, overacting, histrionics, hamming, melodrama, burlesque, travesty **2 enlargement**, magnification, amplification, dilation, maximization, inflation, expansion, aggrandizement, heightening, blowing up **3 extravagance**, excessiveness, flamboyance, ostentation, outrageousness, profuseness, lavishness, overindulgence, overspending, pound-foolishness, intemperance, inordinacy, exorbitance, overdoing it **4 bombast**, pomposity, inflatedness, magniloquence, grandiloquence, boasting, bragging, self-glorification, ranting, raving, huckstering, hype, overpraise, flattery, overrating, purple prose **5 tall story**, traveller's tale

VERBS 6 exaggerate, overemphasize, intensify, overstate, overenthuse, overstress, hyperbolize, sensationalize, overdo, hype, embellish, embroider, touch up, varnish, overexpose, exacerbate, overkill, aggravate, overreact, fuss, pother, stretch, strain, labour, overestimate, overvalue, overcompensate, enhance, overact, have histrionics, overdraw, overwrite **7 enlarge**, magnify, amplify, dilate, maximize, inflate, expand, distend, aggrandize, heighten, blow up **8 be extravagant**, overdo, lavish, overindulge, overspend, run riot **9 boast**, brag, bombast, rant, rave, huckster, hype, oversell, overrate, overpraise, flatter, inflate **10 tell a tall story**, fantasize

ADJECTIVES 11 exaggerated, overemphasized, overstated, sensationalized, overdone, inflated, hyped, puffed, overrated, overpraised, oversold, flattered, embellished, embroidered, varnished, highly coloured, far-fetched, excessive, intensified, overstressed, overenthusiastic, overemphatic, hyperbolic, exacerbated, exorbitant, extreme, inordinate, aggravated, superlative, prodigious, stretched, strained, laboured, overestimated, overvalued, overcompensated, enhanced, overacted, histrionic, melodramatic **12 enlarged**, magnified, amplified, dilated, maximized, inflated, expanded, aggrandized, heightened, blown-up **13 extravagant**, excessive, flamboyant, ostentatious, outrageous, profuse, lavish, grandiose, overindulgent, overspending, pound-foolish, intemperate, inordinate, exorbitant, overdone, overshot, overstepped **14 bombastic**, boasting, bragging, raving, inflating, self-glorifying, hyping, magniloquent, grandiloquent

247 Excess

NOUNS 1 excess, redundance, overspill, overflow, inundation, flood, outflow, deluge, abundance, glut, exuberance, luxuriance, riot, profusion, plenty, richness, lion's share, most, upsurge, avalanche, spate, plethora, congestion, mob, crowd, overpopulation, saturation, plenitude, waste, excessiveness, nimiety, exorbitance **2 overdoing it**, overstretching oneself, overextension, overexpression, overactivity, overpoliteness, officiousness, red tape, overpraise, effusiveness, overoptimism, overestimation, overmeasure, overpayment, overweight, overload, last straw, overindulgence, intemperance, immoderation, gluttony, drunkenness, engorgement, satiety, bellyful, obesity **3 superfluity**, luxury, nonessential, extra, frill, perquisite, overfulfilment, overkill, duplication, supererogation, bonus, spare cash, surplus, leftovers, balance, remainder, spare, accessory, excrescence, parasite, uselessness, inutility, expletive, pleonasm, diffuseness, tautology, redundancy, overemployment, glut, oversupply, product dumping, inflation

VERBS 4 be excessive, overspill, overflow, flood, engulf, stream, deluge, overwhelm, abound, luxuriate, run riot, overproduce, overpopulate, bristle with, teem with, swarm with, crawl with, outnumber, overextend, overexpand, overstep, overlap, soak, saturate, drench, stuff, cram, fill, congest, choke, suffocate, glut, cloy, satiate, sate, sicken, gorge, overindulge oneself, overdose, overfulfil, oversubscribe, go overboard, oversell, overstock, overdo, overact, exaggerate, overload, overburden, overcharge, overspend, lavish, pamper **5 be superfluous**, go begging

ADJECTIVES 6 excessive, redundant, overflowing, brimming over, overfull, flooding, streaming, flowing, overwhelming, saturated, supersaturated, drenched, soaked, abundant, exuberant, luxuriant, riotous, profuse, plentiful, plethoric, overpopulated, bristling, teeming, swarming, crawling, outnumbered, too much, exorbitant, extreme, inordinate, disproportionate, cloying, satiating, nauseating, replete, overfed, gorged, crammed, stuffed, bloated, congested, bursting, overstretched, overburdened, overcharged, exaggerated, overdone, overacted, effusive, gushing, overpolite **7 superfluous**, supererogatory, excess, extra, spare, surplus, leftover, remaining, nonessential, luxury, unnecessary, needless, rambling, circuitous, tautologous, otiose, pleonastic, redundant

248 Exchange

NOUNS 1 exchange, interchange, trade, barter, conversion, commutation, permutation, substitution, transposition, shuffle, switch, swap, pawning, mutuality, reciprocity, give-and-take, retaliation, cooperation, interplay, two-way traffic, repartee, equivalent, correlation, compensation, consideration, redemption, ransom, trade-off, dealing **2 place of exchange**, marketplace, stock exchange, Bourse, rialto, bank **3 something in exchange**, pawn ticket, change, cash

VERBS 4 exchange, interchange, shuffle, switch, swap, reciprocate, cooperate, correlate, requite, answer back, retort, compensate, recompense, change places, transpose, shuttle, commute, substitute, convert, pawn, convert into, change money, barter, trade, traffic, truck

ADJECTIVES 5 in exchange, equivalent, complementary, reciprocal, mutual, two-way, tit-for-tat, retaliatory, compensatory, exchangeable, interchangeable, convertible, commutative **6 exchanged**, interchanged, substituted, transposed, traded, bartered, converted, switched, swapped, pawned, reciprocated, requited

249 Exclusion

NOUNS 1 exclusion, omission, suppression, rejection, refusal, denial, forbiddance, prohibition, veto, proscription, interdiction, ban, taboo, embargo, bar, exception, exemption, special case, dispensation, relegation, lockout, picket line, closed door, nonadmission, shunning, blacklisting, blackball, limitation, circumscription, segregation, sequestration, seclusion, ghettoization, discrimination, boycott, ostracism **2 ejection**, eviction, expulsion, dismissal, redundancy, suspension, disqualification, disbarment, removal, riddance, deletion, elimination, obliteration, censorship, bowdlerization, expurgation, eradication, excommunication, deportation, extradition, banishment, exile **3 exclusion zone**, ghetto, no-go area, no-man's-land, pale, enclosure, dam, wall, fence, partition, screen, Iron Curtain, barricade, ditch, moat, rampart, barrier, tariff wall, economic zone, quarantine **4 exclusiveness**, restrictiveness, closed shop, private club, clique, inner circle, members only, sole rights, monopoly, discrimination, apartheid, colour bar, racial dis-

crimination **5 thing excluded**, foreign body, contaminant
VERBS 6 exclude, leave out, omit, miss out, disregard, ignore, pass over, exempt, excuse, except, keep out, warn off, forbid, prohibit, disallow, veto, proscribe, interdict, ban, taboo, embargo, bar, suppress, stifle, relegate, put aside, leave, give up, abandon, reject, refuse, deny, vote against, shut out, deny entry, spurn, blacklist, blackball, rule out, limit, circumscribe, enclose, wall off, screen off, segregate, discriminate against, sequester, quarantine, isolate, seclude, ghettoize, boycott, shun, cold-shoulder, ostracize, preclude, forestall **7 eject**, evict, expel, throw out, cast out, dismiss, make redundant, suspend, disqualify, disbar, unfrock, strike off, remove, dispense with, oust, delete, cross out, cancel, eliminate, obliterate, censor, edit out, blue-pencil, bowdlerize, expurgate, eradicate, uproot, excommunicate, deport, extradite, banish, exile, outlaw **8 be excluded**, not belong
ADJECTIVES 9 excluding, closed, close-knit, clannish, cliquish, narrow, restrictive, xenophobic, racist, sexist, restricted, limited, private, elite, select, choice, unique, sole, exemptive, interdictory, prohibitive, preventive, preemptive, preclusive **10 excluded**, absent, missing, left out, omitted, excepted, excused, exempt, barred, banned, embargoed, forbidden, taboo, rejected, deleted, dismissed, evicted, expelled, shut out, shunned, blackballed, blacklisted, disbarred, struck off, outcast, exiled, unsaid, inadmissible, peripheral, extra, foreign, not considered, disregarded, outclassed

250 Excretion

NOUNS 1 excretion, egestion, elimination, expulsion, discharge, ejection, extrusion, emission, emanation, secretion, transudation, exudation, extravasation, flux, flow, expectoration, ejaculation, ecchymosis **2 defecation**, evacuation, voidance, dejection, purge, catharsis, clearance, motion, diarrhoea, bloody flux, dysentery, lientery, copremesis **3 urination**, micturation, incontinence, weak bladder, enuresis **4 excrement**, excreta, egesta, ejecta, waste, dejection, exudation, transudation, extravasation, effluent **5 faeces**, stool, motion, feculence, ordure, night soil, dung, muck, manure, cow pats, buffalo chips, guano, dirt, droppings, sheep's currants **6 urine**, water **7 pus**, discharge, matter, pustule, mucopus, seropus, ichor, sanies, purulence, pussiness, suppuration, festering, mattering, running, weeping, rankling, gleet **8 sweat**, perspiration, sudor, sudation, diaphoresis **9 saliva**, spit, salivation, ptyalism, sialorrhoea, dribble, drivel, slaver, slobber, slabber, froth, foam, cough, expectoration, spitting, phlegm, catarrh, mucus, rheum **10 bleeding**, nosebleed, ecchymosis, petechia, bruising, haemorrhage, haematemesis, haemoptysis, haematuria **11 menstruation**, menses, menstrual flow, catamenia, monthlies, courses, the curse, menopause, menarche, amenorrhoea, dysmenorrhoea, epimenorrhoea, hypomenorrhoea, menorrhagia **12 dead tissue**, slough, cast, exuviae, ecdysis, moulting **13 lavatory**, toilet, public convenience, latrine, bathroom, washroom, rest room, ladies, powder room, gents, urinal, privy, outhouse, earth closet **14 toilet**, stool, throne, commode, closestool, chamber pot

VERBS 15 excrete, egest, eliminate, pass, expel, discharge, eject, extrude, emit, give off, secrete, transude, exude, extravasate, weep, expectorate, ejaculate, relieve oneself **16 defecate**, pass, evacuate, void, purge, shit, shit oneself, foul **17 urinate**, micturate, pass water **18 fester**, suppurate, run, weep, rankle **19 sweat**, perspire, exude, swelter, wilt, steam **20 salivate**, spit, splutter, slobber, slabber, slaver, dribble, drivel, drool, cough, expectorate **21 bleed**, spill blood, bloody, ecchymose, extravasate **22 menstruate**, bleed, be on, come on **23 cast**, slough, ecdyse

ADJECTIVES 24 excretory, egestive, eliminative, ejective, exudative, transudative **25 faecal**, feculent, excremental, scatologic, stercoral, shitty, dungy, cathartic, purgative, laxative **26 urinary**, diuretic, enuretic, incontinent, continent, potty-trained, toilet-trained **27 purulent**, suppurative, festering, pussy, mattering **28 sweaty**, sudatory, sudoric, diaphoretic, sweating, perspiring, clammy, sticky, wilting **29 salivating**, spitting, coughing, spluttering, slobbering, slavering, dribbling, drooling, frothing, foaming, rheumy, watery, mucous **30 bleeding**, haemorrhaging, bloody **31 menstrual**, catamenial, monthly, menopausal, menstruating **32 cast-off**, shed, exuvial, moulting

251 Exemption

NOUNS 1 exemption, immunity, impunity, nonliability, nonresponsibility, dispensation, special treatment, privilege, exception **2 acquittal**, absolution, pardon, exoneration, excuse, discharge, release, liberation, freedom, liberty **3 self-exemption**, self-certification **4 licence**, permission, permit, charter, franchise, patent, privilege

ADJECTIVES 5 exempt, immune, nonliable, not responsible, unaccountable, unanswerable, privileged, excepted, excluded, shielded, protected **6 acquitted**, absolved, pardoned, exonerated, excused, let off, spared, clear, discharged, released **7 independent**, free, unrestricted, unbound, unconstrained **8 tax-free**, duty-free

VERBS 9 exempt, exclude, except, leave out, set apart, privilege, grant immunity **10 acquit**, exonerate, exculpate, absolve, grant absolution, pardon, excuse, let off, spare, show mercy, forgive, dismiss, discharge, release, liberate **11 be exempt**, enjoy immunity **12 exempt oneself**, excuse oneself

252 Existence

NOUNS 1 existence, being, life, subsistence, coexistence, entity, ens, esse, occurrence, presence, metaphysics, monadism **2 thing**, something, entity, being, body, object, substance, item, monad, phenomenon **3 nature**, essence, quiddity, innateness, ontology, materiality **4 demonstrable existence**, reality, actuality, factuality, truth, authenticity, necessity **5 fact**, the case, the realities, the specifics, the fundamentals **6 continuing existence**, duration, endurance, persistence, continuance, survival **7 self-existence**, aseity, uncreated being, deity **8 creation**, materialization, actualization, birth, evolution, big-bang theory **9 mere existence**, vegetable existence, stagnation, inertia, indolence

ADJECTIVES 10 existing, being, living, subsistent, coexistent, occurring, present, prevalent, current, extant, manifest, necessary, obvious, in force **11 intrinsic**, innate, inherent, essential, basic, fundamental, natural, material, substantial, substantive, concrete **12 lasting**, enduring, persisting, persistent, abiding, continual, continuous, surviving **13 real**, actual, factual, de facto, true, authentic, veritable, undeniable, indisputable, positive, provable, empirical, historical, phenomenal **14 self-existent**, self-existing, uncreated, god-like **15 created**, materialized, made, actualized **16 vegetating**, stagnating, inert, torpid

VERBS 17 exist, be, live, breathe, coexist, subsist, live in, inhabit, dwell, occur, be there, be found **18 come to be**, become, materialize, take shape, be born, evolve, arise, come about, grow, develop **19 continue to be**, endure, last, persist, continue, survive, prevail, live on, stand, hold, remain **20 bring into being**, create, make, form, compose, devise, invent, cause, realize, actualize, factualize **21 merely exist**, vegetate

253 Exit

NOUNS 1 exit, egress, going out, coming out, emergence, emertion, issue, extrusion, exodus, departure, walk-out, evacuation, breakout, eruption, proruption **2 outflow**, outpouring, flood, inundation, spill, waste, effluence, effusion, outflux, efflux, outfall, waterfall, gush, stream, jet, fountain, well, spring, gusher, exhaust, emission, discharge, emanation, exudation, secretion, voidance, excretion, evaporation, perspiration, sweating, transudation, diaphoresis, running sore, streaming eyes, runny nose **3 leakage**, seepage, dripping, dribbling, trickling, filtration, straining, percolation, leaching, lixiviation, effusion, extravasation, oozing **4 emigration**, migration, expatriation, deportation, exile, expulsion **5 export**, transference, outgoings, outlay, expenditure **6 way out**, exit, egress, door, gate, port, emergency exit, fire escape, escape hatch, escape route, path, avenue, channel **7 outlet**, outfall, chute, spout, tap, drain, drainpipe, gutter, conduit, gargoyle, overflow, flume, sluice, weir, floodgate, orifice, vent, pore, blowhole

VERBS 8 exit, egress, go, leave, depart, withdraw, go out, get out, walk out, pop out, march out, bow out, walk off, die **9 emerge**, come out, issue, debouch, sally forth, emanate, effuse, appear, surface, arise, erupt, break out, project, protrude, jut, break cover, burst out, escape, evacuate, bale out **10 run out**, drain, flow out, flood out, inundate, pour, disembogue, surge, well out, gush out, jet, spurt out, spout, vomit, spew, blow out, overflow, spill **11 leak**, drip, dribble, trickle, seep, weep, ooze, extravasate, filter, exfiltrate, strain, percolate, leach, lixiviate, effuse, drivel, drool, slaver, slobber, salivate, emanate, exude, emit, discharge, secrete, excrete, exudate, perspire **12 emigrate**, outmigrate, migrate, expatriate, deport, exile, expel, dismiss, export **13 be dismissed**, leave, resign

ADJECTIVES 14 outgoing, outward-bound, going, departing, leaving, forthcoming, issuing, egressive, emerging, coming out, arising, surfacing, erupting, volcanic, explosive, expulsive, emanating, transeunt **15 outflowing**, outpouring, effluent, effusive, extravasated, expended **16 leaky**, oozy, weeping, runny, excretory, porous, permeable

254 Expansion

NOUNS 1 growth, enlargement, extension, lengthening, drawing out, stretching, spreading, sprawling, splaying, branching, ramification, fanning out, dispersion, expansion, widening, broadening, flaring, dilation, diastole, opening, unfolding, distension, swelling, bloating, tumefaction, tumescence, tumidness, turgidity, dropsy, oedema, puffiness, inflation, blowing up, bulging, bulbousness, stuffing, fattening, increase, build-up, augmentation, addition, heightening, rising, raising, magnification, aggrandizement, amplification, development, hypertrophy, waxing, crescendo, germination, budding, sprouting, burgeoning, blossoming, blooming, flowering, maturation, flourishing, thriving, multiplication, reproduction, procreation **2 enlargeability**, extendability, extensibility, stretchability, elasticity, spreadability, expansibility, dilatability **3 enlarged thing**, enlargement, extension, swelling, tumour, bulge, balloon

VERBS 4 make bigger, enlarge, extend, lengthen, draw out, stretch, spread out, sprawl, splay, ramify, fan, disperse, expand, widen, broaden, flare, dilate, open, distend, swell, bloat, puff up, inflate, blow up, pump up, stuff, pad, fatten, plump up, increase, build up, augment, add to, heighten, raise, elevate, hike up, up, magnify, aggrandize, amplify **5 become bigger**, grow, enlarge, extend, lengthen, draw out, stretch, spread, sprawl, splay, branch, ramify, fan, disperse, expand, widen, broaden, flare, dilate, open up, unfold, distend, swell, bloat, tumify, puff up, inflate, balloon, belly, bulge, fatten, plump out, fill out, increase, build up, augment, mushroom, snowball, overdevelop, hypertrophy, magnify, amplify, wax, crescendo, shoot up, spring up, germinate, bud, sprout, burgeon, blossom, bloom, flower, flourish, thrive, multiply, reproduce, procreate

ADJECTIVES 6 bigger, larger, extended, lengthened, drawn-out, stretched, spread-out, widespread, splayed, fanned out, dispersed, expanded, widened, broadened, flared, dilated, distended, swollen, bloated, tumid, turgid, incrassate, dropsical, oedematous, puffed-up, inflated, blown-up, pumped-up, stuffed, padded, fatter, overweight, increased, built-up, augmented, heightened, raised, magnified, amplified, developed, mature, fully fledged, full-blown, fully developed, hypertrophied **7 growing**, crescent, extending, lengthening, stretching, spreading, sprawling, splaying, patulous, branching, fanning, flabellate, deltoid, expanding, widening, broadening, flaring, dilating, opening, unfolding, swelling, tumescent, turgescent, bulging, bulbous, increasing, waxing, mushrooming, snowballing, rising, developing, germinating, budding, shooting, sprouting, burgeoning, blossoming, blooming, flowering, flourishing, thriving, multiplying **8 enlargeable**, extendable, extensile, stretchable, elastic, spreadable, dispersive, expandable, expansile, expansionary, dilatable, distensible, inflatable, augmentative, multipliable

255 Expectation

NOUNS 1 expectation, anticipation, contemplation, prospect, hopefulness, optimism, presumption, assumption, confidence, assurance, reliance, trust, belief, waiting, suspense, apprehension, pessimism, dread, fear, foreboding, anxiety, uncertainty, possibility, probability, likelihood **2 expectations**, demands, desires, hopes, prospects, outlook, forecast, prognosis, prediction, accountability, responsibility, contingency, possibility, dream, aspiration **3 the expected thing**, the usual, the normal, custom

ADJECTIVES 4 expecting, hopeful, confident, sanguine, optimistic, desiring, wanting, sure, certain, anticipating, prepared, ready, waiting, on stand-by, forewarned, forearmed, unsurprised, vigilant, watchful, on tenterhooks, in suspense, excited, eager, prognostic, apprehensive, dreading, pessimistic **5 expectant**, pregnant, gravid **6 expected**, predicted, foreseen, unsurprising, designated, chosen, promised, due, anticipated, probable, likely, apparent, predictable, foreseeable, sure, certain, long-awaited, prospective, contemplated, impending, imminent, hoped for, desired

VERBS 7 expect, anticipate, see coming, contemplate, face, intend, plan, envisage, hope for, apprehend, dread **8 predict**, foresee, forecast, think, believe, estimate, reckon, calculate, bargain for, count on, bank on, assume **9 wait**, await **10 demand**, insist on, call for, require, need

256 Expenditure

VERBS 1 expend, spend, disburse, pay, pay out, shop, buy, purchase, incur costs, invest, sink money, afford, splurge, overspend, squander, fritter away, throw away **2 consume**, use, exhaust, deplete, go through, run through **3 donate**, give, contribute, support, back, finance, pay for

NOUNS 4 expenditure, spending, disbursement, payment, shopping, buying, buy **5 expense**, extras, outlay, investment, outgoings, overheads, fee, charge, price, rate **6 extravagance**, prodigality, spending spree, splurge, dissaving **7 donation**, giving, contribution, support, backing, finance

ADJECTIVES 8 expending, spending, sumptuary, out-of-pocket, generous **9 spendthrift**, extravagant, profligate **10 expended**, spent, disbursed, paid, paid out, invested **11 used**, exhausted

257 Experiment

NOUNS 1 experiment, investigation,

probe, analysis, diagnosis, assay, essay, test, trial, inquiry, probation, sounding out, feeler, check, tentation, venture, bid, endeavour, effort, gambit, risk **2 rehearsal**, practice, audition, hearing, model, mock-up, rough draft, sketch, trial run, tryout, dummy run, dry run, road test **3 experimentation**, empiricism, pragmatism, instrumentalism, testing, trying, research, vivisection, investigation, examination, exploration, verification, determination, ascertainment, speculation, conjecture, guesswork **4 originality**, inventiveness, creativity, innovation, novelty, newness, unfamiliarity, strangeness, avant-garde, modernism, daring, recklessness **5 place of experimentation**, laboratory, research establishment, field station, proving ground, think tank

ADJECTIVES 6 experimental, empirical, pragmatic, scientific, analytic, instrumental, probational, exploratory, investigative, experimenting, inquiring, trying, testing, researching, verifying, determining, speculative, conjectural, tentative, provisional, mock, rough, trial, test, dummy, practice, model **7 original**, experimental, inventive, creative, innovative, novel, modern, new, unfamiliar, strange, avant-garde, venturesome, daring, enterprising, reckless, risky **8 tested**, tried, researched, determined, verified, checked, essayed, ventured, estimated

VERBS 9 experiment, test, try, essay, assay, try out, research, sound out, explore, analyse, investigate, probe, sample, examine, inquire, verify, substantiate, confirm, check, determine, prove, ascertain, speculate, prospect, conjecture, guess **10 rehearse**, practise, audition, mock up, sketch, try out, road-test, flight-test, simulate **11 invent**, create, innovate, dare, risk, chance, gamble, venture, attempt

258 Expulsion

VERBS 1 expel, eject, put out, turn out, throw out **2 dismiss**, discharge, disemploy, suspend, lay off, make redundant, drop, let go, release, retire, superannuate **3 disbar**, excommunicate, unfrock, strip, deplume, disqualify, strike off, drum out, cashier, depose, dethrone, expel, suspend, send down, rusticate, demote, downgrade **4 ostracize**, exclude, seclude, blackball, spurn, snub, cut, brush off, make unwelcome, outlaw, fugitate, ban, proscribe, prohibit, banish, rusticate, exile, expatriate, deport, transport **5 send away**, see off, turn away, bundle away, pack off, shake off **6 drive out**, drum out, chase out, rout out, push out, force out, hunt out, smoke out **7 evict**, oust, remove, dispossess, repossess, expropriate, deprive, dislodge, extirpate, uproot, put out, unhouse **8 exterminate**, purge, liquidate, dispel, eradicate, deracinate, eliminate, destroy, rub out, erase, obliterate **9 void**, evacuate, eliminate, remove, deplete, exhaust, empty, vent, siphon off, pump out, clear out, clean out, curette, purge, gut, disembowel, eviscerate, bone, fillet, unclog, unfoul **10 unload**, unburden, unlade, unpack, discharge, dump **11 throw away**, jettison, discard, scrap, precipitate **12 let out**, give out, emit, send out, radiate, perfume, scent, exhaust, exhale, expire, breathe out, puff, fume, smoke, reek, steam, vaporize, stream, disgorge, debouch, disembogue, discharge, ejaculate, cast forth, send forth, extrude, erupt, eruct, blow out, pour out, spew, spout, jet, spurt, squirt, extravasate, bleed, defecate, urinate, excrete, egest, secrete, sweat, ooze, suppurate, dribble, drool, slaver **13 vomit**, spew, regurgitate, spit, bring up, be sick, retch, heave **14 belch**, hiccup, eruct

NOUNS 15 expulsion, ejection, throwing out, rejection **16 dismissal**, discharge, congé, suspension, laying off, redundancy, drumming out, cashiering, demotion, degradation, relegation, stripping, depluming, externment, exclusion, excommunication, unfrocking, disqualification **17 ostracism**, exclusion, seclusion, blackballing, the brushoff, outlawing, fugitation, proscription, banishment, rustication, exile, expatriation **18 eviction**, ousting, removal, dispossession, repossession, expropriation, deprivation, dislodgment, jettison, precipitation, defenestration **19 removal**, elimination, evacuation, voidance, clearance, cleaning out, scouring out, purging, catharsis, unfouling, emptying, depletion, exhaustion, draining **20 disgorgement**, disemboguement, ejaculation, extrusion, obtrusion, eruption, blowout, outburst, outpour, effusion, jet, spout, spurt, squirt, excretion, secretion, extravasation, blood-letting, cupping, venesection, phlebotomy, paracentesis, tapping, spilling, shedding, libation **21 vomiting**, sickness, regurgitation, egestion, emesis, heaving, retching, gagging **22 belch**, hiccup, ructation, eructation, wind, gas, flatulence, fart **23 emission**, emissivity, radioactivity **24 propellant**, explosive, emitter, radiator, ejector seat, volcano, emetic, aperient

ADJECTIVES 25 expulsive, expellent, ejective, ejaculative, eliminant, explosive, eruptive, radiating, emitting, secretory, sweaty, sudatory, salivary, sickening, emetic, purgative, laxative, cathartic, sialagogue **26 vomiting**, sick, nauseated, seasick, travel-sick **27 eructative**, flatulent

259 Exterior

NOUNS 1 exterior, external, surface, façade, front, face, facet, shell, rind, pod, crust, covering, coating, outer wall, envelope, integument, superstratum, superficies, outer layer, skin, epidermis, cuticle, exoskeleton, cortex, hull, husk, periphery, circumference, outline, fringe, surroundings **2 outside**, outwardness, open air, hinterland **3 appearance**, apparentness, aspect, mien, image, impression, public persona, guise, seemingness, superficiality **4 externalization**, exteriorization, projection, openness, outwardness **5 extraneousness**, foreignness, strangeness, otherworldliness, others, outsiders

ADJECTIVES 6 exterior, external, surface, outer, front, facing, faceted, crusty, covered, enveloped, integumental, epidermal, cuticular **7 outside**, outward, out-of-doors, open-air, alfresco, outermost, outlying **8 apparent**, surface, outward, ostensible, superficial, shallow, seeming, imaginal **9 externalized**,

exteriorized, projected, open, outward **10 extraneous**, foreign, alien, exotic
VERBS 11 be exterior, cover, surface, overlie, front, face, encrust, skin over, envelop, outline, fringe, surround **12 be outside**, be out-of-doors, dine alfresco **13 appear outwardly**, seem **14 externalize**, exteriorize, project

260 Extraction

NOUNS 1 extraction, removal, withdrawal, pulling out, drawing, tugging out, wrenching out, wresting out, evulsion, avulsion, ripping out, tearing out, rooting out, deracination, eradication, elimination, dredging, extrication, disengagement **2 displacement**, dislodgment, expulsion, expression, squeezing out, pruning, thinning, weeding **3 digging out**, unearthing, disinterment, exhumation, disentombment, grave-robbing, cutting out, excision, exsection, excavation, mining, quarrying **4 sucking**, drawing, drawing off, draught, aspiration, vacuuming, pumping, siphoning, tapping, milking, pipetting, broaching, emptying, draining, cupping, bleeding, blood-letting, phlebotomy, venesection, evisceration, gutting, disembowelment **5 drawing out**, bringing forth, elicitation, evocation, eduction, calling forth, arousal, stimulation, obtaining **6 extorsion**, wresting, wrenching, wringing, tearing, ripping, wrest, wrench, wring, exaction, demand **7 obtaining an extract**, extraction, separation, refinement, purification, distillation, sublimation, condensation, vaporization, decoction, infusion, squeezing, pressing, expressing, rendering, steeping, soaking **8 extract**, essence, quintessence, spirit, elixir, decoction, infusion, distillate, sublimate, concentrate **9 extractor**, separator, siphon, pump, syringe, pipette, aspirator, vacuum pump, press, wringer, mangle, lemon squeezer, juice extractor, cherry stoner **10 excavator**, miner, quarrier, digger, JCB, shovel, pickaxe, toothpick, rake, dredge, dredger, shadoof, Persian wheel, scoop, spoon, lever, crowbar, wrench, corkscrew, screwdriver, forceps, pliers
VERBS 11 extract, remove, withdraw, pull out, draw out, tug out, wrench out, wrest out, evulse, avulse, rip out, tear out, root out, eradicate, eliminate, pluck out, pick out, rake out, dredge, fish out, grub out, winkle out, extricate, disengage, free **12 displace**, dislodge, lever out, smoke out, expel, express, squeeze out, wring out, prune, thin, thin out, weed out **13 dig out**, unearth, disinter, exhume, disentomb, gouge out, cut out, excise, excavate, mine, quarry **14 suck**, draw off, aspirate, vacuum, pump, siphon off, tap, milk, pipette, broach, empty, drain, cup, bleed, eviscerate, gut, disembowel **15 draw out**, bring forth, elicit, evoke, educe, worm out, summon up, call up, rouse, stimulate, procure, induce **16 extort**, wrest, wrench, wring, force out, tear out, rip out, exact, demand **17 obtain an extract**, separate, refine, purify, cream off, distil, condense, vaporize, decoct, infuse, squeeze, press, melt down, render, steep, soak, marinate
ADJECTIVES 18 extractive, eductive, eradicative, removable, uprooting, elicitory, evocative, arousing **19**

dislodged, displaced, uprooted, deracinated, extricated, disengaged, liberated

261 Extraneousness

NOUNS 1 extraneousness, irrelevance, immateriality, inessentiality, superfluity, pleonasm, superficiality, redundancy, pointlessness, inapplicability, incidentalness, secondariness, insignificance **2 foreignness**, alienism, unrelatedness, unconnectedness, difference, otherness, exoticness, strangeness **3 separateness**, segregation, dissociation, disaffiliation, nonassimilation, discreteness, apartheid, isolation, insularity, detachment, noninvolvement, independence **4 externality**, extrinsicality, exteriority, outside, outwardness, surface, periphery, circumference, the external, foreign product, importation, incoming, invasion, infringement, interloping, intrusion, trespassing, gate-crashing, externalization, projection

ADJECTIVES 5 extraneous, irrelevant, irrelative, immaterial, inessential, superfluous, extra, superficial, redundant, pleonastic, pointless, inapplicable, unrelated, unconnected, incidental, adventitious, secondary, insignificant **6 foreign**, alien, unrelated, other, continental, overseas, transatlantic, tramontane, strange, different, deviating, outlandish, unknown, exotic, barbaric, wandering, travelling, rambling, roaming, nomadic, gypsy, migrant, homeless **7 separate**, apart, dissociated, unaffiliated, nonassimilated, segregated, removed, isolated, discrete, detached, independent, nonconforming, anarchic **8 external**, extrinsic, exterior, extraterrestrial, distant, outward, outer, outside, ulterior, peripheral, superficial, foreign-made, imported, incoming, invading, infringing, interloping, intrusive, trespassing, gatecrashing, externalizing, projecting

VERBS 9 be extraneous, be irrelevant, digress, ramble, not apply **10 be foreign**, emigrate, immigrate, travel, wander, ramble **11 separate**, keep apart, segregate, isolate, remove, detach **12 be external**, exist outside, import, invade, infringe, interlope, squat, intrude, trespass, stowaway, gate-crash, externalize **13 not conform**, be different

262 Extravagance

ADJECTIVES 1 extravagant, wasteful, lavish, uneconomic, spendthrift, prodigal, profligate, thriftless, unthrifty **2 unrestrained**, excessive, inordinate, immoderate, extreme, wild, exaggerated, hyperbolic, magnified, profuse, ostentatious, showy, preposterous, outrageous **3 costly**, high-priced, expensive, dear, overpriced, exorbitant, inflationary, sky-high

NOUNS 4 extravagance, prodigality, lavishness, wastefulness, profligacy, conspicuous consumption, unthriftiness, improvidence, squandering **5 unrestrainedness**, immoderation, exaggeration, hyperbole, profusion, superfluity, dissipation **6 spendthrift**, prodigal, profligate, wastrel

VERBS 7 waste, squander, fritter away, misspend, dissipate, lavish, go through, use up **8 overspend**, overdraw,

263 Fabrics

NOUNS 1 fibre, thread, filament, yarn, natural fibre, synthetic fibre, braided fibre, monofilament **2 spinning**, twining, intertwining, braiding, interbraiding, plaiting, spinning wheel, spinning mule, spinning jenny, spinner, extruder **3 fabric**, cloth, textile, material, drapery, rag, synthetic, woven fabric, knitted fabric, soft furnishing, print, screen print, carpeting, Axminster, Wilton, broadcloth **4 weaving**, weave, plain weave, twill weave, warp, weft, selvage, list, webbing, lacing, interweaving, shoot, weaving frame, loom, shuttle, bobbin, weaver, texture, nap **5 knitting**, stitch, interlock stitch, plain stitch, purl stitch, cable stitch, moss stitch, stocking stitch, knitting machine, pattern, needle **6 dye**, colourant, dyestuff, natural dye, chemical dye, mordant, lake, fast dye, absorption, chromophore, crocein, eosin, fuchsine, madder, mauveine, Tyrian purple, woad, bleach, chromotrope, garance, lake naphthol **7 dyeing**, colouring, staining, patterning, printing, screen printing, tie dyeing **8 fabric treatment**, cleaning, washing, laundering, dry cleaning, stain removal, bleaching, flameproofing, preshrinking, wrinkleproofing

ADJECTIVES 9 spun, twisted, braided, twined, plaited **10 woven**, knitted, fine, sheer, coarse, netted, fine-weave, open-weave, ikat weave, twill, felted, brushed, napped **11 treated**, washed, bleached, dyed, coloured, dyed-in-the-wool, dyed-in-the-yarn, tie-dyed, coated, flameproof, preshrunk, waterproof, showerproof, drip-dry, crease-resistant

VERBS 12 spin, twist, braid, plait **13 weave**, knit, felt, mat, brush **14 treat**, wash, bleach, dye, tie-dye, flameproof, preshrink, waterproof, showerproof

264 Failure

• *She knows there's no success like failure/ And that failure's no success at all.* Bob Dylan.

NOUNS 1 failure, nonfulfilment, negative result, fallibility, inability, inefficiency, weakness, unproductiveness, noncompletion, dereliction, withdrawal, setback, error, mistake, mess, collapse, debacle, fiasco, botch, bungle, blunder, omission, negligence, default, miss, vain attempt, futility, frustration, disappointment, misfortune, uselessness, discontinuance, stoppage, shutdown, closure, stalling, breakdown, halt, fall, crash, decline, deterioration, failing, ailing, downfall, comedown, shortage, incapacity, insufficiency, insolvency, bankruptcy **2 defeat**, loss, collapse, reversal, retreat, trashing, rout, beating, drubbing, hiding, thrashing, trouncing, subjugation, submission, deathblow, Waterloo, lost cause, fatal move **3 personal fault**, foible, failing, weakness, disloyalty, unfaithfulness, promiscuity, peccadillo, vice **4 unsuccessful thing**, bankruptcy, bad idea, lost bet, wasted day, wild-goose chase, miscarriage, engine failure, electrical fault, crop failure, damp squib **5 failing person**, failure, loser, unsuccessful candidate, nonpayer, debtor, insolvent, bankrupt, underachiever, slow learner, born loser, misfit, bun-

gler, reject, second-rater, underling, underdog, unfortunate
VERBS 6 fail, not succeed, lose out, not pass, do badly, blunder, bungle, collapse, discontinue, shut down, close up, disappoint, disillusion, fall short, return empty-handed, tire, sink, flag, ail, decline **7 be defeated**, lose, retreat, run away, surrender, lose out, be eliminated **8 miscarry**, abort, go wrong, go amiss, go awry **9 malfunction**, not start, fail, stall, misfire, jam, seize up, overheat, lose power, go wrong
ADJECTIVES 10 failed, unsuccessful, ineffective, insufficient, unproductive, hopeless, insolvent, bankrupt, negligent, neglectful, unlucky, unfortunate, bungling, blundering, stillborn, abortive, weak, ailing, fruitless, bootless, profitless, useless **11 defeated**, beaten, bested, lost, outmanoeuvred, outclassed, outmatched, outgunned, outplayed, outshone, outvoted, outwitted, thrashed, in retreat, routed

265 Faintness

NOUNS 1 faintness, softness, soft sound, low volume, noise abatement, mutedness, indistinctness, inaudibility, soundproofing, clunk, plunk, thud, thump, bump, plonk, nonresonance, voicelessness, hoarseness, whisper, susurration, bated breath, soft voice, muffled tones, hushed tones, murmur, hum, drone, roll, sigh, sough, moan, scratch, squeak, creak, pop, tick, click, tinkle, clink, chink, buzz, whirr, purr, purl, ripple, plash, plop, babble, burble, gurgle, rustle, swoosh, swish, froufrou, squish, squash, fizz, sizzle, hiss, pitter-patter **2 sound reducer**, silencer, soft pedal, mute, damper, filter, cork, double-glazing, soundproofing, rubber soles, lubricant **3 faint-sounding thing**, bare feet, heartbeat, raindrops, light breeze, rustling leaves
ADJECTIVES 4 faint, soft, quiet, low, gentle, distant, indistinct, inaudible, soundproof, just caught, half-heard, weak, feeble, dying away, unemphatic, unstressed, unaccented, piano, hushed, muted, muffled, damped, nonresonant, dead, dull, soft-pedalled, subdued, suppressed, stifled, bated, voiceless, whispered, hoarse, husky, wheezy, rasping, gravelly, murmuring, sighing, purring, gurgling, rustling, hissing
VERBS 5 sound faint, speak softly, play piano, breathe, whisper, murmur, mutter, hum, croon, drone, purr, buzz, whirr, purl, ripple, plash, splash, lap, plop, babble, burble, gurgle, flow, sputter, splutter, patter, squeak, creak, tick, click, tinkle, clink, chink, clunk, plunk, thud, thump, bump, plonk, moan, sigh, sough, hiss, wheeze, blow, rustle, swish, swoosh, squish, squash, fizz, sizzle, tremble, become inaudible, melt, die away, fade away **6 mute**, soften, dull, deaden, dampen, damp down, soft-pedal, soundproof, muffle, stifle, hush

266 Falsehood

NOUNS 1 falsehood, error, mendaciousness, inveracity, untruth, truthlessness, unverity, fallaciousness, erroneousness, ungenuineness, spuriousness, false conduct, improbity, dissemblance, dishonesty, bad faith, deception, delusion

2 duplicity, doubleness, two-facedness, forked tongue, double-dealing **3 hypocrisy**, insincerity, deception, delusion, disguise, camouflage, concealment, sanctimony, religiosity, ostentatiousness, uncandidness, unfrankness, tokenism, flattery, unctuousness, oiliness, cant, lip service, mummery, mouthing, mealy-mouthedness, empty gesture, disingenuousness, mockery, meretriciousness, cupboard love, crocodile tears, Tartuffery, Pecksniffery, Pharisaism, blandishments **4 spuriousness**, bogusness, falseness, ungenuineness, unauthenticity, unrealness, forgery, counterfeiting, artificiality, factitiousness, hollowness, humbug, speciousness, sophistry, casuistry, Jesuitism, charlatanism, quackery, mountebankery, imposture **5 deceitfulness**, duplicity, fraudulence, falseheartedness, cunning, sneakiness, artfulness, artifice, guile, wile, malingering, improbity, lying, treason, treachery **6 lying**, fibbing, fabrication, pseudology, mythomania, perjury, false witness, forswearing, perfidy, defamation, libel **7 pretence**, dissimulation, impersonation, imitation, play-acting, representation, feigning, pretext, posture, pose, affectation, apparentness, ostensibility **8 fraud**, swindle, dishonesty, cheating, trickery, fakery, falsity, imposture, sharp practice, confidence trick, insider dealing, adulteration, packed jury, stacked deck, loaded dice, salted mine, juggled figures, counterfeiting, forgery, put-up job, hoax **9 falsification**, faking, misrepresentation, misstatement, misquote, misinterpretation, misreporting, misciting, perversion, distortion, straining, warping, slanting, twisting, garbling, sharp practice, collusion, manipulation, tampering with, doctoring, rigging, juggling, retouching, counterfeiting, forgery, fabrication, trumping up, confabulation, invention, imagination, concoction, canard, fiction, figment, myth, legend **10 fake**, sham, mock, imitation, copy, counterfeit, bootleg, dummy, tinsel, paste, rubbish **11 evasion**, equivocation, ambivalence, double-talk, shiftiness, dodging, shuffling **12 facade**, front, mask, show, masquerade, disguise, ostentation, false front, face, appearance, fanfaronade, semblance, seeming, sham, fake, act, bluff, simulation, dissemblance, dressing-up, window-dressing, whitewash, gloss, varnish, gild, embellishment, embroidery, touch-up, deodorization **13 false thing**, forged passport, counterfeit note, fool's gold, nine-bob note, Trojan horse

VERBS 14 be false, lie, dissemble, lack integrity, deceive **15 double-deal**, two-time **16 be hypocritical**, be insincere, deceive, delude, act sanctimoniously, disguise, camouflage, conceal, lack candour, cant, mouth, flatter, mock **17 be deceitful**, malinger, sneak **18 pretend**, dissimulate, impersonate, imitate, play-act, dissemble, represent, feign, feint, posture, pose, affect, attitudinize, put on **19 be fraudulent**, swindle, cheat, trick, fake, copy, falsify, deal underhandedly, stack, juggle, load, salt, adulterate, counterfeit, forge, hoax **20 falsify**, fake, misrepresent, misstate, misquote, misinterpret, misreport, miscite, pervert, distort, strain, warp, slant, twist, garble, collude, manipulate, tamper with, retouch, counterfeit, forge, fabricate, trump up, confabulate, invent, imagine, cry wolf, concoct, mythologize, fable, doctor **21 evade**, equivocate, be ambivalent, double-talk, shuffle **22 mask**, show, masquerade, disguise, impersonate, face, appear, seem, fake, act, bluff, simulate, dissemble, window-dress, embellish, embroider, touch up, dress up, overdo, deodorize, gloss over, whitewash, varnish

ADJECTIVES 23 false, fallacious, erroneous, mendaceous, inveracious, untrue, ungenuine, spurious, dissembling, dishonest, deceptive, delusive **24 duplicitous**, two-faced, Janus-faced, double-dealing **25 hypocritical**, insincere, disingenuous, meretricious, deceptive, delusive, sanctimonious, religiose, falsely pious, empty, Pharisaic, uncandid, unfrank, unctuous, oily, mealy-mouthed, flattering, Pecksniffian, mocking, unserious, tongue-in-cheek **26 spurious**, bogus, ungenuine, unauthentic, unreal, apocryphal, forged, artificial, factitious, hollow, humbug, specious, sophistic, casuistic, charlatan, quackish, imposturous **27 deceitful**, duplicitous, fraudulent, fake, artificial, false-hearted, cunning, sneaky, artful, guileful, wily, crafty, manipulative, malingering, lying, fibbing, fabricating, prevaricating, slandering, libelling, perjuring, forswearing, perfidious, collusive, treasonous **28 pretending**, dissembling, dissimulating, play-acting, masquerading, feigning, bluffing, affecting, attitudinizing, posturing, posing, seeming, apparent, so-called **29 fraudulent**, swindling, dishonest, cheating, tricky, false, fake, imposturous, illicit, underhanded, counterfeit, forged, copied, put-up **30 falsified**, faked, misrepresented, exaggerated, distorted, twisted, stretched, half-true, counterfeit, fabricated, confabulated, invented, slanderous, libellous, perjurious, manipulated, concocted, fictional, imaginative, mythologized, fabled, legendary, made-up, cock-and-bull, trumped-up **31 fake**, sham, mock, artificial, imitative, counterfeit, bogus, tinselled, rubbishy **32 evasive**, equivocal, ambivalent, double-talking, shifty, shuffling, dodging **33 disguised**, false, seeming, sham, fake, imitation, simulated, dissembled, glossed, varnished, gilded, embellished, embroidered, overdone, dressed-up

267 Fashion

NOUNS 1 fashion, style, mode, vogue, look, new look, craze, set, rage, the latest, haute couture, high fashion, elegance **2 fashionableness**, chic **3 fashion business**, rag trade **4 design**, mode, style, structure, set, mould, aspect, light, appearance, tendency, convention, protocol **5 fashion model**, model, mannequin, fashion plate, clothes' horse **6 fashionable élite**, high society

ADJECTIVES 7 fashionable, smart, stylish, snazzy, clothes' conscious, well-dressed, dressy, tasteful, classy, posh, glamorous

VERBS 8 fashion, shape, produce, figure, turn, round, cut, style, tailor, cut out, create, model, chisel, carve, sculpt, hew, mould, cast, hammer out, forge, build, formulate

268 Fasting

NOUNS 1 fasting, abstinence, abstemiousness, austerity, atrophy, Lenten fare, dieting, starvation diet, weight loss, lean cuisine, slimming, reducing, Weightwatchers **2 short rations**, iron rations, short commons, asceticism, Spartan fare, hunger striking, bare subsistence, hunger, famishment **3 fast day**, Lent, Good Friday, Yom Kippur

VERBS 4 fast, abstain, eat nothing, hunger, avoid food, eat sparingly, keep Lent, diet, slim, reduce, count calories, half starve

ADJECTIVES 5 fasting, abstinent, abstemious, anorexic, unfed, empty, Lenten, Quadragesimal, Spartan, dieting, slimming, reducing, austere, ascetic, underfed, thin, half-starved, starving, famished, ravenous, hungry

269 Fatigue

ADJECTIVES 1 fatigued, tired, weary, sleepy, drowsy, nodding, yawning, dozy, half-asleep, exhausted, tired out, worn out, spent, weak, drained, dull, stale, strained, overworked, overtired, overfatigued, overstrained, overwrought, burned out, weakened, enervated, fainting, swooning, stiff, footsore, footweary, travel-weary, jet-lagged, hollow-eyed, haggard, worn, drooping, flagging, languid, listless **2 bored**, tired, weary, jaded, satiated **3 panting**, wheezing, snorting **4 fatiguing**, tiring, exhausting, laborious, tiresome, wearying, wearing, gruelling, punishing, exacting, tough, demanding, irksome, vexatious, annoying, trying, tedious

VERBS 5 be fatigued, be tired, flag, droop, languish, fail, sink, stagger, faint, swoon, feel dizzy, yawn, nod, drowse, sleep, succumb, drop, collapse, overdo it, overwork, overexert, gasp, pant, puff, blow, grunt, breathe heavily **6 fatigue**, exhaust, tire, wear out, weary, prostrate, double up, wind, tax, strain, overwork, overdrive, overtask, overtax, overburden, overload, burn out, weaken, debilitate, enervate, drain, distress, trouble, bother, harass, annoy

NOUNS 7 fatigue, tiredness, weariness, sleepiness, drowsiness, exhaustion, lassitude, languor, listlessness, lethargy, dullness, staleness, jadedness, boredom, aching muscles, collapse, prostration, strain, exertion, work, overtiredness, overexertion, overwork, overdoing it, panting, gasping, palpitations, languishment, weakness, enervation, debilitation, faintness

270 Fear

• *Fear has many eyes and can see things underground.* Miguel de Cervantes.

NOUNS 1 fear, fright, terror, horror, dread, awe, panic, phobia, aversion, mortal fear, unholy terror, blind panic, icy fingers, cold sweat, chattering teeth **2 fearfulness**, nervousness, timorousness, apprehension, anxiety, uneasiness, tension, trepidation, consternation, perturbation, alarm, unease, disquiet, dismay, foreboding, misgivings, qualms, agitation, nerves, palpitations, shivers, quaking, shaking, trembling, gooseflesh, sinking stomach **3 worry**, anxiety,

uneasiness, angst, fretting, concern, care **4 intimidation**, frightening, terrorism, threatening, cowing, bullying, hectoring
ADJECTIVES **5 frightened**, afraid, scared, fearing, fear-stricken, terrified, terror-struck, horrified, horror-struck, aghast, petrified, panic-stricken, terrorized, intimidated, cowed, demoralized **6 fearful**, nervous, timorous, apprehensive, anxious, uneasy, alarmed, disquieted, agitated, jittery, jumpy, timid, tremulous, trembling, shaky, quaking, twitchy, tense, strained, highly strung, nervy, panicky, distressed, on edge **7 worried**, troubled, concerned, solicitous, caring, anxious, fretting, harassed, plagued, haunted **8 frightening**, fearsome, awesome, daunting, dismaying, formidable, menacing, intimidating, alarming, unnerving, startling, scaring, enervating, shocking, horrifying, terrifying, petrifying, terrible, frightful, fearful, dreadful, dire, grim, horrible, horrific, horrendous, ghastly, hideous, awful
VERBS **9 be afraid**, fear, dread, stand aghast, take fright, panic, tremble, shake, shiver, shudder, quiver, flinch, shrink, draw back, recoil, quail, blench, turn pale **10 be fearful**, be nervous, shrink, start, flutter, palpitate, twitch, have qualms **11 frighten**, scare, daunt, dismay, distress, alarm, menace, intimidate, cow, bully, terrorize, browbeat, bulldoze, unnerve, enervate, shake, shock, stagger, startle, panic, horrify, appal, terrify **12 worry**, concern, trouble, harass, fret, plague, haunt, torment

271 Feeling

NOUNS **1 feeling**, perception, sensation, sense, experience, aesthesia, awareness, consciousness, realization, understanding, knowledge **2 impression**, fancy, belief, idea, notion, inkling, intimation, suggestion, hint, nuance, undercurrent, intuition, sixth sense, insight, clairvoyance, presentiment, divination, instinct, impulse, reflex **3 feelings**, sentiments, sensibilities, susceptibilities, affections, sympathies, finer feelings, attitudes, beliefs, opinion, view **4 emotion**, mood, attitude, passion, ardour, fervour, fire, heat, verve, ecstasy, rapture, zeal, intensity, vehemence, obsession, fanaticism **5 good feeling**, fondness, sympathy, empathy, identification, cordiality, warmth, friendliness, amicability, responsiveness, involvement, liking, love **6 bad feeling**, animosity, resentment, bitterness, ill will, offence, dislike, intolerance, spite, jealousy, grudge, envy, hatred, fury, rage **7 emotionalism**, emotiveness, nostalgia, romanticism, sentimentality, mawkishness, bathos **8 seat of feelings**, secret places, heart, bosom, soul
ADJECTIVES **9 feeling**, sensing, sentient, sensible, perceptive, aware, conscious, knowing, realizing, understanding, responsive, sensitive, impressionable **10 intuitive**, instinctive, impulsive, inspirational, clairvoyant **11 sensitive**, sympathetic, empathetic, feeling, caring, fond, cordial, friendly, amicable, warm, soft-hearted, tender, romantic, nostalgic, sentimental, bathetic, maudlin, mawkish, emotional, tearful, overcome, overwhelmed, overwrought **12 pas-**

sionate, intense, effusive, ardent, fervent, zealous, vehement, rapturous, ecstatic, fiery, heated, inflamed, excitable, impetuous, hotheaded, temperamental, touchy, volatile, mercurial, unstable, melodramatic, hysterical, obsessed, jealous, envious, fanatical, manic, raving **13 emotive**, affecting, touching, moving

VERBS 14 feel, experience, sense, perceive, realize, understand, live through **15 feel in one's bones**, sense, intuit **16 feel deeply**, have hysterics, go mad, see red, run amok **17 feel for**, empathize, relate to, sympathize, commiserate, pity, grieve for **18 believe**, think, opine

272 Female

NOUNS 1 female sex, womankind, womanhood, femininity, womanliness, muliebrity, girlishness, feminism, women's rights, gynography, matriarchy, gynarchy, gynocracy, gynaecology, gyniatrics **2 female**, woman, lady, matron, dowager, girl, she, her, herself, Eve, colleen, grisette, midinette, virago **3 female title of address**, Miss, Mrs, Ms, Madam, ma'am, marm, mistress, missus, Dame, Lady, lady, milady, her ladyship, mademoiselle, madame, Frau, Fraulein, Donna, signora, signorina, señora, señorita **4 womenfolk**, women, the girls, the sisterhood, matronage, distaff side, women's quarters, harem, seraglio, zenana **5 female animal**, lioness, tigress, cow, heifer, mare, filly, hind, doe, vixen, sow, gilt, ewe, ewe-lamb, she-goat, nanny goat, bitch

ADJECTIVES 6 female, feminine, womanly, womanish, ladylike, girlish, maidenly, matronly, child-bearing, feminist

273 Fertility

NOUNS 1 fertility, fecundity, fruitfulness, exuberance, luxuriance, lushness, richness, abundance, plenty, plenitude, wealth, riot, profusion, rich harvest, Mother Earth, hotbed, seedbed, nursery, cornucopia **2 productiveness**, mass production, boom, economic upturn, prosperity, overproductiveness, superabundance, superfluity, glut, butter mountain, wine lake, population explosion, baby boom, biotic potential, menarche, menstruation, procreation, reproduction, propagation, fructification, fecundation, fertilization, pollination, resourcefulness, inventiveness **3 fertilizer**, manure, dung, guano, compost, bonemeal, fishmeal, slurry, phosphates, nitrates, potash, ammonium salts, sulphates, lime, marl, dressing, topdressing, mulch, seed, semen, sperm, fertility drug **4 fertility cult**, rite, phallic symbol, phallus, lingam, yoni, Earth Goddess, Earth Mother

ADJECTIVES 5 fertile, fecund, fruitful, fructiferous, productive, profitable, paying, lucrative, remunerative, high-yielding, generative, prolific, multiparous, teeming, streaming, pouring, copious, abundant, plentiful, profuse, bountiful, fat, lush, verdant, luxuriant, rich, rife, exuberant, thriving, flourishing, prosperous, booming, pregnant, parturient, procreant, propagatory, regenerative, creative

VERBS 6 be fertile, thrive, flourish, burgeon, bloom, blossom, fructify, germinate, conceive, give birth, bear, teem, swarm, pullulate, proliferate, mushroom, multiply, boom, populate **7 make fertile**, fecundate, fructify, plant, fertilize, manure, compost, top-dress, mulch, marl, enrich, feed, water, irrigate, impregnate, inseminate, pollinate, propagate, produce

274 Few

NOUNS 1 few, not many, some, couple, handful, almost none, poor turnout, low attendance, scattering, sprinkling, trickle, small quantity, little, soupçon, derisory amount, dash, hint **2 least**, minimum, less, minority **3 fewness**, sparsity, scarcity, scantiness, exiguity, paucity, dearth, lack, deficiency, skimpiness, meagreness, shortage, undersupply, underpopulation **4 rarity**, infrequency

ADJECTIVES 5 few, some, not many, hardly any, little, not much **6 sparse**, scant, light, thin, little, minimal, meagre, exiguous, measly, niggardly, infrequent, occasional, sporadic, intermittent, rare, uncommon, scarce, strung out, widely spaced, dispersed, scattered, sprinkled, dotted about, underpopulated, low-density **7 fewer**, less, reduced, diminished, least, minimum, minimal

VERBS 8 reduce, diminish, rarefy, thin, weed out, eliminate, decimate, pare down, scale down, cut back, prune, trim, rationalize **9 scatter**, sprinkle, dot about, string out, space out

275 Fishes

NOUNS 1 fishes, fish, Pisces, shoal **2 fish**, jawless fish, cyclostome, cartilaginous fish, Chondrichthyes, elasmobranch, selachian, holocephalan, bony fish, lobe-finned fish, crossopterygian, dipnoan, ray-finned fish, teleost fish, flying fish, mouthbrooder, flatfish, food fish, game fish, aquarium fish **3 young fish**, fry, elver, alevin, fingerling, parr, smolt **4 fossil fish**, placoderm, arthrodire, ostracoderm, Pteraspis, crossopterygian, Osteolepis, living fossil **5 fish anatomy**, fin, scale, gill, gill cover, operculum, gill slit, spiracle, swim bladder, air bladder, lateral line **6 study of fish**, ichthyology, fish breeding, aquarium, fish pond, fishtank **7 fishing**, piscatology, angling, game fishing, coarse fishing, fly fishing, sea fishing, big-game fishing, deep-sea fishing, shark fishing, whaling, fish farming, pisciculture, fishery, fishing bank, fishing ground, piscary, fishing fleet, trawler, shrimper, fish-finder, fish-hold, fishing line, fishnet, trawl, drift net, seine, catch, tonnara, eel basket, fishgig, fishtrap, fish weir, fish ladder, gill net, shark net **8 food fish**, cod, haddock, mackerel, herring, whitebait, sprat, sardine, flatfish, plaice, sole, halibut, turbot, game fish, salmon, trout, wet fish, pan fish, preserved fish, smoked fish, kipper, bloater, brisling, smoked haddock, finnan haddock, stockfish, jellied eel **9 fish product**, roe, caviar, cod-liver oil, fishmeal, fish glue **10 fisher**, angler, whaler, fisherman, trawlerman, piscator, pisciculturalist, fishmonger, fishman **11 ichthyologist**, aquarist

ADJECTIVES 12 fishlike, fishy, piscine, pisciform, piscatorial, ichthyic, ichthyomorphic, sharklike, sharkish, selachian, clupeoid, gadoid,

percoid, cyprinoid **13 ichthyological**, piscicultural, piscatorial
VERBS 14 fish, angle, fly-fish, trawl, net

276 Five and Over

NOUNS 1 five, cinque, quintet, fivesome, quintuplicate, quintuplet, quin, fifth, pentagon, pentahedron, pentagram, pentacle, pentameter, pentastich, Pentateuch, pentarchy, pentathlon, pentachord, quint, quinquereme, quincunx, cinquefoil, five-finger, quinquennium, pentathlon, five-a-side, five-by-five, five stones **2 six**, half-a-dozen, hexad, sextet, sextuplicate, sextuplet, sixth, sextile, hexagon, hexahedron, hexagram, hexameter, sixain, Hexateuch, hexachord, hexapod, sixth sense, six-footer, six-shooter **3 seven**, heptad, septet, septenary, septuplicate, septuplet, seventh, heptagon, heptahedron, heptameter, Heptateuch, diminished seventh, seven days **4 eight**, octad, octet, octonary, octuplet, octagon, octahedron, octave, Octateuch, octopus, octarchy **5 nine**, ennead, nonet, nonary, novena, nonuplet, nonagon, enneagon, enneahedron **6 ten**, decade, decennium, decagon, decahedron, decapod, decagram, decathlon, Decalogue, Ten Commandments, tenth **7 double figures**, eleven, undecagon, hendecagon, hendecahedron, twelve, dozen, dodecagon, dodecahedron, duodecimal, duodecimo, twelfth man, Twelfth Night, Twelfth Day, twelvemonth, teens, teenager, thirteen, baker's dozen, long dozen, fourteen, two weeks, fortnight, fifteen, quindecaplet, quindecagon, quindecennial, sixteen **8 twenty and over**, score, twenty-four, two dozen, twenty-five, pony, silver jubilee, forty, twoscore, quadragenarian, fifty, half century, jubilee, quinquagenarian, sixty, threescore, sexagenary, sexagenarian, seventy, septuagenarian, eighty, fourscore, octogenarian, ninety **9 treble figures**, one hundred, century, one hundredfold, centuple, centuplicate, hundred percent, centennial, centenary, centennium, centenarian, centurion, centimetre, centigrade, centipede, gross, two-hundred, bicentennial, bicentenary, three hundred, tercentennial, tercentenary, four hundred, quatercentenary, five hundred, quincentenary, six centuries, sexcentenary, seven centuries, eight centuries, octocentenary, nine centuries, ten centuries **10 thousand**, K, chiliad, millennium, millenary, milligram, millilitre, millimetre, kilometre, kilogram, kilo, kilobyte, gigabyte, millipede, ten thousand, myriad, hundred thousand **11 million**, crore, billion, milliard, trillion, quadrillion, quintillion, sextillion, septillion, octillion, nonillion, decillion, undecillion, duodecillion, tredecillion, quattuordecillion, quindecillion, sexdecillion, septendecillion, octodecillion, novemdecillion, vigintillion, centrillion
ADJECTIVES 12 fifth, fivefold, quintuple, quintuplicate, quinary, quinquennial, quintic, quinquepartite, pentadic, pentagonal, pentangular, pentahedral **13 sixth**, sixfold, sextuple, sextuplicate, sexennial, sexpartite, hexadic, hexagonal, hexangular, hexahedral **14 seventh**, sevenfold, septuple, septuplicate,

septenary, septennial, heptadic, heptagonal, heptangular, heptahedral **15 eighth**, eightfold, octuple, octonary, octennial, octadic, octagonal, octangular, octahedral **16 ninth**, ninefold, nonuple, novenary, nonary, enneadic, nonagonal, enneagonal **17 tenth**, tenfold, decuple, decimal, denary, decennial, decagonal **18 eleventh**, undecennial, hendecagonal, twelfth, duodenary, duodecimal, fifteenth, quindecagonal, quindecennial, sixteenth, hexadecimal **19 twentieth**, vigesimal, vicenary **20 hundredth**, centesimal, centennial, centenary, centenarian, hundredfold, centuple **21 thousandth**, millenary, millenarian, millenial **22 millionth**, billionth

VERBS 23 quintuple, quintuplicate, sextuple, sextuplicate, septuple, octuple, centuple, centuplicate

277 Flattery

NOUNS 1 flattery, adulation, compliments, praise, overpraise, overlaudation, overcommendation, hagiography, panegyric, hype, insincerity **2 blarney**, honeyed words **3 cajolery**, wheedling, inveiglement, blandishments **4 unctuousness**, oiliness, smarminess **5 sycophancy**, servility, toadyism, fawning

VERBS 6 flatter, adulate, compliment, overpraise, overlaud, overcommend, overesteem, overestimate, hype **7 blarney**, sugar, charm, smarm, oil **8 cajole**, wheedle, inveigle, blandish, coax, court, ingratiate oneself **9 be sycophantic**, insinuate oneself, toady, fawn, creep, crawl

ADJECTIVES 10 flattering, adulatory, complimentary, laudatory, praising, insincere, hypocritical **11 honeyed**, sugary, saccharine, blarneying, honey-tongued, smooth-tongued **12 cajoling**, wheedling, inveigling, blandishing, coaxing **13 unctuous**, oily, smarmy, slimy **14 sycophantic**, servile, obsequious, toadyish, fawning, creeping, crawling

278 Flowers

NOUNS 1 flower, floweret, floret, bloom, blossom, wild flower, garden flower, pot plant, flower arrangement, spray, cut flowers, posy, bouquet, garland, wreath, nosegay, daisy chain, buttonhole, boutonniere, dried flower, everlasting flower **2 flowering plant**, flowerer, bloomer, annual, biennial, ephemeral **3 flower part**, sepal, calyx, petal, nectary, corolla, perianth, floral envelope, epicalyx, involucre, bract, whorl, spathe, stamen, filament, anther, androecium, pollen, stigma, style, ovary, carpel, gynoecium, pistil, ovule, micropyle, receptacle, floral diagram **4 flower head**, inflorescence, raceme, panicle, corymb, spadix, spikelet, catkin, ament, umbel, capitulum, cyme, monochasium, dichasium, thyrse **5 flowering**, florescence, efflorescence, blossoming, blooming, flowerage, unfolding, anthesis, blow **6 pollination**, cross-pollination, self-pollination **7 flower culture**, floriculture, floristics, floriculturist, florist, flower seller **8 flower product**, nectar, rose water, rose oil, lavender water

ADJECTIVES 9 floral, flowered, flowery, bloomy, floristic, flower-like, fragrant, florid, ornate **10 flowering**, in flower, in bloom, blossoming, blooming, flourishing, florescent

VERBS 11 flower, bud, bloom, blossom, blow

279 Fluid

NOUNS 1 fluid, liquid, liquor, water, drink, beverage, liquid extract **2 juice**, sap, extract, latex, milk, whey, buttermilk, ghee, water, gravy, stock, meat juice, sauce, gippo **3 body fluid**, lymph, plasma, blood, humour, chyle, rheum, serum, pus, matter, purulence, suppuration, ichor, sanies, discharge, gleet, leukorrhoea, mucus, mucor, phlegm, saliva, spittle, urine, excrement, semen, menstrual flow, sweat, perspiration, tears, milk, colostrum, lactation, dropsy, oedema **4 blood**, lifeblood, gore, claret, serum, plasma, synthetic plasma, dextran, blood cell, erythrocyte, leucocyte, lymphocyte, neutrophil, phagocyte, blood platelet, haemoglobin, clot, thrombosis, blood pressure, blood group, Rhesus factor, antigen, antibody, globulin, opsonin, blood count, circulation, bloodstream, blood bank **5 fluidity**, liquidity, fluxure, liquefaction, colliquation, juiciness, sappiness, pulpiness, wateriness, runniness, rheuminess, nonviscosity, noncoagulation, haemophilia, solubleness, liquidescence, bloodiness, goriness **6 flow**, fluency, flux, haemorrhage, suppuration **7 juiciness**, sappiness, milkiness, succulence, lactescence, chylifaction, serosity **8 fluidification**, liquefaction, colliquefaction, solubility, deliquation, liquescency, deliquescence, fluxibility, solution, dissolving, decoagulation, melting, thawing, unfreezing, running, fusing, solubilization, lixiviation, percolation **9 solvent**, liquifier, dissolvent, dissolving agent, menstruum, anticoagulent, hydragogue, resolvent, thinner, diluent, flux **10 solution**, infusion, decoction, suspension, emulsion, apozem, flux, lixivium **11 liquidizer**, blender, food processor **12 flowmeter**, fluidmeter **13 fluid mechanics**, hydraulics, hydrogeology, hydrology, hydrometry, hydrostatics

ADJECTIVES 14 fluid, liquid, fluidic, liquiform, uncongealed **15 flowing**, fluent, fluxive, watery, runny, juicy, sappy, moist, succulent **16 rheumy**, weeping, pussy, purulent, suppurating, sanious, ichorous, phlegmy, humoral, serous, chylific, tearlike **17 milky**, lacteal, lacteous, lactic, lactescent **18 bloody**, gory, bleeding, sanguineous, haemic, haemal, haemogenic **19 liquefied**, dissolved, deliquescent, melted, molten, thawed, decoagulated, liquescent, liquefacient **20 liquefying**, colliquative, thawing, melting, fusing, dissolving, dissolutional **21 liquefiable**, soluble, meltable, fusible, thawable

VERBS 22 make fluid, liquefy, liquidize, fluidize, fluidify, blend **23 dissolve**, solve, thin, solubilize, decoagulate, unclot, leach, lixiviate, percolate, decoct, infuse **24 melt**, run, thaw, smelt, defrost, unfreeze, render, clarify, deliquesce, fuse **25 flow**, run, stream, pour, well up, gush, spout, vomit forth, spew out, bleed, flood, weep, seep

280 Fold

NOUNS 1 fold, bend, turn, overlap, layer, roll, furl, coil, doubling, dog-ear, plication, plica, flexure, flection, buckling, anticline **2 pleat**, plait, crease, pucker, tuck, gather, ruche, ruffle, shirr, flounce, ruck, rumple, wrinkle, crinkle, crumple, crimp, ripple, furrow **3 enfoldment**, envelopment, enclosure, wrapping, swathing, entwining, hug, embrace **4 closure**, closing, shutting, financial failure

ADJECTIVES 5 folded, bent, pleated, plicate, flexuous, doubled over, turned over, dog-eared, rolled, creased, rucked up, flexed **6 closed**, close-down, shut-down

VERBS 7 fold, lap, double over, turn over, turn up, dog-ear, bend, buckle, overlap, layer, roll, furl **8 pleat**, crease, pucker, tuck up, gather, ruffle, shirr, flounce, ruck, rumple, wrinkle, crinkle, crumple, crimp, ripple, furrow **9 enfold**, envelop, enclose, wrap, swathe, entwine, intertwine, hug, embrace **10 close**, shut down

281 Folly

NOUNS 1 folly, foolishness, stupidity, ineptitude, inanity, rashness, recklessness, madness, senselessness, silliness, absurdity, ridiculousness, ludicrousness, asininity, childishness, puerility, fatuousness, pointlessness, extravagance, frivolity, flippancy, conceit, giddiness, irresponsibility, imprudence, indiscretion, heedlessness, thoughtlessness, ignorance, unintelligence, eccentricity, insanity, lunacy, idiocy, imbecility, feeble-mindedness, empty-headedness, senility **2 act of folly**, foolery, tomfoolery, mistake, error, misjudgment, gaffe **3 foolish person**, fool, simpleton, imbecile, idiot, moron, cretin, halfwit, ass, jackass, dolt, blockhead, dunce **4 rash person**, hothead, daredevil, adventurer

ADJECTIVES 5 foolish, stupid, inept, inane, mad, ill-advised, ill-considered, unwise, imprudent, injudicious, uncircumspect, incautious, rash, reckless, foolhardy, harebrained, heedless, inattentive, hotheaded, hellbent, headstrong, prodigal, devil-may-care, frivolous, flippant, silly, asinine, idiotic, imbecilic, moronic, lunatic, insane, senseless, brainless, ignorant, unintelligent, dim-witted, feeble-minded, empty-headed, simple, slow, doltish, dull, gormless, fatuous, pointless, absurd, ludicrous, ridiculous, nonsensical, preposterous, childish, puerile

VERBS 6 be foolish, go mad, tempt fate **7 play the fool**, clown around

282 Foresight

VERBS 1 foresee, see ahead, foreknow, predict, forecast, prophesy, divine, augur, forewarn, be clairvoyant, scent, expect, envisage, anticipate, forestall, surmise, suppose, presume, forejudge, portend, foreshadow, forebode, promise, presage, foretell, predetermine **2 show prudence**, be cautious, plan ahead, guard against

NOUNS 3 foresight, prevision, prediction, forecast, prophecy, prognosis, certainty, expectation, anticipation, foretaste, precognition, foreknowledge, prescience, second sight, clairvoyancy, telepathy, premonition, presentiment, foreboding, forewarning, divination, augury, portent, omen, astrology, horoscope, fortune-telling, palmistry, crystal-gazing **4 prudence**, caution, care, circumspection, wisdom, sagacity, forethought,

precaution, plan, longsightedness, farsightedness, providence, readiness, preparation, intelligent anticipation, perspicacity, insight, vision, futurology, premeditation, predetermination, predestination
ADJECTIVES 5 foreseeing, predictive, prophetic, prognostic, precognitive, prospective, clairvoyant, intuitive, telepathic, second-sighted, prescient, farsighted, longsighted, weather-wise, expectant, anticipant, anticipatory, prudent, provident, cautious, careful, circumspect, wise **6 foreseeable**, predictable

283 Forgiveness

• *To err is human, to forgive, divine.* Alexander Pope.

NOUNS 1 forgiveness, pardon, amnesty, excuse, reprieve, sparing, indemnity, exemption, immunity, grace, dispensation, absolution, remission **2 forgivingness**, mercifulness, clemency, compassion, kindness, benevolence, magnanimity, unresentfulness, unrevengefulness, placability, lenity, long-suffering, forbearance, patience, tolerance, indulgence, stoicism, overlooking **3 absolution**, acquittal, cancellation, discharge, release, deliverance, freeing, exoneration, condonation, exculpation, vindication, justification, reconciliation, conciliation, redemption, pacification
ADJECTIVES 4 forgiving, pardoning, excusing, reprieving, sparing, absolving, shriving, exonerating, condoning, vindicating, justifying, reconciling, conciliatory, redeeming, pacifying **5 merciful**, compassionate, kind, clement, benevolent, magnanimous, unresentful, unrevengeful, unreproachful, placable, lenient, long-suffering, forbearing, patient, tolerant, indulgent **6 forgiven**, pardoned, excused, granted amnesty, reprieved, spared, absolved, shriven, indulged, remitted, acquitted, cancelled, discharged, released, delivered, freed, let off, exonerated, condoned, exculpated, vindicated, justified, reconciled, redeemed, pacified, rehabilitated, atoned, restored, reinstated **7 forgivable**, pardonable, venial, excusable **8 overlooked**, disregarded
VERBS 9 forgive, pardon, excuse, reprieve, spare, indemnify, exempt, absolve, grant absolution, shrive, forget, reconcile, conciliate, redeem, make peace **10 absolve**, acquit, vindicate, cancel, discharge, release, deliver, free, let off, exonerate, exculpate, remit, dismiss **11 condone**, overlook, disregard, connive, justify, wink at, ignore, let pass **12 show mercy**, show compassion, leave unavenged, be lenient, tolerate, endure, bear with, unbend, soften **13 ask forgiveness**, beg pardon

284 Form

NOUNS 1 form, structure, order, system, conformation, format, configuration, construction, composition, composure, gestalt, shape, figure, profile, contour, frame, lines, outline, silhouette, relief, pattern, arrangement, design, essence, substance, nominalism, Platonism, idea, morphology **2 prototype**, formula, format, model, dummy, mould, example, paradigm, pattern, jig, template, stencil, matrix, frame, blank, punch, stamp, cast, die **3 kind**, type, sort, variety, character, order, genre **4 forming**, formulation, creation, morphogenesis, construction, production, expression, fashioning, modelling, moulding, tailoring, knitting, weaving, shaping, setup, makeup **5 formality**, decorum, etiquette, protocol, behaviour, conduct, practice, routine, habit, fashion, trend, style, custom, tradition, convention, procedure, litigation, ceremony, ritual **6 nature**, health, fitness, condition, shape, fettle, soundness, character, attitude, turn, appearance, features, lineament, face, expression, look, mein, aspect, demeanour, cast, set, physiognomy, physique, anatomy, body, build, ectomorph, figure, trim

VERBS 7 form, structure, order, systematize, formalize, arrange, pattern, figure, design, draft, sketch, formulate, draw, format, lay out, shape, turn, round, square, frame, outline, silhouette, cut out, whittle, hew, carve, chisel, sculpt, mould, model, knead, cast, coin, mint, stamp, found, hammer out, punch out, forge, smith, fashion, work, build, construct, create, make, produce, express **8 be formal**, conform, comply, follow protocol, practise etiquette, behave well

ADJECTIVES 9 formed, orderly, systematic, conformable, configurational, creative, made, constructed, produced, shaped, sculptured, carved, moulded, modelled, tailored, turned, rounded, squared, fashioned, set-up, composed, styled, stylish, expressive, morphologic, morphogenic, isomorphic, Platonic, concrete, solid, plastic **10 prototypical**, original, exemplary, dummy, paradigmatic, generic, model, custom-built, ready-made, tailor-made **11 formal**, conventional, procedural, protocol, decorous, behavioural, traditional, ceremonial, solemn, ritual, customary, routine, habitual, litigious, ritualistic, fashionable, trendy **12 on form**, fit, able, capable, healthy, salubrious

285 Formality

NOUNS 1 formality, state, dignity, ceremoniousness, stiffness, sedateness, staidness, starchiness, solemnity, royal we, etiquette, correct behaviour, protocol, smartness, correctness, fastidiousness, decorum, stiff-neckedness, straitlacedness, hideboundness, stuffiness, preciseness, red carpet, conventionality, propriety, stylization, primness, rigidness, pomp, circumstance, pride, gravity **2 formalism**, ritualism, ceremonialism, pedantry, preciseness, preciousness, purism, punctiliousness, scrupulousness, conventionalism, over-refinement, over-preciseness **3 formal occasion**, ceremony, procedure, ritual, drill, practice, routine, celebration, spectacle, tableau, scene, show, turnout, review, march past, pageant, fête, gala, tournament, tattoo, field day, red-letter day, rite, liturgy, service, Christening, wedding, funeral, coronation, convocation, graduation, inauguration, initiation **4 etiquette**, formalities, social graces, custom, good manners, politeness, civilities, comity, decencies, elegancies, mores, proprieties, decorum, right form, protocol, diplomatic code

ADJECTIVES 5 formal, formulary, for-

malistic, legalistic, pedantic, stately, dignified, ceremonious, stiff, refined, starchy, sedate, staid, stilted, rigid, solemn, royal, correct, smart, precise, conventional, ritual, procedural, official, stylized, prim, punctilious, precise, scrupulous, fastidious, precious, puristic, exact, meticulous, orderly, methodical, elegant, decorous, proud, grave, pompous **6 dressed up**, uniformed, black-tie, white-tie, chic, soignée, stylish, modish, fashionable, dolled up **7 ceremonious**, ritual, solemn, pompous
VERBS 8 formalize, ritualize, solemnize, conventionalize **9 celebrate**, dignify **10 be formal**, follow protocol

286 Forward Motion

VERBS 1 go forward, proceed, progress, advance, go forward, pass on, move, travel, get along **2 start**, set off, embark **3 press on**, push, drive on, keep on, make leeway, push on, gain ground, gather way, forge ahead, climb, gain height **4 make good time**, recoup **5 develop**, evolve, show promise, come on, get on, do well **6 march on**, rub on, jog on, roll on, flow **7 make one's way**, inch forward, muddle through, further oneself, get somewhere, climb, reach towards **8 further**, bring on, foster, contribute to, advance, aid, raise, lift, elevate, bounce up, promote, upgrade, improve, better, forward, hasten, modernize, push, force, develop, grow, augment, step up, accelerate, propose, favour, make for **9 maintain progress**, overtake, gain on, distance, outstrip, leave behind
NOUNS 10 forward motion, progress, advance, headway, rolling on **11 course**, march, passage, way, ongoing, career, tide, current, flood, ongo, go ahead **12 advance**, promotion, preferment, leg-up, furtherance, rise, lift, ascent, elevation, gain, enterprise, success, achievement, economic progress **13 step**, stride, jump, leap, spurt **14 development**, growth, evolution, furtherance **15 improvement**, betterment, reform, perfectability, irreversibility, getting ahead, overtaking
ADJECTIVES 16 forward, progressive, advanced, up-to-date, forward-looking, go-ahead, enterprising **17 ongoing**, continuing, inexorable, irreversible, onward, oncoming, proceeding, moving, profluent

287 Four

NOUNS 1 four, quatre, quartet, foursome, tetrad, quaternity, quadruple, quadruplet **2 quadrilateral**, tetragon, quadrangle, square, rectangle, oblong, parallelogram, rhombus, trapezium, trapezoid **3 foursome**, quadruped, tetrapod, tetradactyl, quadrennium, quadrille, square dance, quatrefoil, four-leaf clover, four-in-hand, four-poster, four winds, four seasons, tetrameter, quatrain, tetragram, tetragrammation, tetralogy **4 quadruplication**, quadruplicature, quadrupling **5 quadrisection**, quadripartition **6 quarter**, fourth
ADJECTIVES 7 four, quaternary, quadratic, quadruple, quadruplex, fourfold **8 quadrilateral**, four-sided, square, rectangular, quadrate, tetrahedral **9 tetramerous**, quadruped, four-legged, four-footed, quadraphonic, quadrennial, tetravalent **10 quartered**,

quadrisected, quadripartite, four-part, four-handed, four-stroke
VERBS 11 quadruple, quadruplicate, increase fourfold **12 quadrisect**, quarter

288 Fraction

NOUNS 1 fraction, simple fraction, common fraction, vulgar fraction, compound fraction, proper fraction, improper fraction **2 fractional part**, part, percentage, proportion, portion, share, piece, section, segment, division, subdivision **3 fragment**, particle, sliver, shred, bit, atom, iota, whit, jot **4 less than one**, half, third, quarter, fourth, fifth, sixth, seventh, eighth, ninth, tenth, eleventh, twelfth, thirteenth, fourteenth, fifteenth, sixteenth, seventeenth, eighteenth, nineteenth, twentieth, thirtieth, fourtieth, fiftieth, sixtieth, seventieth, eightieth, ninetieth, hundredth, thousandth
ADJECTIVES 5 fractional, half, quarter, partial, fragmentary, incomplete, proportional, sectional, segmental, divisional **6 small**, tiny

289 Fragrance

NOUNS 1 fragrance, sweet smell, bouquet, aroma, scent, perfume, muskiness, spiciness, balminess **2 fragrant thing**, new-baked bread, fresh coffee, wax polish, sea air, new-mown hay, flower garden, herbs, spices, flower, bouquet, posy, nosegay, buttonhole, corsage, orange blossom, honeysuckle, lily, sweet pea, gardenia, lavender, jasmine, rose, stephanotis, violet, carnation, tuberose, cloves, vanilla, sweet cicely, essence, essential oil, fixative, toiletries, body lotion, talcum powder, bath oil, scented soap, rose water, lavender water, scent, perfume, aftershave, pomade, atomizer, lavender bag, pomander, potpourri, pastille **3 incense**, frangipani, resin, olibanum, frankincense, myrrh, camphor, eucalyptus, spikenard, musk, civet, otto, ambergris, patchouli, sandalwood, vetiver, chypre, censer, thurible
ADJECTIVES 4 fragrant, sweet-smelling, scented, perfumed, aromatic, flowery, floral, spicy, musky, fruity, pungent, heady, camphorated, balmy
VERBS 5 be fragrant, smell sweet **6 perfume**, scent, aromatize, spray, burn incense, cense

290 Freedom

• *Man was born free and everywhere he is in chains.* Jean Jacques Rousseau.

NOUNS 1 freedom, liberty, unrestraint, noncoercion, nonintimidation, option, choice, prerogative, discretion, initiative, pwn responsibility, own volition, liberation, licence, privilege, exemption, nonliability, exception, immunity, discharge, release, deliverance, emancipation, broad-mindedness, open-mindedness, toleration, liberalism, libertarianism, latitudinarianism, freethinking, bohemianism, nonconformity, noninterference, nonintervention, high seas, self-regulating market, open market, capitalism, noninvolvement, seclusion, nonalignment, neutrality **2 free speech**, rights, First Amendment, civil rights **3 independence**, own authority, self-determination, individualism, self-expression, self-reliance, self-sufficiency, independent means, wealth, no allegiance, umarried state, bachelorhood, maidenhood, franchisement, citizenship, authority, statehood, national status, unilaterality, autonomy, autarky, self-government **4 informality**, ease, familiarity, frankness, candidness, relaxation, friendliness, casualness, candour, openness **5 scope**, play, full opportunity, wide range, manoeuvrability, room, elbowroom, wide berth, leverage, leeway, latitude **6 liberality**, carte blanche, blank cheque, free hand, laxness, laxity, licence, excess, libertinism, immoderation, uninhibitedness, intemperance, incontinence, free love, unruliness, abandon, licentiousness

ADJECTIVES 7 free, emancipated, liberated, franchised, authorized, constitutional, inalienable, national, unilateral, autonomous, self-governing, autarkic, self-determining, unconfined, unrestrained, unregulated, unhindered, unimpeded, unshackled, unfettered, unbridled, uncurbed, unbound, unchecked, ungoverned, acquitted, at large, discharged, released, privileged, exempt, nonliable, excepted, immune, noninvolved, secluded, nonaligned, nonpartisan, neutral, isolationist, noninterventional, free-trade, self-regulating, open, capitalistic, broad-minded, unbiased, unprejudiced, uninfluenceable, cross-bench, undecided, floating, moderate, just, tolerant **8 independent**, individual, self-employed, freelance, wildcat, free-minded, maverick, individualistic, self-reliant, self-sufficient, self-contained, self-supporting, self-motivated, inner-directed, unsubjected, freewheeling, ungoverned, anarchic, uncontrolled, uncompelled, uninfluenced, unattached, indifferent, unconventional, breakaway, dissenting, rationalist, humanist, nonbelieving, latitudinarian, bohemian, nonconforming, eccentric **9 ranging**, travelling, free-range, unconfined, untethered, unfettered **10 unconditional**, unrestricted, unlimited, without strings, anything goes, absolute, discretionary, arbitrary, liberated, lax, excess, immoderate, loose, uninhibited, unbridled, intemperate, incontinent, unruly, abandoned, licentious, wanton, impure **11 informal**, relaxed, casual, easygoing, at home, retired, familiar, frank, candid, open, self-expressive, plain-spoken, uninhibited, unconstrained, spontaneous

VERBS 12 be free, escape, enjoy liberty **13 set free**, emancipate, manumit, enfranchise, liberate, release, let go, let off, excuse, grant immunity, exempt, except, loose, unchain, untie, rescue, deliver, extricate, give scope, allow initiative, facilitate, not interfere, not tamper **14 be independent**, freelance, have authority, have self-reliance, stay unmarried, please oneself, roam, stray, drift **15 be informal**, show candour **16 have scope**, range **17 liberalize**, live immoderately, lack restraint, take liberties, presume, cut loose

291 Friction

NOUNS 1 friction, rubbing, drag, force, resistance, viscosity, roughness, rub, affriction **2 wearing away**, attrition, abrasion, erosion, wear, corrosion, detrition, ablation, collision, rubbing out, erasure, obliteration **3 grinding**, filing, rasping, fretting, limation, chafing, galling, chafe **4 scraping**, scratching, grazing, scuffing, scrubbing, scouring, scratch **5 polishing**, rubbing, burnishing, sanding, smoothing, buffing, shining, dressing **6 massage**, massotherapy, stroking, rubdown, kneading, facial, shampoo, whirlpool bath **7 eraser**, rubber, scraper, sander, sanding disc, sandpaper, glasspaper, emery paper, emery board, nailfile, file, rasp, face mask **8 irritation**, grating, prickliness

ADJECTIVES 9 frictional, abrasive, anatriptic, irritant, rubbing, attritive, erosive, ablative **10 rough**, rasping, grating, grinding, chafing

VERBS 11 rub, smooth, polish, wax, levigate, burnish, furbish, buff, scour, scrub, sandpaper, sand, sandblast, dress, brush **12 abrade**, frictionize, abrase, rub against, scrape, scuff, graze, raze, bark, scratch **13 erode**, corrode, wear, fray, frazzle, skin, erase, rub out **14 grind**, rasp, file, plane, grate, catch, stick, chafe, gall, fret **15 massage**, knead, rub down, pulverize, shampoo, smooth, iron out, stroke

292 Friendship

NOUNS 1 friendship, fellowship, companionship, amicableness, amiableness, amity, acquaintanceship, camaraderie, fraternization, comradeship, colleagueship, togetherness, solidarity, cooperation, concord, harmony, sociability, neighbourliness, good will, benevolence, philanthropy, kindness, hospitality, warmth, ardency, love, cordiality, courtesy, regard, heartiness, bonhomie, geniality, brotherhood, fraternalism, sodality, confraternity, freemasonry, sorority, sisterhood, partiality, prejudice, favouritism, partisanship **2 friendly relations**, compatibility, harmony, rapport, sympathy, understanding, fellow feeling, mutual support, mutual respect, entente cordiale **3 familiarity**, intimacy, closeness, nearness, inseparability, affinity, devotion, dedication, steadfastness, commitment, firmness, staunchness, constancy, trueness **4 act of friendship**, toast, handshake, embrace, hug, kiss, rubbing noses, open arms, holding hands **5 friend**, acquaintance, companion, fellow, colleague, comrade, shipmate, messmate, playmate, roommate, classmate, schoolmate

ADJECTIVES 6 friendly, cordial, courteous, amicable, amiable, kindly, peaceable, unhostile, sociable, affectionate, gracious, harmonious, pleasant, congenial, compatible, cooperative, agreeable, favourable, hospitable, demonstrative, effusive, back-slapping, ardent, warm, genial, well-meaning, well-disposed, well-intended, generous, benevolent, philanthropic, companionable, fraternal, confraternal, neighbourly, welcoming, receptive, hearty, sympathetic, understanding **7 friends with**, acquainted **8 familiar**, intimate, close, near, inseparable, favourite **9 devoted**, dedicated, supportive, loyal, true, tried-and-true, tested, faithful, steadfast, constant, committed, firm, fast, staunch **10 favourable**, beneficial, helpful, promising, auspicious, propitious, advantageous

VERBS 11 befriend, fraternize with, hobnob with, get acquainted, make overtures, warm to, show benevolence **12 seek the friendship of**, make advances, court, woo, run after, date **13 be hospitable**, entertain, greet, shake hands, embrace, introduce, acquaint, present, carve **14 be favourable**, help, promise

293 Front

NOUNS 1 front, forefront, fore, frontage, facade, foreground, entrance, foyer, vestibule, lobby, forecourt, antechamber, anteroom, proscenium, seafront, shore, marina, promenade, esplanade, strand, battlefront, first, beginning, introduction, preliminaries, prefix, preface, foreword, frontispiece, prelims, prologue, avant-garde, vanguard, spearhead, figurehead, prow, bowsprit, forecastle, foredeck **2 face**, visage, facade, physiognomy, countenance, profile, fullface picture **3 show**, outward appearance, projected image, persona, mask, façade **4 assurance**, confidence, self-confidence, composure, equanimity **5 boldness**, cheek, nerve, audacity, brazenness, brassiness, arrogance

ADJECTIVES 6 front, fore, foreground, frontal, entrance, obverse, anterior, preceding, forward, physiognomic, full-faced **7 outward**, surface, facial, superficial, displayed, projected **8 assured**, self-confident, composed **9 arrogant**, overconfident

VERBS 10 be in front, come forward, be first, ante, lead, head, introduce, prefix, preface, prelude, spearhead, challenge

294 Fruits

NOUNS 1 fruits, produce, crop, yield, soft fruit, stone fruit, citrus fruit, dried fruit, nuts, kernels, grain, seeds, pulses, vegetables, legumes, roots, tubers, green vegetables **2 botanical fruit**, simple fruit, true fruit, composite fruit, aggregate fruit, multiple fruit, false fruit, succulent fruit, citrus fruit, drupe, berry, pome, pepo, sorosis, syconus, hesperidium, dry fruit, dehiscent fruit, legume, pod, capsule, follicle, siliqua, silicula, pyxidium, indehiscent fruit, nut, achene, samara, caryopsis, cypsela, schizocarp, carcerulus, cremocarp, lomentum, regma **3 fruit structure**, pericarp, exocarp, skin, rind, peel, shell, shuck, husk, seed pod, mesocarp, endocarp, flesh, pulp, meat, pith, stone, nutlet, seed, pip, kernel **4 fruit eating**, fruit bat, frugivore, fruitarian, vegetarian, vegan, frugivorousness, fruitarianism, vegetarianism, market gardening

ADJECTIVES 5 fruiting, fructiferous, pomiferous, leguminous, fructuous, fruitful, productive **6 fruitlike**, fruity, citrus, citrous, citric **7 fruit-eating**, frugivorous **8 of a fruit**, fleshy, succulent, ripe, unripe, indehiscent, dehiscent, monocarpellary, bicarpellary, polycarpellary, syncarpous, apocarpous, monocarpic

VERBS 9 fruit, bear fruit, fructify, ripen, be fruitful, yield

295 Fuel

NOUNS 1 fuel, fossil fuel, gas, oil, solid fuel, coal, wood, charcoal, peat, peat bog, peat moss, electricity **2 lighter**, firelighter, tinder, kindling, firewood, log, faggot, brushwood, spunk, punk, touchpaper, taper, match, spill, vesta, lucifer, wick, spark, scintilla, flint, burning glass, torch, firebrand, cigarette lighter, cap, percussion cap, ignition system, sparking plug, detonator, fuse, explosive **3 gas**, coal gas, natural gas, town gas, producer gas, Calor gas, propane, butane, methane, lighter fuel, gasfield, gasworks, gasholder, gasometer, gas tank, gas main, gas pipe, gas meter, gas poker, gas burner, gas turbine, rocket fuel, liquid oxygen **4 coal**, bituminous coal, brown coal, cannel coal, lignite, coke, anthracite, briquette, coal dust, slack, coal-bed, Coal Measures, coalfield, coalmine, pit, coalface, coal cellar, coal bunker, coal scuttle **5 oil**, mineral oil, crude oil, diesel oil, derv, paraffin, aviation fuel, methylated spirits, naphtha, gas oil, oil reserves, oil field, oil well, oil rig, offshore rig, oil platform, oil refinery, fractionation, cracking, oil pipeline, oil tanker, oil drum, oilcan, petrol can, octane number, petrol station, filling station, petrol pump, oil shale, oil slick **6 nuclear power**, nuclear energy, nuclear reactor, thermal reactor, gas-cooled reactor, magnox reactor, water-cooled reactor, fast-breeder reactor, nuclear fuel, core, fuel rod, uranium, enriched uranium, plutonium, nuclear fission, nuclear fusion, nuclear waste, nuclear accident **7 renewable energy**, solar energy, photovoltaic cell, wind power, windmill, wind pump, wind generator, wind turbine, geothermal energy, water mill, water turbine, wave power, tidal power, tidal energy, biomass, biofuels **8 power-worker**, stoker, charcoal-burner, coal merchant, coal miner, gas-fitter, gasman, boilermaker, meter-reader, electrician, oil-worker, oilman, lumberjack

ADJECTIVES 9 powered, charged, combustible, inflammable, flammable, explosive, incendiary, carbonaceous, carboniferous, coaly, bituminous, lignitic, coal-fired, gaseous, gas-fired, electric, hydroelectric, electrical, woody, ligneous, wood-burning, oil-fired, thermal, nuclear, thermonuclear, geothermal

VERBS 10 fuel, stoke, fill up, refuel, strike, kindle, fire, detonate, set off, explode, power, charge, recharge, electrify, plug in

296 Furniture

NOUNS 1 furniture, furnishings, veneering, lacquering, painting, trompe l'œil, chinoiserie, japanning, marquetry, parquetry, upholstery, soft furnishings, built-in furniture, unit furniture **2 chair**, bentwood chair, captain's chair, cane chair, box chair, barrel chair, straight chair, Shaker chair, ladder-back chair, wheel-back chair, panel-back chair, rocking chair, nursing chair, bucket seat, dining chair, armchair, easy chair, Morris chair, Queen-Anne chair, Sheraton chair, Windsor chair, wing chair, club chair, recliner, carver chair, folding chair, swivel chair, deck chair, high chair, camp chair, stool, stall, bench, settle, couch, Grecian couch, sofa, chesterfield, chaise longue, settee, divan **3 table**, pier table, drop-leaf table, Pembroke table, gate-leg table, console table, bedside table, pedestal table, card table, desk, writing desk, escritoire, secretaire, davenport, roll-top desk, slant-top desk, knee-hole desk, bureau, reading desk **4 cabinet**, dresser, Welsh dresser, chest, cassone, tallboy, highboy, lowboy, commode, wardrobe, drinks cabinet, sideboard, canterbury, cupboard, corner cupboard, press, bookcase, shelves, bookshelf **5 bed**, panelled bed, four-poster bed, feather bed, Colonial bed, canopied bed, Empire bed, day bed, chaise longue, sofa bed, futon, divan, bunk bed, crib, cot, cradle, berth, hammock, foldaway bed, zed bed, camp bed, truckle bed, water bed, bedstead, headboard **6 furniture style**, Louis Quatorze, Louis Quinze, Louis Seize, Tudor, Elizabethan, Jacobean, Queen-Anne, Chippendale, Adam Hepplewhite, rococo, Georgian, French provincial, colonial, Early American, Early Federal, Shaker, Empire, Sheraton, Regency, chinoiserie, boulle, gothic, baroque, Biedermeier, Victorian, Art Nouveau, Bauhaus, Scandinavian **7 woodwork**, woodworking, woodcraft, timberwork, carpentry, joinery, cabinet-making, woodcarving, wood turning, wood sculpting, treen, whittling, woodburning, pyrography, xylopyrography, woodcut, black-line woodcut, white-line woodcut, woodblock printing, relief printing, xylography, lignography, wood engraving, woodprint, xylograph **8 decorative woodwork**, wood inlay, Certosina work, intarsia, true inlay, marquetry **9 carpenter's term**, joint, bevel, mitre joint, timber joint, housed joint, lap joint, fish joint, scarf joint, flitched joint, birdsmouth joint, dovetailing, cogging, trimming, framing, joist, strut, truss, laths **10 woodworking tool**, lathe, saw, plane, drawknife, spokeshave, adze, band saw, jigsaw, circular saw, power-driven saw, planer, jointer, shaper, router, sander, mortiser, tenoner, borer, drill, wood-engraving tool, chisel, burin, graver, tint tool, velo, lamina **11 wood**, timber, lumber, softwood, hardwood, heartwood, sapwood, boarding, plank, deal, stick, stave, pole, post, two-by-four, slab, puncheon, slat, splat, lathwork, timberwork, sheeting, panelboard, panelwork, plywood, sheathing, siding, weatherboard, clapboard, hardboard, blockboard, chipboard, shingle, shake, log, cordwood, woodgrain, wood texture **12 carpenter**, joiner, cabinet-maker, furniture-maker, coachbuilder, wheelwright, turner, sawyer, cooper, woodcarver

ADJECTIVES 13 wooden, lacquered, painted, inlaid, marquetried, parquetried, upholstered, built-in, straight, ladder-back, panel-back, rocking, reclining, folding, drop-leaf, gate-leg, roll-top, slant-top, knee-hole, panelled, canopied, convertible **14 woodcrafted**, carved, woodcarved, wood-turned, wood-sculpted, whittled, woodburned, woodcut, black-line, white-line, wood-engraved, woodblocked **15 joined**, joining, jointed, mitred, timbered, housed, flitched, mortised, dovetailed, dovetailing, cogged, cogging, trimmed, trimming, framed, framing, joisted, herringbone, beamed, boarded, boarding

VERBS 16 carpenter, mitre, mortise, dovetail, cog, trim, frame, joist, strut, truss, lathe, saw, cut, cross-cut, rip, drill, screw, plane, shape, sand, tenon, bore, chisel, board, plank, post, slat, lath, timber, sheet, panel **17 work wood**, laminate, veneer, lacquer, paint, inlay, build in, upholster, carve, turn wood

297 Furrow

NOUNS 1 furrow, trench, trough, scratch, seam, groove, wheel-track, slot, fissure, chink, cut, slit, channel, conduit, rut, ditch, gutter, canal, flute, score **2 wrinkle**, crinkle, crease, pucker, line, laugh-line, crow's-foot **3 furrowed thing**, corduroy material, pleated dress, washboard, corrugated paper, corrugated iron, etching, engraving

ADJECTIVES 4 furrowed, scratched, grooved, wheel-tracked, slotted, chinky, rutty, rimose, fluted, scored, corrugated, etched, engraved **5 wrinkly**, crinkly, creased, puckered, lined

VERBS 6 furrow, trench, trough, scratch, seam, groove, track, slot, fissure, cut, etch, engrave, slit, channel, rut, plough, ditch, gutter, canal, flute, score **7 wrinkle**, crinkle, crease, pucker

298 Future Time

NOUNS 1 future time, tomorrow, next week, next year **2 future generation**, descendants, heirs, inheritors, successors **3 future condition**, better days, jam tomorrow, fate, destiny, coming events, latter days, doomsday, the millennium, Judgment Day, post-existence, the hereafter, kingdom come, paradise, nirvana, heaven, damnation, the underworld, hell **4 looking to the future**, eschatology, teleology, waiting, expectancy, anticipation, foresight, foreknowledge, prescience, preparation, prospects, likelihood, outlook, forecast, prediction, prophecy, premonition, astrology, horoscope, fortune-telling

VERBS 5 be in the future, lie ahead, draw near, approach, come soon, overhang **6 intend**, plan to, mean to, shall **7 look ahead**, hope for, foresee, predict, presage, prophesy, divine, foretell, augur, cast bones **8 expect**, await, wait for, prepare for, have prospects, anticipate

ADJECTIVES 9 future, forthcoming, coming, to come, to be, eventual, later, ahead, approaching, oncoming, due, fated, destined, imminent, threatening, overhanging, impending **10 predictable**, foreseeable, probable, possible, potential, likely, certain **11 foreseen**, foretold, predicted, expected, anticipated, awaited, looked for, hoped for, promised

299 Gain

NOUNS 1 gain, getting, receiving, taking, winning, acquisition, acquirement, obtainment, attainment, benefit, securement, procurement, moneymaking, breadwinning, profitableness, fund-raising, profiteering, usury **2 augmentation**, increase, appreciation, rise, increment, growth, expansion, escalation, inflation, dilation, advance, improvement **3 acquisition**, collection, gathering, gleaning, assembling, accumulation, amassment, accretion, catch, hoard, store, heap, stack, stockpile, mountain **4 earnings**, income, advance, royalty, privy purse, revenue, wages, salary, pay, takings, makings, receipts, turnover, return, proceeds, gate money, winnings, pickings, pension, stipend, annuity, tontine, fee **5 profit**, gains, gross, net, emolument, interest, percentage, dividends, inheritance, bequest, legacy, grant, subsidy, compensation, scholarship, benefit, extra, bonus, perquisite, perk, commission, expense account, allowance, filthy lucre, savings, reward, gratuity, tip, baksheesh, award, trophy, prize, gift, find, treasure trove, windfall, theft, bribe **6 yield**, output, production, proceeds, produce

VERBS 7 gain, get, win, acquire, obtain, appropriate, annex, attain, benefit, come by, gather in, bring in, secure, procure, earn, make, profit, realize, raise funds **8 augment**, increase, escalate, appreciate, grow, develop, proliferate, mushroom, flower, expand, snowball, broaden, widen, spread, inflate, dilate, advance, approach, make headway, gain ground **9 acquire**, collect, glean, harvest, assemble, accumulate, accrete, amass, save, catch, hoard, heap, stack, stockpile **10 earn**, receive royalties **11 be profitable**, pay, yield, produce, gross, pay interest, accrue **12 profit**, capitalize on, clear, prosper, pay dividends, inherit, save, steal

ADJECTIVES 13 gainful, beneficial, acquiring, obtainable, attainable, available, procurable, inheriting, beneficiary, compensatory, fund-raising, moneymaking, capitalistic, profitable, gross, net, gratuitous, windfall, useful, paid, lucrative, remunerative **14 greedy**, avaricious, acquisitive, grasping **15 well-off**, well-to-do, solvent, affluent, prosperous, rich, wealthy **16 acquisitional**, collective, accumulative, cumulative, mountainous, augmentative, expansive, gaining, widening, inflationary, improvable **17 yielding**, productive, fruitful, fertile, prolific

300 Games

NOUNS 1 game, ball game, board game, cards, darts, dice, billiards, word game, children's game, gambling game, computer game **2 card game**, pack, playing card, heart, club, diamond, spade, picture card, face card, court card, one-eyed jack, ace, deuce, joker, wildcard, cut, shuffle, deal, shoe, misdeal, hand, banker, pot, ante, limit, raise, cull, kicker, hold, stack, pair, trey, prial, full house, flush, run, straight, trump, bid, pass, fold, undertrick, finesse, contract, rubber, slam **3 chess**, board, square, piece, chessman, pawn, castle, rook, knight, bishop, king, queen, opening, fork, pin, castling, check, end game, checkmate **4 dice**, die, spots, throw, double, snake eyes **5 darts**, arrow, flight, board, bull, top, double top, treble top, oche, shanghai **6 pastime**, hobby, activity, recreation

ADJECTIVES 7 recreational, entertaining

VERBS 8 play, compete, gamble, join in, shuffle, cut, deal, misdeal, bank, raise, call, hold, pass, stack, throw in, fold, bid, double, pre-empt, ruff, finesse, open, move, castle

301 Gas

NOUNS 1 gas, rare gas, air, atmosphere, vapour, elastic fluid, ether **2 exhalation**, breath, expiration **3 miasma**, mephitis, reek, smoke, smog, damp **4 water vapour**, steam, cloud, mist **5 belch**, ructation, eructation, hiccup, flatulence, flatus, wind **6 aerogastria**, aerogenesis, aerodontalgia, aeroneurosis, aerophagia **7 gaseousness**, gassiness, fizziness, effervescence, fermentation, vaporousness, vapour **8 volatility**, vapourability **9 aeriness**, etherealism **10 vaporization**, evaporation, volatilization, gasification, aeration, etherification, sublimation, distillation, fractionation, atomization, exhalation, etherealization, steaming, smoking **11 vaporizer**, spray, aerosol, propellant, atomizer, condenser, retort **12 aerostatics**, aerodynamics, pneumatostatics, pneumatics **13 vaporimeter**, manometer, pressure gauge, gasometer, gas meter, airometer, aerometer, spirometer

ADJECTIVES 14 gaseous, gassy **15 airy**, aery, aerial, ethereal **16 miasmic**, mephitic, foetid, reeking, fumy **17 smoky**, smoggy, steamy, vaporing, cloudy, misty **18 flatulent**, windy **19 gassy**, fizzy, effervescent, bubbly, sparkling, carbonated **20 aerostatic**, aerodynamic **21 volatile**, vapourable

VERBS 22 gasify, evaporate, vaporize, volatilize, atomize, sublimate, distil, fractionate **23 aerate**, fumigate, aerify, etherize, carbonate, oxygenate, hydrogenate, atomize, spray, perfume **24 give off**, emit, exhale, reek, fume

302 Generality

NOUNS 1 generality, universality, comprehensiveness, inclusiveness, globality, cosmopolitanism **2 catholicity**, ecumenicalism, Broad Church **3 nonspecificness**, broadness, looseness, sweepingness, imprecision, inexactitude, broad spectrum, blanket coverage, dragnet, catch-all, open house **4 widespreadness**, extensiveness, rifeness, rampantness, pervasiveness, ubiquity **5 averageness**, ordinariness, standardness, rule, commonness, routineness, habitualness **6 average**, ruck **7 global view**, world view, panorama, bird's-eye view **8 generalization**, abstract, sweeping statement, cliché, platitude **9 everyman**, everywoman, common type, Mr Average, Joe Bloggs **10 everyone**, everybody, everything **11 general public**, populace, common people, grass roots, masses, multitude, hoi polloi, vox populi

ADJECTIVES 12 general, universal, whole, comprehensive, inclusive, all-embracing, all-encompassing, all-covering, all-comprehending, all-pervading, overall, synoptic, heterogenous, diversified, miscellaneous, eclectic, liberal, catholic, ecumenical, cosmopolitan, broad-based, encyclopedic, blanket, extensive, wide, broad, sweeping, across-the-board, panoramic **13 universal**, cosmic, galactic, planetary, worldwide, global, international, cosmopolitan, national **14 widespread**, extensive, rife, rampant, pervasive, ubiquitous, omnipresent, endemic, epidemic **15 far-reaching**, far-ranging, wide-ranging **16 prevailing**, prevalent, widespread, common, popular, accepted, predominant, dominant, public, communal **17 generalized**, nonspecific, generic, approximate, inexact, imprecise, indefinite, indeterminate, undetermined, unspecified, ill-defined, broad, loose, vague, sweeping, abstract **18 common**, regular, standard, normal, usual, ordinary, average, unexceptional, run-of-the-mill, customary, habitual, routine, everyday, equotidian, familiar, accustomed, middlebrow, middle-of-the-road, conventional, pedestrian, vernacular, vulgar, downmarket **19 commonplace**, trite, platitudinous, hackneyed, uninspired, unimaginative, jaded

VERBS 20 generalize, universalize, globalize, catholicize **21 broaden**, widen, spread, expand **22 broadcast**, diffuse, disperse, disseminate **23 popularize**, vulgarize **24 make a generalization**, generalize **25 prevail**, predominate, dominate, obtain, reign

303 Generosity

ADJECTIVES 1 generous, liberal, openhanded, hospitable, giving, unstinting, ungrudging, beneficent, munificent, bountiful, lavish, princely **2 magnanimous**, charitable, benevolent, humanitarian **3 abundant**, plentiful, ample, lavish, copious, overflowing, profuse **4 big**, roomy, large, capacious

NOUNS 5 generosity, liberality, charity, open-handedness, beneficence, bounty, munificence, bounteousness **6 magnanimity**, charitableness, benevolence **7 gift**, contribution, subscription, donation, covenant, bonus, tip, handout, alms **8 abundance**, plenty

VERBS 9 be generous, give generously, pay towards **10 give**, contribute, subscribe, donate, covenant, bequeath, endow, finance, fund

304 Geography

NOUNS 1 continent, Africa, Europe, Asia, Antarctica, landmass, North America, South America, Eurasia, Oceania, Australasia, subcontinent **2 island**, isle, islet, river island, coral island, lagoon, atoll, reef, cay, key, Key West, sandbank, sandbar, floating island, iceberg, ice floe, island continent, archipelago **3 marsh**, marshland, wetlands, fen, fenland, flat, mud flat, salt marsh, saltpan, salina, playa, bog, peat bog, moss, moor, carr, swamp, swampland, the Everglades, swamp-forest, morass, quag, quagmire, quicksand, mudhole, mud, mire, ooze, wallow, slough, sudd **4 coast**, coastline, shoreline, coastland, rocky coast, ironbound coast, sea wall, sea cliff, beach, shore, seaboard, seaside, strand, sand, pebbles, shingle, submerged coast, continental shelf **5 peninsula**, point, tongue, neck, spit, sandspit, hook, spur, cape, promontory, bill, foreland, headland, head, projection, Cape Horn **6 lowland**, flat country, flats, level, meadow, field, lea, water meadow, plain, alluvial plain, flood plain, polder, vale, range, heath, grassland, prairie, pampas, llano, veld, savanna, campos **7 upland**, high country, highland, heights, plateau, mesa, tableland **8 valley**, vale, dale, dell, dingle, dip, coomb, cirque, glen, ravine, gorge, canyon, gully, crevasse, chimney, ditch, chine, clough **9 inlet**, bay, gulf, natural harbour, port, bight, cove, fiord, sound, backwater, outlet, estuary, mouth, delta, channel, gut **10 miscellaneous**, desert, desert sands, sands, geyser, Old Faithful, hot spring, warm spring, thermal spring, thermae, fault, volcano

ADJECTIVES 11 continental, Australasian, Asian, European, African, American, subcontinental, insular, islander, isleted, archipelagic, estuarial, coastal, littoral, ashore, sandy, pebbled, shingled, swampy, boggy, marshy, paludal, deltaic, flat, plain, rocky, peninsular, isthmian, promontory, campestral

305 Giving

NOUNS 1 giving, donation, bestowal, charity, almsgiving, benevolence, benefaction, philanthropy, subvention, subsidization, generosity, liberality, largess, bounty, contributing, offering, tithing, subscription, prize-giving, presentation, awarding, service, commitment, voluntary work, consignment, conveyance, imparting, delivery, supplying, transfer, provision, concession, surrender, endowing, settlement, dowry, grant, conferral, investment, bequeathal, leaving, will, testament, gifting **2 gift**, present, box, souvenir, memento, keepsake, token, tip, fee, honorarium, incentive pay, subsidy, subvention, support, tax benefit, grant, allowance, pocket money, stipend, allotment, aid, help, scholarship, fellowship, welfare, relief, alimony, annuity, pension, bequest, legacy, inheritance, gratuity, consideration, bribe, kickback, inducement, prize, reward, award, presentation, trophy, bonus, bonanza, something extra, perquisite, benefit, blessing, boon, grace, favour, windfall, conscience money, payment **3 offering**, dedication, consecration, offertory, collection, sacrifice, oblation, Peter's pence, tithe, widow's mite, contribution, subscription, flag day, appeal, benefit match, alms, Maundy money, dole, food parcel, meal ticket, free meal, bounty, manna, largess, donation **4 giver**, philanthropist, provider, benefactor, donor, bestower, rewarder, tipper, briber, grantor, conferrer, awarder, imparter, presenter, prize-giver, bequeather, subscriber, contributor, sacrificer, worshipper, tributary, almoner, almsgiver, saint, good Samaritan, helper, saviour, supporter, backer, patron, rich uncle, fairy godmother

VERBS 5 give, give away, treat, entertain, pour out, lavish upon, enrich, subscribe to, present, transmit, impart, convey, deliver, supply, consign, lend, render, provide, honour with, grant, vouchsafe, bestow upon, award, accord, will, bequeath, leave, provide for, endow, tender, transfer, mete out, share, dispense, delegate, allot, commission, dispatch, cede, yield, entrust, vest, subsidize, pay, finance, reward, dedicate, devote, consecrate, vow, offer, sacrifice, tip **6 give to charity**, philanthropize, donate, tithe, contribute to, volunteer, give alms, help

ADJECTIVES 7 given, bestowable, impartable, available, saleable, subventionary, bequeathed, willed, transferable, granted, accorded, bestowed, bonus, gratis, for nothing, voluntary, complimentary, courtesy, sacrificial, votive, oblatory, gratuitous, God-given, donative, contributory, tributary, endowed, subsidized, dowered, stipendiary, pensionary, insurable **8 giving**, bestowing, imparting, granting, transferring, alms-giving, charitable, benevolent, philanthropic, generous, open-handed

306 Giving Back

NOUNS 1 giving back, returning, extradition, restitution, reversion, repatriation, reinstatement, reappointment, reenthronement, reestablishment, restoration, recycling, retrocesson, reinvestment, rehabilitation, replacement, redemption, atonement, deliverance, requital, ransom **2 compensation**, repayment, recoupment, refund, reimbursement, indemnification, indemnity, damages, penalty, amends, making good, reparation, recompense, paying back

VERBS 3 give back, return, extradite, make restitution, repatriate, reinstate, reappoint, reenthrone, reestablish, restore, recycle, retrocede, reinvest, rehabilitate, replace, redeem, atone, deliver, requite, ransom **4 compensate**, repay, refund, reimburse, indemnify, pay damages, make redress, make good, make reparations, recompense

ADJECTIVES 5 restoring, restitutive, restorable, redemptive, redeeming, atoning, refunding, compensatory

307 Gluttony

NOUNS 1 gluttony, greediness, greed, overeating, self-indulgence, overindulgence, intemperance, insatiability, voraciousness, ravenousness, rapacity, edaciousness, polyphagia, hedonism, concupiscence, big appetite **2 epicurism**, gourmandise **3 act of gluttony**, banquet, feast **4 glutton**, guzzler, gorger, trencherman, trencherwoman, omnivore, bacchanal, Lucullus, gourmet, gourmand, gastronome, epicurean

VERBS 5 be greedy, gluttonize, gormandize, hedonize, overeat, self-indulge, overindulge, set to, devour, bolt, guzzle, gobble, gulp, snap up, wolf, stuff, cram

ADJECTIVES 6 gluttonous, greedy, insatiable, intemperate, hedonistic, overeating, self-indulgent, overindulgent, voracious, ravenous, rapacious, well-nourished, edacious, polyphagous, epicurean, gastronomic, omnivorous, devouring, stuffing, cramming, bolting, gobbling, gulping, glutting, gorging, guzzling

308 Good

ADJECTIVES 1 good, excellent, first-rate, superior, better, superb, splendid, great, famous, fine, exquisite, high-class, wonderful, magnificent, terrific, impressive, meritorious, praiseworthy, admirable, worthy, valuable, profitable, sound, healthy, salubrious, salutary, favourable, propitious, auspicious, heaven-sent, lucky, suitable, apt **2 best**, top, essential, choice, elite, unequalled, nonpareil, peerless, matchless, record-breaking, class A, perfect, flawless, supreme **3 kind**, goodly, nice, gracious, fair, virtuous, righteous, moral, honest, honourable, benevolent, helpful, good-natured, friendly, well-wishing, thoughtful **4 well-behaved**, obedient, compliant, docile, willing, biddable **5 proficient**, efficient, competent, accomplished, expert, handy, skilled, deft, versatile, dexterous, adroit, talented, gifted **6 beneficial**, useful, advantageous, worthwhile, profitable, improving, bettering

NOUNS 7 good, goodness, excellence,

first class, quality, superiority, superbness, splendidness, greatness, fame, wonderfulness, magnificence, merit, worth, praiseworthiness, value, soundness, healthiness, favourableness, propitiousness, auspiciousness, suitableness, appropriateness, aptness **8 the best**, tops, essence, choice, pick, elite, cream, flower, paragon, nonpareil, top marks, class A, superlative, perfection, flawlessness **9 kindness**, kindliness, goodliness, niceness, graciousness, fairness, virtue, righteousness, rectitude, morality, honesty, honourableness, benevolence, thoughtfulness, helpfulness, grace, friendliness, well-wishing, generosity, kind act **10 proficiency**, efficiency, competence, accomplishment, expertise, skilfulness, deftness, versatility, dexterousness, adroitness, handiness, ability, talent, gift **11 benefit**, well-being, welfare, interest, behalf, happiness, blessing, benediction, betterment, improvement, advantage, worthwhileness, profitability, prosperity, boon, gift, profit, gain, usefulness, advantage **12 good person**, saint, priest, nun, monk, Good Samaritan, altruist, philanthropist, friend, good neighbour, well-wisher, helper

VERBS 13 be good, behave well, obey, comply, conform **14 be good at**, master, excel, qualify for, pass, transcend **15 do good**, help, serve, benefit, avail, make better, bless, better, improve, advance, profit **16 do well**, thrive, flourish, prosper, succeed, improve, get better, gain

309 Government and Politics

- *Every country has the government it deserves.* Joseph de Maistre.
- *The ballot is stronger than the bullet.* Abraham Lincoln.
- *That government of the people, by the people, and for the people, shall not perish from the earth.* Abraham Lincoln.
- *Politics is not an exact science.* Bismarck.
- *Politics is the art of the possible.* R. A. Butler.

NOUNS 1 government, direction, management, administration, executive, local government, national government, world government, parliament, political system, hierarchy, polity, politicking, tribalism, feudalism, physiocracy, Poujadism, benevolent despotism, paternalism, squirearchy, patriarchy, matriarchy, gynocracy, constitutionalism, theocracy, thearchy, hierocracy, clericalism, ecclesiasticism, monarchy, monarchical absolutism, constitutional monarchy, kingship, republicanism, federalism, aristocracy, meritocracy, oligarchy, elitism, gerontocracy, duumvirate, triumvirate, plutocracy, party system, democracy, egalitarianism, majority rule, proportional representation, isocracy, pantisocracy, pluralism, collectivism, proletarianism, communism, Leninism, Marxism-Leninism, Maoism, Titoism, Bolshevism, totalitarianism, Fascism, Nazism, National Socialism, demagoguery, puppet government, sovietism, stratocracy, military government, martial law, ochlocracy, mobocracy, mob rule, anarchy, syndicalism, socialism, Fabianism, statism, technocracy, autocracy, autarchy, self-rule, autonomy **2**

politics, political science, public affairs, statecraft, statesmanship **3 governance**, rule, sway, direction, command, directorship, control, hold, grip, clutches, domination, mastery, whip hand, condominium, sovereignty, suzerainty, raj, overlordship, presidency, supremacy, superiority, reign, regency, heteronomy, empery, subjection, imperialism, colonialism, neocolonialism, white supremacy, black power, regime, statism, dirigisme, paternalism, apparat, civil service, officialism, beadledom, bumbledom **4 political organization**, body politic, state, commonwealth, country, realm, kingdom, republic, city-state, federation, confederation, principality, duchy, archduchy, dukedom, palatinate, empire, dominion, colony, dependency, protectorate, mandate, territory, superpower, buffer state, county, region, province, district, laws **5 political party**, right, left, centre, Conservative Party, Labour Party, Green Party, ecologist, liberal, radical, socialist, nationalist, Trotskyist, Marxist, communist, fascist, Nazi, neo-Nazi, syndicalist, anarchist, anarcho-syndicalist, revolter, right-winger, rightist, tory, reactionary, hard-liner, left-winger, leftist, leftie, populist, democrat, centrist, moderate, party member, party worker **6 governor**, controller, legislator, lawmaker, statesman, stateswoman, president, vice president, prime minister **7 politician**, Parliamentarian, backbencher, peer, life peer, cabinet minister, secretary, minister, undersecretary, junior minister, party chairman, party manager

ADJECTIVES 8 governmental, political, presidential, parliamentary, democratic, republican, independent, constitutional, federal, civic, administrative, executive, ministerial, senatorial, official, bureaucratic, centralized, technocratic, matriarchal, patriarchal, theocratic, monarchical, feudal, aristocratic, meritocratic, oligarchic, plutocratic, dictatorial, totalitarian, classless, self-governing, self-ruling, autonomous, autarchic, anarchic, socialistic **9 governing**, ruling, controlling, dictating, in charge, in power, regnant, regnal, royal, regal, majestic, monarchical

VERBS 10 govern, rule, command, control, lead, hold sway, reign, direct, manage, hold office, wield power, exert authority, tyrannize, oppress, dictate, legislate, Balkanize **11 take authority**, seize power, take control, assume command

310 Grasses

NOUNS 1 grass, true grass, graminaceous plant, ornamental grass, mowing grass, lawn grass, fodder grass, meadow grass, pasture grass, ley grass, cereal grass, rush **2 grassland**, meadow, field, pasture, pasturage, herbage, verdure, ley, grazing, plain, common, moor, heath, downs, park, lawn, green, turf, sod, tussock, tuft **3 cereal grass**, cereal, grain, corncob, barleycorn, husk, bran, chaff

ADJECTIVES 4 grasslike, gramineous, graminaceous, poaceous, gramíniferous, farinaceous, wheaten **5 grassy**, verdant, verdured, meadowy, swardy, turfy, reedy, rushy **6 grass-eating**, graminivorous, herbivorous

VERBS 7 eat grass, graze, browse,

crop, forage, pasture, ruminate, forage **8 manage grassland**, cut, mow, scythe, top, grass over, turf, seed, fertilize, weed, top-dress

311 Gratitude

NOUNS 1 gratitude, gratefulness, thankfulness, appreciation, obligation, awareness, mindfulness **2 thanks**, thanksgiving, Eucharist, blessing, benediction, Magnificat, Te Deum, prayer, paean, praise, hymn **3 recognition**, acknowledgment, credit, by-line, thank-you letter, reward, tip, bonus, gratuity, leaving present, gold watch, tribute, praise

ADJECTIVES 4 grateful, thankful, appreciative, pleased, gratified, indebted, beholden **5 thanking**, blessing, praising, crediting

VERBS 6 be grateful, be thankful, appreciate, thank, show appreciation, reward, tip, acknowledge, pay tribute, praise, recognize, applaud, give credit **7 give thanks**, say grace, bless

312 Greenness

ADJECTIVES 1 green, emerald, jade, vert, greenish, virescent, chartreuse, eau-de-nil, avocado, celadon, reseda, mignonette, glaucous **2 verdant**, grassy, leafy, green, fresh **3 raw**, unripe, unseasoned, immature, callow, green, inexperienced, unskilled, inexpert, untrained, untried, untested, unsophisticated, naive, ingenuous, artless, innocent, credulous, gullible, gauche **4 fresh**, new, young, youthful, evergreen, sappy, springlike, vernal, vigorous, flourishing **5 environmental**, conservationist, green

NOUNS 6 greenness, viridity, verdancy, verdure, greenery, woodland, evergreen, grass, moss, turf, sward, grassland, pasture, common, green belt **7 greenstuff**, greens, cabbage, lettuce, broccoli, greengage, lime **8 green pigment**, chlorophyll, terre verte, celadonite, viridian, verditer, Paris green **9 green thing**, greenstone, jade, emerald, malachite, beryl, olivine, aquamarine, greensand, verdigris, patina, greenfinch, greenfly **10 figurative green thing**, Greenland, Green Mountains, Green Berets, greenhouse effect **11 green-eyed monster**, jealousy, envy **12 green light**, go-ahead, all clear, permission, approval **13 green politics**, Green Party, Greens, environmentalist, preservationist

313 Guilt

NOUNS 1 guilt, culpability, liability, red-handedness, delinquency, illegality, criminality, implication, complicity, responsibility, reproach, censure, blame, peccancy, inculpation, reprehensibility, blameworthiness, impeachability, indictability, accusation **2 signs of guilt**, guilt complex, guilty conscience, qualms, remorse, shame, contrition, regret, self-reproach, penitence, blush, stammer, embarrassment, dirty hands, bloody hands **3 sin**, sinfulness, vice, iniquity, wickedness, guilty act, wrongdoing, misconduct, slip, faux pas, blunder, mistake, fault, failure, injury, wrong, negligence, indiscretion, impropriety, peccadillo, transgression, trespass, injustice, illegality, crime, misdemeanour, malpractice, felony, atrocity

ADJECTIVES 4 guilty, responsible, reprehensible, censurable, inexcusable, unjustifiable, unpardonable, unforgivable, reproachable, reprovable, at fault, culpable, impeachable, chargeable, accusable, blameworthy, implicated, censured, peccant, condemned **5 appearing guilty**, shamefaced, ashamed, sheepish, blushing, stammering, hangdog, red-handed, contrite, conscience-stricken, remorseful, regretful **6 sinful**, wicked, illegal, criminal, trespassing, transgressing, heinous, mortal

VERBS 7 be guilty, plead guilty, confess **8 appear guilty**, look ashamed, look embarrassed, look sheepish, blush, stammer, accuse oneself, torture oneself **9 sin**, trespass, transgress, rob, steal, kidnap, murder, assassinate

314 Habit

• *Men's natures are alike; it is their habits that carry them far apart.* Confucius.

NOUNS 1 habit, second nature, custom, use, wont, pattern, praxis, regularity, familiarity, inveteracy, addiction, compulsion, cacoethes, mania, obsession, fixation **2 tendency**, habitude, leaning, bent, propensity, proclivity, instinct, knack, trick, trait, idiosyncrasy **3 way**, lifestyle, constitutional, routine, run, round, groove, rut, tramlines, beaten track **4 custom**, usage, tradition, lore, folklore, mores, behaviour patterns, institution, ritual, rite, ceremony, observance, religion, cult, trend, fashion **5 tradition**, consuetude, law, prescription, legal precedent, convention, protocol, unwritten law, formality, etiquette, manners, conduct **6 procedure**, policy, practice, routine, system, drill, bureaucracy, red tape, beadledom, petty officialdom, conventionalism, traditionalism, conservatism, old school **7 habituation**, training, drilling, memorization, rote, indoctrination, brainwashing, inurement, institutionalization, hardening, seasoning, maturing, naturalization, acclimatization, adaptation, orientation, conditioning

ADJECTIVES 8 habitual, customary, accustomed, wonted, predictable, invariable, usual, regular, routine, everyday, quotidian, annual, professional **9 familiar**, known, everyday, household, ordinary, commonplace, unexceptional, unoriginal, stock, trite, banal, hackneyed, clichéd, well-worn, trodden, beaten, current, prevalent, widespread, obtaining **10 normal**, natural, in character, typical, stereotyped, conventional, orthodox, traditional, ritual, time-honoured, old-fashioned, old-world, permanent **11 established**, official, de rigueur, done, practised, approved, accepted, received, admitted, acknowledged, recognized, understood, accredited, instituted, institutionalized, hallowed in, fashionable **12 fixed**, staunch, true-blue, dyed-in-the-wool, ingrained, implanted, deep-rooted, deep-seated, imbued, permeated, soaked **13 habituated**, used, accustomed, familiar, conversant, practised, trained, tamed, broken in, acclimatized, naturalized, conditioned, inured, seasoned, hardened, confirmed, chronic, inveterate, addicted, given, dedicated, devoted, wedded, frequent, recurrent, constant **14**

habit-forming, addictive, obsessive, haunting
VERBS 15 have a habit, do regularly, haunt, frequent, take up, never vary, observe routine **16 become a habit**, become acceptable, catch on, stick, cling, adhere, settle, take root, obtain **17 habituate**, accustom, inure, season, harden, teach, train, domesticate, tame, break in, naturalize, acclimatize, adapt, orient, implant, ingraft, imbue, indoctrinate, brainwash, condition, accustom oneself, warm up

315 Habitat

NOUNS 1 habitat, habitation, abode, dwelling place, domicile, house, home, accommodation, living quarters, lodgings, billet, rooms **2 environment**, surroundings, habitat, microhabitat, ecosystem, niche, locality, haunt, domain, range, territory, element, home ground, base, bailiwick **3 home**, homestead, hearth, fireside, inglenook, base, home town, birthplace, cradle, homeland **4 house**, town house, semi, detached house, terraced house, two-up-two-down, farmhouse, villa, bungalow, chalet, cottage, cabin, flat, apartment, maisonette, penthouse, bedsit, studio, snuggery **5 shelter**, shed, shack, hut, lean-to, outhouse, hutch, booth, shanty, hovel, squat **6 mobile home**, caravan, trailer, camper, campervan, houseboat, tent, tepee, wigwam **7 hotel**, motel, inn, hostelry, guest house, boarding house, hostel **8 retreat**, haven, refuge, sanctuary, hideaway **9 stall**, fold, barn, stable, byre, sty, cowshed, kennel, pound, cattery, coop, henhouse, run, battery, cage, zoo, menagerie, aquarium, aviary, bird cage, dovecote **10 lair**, den, cave, hole, covert, sett, holt, burrow, warren, tunnel, earth, drey, nest, eyrie, perch, roost
ADJECTIVES 11 inhabiting, residential, at home, dwelling, domiciled, housed, roofed, lodged, billeted **12 environmental**, territorial **13 manorial**, palatial, presidential, detached, semidetached, terraced, back-to-back, duplex, split-level, single-storey
VERBS 14 inhabit, abide in, dwell in, reside in, live in, occupy, squat, stay, sojourn, settle, colonize **15 take up residence**, move in, nest, nestle, perch, roost, burrow, stable, encamp, quarter, board **16 frequent**, haunt

316 Hardness

ADJECTIVES 1 hard, steely, diamondlike, iron, stone, lithic, granite, marble, rocky, rock-hard, lapideous, lithoid, flinty, pebbly, gravelly, gritty, lumpy, horny, corneous, callous, leathery, bony, osseous, cartilaginous, gristly, sclerotic, crusty, glassy, crystalline, vitreous **2 tough**, strong, firm, solid, unbreakable, adamant, indestructible, shatterproof, resistant, starchy, boned, stark, stiff, rigid, inflexible, inelastic, unsprung, unrelaxed, tight, taut, tense, pokerlike **3 hardened**, toughened, fortified, strengthened, stiffened, reinforced, backed, braced, buttressed, proofed, tempered, heat-treated, annealed, indurate, hard-boiled, steeled, armoured, calloused, ossified, hornified, calcified, crusted, crystallized, granulated, vitrified, petrified, fossilized, sun-baked, solidified, set, frozen **4**

mentally hard, inflexible, stubborn, obdurate, obstinate, firm, tough, intransigent, unadaptable, unpliable, unmalleable, intractable, unbending, unyielding, ungiving, unalterable, immutable, difficult, callous, case-hardened, hard-hearted, stony-hearted, heartless, insensitive

NOUNS 5 hardness, strength, firmness, solidity, impenetrability, resistance, density, toughness, steeliness, stoniness, rockiness, cragginess, grittiness, lumpiness, nodularity, nodosity, rigidity, rigour, temper, stiffness, starchiness, tautness, tightness, inflexibility, inelasticity, inextensibility, tension **6 solidification**, hardening, setting, crystallization, granulation, petrifaction, fossilization, lapidification, ossification, vitrification, glaciation, steeling, tempering, vulcanization, calcification

VERBS 7 harden, case-harden, strengthen, toughen, steel, temper, reinforce, brace, buttress, shore, back, tighten, stiffen, tauten, starch, wax, tense, vulcanize, crisp, bake, heat-treat, hard-boil, anneal **8 solidify**, petrify, fossilize, ossify, calcify, vitrify, crystallize, glaciate, granulate, candy, set, firm, stiffen, condense, thicken **9 be stubborn**, remain intransigent, not yield, not bend

317 Harsh Sound

NOUNS 1 stridency (*or* stridence), harshness, discordance, clamour, stridor, cacophony, raucousness, dissonance, squawk, yawp, yelp, yell, howl, wail, ululation, bray, brassiness, blare, skirl, blast **2 hoarseness**, roughness, huskiness, gruffness, lowness, gutteralness, throatiness, caw, croak, grunt, snort, snore, stertor, cough, belch, cracked voice, rustiness, friction, scrape, scratch, nasality, twang **3 shrillness**, high pitch, shriek, scream, squeal, screech, squeak, piping, whistling, whistle, catcall, wolf whistle, bleep, high note

VERBS 4 be strident, jar, clash, discord, jangle, rasp, grind, squawk, yawp, yelp, yawl, yell, howl, wail, ululate, bray, blare, skirl **5 sound hoarse**, rasp, grate, grind, crunch, scrunch, gutteralize, caw, croak, grunt, snort, snore, cough, hawk, hem, belch, choke, gasp, scrape, saw, scratch, twang, drone, clank **6 be shrill**, shriek, scream, screech, squeal, squeak, creak, pipe, whistle

ADJECTIVES 7 strident, harsh, raucous, discordant, grating, jarring, flat, inharmonious, unmelodious, unmusical, twangy, metallic, penetrating, loud, clamorous, cacophonous, dissonant, ear-splitting, squawky, howling, ululant, brassy, braying **8 hoarse**, husky, rough, gruff, low, gutteral, throaty, gravelly, rasping, cawing, croaky, croaking, grunting, snorting, snoring, stertorous, cracked, nonresonant, dry, rusty, scraping, scratchy, droning, clanking **9 shrill**, high-pitched, sharp, acute, ear-piercing, squeaky, creaky, tinny, reedy, piping

318 Haste

• *For fools rush in where angels fear to tread.* Alexander Pope.

VERBS 1 hasten, speed up, accelerate, quicken, precipitate, hurry, rush, expedite, dispatch, urge, impel, propel, drive, stampede, spur, goad, whip, lash, flog, incite, hustle, bundle out, rush along, push **2 make haste**, move fast, speed, rush, spurt, sprint, dash, bolt, race, fly, run, rush headlong, run helter-skelter, run pell-mell, scurry, scuttle, scamper, dash off, tear off, hurry, catch up, overtake, whirl by, zoom past, accelerate, hustle, bustle, fret, fume, fidget, ignore formalities, brush aside, rush through

ADJECTIVES 3 hasty, rushed, speedy, prompt, brisk, quick, presto, allegro, swift, rapid, fast, fleet, expeditious, impetuous, impulsive, precipitant, headlong, reckless, heedless, rash, hot-headed, feverish, impatient, thoughtless, unthinking, ill-considered, ardent, fervent, rushing, scampering, pushing, shoving, elbowing, uncontrolled, boisterous, furious, violent, breathless, breakneck, urgent, immediate, hotfoot, running, racing, speeding, hard-pressed, driven, hurried, haphazard, slapdash, careless, negligent, cursory, perfunctory, superficial, fleeting, last-minute, rough-and-tumble, unprepared, forced

NOUNS 4 haste, hurry, rush, speed, promptness, briskness, quickness, swiftness, rapidity, alacrity, celerity, expeditiousness, urge, impulsion, drive, stampede, push, spur, goad, whip, activity, scurry, hustle, bustle, hassle, flurry, whirl, scramble, flutter, fidget, fuss, agitation, distress, panic, nonpreparation, deadline, pressure, lateness, urgency, immediacy, importance, expedition, dispatch, velocity, acceleration, dash **5 hastiness**, precipitance, impetuosity, impulsiveness, recklessness, rashness, impatience, thoughtlessness

319 Hate

NOUNS 1 hate, hatred, dislike, aversion, loathing, detestation, spleen, disfavour, displeasure, disaffection, disapproval, disapprobation, repugnance, revulsion, repulsion, disgust, abhorrence, abomination, antipathy, antagonism, animosity, enmity, hostility, odium, execration, spite, malice, malevolence, malediction, malignity, bitterness, gall, rancour, acrimony, ill feeling, ill will, sullenness, resentment, grudge, jealousy, envy, venom, virulence **2 curse**, spell, evil eye, hex **3 race hatred**, racism, colour prejudice, segregation, apartheid, bigotry, anti-Semitism **4 hatefulness**, loathesomeness, obnoxiousness, despicability, contemptibility, unpopularity, alienation, estrangement, discredit, disrepute, black books **5 anger**, wrath, rage, ire, fury, temper, crossness **6 swearing**, cursing, profanity, shouting **7 hated thing**, pet hate, abomination, anathema, bugbear, bitter pill, unwelcome necessity, embarrassing situation, phobia, fear, filth, illness, injury **8 hater**, misanthrope, misanthropist, misogamist, misogynist, misandrist, racist, bigot, anti-Semite, xenophobe

ADJECTIVES 9 hating, loathing, detesting, abhorring, antipathetic, antagonistic, hostile, execrative, averse, spiteful, spleenful, vindictive, vicious, contemptuous, malicious, malevolent, maledictive, malignant, rancorous, acrimonious, poisonous, bitter, ill-natured, resentful, grudging, sour, sullen, jealous, envious, green-eyed, venomous **10 hated**, loathed, detestable, disgusting, abhorrent, odious, obnoxious, despicable, contemptible, execrable, accursed, unlovable, invidious, unpopular, discredited, disliked, unwelcome, unwanted, baneful, nasty, horrid, repugnant, revolting, repelling, abominable, disgusting, vile, repulsive, nauseous, alien, strange, foreign, unloved, scorned, jilted, unvalued, unmissed, unlamented, unmourned, unchosen, spurned **11 angry**, wrathful, irate, furious, bad-tempered, cross, choleric, implacable, profane, evil-speaking, cursing

VERBS 12 hate, dislike, detest, loathe, abhor, execrate, despise, abominate, disapprove, shudder at, recoil at, shrink from, reject, spurn, refuse, resent, envy, disrelish, condemn, denounce, avoid **13 curse**, execrate **14 cause hate**, antagonize, aggravate, exacerbate, alienate, estrange, sour, envenom, embitter, poison, incense, enrage, disgust, repel, nauseate, grate **15 anger**, rage, show ire

320 Health

ADJECTIVES 1 healthy, fit, well, fine, sound, fighting fit, eupeptic, fresh, thriving, flourishing, blooming, glowing, ruddy, rosy, rosy-cheeked, bouncing, bonny, lusty, energetic, vigorous, strapping, robust, hardy, sturdy, stalwart, great, convalescent, cured **2 healthful**, wholesome, nutritious, nourishing, tonic, bracing, invigorating, hygienic, sanitary, salubrious

NOUNS 3 health, fitness, well-being, soundness, trim, form, condition, heartiness, constitution, strength, vigour, energy, vitality, robustness, bloom, rosy cheeks, eupepsia, haleness, incorruption, longevity, shape, tone, fettle, state, Hygeia, recuperation **4 healthfulness**, wholesomeness, goodness, nutritiousness

VERBS 5 be healthy, feel well, feel fine, wear well, be well-preserved, bloom, thrive, flourish, keep fit **6 get healthy**, get well, recover, recuperate, mend **7 make healthy**, make well, treat, cure, heal

321 Hearing

NOUNS 1 hearing, audition, sharp ear, good ear, musicality, perfect pitch, poor ear, earshot, auditory range, audibility, listening, listening in, eavesdropping, attention, heed, mind, auscultation, sounding, acoustics **2 hearer**, listener, auditor, hearkener, ear witness, audience, congregation, house, audiophile, hi-fi enthusiast, eavesdropper, listener in, telephone tapper **3 auditorium**, concert hall, opera house, music room **4 ear**, outer ear, earlobe, earhole, cauliflower ear, jug ears, bat ears **5 internal ear**, middle ear, eardrum, tympanic membrane, auditory ossicle, incus, anvil, malleus, hammer, stapes, stirrup bone, Eustachian tube, inner ear, labyrinth, cochlea **6 otology**, otolaryngology, otorhinolaryngology, audiology, ear wax, ear drops, earache, otalgia, otitis, labyrinthitis, otologist, otolaryngologist, otorhinolaryngologist, audiologist, aurist

ADJECTIVES 7 aural, auditory, acoustic, audio, radio, transmitted, telephone, audiovisual, audient, listening, attentive **8 otological**, audiological, otolaryngological, otorhinolaryngological, nose, and throat), otalgic **9 hearable**, audible, reachable, within earshot,

loud, soft, resonant, sonorous, echoing, carrying, listenable
VERBS 10 hear, perceive, catch, listen, hearken, hark, attend, pay attention, concentrate, heed, mind, learn, gather, auscultate, sound, tune in, pick up, eavesdrop, tape, tap, intercept **11 be heard**, reach, carry, sound, reverberate, echo

322 Heat

NOUNS 1 heat, hotness, warmness, tepidity, temperature, radiant heat, body heat, warm-bloodedness, calescence, high temperature, fever, pyrexia, inflammation, flush, blush, fug, stuffiness, steam, overheating, sweatiness, perspiration, white heat, incandescence, flash point, melting point, boiling point **2 heat measurement**, temperature, calorific value, joule, calorie, heat unit, therm, calorimeter, thermometer, thermograph, Fahrenheit scale, Celsius scale, centigrade scale, Réaumur scale, specific heat **3 heater**, warmer, heating element, fan heater, central heating, radiator, hot-water tank, boiler, copper, immersion heater, geyser, thermostat, hypocaust, solar heating, antifreeze, ethylene glycol, de-icer, double glazing, lagging, insulation, polystyrene, winter woollies, overcoat, parka, poultice, fomentation, hot-water bottle, electric blanket, duvet, quilt, iron, soldering iron **4 burner**, cooker, stove, hob, hotplate, grill, griddle, kitchen range, oven, kettle, toaster, barbecue, spit, microwave oven, haybox, Dutch oven **5 hot weather**, summer, flaming June, dog days, hot spell, heat-haze, midday sun, sunbathing, sun-bed, suntan, browning, sunburn, heat rash, sunstroke, heatstroke, sunbather, nudist, heat wave, sultriness, Indian summer, thaw, melting, global warming, greenhouse effect **6 fire**, combustion, fireplace, hearth, inglenook, grate, flue, chimney, brazier, flame, blaze, glow, conflagration, holocaust, fireball, smoke, embers, clinker, coke, charcoal, bonfire, kiln, furnace, forge, oasthouse, incinerator, torch, pyre, campfire, paraffin stove, Bunsen burner, arson, pyromania, firebomb, incendiary bomb, Greek fire, wildfire, firestorm, towering inferno, flammability, combustibility, ignition
ADJECTIVES 7 hot, thermal, warm, mild, tepid, lukewarm chambré, snug, fuggy, stuffy, stifling, sultry, subtropical, tropical, equatorial, warming, calefacient, calorific, suffocating, piping hot, fiery, scalding, searing, scorching, blistering, cauterizing, roasting, boiling, simmering, steaming, sizzling, sweltering, smoking, red-hot, incandescent, molten **8 on fire**, alight, flaming, burning, ablaze, flaring, inflammable, flammable, combustible, incendiary, igneous, caustic, thermonuclear, volcanic **9 warm**, balmy, temperate, mild, fair, clement, summery, humid, muggy, close **10 warm-hearted**, cordial, hot-blooded, ebullient, homoiothermic, blushing, pyrexial, fevered, flushed, passionate, ardent, vehement, hot-tempered, burning, torrid, seething **11 heated**, insulated, lined, padded, double-glazed, lagged, centrally heated, warmed up, defrosted, heated up, preheated, baked, roasted, boiled, toasted, burnt, singed

VERBS 12 be hot, heat up, glow, defrost, thaw, melt, warm, reheat, cook, roast, toast, simmer, boil, scald, steam, bake, stew, braise, grill, fry, parch, wither, smelt, solder, weld, fuse, lag, insulate, line, pad, double-glaze, rub **13 burn**, fire, set alight, torch, kindle, ignite, flame, flare, blaze, crackle, smoke, fume, smoulder, burn up, singe, scorch, sear, calcine, char, carbonize, cremate, incinerate, vaporize, cauterize **14 feel hot**, keep warm, dress warmly, get overheated, blush, flush, sweat, perspire, be feverish, swelter, bask, sunbathe, tan, brown, burn

323 Heaviness

ADJECTIVES 1 heavy, weighty, weighing, weighed, heavyweight, middleweight, lightweight, featherweight, leaden, solid, dense, massive, considerable, great, stout, large, lumpish, bulky, fat, overweight, obese **2 loaded**, laden, charged, overloaded **3 ponderous**, onerous, heavy-handed, cumbersome, weighed down, burdensome, taxed, saddled, overburdened, overloaded, overladen, oppressive, taxing, overbalanced, top-heavy, unwieldy, pressing, incumbent on

NOUNS 4 heaviness, weightiness, weight, poundage, tonnage, solid body, massiveness, mass, lumpiness, bulkiness, fatness, obesity, corpulence **5 gravity**, specific gravity, gravitation, gravitational pull, G **6 displacement**, draught, sinkage, load, freight, cargo, bale, ballast, lading, charging, overloading, overweighting **7 weighing**, weighing-in, dead weight, dead load, live load, gross weight, net weight, overweight **8 weighing down**, saddling, burdensomeness, ponderousness, incubus, onerousness, oppressiveness, taxing, overtaxing, overbalance, unwieldiness, pressure, cumbersomeness, cumbrance, handicap, drag **9 avoirdupois weight**, troy weight, apothecaries' weight, atomic weight, molecular weight, ounce, pound, stone, ton, pennyweight, hundredweight, milligram, gram, kilogram, kilo, dram, drachm, carat, scruple, axle load **10 scales**, scale, calibrator, weighing machine, weighbridge, steelyard, balance, counterbalance, counterpoise, makeweight **11 weight**, sinker, lead, plumb, plummet, plumb bob

VERBS 12 be heavy, gain weight, balance, counterweigh, counterpoise, outweigh, overbalance, wallow, sink, gravitate, settle, founder **13 weigh on**, press upon **14 make heavy**, load, lade, weigh down, ballast, burden, overburden, overload, encumber, charge, tax, hinder, handicap, hamper, saddle, oppress, overweigh **15 weigh**, measure

324 Height

NOUNS 1 height, altitude, highness, tallness, stature, lankiness, ranginess, pitch, loftiness, elevation, rise, lift, exaltation, eminence, prominence **2 heights**, moorland, wold, fell, foothills, acclivity, incline, escarpment, climb, zenith, acme, apex, pinnacle, summit, peak, top, knap, plateau, tableland **3 mountain**, mount, alp, tor, ben, Olympus, Everest, hill, brae, pike, butte, cliff, bluff, crag, scar, precipice, hillock, hummock, monticule, knoll, kop, kopje, inselberg, roche moutonnée, drumlin, knob, hump, dune, mound, tump, barrow, tumulus **4 mountain range**, massif, sierra, chain, cordillera, Himalayas, Alps, Andes, Rockies, ridge, arête, chine, spur, kame, esker, os, moraine, col, saddleback, hogback, watershed, divide, bank, bench, crest, spine, comb **5 height measure**, relief, topography, orography, hypsography, hypsometry, altimetry, altimeter **6 tall thing**, telegraph pole, steeple, spire, flèche, tower, turret, campanile, belfry, watchtower, barbican, minaret, pagoda, ziggurat, lighthouse, windmill, pile, skyscraper, tower block, high-rise flats, mast, chimney, smokestack, pillar, column, shaft, pilaster, maypole, flagstaff, lamppost, pylon, crane, derrick, obelisk, monument, sequoia, redwood, giraffe **7 high thing**, ceiling, roof, vault, cupola, dome, lantern, attic, garret, loft, cockloft, mansard, penthouse, top floor, clerestory, weathercock, topmast, masthead, crow's-nest, eyrie, vantage point, triangulation station, sky, heaven, ether, stratosphere, mesosphere, thermosphere, exosphere, highchair, ladder, steps, stilts, high heels, high tide, flood tide, spring tide, equinoctial tide

ADJECTIVES 8 high, tall, altitudinal, high-up, sky-high, lofty, elevated, uplifted, upreared, upraised, high-rise, multistorey, towering, sky-scraping, ascending, rising, uprising, mounting, aspiring, soaring, flying, hovering, topping, overlooking, dominating, overshadowing, overhanging, beetling, cloud-topped, aerial, supernal, ethereal, airy, vertiginous, dizzy **9 higher**, taller, highest, tallest, superior, upper, upmost, uppermost **10 exalted**, elevated, eminent, prominent, sublime, supreme **11 tall**, lanky, rangy, leggy, long-legged, long-limbed, long-necked, giant, gigantic, colossal, statuesque, monumental, Amazonian, Olympian, knee-high **12 mountainous**, hilly, rolling, undulating, hillocky, hummocky, orogenic, alpine, Himalayan, Andean, mountain-dwelling **13 altimetric**, topographic, orographic

VERBS 14 be high, tower, tower above, spire, aspire, soar, fly, hover over, top, overtop, clear, surmount, overlook, dominate, command, overshadow, overarch, bestride, overhang **15 rise**, rise up, uprise, climb, ascend, mount, rear, rear up, uprear, grow, shoot up, culminate **16 raise**, heighten, elevate, hoist, lift, lift up, uplift, exalt **17 erect**, construct

325 Help

NOUNS 1 help, aid, assistance, hand, springboard, instrument, avail, use, benefit, advantage, improvement **2 support**, succour, relief, comfort, ease, remedy, ministration, offices, service, benefit, advice, counsel, guidance, constructive criticism, intercession, prayer, benediction, lift, boost, good turn, favour, kindness, rescue **3 sustenance**, support, subsistence, sustainment, maintenance, upkeep, livelihood, living, keep, daily bread, manna, provision, nourishment, nurture, mothering, care **4 medical assistance**, therapy, treatment, remedy, cure, medicine, first aid **5 financial assistance**, subsidy, subvention, grant, allowance, aid, stipend, donation, contribution, endowment, settlement, bestowal, dowry, scholarship, bursary, fellowship, sponsorship, funding, loan, advance **6 convenience**, facility, amenity, accommodation, appliance, aid, tool, labour-saving device **7 furtherance**, advancement, facilitation, expediting, forwarding, promotion, preferment **8 patronage**, fosterage, tutelage, auspices, aegis, championship, sponsorship, subsidization, seconding, advocacy, encouragement, backing, support, abetment **9 helpfulness**, cooperation, collaboration, willingness, usefulness, utility, benevolence, kindness, goodwill, advantageousness **10 helper**, assistant, aid, enabler, aide, mate, abettor, collaborator, colleague, partner, ally, attendant, adjutant, adjuvant, facilitator, auxiliary, second, subordinate, deputy, lieutenant, backup, standby, henchman, right-hand man, man Friday, girl Friday, support, backing, backroom boys, reinforcements, reserves, staff **11 recipient**, beneficiary **12 supporter**, mainstay, comfort, prop, succourer, good neighbour, good Samaritan, ministering angel, carer **13 adviser**, mentor, guide, cousellor, minister, pastor, consultant, arbitrator, advocate **14 benefactor**, well-wisher, philanthropist, patron, sponsor, promoter, backer, guardian angel, patron saint, tutelary, fairy godmother **15 home help**, housekeeper, daily help, domestic, cleaner

VERBS 16 help, aid, assist, abet, proffer aid, rescue, deliver **17 receive help**, accept aid, collect unemployment **18 support**, succour, comfort, hearten, minister to, care for, tend, look after, nurse, alleviate, relieve, ease, remedy, treat, doctor, bolster, strengthen, reinforce, buttress, shore up, prop up, boost, lift, revive **19 sustain**, support, maintain, keep, provide for, nourish, nurture, mother, pamper, coddle, cosset, protect **20 be helpful**, benefit, advantage, serve, avail, profit **21 improve**, better, ameliorate, enhance, accommodate, oblige, indulge, favour, collaborate, cooperate **22 advise**, counsel, guide, countenance, encourage, uphold, support, subscribe to, cultivate, give support, lend oneself, endorse, sanction, advocate, champion, argue for, intercede, patronize, sponsor, propose, second, back **23 back**, stand behind, get behind, stand by, side with, align with **24 serve**, attend, wait on, tend, look after, work for, cater for **25 be useful**, augment **26 find useful**, need **27 further**, advance, forward, promote, prefer, favour, advantage, facilitate, expedite, subserve, subvene, contribute to, help along, boost, conduce to, quicken, hasten **28 finance**, fund, sponsor, back, support, subsidize, subventionize, guarantee, endow, settle, bestow, donate, contribute to, pitch in, lend, loan, advance, set up

ADJECTIVES 29 helping, aiding, assisting, adjuvant, serving, supporting, supplementing, facilitative, instrumental, promoting **30 supplementary**, auxiliary, subsidiary, ancillary, accessory **31 supportive**, comforting, reassuring, succouring, morale-boosting, caring, tending, ministering, encouraging, heartening, sustaining, fostering **32 helpful**, useful, utilitarian, serviceable, convenient, handy, informative, practical, constructive, positive, furthering, promoting, contributory **33 beneficial**, good, salutary, advantageous, favourable, propitious, expedient, profitable, gainful, valuable, remedial **34 benevolent**, kind, considerate, benign, sympathetic, friendly, neighbourly, cooperative, willing, accommodating, obliging, generous, charitable, beneficent, philanthropic, indulgent, well-disposed

326 Hindrance

NOUNS 1 hindrance, impediment, encumbrance, obstruction, restriction, circumscription, restraint, retardation, control, curb, detention, detainment, limitation, friction, interruption, interference, interception, interposition, intervention, meddling, opposition, contrariness, unwillingness, refusal, interdiction, injunction, resistance, counteraction, countermeasure, obviation, determent, dissuasion, discouragement, frustration, foiling, prevention, repression, preclusion, prohibition, stopping, forestalling **2 obstacle**, block, blockade, lockout, stoppage, tollgate, strike, barrier, bar, picket line, embargo, intervention, impediment, turnstile, bottleneck, jam, difficulty, deterrent, drawback, inconvenience, bureaucracy, hazard, hurdle, hitch, snag, drag, rub, catch, vicious circle, check, stay, arrest, sabotage, filibuster, delay, trouble, contretemps, accident, breakdown, technical hitch, malfunction, glitch, teething troubles, flaw, impasse, deadlock, botch **3 barrier**, wall, fence, barbed wire, portcullis, jetty, mole, breakwater, levee, dam, dike, bulwark, rampart, bunker, buffer, parapet, earthwork, embankment, moat, ditch, weir, contraceptive **4 restraint**, curb, check, shackles, chains, tether, fetter, bond, tie, apron strings, knot, rein, leash, lead, brake, wheel clamp, doorstop **5 inhibition**, introversion, conservativeness, embarrassment, shyness, negativism **6 burden**, inconvenience, handicap, encumbrance, debts, dependents, white elephant, overload

VERBS 7 hinder, impede, encumber, obstruct, restrict, circumscribe, choke, stifle, restrain, disable, incapacitate, undermine, impair, control, curb, detain, hold back, limit, retard, stall, interrupt, interfere, intercept, upset, interpose, intervene, meddle, bother, heckle, barrack, oppose, refuse, resist, counteract, obviate, deter, dissuade, frustrate, thwart, spike, foil, foul up, prevent, repress, preclude, prohibit, forbid, stop, scotch, forestall, hamper, stymie **8 block**, blockade, wall, fence, dam, strike, picket, bar, lock out, embargo, intervene, impede, trip, bottleneck, deter, inconvenience, snag, sabotage, filibuster, delay, stall, protract, malfunction **9 restrain**, curb, check, shackle, chain, tether, fetter, bind, tie, rein, leash, brake **10 be inhibited**, be introverted, embarrass, shy **11 burden**, inconvenience, handicap, encumber

ADJECTIVES 12 hindering, hindered, impeding, held back, unhelpful, uncooperative, unwilling, contrary, encumbering, obstructive, restrictive, cramping, circumscriptive, limited, interfering, intrusive, interventional, meddling, deterrent, dissuasive, discouraging, off-putting, preventive, defensive, prophylactic, counteractive, repressive, preclusive, prohibitive **13 blocked**, barred, walled in, fenced in, restrained, anchored, curbed, shackled, chained, tethered, leashed, deterrent, interventional, inconvenient, bureaucratic, regulatory, deadlocked, burdened, handicapped, saddled with **14 inhibitive**, introversive, conservative, embarrassing

327 Hissing Sound

NOUNS 1 hiss, sibilation, assibilation, susurration, rustle, swish, swoosh, froufrou, sputter, splutter, splash, plash, wheezing, whistling, white noise, rhonchus, rale, sneeze, wheeze, effervescence, sizzling, squish, squash **2 catcall**, jeer, boo, hoot

VERBS 3 hiss, sibilate, assibilate, lisp, whisper, shush, hush, rustle, susurrate, swish, swoosh, sputter, splutter, splash, plash, wheeze, rasp, whistle, snuffle, sneeze, fizz, effervesce, sizzle, whiz, squish, squash **4 catcall**, jeer, boo, hoot

ADJECTIVES 5 hissing, sibilant, rustling, whispering, sneezing, wheezy, asthmatic, fizzy, effervescent **6 catcalling**, jeering, booing, hooting, disapproving

328 History

• *History is more or less bunk.* Henry Ford.

NOUNS 1 history, historiography, social history, economic history, religious history, political history, constitutional history, legal history, local history, counterfactual history, historical materialism, revisionist history **2 archaeology**, fossilology, Assyriology, Egyptology, Sumerology, palaeology, palaeontology **3 historian**, recorder, biographer, archivist, historiographer, archaeologist, Assyriologist, Egyptologist, Sumerologist, palaeologist, palaeontologist, palaeographer **4 chronicle**, history, account, record, biography, diary, autobiography, memoirs, life story, journal, log, recollection, report, documentary, annals, archive, minutes, notes, track record, file, dossier, background, information, narration, description, tradition, legend, myth **5 past time**, history, the past, yesteryear, olden days, former times, bygones, long ago, ancient history, antiquity, prehistory, protohistory **6 looking back**, remembrance, reminiscence, flashback, recalling, reviewing, harking back

ADJECTIVES 7 historic, ancient, old, ancestral, prehistoric, protohistoric, diachronic, antediluvian, primordial, primal, aboriginal, antiquated, dated, archaic, former, prior, Classical, Hellenistic, Medieval, Elizabethan, Renaissance, Victorian, atavistic, vestigial, remaining **8 historical**, historiographical, prehistorical, protohistorical, archaeological, Assyriological, Egyptological, Sumerological, palaeological, palaeographical **9 in the past**, over, finished, old hat, yesterday's news, extinct, defunct, obsolete, expired, lapsed, passé, has been, retroactive **10 chronicled**, recorded, logged, documented, minuted, archival, reported, biographical, autobio-

graphical, factual, actual, authentic, genuine, valid, verifiable, traditional
VERBS 11 chronicle, record, log, report, document, register, minute, file, narrate, relate **12 antiquarianize**, archaize, excavate, exhume, look back **13 remember**, reminisce, recall, recollect, review **14 turn back time**, reconstruct

329 Hope

- *Still nursing the unconquerable hope,/ Still clutching the inviolable shade.* Matthew Arnold
- *Hope springs eternal in the human breast;/ Man never is, but always to be blest.* Alexander Pope.

NOUNS 1 hope, optimism, cheerfulness, buoyancy, positive thinking, bright side, silver lining, rose-coloured glasses **2 expectation**, anticipation, assumption, presumption, trust, confidence, faith, belief **3 aspiration**, ambition, dream, vision, high hopes, great expectations, aim, intention, wish, desire, longing, yearning, pipe dream, fool's paradise, Utopia, Erewhon, promised land, dream world **4 comfort**, cheer, reassurance, encouragement, support, security, promise, auspiciousness
VERBS 5 hope, count on, rely on, bank on, believe, feel confident, rest assured, assume **6 aspire**, aim, dream, wish, desire, long, yearn, expect, await **7 be optimistic**, think positively **8 be hopeful**, touch wood, take heart, cheer up, buck up **9 inspire hope**, comfort, cheer, reassure, encourage, promise
ADJECTIVES 10 hopeful, optimistic, sanguine, cheerful, buoyant, positive **11 expectant**, anticipating, confident **12 aspirant**, ambitious, go-getting, dreaming, wishful, desirous, longing **13 cheering**, heartening, reassuring, encouraging, promising, auspicious, propitious, favourable, bright, sunny, golden, rosy

330 Hopelessness

NOUNS 1 hopelessness, no hope, despondency, discouragement, defeatism, scepticism, negativism, pessimism, cynicism, dejection, despair, melancholy, depression **2 hopeless situation**, lost cause, quandary, predicament
ADJECTIVES 3 hopeless, forlorn, despondent, comfortless, cheerless, discouraged, defeated, negative, sceptical, pessimistic, cynical, dejected, downcast, despairing, desperate, suicidal, desolate, disconsolate, melancholic, depressed **4 past hope**, terminal, incurable, inoperable, irremediable, irreparable, irrevocable, irreversible, incorrigible, irredeemable, irretrievable, beyond recall, lost **5 inauspicious**, unpropitious, ill-omened, ill-starred, doomed, ominous **6 futile**, useless, worthless, pointless, vain **7 bad**, poor, inferior, incompetent, lamentable, awful, terrible
VERBS 8 be hopeless, give up, despair, doubt, lose heart **9 disappoint**, crush

331 Horizontality

NOUNS 1 horizontality, flatness, levelness, planeness, plainness, evenness, smoothness, flushness, lying, reclining, recumbency, prostration, proneness, supineness **2 horizontal surface**, flat, level, plane, homaloid, water level, sea level **3 flat thing**, disc, slab, layer, stratum, tablet, pancake, flatfish, flounder, flatware, saucer, plate, platter, tray, gridiron, flat tyre, flats, plain, prairie, pampas, steppe, green, bedding plane, bed, esplanade, plateau, tableland, terrace, ledge, platform, table, floor, ceiling, horizon **4 flattener**, plane, press, iron, mangle, rolling pin, steamroller **5 planometer**, planimeter

VERBS 6 be horizontal, recline, lie down, sprawl, spread-eagle, prostrate oneself **7 make horizontal**, level, flatten, grade, plane, flush, even, equalize, smooth, iron, press, roll, beat flat, trample down, lay down, spread, knock down, knock flat, prostrate

ADJECTIVES 8 horizontal, flat, level, plane, plain, planar, two-dimensional, tabular, homaloidal, even, smooth, unwrinkled **9 flattened**, levelled, smoothed, pressed, ironed, rolled, consolidated, beaten flat, squashed flat, well-trodden, trampled down **10 lying**, lying down, flat out, recumbent, decumbent, accumbent, prostrate, prone, procumbent, face down, supine, couchant, reclining, sprawling

332 Horses

NOUNS 1 horse, equine species, quadruped, horseflesh, dobbin, pony, mount, warhorse, charger, courser, steed, stallion, gelding, mare, sire, dam, foal, colt, yearling, filly, mustang, bronco, roadster, ambler, jennet, nag, jade, hack, stud, brood mare, packhorse, strawberry roan, dapple-grey, bay, chestnut, sorrel, black, piebald, skewbald, pinto, mustang, dun, bayo coyote, bangtail, cayuse, palomino, cob, garroway, garron, sheltie, montura, hackney, hunter, Pegasus, Black Bess, Black Beauty, Trigger, Champion, Silver **2 thoroughbred**, purebred, pacer, stepper, trotter, courser, racehorse, steeplechaser, hurdler, foxhunter, draught horse, plough horse, cart horse, drayhorse, coach horse **3 horsemanship**, horsewomanship, equitation, equestrianism, riding, manège, dressage, show jumping, eventing, gymkhana, horseracing, steeplechasing, point-to-point racing, polo, bareback riding **4 horse person**, horseman, equestrian, equestrienne, postilion, postboy, sowar, hussar, lancer, dragoon, Cossack, cavalier, knight errant, huntsman, kennel man, racing steward, jockey, steeplechaser, bookmaker, show jumper, eventer, trainer, breaker, roughrider, bronco-buster, buckaroo, cowboy, cowgirl, gaucho, saddler, black saddler, loriner, farrier, blacksmith, vet, horse doctor

VERBS 5 ride, saddle, mount, trot, canter, gallop, break in, train, race, steeplechase, hunt, jump, groom

ADJECTIVES 6 equine, equestrian, horse-riding, horseracing, hunting, show-jumping, mounted

333 Horticulture

NOUNS 1 horticulture, gardening, landscape gardening, floriculture, market gardening, pomiculture, citriculture, fruitage, viticulture, viniculture, arboriculture **2 garden**, flower garden, rock garden, rose garden, water garden, parterre, Japanese garden, sunken garden, indoor garden, winter garden, bottle garden, hanging garden, bonsai, herb garden, vegetable garden, kitchen garden, allotment, cabbage patch, market garden, fruit farm, orchard, hop garden, vineyard, arboretum, roof garden, flowerbed, rosery, rockery, lawn, shrubbery, hedge, topiary, bower, arbour, grotto, patio, terrace, window box, zoological garden, garden city **3 nursery**, glasshouse, greenhouse, conservatory, orangery, potting shed, polytunnel, hothouse, coolhouse, forcing house, forcing bed, cold frame, propagator, cloche, module, seed tray, grow bag, compost heap, flowerpot, planter **4 horticulturist**, gardener, plantsman, landscapist, topiarist, floriculturist, flower grower, rosarian, seedsman, nurseryman, market gardener, fruiter, fruit farmer, pomologist, orchardist, viniculturist

VERBS 5 practise horticulture, garden, landscape, cultivate **6 cultivate**, plant, pot, sow, seed, dib, dibble, puddle in, transplant, pot on, prick out, plant out, bed out, dig, trench, delve, spade, fork, rotavate, hoe, rake, weed, thin, train, tie in, stake, prune, mow, crop, lop, deadhead, debud, deblossom, mulch, topdress, fertilize, compost, water, dust, propagate, breed, pollinate, graft

ADJECTIVES 7 horticultural, floricultural, ornamental, herbaceous, herbal, vegetal, vegetative, leguminous, cereal, arboricultural, arboreal, silvicultural, pomological, viticultural, vinicultural, aquicultural **8 herbicidal**, pesticidal

334 Human Cry

NOUNS 1 cry, call, outcry, outburst, battle cry, vociferation, clamour, uproar, hullabaloo, hubbub, shout, scream, screech, shriek, yell, roar, bellow, bawl, yawl **2 cry of joy**, laugh, cachinnation, guffaw, hoot, whoop, yippee, chortle, chuckle, giggle, titter **3 cry of praise**, acclamation, paean, hallelujah, hosanna, glossolalia, applause, cheer, whoop, bravo **4 cry of greeting**, hello, hail, greetings **5 hunting cry**, whoa, view halloo **6 cry of pain**, scream, shriek, squeal, gasp, whine, whimper, groan, moan, keening, ululation, lamentation, wail, howl, bawl, sob, sigh, boohoo, ouch **7 cry of disapproval**, exclamation, ejaculation, interjection, expoetive, hoot, jeer, boo, hiss, catcall, curse **8 musical cry**, song, yodel, chant

VERBS 9 cry out, call, call out, vociferate, shout, blast out, thunder out, explode, scream, shriek, yell, roar, bellow, bawl, yawl, yowl, squall **10 laugh**, cachinnate, guffaw, hoot, whoop, chortle, chuckle, giggle, titter **11 cheer**, hurrah, horray **12 cry**, sob, sigh, groan, moan, whine, whimper, yammer, mewl, pule, gasp, fret, lament, weep, wail, keen, ululate, howl, bawl **13 hiss**, hoot, boo, jeer, catcall, exclaim, ejaculate, curse, tell off, shout down **14 sing out**, give voice, yodel

ADJECTIVES 15 vociferous, noisy, loud, vocal, stentorian, full-throated, thundering, booming, deafening, shouting, screaming, yelling, bellowing, roaring, uproarious, clamorous **16 cheering**, rousing, shooping, laughing, chuckling **17 crying**, sobbing, sighing, groaning, moaning, whimpering, weeping, wailing, howling, ululant **18 hissing**, booing, jeering, cursing

335 Humankind

NOUNS 1 humankind, mankind, womankind, humanity, Homo sapiens, hominid, man, earthlings, everyone, everybody, the living, us **2 human nature**, mortality **3 uncivilized human**, primitive humanity, backward peoples, barbarians, pagans, savages, bushmen, aborigines, ancient man, early man, primeval man, Homo erectus, Stone-age man, Neanderthal man, apeman, caveman **4 civilized human**, modern man, well-bred person, gentleman, lady, political animal, culture, civilization, the ancients, Sumerian, Egyptian, Persian, Greek, Roman, Mogul, Chinese **5 study of mankind**, anthropology, craniometry, anthropogenesis, somatology, demography, sociology, humanitarianism, humanism, anthroposophy, anthropomorphism, ethnology, folklore **6 person**, individual, human, Adamite, mortal, creature, body, soul, everyman, John Doe, earthling, tellurian, I, one, somebody, party, customer, character, type, element, personage, VIP, celebrity, star, favourite, personnel, cast **7 humanlike machine**, robot, automaton, android, humanoid, cyborg **8 group**, kinship group, family, clan, brotherhood, clique, set, society, class, nobility, aristocracy, gentility, bourgeoisie, public, populace, citizenry, inhabitants, the masses, commonalty, plebs, hoi polloi, people, folk, community, neighbourhood, ghetto, ethnic group, race **9 member of society**, citizen, nobleman, aristocrat, patrician, gentleman, lady, bourgeois, white-collar worker, commoner, blue-collar worker, colleague **10 nation**, people, state, country, realm, kingdom, nationality, statehood, civil society, body politic, demos, city state, welfare state, nation state, isolationism, neutrality, commonwealth, polity, democracy, republic, socialism, communism, totalitarianism, dictatorship, nationalism, Pan-Africanism, chauvinism, jingoism, expansionism, imperialism

ADJECTIVES 11 human, mortal, creaturely, fleshly, earthborn, tellurian, anthropoid, humanoid, hominoid, humanlike, subhuman, civilized, anthropological, ethnographical, racial, ethnic, anthropocentric, anthropomorphic, personal, individual, humanistic **12 national**, state, civic, governmental, democratic, republican, socialistic, communistic, totalitarian, public, general, communal, tribal, social, societal, cosmopolitan

VERBS 13 make human, humanize

336 Humility

• *Blessed are the meek: for they shall inherit the earth.* Bible: Matthew.

ADJECTIVES 1 humble, meek, unpretentious, unassuming, modest, mouselike, harmless, inoffensive, undistinguished, unimportant, without airs **2 lowly**, low, poor, mean, small, plebeian **3 humbled**, humiliated, embarrassed, mortified, deflated, wounded, shamed, scorned, abject, chagrined, crushed, hangdog, put down, squashed, debunked, slapped down, rebuked, disapproved, discomfited, defeated, reduced, diminished, dejected, degraded, deflated, lowered, brought down, laid low, shamefaced, crestfallen, disconcerted, broken-spirited, dashed, abashed **4 self-abasing**, self-effacing, deferent, self-submitting, diminished, self-abnegating, dispirited, self-doubting, self-deprecating, condescending **5 submissive**, subservient, obedient, resigned **6 humiliating**, embarrassing, mortifying, wounding

NOUNS 7 humility, humbleness, meekness, modesty, unpretentiousness, simplicity, undistinguished **8 lowliness**, poorness, meanness **9 humiliation**, embarrassment, mortification, comedown, descent, deflation, wounded pride, kenosis, hangdog look **10 abasement**, debasement, degradation, putdown **11 self-abasement**, self-effacement, deference, self-submission, diminishment, self-abnegation **12 submissiveness**, subservience, obedience, resignation **13 disrepute**, shame, disgrace, mortification, shamefacedness **14 rebuke**, retort, crushing reply, reprimand **15 condescension**, deigning

VERBS 16 humiliate, humble, mortify, embarrass, put out, chasten, disconcert, abash, snub, crush, squash, slight **17 condescend**, deign, stoop, lower oneself, demean oneself, unbend **18 be humble**, succumb **19 submit**, crawl, knuckle under, eat dirt **20 humble oneself**, resign oneself, demean oneself, genuflect, bow, scrape, crawl, climb down **21 shame**, disgrace **22 abase**, debase, crush, degrade, abash, reduce, diminish, demean, bring low, trip up, take down, set down **23 be humiliated**, feel small, look foolish **24 outdo**, outstare, frown down, daunt

337 Humour

• *True wit is nature to advantage dress'd;/ What oft was thought, but ne'er so well express'd.* Alexander Pope.

NOUNS 1 humorousness, funniness, wit, jokiness, drollery, dryness, facetiousness, flippancy **2 amusement**, entertainment, diversion, fun, merriment, mirth, laughter, enjoyment **3 wit**, joking, jesting, joshing, teasing, kidding, clowning, buffoonery, quipping, wordplay, banter, badinage, repartee, sarcasm **4 entertainment**, comedy, satire, parody, caricature, send-up, take-off, farce, lampoon, burlesque, slapstick, cartoon **5 joke**, jest, jape, caper, prank, trick, witticism, gag, pun, one-liner, wisecrack, quip, pleasantry, funny story, yarn, old chestnut, tall story, dirty story **6 humorist**, wit, wag, joker, jester, tease, teaser, gagster, wisecracker, jokesmith, comic, comedian, stand-up comic, alternative comedian, straight man, clown, buffoon, gag writer, ironist, satirist, lampooner

ADJECTIVES 7 funny, amusing, diverting, entertaining, laughable, risible, hilarious, uproarious **8 humorous**, witty, funny, jocular, jocose, joking, slapstick, waggish, nimblewitted, quick-witted, smart, comic, droll, amusing, whimsical, quirky, zany, merry, pawky, dry, facetious, farcical, sarcastic, ironic, satirical, flippant **9 humouring**, pleasing, placating, indulging, pampering, cossetting, spoiling, cajoling, flattering, sycophantic, servile, ingratiating, toadying, unctuous **10 four humours**, phlegmatic, sanguine

VERBS 11 be humorous, entertain,

amuse, regale, divert, joke, josh, jest, banter, pun, quip, wisecrack, clown, tease, rag, twit, kid, rib, scoff, mock, satirize, parody, send up, take off, lampoon **12 laugh**, giggle, snigger, snicker, titter, chuckle, chortle, guffaw, howl **13 humour**, gratify, please, placate, indulge, pamper, cosset, spoil, cajole, flatter, patronize, condescend, smarm

338 Hygiene

NOUNS 1 hygiene, sanitation, cleanliness, asepsis, antisepsis, disinfection, sterilization, chlorination, pasteurization, preventive medicine, prophylaxis, quarantine, isolation, protection, immunity, inoculation, vaccination, fumigation, decontamination, purification, sanatorium, spa, hot springs, thermae, health farm, keeping fit, exercise, sport, working-out **2 salubrity**, healthiness, health, well-being, fitness, wholesomeness, nutritiousness, healthy diet, smokeless area, ventilation, fresh air, open air, sea air

ADJECTIVES 3 hygienic, sanitary, disinfected, chlorinated, pasteurized, sterilized, clean, pure, aseptic, antiseptic, germ-free, sanative, prophylactic, immunizing, protective, remedial, salubrious, healthy, ventilated, refreshing, restorative, salutary, beneficial, wholesome, nutritious, nourishing, body-building, noninjurious, benign, uninfectious, innocuous, immune, vaccinated

VERBS 4 be hygienic, prevent disease **5 make hygienic**, sanitate, disinfect, chlorinate, pasteurize, boil, sterilize, antisepticize, immunize, inoculate, vaccinate, quarantine, isolate, ventilate, aerate, freshen, fumigate, decontaminate, purify, cleanse, drain, dry, conserve, preserve

339 Idea

NOUNS 1 idea, notion, abstraction, thought, thinking, concept, observation, perception, understanding, awareness, apprehension, comprehension, reflection, assumption, presumption, reaction, estimation, feeling, sentiment, memory, construct, mental picture, imago, ideatum, noumenon **2 theory**, hypothesis, suggestion, conjecture, speculation, supposition, suspicion, indication, fancy, clue, hint, guess, feeling **3 plan**, intention, scheme, project, proposal, invention, idea, brainwave, brainstorm **4 purpose**, aim, design, function, goal, object, target, end, point, reason, significance **5 ideology**, opinion, view, stand, stance, position, philosophy, beliefs, principles, creed, credo, teachings, tenets, ideals, morals, standards **6 ideal**, model, example, paragon, paradigm, standard, pattern, quintessence, epitome, prototype, archetype, vision, dream, Utopia, fantasy, fancy **7 idealism**, idealization, optimism, visionariness, utopianism, romanticism, daydreaming, wishful thinking, impracticality **8 imagination**, inventiveness, originality, creativity, ingenuity, inspiration, perception

ADJECTIVES 9 theoretical, notional, abstract, putative, conceptual, perceptual, philosophical, hypothetical, conjectural, speculative, suppositional, propositional, suggestive, indicative, suspected, assumed, presumed **10 ideational**, mental, cerebral, intellectual, imagined, visualized, conceived, conceptualized, inspired, aware, reflective, inventive, creative, original, ingenious **11 purposive**, functional, teleological, aiming, functioning, targeting, intentional, proposed, aimed, schematic, designed, planned, reasoned, significant **12 ideal**, model, exemplary, paradigmatic, epitomical, quintessential, prototypical, archetypical, visionary, fantastic, idealistic, optimistic, utopian, romantic, sentimental, dreamy

VERBS 13 have an idea, suggest itself, dawn upon, realize, perceive, remember, hit one, strike one, deduce, understand, apprehend, intuit, see **14 imagine**, ideate, think, reflect, deliberate, feel, conceive, visualize, conceptualize, picture, envision, formulate, create, invent, originate, think up, conjure up, dream, fancy, fantasize, idealize, romanticize, daydream **15 inspire**, inspirit, animate, exhilarate **16 theorize**, hypothesize, conjecture, suggest, suspect, guess, reckon, estimate, suppose, opine, believe, assume **17 aim**, plan, plot, scheme, design, propose, intend, target, point to, head for, aspire **18 epitomize**, exemplify, model, pattern, indicate, represent

340 Identification

NOUNS 1 identification, recognition, detection, differentiation, diagnosis, indication, pinpointing, designation, naming, labelling, characterization, characteristic, form, shape, outline, size, colour, mannerism, trait, denomination, classification, categorization, cataloguing, analysis, establishing, authentication, verification, substantiation **2 identity**, particularity, individuality, distinctiveness, uniqueness, personality, self **3 means of identification**, ID, name, title, signature, autograph, initials, mark, monogram, identity card, passport, visa, permit, credentials, endorsement, fingerprint, dental record, genetic fingerprinting, passport photograph, Identikit, identity number, telephone number, call sign, password, token, shibboleth, trademark, brand name, tradename, copyright, logo, hallmark, cachet, seal, signet, sigil, superscription, impress, imprint, watermark, letterhead, colophon, bookplate, ex-libris, caste mark, tattoo, birthmark, label, tag, tally, tessera, sticker, badge, emblem, nameplate, card, pub sign, certificate, ticket, chit, docket, invoice, bill **4 insignia**, badge, markings, throne, sceptre, orb, crown, regalia, gavel, mace, staff, military insignia, star, bar, stripe, chevron, wings, epaulette, brassard, aiguillette, cockade, hackle, sash, medal, ribbon, decoration, victory laurels, garland, wreath, bays, chaplet, trophy, medal, cup, rosette **5 uniform**, military uniform, regimentals, school uniform, sports outfit, livery, national dress, prison clothes, widow's weeds, lapel pin **6 flag**, standard, banner, ensign, bunting, colours, regimental colours, ship's colours, military flag, vexillum, labarum, gonfalcon, guidon, oriflamme, bannerette, streamer, pennon, banderole, pennant, swallowtail, burgee, flagpole, flagstaff, canton, hoist, fly, grommet, halyard, heading, sleeve, truck **7 heraldic device**, arms, crest, crown, motto, device, fleur-de-lis, Tudor rose

VERBS 8 identify, recognize, detect, distinguish, differentiate, diagnose, analyse, indicate, show, exhibit, point out, pinpoint, establish, substantiate, corroborate, designate, name, specify, hallmark, earmark, label, docket, tag, tab, classify, categorize, catalogue, reference, record, photograph, register, ticket, limit, annotate, underline, underscore, tick, mark off, etch, engrave, imprint, tattoo, pierce, notch, chalk, scar, disfigure, blaze, brand, burn in, stamp, seal, punch, impress, emboss, overprint **9 identify oneself**, sign, ratify, countersign, endorse, autograph, inscribe, undersign, initial, be conspicuous

ADJECTIVES 10 identified, recognized, substantiated, corroborated, identifiable, recognizable, known, designated, denoted, labelled, tagged, marked, hallmarked, trademarked, earmarked, characterized, classified, categorized, referenced, signatory, sigillary, fingerprinted, photographed, branded **11 heraldic**, emblematic

341 Ignorance

• *No more; where ignorance is bliss,/ 'Tis folly to be wise.* Thomas Gray.

NOUNS 1 ignorance, nescience, incognizance, incomprehension, unawareness, insensibility, unconsciousness, blankness, nonrecognition, unfamiliarity, awkwardness, gaucherie, uncertainty, illiteracy, backwardness, unenlightenment, unskilfulness, artlessness, naivety, innocence, unintelligence, empty-headedness, folly **2 half-knowledge**, inexperience, inexpertness, amateurism, semi-literacy, dabbling, superficiality, sciolism, dilettantism, quackery, charlatanism **3 unknown thing**, mystery, enigma, secret, anonymity, guesswork, complete blank, closed book, all Greek **4 unknown person**, John Doe, dark horse, anon.

ADJECTIVES 5 ignorant, unknowing, nescient, incognizant, unwitting, unaware, oblivious, unconscious, blank, uninformed, misled, unskilled, uninitiated, green, naive, simple, innocent, gauche, awkward, unenlightened, backward, illiterate, uneducated, low-brow, Philistine, stupid, dull, dim-witted, slow-witted, thick **6 semi-skilled**, semi-literate, semi-schooled, lay, amateur, inexperienced, unqualified, quack, shallow, superficial **7 unknown**, mysterious, strange, unfamiliar, unrecognized, unidentified, anonymous, secret, obscure, unseen, ineffable, unperceived

VERBS 8 be ignorant, not know, know nothing, lack information, be stumped **9 know little**, dabble in **10 make ignorant**, mystify

342 Ill Health

NOUNS 1 ill health, poor health, failing health, unhealthiness, delicacy, weakness, infirmity, debility, diathesis, sickiness, manginess, morbidity, illness, sickness, indisposition, cachexia, chronic complaint, allergy, hay fever, catarrh, invalidism, valetudinarianism, hypochondria, nerves **2 illness**, disease, disorder, sickness, cold, influenza, fever, nausea, malaise, ailment, indisposition, malady, distemper, affliction, complaint, disability, handicap, condition, visitation, attack, spasm, stroke, seizure, apoplexy, fit, shock, virus, poisoning, complication, infection, contagion, eating disorder, malnutrition, addiction, cancer, terminal illness, fatal illness, coma, death, sickbed, deathbed, epidemic, plague **3 sick person**, invalid, patient, in-patient, out-patient, sufferer, case, valetudinarian, hypochondriac, malingerer, weakling, consumptive, asthmatic, bronchitic, dyspeptic, diabetic, haemophiliac, bleeder, insomniac, neuropath, addict, alcoholic, spastic, arthritic, paralytic, paraplegic, quadriplegic, hemiplegic, disabled person **4 pathology**, forensic pathology, diagnosis, prognosis, etiology, nosology, epidemiology, bacteriology

ADJECTIVES 5 unhealthy, ill, unfit, unsound, sickly, infirm, decrepit, weak, tired, run down, delicate, invalid, valetudinarian, hypochondriac, mangy, undernourished, anorexic, malnourished, emaciated, peaky, anaemic, jaundiced **6 sick**, ill, unwell, poorly, indisposed, off-colour, wasting away, queasy, feverish, headachy, confined, quarantined, bedridden, prostrate, hospitalized, taken ill, comatose, serious, critical, chronic, incurable, terminal, inoperable **7 diseased**, infected, contaminated, tainted, stricken, distempered, pathological, pathogenic, morbid, morbific, peccant, insalubrious, unhygienic, iatrogenic, psychosomatic, gangrenous, infectious, contagious, poisonous, toxic, purulent, degenerative, consumptive, phthistic, tuberculous, diabetic, hydrocephalic, anaemic, leukaemic, haemophilic, arthritic, rheumaticky, rickety, palsied, paralytic, spastic, epileptic, leprous, carninomatous, cancerous, oncogenic, carcinogenic, syphilitic, venereal, oedematous, gouty, bronchial, croupy, sniffly, snuffly, asthmatic, allergic, pyretic, febrile, feverish, delirious, shivering, aguish, sore, tender, painful, ulcerous, inflamed, rashy, spotty, erysipelatous

VERBS 8 be unhealthy, ail, suffer, feel ill, complain of, feel sick, vomit, sicken, collapse, faint, languish, pine, peak, droop, weaken, fail, flag, drop

343 Imagination

NOUNS 1 imagination, vision, perception, creativity, invention, originality, ingenuity, resourcefulness, enterprise, skill, fancifulness, fantasy, visualization, objectification, conceptualization, imagery, word-painting, artistry **2 inspiration**, muse, afflatus, frenzy, ecstasy **3 insight**, understanding, empathy, sympathy, moral sensibility **4 ideality**, impression, concept, thought, idealization, appearance, image, picture, projection, brainchild, notion, idea, whim, maggot, vagary, caprice, whimsy, crinkum-crankum, absurdity, unreality, figment, fiction, creative writing, story, novel, romance, fantasy, fairy tale, daydream, extravaganza, rhapsody, exaggeration, falsehood, poetic licence, quixotry, shadow-boxing **5 fantasy**, fabrication, improvisation, make-believe, vision, dream, nightmare, bogey, phantom, ghost, apparition, spectre, shadow, dimness, mirage, fancy, illusion, trompe l'oeil, delusion, hallucination, chimera **6 reverie**, daydream, brown study, abstractedness, sleepwalking, somnambulism, trance, insensibility, delirium, frenzy, subjectivism, autosuggestion, wishful thinking, sophistry, window-shopping, pipe dream, fantasia, wish, desire, romanticism **7 idealism**, Utopianism, millennium, idle fancy, myth **8 dreamland**, dream world, Utopia, Erewhon, promised land, El Dorado, Arcadia, Shangri-la, never-never land, wonderland

ADJECTIVES 9 imaginative, creative, inventive, innovative, original, ingenious, resourceful, enterprising, skilful, clever, eidetic, visualizing, perceptive, fertile, fecund, productive, inspired, fancy-led, romancing, high-flown, rhapsodic, enthusiastic, exaggerated, lively, vivid, poetic, fictional, Utopian, idealistic **10 fantastical**, unreal, bizarre, grotesque, extravagant, whimsical, fanciful, preposterous, absurd, outlandish, impractical, Heath Robinson, visionary, otherworldly, starry-eyed, quixotic **11 imaginary**, unreal, abstract, illusory, fanciful, chimerical, ethereal, unsubstantial, subjective, hypothetical, suppositional, conceptual, notional, ideal, dreamy, visionary, shadowy, fictitious, fictional, storybook, make-believe, created, invented, fabricated, contrived, devised, pretend, simulated, imitated, nonexistent, untrue, unhistorical, mythical, legendary **12 imaginable**, conceivable

VERBS 13 imagine, perceive, conceive, create, invent, think, suppose, think of, conjure up, fancy, dream up, make up, devise, concoct, coin, hatch, produce, fabricate, originate, excogitate, improvise, visualize, envisage, picture, conceptualize, represent, paint, write, compose, realize, objectify, capture, summon up, exaggerate, pretend, make believe **14 fantasize**, see visions, daydream, muse, idealize, romanticize, poeticize, fictionalize, rhapsodize **15 have insight**, understand

344 Imitation

• *Imitation is the sincerest form of flattery.* Charles Caleb Colton.

NOUNS 1 imitation, copying, simulation, repetition, mimesis, parody, onomatopoeia, emulation, impersonation, imposture, conformity, slavishness, literalism, representation, reflection, echo, canon, fugue, mirroring **2 copy**, reproduction, image, likeness, replica, model, duplication, imitation, dummy, mock-up, facsimile, photocopy, picture, portrait, pastiche, clone, doppelgänger, simulation, fake, forgery, sham, bootleg, counterfeit, plagiarism, disguise **3 mockery**, mimicry, pantomime, mime, satire, caricature, travesty, burlesque, impersonation, parody, apery **4 camouflage**, protective colouration, mimicry, simulation, cosmetics, make-up, disguise, dissimulation, playing possum **5 duplicate**, photocopy, pantograph, graph, stencil, facsimile, fax, carbon copy, replica, model, tracing, rubbing, transfer, transcript, video recording, tape recording, print, offprint, Photostat, photograph

VERBS 6 imitate, emulate, follow, ape, parrot, flatter, mirror, repeat, echo, reflect, pattern after, mimic, mock, caricature, satirize, burlesque, parody, travesty, impersonate **7 copy**, reproduce, duplicate, clone, photocopy, Mimeograph, stencil, plagiarize, borrow, replicate, counterfeit, fake, forge **8 emulate**, follow

ADJECTIVES 9 imitative, derivative, unoriginal, parodied, transcribed, mimetic, onomatopoeic, emulating, echoing, aping, parrot-like, following, posing, apish, echoic **10 imitation**, mock, sham, fake, forged, plagiarized, copied, counterfeit, ersatz, artificial, synthetic, cultured

345 Immediacy

NOUNS 1 immediacy, instantaneousness, directness, urgency, emergency, exigency **2 closeness**, nearness, proximity **3 instant**, second, split second, moment **4 point in time**, moment, juncture

ADJECTIVES 5 immediate, instantaneous, prompt, quick, fast, rapid, swift, speedy, direct, split-second, urgent **6 allowing no delay**, demanding, importunate, burning, imperative, exigent **7 prepared for immediate use**, precooked

346 Immorality

NOUNS 1 immorality, amorality, unscrupulousness, unethicalness, moral turpitude, badness, wickedness, vice, viciousness, evil, wrong, criminality **2 indecency**, salaciousness, prurience, lewdness, filthiness, defilement, uncleanness, indelicacy, bad taste, coarseness, vulgarity, grossness, nastiness, ribaldry, bawdiness, loose talk, dirty joke, double entendre, filth, dirt, smut, obscenity, corruption, depravity, erotica, facetiae, pornography, blue movie, voyeurism, sexploitation **3 sexual immorality**, unchastity, promiscuity, wantonness, incontinence, easy virtue, lightness, shamelessness, immodesty, laxity, amorality, permissive society, free love, wife swapping, roving eye, libido, lust, lecherousness, concupiscence, carnality, eroticism, fleshliness, sexiness, lasciviousness, salaciousness, lubricity, dissoluteness, decadence, degeneracy, profligacy, dissipation, debauchery, depravity, licentiousness, libertinism, seduction, defloration, venery, satyriasis, priapism, nymphomania, fornication, whorishness, harlotry, womanizing **4 illicit love**, forbidden fruit, adultery, unfaithfulness, infidelity, extramarital relations, eternal triangle, liaison, intrigue, amour, irregular union, concubinage **5 prostitution**, vice, soliciting, importuning, kerb crawling, streetwalking, harlotry, whoredom, oldest profession, pimping, pandering, procuring **6 brothel**, bordello, bagnio, whorehouse, massage parlour **7 sexual assault**, incest, buggery, sodomy, bestiality, sadism, sado-masochism, child abuse, pederasty, rape, ravishment, violation, gang rape

ADJECTIVES 8 immoral, amoral, unethical, unprincipled, unscrupulous, bad, wicked, wrong, evil, criminal, illegal **9 indecent**, salacious, prurient, lewd, lubricious, indelicate, improper, suggestive, provocative, risqué, titillating, arousing, erotic, naughty, blue, coarse, crude, vulgar, ribald, strong, racy, louche, bawdy, Rabelaisian, unwholesome, insalubrious, defiling, corrupting, depraving, impure, unclean, dirty, smutty, filthy, scrofulous, scabrous, scatological, stinking, rank, offensive, shocking, obscene, pornographic, uncensored **10 unchaste**, unvirtuous, wanton, light, loose, frail, fallen, seduced, prostituted, fast, naughty, immodest, unblushing, shameless, flaunting, brazen, amoral, promiscuous, sex-mad, nymphomaniac, scarlet, whorish **11 lecherous**, carnal, fleshly, voluptuous, libidinous, lustful, concupiscent, incontinent, Paphian, sexy, hot, rampant, rutting, sex-mad, priapic, lewd, lascivious, licentious, libertine, wild, rakish, amoral, adulterous, unfaithful, dissolute, dissipated, profligate, whoremongering, debauched, depraved **12 unlawful**, abnormal, incestuous, sadistic, sado-masochistic, perverted

VERBS 13 do wrong, err, sin, stray, fall, lapse, sink **14 be sexually immoral**, commit adultery, cuckold, fornicate, womanize **15 prostitute**, solicit, importune, streetwalk, pimp, pander **16 corrupt**, debase, demoralize, lead astray, ruin, wreck, disgrace, shame, dishonour, defile, smirch, sully, soil, debauch, deprave, vitiate **17 seduce**, deflower, ravish, rape, force, violate, indecently assault

347 Impenitence

NOUNS 1 impenitence, nonrepentance, incorrigibility, obstinacy, stubbornness, obduracy, hardness, cold-heartedness, callousness, induration, remorselessness, pitilessness

ADJECTIVES 2 impenitent, unrepentant, incorrigible, inveterate, obdurate, obstinate, brazen, shameless, unreformed, unregretting, unsorry, unapologetic, uncontrite, unmoved, unashamed, unblushing, remorseless, unsorrowful, unregretful, regretless, without compunction, conscienceless, heartless, cold-hearted, hard-hearted, hardened, callous, indurative, untouched, hopeless, lost, irreclaimable, irredeemable, unreconciled, unreformed, unregenerated, unchastened, unrecanting, unshriven **3 unatoned**, unrepented

VERBS 4 be impenitent, not reform, feel nothing, remain obstinate, not confess

348 Imperfection

ADJECTIVES 1 imperfect, flawed, faulty, defective, fallible, peccable, irregular, uneven, patchy, unsteady, weak, vulnerable, bungled, botched, damaged, broken, cracked, leaky, unsound, soiled, stained, spotted, marked, scratched, chipped, blemished, tainted, corked, stale, overripe, bad, off, off-colour, below par, off form, unfit, unhealthy, unsatisfactory, unacceptable, second-best, second-rate, inferior, poor, unimpressive **2 incomplete**, deficient, wanting, lacking, inadequate, insufficient, perfunctory, cursory, partial, fragmentary, unfilled, half-filled, unequipped, undermanned, unfinished, makeshift, jerry-built, provisional, raw, crude, untrained, scratch, immature, undeveloped, unpolished, unrefined, overwrought **3 deformed**, distorted, warped, twisted, handicapped, disabled, blind, deaf, dumb, mute, mutilated, maimed, lame **4 ordinary**, middling, average, median, everyday, commonplace, mediocre, middle-of-the-road, moderate, unheroic, only passable

NOUNS 5 imperfection, faultiness, defectiveness, perfectibility, fallibility, peccability, erroneousness, peccadillo, bungle, botch, irregularity, unevenness, patchiness, curate's egg, adulteration, weakness, vulnerability, frailty, failure, damage, unsoundness, staleness, overripeness, unfitness, infirmity, ill health, inferiority, worthlessness, second class, second rate, low standard, minimum requirement, incompleteness, deficiency, want, lack, need, requirement, shortfall, inadequacy, insufficiency, perfunctoriness, cursoriness, carelessness, underachievement, immaturity, unripeness, rawness, crudeness, undevelopment, deformity, distortion, blindness, deafness **6 imperfect item**, second, reject, misshape, poor effort, inferior version, poor relation, missing link, incomplete set, makeshift, stopgap, consolation **7 defect**, fault, flaw, blemish, mark, taint, stain, blot, spot, smudge, scratch, chip, error, rift, leak, loophole, crack, chink, lacuna, deficiency, lack, limitation, shortfall, kink, quirk, failing, shortcoming, weakness, blind spot, soft spot, Achilles' heel, disability, handicap, disadvantage, difficulty, drawback, catch, snag, hindrance **8 ordinariness**, averageness

VERBS 9 be imperfect, fall short, not impress, fail, dissatisfy, not suffice, barely pass, scrape through **10 leave imperfect**, finish halfway

349 Importance

• *In heaven an angel is nobody in particular.* George Bernard Shaw.

NOUNS 1 importance, primacy, pre-eminence, priority, urgency, precedence, prominence, distinction, eminence, reputation, paramountcy, supremacy, superiority, essentiality, irreplaceability, import, consequence, significance, weight, gravity, seriousness, solemnity, materiality, substance, interest, consideration, concern, business, matter, account, note, noteworthiness, memorability, mark, influence, prestige, size, magnitude, greatness, degree, rank, rating, standing, status, value, worth, excellence, merit, use, power, stress, emphasis, insistence **2 important matter**, vital concern, crisis, no joke, key point, memorandum, reminder, news, exploit, deed, big deal, landmark, milestone **3 chief thing**, what matters, the thing, main thing, issue, main topic, fundamentals, basics, grass roots, bedrock, core, hard facts, reality, essential, requirement, priority, first choice, highlight, main attraction, pick, elite, gist, substance, essence, heart, kernel, nucleus, nub, centre, hub, nexus, fulcrum, pivot, keynote, cornerstone, mainstay, linchpin, kingpin, head, cardinal point, chief hope, secret weapon

ADJECTIVES 4 important, primary, pre-eminent, urgent, imperative, prominent, distinct, eminent, weighty, grave, solemn, serious, pregnant, big, consequential, significant, considerable, world-shattering, earth-shaking, momentous, critical, crucial, fateful, chief, cardinal, capital, staple, major, main, top, paramount, supreme, prime, foremost, leading, overriding, overruling, uppermost, superior, essential, material, relevant, pivotal, central, basic, fundamental, bedrock, radical, worthwhile, valuable, necessary, vital, indispensable, irreplaceable, key, required, helpful, useful, telling, trenchant, meaningful, high-priority, high-level, top-level, summit, top-secret, confidential, high, grand, noble **5 notable**, noteworthy, remarkable, memorable, unforgettable, signal, first-rate, A1, gold-medal, outstanding, sterling, excellent, superior, top-rank, top-ten, top-flight, high-ranking, prestigious, conspicuous, prominent, eminent, distinguished, exalted, august, dignified, imposing, commanding, leading, impressive, formidable, powerful, influential, newsworthy, front-page, eventful, stirring, breathtaking, shattering, monumental, world-shattering, earth-shaking

VERBS 6 be important, matter, weigh, carry, carry weight, tell, count, influence, motivates, signify, represent, import, mean, concern, interest, affect, have priority, precede, come first, predominate, command respect **7 make important**, build up, seize on, fasten on, enhance, highlight, stress, emphasize, underline, labour, publicize, promote, advertise, headline, splash, proclaim, announce, celebrate, lionize, honour, glorify, exalt, respect, value, esteem, regard, magnify

350 Impossibility

ADJECTIVES 1 impossible, inconceivable, unthinkable, unimaginable, unquestionable, unreasonable, absurd, ridiculous, preposterous, illogical, irrational, paradoxical, self-contradictory **2 unbelievable**, incredible, counterintuitive, beyond belief, fantastic, miraculous, fabulous, bizarre, weird, ineffable, mysterious **3 hopeless**, impractical, unfeasible, unworkable, unachievable, untenable, unviable, inoperable, broken, irreparable, irrecoverable, irrevocable, unattainable, insurmountable, insuperable, inaccessible, unapproachable, unreachable, impenetrable, impervious, unobtainable, unavailable, out **4 forbidden**, prohibited, denied, disallowed, blocked, barred, banned, stopped

NOUNS 5 impossibility, inconceivability, unthinkability, unimaginability, nonexistence, unreality, self-contradiction, absurdity, paradox **6 hopelessness**, impracticability, unfeasibility, unworkability, inoperability, unattainability, insurmountability, insuperability, inaccessibility, impenetrability, imperviousness, unobtainability **7 obstacle**, prohibition, no-go area, deadlock, block, impasse, barrier

VERBS 8 make impossible, prohibit, block, bar, ban, forbid, rule out, disqualify, exclude, deny, withhold, negate

351 Improbability

ADJECTIVES 1 improbable, unlikely, uncertain, doubtful, dubious, unpromising, inauspicious, unrealistic, remote, far-fetched **2 questionable**, implausible, unbelievable, fanciful, extraordinary, exceptional, wild, incredible **3 unexpected**, unforeseeable, unpre-

dictable, unanticipated, unguessed, unpredicted, unforeseen, fortuitous, rare, accidental
NOUNS 4 improbability, unlikeliness, uncertainty, doubt, pipe dream, outside chance, slim chance, long shot, long odds **5 unexpectedness**, unforeseeableness, unpredictability, miraculousness, rarity, oddity, the unforeseen, freak accident, miracle, prodigy, wonder, surprise, lucky shot, fluke **6 implausibility**, incredibility, unbelievability, questionableness, tall story
VERBS 7 be improbable, dream, fib

352 Improbity

NOUNS 1 improbity, dishonour, dishonesty, disrepute, shame, worthlessness, evilness, wickedness, badness, villainy, corruption, depravity, venality, turpitude, knavery, disrespect, disgrace, debasement, baseness, indecency, immorality, unscrupulousness, deviousness, opportunism, unfairness, partiality, bias, prejudice, injustice, insincerity, hypocrisy, disingenuousness, untruthfulness, falsehood, lie, foul play, contrivance, chicanery **2 faithlessness**, infidelity, perfidy, deceit, falseness, broken promise, untrustworthiness, unreliability, undependability, disloyalty, disobedience, double-dealing, double-crossing, duplicity, U-turn, volte-face, tergiversation, defection, desertion, betrayal, treachery, Judas kiss, treason, sedition **3 criminality**, crime, law-breaking, felony, racketeering, fraudulency, thieving, embezzlement, bribery, tax evasion, graft, sharp practice, swindle, confidence trick
ADJECTIVES 4 dishonourable, dishonest, disreputable, shameful, worthless, good-for-nothing, evil, wicked, bad, villainous, nefarious, corrupt, unprincipled, unethical, bribable, depraved, venal, disrespectful, disgraceful, ignoble, contemptible, debased, base, indecent, immoral, rotten, unscrupulous, ungentlemanly, unsportsmanlike, devious, opportunistic, scheming, unfair, biased, prejudiced, unjust, insincere, hypocritical, disingenuous, uncandid, untruthful, lying, tricky, foxy, vulpine **5 faithless**, unfaithful, perfidious, deceitful, false, two-faced, untrustworthy, unreliable, undependable, questionable, shaky, disloyal, disobedient, double-crossing, duplicitous, deserting, betraying, treacherous, treasonous, seditious **6 criminal**, lawbreaking, felonious, fraudulent, underhanded, thieving, light-fingered, embezzling
VERBS 7 be dishonourable, be dishonest, evade, falsify, lie **8 prove false**, dissemble, deceive, double-cross, let down, turn against, forsake, betray **9 be criminal**, smuggle, defraud, cheat, rob, embezzle, racketeer, fence, swindle, steal, thieve

353 Improvement

VERBS 1 improve, better, ameliorate, reform, polish, perfect, elaborate, enrich, enhance, transform, transfigure, convert, redeem, rehabilitate, make, raise, uplift, regenerate, refine, upgrade, elevate, sublimate, purify, civilize, socialize, mend, repair, straighten, rectify, restore, cure, recruit, revive, refresh, soften, lessen, alleviate, mitigate, palliate, moderate, forward, further, advance, promote, market, hype, foster, encourage, mature, use, exploit, develop, open up, reclaim, cultivate, tidy, neaten, spruce up, clean, do up, vamp up, shape up, rationalize, renovate, refurbish, recondition, renew, modernize, beautify, dress up, titivate, prink, primp, embellish **2 get better**, improve, mend, pick up, rally, revive, recover, recuperate, convalesce, make progress, make headway, advance, develop, evolve, progress, mellow, ripen, mature, increase, graduate, succeed, prosper, reform, learn **3 rectify**, put right, remedy, straighten, adjust, repair, mend, patch, fix, correct, blue-pencil, proofread, revise, redact, edit, amend, alter, rewrite, redraft, retell, recast, remould, refashion, remodel, recreate, reform, reorganize, regularize, fine-tune, streamline, rationalize, review **4 reconsider**, redo

NOUNS 5 improvement, betterment, amelioration, sea change, transfiguration, transformation, conversion, redemption, rehabilitation, reform, penitence, new leaf, new resolution, polish, perfection, elaboration, enrichment, enhancement, rise, uplift, upturn, upswing, graduation, success, prosperity, self-improvement, regeneration, refinement, upgrading, elevation, sublimation, purification, civilization, education, repair, rectification, restoration, cure, remedy, recruitment, revival, recovery, recuperation, refreshment, alleviation, mitigation, palliation, furtherance, advancement, progress, headway, promotion, rationalization, renovation, refurbishment, reconditioning, renewal, modernization, face-lift, beautification, titivation, embellishment, ornamentation, decoration, finishing touch, last word, completion, perfectionism **6 rectification**, adjustment, repair, mending, correction, revision, recension, redaction, editing, amendment, alteration **7 reconsideration**, re-examination, review **8 better thing**, new idea, second thought, updated model, revised edition, improved version, corrected copy **9 physical improvement**, exercise, aerobics, callisthenics, eurhythmics, jogging **10 reformatory**, borstal **11 reformism**, humanism, meliorism, perfectionism, idealism, Utopianism, millenarianism, chiliasm, liberalism, socialism, progressivism, gradualism, Fabianism, radicalism, extremism, revolution, communism, Marxism, feminism, suffragism, antiracism, Black Power, antifascism, prohibitionism, peace movement

ADJECTIVES 12 improved, better, superior, enhanced, beautified, reformed, transformed, revised, edited, rewritten, repaired, restored, renovated, modernized, recovering, recuperating, rising, increasing **13 improvable**, perfectible, ameliorable, reformable, corrigible **14 improving**, advancing, ameliorative, remedial, restorative, reformative, progressive, radical, extreme, civilizing, cultural, idealistic, perfectionist, Utopian

354 Improvisation

ADJECTIVES 1 improvised, makeshift, jury-rigged, inventive, ad hoc, impromptu, ad-lib, extemporaneous, unrehearsed, unprepared, unpremeditated, uncalculated **2**

spontaneous, sudden, snap, spur-of-the-moment, unprompted, unmotivated, unprovoked, unforced, voluntary, willing, unguarded, incautious, rash, impetuous, impulsive, natural, instinctive, involuntary, automatic, kneejerk, intuitive

VERBS **3 improvise**, invent, devise, contrive, think up, ad-lib, extemporize

NOUNS **4 improvisation**, invention, extemporization, jam session, cadenza, ad-libbing, impromptu talk, unpremeditation **5 spontaneity**, involuntariness, reflex, knee-jerk reaction, impulsiveness, instinct, intuition, hunch, idea, flash

355 Impulsion

VERBS **1 impel**, accelerate, drive, propel, compel, motivate, incite, urge, spur, start, run, move, animate, actuate, galvanize, power, goad, drive on, project, traject, thrust, press, stress, push, shove, heave, prod, poke, dig, jostle, jolt, jog, tug, wrench, joggle, jerk, elbow, shoulder, hustle, butt, thwack, press on, expel, eject **2 collide**, impact, crash, bump into, smash, impinge upon, crunch, crump, clash, cannon into, jolt, nudge, bump, meet, encounter, confront, charge, attack, converge, careen, bang, percuss, hurtle, fence, ram, tamp, hammer, bulldoze, shoulder, butt, bash **3 hit**, strike, stroke, rap, punch, thwack, pound, slam, bang, smack, swipe, dash, belt, clout, swat, swing, buffet, box, jab, knock, bat, poke, thump, pelt, biff, sock, cut, slog, slug, bash, bonk, dent **4 throw**, fling, hurl, toss, launch, propel, pitch, cast, hurtle, heave, lob, fire **5 beat**, trounce, leather, hammer, spank, pound, pummel, whip, flog, flail, thrash, cut, lash, stripe, cane, lambaste, batter **6 tap**, rap, touch, tip, pat, dab, flick, flip, peck, pick, brush **7 kick**, boot, punt, knee, stamp, clump, clop, drub, trample **8 club**, cudgel, blackjack, sandbag, cosh, crown, concuss, assail **9 fight**, box **10 bat**, drive, hit, lift, smash, volley, slice

NOUNS **11 impulsion**, impellent, impetus, momentum, force, power, propulsion, compulsion, incentive, incitement, mechanics **12 collision**, meeting, encounter, charge, attack, convergence, multiple collision, pile-up, smash-up, percussion, concussion, scrape, friction, crash, impact, shock, smash, crunch, cannon, jolt, nudge, bump, ramming, hammering, drumming, rapping, tapping, beating, thrusting, bulling, bulldozing, smashing, sledgehammering, butting, bashing, spanking, trouncing, leathering, paddling, pummelling, hiding, whipping, flogging, thrashing, assault, attack, fisticuffs **13 blow**, hit, strike, stroke, rap, punch, thwack, pound, slam, bang, butt, smack, swipe, dash, belt, clout, swat, swing, buffet, jab, knock, poke, thump, pelt, cut, slog, slug, bash, bonk, dent, thrust, press, stress, push, shove, heave, prod, nudge, dig, biff, jostle, jolt, jog, hustle, tap, touch, chuck, tip, pat, dab, flick, flip, fillip, peck, brush, whisk, slap, spank, cuff, kick, punt, stamp, clump, clop **14 weapons**, cudgel, mace, truncheon, whip, flail, cosh, knuckle-duster

ADJECTIVES **15 impelling**, impellent, impulsive, pulsive, dynamic, motive, moving, thrusting, thrustful, driving, ramming, smashing

356 Inaction

NOUNS 1 inaction, inertia, impotence, neglect, negligence, abstention, refraining, avoidance, passive resistance, suspension, abeyance, dormancy, inactivity, nonuse, deadlock, stalemate, stop, standstill, immobility, motionlessness, paralysis, impassivity, insensibility, passivity, apathy, stagnation, vegetation, doldrums, stillness, quiet, calm, tranquillity, quiescence, leisure, rest, repose, relaxation, laziness, loafing, idleness, indolence, unemployment, redundancy, sinecure, Fabianism, do-nothingism, delay, procrastination, noninterference, nonintervention, defeatism

ADJECTIVES 2 inactive, inert, impotent, powerless, negligent, abstaining, suspended, dormant, inoperative, deadlocked, stalemated, stationary, immobile, motionless, still, calm, tranquil, quiet, stagnant, half-dead, dead, extinct, benumbed, frozen, paralysed, impassive, insensible, passive, apathetic, phlegmatic, dull, sluggish, leisured, relaxed, lazy, indolent, idle, fallow, unoccupied, unemployed, laid off, redundant, jobless, ostrich-like, Fabian, refraining, procrastinating, cunctative, indifferent, neutral, hands-off

VERBS 3 not act, do nothing, be inert, refrain, avoid, abstain, pass up, stand by, look on, watch, loaf, idle, sit tight, delay, procrastinate, defer, stay neutral, tolerate, disregard, ignore, stagnate, vegetate, tread water, drift, glide, freewheel, neglect, sit back, relax, unwind, rest, repose, be redundant, be superfluous, kill time, stop, gather dust, lie idle

357 Inactivity

ADJECTIVES 1 inactive, quiescent, still, motionless, immobile, stationary, static, sedentary, stagnant, inert, passive, extinct, lifeless **2 not working**, unemployed, unengaged, laid off, redundant, on strike, jobless, resting, free, broken down, unused, fallow, idle, disengaged **3 not participating**, lazy, idle, indolent, slothful, work-shy, bone idle, loafing, lolling, parasitic, slack, lax, slow, dilatory, dawdling, tardy, procrastinating, laggard, sluggish, lethargic, languid, dull, listless, torpid, apathetic, indifferent, uninterested, phlegmatic **4 not awake**, somnolent, drowsy, dozy, sleepy, soporific, heavy-eyed, slumberous, yawning, dozing, resting, dopy, drugged, sedated, narcotized, anaesthetized, hypnotized, dormant, torpid, hibernating, aestivating, dreaming, unconscious, insensible

NOUNS 5 inactivity, quiescence, stillness, quietness, silence, immobility, inertia, passivity, inertness, lull, suspension, cessation, extinction **6 unemployment**, shutdown, lay-off, slump, recession, depression **7 idleness**, laziness, indolence, sloth, absenteeism, slowness, dawdling, delay, procrastination, sluggishness, lethargy, languor, dullness, listlessness, torpor, apathy, indifference, phlegm **8 sleep**, somnolence, doziness, drowsiness, heaviness, oscitancy, slumber, rest, repose, Morpheus, dreamland, sandman, dormancy, hibernation, aestivation, unconsciousness, coma, stupor, trance, catalepsy, hypnosis, oblivion, insensibility, nap, catnap, snooze, doze **9 soporific**, somnifacient, sleeping pill, nightcap, sedative, barbiturate, narcotic, opiate, morphine

VERBS 10 be inactive, stagnate, vegetate, do nothing, idle, laze, skive, loaf, lounge, cadge, sponge, slouch, mooch, kill time, waste time, hang about, lie around, delay, procrastinate, hang fire, dawdle **11 sleep**, snooze, doze, drowse, yawn, nod off, nap, rest, slumber, hibernate **12 make inactive**, dismantle, defuse, neutralize, extinguish, shut down, suspend, lay up, lay off, dismiss, fire, sack, demobilize, incapacitate, disable, deaden, drug, dope, sedate, narcotize, knock out

358 Inattention

NOUNS 1 inattention, incuriosity, thoughtlessness, unmindfulness, forgetfulness, aberration, heedlessness, unconcern, detachment, obliviousness, apathy, disregard, distraction, nonobservance, carelessness, rashness, desultoriness, superficiality, indifference **2 impetuosity**, precipitance, impulsiveness, rashness, recklessness, foolhardiness **3 absent-mindedness**, daydreaming, dizziness, frivolity, woolgathering, stargazing **4 thoughtlessness**, inconsideration, disregard, indifference, ignoring, insensitivity **5 inattentive act**, oversight, lapse, slip, error, mistake, blunder

ADJECTIVES 6 inattentive, thoughtless, unthinking, incurious, unmindful, forgetful, heedless, unconcerned, detached, oblivious, apathetic, listless, disregarding, distracted **7 absent-minded**, daydreaming, woolgathering **8 thoughtless**, inconsiderate, uncaring, selfish, insensitive **9 careless**, negligent, neglectful, slack, remiss, sloppy, slapdash, slipshod, hit-or-miss, dizzy, flighty, rash **10 perfunctory**, casual, lackadaisical

VERBS 11 be inattentive, disregard, ignore, overlook, daydream, stargaze **12 be thoughtless**, disregard, ignore, slight

359 Inclusion

NOUNS 1 inclusion, enclosure, encirclement, encapsulation, containment, comprisal, comprehension, involvement, implication, concern, reception, admission, elegibility, participation, membership, presence, accommodation, room, space, capacity, volume, coverage, universality, generality, versatility, comprehensiveness, complete set, package, complement, full quota, allowance, comprising, composition, construction, make-up, constitution, incorporation, integration **2 thing included**, enclosure, ingredient, constituent, factor, additive, appurtenance, feature, component, item, element, part, piece

VERBS 3 include, contain, hold, have, enclose, encircle, envelop, encapsulate, comprehend, involve, implicate, embrace, cover, encompass, receive, admit, accommodate, count, number, boast, allow for, recognize, admit of, consist of, comprise, compose, incorporate, integrate, embody, constitute **4 be included**, make up, belong, enter into, participate, share, merge, appertain to **5 subsume**, place under,

count with, reckon among, number with, enumerate with, class with, categorize as, enter, list
ADJECTIVES 6 including, containing, holding, accommodating, having, allowing, considering, counting, consisting of, comprising, composed of, incorporating, all-in, comprehensive, wholesale, blanket, extensive, widespread, across-the-board, wall-to-wall, sweeping, global, expansive, broad-based, umbrella, overall, general, encyclopedic, nonexclusive **7 included**, built-in, integrated, unsegregated, unseparated, constituent, component, inherent, intrinsic, belonging, pertinent, appurtenant, admissible, allowed, eligible, classed with, related, akin, congenerous, entered, listed, noted, recorded, added, linked, joined

360 Incompleteness

NOUNS 1 incompleteness, partialness, defectiveness, insufficiency, poverty, scantness, inadequacy, lack, want, need, ineffectiveness, imperfection, unpreparedness, unreadiness, under-development, unripeness, immaturity, rawness, roughness, sketchiness, scrappiness, bittiness, hollowness, superficiality, insubstantiality, perfunctoriness, half-heartedness, negligence, default, arrears, nonfulfilment, mutilation, impairment **2 omission**, gap, lacuna, void, interval, break, loss, deficit, lack, want, need, deficiency, insufficiency, shortfall, slippage, ullage, defalcation, arrears, default **3 incomplete thing**, part, fraction, proportion, instalment, sketch, draft
ADJECTIVES 4 incomplete, defective, scant, skimpy, short, insufficient, inadequate, ineffective, ineffectual, missing, omitting, lacking, wanting, needing, requiring, short of, shy of, shortened, abbreviated, abridged, truncated, curtailed, cropped, docked, lopped, maimed, mutilated, mangled, marred, spoiled, impaired, garbled, broken, fragmentary, unsatisfactory, blemished, stained, flawed, imperfect, half, partial, unfinished, developing, in progress, in embryo, in preparation, half-finished, neglected, under-developed, unprepared, unready, unripe, immature, raw, underdone, undercooked, rude, rough, crude, rough-hewn, sketchy, scrappy, bitty, thin, poor, meagre, hollow, superficial, insubstantial, perfunctory
VERBS 5 be incomplete, need, want, lack, miss, fall short, skimp on, default, sketch, draft, leave unfinished, interrupt, leave hanging, neglect, omit

361 Inconvenience

ADJECTIVES 1 inconvenient, discommodious, disadvantageous, detrimental, inexpedient, inadvisable, undesirable, uncommendable, ill-advised, ill-considered, impolitic, imprudent, injudicious, unwise, inappropriate, unfitting, misapplied, malapropos, improper, unseemly, undue, objectionable, offensive, wrong, unfit, unsuitable, ineligible, unqualified, inadmissible, unfortunate, infelicitous, inept, unapt, inopportune, unseasonable, untimely, disruptive, disturbing, unsettling, useless, unprofitable, unhelpful, hindering, untoward, adverse, unprofessional, ill-contrived, ill-planned, awkward, clumsy, cumbersome, lumbering, hulking, unwieldy, burdensome, onerous, troublesome, bothersome, annoying, irritating, irksome, boring, tiresome, vexatious **2 distant**, remote, innaccessible

NOUNS 3 inconvenience, disadvantage, drawback, detriment, hurt, harm, inexpedience, Pyrrhic victory, two-edge sword, inadvisability, undesirability, imprudence, inappropriateness, unfittingness, impropriety, unseemliness, undueness, wrongness, unfitness, unsuitability, inaptitude, inopportuneness, untimeliness, disruption, disturbance, disability, handicap, impediment, obstacle, hindrance, nuisance, bother, trouble, upset, discomfort, incommodiousness, pain, difficulty, annoyance, irritation, vexation, awkwardness, burden, cumbersomeness, unwieldiness **4 distance**, remoteness, inaccessibility

VERBS 5 be inconvenient, go amiss, trouble, bother, disturb, disrupt, upset, discommode, put out, annoy, irritate, vex, irk, embarrass, hinder, obstruct, handicap, disadvantage, penalize, work against, hurt

362 Increase

NOUNS 1 increase, addition, increment, augmentation, enlargement, growth, development, progress, advancement, accumulation, build-up, accretion, snowballing effect, gain, waxing, bulging, swelling, dilation, expansion, fattening, thickening, broadening, widening, deepening, improvement, prosperity, profitability, appreciation, excess, overenlargement, magnification, duplication, multiplication, reproduction, propagation, proliferation, amplification, extension, prolongation, protraction, intensification, escalation, acceleration, speeding, stepping up, concentration, condensation, enrichment, supplement, added contribution, accrual, heightening, enhancement, exaltation, elevation, aggrandizement, exaggeration, invigoration, stimulation, spur, aggravation, exacerbation **2 spread**, spiral, upswing, upturn, upsurge, uprush, push, swell, intumescence, surge, gush, boost, boom, rise, climb, crescendo, leap, jump **3 increasing thing**, snowball, spring tide, waxing moon, bull market, inflation

VERBS 4 increase, grow, gain, develop, escalate, wax, bulge, swell, dilate, distend, expand, fill out, fatten, thicken, broaden, bud, sprout, burgeon, blossom, flower, flourish, thrive, breed, swarm, spawn, proliferate, mushroom, multiply, spread, swell, intumesce, climb, spiral, mount, rise, soar, accumulate, snowball, rocket, improve, prosper, profit, appreciate, boom, surge, exceed, crescendo, progress, gain ground **5 make bigger**, augment, supplement, increase, enlist, recruit, enlarge, magnify, double, triple, quadruple, multiply, duplicate, square, cube, reproduce, propagate, breed, develop, build up, fill up, pad out, expand, amplify, extend, prolong, stretch, lengthen, broaden, thicken, deepen, enrich, widen, inflate, blow up, heighten, enhance, raise, exalt, elevate, ag-

grandize, glorify, overrate, exaggerate, spur on, accelerate, intensify, escalate, energize, stimulate, invigorate, reinforce, boost, maximize, stoke, aggravate, exacerbate
ADJECTIVES 6 increasing, progressive, expanding, growing, spreading, escalating, crescent, waxing, filling, ever-increasing, cumulative, snowballing, augmentative, prolific, additional **7 increased**, enlarged, magnified, accelerated, swollen, bloated, expanded, extended, stretched, intensified, heightened, enhanced

363 Indifference

• *At length the morn and cold indifference came.* Nicholas Rowe.

NOUNS 1 indifference, unconcern, apathy, disinterestedness, incuriosity, aloofness, detachment, dispassion, noninvolvement, inertia, inactivity, passiveness, ataraxia, phlegmaticalness, phlegmaticness), lethargy, listlessness, dispiritedness, sluggishness, oscitation, inappetance, lethargy, half-heartedness, perfunctoriness, inexcitability, calmness, lukewarmness, coolness, coldness, cold-heartedness, nonchalance, insouciance, lackadaisicalness, insensibility, insensitivity, dullness **2 carelessness**, disregard, inattention, laxity, heedlessness, negligence, recklessness, rashness, promiscuousness **3 impartiality**, indiscrimination, disinterest, objectivity, open mind, neutrality, middle way, moderation, justice **4 mediocrity**, averageness, ordinariness, tolerability **5 insignificance**, unimportance, triviality, irrelevance
ADJECTIVES 6 indifferent, disinterested, incurious, uninquisitive, apathetic, detached, dispassionate, uninvolved, withdrawn, aloof, carefree, fancy-free, noncommittal, impersonal, matter-of-fact, unconcerned, uncaring, unresponsive, unaware, oblivious, insensible to, blind to, deaf to, dead to, lost to, unconscious, inert, inactive, ataractic, listless, dispirited, sluggish, inappetant, lethargic, half-hearted, perfunctory, impassive, pococurante, blasé, easy-going, unsurprised, inexcitable, unimpressed, unaffected, unfeeling, untouched, unemotional, unmoved, unruffled, calm, lukewarm, cool, cold, frigid, frosty, cold-hearted, cold-blooded, unmoved, nonchalant, insouciant, unaffectionate, undesirous, passionless, lackadaisical, insensible, insensitive, thick-skinned, dull, deadpan, numb **7 careless**, disregarding, negligent, inattentive, lax, heedless, reckless, rash, devil-may-care, promiscuous **8 impartial**, indiscriminate, disinterested, objective, unbiased, unprejudiced, open-minded, neutral, moderate, just **9 mediocre**, average, middling, ordinary, fair, unexceptional, unaspiring, tolerable, passable **10 insignificant**, unimportant, trivial, irrelevant, inconsequential
VERBS 11 be indifferent, disregard, dismiss, not care, shrug off, detach oneself, withdraw, yawn, oscitate, remain unmoved, lose interest **12 make indifferent**, make insensitive, dull, blunt, desensitize, numb, deaden **13 be careless**, disregard **14 be impartial**, be objective **15 be mediocre**, get by

364 Inelegance

NOUNS 1 inelegance, gracelessness,

clumsiness, awkwardness, gaucheness **2 impropriety**, indelicacy, crudeness, vulgarity, tastelessness, rudeness, discourtesy, grossness, coarseness, roughness, boorishness, churlishness, uncouthness **3 ugliness**, plainness, drabness, shabbiness, garishness, gaudiness, loudness, tawdriness, vulgarity **4 inelegance of speech**, incorrectness, bad grammar, solecism, vulgarism, dysphemism, clumsiness, long-windedness, sesquipedalianism, stiffness, stiltedness, cumbrousness, ponderousness, turgidity, bombast, pomposity, grandiloquence, cacology **5 blunder**, faux pas

ADJECTIVES 6 graceless, inelegant, clumsy, awkward, ungainly, cumbersome, ill-proportioned, dumpy, clownish, gauche, gawky, undignified, ham-fisted **7 indecorous**, unseemly, improper, indelicate, crude, vulgar, tasteless, rude, discourteous, impolite, gross, coarse, boorish, churlish, uncouth, barbaric, unrefined, unpolished, *infra dignitatem infra dig* **8 inelegant**, dysphemistic, cacological, turgid, pompous, rhetorical, grandiloquent, formal, stiff, stilted, wooden, unfluent, ill-sounding, cacophonous, uneuphonious, jarring, grating, incorrect, solecistic, doggerel, artless, unnatural, artificial, affected, laboured, tortuous, ludicrous **9 ugly**, unattractive, unaesthetic, plain, drab, dingy, dreary, dull, shabby, seedy, squalid, rough, mousy, lank, dowdy, unfashionable, tasteless, common, vulgar, garish, gaudy, loud, tawdry

365 Inequality

NOUNS 1 inequality, disparity, difference, discrepancy, disproportion, heterogeneity, imparity, dissimilarity, nonuniformity, diversity, variability, patchiness, imbalance, odds, overload, overkill, top-heaviness, extra, shortage, shortfall, deficiency, tilt, camber, list, superiority, inferiority, unevenness, oddness, distortion, roughness, irregularity, asymmetry, lopsidedness, skewness, obliquity, disequilibrium, dizziness, the staggers, preponderance, overweight, lightness, insufficiency, disadvantage, handicap **2 injustice**, inequity, discrimination, prejudice

ADJECTIVES 3 unequal, disparate, different, disproportionate, incongruent, dissimilar, diverse, disagreeing, unlike, uneven, odd, asymmetrical, distorted, irregular, scalene, unique, unequalled, inferior, below par, unequable, variable, variegated, deficient, patchy, inadequate, insufficient, mismatched, ill-matched, ill-sorted, unbalanced, lopsided, unwieldy, listing, leaning, canting, heeling, off balance, overbalanced, top-heavy, overweight, underweight, askew, awry, swinging, swaying, rocking, unstable, untrimmed, unballasted, uncompensated, dizzy, giddy, toppling **4 unjust**, unfair, inequitable, discriminatory, prejudiced, biased

VERBS 5 be unequal, not match, not equate, not balance, disagree, preponderate, outclass, outstrip, outrank, outvote, outweigh, outdo, surpass, overtop, not suffice, fall short, disadvantage, handicap, overbalance, unequalize, disproportion, skew, destabilize, upset, list, tilt, lean, heel, rock, swing, sway, lilt, fluctuate, vary, change, capsize, miss **6 be unjust**, discriminate, show prejudice, be biased

366 Inertness

NOUNS 1 inertness, inactivity, inaction, stillness, motionlessness, indolence, idleness, lifelessness, deathliness, languor, torpor, torpidity, paralysis, insensibility, numbness, vegetation, stagnation, quiescence, dormancy, latency, fallowness, apathy, indifference, dullness, sloth, slowness, sluggishness, laziness, sleepiness, hibernation, laxity, slackness, passivity, peacefulness, impassivity, immobility, stolidity, inexcitability, indecisiveness

VERBS 2 be inert, sleep, slumber, doze, laze around, lie idle, lurk, smoulder, hang fire, stagnate, vegetate

ADJECTIVES 3 inert, inactive, passive, apathetic, indifferent, unexcitable, pacific, unaggressive, unwarlike, peaceful, unreactive, indecisive, irresolute, unresponsive, stolid, idle, lazy, indolent, slack, lax, limp, flaccid, heavy, slothful, lumpish, doltish, sluggish, slow, dull, numb, dormant, smouldering, latent, dead, lifeless, languid, torpid, insensible, hibernating, sleepy, immobile, unmoving, motionless, still, static, stagnant, vegetating, paralysed, quiet, quiescent **4 suspended**, pending, in abeyance, switched off, on hold, on ice, in reserve, abrogated

367 Inferiority

NOUNS 1 inferiority, secondariness, supporting role, subordinate position, second best, ordinariness, obscurity, lowliness, baseness, subordination, abasement, dependence, humbleness, humility, subservience, insignificance **2 deficiency**, disadvantage, handicap, impairment, stain, blemish, defect, fault, imperfection, failure, decline, worsening, deterioration, reversion, insufficiency, shortfall **3 inferior numbers**, minority, fewness, littleness, smallness, meanness, meagreness **4 poor quality**, badness, cheapness, shoddiness, worthlessness, shabbiness, vulgarity, bad taste **5 inferior state**, reduced circumstances, record low, all-time low, nadir, minimum, floor, base, bottom, trough, depression, lowness, level, flatness **6 inferior**, younger, minor, junior, subordinate, subaltern, assistant, satellite, vassal, underling, henchman, menial, servant, subject, slave, subsidiary, deputy, dupe, pawn, flunky, tool, dependant, follower, nonentity, private, hoi polloi, lower orders, low life, scum, the masses, the mob, rabble, worm, loser, second-rater, reject **7 inferior thing**, sweepings, leavings, remains, left-overs, crumbs, seconds

VERBS 8 be inferior, fail, fall short, lag **9 yield to**, concede, bow to, knuckle under, submit **10 follow**, conform **11 become inferior**, worsen, lack, want, deteriorate, decline, diminish, descend

ADJECTIVES 12 inferior, lesser, lower, bottommost, second-best, second-rate, low-caste, secondary, second-class **13 insignificant**, minimal, small, inconsiderable, diminished, small-time, unimportant, lightweight **14 poor**, worthless, bad, shoddy, substandard, subnormal, tatty, cheap, scratch, makeshift, jerry-built **15 subordinate**, minor, junior, dependent, subsidiary, subject, subservient, humble, tributary, ancillary, auxiliary, untouchable **16 ordinary**, middling, mediocre, common, vulgar, base **17 defective**, deficient, marred, spoilt, shopsoiled, failed, faulty, imperfect **18 outclassed**, outshone, bested, worsted, trounced, beaten, defeated, humiliated

368 Infertility

NOUNS 1 infertility, infecundity, fruitlessness, unproductiveness, barrenness, sterility, impotence, celibacy, childlessness, fallowness, aridity, desert, dustbowl, wasteland, wilderness, desolation, desertification, deforestation, defoliation, dying race, menopause, miscarriage, recession, stagnation, slump, depression, low yield, dearth **2 making infertile**, sterilization, hysterectomy, vasectomy, castration, neutering, spaying **3 birth control**, contraception, prophylactic, family planning, contraceptive, coil, loop, diaphragm, Dutch cap, condom, sheath, femidom, spermicide, the pill

ADJECTIVES 4 infertile, infecund, fruitless, unproductive, unprolific, barren, sterile, impotent, celibate, childless, fallow, arid, dry, drought-stricken, desert, gaunt, bleak, uncultivated, stony, withered, shrivelled, dead, blasted, waste, wild, desolate, stagnant, recessionary **5 rendered infertile**, unfertilized, sterilized, vasectomized, castrated, gelded, neutered **6 having no effect**, unsuccessful, failed

VERBS 7 be infertile, stagnate, rust, rot, hang fire, fail, abort, miscarry **8 make infertile**, sterilize, vasectomize, unman, emasculate, castrate, geld, spay **9 waste**, desolate, deforest

369 Infinity

ADJECTIVES 1 infinite, boundless, limitless, bottomless, endless, interminable **2 immeasurable**, vast, immense, enormous, astronomical, incalculable, uncountable, innumerable, myriad, numberless, untold, indeterminable, inestimable, unfathomable, incomprehensible **3 eternal**, perpetual, everlasting, immortal, undying, forever, ceaseless, endless, unending, never-ending, constant, continual, continuous

NOUNS 4 infinity, boundlessness, limitlessness, endlessness, interminability, infinite supply **5 immeasurability**, incalculability, countlessness, innumerability, numberlessness, indeterminableness **6 vastness**, immenseness, space, outer space **7 eternity**, perpetuity, forever, everlastingness

VERBS 8 be infinite, last forever, never end, never cease, recur, perpetuate

370 Influence

• *How to Win Friends and Influence People.* Dale Carnegie.

NOUNS 1 influence, power, potency, potentiality, ability, capability, strength, might, force, predominance, prevalence, greatness, magnitude, importance, significance, advantage, authority, whip hand, leverage, weight, impact, pressure, magnetism, gravity, drive, push, motivation, vested interest, impression, inspiration, persuasion, atmosphere, fate **2 occult influence**, magic, witchcraft, sorcery, charm, mesmerism, hypnotism, stars, astrology, horoscope, malevolence, curse **3 personal influence**, personality, charisma, reputation, credit, prestige, leadership, ascendancy, hegemony, domination, dominion, tyranny, authority, sway, control **4 indirect influence**, favour, patronage, wires, strings, lever, power broker **5 group influence**, pressure group, self-help group, lobby, public opinion, the Establishment, Big Brother, multinational company **6 sphere of influence**, territory, orbit

VERBS 7 influence, impress, motivate, actuate, activate, encourage, suggest, persuade, carry weight, take root, affect, bear upon, pressurize, lobby, guide, direct, lead, promote, prejudice, bias, brainwash, predispose, colour, lure **8 change**, improve, leaven, discourage, repulse, disgust, repel, put off, militate against, infect, dilute, contaminate, adulterate, mar, spoil, impair **9 be a prevailing influence**, prevail, predominate, fascinate, mesmerize, hypnotize, outweigh, override, overbear, have sway, force, compel, tyrannize, dominate, subdue, subjugate, overcome, master, rule, run, control, monopolize

ADJECTIVES 10 influential, causal, effectual, persuasive, important, significant, contributing, decisive, momentous, world-shattering, telling, prestigious, impressive, potent, powerful, interfering, mighty, forceful, superior, ruling, leading, guiding, directing, instructive, educative, reigning, commanding, authoritative **11 appealing**, emotional, moving, affecting, charming, attractive, gripping, fascinating, irresistible, charismatic, magnetic, mesmeric, hypnotic, compelling, inspirational, encouraging, motivating, suggestive, tempting, seductive, addictive, infectious **12 dominant**, wide-ranging, international, multinational, monopolistic, prevailing

371 Informality

NOUNS 1 informality, unceremoniousness, unconventional, unofficial, indifference, nonconformity, casualness **2 sociability**, affability, graciousness, cordiality, relaxedness **3 familiarity**, naturalness, simplicity, plainness, homeliness, folksiness **4 freedom**, licence, indulgence, toleration, free speech, free will, free-and-easiness, leeway, margin, unconstraint, latitude, independence, laxity, permissiveness, relaxation, forbearance, easygoingness, leave, looseness, irregularity **5 nonobservance**, nonadherence, bad form, gaffe, bad taste, bad manners, incorrectness **6 informal dress**, mufti, casual clothes, leisure wear, slacks, jeans, tracksuits, shellsuits, dishabille, bath robe, smoking jacket

ADJECTIVES 7 informal, unceremonious, unconventional, unofficial, indifferent, nonconformist, casual, offhand, unstuffy, unaffected **8 sociable**, affable, gracious, cordial, relaxed **9 familiar**, natural, simple, plain, homely, folksy, common **10 free**, indulgent, tolerant, unconstrained, independent, lax, permissive, easygoing

VERBS 11 not stand on ceremony, be oneself, be natural

372 Information

NOUNS 1 information, data, knowledge, intelligence, acquaintance, news, tidings **2 communication**, transmission, dissemination, diffusion, notification, announcement, broadcast, publication, narration, eyewitness account, statement, review, report, dispatch, communiqué, bulletin, message, wire, fax, telegram, telex, cable, notice, order, briefing **3 document**, paper, certificate, record, report, review, statement, estimate, specification, tax return, white paper, green paper, file **4 mass communication**, mass media, broadcasting, radio, television, journalism, the press, tabloid press, news, newscast, feature story, scoop, publicity, press release, hand-out, press conference, mention, obituary, advertisement, hatches, matches, magazines, journals, mailing list, circular, mailshot **5 reference book**, encyclopaedia, almanac, yearbook, dictionary, thesaurus, directory, index, guidebook, Baedeker, Fodor, Michelin, travelogue, handbook, manual, vade mecum, ABC, A–Z, timetable, Bradshaw, map, atlas, road map, itinerary, chart, plan, gazetteer, ephemeris, catalogue, telephone directory **6 information technology**, IT, computerized information, data communications, information retrieval, database, data processing, information theory **7 advice**, tip, hint, whisper, aside, suggestion, inference, intimation, insinuation, indication, pointer, tip-off, rumour, leak, gossip, prompt, reminder, signal, nod, wink, caution **8 source of information**, source, authority, grapevine, channel, press office, news agency, Reuters **9 informant**, messenger, herald, eyewitness, broadcaster, newscaster, anchorman, spokesperson, weather forecaster, advertiser, publicizer, publicity agent, press agent, publisher, journalist, correspondent, reporter **10 informer**, contact, source, tipster, telltale, blabber, tattler, gossip, newsmonger

VERBS 11 inform, tell, apprise, acquaint, advise, notify, testify, brief, instruct, teach, enlighten, educate, point out, correct, disabuse **12 communicate**, impart, transmit, disseminate, convey, recount, narrate, describe, publicize, broadcast, announce, televise, publish, report, document, post, wire, telegraph, fax, telex **13 inform on** (*or* **against**), betray, denounce, accuse, tergiversate, tell on **14 tip**, tip off, hint, breathe, whisper, indicate, signal, suggest, imply, intimate **15 be informed**, realize, understand, know, learn, discover, infer

ADJECTIVES 16 informative, revealing, illuminating, enlightening, explicit, clear, definite, expressive, expository, instructive, educational, advisory, cautionary, monitory, communicative, indicating, insinuating, suggesting, candid, plain-spoken, indiscreet **17 newsworthy**, front-page, headline **18 informed**, enlightened, briefed, posted

373 Ingratitude

• *Blow, blow, thou winter wind,/ Thou art not so unkind/ As man's ingratitude.* William Shakespeare.

•*Ingratitude, thou marble-hearted fiend,/ More hideous when thou show'st thee in a child/ Than the sea-monster!* William Shakespeare.

NOUNS 1 ingratitude, ungratefulness, thanklessness, unappreciation, ungraciousness, discourteousness, thoughtlessness, forgetfulness, inconsiderateness, rudeness, selfishness, nonrecognition, nonacknowledgment, no thanks

ADJECTIVES 2 ungrateful, unthankful, unappreciative, ungracious, discourteous, ill-mannered, bad-mannered, forgetful, thoughtless, inconsiderate, unmindful, heedless, rude **3 unthanked**, unrewarded, unacknowledged, unrecognized, uncredited, unrequited, forgotten, neglected **4 thankless**, unrewarding, useless

VERBS 5 be ungrateful, be forgetful, be thoughtless, be rude, begrudge

374 Inhabitant

NOUNS 1 inhabitant, native, aborigine, autochthon, indigene, indian, first comer, local, occupant, dweller, resident, denizen, inmate **2 inhabitants**, population, populace, people, public, citizenry, colony, commune, community, neighbourhood, dwellers, residents, household, family, ménage, tribe **3 householder**, owner-occupier, freeholder, tenant, renter, lessee, leaseholder, lodger, roomer, paying guest, boarder, roommate, flatmate, addressee, guest **4 townsman**, townsfolk, burgess, burgher, oppidan, citizen, city-dweller, metropolitan, urbanite **5 countryman**, country gentleman, country cousin, country bumpkin, ruralist, provincial, rustic, peasant, yokel, villager, parishioner, cottager, farmer, smallholder, crofter, highlander, frontiersman **6 illegal occupant**, squatter, trespasser, uninvited guest **7 settler**, pioneer, precursor, incomer, immigrant, colonizer **8 national**, subject, citizen, compatriot **9 British inhabitant**, Brit, Briton, John Bull, Englishman, Scot, Celt, Gael, cockney, Mancunian, Geordie, Liverpudlian **10 US inhabitant**, American, Uncle Sam

ADJECTIVES 11 inhabited, occupied, populated, lived in, indwelt, residential, tenanted, rented, leased, let, freehold, squatted **12 native**, indigenous, aboriginal, autochthonous, ethnic, tribal, local, metropolitan, urban, rustic **13 resident**, dwelling, settled, domiciled, colonial, colonized

VERBS 14 inhabit, dwell, reside, live in, abide in, occupy, lease, rent, lodge, board, stay, sojourn **15 settle**, move in, domicile, pioneer, immigrate, colonize, people, populate, squat

375 Innocence

NOUNS 1 innocence, virtue, goodness, morality, uprightness, probity, purity, virginity, chastity, saintliness, perfection, immaculacy, spotlessness, stainlessness, whiteness, incorruption, sinlessness, guiltlessness, inculpability, clear conscience, clean hands, faultlessness, impeccability, blamelessness, irreproachability, pure motives, inoffensiveness, harmlessness **2 legal innocence**, acquittal, exoneration, exculpation **3 naivety**, ingenuousness, guilelessness, artlessness, unsophistication, inexperience, immaturity, callow-

ness, greenness, unworldliness, naturalness, simplicity, credulousness, childhood
ADJECTIVES **4 innocent**, virtuous, good, upright, pure, virginal, chaste, saintly, perfect, angelic, immaculate, unblemished, untainted, stainless, spotless, unsullied, undefiled, clean, pristine, white, prelapsarian, faultless, impeccable, unerring, blameless, irreprehensible, inculpable, reproachless, guiltless, uncorrupt, incorrupt, gentle, inoffensive, harmless, innocuous, safe **5 declared innocent**, cleared, acquitted, exonerated, exculpated **6 naive**, ingenuous, guileless, artless, unsophisticated, credulous, inexperienced, immature, callow, green, unworldly, natural, simple
VERBS **7 be innocent**, have clean hands **8 declare innocent**, clear, acquit, exonerate, exculpate **9 be naive**, lack sophistication

376 Insanity

NOUNS **1 insanity**, madness, lunacy, idiocy, irrationality, unsound mind, mental illness, mental instability, unbalanced mind, criminal insanity, McNaghten Rules, diminished responsibility, abnormality, aberration, incoherence, eccentricity, oddness, freakishness, crankiness **2 subnormality**, mental deficiency, amentia, aphrenia, mental handicap, oligophrenia, backwardness, Down's syndrome, autism, cretinism, feeble-mindedness, imbecility **3 mental deterioration**, dementia, confusion, senile dementia, Alzheimer's disease, Pick's disease, encephalopathy, mad-cow disease, Creutzfeld-Jacob disease, kuru, fit, convulsion, paroxysm, seizure, stroke, rabies, hydrophobia **4 delusion**, illusion, hallucination, paraphrenia, personality disorder, paranoia, monomania, hypochondria, obsession, phobia, persecution mania, fixation, compulsion, urge, craving, craze, passion, elation, ecstasy, mania, frenzy, hysteria, ravings, delirium, dipsomania, megalomania, kleptomania, pyromania, agromania, onomatomania, theomania, nymphomania, satyriasis, erotomania, necromania **5 psychosis**, psychopathy, schizophrenia, dementia praecox, hebephrenia, catatonia, manic-depressive psychosis, cyclothymia, alcoholic psychosis **6 mental breakdown**, neurosis, neuroticism, neurasthenia, anxiety, depression, melancholia, hysteria, shell shock **7 mental hospital**, lunatic asylum, madhouse, Bedlam, psychiatric unit, padded cell **8 treatment**, psychoanalysis, psychotherapy, counselling **9 psychiatrist**, psychoanalyst
ADJECTIVES **10 insane**, mad, deranged, demented, abnormal, disturbed, unbalanced, unhinged, alienated, weird, peculiar, odd, anile **11 manic**, ranting, raving, frenzied, frenetic, frantic, hysterical, demented, rabid, wild, berserk, delirious, deluded **12 mentally ill**, disturbed, sick, abnormal, neurotic, depressed, melancholic, paranoid, fixated, psychotic, schizophrenic, catatonic
VERBS **13 become insane**, go mad, be insane, rave, ramble **14 make insane**, madden, derange, dement, unbalance, unhinge **15 certify**, commit

377 Insects and Arachnids

NOUNS 1 insect, winged insect, fly, gnat, midge, mosquito, cranefly, dragonfly, caddis fly, butterfly, moth, bee, wasp, ant, beetle, cockroach, earwig, stick insect, mantis, grasshopper, locust, **2 arachnid**, scorpion, pseudoscorpion, spider, black widow, tarantula, harvestman, acarid, mite, tick **3 pest**, parasite, vermin, weevil, borer, deathwatch beetle, woodworm, bookworm, wireworm, cutworm, screwworm, chafer, scale, bug, aphid, greenfly, blackfly, louse, nit, flea, chigoe, chigger, jigger, bloodsucker **4 social insect**, bee, wasp, ant, termite, queen bee, drone, worker, soldier ant, hive, beehive, apiary, wasps' nest, vespiary, anthill, antheap, termite colony, termitarium, swarm, army **5 larva**, grub, maggot, spiderling, caterpillar, silkworm, antlion, leatherjacket, glowworm, mealworm, nymph, pupa, chrysalis, cocoon, metamorphosis **6 study**, entomology, beekeeping, sericulture, arachnology **7 entomologist**, lepidopterist, bug hunter, beekeeper, apiarist, sericulturalist

ADJECTIVES 8 insectan (*or* **insectean**), insectile, insectiform, thysanuran, dipluran, collembolan, proturan, orthopteran, phasmid, dermapteran, isopteran, hemipteran, homopteran, heteropteran, thysanopteran, grylloblatodean, lepidopteran, hymenopteran, coleopteran **9 arachnidan**, spidery, arachnoid, acarid **10 verminous**, infested, weevilly, maggoty, grubby, lousy, flea-bitten **11 immature**, larval, pupal **12 entomological**, apiarian, sericultural

VERBS 13 infest, invade, swarm, buzz, drone, plague, sting, bite, parasitize, swarm with, crawl with, teem with, contaminate **14 develop**, hatch

378 Insensibility

NOUNS 1 lack of feeling, ignorance, analgesia, paralysis, anaesthesia, clumsiness, heavy-handedness, dullness, insensitiveness **2 unconsciousness**, coma, faint, swoon, sleep, doze, snooze, torpor, daydream, nap, cat-nap, stupor, trance, suspended animation, etherism, sleepiness, somnolence **3 heedlessness**, impassivity, hardness, callousness, hard-heartedness, heartlessness **4 anaesthetic**, painkiller, analgesic, narcotic, opium, laudanum, dope, drug, ether, novocaine, cocaine, pethidine, barbiturate, halothane, lignocaine, acupuncture, hypnosis, Mickey Finn, sleeping pill, somnifer, sleeping draught

ADJECTIVES 5 unfeeling, blind, deaf, insentient, nerveless, senseless, insensitive, clumsy, heavy-handed, unresponsive, impassive, cold-blooded, apathetic, heedless, oblivious, unmindful, forgetful, unwary, impervious, unemotional, hardened, stolid **6 anaesthetized**, etherized, frozen, hypnotized, insensible, numb, deadened **7 unconscious**, stunned, concussed, comatose, asleep, out cold **8 anaesthetic**, analgesic, deadening, numbing, hypnotic, narcotic, soporific **9 sleepy**, somnolent, dopy

VERBS 10 be unfeeling, be impassive, be apathetic, drowse, doze, sleep, sleepwalk, nod off, drop off, faint, pass out, black out, shut off, switch off, ignore **11 anaesthetize**, etherize, put under, desensitize, deaden, blunt, benumb, freeze, hypnotize, mesmerize, narcotize, stun, stupefy, knock out, brain

379 Insensitivity

ADJECTIVES 1 insensitive, insensible, unsusceptible, immune, unresponsive, unimpressionable, unaffected, indifferent, apathetic, impassive, unfeeling, insensate, unemotional, frigid, cold-hearted, cold-blooded, heartless, thick-skinned, impervious, proof against, rhino-hided, obtuse, blunt, tactless, unimaginative, callous, uncaring, tough, hard, blind, deaf, unaware, unconscious, imperceptive **2 desensitized**, numb, frozen, paralysed, anaesthetized, dopey, groggy, torpid, sluggish, drugged, stupefied, comatose, unfeeling, unconscious, quiescent

NOUNS 3 insensitiveness, insensibility, unsusceptibility, unresponsiveness, indifference, apathy, impassivity, coldness, cold-heartedness, heartlessness, callousness, tactlessness, bluntness, hardness, unawareness, dullness **4 desensitization**, narcotization, stupefaction, hypnosis, numbness, paralysis, stupor, torpor, sluggishness, grogginess, trance, coma, catalepsy, catatonia, narcosis, analgesia, anaesthesia, unconsciousness, stagnation **5 desensitizing substance**, narcotic, anaesthetic, drug, soporific, pain-killer, analgesic, sleeping draught, sleeping pill, nepenthes

VERBS 6 render insensitive, desensitize, numb, paralyse, freeze, stupefy, anaesthetize, narcotize, drug, dope, hypnotize, deaden, blunt, concuss

380 Insertion

VERBS 1 insert, put in, stick in, introduce, introject, insinuate, add, interject, interpolate, intercalate, intromit, include, import, drop in, pot **2 inject**, inoculate, vaccinate, implant, impregnate, enter, penetrate, pierce, poke in, squirt in, introduce, pop in, infuse, instil, imbue, perfuse, transfuse, pour in **3 impact**, thrust in, drive in, plunge in, run in, push in, force in, hammer in, knock in, pound in, ram in, jam in, cram in, press in, squeeze in, crowd in, stuff in **4 immerse**, submerge, plunge, dunk, dip, duck, baptize, steep, souse, drench, flood, bury **5 inset**, inlay, slip in, slide in, ease in, wedge in, infix, dovetail, embed, encapsulate, ensheathe, encase, box, cover, mount, frame **6 plant**, implant, transplant, bed out, graft, engraft **7 install**, instate, inaugurate, initiate, invest, ordain, induct, enrol, enlist, sign up

NOUNS 8 insertion, introduction, introjection, insinuation, addition, interjection, interpolation, intercalation, intromission, embolism, parenthesis, import, infixion, impaction, planting, implantation, transplantation, graft, embedment **9 injection**, inoculation, vaccination, implantation, impregnation, entry, ingress, penetration, infusion, perfusion **10 immersion**, submersion, plunge, dip, bath, ducking, baptism, interment **11 thing inserted**, insert, inset, inlay, inclusion, supplement, filling, stuffing, syringe, tampon, suppository

ADJECTIVES 12 inserted, introduced, introjected, insinuated, added, interpolated, intercalated, parenthetical, by-the-by, imported, infixed, impacted, planted, transplanted, grafted, embedded, tessellated, inlaid **13 injected**, inoculated, vaccinated, implanted, impregnated, infused **14 immersed**, submersed, submerged, baptized

381 Insolence

NOUNS **1 insolence**, procacity, effrontery, impudence, impertinence, rudeness, bumptiousness, contumely **2 cheek**, face, mouth, sass, brass, brass neck, nerve, gall, crust, lip, chutzpah **3 audacity**, boldness, assurance, hubris, brazen face, blatancy, flagrancy, presumptiousness **4 arrogance**, loftiness, uppishness, uppitiness, pushiness, haughtiness, pride, tyranny **5 bravado**, defiance, bluster **6 contempt**, disdain, sneer **7 insult**, gesture, taunt, affront, snook, V-sign **8 rudeness**, disrespectfulness, contempt, derision **9 discourtesy**, petulance, defiance, backchat, rejoinder, raillery, banter **10 impudence**, impertinence, flippancy, cockiness, cheek, freshness, brazen-facedness **11 sauciness**, disrespect, impertinence, pertness, impudence

ADJECTIVES **12 insolent**, impudent, malapert, impertinent, bumptious **13 cheeky**, brazen, mouthy, brassy, saucy, sassy, crusty, gally **14 audacious**, bold, assured, brazenfaced, blatant, flagrant, precocious, obtrusive, familiar **15 arrogant**, lofty, haughty, uppish, uppity, pushy, proud, tyrannical, shameless, presumptuous **16 contemptuous**, disdainful, sneering, cool, cold, disparaging **17 insulting**, taunting, uncalled for **18 rude**, disrespectful, contemptuous, derisive, bluff, brash **19 discourteous**, petulant, defiant, backchatting, bantering **20 impudent**, impertinent, pert, flippant, cocky, cheeky, fresh, brazen, brazen-faced, brassy, bold

VERBS **21 be rude**, dare, presume, take liberties **22 be proud**, presume **23 be vain**, brag, swagger, swank, swell, talk big **24 answer back**, cheek, sass, backchat, provoke, retort **25 oppress**, hector, bully, browbeat, grind down **26 dare**, presume, take liberties, outface, lord it, queen it **27 get above oneself**, presume, lord it **28 ridicule**, express contempt, snort, sneer, jeer, taunt, deride, despise, scorn

382 Instrumentality

NOUNS **1 instrumentality**, agency, operation, occasion, opportunity, responsibility, cause, effect, result, influence, significance, power, weight, effectiveness, efficacy, performance, achievement, functionality, service, promotion, advancement, help, aid, assistance, support, midwifery, intermediacy, intervention, interposition, intercession, mediation, interference, pressure, cooperation, subordination, subservience, employment, use, medium, means, instrumentation, mechanization, computerization, automation, application, practicality, serviceability, utility, usefulness **2 instrument**, means, medium, catalyst, vehicle, agency, influence, mechanism, force, factor, organ, implement, device, tool, machine, apparatus, appliance, equipment, gadget, contrivance

VERBS **3 be an instrument**, function, operate, work, act, perform, do, serve, be useful, work for, minister to, pander to, pimp, procure, help, assist, aid, support, cooperate, promote, advance, cause, control, bridge, channel, interpose, intervene, intercede for, mediate, compromise, influence, pressure, pull strings, implement, effect, carry through, carry out, expedite **4 find means**, obtain assistance

ADJECTIVES 5 instrumental, useful, applicable, employable, utilizable, handy, helping, assisting, cooperative, advancing, promoting, aiding, supportive, subordinate, subservient, effective, efficient, effectual, efficacious **6 causal**, responsible, instrumental, central, powerful, weighty, significant, telling, influential, mediative, intermediate, intervening, intercessional, interfering, pressuring, maieutic, Socratic **7 practical**, applied, servicing, general-purpose, working, functioning, operational, manual, mechanical, automatic, automated, electronic

383 Insufficiency

ADJECTIVES 1 insufficient, inadequate, unsatisfactory, disappointing, unacceptable, insubstantial, limited, cramped, slender, meagre, skimpy, scanty, sketchy, deficient, incomplete, lacking, wanting, poor, inferior, incompetent, incapable, unequal to, weak, thin, watery, jejune, undernourished, underfed, niggardly, miserly **2 unprovided**, unsupplied, unfurnished, ill-equipped, absent, vacant, bare, empty, unstocked, unfilled, empty-handed, unsuccessful, unsatisfied, discontented, unfulfilled, unaccommodated, insatiable, greedy, stinted, rationed, skimped, lacking, needing, hard up, poor, undercapitalized, underfinanced, underfunded, underpaid, understaffed, undermanned **3 underfed**, undernourished, hungry, famished, famine-stricken, starved, voracious, ravenous, fasting, emaciated, macerated, thin, lean, spare, skinny, wasting, anorexic, scraggy **4 scarce**, rare, infrequent, sparse, few, short, unavailable, unobtainable

VERBS 5 be insufficient, hinder, restrain, restrict, limit, lack, fail, disappoint **6 be unsatisfied**, feel hungry, feel cheated, want, desire, long for, yearn for, need **7 make insufficient**, overtax, overextend, overwork, overcrop, overgraze, overfish, impoverish, damage, impair, exhaust, drain, deplete, squander, waste, grudge, stint, skimp, ration

NOUNS 8 insufficiency, inadequacy, disappointment, discontent, meagreness, skimpiness, scantiness, deficiency, deficit, shortfall, slippage, incompleteness, incompetence, inferiority, imperfection, defect, nonfulfilment, noncompletion, makeshift, tinkering, failure, weakness, bankruptcy, insolvency, stinginess, meanness, parsimony, low pay, pittance, dole, mite, iron rations, austerity, Spartan fare, starvation diet, fasting, asceticism, anorexia nervosa, malnutrition **9 scarcity**, paucity, dearth, shortage, leanness, drought, famine, starvation, infertility, unproductiveness, energy crisis, decrease, diminution, seller's market, deprivation

384 Intellect

• *We should take care not to make the intellect our god; it has, of course, powerful muscles, but no personality.* Albert Einstein.

NOUNS 1 mind, mentality, rationality, ratiocination, conception, intellectualism, consciousness, awareness, cognition, perception **2 ways of thinking**, logic, deduction, induction, reasoning, insight, acumen, inspiration, instinct, rationale, intuition **3 intelligence**, intellect, understanding, comprehension, sense, judgment, mentality, mind, brain, wit, reason **4 cleverness**, genius, flair, brains, wit, wisdom, sagacity, sapience, erudition, knowledgeableness, brightness, incisiveness, shrewdness, astuteness, aptitude, brilliance, alertness, sharpness, acuity, quick-wittedness, canniness **5 common sense**, sensibleness, sound judgment, discernment, clear thinking, horse sense, native wit **6 thoughtfulness**, judiciousness, consideration, reflection, circumspection, profundity **7 brain**, head

ADJECTIVES 8 mental, intellectual, rational, reasoning, thinking, conceptual, cerebral, cephalic, noetic, phrenic, psychological, logical, deductive, instinctive **9 intelligent**, understanding, clever, learned, erudite, knowledgeable, wise, sage, sagacious, bright, smart, shrewd, astute, brilliant, alert, sharp, acute, quick-witted, keen-witted **10 thoughtful**, judicious, reflective, circumspect, sapient, profound, sensible, reasonable

VERBS 11 think, reason, rationalize, ratiocinate, perceive, conceptualize, cognize, perceive, ideate, deduce, induce

385 Intelligibility

ADJECTIVES 1 intelligible, comprehensible, understandable, knowable, apprehensible, fathomable, penetrable, scrutable, interpretable, realizable, coherent, sane, audible, visible, luminous, unambiguous, unequivocal, univocal, meaningful, explicable, teachable, focused, clear-cut, precise, certain, positive, striking, vivid, graphic, descriptive, illustrative, explanatory, interpretative **2 simple**, clear, plain, explicit, articulate, distinct, direct, straightforward, downright, forthright, uncomplicated, easy, obvious, self-explanatory, self-evident, readable, legible, explained, interpreted, popularized, exoteric, apodictic, limpid, transparent, lucid **3 recognizable**, distinguishable, identifiable, distinct, defined

VERBS 4 be intelligible, make sense, speak volumes, become apparent, dawn on **5 simplify**, make clear, make plain, articulate, repeat, recapitulate, predigest, popularize, spell out, facilitate, explain, explicate, interpret, elucidate **6 understand**, comprehend, know, realize, fathom, penetrate, master, learn, grasp, seize, take in, follow **7 recognize**, detect, identify, spot, distinguish, discern, perceive **8 be recognizable**, stand out

NOUNS 9 intelligibility, comprehensibility, understandability, knowability, apprehensibility, fathomableness, penetrability, scrutability, interpretability, explicability, teachability, coherence, unambiguity, unambivalence, precision, certainty, sense, meaningfulness, informativeness, vividness, graphicness **10 simplicity**, clarity, clearness, plainness, explicitness, articulateness, distinctness, directness, straightforwardness, unadornment, readability, legibility, decipherability, decoding, easiness, facility, obviousness, self-evidence, explanation, amplification, interpretation, simplification, popularization, plain English, mother tongue, limpidity, transparency, lucidity **11 recognizability**, cognizability, distinguishability, distinctiveness **12 understanding**, comprehension, realization, apprehension, mastery, grasp, learning, knowledge

386 Intention

NOUNS 1 intention, meaning, purpose, motive **2 intentionality**, deliberateness, calculation, determination, resolve, predetermination **3 future intention**, prospect, view, purview, plan, proposal, design, project, enterprise, undertaking, pursuit, study, ambition, aspiration, hope **4 formulated intention**, decision, judgment, ultimatum, threat, promise, engagement, bid **5 final intention**, ultimate aim, teleology, God's purpose, eschatology, trend, tendency **6 objective**, end, destination, aim, goal, mark, target, butt, bull's-eye, finishing line, winning post, Mecca, prey, quarry, game, prize, cup, trophy, crown, wreath, laurels, dream, vision, Promised Land, El Dorado, Shangri-La

VERBS 7 intend, mean, purpose, propose, contemplate, think of, ponder, meditate, calculate, reckon on, plan, prepare for, expect **8 resolve**, determine, mean to, premeditate, predetermine, project, design, undertake, engage, shoulder, promise **9 intend for**, predestine, earmark **10 aim**, go for, try for, bid for, aspire to, dream of, strive after, work for

ADJECTIVES 11 intending, resolute, serious, seeking, purposive, teleological, inclined, disposed, prospective, would-be, hopeful, aspiring **12 intended**, meant, deliberate, intentional, voluntary, volitional, wilful, calculated, studied, planned, designed, purposeful, premeditated, aforethought

387 Interface

NOUNS 1 interface, meeting point, contiguity, adjacency, abutment, threshold, battlefront, common boundary, Iron Curtain, Bamboo Curtain, forty-ninth parallel, Mason-Dixon Line **2 interaction**, common ground, cooperation, compatibility, permeation, interpenetration, blend **3 interfacer**, confronter, frontbencher, frontiersman, pioneer, intermediary, middleman, mediator, negotiator, referee, umpire, director

VERBS 4 interface, meet, contact, touch, adjoin, abut, interact, confront, divide, share **5 cooperate**, be compatible, work together, blend, dovetail

ADJECTIVES 6 interfacial, contiguous, adjacent, adjoining, meeting, abutting, liminal, interactive, confrontational, divisive, shared, common, same, cooperative, compatible, blended, dovetailed, permeated

388 Interior

NOUNS 1 interior, internality, inwardness, centrality, inner surface, undersurface, endodermis, subcortex, substratum, subsoil, depth, cave **2 inside**, indoors, home, room, confinement, cell, prison, jail, centre, middle, heart, core, depths, recesses, seclusion, retreat **3 inland**, the interior, hinterland, heartland, upstate, upcountry **4 insides**, contents, internal organs, the vitals, viscera, gland, heart, lung, liver, belly, paunch, womb, entrails, intestines, offal **5 inner nature**, intrinsicality, heart, soul, animus, anima, core, marrow **6 internalization**, secretiveness, privacy, inwardness, self-absorption, engrossment

ADJECTIVES 7 interior, internal, central, inside, inward, inner, undersurfaced, enclosed, endemic, endodermal, subcutaneous, subcortical, intravenous, substrative **8 internal**, inward, indoor, homelike, in-house, domestic, local, civil **9 inland**, landlocked, central, upstate, upcountry, midland **10 visceral**, internal, bodily, vital, spanchnic, cardiovascular, intestinal, enteric, gastric, uterine **11 intrinsic**, innate, inherent, innermost, fundamental, radical **12 internalized**, intimate, personal, private, secret, hidden, veiled, inmost, inward, self-absorbed, engrossed, egocentric

VERBS 13 be interior, lie within **14 go inside**, enter, retreat into, take refuge, seclude oneself **15 keep inside**, internalize, bottle up, contain, absorb, hold within, hide, conceal, confine

389 Interpretation

NOUNS 1 interpretation, construction, rendering, explanation, definition, description, explication, emendation, amendment, editing, simplification, exposition, exegesis, eisegesis, isogesis, judgment, estimate, understanding, insight, enlightenment, clarification, elucidation, illumination, illustration, exemplification, demonstration, example, resolution, solution, answer, key, clue, decipherment, analysis, conflation, application, twist, turn, reading, lection, meaning, subaudition, connotation, euhemerism, demythologization, allegorization, metaphor, accepted reading, vulgate, rendition, deconstruction, version **2 annotation**, gloss, footnote, marginalia, variorum, scholium, apparatus criticus, note, exegesis, legend, appendix, inscription, comment **3 criticism**, critique, review, notice, puff, panning **4 translation**, transcription, rendering, bilingual text, version, rewording, paraphrase, adaptation, simplification, amplification, transliteration, decoding, unscrambling, decipherment, lipreading **5 science of interpretation**, exegetics, hermeneutics, tropology, epigraphy, cryptology, cryptanalysis, palaeography, semiology, lexicography, linguistics, diagnostics, symptomatology, physiognomy, phrenology, graphology, prophecy

VERBS 6 interpret, construe, render, put, explain, explicate, inform, expound, understand, deduce, infer, reason, define, describe, emend, twist, turn, conflate, edit, simplify, spell out, popularize, facilitate, judge, estimate, clarify, disambiguate, analyse, elucidate, illuminate, illustrate, exemplify, demonstrate **7 decipher**, decode, unscramble, read, spell out, work out, solve, resolve, enucleate, unravel, unriddle, demystify **8 annotate**, gloss, footnote, inscribe **9 crit-**

icize, review, critique, evaluate, pan, slate **10 translate**, transcribe, transliterate, render, paraphrase, reword, restate, rehash, adapt, simplify, amplify, encode, decode, cipher, decipher, sign, lip-read **11 interpret news**, report, cover, slant
ADJECTIVES 12 interpretive, constructive, explanatory, explicatory, explaining, descriptive, expositive, insightful, illustrative, demonstrative, definitional, exemplary, exegetic, hermeneutic, clarifying, elucidative, illuminating, semiological, euhemeristic **13 interpreted**, glossed, explained, defined, illustrated, elucidated, clarified, simplified, annotated, edited, emended, amended, conflated, translated, rendered, deciphered, decoded, unscrambled, cracked, unlocked, coded **14 annotative**, glossarial, scholiastic, explanatory, critical, editorial **15 translational**, paraphrastic, metaphrastic, polyglot, multilingual, bilingual, synonymous, equivalent, literal, word-for-word, verbatim, faithful

390 Interval

NOUNS 1 interval, gap, space, distance, room, margin, clearance, headroom, leeway, freeboard, interspace, interruption, daylight, firebreak, passage, separation, discontinuity, hiatus, lacuna, caesura, jump **2 crack**, crevice, cleft, fissure, scissure, interstice, chink, cranny, check, flaw, notch, nick, cut, incision, gash, slit, split, rift, fault, rupture, rent, tear, break, fracture, breach, hole, opening, aperture, orifice, cavity, groove, slot, furrow, trench, ditch, dyke, moat **3 gulf**, abyss, chasm, void, gape, gorge, ravine, canyon, crevasse, chimney, gully, gulch, ghat, pass, defile, col, couloir, flume, draw
VERBS 4 space, interspace, separate, make room **5 crack**, cleave, check, notch, nick, cut, incise, gash, slit, split, rive, rupture, rend, tear, break, fracture, breach, open, gape, groove, slot, furrow
ADJECTIVES 6 spaced, interspaced, interstitial, separate, parted, removed, intervallic **7 cracked**, cleft, cloven, fissured, cut, slit, split, riven, ruptured, rent, torn, broken, fractured, open, gaping, gappy, grooved, furrowed

391 Interweaving

NOUNS 1 interweaving, weaving, crisscross, interlacing, intertexture, interwork, lacing, intertwining, entanglement, webbing, braiding, plaiting, pleaching, interlocking, intercommunication, interfusion, interlineation, interdigitation, reticulation **2 braid**, plait, pigtail, wreath, arabesque, filigree, cat's cradle, web, skein, network, webbing, netting, mesh, spider's web, wickerwork, trellis, espalier, lattice, wattle, grid, tracery, fretwork, knitting, tatting, macramé, crochet, lace **3 weaving**, loom, warp, weft, woof, shuttle, distaff, spinning wheel, sewing machine, weaver, knitter, spinner, spider **4 textile**, cloth, material, fabric, broadcloth, suiting, sackcloth, jute, linen, cheesecloth, muslin, towelling, flannel, wool, mohair, cashmere, tweed, vicuna, alpaca, merino, angora, cotton, khaddar, homespun, drill, twill, moleskin, denim, voile, poplin, madras, seersucker, chintz, silk, satin, tussore, taffeta, shantung, chiffon, velvet, corduroy, lace **5 crossroads**, crossing, intersection, interchange

ADJECTIVES 6 interwoven, crisscross, interlaced, intertwined, webbed, interdigitated, braided, plaited, pleached, wreathed, reticulate, loomed, woollen **7 crossing**, intersecting, interchanging

VERBS 8 interweave, crisscross, interlace, lace, intertwine, entangle, web, braid, plait, pleach, interlock, interdigitate, reticulate, filigree, net, mesh, knit, tat, macramé, crochet, knot, twist, warp, shuttle, spin, sew, intercrop, espalier, interfile, interfuse, intermingle, interlay, interline **9 cross**, intersect

392 Intuition

NOUNS 1 intuition, feeling, insight, perception **2 precognition**, sixth sense, second sight, clairvoyance, divination, telepathy **3 insight**, foreboding, impression, feeling, impulse, hunch **4 instinct**, proclivity, subconscious, unconscious

ADJECTIVES 5 intuitive, insightful, perceptive, sensitive, sensing **6 procognitive**, *a priori*, unmediated, second-sighted, clairvoyant, divinatory, telepathic, extrasensory **7 instinctive**, automatic, spontaneous, reflex

VERBS 8 be intuitive, feel, perceive **9 be instinctive**, react automatically

393 Inversion

NOUNS 1 inversion, reversion, reversal, converse, transposition, contrary, opposite, antithesis, introversion, retroversion, evagination, invagination, capsizing, overturning, upset, spill, cartwheel, somersault, handspring, headstand, undermining

ADJECTIVES 2 inverted, reversed, transpositional, upside-down, head-over-heels, bottom-up

VERBS 3 invert, reverse, transpose, introvert, retrovert, evaginate, invaginate, capsize, overturn, upset, spill, cartwheel, somersault

394 Invertebrates

NOUNS 1 invertebrate, lower animal, protochordate, metazoan, mesozoan, parazoan, protozoan **2 protochordate**, hemichordate, acorn worm, chordate, urochordate, tunicate, ascidian, sea squirt, salp, cephalochordate, lancelet, amphioxus **3 echinoderm**, crinoid, sea lily, feather star, asteroid, starfish, sea star, ophiuroid, brittle star, echinoid, sea urchin, sand dollar, sea biscuit, holothurian, sea cucumber, trepang **4 arthropod**, trilobite, eurypterid, horseshoe crab, limulus, spiders, ticks, mites, etc.), insect, crustacean, branchiopod, shrimp, daphnia, ostracod, copepod, cyclops, branchiuran, fish louse, cirripede, barnacle, malacostracan, amphipod, sand hopper, isopod, water louse, woodlouse, pill bug, gribble, prawn, crab, lobster, crayfish, shellfish, seafood, myriapod, pauropod, symphylan, arthropod-like invertebrate, tardigrade, water bear, pentastomid **5 mollusc**, snails, slugs, etc.), bivalve, clams, mussels, scallops, oysters, etc.), squids, octopods, octopuses, etc.), mollusc-like invertebrate, lampshell **6 invertebrate zoology**, arachnology, entomology, malacology, conchology, helminthology, protozoology **7 invertebrate zoologist**,

arachnologist, entomologist, malacologist, conchologist, helminthologist
ADJECTIVES 8 invertebrate, protochordate, hemichordate, urochordate, cephalochordate, acraniate, coelomate, pseudocoelomate, acoelomate, metazoan, mesozoan **9 echinodermal**, echinodermatous, crinoidal, asteroid, ophiuroid, echinoid **10 arthropodous**, arthropodial, chelicerate, arachnoid, spidery, insectile, crustacean, arachnological **11 molluscan**, gastropodan, bivalvular, cephalopodic, octopod, malcological **12 wormlike**, vermicular, helminthic, fluky, cestoid, annelid, segmented, polychaetous, oligochaetous, lumbricoid, hirudinean, leechlike **13 coelenterate**, hydroid, polypoid, medusoid, hydrozoan, scyphozoan, anthrozoan, coralline **14 spongelike**, poriferan, poriferous, spongy, fibrous **15 protozoan**, protozoic, amoebic, flagellate, ciliate

395 Invisibility

ADJECTIVES 1 invisible, unseeable, unperceivable, imperceptible, indistinguishable, indiscernible, unnoticeable, undetectable, unrecognizable, unidentifiable, unidentified, unmarked, unapparent, inappreciable, immaterial, insubstantial, transparent, unseen, unsighted, unobserved, unwitnessed, eclipsed, latent, buried, submerged **2 difficult to see**, partly visible, half-seen, inconspicuous, infinitesimal, microscopic, subliminal, distant, remote, darkened, faint, pale, indefinite, unclear, indistinct, unfocused, undefined, blurred, bleared, hazy, misty, foggy, filmy, shadowy, obscured, dim, low-definition, ill-defined **3 private**, internal, inward, hidden, concealed, covert, secret, clandestine, disguised, camouflaged, screened, masked, covered, veiled, recondite, dark, obscure, obstructed
NOUNS 4 invisibility, disappearance, vanishing, non-appearance, absence, transparency, insubstantiality, darkness, blackness, obscurity, haze, mist, fog, fuzziness, indistinctness, faintness, paleness, imperceptibility, indistinguishability, indiscernibility, undetectability, latency, concealment, hiding, secrecy **5 invisible thing**, vanisher, blind spot, black hole, black ice, invisible ink, backroom boys, spirit world **6 that which makes invisible**, darkness, night, mist, fog, peasouper, haze, smoke, film, membrane, eraser, rubber, eclipse, distance, remoteness, horizon, veil, yashmak, chador, purdah, mask, domino, disguise, front, camouflage, shroud, curtain, blind, shade, shutter, screen, partition, hide, hidey-hole
VERBS 7 become invisible, disappear, vanish, fade, blur, dim, darken, hide, retreat **8 make invisible**, hide, bury, conceal, mask, screen, cloak, veil, eclipse, obscure, disguise, erase, delete, black out, blank out, blur

396 Irascibility

NOUNS 1 irascibility, irritability, impatience, temperamentalness, touchiness, tetchiness, prickliness, grumpiness, gruffness, peevishness, pepperiness, testiness, petulance, querulousness, fretfulness, resentfulness, sullenness, shrewishness, vixenishness, fractiousness, crankiness, crossness, huffiness, cussedness, cantankerousness, churlishness, sharpness, tartness, acerbity, asperity, gall, bile, vinegar, sourness, acidity, shrewishness, waspishness, meanness, contentiousness, quarrelsomeness, disputatiousness, argumentativeness, belligerence **2 sign of irascibility**, frown, scowl, glare, grimace, glower, lour, growl

ADJECTIVES 3 irascible, irritable, impatient, nervous, jumpy, strained, fretful, oversensitive, touchy, tetchy, thin-skinned, petulant, peevish, querulous, testy, temperamental, short-tempered, highly-strung, short, huffy, annoyed, resentful, sullen, sore, riled, nettled, ill-humoured, snappish, bellicose, waspish, sharp-tongued, tart, acerbic, sour, acid, shrewish, vixenish, crusty, ornery, prickly, peppery, hot-blooded, hot-tempered, quick-tempered, short-tempered, grumpy, gruff, cross, cantankerous, churlish, fractious, bilious, dyspeptic, contentious, quarrelsome, disputatious, argumentative, belligerent, angry, mean **4 showing irascibility**, frowning, scowling, glowering, louring, pouting, grimacing

VERBS 5 be irascible, strain, fret, resent, quarrel, dispute, argue, get angry, turn against, fly at **6 frown**, scowl, glower lour, pout, grimace, growl **7 make irascible**, irritate, vex, annoy, bother, rile

397 Irregularity

NOUNS 1 irregularity, nonuniformity, unequalness, asymmetry, unevenness, roughness, choppiness, spottiness, patchiness, brokenness, disconnection, discontinuation, sporadicalness, infrequency, intermittence, fluctuation, changeableness, wavering, variability, variety, diversity, inconsistency, unpredictability, randomness, fitfulness, capriciousness, restlessness, desultoriness, unmethodicalness, haphazardness, disorder, instability, unsteadiness, oscillation, wobbliness, shakiness, jerkiness, flickering, staggering, lurching, careening, veering **2 unusualness**, uncommonness, exceptionalness, anomalousness, incongruousness, aberrance, abnormality, eccentricity, nonconformity, unconventionality, unorthodoxy, oddness, peculiarity, whimsicality **3 irregular thing**, mountain range, stormy sea, British weather, stock exchange

ADJECTIVES 4 irregular, nonuniform, unequal, asymmetric, uneven, rough, choppy, spotty, patchy, broken, disconnected, discontinuous, sporadic, spasmodic, halting, infrequent, intermittent, fluctuating, changeable, wavering, variable, diverse, inconsistent, erratic, inconstant, unpredictable, random, fitful, capricious, restless, desultory, unmethodically, unsystematic, unrhythmic, haphazard, disorderly, unstable, unsteady, oscillatory, wobbly, shaky, jerky, flickering, staggering, lurching, careening, veering **5 unusual**, uncommon, exceptional, anomalous, incongruous, incoherent, aberrant, erratic, abnormal, eccentric, idiosyncratic, unique, individual, nonconforming, unconventional, unorthodox, odd, peculiar

VERBS 6 be irregular, intermit, break, disconnect, fluctuate, change, vary, waver, oscillate, wobble, shake, jerk, flicker, stagger, lurch, careen, veer **7 be unusual**, be eccentric, act erratic, act odd

398 Jealousy

• *O, beware, my lord, of jealousy;/ It is the green-ey'd monster which doth mock/ The meat it feeds on.* William Shakespeare.

NOUNS 1 jealousy, enviousness, covetousness, heartburn, jaundice, sour grapes, resentment, hostility, possessiveness, rivalry, competition **2 distrust**, mistrust, suspicion, doubt, watchfulness, vigilance, possessiveness, solicitousness

ADJECTIVES 3 jealous, envious, covetous, jaundiced, jaundice-eyed, green, green-eyed, yellow, yellow-eyed, lynx-eyed, sour, resentful, possessive, hostile, invidious, rival, competitive **4 distrustful**, mistrustful, suspicious, doubtful, watchful, vigilant, Argus-eyed, solicitous

VERBS 5 be jealous, envy, covet **6 arouse jealousy**, create resentment **7 distrust**, be suspicious, be wary, doubt

399 Joint Possession

NOUNS 1 joint possession, joint ownership, time sharing, partnership, copartnership, union, association, alliance, stock, profit-sharing, dividend, share, pool, kitty, tontine, store, common, public land, cooperative system, public domain, nationalization, socialism, communism, collectivism, collective, commune, community, communalization, kolkhoz, kibbutz, coalition, federation, confederation, commonwealth, commonweal, international organization, global village, cooperative, dependency, dominion **2 participation**, membership, affiliation, association, collaboration, cooperation, sympathy strike, companionship, fellowship, mutualism, inclusion, involvement, engagement, contribution, partaking, complicity, sharing, co-sharing

VERBS 3 have joint possession, go Dutch, cooperate, contribute, join, partake of, involve oneself, join in, communalize, socialize, communize

ADJECTIVES 4 jointly possessing, joint, united, concerted, associate, corporate, profit-sharing, time-sharing, house-sharing, flat-sharing, cooperative, common, communal, general, public, mutual, collective, socialistic, communistic, global, international, participating, accessory, partaking, sympathetic

400 Joy

NOUNS 1 happiness, contentment, euphoria, gladness, lightheartedness, cheerfulness, merriment, delight, pleasure, enjoyment, delectation, joy, felicity, gaiety, glee, high spirits, gusto, zest, exuberance, ebullience, transport, exaltation, exhilaration, rapture, ecstasy, bliss, enchantment, intoxication **2 fun**, entertainment, party, treat, holiday, celebration, merrymaking, revelry, honeymoon period, halcyon days, heaven, paradise

ADJECTIVES 3 happy, contented, euphoric, pleased, glad, cheerful, joyful, felicitous, gay, blithe, merry, delighted, exuberant, ebullient, blissful, starry-eyed, elated, overjoyed, thrilled, transported, ecstatic, celebratory, jubilant, captivated, enchanted, enraptured, delirious **4 delightful**, lovely, wonderful,

marvellous, heavenly, enchanting, gorgeous, entrancing, charming
VERBS 5 enjoy, have fun, celebrate, relish **6 show joy**, smile, grin, beam, laugh, chuckle, giggle, chortle, guffaw, crow, sing, purr **7 cause joy**, gladden, please, cheer, thrill, delight, charm, enchant, enrapture, enthral

401 Judgment

NOUNS 1 judgment, discrimination, discernment, distinction, differentiation, selection, choice, discretion, taste, wisdom, sense, adjudication, arbitration, umpirage, reasoning, deduction, inference, dissertation, corollary, consideration, view, belief, opinion, assessment, evaluation, speculation, conjecture, surmise, sensibility, guesswork, estimate, calculation, rating, valuation, appraisal, appreciation, survey, inspection, report, review, notice, remark, comment, critique, criticism, censure, vox populi, vote, referendum **2 verdict**, adjudication, summing up, recapitulation, decision, conclusion, ruling, finding, award, sentence, pronouncement, order, edict, decree, acquittal, condemnation, law, canon, act **3 place of judgment**, tribunal, the Woolsack, law court, criminal court, civil court, Star Chamber, High Court, Queen's Bench, circuit court, assizes, quarter sessions, crown court, petty sessions, magistrate's court, police court, coroner's court, court martial, kangaroo court, courtroom, the bench, jury box, dock, witness box **4 judgment day**, Last Judgment, Doomsday, millennium, afterlife **5 judge**, adjudicator, arbitrator, jurist, arbiter, umpire, referee, mediator, assessor, valuer, appraiser, surveyor, inspector, examiner, tester, reporter, commentator, censor, editor, critic, reviewer, expert, connoisseur, adviser **6 justice**, judge, his Lordship, his Worship, chief justice, public prosecutor, procurator fiscal, district attorney, recorder, magistrate, coroner, the bench, the judiciary **7 jury**, juror
ADJECTIVES 8 judging, discriminating, discerning, selecting, criticizing, judgmental, inquisitional, moralistic, sententious, approving, appreciative, disapproving, condemnatory **9 judicious**, discerning, discriminating, sensitive, accurate, right, just, fair, unbiased, dispassionate, wise, shrewd **10 judged**, on trial
VERBS 11 judge, umpire, referee, arbitrate, hear, try, sum up, award, decree, adjudge, adjudicate, decide, conclude, find, determine, settle, rule, pronounce sentence, acquit, condemn, censure, censor, criticize, disapprove of **12 estimate**, judge, gauge, calculate, reckon, size up, evaluate, assess, value, appraise, rate, regard, deem, esteem, think, believe, guess, surmise, conjecture, weigh up, ponder over, consider, reason, deduce, infer, examine, investigate, inspect, survey, vet, review

402 Juxtaposition

NOUNS 1 juxtaposition, apposition, adjacency, nearness, closeness, contiguity, abuttal, tangency, touching, contact, continuity, junction, connection, union, bordering, frontier **2 meeting**, encounter, confrontation, interface,

intercommunication, impingement, touch, nudge, brush
VERBS 3 juxtapose, appose, adjoin, abut, touch, join, connect, border **4 meet**, encounter, confront, interface, intercommunicate, impinge, hit, nudge, jostle, elbow, rub, brush, kiss, graze, scrape, shave
ADJECTIVES 5 juxtaposed, adjacent, near, close, tangential, contiguous, adjoining, abutting, touching, continuous, joined, connecting, intercommunicating, bordering, conterminous, coterminous, side-by-side, cheek-by-jowl, face-to-face, nose-to-nose, eyeball-to-eyeball, end-to-end, elbow-to-elbow, bumper-to-bumper **6 meeting**, impinging, rubbing, brushing, grazing, glancing

403 Killing

NOUNS 1 killing, slaying, murder, manslaughter, destruction, execution, blood-shedding, bloodletting **2 murder**, assassination, manslaughter, unlawful killing, thuggery, shooting, knifing, poisoning, suffocation, asphyxiation, strangulation, garrotting, hanging **3 homicide**, regicide, tyrannicide, parricide, patricide, matricide, uxoricide, fratricide, sororicide, infanticide, genocide **4 slaughter**, massacre, bloodbath, carnage, butchery, noyade, battue, holocaust, pogrom, purge, annihilation, liquidation, decimation, extermination, destruction, genocide, the Holocaust, Final Solution, war **5 execution**, death penalty, legalized killing, judicial murder, auto-da-fé, hanging, rope, scaffold, gallows, gibbet, electrocution, electric chair, shooting, firing squad, lethal injection, gas chamber, beheading, guillotine, axe, the stake, stoning, lynching, dispatch, deathblow, final stroke **6 ritual killing**, sacrifice, martyrdom, immolation, crucifixion **7 suicide**, self-destruction, self-slaughter, felo-de-se, self-immolation, suttee, seppuku, hara-kiri, kamikaze **8 accidental killing**, manslaughter **9 animal killing**, blood sports, bullfighting, hunting, wildfowling, chase, shooting, trapping, cull, extermination, slaughtering, knackery, vivisection, lemmings **10 slaughterhouse**, abattoir, knacker's yard, shambles, bullring, arena, battleground, battlefield, the Alamo, Little Bighorn, Wounded Knee, the Somme, Pearl Harbor, Stalingrad, Mylai, Dresden, Hiroshima, Nagasaki, gas chamber, gas oven, Auschwitz
VERBS 11 kill, slay, murder, dispatch, destroy **12 murder**, assassinate, poison, stab, knife, sabre, spear, lance, bayonet, shoot, pistol, bomb, strangle, garrotte, choke, smother, burke, suffocate, asphyxiate, stifle, drown, bury alive, strike, smite, brain, poleaxe, sandbag, burn, gas **13 slaughter**, butcher, poleaxe, massacre, decimate, mow down, shoot down, gun down, destroy, wipe out, annihilate, exterminate, liquidate **14 execute**, condemn, hang, electrocute, gas, shoot, behead, guillotine, burn alive, lynch **15 kill ritually**, sacrifice, martyr, crucify, immolate **16 commit suicide**, commit hara-kiri, commit suttee, hang oneself, shoot oneself, gas oneself **17 kill animals**, hunt, shoot, trap, fish, angle, poison, cull, exterminate

ADJECTIVES 18 deadly, lethal, killing, mortal, fatal, deathly, life-threatening, capital, death-bringing, malignant, poisonous, toxic, asphyxiant, suffocating, stifling, unhealthy, miasmic, insalubrious, inoperable, incurable **19 murderous**, homicidal, psychopathic, pathological, genocidal, internecine, slaughterous, death-dealing, destructive, trigger-happy, cold-blooded, sanguinary, bloody, gory, bloodthirsty, cruel, savage, brutal, head-hunting, man-eating, cannibalistic

404 Knowledge

•*Nam et ipsa scientia potestas est./ Knowledge itself is power.* Francis Bacon.

NOUNS 1 knowledge, ken, cognition, cognizance, gnosis, realization, perception, understanding, comprehension, apprehension, grasp, mastery, awareness, consciousness, acquaintance, familiarity, illumination, enlightenment, foresight, foreknowledge, intuition **2 information**, data, facts, know-how, expertise, skill, aptitude, forte, métier, touch, technique, accomplishment, smattering, inkling, intimation **3 learning**, lore, erudition, sagacity, wisdom, scholarship, letters, omniscience, polymathy, proficiency, mastery, craftsmanship, literacy, numeracy, cleverness, intelligence, bookishness, schooling, education, instruction, teaching, culture, cultivation, civilization, self-education, self-instruction, autodidactism, accomplishments, acquirements, attainments, experience **4 intellect**, mind, brain, intelligence, wit **5 science**, technology, the arts, the humanities, letters **6 academia**, intelligentsia

ADJECTIVES 7 knowledgeable, well-informed, omniscient, polymathic, encyclopedic, clever, intelligent, sagacious, wise, enlightened, informed, instructed, trained, cognizant, qualified, experienced, practised, versed, competent, skilled, proficient, efficient, expert, well versed, gifted, talented, good at, aware, conscious, mindful, attentive, acquainted with, conversant with, briefed, primed streetwise, shrewd, astute, perceptive **8 literate**, numerate, schooled, educated, erudite, scholarly, donnish, academic, intellectual, highbrow, cultured, cultivated, sophisticated, worldly, pedantic **9 known**, verified, proved, true, certain, discovered, explored, recognized, perceived, seen, heard of, well-known, famous, infamous, notorious, celebrated, renowned

VERBS 10 know, understand, comprehend, apprehend, realize, conceive, appreciate, recognize, identify, distinguish, discern, perceive, see, master **11 know by heart**, memorize **12 get to know**, experience, study, con, learn, discover, find out, take in **13 cause to know**, tell, inform, brief, prime, teach, instruct, train, school, educate, coach

405 Lack of Curiosity

NOUNS 1 incuriousness, total trust, blind faith, credulity **2 lack of interest**, disinterest, unconcern, boredom, insouciance, indifference, apathy, impassivity, imperturbability, uninvolvement, numbness, stupor, insensibility, inactiv-

ity, stagnation, idleness, sluggishness, slowness, mental inertia, complacency
ADJECTIVES 3 incurious, uninquisitive, unquestioning, trusting, credulous **4 uninterested**, unthinking, unconcerned, heedless, nonchalant, bored, insouciant, indifferent, dull, imperturbable, unresponsive, aloof, insensible, apathetic, complacent, phlegmatic, impassive, uninvolved, unmoved, detached, distant, disengaged, unenthusiastic, unstirred, numb, inactive, slow, stagnating, deadpan, idle
VERBS 5 not ask, believe **6 be incurious**, disregard, disengage

406 Lack of Discrimination

ADJECTIVES 1 undiscriminating, unselective, catholic, omnivorous, undiscerning, undifferentiating, colour-blind, tone-deaf, uncritical, indifferent, unfussy, unfastidious, unrefined, tasteless, indelicate, insensitive, coarse, vulgar, promiscuous, unrestrained, lax, loose, sloppy, casual, negligent, thoughtless, indiscreet, slipshod, careless, unmeticulous, inaccurate, cursory **2 impartial**, equanimous, fair, neutral, nonaligned, mugwumpish, nonpartisan, disinterested, unbiased, unprejudiced, nonjudgmental, uncriticizing, tolerant, liberal **3 indiscriminate**, random, haphazard, unsystematic, mixed, assorted, unsorted, unselected, miscellaneous, motley, unorganized, confused, jumbled, muddled, intermingled, disordered, chaotic **4 wholesale**, broad, wide, general, all-embracing, wide-ranging, all-inclusive, comprehensive, catholic, widespread, world-wide, global **5 vague**, indistinct, inexact, desultory, undefined, undifferentiated, undistinguished, interchangeable, standard
NOUNS 6 lack of discrimination, unselectiveness, catholicity, uncriticalness, indifference, tastelessness, insensitivity, indelicacy, vulgarity, promiscuity, negligence, thoughtlessness, indiscretion, carelessness **7 impartiality**, equanimity, fairness, justice, neutrality, nonalignment, mugwumpism, disinterestedness, tolerance, fair-mindedness **8 indiscriminateness**, randomness, generality, universality, vagueness, inexactitude, confusion, muddle, jumble
VERBS 9 not discriminate, disregard, generalize, universalize, muddle up, confound, jumble, mix, heap, lump together **10 be fair**, remain neutral, tolerate

407 Lack of Emphasis

ADJECTIVES 1 unemphatic, unimpassioned, unspirited, unexciting, uninspiring, tame, undramatic, inane, empty, pointless, lame, uninspired, boring, monotonous, stale, prosaic, prosy, commonplace, platitudinous, hackneyed, cliché-ridden, conventional, insipid, wan, colourless, dull, dry, vapid, flat, thin, careless, inexact, slovenly, rambling, prolix, disjointed, disconnected, garbled, amorphous, shapeless, smooth, loose, limp, unconvincing, ineffective, feeble, weak, meagre, languid, flaccid, exhausted
NOUNS 2 lack of emphasis, tameness, emptiness, pointlessness, lameness, boredom, monotony, sameness, staleness, prosiness, plain-

ness, commonplace, platitude, cliché, convention, insipidity, wanness, dullness, vapidity, flatness, thinness, wateriness, carelessness, inexactitude, flatulence, disconnection, garble, looseness, limpness, ineffectiveness, feebleness, weakness, enervation, anticlimax, meagreness

408 Lack of Entitlement

NOUNS 1 lack of entitlement, nonentitlement **2 disentitlement**, disfranchisement, dispossession, expropriation, deprivation, forfeiture, disqualification, disestablishment, unfrocking, deposal, dethronement, denaturalization, deportation **3 arrogation**, presumption, assumption, usurpation, appropriation, seizure, violation, invasion, trespass, encroachment **4 presumptuousness**, familiarity, impertinence **5 undueness**, unwarrantedness, undeservedness, gratuitousness, unfittingness, unworthiness **6 excessiveness**, immoderateness

ADJECTIVES 7 unentitled, unauthorized, unsanctioned, unlicensed, unqualified, unempowered, unfranchised, unchartered, unconstitutional, unlawful, illicit, illegal, illegitimate, unrightful, invalid, false, counterfeit, bogus, spurious **8 presumptive**, usurpative, violative, arrogative, familiar **9 undue**, unwarranted, unjustified, unnecessary, gratuitous, excessive, immoderate, unexpected, uncalled-for, unlooked-for, undeserved, unmerited **10 undeserving**, unworthy **11 disentitled**, disfranchised, dispossessed, deprived, disqualified, disestablished, unfrocked, deposed, dethroned, denaturalized, deported, expelled, criminalized, banned, forbidden, prohibited

VERBS 12 not be entitled, have no right **13 arrogate**, assume, usurp, appropriate, seize, steal, violate, encroach, infringe, invade, trespass **14 presume**, take liberties **15 disentitle**, disfranchise, dispossess, expropriate, deprive, forfeit, disqualify, disestablish, unfrock, depose, dethrone, uncrown, denaturalize, deport **16 criminalize**, illegalize, ban, forbid, prohibit

409 Lack of Hygiene

NOUNS 1 lack of hygiene, uncleanliness, insanitariness, verminousness, infestation, dirtiness, filth, squalor, uncleanness, insalubrity, unhealthiness, unwholesomeness, slum, squalor, mephitis, pollution, miasma, smoke, smog, fog, radioactivity, fallout, deadliness, poisonousness, bane, infectiousness, contagiousness, sepsis, purulence, suppuration, decay, mould **2 germ**, bacterium, virus, microbe, contagium, microorganism

ADJECTIVES 3 unhygienic, unhealthy, unwholesome, unsanitary, insalubrious, verminous, dirty, filthy, unclean, squalid, sordid, bad, nasty, noxious, miasmal, dangerous, injurious, harmful, corrupting, polluting, deadly, poisonous, rat-infested, flea-bitten, flyblown, undrained, marshy, stagnant, foul, polluted, undrinkable, inedible, indigestible, unnutritious, unsound, stale, bad, off, rotten, decayed, mouldy, unventilated, windowless, airless, musty, fusty, smoke-filled, humid, stuffy, muggy, fuggy, overheated, steaming **4**

contagious, infectious, catching, communicable, infective, morbific, pathogenic, germ-carrying, zymotic, pestiferous, plague-stricken, malarious, aguish, epidemic, pandemic, endemic, epizootic, enzootic, sporadic, unsterilized, insterilized, nonsterile, infected, septic, contaminated **5 toxic**, poisonous, mephitic, pestilent, germladen, venomous, poisoned, gathering, festering, septic, pussy, purulent, suppurating

410 Lack of Intellect

NOUNS 1 lack of intellect, low IQ, feeble-mindedness, simple-mindedness, backwardness, slowness, imbecility, idiocy, mindlessness, senselessness, brainlessness, vacancy, vacuity, senility, dementia, unreason, irrationality **2 unintelligence**, ignorance, stupidity, denseness, foolishness, folly, thoughtlessness, illogicality, empty-headedness, inanity, fatuity, puerility, childishness, immaturity, incomprehension, unperceptiveness, obtuseness, stolidity, thickheadedness, hebetude, oafishness, boorishness, witlessness, dimwittedness, dimness, unoriginality, uninventiveness, unimaginativeness **3 nonhuman existence**, irrationality, unreason, animality, instinct

ADJECTIVES 4 lacking intellect, feeble-minded, simple, slow, backward, dull, vacuous, vacant, mindless, senseless, brainless, imbecilic, idiotic, cretinous, moronic, brain-damaged, senile, demented, insane **5 unintelligent**, ignorant, stupid, dense, foolish, thoughtless, unthinking, illogical, inane, fatuous, empty-headed, puerile, childish, infantile, immature, unwise, unperceptive, obtuse, stolid, thickheaded, blockheaded, oafish, boorish, doltish, witless, unoriginal, uninventive, unimaginative **6 intellectually subnormal**, subnormal, retarded, backward, simple-minded, feebleminded, imbecilic, idiotic, moronic, cretinous, autistic, brain-damaged, senile, confused, incoherent **7 nonhuman**, irrational, dumb, brute, animal, instinctive, vegetable, inanimate

VERBS 8 lack intellect, lack reason, show ignorance **9 bemuse**, confound, confuse, muddle, bewilder, mystify, perplex, flummox, baffle, bedazzle, addle, stump, stun, knock out, paralyse, blunt, dull, obscure

411 Lack of Meaning

NOUNS 1 lack of meaning, meaninglessness, irrelevance, insignificance, unimportance, nonsense, amphigory, absurdity, inanity, vacuity, emptiness, triteness, truism, platitude, commonplace, cliché, verbalism, unreason, illogicality, sophistry, invalidity, nullity, ineffectuality, illegibility, scribble, doodle, scrawl, daub, misrepresentation, strumming, loudness, jargon, mystification, abracadabra, hocus-pocus, mumbo jumbo, unintelligibility, incoherence, raving, delirium **2 aimlessness**, purposelessness, pointlessness, futility **3 meaningless thing**, empty gesture, insincerity, flattery, liar's promise **4 senseless talk**, nonsense, absurdity, balderdash, gibberish, gobbledygook, rigmarole, double talk, Babel, rubbish, drivel **5 empty talk**, verbiage, diffuseness, jabber, jaw, babble, gabble, prattle, prate, sweet nothings, endearments, flattery, blarney, flummery, trumpery, bunkum, moonshine, humbug, claptrap, drivel, wind, vapouring, galimatias, fable, falsehood, exaggeration, blether, patter, spiel **6 aimlessness**, purposelessness

VERBS 7 mean nothing, scribble, daub, fiddle, tap, drum, strum **8 not understand**, misinterpret, puzzle **9 talk nonsense**, twaddle, jabber, jaw, babble, gabble, blather, prattle, prate, gibber, drivel, flatter, blarney

ADJECTIVES 10 meaningless, senseless, unmeaning, irrelevant, nonsignificant, unimportant, trite, commonplace, platitudinous, hackneyed, clichéed, banal, trivial, trifling, nonsense, amphigoric, absurd, inane, foolish, fatuous, illogical, sophistic, incoherent, unintelligible, illegible, mystifying, piffling, ineffectual, ineffective, invalid, null, empty, vacuous, hollow, unexpressive, unidiomatic, unapt, rubbishy, trashy, delirious, frenzied, ranting, raving, prattling, gibbering, blithering, windy, exaggerated **11 aimless**, purposeless, pointless, futile, vain, worthless **12 unmeant**, unintentional, unintended, involuntary, unimplied, misunderstood, misread, mistranslated, misinterpreted, misrepresented, mistaken, insincere

412 Lack of Motive

NOUNS 1 lack of motive, nonintention, aimlessness, haphazardness, randomness, purposelessness, arbitrariness, fortuity, indeterminacy, unpredictability, uncertainty, inexplicability, unaccountability, inconsistency, illogicality, irrationality **2 chance**, lot, luck, fortune, misfortune, ill-fortune, risk, fifty-fifty chance, toss-up, random sample, gamble, raffle, lottery, bingo, tombola, sweepstake, long shot, long odds, short odds, safe bet **3 coincidence**, chance encounter, lucky strike, lucky break, fluke, wild guess, serendipity, misadventure

VERBS 4 chance, risk, toss up, gamble, bet **5 happen by chance**, happen, befall, light upon, blunder into

ADJECTIVES 6 motiveless, groundless, unintended, unmeant, noncausal, aimless, purposeless, unplanned, unmotivated, arbitrary, fortuitous, indeterminant, random, stochastic, unpredictable, haphazard, uncertain, inexplicable, unaccountable, unexpected, unreasonable, inconsistent, hit-or-miss, illogical, irrational, coincidental, accidental, chance, casual, stray, incidental, adventitious, serendipitous, aleatory, quirky, risky, fifty-fifty **7 adventurous**, gambling, lucky, fortunate

413 Lack of Preparation

ADJECTIVES 1 unprepared, unready, backward, behind, late, slow, disorganized, unarranged, surprised, caught unawares, caught napping, inexpectant, unguarded, exposed **2 spontaneous**, ad hoc, extemporized, improvised, impromptu, ad lib, unrehearsed, snap, uncontrived **3 without preparation**, unpremeditated, unplanned, inadequate, careless, negligent, rushed, makeshift, jerry-built, temporary, hasty, rash, reckless, precipitant, shiftless, improvident, unthrifty, thoughtless, carefree, easygoing, happy-go-lucky **4 untrained**,

scratch, untaught, untutored, ignorant, uninstructed, undrilled, unexercised, unpractised, inexperienced, unskilled, apprentice, natural, simple, unsophisticated, artless, uncultivated, unrefined, unworked, unprocessed, untilled **5 immature**, ungrown, unripe, green, unmellowed, unseasoned, unblown, unfledged, unlicked, callow, nonadult, adolescent, young, juvenile, childish, puerile, undeveloped, backward, retarded, unhatched, unborn, inchoate, embryonic, rudimentary, elementary, unformed, unfashioned, unhewn, unwrought, unworked, uncut, rough-hewn, unpolished, unfinished, raw, crude, imperfect, coarse, boorish, rude, savage, uncivilized, premature, forward, precocious, forced **6 uncooked**, raw, red, pink, rare, bloody, underdone, half-cooked, half-baked, cold, unwarmed, unprepared, undressed, ungarnished, indigestible, inedible **7 unequipped**, untrimmed, unrigged, dismasted, dismantled, undressed, uncovered, unfurnished, ill-provided, deficient, incompetent, incapable
NOUNS 8 lack of preparation, unreadiness, backwardness, belatedness, lateness, disorganization, rustiness, unfitness, incompetence, disqualification, unskilfulness, nonpreparation, unpremeditation, thoughtlessness, improvidence, nonprovision, neglect, rashness, hastiness, impetuousness, precipitance, rush **9 spontaneity**, improvisation, extemporization, impromptu **10 immaturity**, unripeness, greenness, youth, childishness, newness, undevelopment, rawness, crudeness, coarseness, imperfection, incompleteness, prematurity, forwardness **11 natural state**, native state
VERBS 12 be unprepared, lack planning, lie fallow, rust, catch unawares **13 improvise**, extemporize

414 Lack of Thought

NOUNS 1 lack of thought, mindlessness, vacancy, inanity, fatuity, vacuity, blankness, empty-headedness, absent-mindedness, folly, tranquillity, calm **2 ignorance**, unintelligence, unawareness, nescience **3 instinct**, intuition, conditioned reflex, kneejerk response **4 inconsideration**, thoughtlessness, insensitivity, inattention, neglect, selfishness, unkindness **5 mental block**, blank spot, blind spot, brainstorm **6 daydream**, reverie, fantasizing, pensiveness, deep thought
ADJECTIVES 7 thoughtless, mindless, unthinking, unreflective, inane, fatuous, vacuous, vacant, blank, empty-headed, absent-minded, abstracted, fallow, oblivious, ignorant, foolish, carefree, easygoing, happy-go-lucky **8 instinctive**, intuitive, automatic, involuntary, reflex **9 inconsiderate**, thoughtless, insensitive, heedless, inattentive, neglectful, uncaring, selfish, oblivious to, unkind, tactless, pestering, bothering **10 unthought**, unconsidered, unconceived
VERBS 11 lack thought, forget, blank out **12 be inconsiderate**, pester

415 Lack of Wonder

NOUNS 1 lack of wonder, irreverence, indifference, blankness, serenity, tranquillity, calmness, coolness, collectedness, composure, inexcitability, imperturbability,

unimaginativeness, nonchalance, insouciance, disinterest, unconcern, dullness, impassivity, sanguinity, apathy, phlegmaticalness **2 predictability**, unimpressiveness, customariness, ordinariness, commonness, straightforwardness
ADJECTIVES 3 unmoved, uninspired, wonderless, unamazed, unawed, unimpressed, unadmiring, irreverent, indifferent, blank, serene, tranquil, calm, cool, collected, composed, unsurprised, unexcited, imperturbed, sanguine, unimaginative, nonchalant, insouciant, disinterested, unconcerned, dull, impassive, apathetic, phlegmatic, blasé, unenthusiastic, unimaginative, unaroused, spiritless, cold-hearted **4 predictable**, unsurprising, unimpressive, customary, ordinary, common, expected, straightforward, run-of-the-mill
VERBS 5 not wonder about, accept, see through, expect, calm oneself, collect oneself

416 Lakes

NOUNS 1 lake, natural lake, artificial lake, man-made lake, reservoir, freshwater lake, mountain lake, tarn, volcanic lake, glacial lake, oxbow lake, broad, sea loch, salt lake, salina, lagoon **2 small lake**, lakelet, pool, tidal pool, clear pool, muddy pool, pond, millpond, farm pond, village pond, fishpond, dew pond, water hole, landlocked water, standing water, backwater, water pocket, still water, stagnant water, dead water, bayou, wash, marsh **3 limnology**, limnologist, limnometer
ADJECTIVES 4 lakelike, pondlike, landlocked, tidal, clear, muddy, stagnant, marshy, lake-dwelling, lacustrine, lacustrian, lacustral

417 Lamentation

NOUNS 1 lamentation, grieving, crying, weeping, wailing, keening, mourning, wake, last rites, widow's weeds, dolefulness, tearfulness, sobbing, sadness, sorrow, plangency, wretchedness **2 lament**, requiem, obsequies, dirge, elegy, swansong, threnody, coronach, knell, funeral oration, thanatopsis, last post, keen, howl, ululation, cry, moan, groan, sigh
ADJECTIVES 3 lamenting, grieving, crying, weeping, lachrymose, tearful, wailing, keening, mourning, miserable, doleful, wretched, woebegone, disconsolate, unhappy, sad, sorrowful, wet-eyed, red-eyed, plaintive, plangent, dirgelike, elegiac, threnodic **4 lamentable**, pitiful, tear-jerking, distressing, depressing
VERBS 5 lament, grieve, sorrow, mourn, elegize, threnodize, weep for, wail, keen, bemoan, bewail, complain, deplore, regret **6 weep**, cry, sob, wail, weep over, howl, ululate, sigh

418 Latency

ADJECTIVES 1 latent, dormant, sleeping, hibernating, aestivating, inactive, passive, quiescent, inert, delitescent, undeveloped, potential, possible, virtual, subconscious, subliminal, submerged, underlying, unacknowledged, subterranean **2 concealed**, hidden, covert, unseen, unmanifested, unexposed, invisible, screened, backroom, underground, skulking, lurking, stealthy, hiding, private, secluded, sequestered, unspied, undetected, undisclosed, undercover, veiled, muffled, masked, disguised, coded, cryptographic, secret, classified, restricted, off-the-record, obscure, murky, dark, arcane, unintelligible, impenetrable, undiscoverable **3 unsolved**, unknown, undiscovered, unexplained, unrevealed, undivulged, unguessed, unsuspected, untold, unspoken, unexplored, untracked, untraced **4 unsaid**, unspoken, unvoiced, unpronounced, unuttered, unexpressed, unarticulated, unmentioned, untold of, undivulged, unsung, unpromoted, unproclaimed, undeclared, unprofessed, unwritten, unpublished, tacit, half-spoken, understood, implied, inferred, inferential, implicit, meant, indicated, suggested, hinted, intimated, insinuated, implicative, suggestive, allusive **5 mysterious**, mystic, occult, symbolic, allegorical, tropic, anagogical, metaphorical, figurative, cryptic, esoteric, secret, cabbalistic, gnostic, indirect, oblique, clandestine, insidious, treacherous

NOUNS 6 latency, dormancy, sleep, hibernation, aestivation, inactivity, passivity, quiescence, abeyance, inertness, delitescence, underdevelopment, potentiality, possibility, virtuality, subconsciousness, sublimity, anonymity, cabal, clandestineness, depth, trope, figure, metaphor, allegory **7 latent things**, cancer, sleeping dog, sleeping giant, dark horse, undercurrent **8 concealment**, hiding, invisibility, imperceptibility, submergence, skulking, lurking, stealth, privacy, seclusion, sequestration, secrecy, restriction, obscurity, code, cryptography, intrigue, undercurrent, plot **9 quietness**, taciturnity, muteness, half-spoken word, whisper, undertone, nuance, faintness, mutter, aside, hint, suggestion, innuendo, insinuation, connotation, adumbration, implication **10 mysteriousness**, mysticism, occultism, symbolism, allegory, anagoge, metaphor, esotericism, cabbala, unintelligibility, oracle, secret, mystery, dimness

VERBS 11 be latent, sleep, hibernate, smoke **12 hide**, conceal, submerge, skulk, lurk, creep, slink, tiptoe, burrow, lie low, dissemble, underlie **13 imply**, mean, indicate, spell, suggest, connote, hint, intimate, insinuate, whisper, murmur, understand, allude, symbolize

419 Lateness

NOUNS 1 lateness, unpunctuality, belatedness, tardiness, slowness, retardation, lag, delay, unreadiness **2 late hour**, day's end, sunset, nighttime, last minute **3 delayed action**, delay, wait, dilatoriness, procrastination, pigeonholing, tabling, postponement, deferment, adjournment, prorogation, prolongation, extension, protraction, filibuster, stonewalling, prevention, hindrance, obstruction, jam, suspension, hold-up, red tape, blockage, restraint, detention, remand, moratorium, halt, pause, truce, cease-fire, lull, respite, stay, reprieve, last-ditch stand, afterthought

VERBS 4 be late, oversleep, lag **5 wait**, pause, stop, stay, tarry, linger, dawdle, waste time, loiter, hang around, hang about, await, delay, dally, dilly-dally, hang fire **6 delay**, stall, retard, hold up, obstruct, jam, suspend, halt, block, stonewall, prevent, hinder, restrain, remand, detain, postpone, reprieve, stay, adjourn, prorogue, defer, filibuster, prolong, extend, protract, spin out, procrastinate, temporize, reserve, withhold, file, shelve, pigeonhole, table, hold, hang on

ADJECTIVES 7 late, delayed, overdue, unpunctual, dilatory, unready, unprepared, tardy, behindhand, slow **8 held up**, postponed, deferred, adjourned, prorogued, prolonged, extended, protracted, stonewalled, hindered, obstructed, suspended, held-up, blocked, tabled, stalled, restrained, detained, remanded, halted, jammed **9 late in the day**, last-minute, eleventh-hour **10 delaying**, slowing, procrastinating, obstructive, hindering, retarding, blocking, restraining, detaining, lagging, late-running **11 later**, future, distant **12 dead**, deceased, late, former, previous, past, erstwhile, sometime

420 Law

- *The law does not concern itself with trifles.* Saying.
- *The good of the people is the chief law.* Cicero.

NOUNS 1 the law, law, corpus juris, constitution, charter, institution, codified law, statute book, legal code, pandect, penal code, civil code, Napoleonic code, lex scripta, statute law, common law, equity law, personal law, private law, canon law, jus canonicum, ecclesiastical law, international law, commercial law, business law, lex mercatoria, criminal law, civil law **2 jurisdiction**, portfolio, function, judicature, magistracy, mayoralty, shrievalty, bumbledom, competence, legal authority, cognizance, mandate, legal administration, Home Office, Justice Department, local jurisdiction, local authority, corporation, municipality, council, county board, bailiwick, vigilance committee, watch committee, tribunal, office, bureau, secretariat **3 law**, bylaw, statute, decree, ordinance, edict, order, standing order, canon, rule, rescript **4 litigation**, legal action, legal case, legal dispute, legal issue, legal remedy, cause, contest, lawsuit, suit, seeking justice, litigiousness, quarrelsomeness, test case, prosecution, arraignment, impeachment, charge, accusation, claim, counter claim, plea, petition, request, objection, demurrer, affirmation, affidavit, written statement, averment **5 legal process**, legal proceedings, legal procedure, due process, citation, subpoena, summons, warrant, apprehension, arrest, detention, questioning, committal, restraint, habeas corpus, bail, surety, security, recognizance, injunction, stay, order, writ, certiorari, mandamus **6 legal trial**, fair trial, assize, court sessions, court sitting, military court, military justice, inquest, inquisition, inquiry, hearing, prosecution, defence, plea-bargaining, examination, cross-examination, re-examination, objection sustained, objection overruled, testimony, pleadings, rebuttal, rejoinder, proof, demonstration, disproof, confutation, summing-up, ruling, finding, decision, judgment, verdict, hung jury, not guilty, acquittal, guilty, condemnation, sentence, prison term, execution, appeal, retrial, precedent, case law, law reports, cause list, case record **7 litigant**, litigator, libellant, suitor, petitioner, suer claimant, plaintiff, pursuer, defendant, appellant, libellee, respondent, objector, intervener, accused, prosecutor, accuser **8 lawmaker**, lawgiver, legislator, Law Lord, Solon, Draco, Moses **9 law officer**, legal administrator, public prosecutor, judge advocate, district attorney, judge, mayor, provost general, sheriff, court officer, bailiff, procurator fiscal, summoner, process-server, macebearer, official, apparitor **10 lawyer**, solicitor, barrister, counsel, Queen's counsel, legal adviser, legal representative, advocate, jurist, legal practitioner, judge, recorder, magistrate, jury **11 police**, constabulary, gendarmerie, airport police, mounted police, international police **12 police officer**, policeman, law-enforcer, constable, patrolman, police sergeant, police lieutenant, police inspector, police superintendent, chief constable, police commissioner, provost marshal, detective, plainclothes officer, private detective, private police **13 tribunal**, throne, confessional, forum, ecclesia, wardmote, council, public opinion, vox populi, electorate, judicatory, bench, board, judicial assembly **14 lawcourt**, open court, high court, criminal court, civil court, appellate court, county court, probate court, divorce court, assizes, police court, juvenile court, children's court, coroner's court, sheriff court, feudal court, manorial court, court-martial, drumhead court-martial, summary court-martial, summary court, kangaroo court **15 judge**, justice, justiceship, justiciary, verderer, military judge, chief justice, recorder, sessions judge, subordinate judge, magistrate, district magistrate, city magistrate, police magistrate, coroner, bench, judiciary, magistracy, hanging judge, umpire, referee, arbitrator, ombudsman, assessor, estimator, recorder, Recording Angel, Solomon **16 jury**, assize, grand jury, special jury, common jury, petit jury, trial jury, jury panel, juror's panel, jury list, juror, jury man, jurist **17 courtroom**, courthouse, bench, jury box, judgment seat, woolsack, mercy seat, dock, bar **18 legislation**, nomology, lawmaking, lawgiving, codification, ratification, enactment, validation, confirmation, affirmation, regulation, constitutionalism **19 jurisprudence**, nomology **20 litigation**, lawsuit, legal action, writ, summons, trial, verdict, sentence **21 legal formality**, procedure **22 criminology**, penology

ADJECTIVES 23 legal, lawful, licit, legitimate, valid, just, right, proper, sanctioned, allowable, permissible, permitted, authorized, licensed, warranted, legalized, legitimized, legitimatized, decriminalized, by right **24 legislative**, nomothetic, legislatorial, legislational, decretal, nomological **25 legislated**, made law, enacted, passed, decreed, ordained, codified, ratified, constitutional **26 liable to law**, justiciable, cognizable, triable, actionable **27 jurisdictional**, directive, judiciary, juridical, justiciable, judicatory, judicatorial, judicial, judicative, jurisdictive, jural, jurisprudential, justiciary, curial, inquisitional, forensic, Rhadamanthine, original, appellate, tribunal, magisterial, judicious **28 legalistic**, litigious, disputatious, contentious **29 litigating**, litigant, suing, accusing, claiming, contesting, objecting, disputing, litigious, quarrelsome **30 litigated**, on trial, sub judice, litigable, actionable, justiciable, disputable, arguable

VERBS 31 make legal, legalize, legitimize, decriminalize, validate, sanction, allow, permit, authorize, license **32 follow the law**, obey **33 legislate**, enact, pass, vote, decree, ordain, order, codify, ratify, confirm, affirm, formalize, endorse, vest **34 litigate**, seek justice, petition, request, brief counsel, claim, have up, sue, implead, arraign, impeach, accuse, charge, press charges, indict, cite, summon, prosecute, try, advocate, plead, call evidence **35 stand trial**, give evidence **36 make illegal**, outlaw, criminalize, illegalize, ban, proscribe, veto, prohibit, forbid, punish, bastardize **37 judge**, administer justice, exercise judgment, adjudge, adjudicate, hold court, preside, pass judgment, decide, pass sentence

421 Layer

NOUNS 1 layer, stratum, seam, zone, vein, lode, bed, belt, strip, band, course, table, thickness, ply, interlining, fold, pleat, lap, flap, superstratum, overlayer, topcoat, topsoil, overlap, substratum, underlayer, lining, undercoat **2 level**, tier, row, storey, floor, landing, deck, terrace, ledge, shelf, step **3 coat**, covering, sheet, blanket, foil, leaf, lamina, lamella, plate, veneer, facing, fascia, overlay, sheathe, bark, membrane, skin, peel, pellicle, film, patina, bloom, scum **4 slice**, sliver, wafer, disc, chip, rasher, cut, slab, tablet, plaque, plank, slat, lath, panel, pane, tile, slate, shaving, paring, scale, squama, flake, dandruff, scurf, flock **5 layered thing**, laminate, plywood, sandwich, double-decker, layer cake, onion, Russian doll, shingled roof **6 layering**, stratification, lamination, lamellation, foliation, scaliness, flakiness, squamation, delamination

ADJECTIVES 7 layered, stratified, straticulate, foliated, laminate, two-ply, three-ply, two-tiered, two-storeyed, double-decker, terraced **8 coated**, plated, veneered, faced, lined, overlaid, overlaying, overlapped, sheathed **9 platelike**, leaflike, foliate, lamellar, placoid, membranous, pellicular, filmy, scummy, drossy, scaly, furfuraceous, squamous, flaky

VERBS 10 layer, lay, stratify, laminate, tier, deck, shingle, sandwich, coat, spread, cover, plate, veneer, face, line, overlay **11 scale**, peel off, flake off, strip, shave, delaminate

422 Leisure

• *If all the year were playing holidays, To sport would be as tedious as to work.* William Shakespeare.

NOUNS 1 leisure, free time, spare time, idle moments, freedom, liberty, convenience, opportunity, sinecure, idleness, inactivity, rest, repose, ease **2 time off**, holiday, vacation, leave, day off, half-holiday, sabbatical, furlough, break, recess, respite, relief, peace, quiet **3 unemployment**, joblessness, redundancy, lay-off, dismissal, discharge

VERBS 4 have leisure, spend, pass, take leave, rest, repose, resign **5 dismiss**, discharge
ADJECTIVES 6 leisure, free, spare, unoccupied **7 leisurely**, unhurried, slow, deliberate, relaxed, easy, labour-saving, idle, inactive, resting, reposeful, leisured, unoccupied, free, available, disengaged, retired, redundant, dismissed, discharged, unemployed, jobless, non-working, sackedfavour, concession, sop, humouring, consideration, leave, allowance, permission, indulgence, spoiling
VERBS 8 be lenient, moderate, treat kindly, tolerate, forbear, bear with, give quarter, pity, forgive, forget, pardon, spare, grant amnesty, favour, concede, humour, show consideration, allow, permit, indulge
ADJECTIVES 9 lenient, lax, easy, easygoing, mild, moderate, clement, gentle, soft, tender, patient, tolerant, forbearing, long-suffering, compassionate, pitying, merciful, forgiving, reasonable, considerate, humane, benevolent, kind, gracious, charitable, accepting, magnanimous, accommodating, generous, permissive, indulgent, spoiling, kid-glove **10 given consideration**, allowed, permitted, pardoned, forgiven, indulged, gratified

423 Lending

NOUNS 1 lending, loaning, giving, moneylending, advancing, advance, accommodation, grant, usury, extortion **2 loan**, unsecured loan, secured loan, bank loan, personal loan, foreign loan **3 lending institution**, building society, friendly society, credit-card company, finance company, mortgage company, bank
VERBS 4 lend, loan, lend money, advance, accommodate, grant, give credit
ADJECTIVES 5 loaned, lent, accommodative, secured, unsecured, unsurious

424 Length

ADJECTIVES 1 long, lengthy, tall, high, extended, prolonged, protracted, drawn out, dragged out, stretched, spun out, strung out, straggling, overlong, extensive, far-reaching, sustained, polysyllabic, sesquipedalian, interminable, endless, long-winded, verbose, shoulder-length, full-length **2 elongated**, oblong, rectangular **3 longitudinal**, lengthways, longways
NOUNS 4 length, longitude, lengthiness, tallness, height, distance, measure, mileage, yardage, footage, extent, reach, span, stretch, duration, elongation, extension, prolongation, protraction, sesquipedalianism, infinity, interminability **5 piece**, portion, section, measure, roll, bolt, coil, run, strip, band, stripe, bar, streak, line, string, queue **6 oblong**, rectangle **7 measure of length**, inch, foot, yard, mile, knot, metre, light-year **8 measure of time**, millisecond, second, minute, hour, day, week, month, year, decade, lifetime
VERBS 9 be long, extend, stretch, outreach, spreadeagle **10 lengthen**, extend, stretch, produce, continue, increase, elongate, unroll, uncoil, unfurl, unfold, drop, prolong, protract, draw out, drag out

425 Liberation

NOUNS 1 liberation, freedom, deliverance, release, disencumberment, emancipation, manumission, unbinding, unchaining, unfettering, unknotting, unleashing, unburdening, loosing, disengagement, decontrol, deregulation, relaxation, discharge, dismissal, extrication, parole, bail, demobilization, disbanding, escape, rescue, redemption, pardoning, absolving, salvation, relief, reprieve, exemption, absolution, forgiveness, acquittal, quittance **2 equal opportunity**, equal rights, civil rights, women's liberation, feminism, minority rights

VERBS 3 liberate, free, deliver, release, emancipate, manumit, disencumber, unbind, unchain, unlock, unshackle, unfetter, unknot, unleash, unburden, loose, let out, disengage, decontrol, deregulate, discharge, dismiss, extricate, parole, bail, discharge, demobilize, disband, release, escape, rescue, redeem, save, deliver, relieve, exempt, reprieve, acquit, pardon **4 be liberated**, go free, extricate oneself

ADJECTIVES 5 liberated, free, emancipated, unshackled, unfettered, independent-minded, deregulated, liberalized, released, paroled, bailed, redemptive, absolving, saved, rescued, exemptible

426 Life

- *Life is as tedious as a twice-told tale/ Vexing the dull ear of a drowsy man.* William Shakespeare.
- *Lift not the painted veil which those who live/ Call life.* Percy Bysshe Shelley.
- *Oh, isn't life a terrible thing, thank God?* Dylan Thomas.

NOUNS 1 life, being, existing, subsistence, entity, animation, humankind, mankind, human being, person, individual, survivor, soul, spirit, vital force, liveliness, vivacity, energy, sprightliness, vitality, vivification, sensation, sentience, sensibility, symbiosis **2 living matter**, protoplasm, bioplasm, tissue, macromolecule, bioplast, cell, gene **3 life requirements**, subsistence, sustenance, nourishment, food, bread, manna, water, oxygen, air, lifeblood **4 biological function**, sight, smell, touch, taste, hearing, breathing, respiration, biological clock, fertility, parenthood, procreation, propagation, reproduction, sex, coition, copulation, conception, pregnancy, confinement, delivery, birth, nativity, viability **5 life cycle**, birth, childhood, youth, adolescence, adulthood, middle age, old age, death, lifetime, life span, biometry, longevity, survival, renaissance, revivification, revival, reanimation, reincarnation, resurrection, immortality, eternity, afterlife, heaven **6 studies of life**, life sciences, biology, genetics, botany, zoology, anthropology, humanities **7 theories of life**, creation, evolution, Bhavachakra, reincarnation **8 classifications of life**, taxonomy, viruses, bacteria, plants, algae, fungi, bryophytes, pteridophytes, spermatophytes, animals, protozoa, parazoa, metazoa, vertebrates, amphibians **9 lifestyle**, existence **10 life story**, history, biography

ADJECTIVES 11 alive, living, animate, conscious, breathing, incarnate, existent, extant, surviving, ongoing, long-lived, old, aged, ancient, lasting, lifelong, viable, vital, vivifying, life-giving, Promethean, enlivened, revived, restored **12 lively**, animated, vivacious, spirited, energetic, vigorous, dynamic, active **13 biotic**, symbiotic, biological, biogenetic, protoplasmic, protoplastic **14 born**, newborn, begotten, by, fathered, sired, mothered, dammed, foaled, dropped, spawned, littered, laid

VERBS 15 live, be, exist, breathe, respire, subsist, quicken, revive, survive, endure, carry on, continue, last, persist **16 dwell**, live at, reside at, inhabit, lodge, stay **17 be born**, begin **18 give birth to**, beget, breed, spawn, procreate, reproduce, conceive, generate, vitalize, vivify, resuscitate **19 support life**, maintain, feed **20 invigorate**, revitalize, rejuvenate, reanimate

427 Life Science

NOUNS 1 life science, biological science, natural science, biology, zoology, botany, palaeobotany, dendrology, pomology, phytochemistry, phytoecology, phytobiology, phytography, phytology, vegetable pathology, vegetable physiology, microbiology, algology, bryology, fungology, epidemiology, bacteriology, virology, gnotobiotics, parasitology, anatomy, morphology, physiology, biochemistry, enzymology, endocrinology, neuroscience, immunology, histology, cytology, biogenetics, biotechnology, embryology, palaeontology, natural history, marine biology, bioecology, bionomics, biophysics, biometry, bionics, cybernetics, cryobiology, electrobiology, radiobiology, astrobiology, exobiology, xenobiology, ethnobiology **2 living world**, natural world, nature, biota, biosphere **3 organism**, creature, entity, body, animal, plant, eukaryote, prokaryote, aerobe, anaerobe, microorganism, microbe, animalcule, microphyte, protist, monad, germ, bacterium, coccus, bacillus, spirillum, rickettsia, mycoplasma, virus, filtrable virus, bacteriophage, phage, retrovirus, virion, viroid, plasmid, provirus, organic remains **4 anatomy**, form, structure, morphology, comparative anatomy, dissection, zootomy, tissue structure **5 physiology**, vital functions, nutrition, absorption, respiration, photosynthesis, metabolism, anabolism, catabolism, transpiration, guttation, osmoregulation, secretion, excretion, sensation, reproduction, growth **6 cell biology**, cytology, cell structure, ultrastructure, light microscopy, electron microscopy, phase-contrast microscopy, fixation, sectioning, staining, counterstaining, cytochemistry, histochemistry, tissue culture, histology, cytological test, smear test, cell physiology **7 cell**, prokaryotic cell, eukaryotic cell, protoplast, cellule, germen, gamete, spore, blood cell, corpuscle, unicellular organism, unicell, cell membrane, plasma membrane, plasmalemma, microvillus, cell wall, cellulose, lignin, chitin, cell plate, middle lamella, plasmodesma, protoplasm, cytoplasm, bioplasm, cytosome, hyaloplasm, energid, trophoplasm, ectoplasm, endoplasm, reticulum, coenocyte, syncytium, idioplasm **8 genetics**, classical genetics, Mendelian genetics, Mendel's laws, heredity, inheritance, factor, gene, chromosome, dominance, recessiveness, genotype, biotype, phenotype, genecology, gene flow, gene frequency, gene pool, genetic drift, gene complex, cytogenetics, molecular genetics, biochemical genetics, microbial genetics, genetic engineering **9 molecular biology**, macromolecule, protein, nucleic acid, polypeptide chain, amino-acid sequence, protein sequencing, nucleic-acid structure, nitrogenous base, adenosine, cytosine, guanine, thymine, uracil, nucleoside, nucleotide, polynucleotide, gene sequencing, genetic mapping, biotechnology, genetic engineering, genetic fingerprinting, gene probe, restriction enzyme, gene cloning, cloning vector, gene splicing, designer gene, genotype, phenotype, genetic material, DNA, RNA, genome, codon, anticodon, ribosomal RNA, exon **10 chromosome**, heterosome, autosome, heterochromosome, allerome, idiochromosome, sex chromosome, W chromosome, X chromosome, Y chromosome, Z chromosome, euchromosome, homologous chromosome, univalent chromosome, chromatid, centromere, kinetochore, chromomere, chromonema, gene string, chromatin, complement, chromosome number, diploidy, haploidy, polyploidy, autopolyploidy, allopolyploidy **11 developmental biology**, embryology, ontogeny, embryogenesis, embryogeny, germination, cleavage, blastulation, gastrulation, induction, evocation, metamorphosis, paedogenesis **12 evolution**, phylogeny, speciation, convergent evolution, parallel evolution, natural selection, Darwinism, Weismannism, neo-Darwinism, Lamarckism, neo-Lamarckism, Lysenkoism, uniformitarianism, catastrophism, palaeontology **13 taxonomy**, systematics, biological classification, cytotaxonomy, biosystematics, cladistics, taxon, kingdom, subkingdom, division, subdivision, phylum, subphylum, superclass, class, subclass, order, suborder, superfamily, family, subfamily, tribe, subtribe, genus, section, series, species, subspecies, variety, cultivar, race, form, binomial nomenclature **14 ecology**, synecology, autecology, phytoecology, zooecology, ecosystem, ecophysiology, food chain, food web, food pyramid, parasitism, mutualism, symbiosis, commensalism, competition, conservation **15 life scientist**, biologist, zoologist, botanist, bacteriologist, virologist, parasitologist, anatomist, morphologist, physiologist, biochemist, endocrinologist, immunologist, histologist, cytologist, geneticist, embryologist, palaeontologist, evolutionist, Darwinist, Neo-Darwinist, taxonomist, cladist, naturalist, ecologist

ADJECTIVES 16 biological, zoological, botanical, bacteriological virological, gnotobiotic, parasitological, anatomical, morphological, physiological, biochemical, endocrinological, immunological, histological, cytological, genetic, biotechnological, embryological, palaeontological, taxonomic, systematic, ecological, bionomic, biophysical, biometric **17 living**, animate, vital, viable, organic, biotic, microbial, bacterial **18 physiological**, metabolic, anabolic, catabolic, alimentary, respiratory, aerobic, anaerobic, photosynthetic, secretory, excretory, reproductive **19 cellular**, multicellular, unicellular, single-celled, acellular, plasmic, protoplasmic, cytoplasmic, ectoplasmic, endoplasmic, reticular, coenocytic, syncytial, mitochondrial **20 genetic**, genomic, factorial, hereditary, Mendelian, dominant, recessive, mutant, chromosomal, mitotic, meiotic, haploid, diploid **21 developmental**, ontogenic, germinal, embryonic, ectodermal, endodermal, mesodermal, fetal, amniotic, chorionic, allantoic, juvenile, larval, pupal, neotenous **22 taxonomic**, systematic, biosystematic, cladistic, generic

428 Light

NOUNS 1 light, luminosity, lucency, phosphorescence, fluorescence, luminescence, illumination, incandescence, lustre, radiance, radiation, refulgence, splendour, resplendence, brightness, brilliance, vividness, visible radiation, light wave, ray, beam, sunbeam, ultraviolet light, infrared radiation, photon, monochromatic light **2 quality of light**, glow, shimmer, gleam, glint, glister, sheen, gloss, patina, polish, lustre, iridescence, opalescence, shine, glassiness, glistening, beam, brightness, effulgence, glare, dazzle, flare, brilliance, sparkle, twinkle, scintillation, glitter, spangle, tinsel, spark, flash, coruscation **3 lightening**, illumination, brightening, bleaching **4 natural light**, daylight, sunlight, sunshine, sunbeam, moonlight, moonshine, starlight, nova, supernova, Pole Star, North Star, Milky Way, meteor, comet, northern lights, aurora borealis, aurora australis, streamers, counterglow, earthshine, lightning, flash, thunderbolt **5 highlight**, downlight, uplighter, reflection, chiaroscuro, black-and-white, half-tone, laser, hologram, halo, aureole, gloriole, nimbus, corona, rainbow **6 enlightenment**, elucidation, illumination, clarification, knowledge, understanding, comprehension, insight, clue, star **7 light colour**, lightness, colourlessness, paleness, pallor, pastiness, blondness, fairness, cream

ADJECTIVES 8 lucent, luminous, radiant, refulgent, glowing, glimmering, burning, candescent, incandescent, aglow, phosphorescent, fluorescent, shining, lambent, flickering, blinking, winking, flashing, occulting, stroboscopic, illuminating, brightening **9 bright**, vivid, brilliant, flamboyant, garish, lurid, flashy, effulgent, splendid, resplendent, kaleidoscopic, shining, dazzling, fluorescent, blinding, glaring, flashing, sparking, coruscating, glinting, sparkling, scintillating, twinkling, glittering, fiery, flaming, blazing **10 lustrous**, glossy, gleaming, shiny, polished, burnished, glassy, glistening, shimmering, opalescent, iridescent, pearly **11 lit**, illuminated, brightened, bright, lamplit, candlelit, torchlit, firelit, spotlit, floodlit, highlighted, sunlit, starlit **12 sunny**, daylight, cloudless **13 starry**, starbright, star-spangled **14 light**, pale, pastel, cream-coloured, ivory, pallid, pasty, colourless, white, albino, blond, fair, flaxen, tow-headed, faded, bleached, peroxided, lightened **15 enlightened**, elucidated, clarified, lucid, illuminated, bright, brilliant **16 photoelectric**, photoconductive, photoemissive, photometric, photosensitive, phototropic, photophobic, spectral

VERBS 17 light, illuminate, brighten, switch on, turn on, put on, strike, ignite, kindle, fire, floodlight, spotlight, highlight, irradiate, dazzle **18 light up**, gleam, glint, glance, glisten, glimmer, blink, wink, flicker, twinkle, sparkle, flash, coruscate, scintillate, glitter, spangle, shine, glow, glare, flare, flame, blaze, burn, incandesce, radiate, beam, fluoresce, phosphoresce **19 grow light**, dawn, break **20 glaze**, polish, burnish, reflect **21 bleach**, lighten, whiten, dye, peroxide, overexpose, fade, pale, blench **22 clarify**, elucidate

429 Lightness

ADJECTIVES 1 light, unheavy, portable, handy, lightweight, featherweight, bantamweight, light-footed, light-fingered, weightless, unweighable **2 insubstantial**, ethereal, rare, sublime, airy, gaseous, volatile, frothy, foamy, whipped, whisked, bubbly, effervescent, sparkling, downy, feathery, cobwebby, gossamery, fluffy, soft, gentle, delicate, dainty, tender, flimsy, floaty, buoyant, unsinkable **3 lightening**, unloading, off-loaded, aerating, easing, relieving, alleviating, disburdening **4 leavening**, fermenting, raising, self-raising, yeasty, enzymic

NOUNS 5 lightness, rarity, thinness, unheaviness, portability, airiness, ethereality, gaseousness, volatileness, vaporization, foaminess, frothiness, bubbliness, effervescence, sparkling, yeastiness, downiness, fluffiness, softness, gentleness, tenderness, flimsiness, delicacy, daintiness, unweighableness, imponderableness, weightlessness, levitation, floating, ascent **6 lightening**, easing, easement, aeration, alleviation, relief, unburdening, unloading, unlading, unsaddling **7 light thing**, air, helium, ether, bubble, balloon, snowflake, feather, down, thistledown, fluff, fuzz, gossamer, cobweb, straw, dust, mote, cork, froth, foam, spume, soufflé, mousse, sponge, float, life buoy **8 leavening**, fermentation, raising agent, yeast, enzyme

VERBS 9 be light, weigh little, defy gravity, levitate, ascend, rise, elevate, surface, float, swim, drift, waft, glide, soar **10 lighten**, gasify, vaporize, aerate, volatilize, buoy, uplift, fluff, leaven, ferment, raise, unload, unlade, unballast, jettison, disencumber, disburden, unsaddle, untax, relieve

430 Liking

NOUNS 1 liking, attachment, tenderness, fondness, affection, attraction, affinity, friendship, intimacy, empathy, sympathy, approval, admiration, infatuation, titillation, fascination, temptation, allurement, devotion, patriotism, adoration, love, desire, passion, appetite, weakness, zest, wishing, longing, yearning **2 inclination**, tendency, penchant, propensity, proclivity, preference, favour, predilection, predisposition, intention, partiality, prejudice, bias, leaning, selection, choice, readiness, willingness, eagerness, mind, turn, bent **3 likes**, hobby, fancy,

caprice, whim, phase, trend, craze, pleasure, relish, taste, mania, wish, craving, infatuation, soft spot
ADJECTIVES 4 likable, favoured, admired, appreciated, popular, good, amicable, congenial, friendly, affectionate, appealing, fascinating, adorable, lovely, attractive, pleasing, endearing, captivating, infatuating, titillating, tempting, alluring, lovable **5 liking**, admiring, fascinated, devoted, empathetic, sympathetic, tending, turning, bending, leaning, predisposed, prejudiced, biased, favouring, preferring, approving, wishing, hankering, longing, yearning, loving
VERBS 6 like, care for, sympathize with, hold dear, cherish, appreciate, esteem, treasure, prize, enjoy, delight in, adore, admire, relish, savour, take to, love, desire, wish, long, yearn **7 prefer**, want, approve, favour, predispose oneself, lean towards, intend, select **8 like to**, want to, wish to, love to

431 Limit

NOUNS 1 limitation, restriction, proscription, circumscription, demarcation, definition, moderation, mitigation, exclusion, restraint, constraint, control, containment **2 limiting factor**, self-control, self-restraint, check, prohibition, restricted area, no-go area, specification, ceiling, high-water mark, bottom, threshold, hindrance, brake, censorship, veto, ban, stricture, rationing, curtailment, curb, curfew, closed shop, monopoly, cartel, trust, quota, embargo, tariff, allotment, extent, measure, dose, lot, copyright **3 furthest point**, extremity, farness, boundary, verge, margin, edge, brink, frontier **4 boundary marker**, partition wall, fence, hedge, river, checkpoint, time zone
ADJECTIVES 5 limited, restricted, proscripted, prohibitive, repressive, inhibiting, no-go, exclusive, definite, confined, frozen, curtailed, finite, narrow, cramped, hidebound, copyrighted **6 furthest**, extreme, far, verging, boundary, border
VERBS 7 limit, restrict, proscribe, circumscribe, demarcate, define, moderate, exclude, restrain, constrain, control, mitigate, inhibit, check, hamper, hold in, confine, prohibit, specify, hinder, repress, curb, censor, veto, ban, ration, curtail, contain, monopolize, embargo, allot

432 Linguistics

- *In the beginning was the Word, and the Word was with God, and the Word was God.* Bible: John.
- *Word's are men's daughters; but God's sons are things.* Samuel Madden.

NOUNS 1 linguistics, linguistic geography, syntactics, phonetics, pronunciation, phonology, phonography, phonemics, orthoepy, morphophonemics, morphology, morphophonology, lexicology, lexicography, lexicostatistics, philology, grammatology, etymology, semantics, semasiology, graphemics, comparative linguistics, contrastive linguistics, structuralism, psycholinguistics, geolinguistics, dialectology, onomastics, nomenclature, sociolinguistics, stylistics, glottochronology, palaeography, bilingualism, multilingualism **2 linguist**, grammarian, phonetist, phonemicist, phonologist, orthoepist, morphologist, lexicologist, lexicographer, etymologist, semanticist, semasiologist, philologist, grammatologist, structuralist, psycholinguist, geolinguist, dialectician, onomasiologist, epigrammatist, palaeographer, epigraphist, classicist, polyglot, translator, interpreter, clarifier, expositor, exegete, orthographer, neologist, logophile, phrasemonger, phrasemaker, writer, poet, proverbialist, nomenclator, terminologist, namegiver, christener, baptizer **3 spoken language**, tongue, speech, vocalism, talk, parlance, vernacular, phraseology, colloquialism, conversationalism, idiom, slang, jargon, argot, patois **4 parent language**, mother tongue **5 nonstandard language**, body language, signal, code, parole, patter, idiolect, idioglossia, baby talk, empty words, illiterate speech, barbarism, corruption, gobbledegook, polyglot medley, glossolalia, vocalise semiotics, Babel, babble, jabber **6 official language**, standard usage, Queen's English, BBC English, Oxford English, literary language **7 international language**, trade language, lingua franca, koine, Esperanto **8 artificial language**, sign language, semaphore, Morse code, computer language **9 ancient language**, classical language, dead language, lost language, archaism, **10 translation**, rendering, literal translation, loose translation, paraphrase, restatement, edition, redaction, transliteration, abridgment, epitome, exegesis, hermeneutics, exegetics, epigraphy, palaeography, decipherment **11 letter**, writing, lexigraphy, lettering, print, type, symbol, character, grapheme, digraph, sign, ideogram, ideograph, pictogram, pictograph, cuneiform, hieroglyph, Pinyin, Kanji, Devanagari, Nagari, rune, wen, initial, monogram, anagram, acronym **12 alphabet**, ABC, Roman alphabet, Cyrillic alphabet, Hebrew alphabet, Arabic alphabet, Cherokee alphabet, Greek alphabet, runic alphabet, ogham alphabet, phonetic alphabet, futhark **13 spoken letter**, speech sound, phoneme, grapheme, syllable, vowel, consonant, guttural, nasal, frictionless continuant, labial, labiodental, labionasal, liquid, spirant, sibilant, aspirate, glottal stop, fricative, sonant, polyphone, digraph, diphthong, stress, pitch **14 word**, Logos, term, name, glosseme, sememe, synonym, cognate, paronym, metonym, antonym, homonym, homograph, homophone, tautonym, doublet, palindrome, root, etymon, morpheme, stem, enclitic, pejorative, intensive, polysyllable, sesquipedalian, monosyllable, neologism, coinage, nonce word, loan word, calque, hybrid, ghost word, rhyming word, onomatopoeic word **15 slang**, back slang, rhyming slang, dog Latin **16 swearword**, rude word, vulgarism, coprolalia, billingsgate, scatology, expletive, four-letter word **17 jargon word**, officialese, legalese, journalese, newspeak, telegraphese, technospeak, argot, cant **18 catchword**, jingo, cliché, catchphrase, maxim, adage, moral, proverb, quotation, slogan **19 phrasing**, phraseology, wording, rounded phrase, well-turned phrase, set phrase, locution, trope, metaphor, compliments, elegance, circumlocution, periphrasis, diffuseness, paraphrase, translation, phraseogram **20 inscription**, epitaph, obsequies, legend **21 dialect**, idiom, patois, speech community, argot, isogloss, isophone, isolex, localism, regionism, provincialism, vernacularism, accent, brogue, broagh, burr, Africanism, Americanism, Briticism, Anglicism, Scotticism, Irishism, Hibernicism, Teutonism, Gallicism, dialectology, broken English, pidgin English, lingua franca, Strine **22 spelling**, orthography, spelling bee, spelling game, phonetic spelling, misspelling **23 dictionary**, lexicon, wordbook, school dictionary, monolingual dictionary, bilingual dictionary, multilingual dictionary, concise dictionary, compact dictionary, biographical dictionary, rhyming dictionary, *Webster's Dictionary*, glossary, gloss, gradus, concordance, synonym dictionary, thesaurus, *Roget's Thesaurus*, *Bloomsbury Thesaurus*, lexicography **24 grammar**, grammatical rules, grammaticalness, formal language, structural linguistics, traditional grammar, descriptive grammar, systemic grammar, case grammar, transformational grammar, transformation-generative grammar, syntax, word order, agreement, number, gender, case, inflection, declension, conjugation, paradigm, mood, voice, tense, parsing, construing, punctuation, accentuation, bad grammar, solecism, malapropism **25 part of speech**, noun, pronoun, adjective, verb, participle, adverb, preposition, copula, conjunction, interjection, modifier, article **26 accent**, diacritical mark, umlaut, diaeresis, ablaut, grave, acute, circumflex, breve, cedilla, macron, tilde, hacek, ogonek, caron, alif, hamzah, horn, rude

ADJECTIVES 27 linguistic, grammatical, descriptive, structural, phonetic, pronounced, phonological, phonemic, orthoepic, orthographic, morphophonemic, diachronic, synchronic, lexicological, etymological, semantic, semasiological, glottological, glottochronological, lexicostatistical, philological, psycholingustic, geolinguistic, dialectological, onomastic, onomasiological, sociolinguistic, bilingual, multilingual **28 of language**, written, spoken, educated, standard, official, formal, literary, politically correct, informal, common, vernacular, colloquial, conversational, childish, holophrastic, dialectal, guttural, burring, slangy, jargonish, journalistic, jingoistic, idiomatic, scatological, blasphemous, nonstandard, substandard, inflected, affixing, analytic, agglutinative, polysynthetic, monosyllabic, polysyllabic, symbolic, tonal **29 translated**, rendering, word-for-word, paraphrased, reworded, restated, transliterated, abridged, edited, redacted, ciphered, deciphered **30 lettered**, lexicographical, literal, printed, typed, syllabic, phonogramic, phonographic, pictographic, ideographic, cuneiform, capital, upper-case, majuscule, uncial, lower-case, minuscule, bold, italic, sans serif, cursive, initial, acronymic, acrostic, voiced, vocal, vocalic, consonantal, guttural, polyphonic, polyphonous **31**

worded, verbal, vocabular, lexical, glossarial, paronymic, antonymous, homonymic, homographic, homophonic, tautonymic, palindromic, morphological, inflectional, enclitic, sesquipedalian, onomatopoeic, argotic, canting, clichéd, proverbial, pleonastic, wordy, verbose **32 phrasal**, phraseological, clausal, sentential, collocating, locutionary, circumlocutory, periphrastic, diffuse, paraphrastic, phraseographic **33 grammatical**, pronominal, adjectival, verbal, copular, reflexive, transitive, intransitive, participial, adverbial, prepositional, conjunctive, coordinate, interjectional, objective, subjective, direct, indirect, modifying, definite, indefinite, inflectional, inflected, formative, morphemeic, diminutive, intensive, attributive, augmentative, comparative, superlative, masculine, feminine, neuter

VERBS 34 use language, communicate, write, speak, pronounce, vocalize, voice, articulate, rhyme, phrase, express, formulate, anagrammatize, neologize, colloquialize, vernacularize, jargonize, cant, patter, swear, blaspheme **35 translate**, interpret, paraphrase, reword, restate, abridge, edit, redact, decipher, decode, transliterate, transcribe, read **36 word**, verbalize, define, syllabify, alphabetize, rewrite, rephrase, initial, inscribe

433 Lining

NOUNS 1 lining, coating, undercoating, facing, interfacing, interlining, insulation, soundproofing, double glazing, wallpaper, panelling, wainscot, backing, petticoat **2 filling**, stuffing, padding, packing, packaging, filler, wadding, quilting, foam, polystyrene, kapak

VERBS 3 line, interline, coat, undercoat, face, interface, insulate, soundproof, double glaze, wallpaper, panel, wainscot **4 fill**, stuff, pad, pack, package

434 List

NOUNS 1 list, enumeration, series, items, itemization, inventory, tally, stock, repertory, register, registry, table, chart **2 table**, contents, index, file, filing system, catalogue, reference list, bibliography, reading list, syllabus, filmography, discography, menu, window, database **3 dictionary**, lexicon, glossary, vocabulary, terminology, nomenclature, thesaurus, gazetteer, atlas, encyclopedia, almanac, yearbook, reference book, directory, guidebook, who's who, telephone directory, yellow pages **4 bill**, invoice, account, statement, ledger, books, daybook, journal, manifest, docket, price list, tariff, menu **5 list of appointments**, diary, engagement book, day book, calendar, agenda, programme, timetable, schedule, itinerary, prospectus, syllabus, curriculum, synopsis **6 list of names**, roll, register, rota, roster, scroll, panel, census, poll, head count, roll call, electoral roll, voting list, cadaster, payroll, civil list, waiting list, sick list, short list, blacklist, dramatis personae, credits **7 listing**, enumeration, itemization, registration, filing, indexing, cataloguing, tabulation, charting

VERBS 8 list, enumerate, itemize, inventory, register, record, note, write down, chronicle, enter,

book, post, file, pigeonhole, classify, catalogue, index, tabulate, chart, diarize, timetable, schedule, bill, invoice, short-list **9 enlist**, enrol, matriculate **10 score**, tally
ADJECTIVES 11 listed, enumerated, itemized, inventoried, registered, recorded, entered, noted, filed, catalogued, taxonomic, classificatory, indexed, tabulated, charted, scheduled, programmed **12 inventorial**, glossarial

435 Literature

• *The reading of all good books is like a conversation with the finest men of past centuries.* René Descartes.

NOUNS 1 literature, letters, belles-lettres, underground literature, popular literature, folk literature, oral literature, the classics, the arts **2 fiction**, novel, novella, novelette, story, short-story, vignette, sketch, thriller, stream-of-consciousness novel, antinovel, metafiction, epistolary novel, erotic novel, pornographic novel, autobiographical novel, fictional biography, historical novel, social novel, love story, adventure story, western, science-fiction novel, utopia, dystopia, gothic horror, crime story, spy story, detective story, ghost story, fairy tale, legend, myth, folk tale, fable, parable, conte, geste **3 aspect of fiction**, storyline, narrative, plot, subplot, scenario, subject, theme, motif, leitmotiv, development, structure, action, incident, episode, complication, turning-point, dénouement, peripeteia, recognition, anagnosis, description, symbolism, characterization, dramatic irony, comic relief, catharsis, digression, metanarrative **4 non-fiction**, descriptive writing, travelogue, history, annals, diary, memoir, confessions, kiss-and-tell confession, autobiography, biography, hagiography, historiography, homily, apology, treatise, discourse, thesis, dissertation, essay, study, commentary, critique **5 poetry**, poesy, verse, rhyme, song, balladry, versification, poetics, light verse, folk poetry, doggerel, jingles, ditties **6 poem**, verse, rhyme, ballade, ballad, epic, lay, saga, dithyramb, epigram, cento, limerick, clerihew, lyric, madrigal, nursery rhyme, ode, epode, palinode, verse epistle, complaint, encomium, satire, sonnet, sestina, chanson, tenzone, rondeau, rondel, roundel, roundelay, alba, aubade, reverdie, virelay, triolet, eclogue, idyll, pastoral, georgic, bucolic, prothalamion, epithalamium, elegy, threnody, elegiac poem, monody, dirge, song, villanelle, hymn, psalm, haiku **7 metre**, metrics, measure, rhythm, scansion, prosody, accentuation, stress, beat, emphasis, quantity, metrical unit, foot, dipody, iamb, spondee, trochee, dactyl, anaepest, pyrrhic, tribrach, amphibrach, amphimacer, cretic, ionic, paeon, choriamb, dimeter, trimeter, tetrameter, pentameter, hexameter, heptameter, octameter, iambic pentameter, elegiac pentameter, Alexandrine, dactylic hexameter, heroic couplet, elegiac couplet, elegiac distich, distich, sprung rhythm, counterpoint, anacrusis, catalexis, caesura **8 poetic language**, poeticism, archaicism, alliteration, repetition, anaphora, epistrophe, assonance, consonance, onomatopoeia, euphony, elision, inversion, chiasmus, peraphrasis, imagery, conceit, trope, metaphor, simile, compound epithet, transferred epithet, kenning, personification, prosopopoeia, apostrophe, metonymy, synecdoche, antonomasia, paronomasia, parallelism, synaesthesia, pathetic fallacy, poetic licence, pseudostatement, irony **9 author**, writer, storyteller, novelist, fabler, fabulist, mythologist, allegorist, romancer, novelettist, diarist, chronicler, historian, historiographer, biographer, autobiographer, annalist, poet, poetess, minnesinger, Meistersinger, rhapsodist, dithyrambist, elegist, satirist, sonneteer, symbolist, modernist, beat poet, rap poet, librettist, lyricist, vers-librist, rhymer, rhymester, versemonger, versifier, versesmith, versemaker, poetaster, balladeer, bard, minstrel, jongleur, trouveur, troubadour, scop, skald, comic poet, tragic poet, dramatic poet, playwright, dramatist, dramaturge **10 literary person**, belletrist, literary critic, structuralist, post-structuralist, deconstructor, book reviewer anapaestic, catalectic, rhyming, assonant, alliterative

VERBS 11 write, compose, dramatize, poetize, versify, compose, elegize, rhyme, prosify, describe, portray, represent, express

436 Littleness

NOUNS 1 littleness, smallness, diminutiveness, shortness, petiteness, squatness, dumpiness, dwarfishness, daintiness, dinkiness, compactness, handiness, portability, tininess, minuteness, fineness, thinness, slightness, exiguity, tenuousness, imperceptibility, intangibility, impalpability, imponderability, inappreciability, invisibility, undersize, stuntedness, puniness, runtiness, shrunkenness, scrubbiness, scrawniness, scragginess, meagreness, scantness, skimpiness, paltriness, pettiness, miniaturization, microscopy **2 little thing**, particle, grain, seed, granule, corpuscle, molecule, cell, nucleus, monad, atom, ion, electron, proton, neutron, neutrino, parton, meson, muon, quark, point, pinpoint, pinhead, dot, microdot, pixel, microbe, bacterium, virus, germ, bacillus, microorganism, animalcule, protozoan, amoeba, miniature, mini, baby, model, microcosm, microphotograph, microfiche, duodecimo **3 little piece**, bit, fragment, sliver, shaving, filing, jot, tittle, iota, speck, fleck, mote, scrap, crumb, morsel, snippet, minutia, minim **4 little space**, pigeonhole, cubbyhole, doll's house, tight squeeze

VERBS 5 be little, be small

ADJECTIVES 6 little, small, diminutive, short, petite, squat, dumpy, dwarfish, elfin, dainty, dinky, Lilliputian, miniature, mini, bantam, baby, small-scale, miniaturized, microcosmic, duodecimo, tiny, minute, minuscule, infinitesimal, microscopic, rudimentary, incipient, embryonic, fine, thin, slight, exiguous, tenuous, imperceptible, intangible, impalpable, negligible, indiscernible, stunted, puny, shrunk, contracted, meagre, scant, skimpy, poky, cramped, limited, snug, cosy, bijou, paltry, petty, trifling, insignificant, minimal, molecular, subatomic, microbic, diminutively, daintily, slightly, minimally, tinily, minutely, finely, tenuously, inappreciably, negligibly **7 microscopically**, microcosmically, subatomically, infinitesimally, indiscernibly, imperceptibly, invisibly, intangibly

437 Location

NOUNS 1 location, locality, situation, place, site, position, whereabouts, spot, setting, environs, environment, habitat, haunt, patch, pitch, beat, territory, seat, station **2 exact location**, spot, point, dot, bench mark, grid reference, coordinates, bearings, compass direction, declination, chart, map, plan, address **3 locating**, pinpointing, finding, discovering, detecting, unearthing, turning up, tracking down, pinning down, coming across, chancing upon **4 placing**, locating, situating, siting, placement, establishment, installation, settling, fixation, posting **5 topography**, geography, cartography, chorography, surveying, triangulation, navigation

ADJECTIVES 6 located, situated, placed, positioned, sited, set, stationed, posted, established, installed, settled, fixed, emplaced, planted **7 found**, discovered, pinpointed, detected, unearthed, tracked down **8 locational**, situated, positional, topographical, geographical, cartographical, navigational

VERBS 9 locate, situate, place, site, position, emplace, install, establish, plant, ensconce, station, post, billet, quarter, base **10 settle**, move in, ensconce oneself, inhabit, dwell, reside in **11 find**, pinpoint, discover, detect, turn up, track down, pin down, come across, chance upon

438 Loss

- *'Tis better to have loved and lost than never to have lost at all.* Samuel Butler.
- *To lose one parent, Mr Worthing, may be regarded as a misfortune; to lose both looks like carelessness.* Oscar Wilde.

NOUNS 1 loss, misplacing, mislaying, decrease, subtraction, deprivation, dispossession, eviction, expropriation, divestment, robbery, stripping, detriment, disadvantage, setback, check, reverse, failure, defeat, penalty, forfeiture, disentitlement, disenfranchisement, disqualification, coma, death, bereavement, perdition, sacrifice, denial, dieting, slimming, fasting, weight-watching, anorexia **2 financial loss**, poor return, cut price, loss leader, diminishing returns, cost, expense, expenditure, deficit, shortfall, overspending, overdraft, debit, insolvency **3 waste**, squandering, dissipation, misuse, losing battle, unproductiveness, fruitlessness, spilt milk, fool's errand **4 lessening**, dwindling, falling off, waning, fading out, dimming, wearing away, erosion, depletion, shrinkage, depreciation, diminution, outflow, draining, leakage, haemorrhage, evaporation, impoverishment **5 destruction**, denudation, spoiling, despoilment, sabotage, harm, injury, impairment, damage

VERBS 6 lose, misplace, mislay, miss, forget, decrease, subtract, consume, deprive, dispossess, evict, expropriate, divest, rob, strip, fail, face defeat, forfeit, sacrifice, relinquish, die, diet, slim **7 have a financial loss**, fall short, overspend, overdraw **8 be wasteful**, squander, dissipate, throw away **9 lessen**, dwindle, wane, fade out, dim, deplete, depreciate, diminish, deteriorate, wear away, drain, dribble away, leak, haemorrhage, seep away, evaporate **10 destroy**, misuse, despoil, spoliate, denude, sabotage, harm, injure, impair, damage, ruin **11 go to waste**, dissipate **12 lose someone**, avoid, evade, elude, dodge, escape, outrun, outstrip

ADJECTIVES 13 losing, lost, missing, misplaced, mislaid, astray, lacking, forgotten, irrecoverable, irretrievable, incorrigible, irredeemable, hopeless, depriving, failing, squandered, depleted, stripped of, shorn of, bereft, spent **14 unprofitable**, cut-price, out-of-pocket, deficient, prodigal, wasteful, overspent, overdrawn, insolvent, impoverished, ruined **15 at a loss**, off course, disoriented, confused, bewildered, astonished, dumbstruck

439 Loudness

NOUNS 1 loudness, high volume, loud noise, report, explosion, bang, blast, boom, burst, alarm, siren, honk, toot, reverberation, cachinnation, stertorousness, snoring, rumble, roll, rattle, thunder, sibilation, gunfire, blitz, dissonance, cacophony, stridency, brassiness, shrillness, blare, bray, fanfare, clarion call, sonority, clang, plangency, resonance, bells, peal, chimes, diapason, crescendo, forte, fortissimo **2 outcry**, vociferation, clamour, shouting, screaming, roaring, bawling, yelling, hooting, chanting, shriek, roar, whoop, howl, ululation, hubbub, hullabaloo, slamming, banging, stamping, crash, clash, clatter, din, row, uproar, tumult, noisiness, racket, bedlam, pandemonium, turmoil **3 audibility**, distinctness, sound, noise **4 sound maker**, voice, larynx, voice box, vocal chords, loud pedal, amplifier, public-address system, loudspeaker, megaphone, loudhailer, microphone, ear trumpet, hearing aid, gong, whistle, siren, horn, hooter, klaxon, rattle, bullroarer, buzzer, bell, alarm, door knocker

ADJECTIVES 5 loud, noisy, booming, ringing, carrying, deafening, earsplitting, thundering, rattling, crashing, pealing, clangorous, dinning, rackety, shrill, piercing, strident, braying, blaring, brassy, echoing, resonant, sonorous, plangent, cacophonous, shouting, yelling, whooping, bellowing, lusty, powerful, stentorian, rowdy, rumbustious, rambunctious, boisterous, vociferous **6 heard**, hearable

VERBS 7 be loud, sound, speak, vociferate, shout, yell, roar, bellow, catcall, caterwaul, yowl, howl, ululate, shriek, cry, scream, squawk, trumpet, blare, whistle, shrill, bray, cachinnate, clap, stamp, reverberate, resound, clang, rattle, thunder, fulminate, storm, clash, crash, clatter, slam, bang, blast, burst, boom, explode, hammer, drill, din, deafen, swell

440 Love

NOUNS 1 love, affection, sentiment, fondness, liking, attachment, devotion, adoration, worship, admiration, fascination, idolization, regard, popularity, respect, charity, Agape, friendship, loyalty, compatibility, fellow feeling, understanding, mutual attraction, patriotism, narcissism **2 romantic love**, ardour, fervour, ecstasy, transport, fancy, fascination, enchantment, bewitchment, possessiveness, jealousy, lust, uxoriousness, Cupid's string, Oedipus complex **3 lovingness**, amorousness, amativeness, affectionateness, tenderness, kindness, sentiment, demonstrativeness, feeling, susceptibility, emotion, romanticism, lovesickness **4 loveability**, likeability, amiability, agreeability, attractiveness, beauty, appeal, sweetness, charm, endearment, adorability, desirability, sexiness, flirtatiousness, coquetry, enchantment, allurement **5 desire**, lust, passion, yearning, longing, itching, amorousness, aphrodisia, lasciviousness, licentiousness, caprice, ecstasy, intimacy, lovemaking, sex, libido, sexual relations, coupling, copulation, coition, cohabitation, fornication, carnal knowledge, mating, consummation, eroticism, wantonness, libertinage **6 courtship**, wooing, dating, suit, going out, flirtation, coquetry, coyness, dalliance, toying, sheep's eyes, ogle, flattering, honeying, gallantry, advances, addresses, sighing, proposing **7 choice**, preference, sympathy, predilection, inclination **8 love affair**, romance, relationship, amour, liaison, intrigue, flirtation, seduction, eternal triangle, affair, adultery, infidelity, unfaithfulness, cuckoldry, entanglement, amourette, flirtation, betrothal, engagement **9 lover**, wooer, suitor, paramour, sweetheart, conquest, admirer, adorer, aficionado, fan, date, girlfriend, temptress, flirt, coquette, fiancée, bride-to-be, mistress, boyfriend, beau, fiancé, escort, gigolo, seducer, lecher, libertine, womanizer, Casanova, Don Juan **10 abode of love**, love nest, bower, boudoir, honeymoon suite, honeymoon cottage, bridal suite, nuptial chamber, bridal bed, woman's quarters, gynaeceum, zenana, harem **11 communication of love**, sweet talk, sweet nothings, flattery, blandishments, pet names, ogle, sheep's eyes, wink, cuddling, tickling, snuggling, hugging, embracing, nuzzling, squeezing, caressing, fondling, bundling, kissing, osculation, lovebite, bearhug, stroke, caress **12 love item**, ribbon, pin, love letter, billet-doux, love poem, love song, serenade, caterwauling, valentine **13 gods and goddesses of love**, Venus, Aphrodite, Astarte, Freya, Cupid, Eros

ADJECTIVES 14 loving, amorous, affectionate, demonstrative, fond, attached, devoted, kind, friendly, amicable, sympathetic, charitable, agapistic, sentimental, faithful, loyal, uxorious, motherly, paternal, fraternal, platonic, charitable **15 in love**, infatuated with, enamoured of, fond of, sweet on, keen on, mad about, set on, engaged to, wedded to **16 enamoured**, attracted, charmed, fervent, doting, devoted, gallant, enslaved, ensnared, enraptured, infatuated, enchanted, captivated, fascinated, bewitched, besotted, mad, insane, crazed, lovesick, lovelorn, languishing **17 amorous**, romantic, sentimental, emotional, tender, soft, adoring, melting, flirtatious, coquettish, seductive, coy, passionate, lustful, ardent, yearning, longing, moping, mooning, desirous, lascivious, capricious, ecstatic, excited, erotic, sexy, alluring, erogenous, ensnaring, possessive **18 beloved**, cherished, adored, esteemed, revered, preferred, fancied, favourite, chosen, pet, darling, dear, admired, regarded, respected **19 loveable**, endearing, adorable, appealing, interesting, intriguing, enchanting, captivating, beguiling, desirable, tempting, alluring, seductive, beautiful, winsome, sweet, winning, pleasing, engaging, graceful, angelic, divine, kissable, cuddly

VERBS 20 love, adore, cherish, relish, treasure, prize, value, esteem, appreciate, like, desire, fancy, revere, admire, idolize, worship, delight in **21 be in love**, dote on, fall for, yearn for **22 be loved**, be courted, break hearts, arouse, rouse, stir, excite, warm, heat up, inflame, draw interest **23 court**, woo, squire, escort, pursue, chase, date, philander, tempt, lure, flirt, tease, trifle, dally, toy, lead on, coquet, vamp, make eyes, ogle **24 kiss**, smack, osculate, caress, cuddle, enfold, embrace, stroke, fondle, drool over, slobber over **25 win the love of**, enamour, enchant, becharm, beguile, captivate, fascinate, enrapture, enthral, bewitch, allure, attract, endear oneself, ingratiate oneself, flatter, curry favour, dazzle, ensnare, catch **26 make love**, have sex, have intercourse, sleep with, mate, couple, copulate

441 Lowering

VERBS 1 lower, depress, deflate, reduce, decrease, deteriorate **2 flatten**, level, demolish, rase, raze, fell, hew, chop, mow down, lumber, ground, tear down, dent **3 bring down**, overthrow, overturn, couch, topple, subvert, floor, deck, lay out, bowl over, spreadeagle, torpedo, scuttle, sink, drown **4 debase**, abase, degrade, downgrade, demote, humble, cashier, humiliate, snub, deflate, debunk, water down, dilute **5 bear down on**, push down, weigh on, press, suppress **6 throw down**, cast down, fling, pitch, drop, shed, scatter, dust, sow, broadcast, disperse, pour, void, spill **7 lean**, incline, bend over, trip, topple, tumble, fall headlong, capsize, roll over, tip **8 sit**, seat oneself, park oneself, perch, alight, squat, crouch, hunch, stoop, bend, duck, scrooch down, prostrate, supinate, lie down, recline, drape oneself **9 bow**, bend, genuflect, kneel, kowtow, salaam, kiss hands, revere, pay respects, do reverence, curtsy, bob, duck, nod, make obeisance, prostrate oneself, grovel, cower, cringe

NOUNS 10 lowering, depression, deflation, sinking, levelling, demolition, reduction, decrease, deterioration, worsening, diminution, deescalation, descent, drop, downfall, rainfall, fall, trip, tumble **11 downthrow**, downcast, flattening, levelling, grounding, overthrow, overturn, overset, upset, toppling, subversion, revolution, precipitation **12 submergence**, sinking, ducking, sousing, pushing under, detrusion, plunging, suppression **13 depression**, indentation, hollow, cavity, concavity, dip, dent, sinkhole **14 debasement**, degradation, downgrading, demotion, deterioration, humiliation, grovelling **15 courtesy**, deference, respect, comi-

ty, bow, genuflect, kneeling, kowtow, salaam
ADJECTIVES 16 lowered, depressed, deflated, flattened, grounded, levelled, demolished, reduced, decreased, deteriorated **17 lowering**, descendent, depressing, humiliating, demeaning **18 fallen**, sunk, soused, submerged, downcast, downthrown **19 falling**, toppling, tumbling, tripping, showering, sprinkling, scattering, spilling, dropping **20 degraded**, debased, downgraded, demoted, humiliated, downcast, depressed, kowtowing, kneeling, grovelling, courteous **21 overthrown**, overturned, overset, upset, toppled, subverted, suppressed, oppressed, subversive **22 sedentary**, sitting, crouching, stooping, squatting, hunched, bent

442 Lowness

NOUNS 1 lowness, shortness, squatness, stumpiness, stuntedness, shallowness, flattening, lying down, prostration, proneness, supineness, recumbency, reclining, subordination **2 lowland(s)**, foothills, hillock, hummock, molehill, nursery slope, plain, flats, level ground, flatness, sea level, depression, hollow **3 lowest point**, nadir, low tide, low water, ebb **4 low thing**, nether regions, subjacency, subscript, subcortex, submucosa, hypolimnion, underlay, underfelt, substratum, subsoil, bedrock, floor, bottom, foot, base, subgrade, basement, cellar, underneath, underside, undersurface, underbelly, underpart, underbody, undercarriage, bungalow, coffee table, décolletage, dachshund
ADJECTIVES 5 low, short, squat, stumpy, stunted, shallow, knee-high, low-slung, flattened, knocked flat, reclining, couchant, crouched, stooped, décolleté **6 lower**, inferior, nether, bottom, undermost, subjacent, underlying, underlaid, **7 lowland**, subalpine, submontane, piedmont, low-lying, flat, submerged
VERBS 8 be low, bottom out, underlie, underlay, creep **9 lower**, flatten, depress, knock over

443 Lubrication

NOUNS 1 lubrication, nonfriction, smoothness, slickness, sleekness **2 oiliness**, greasiness, waxiness, unctuousness, soapiness, saponacity, fattiness **3 anointment**, unction, oiling, inunction **4 lubricant**, lubricating agent, antifriction, graphite, plumbago, black lead, silicone, glycerine, wax, grease, tallow, oil, oleum soap, lather, mucilage, mucus, synovia, saliva **5 ointment**, salve, balm, lotion, cream, unguent, inunction, unction, chrism, emollient, lenitive, soothing syrup, embrocation, demulcent, spikenard, nard, balsam **6 pomade**, pomatum, brilliantine, hair conditioner, setting lotion, styling mousse, cleanser, cold cream, hand lotion, lanolin, eyewash, collyrium **7 lubricator**, oil can
ADJECTIVES 8 lubricated, oiled, greased, smooth-running **9 lubricant**, lenitive, emollient **10 oily**, greasy, waxy, slippery **11 unguent**, chrismal **12 smooth**, slick, sleek, slippery
VERBS 13 lubricate, oil, grease **14 anoint**, salve, unguent

444 Male

NOUNS 1 male sex, masculine gender, man, mankind, manhood, masculinity, manliness, virility, machismo, misogyny **2 male**, man, gentleman, youth, boy, lad, fellow, he, him, himself **3 boyfriend**, boy, sweetheart, fiancé, bridegroom, beau, escort, date, partner, lover, Adonis **4 single man**, bachelor, divorcee, ex-husband **5 macho man**, muscleman **6 libertine**, rake, cad, bounder, philanderer, heartbreaker, Casanova, Don Juan, buck, stallion, gigolo, ladies' man **7 man in the family**, married man, husband, spouse, live-in lover, widower, house husband, father, patriarch, paterfamilias, paternity, fatherhood, son, boy, brother, uncle, nephew, godfather, godson, grandfather **8 male animal**, lion, tiger, bull, bullock, ox, steer, stallion, stud, colt, gelding, stag, buck, hart, boar, hog, ram, tup, billy goat, dog, tom cat, jack, cockerel, rooster, capon

ADJECTIVES 9 male, masculine, manly, macho, virile, muscular, gentlemanly, chivalrous, mannish, unmanly, effeminate

445 Malevolence

NOUNS 1 malevolence, evilness, badness, ill will, malignity, hate, loathing, blind fury, misanthropy, misandry, misogyny, malice, malice aforethought, maleficence, wickedness, devilry, enmity, truculence, hostility, animosity, antagonism, meanness, nastiness **2 cruelness**, inhumanity, barbarism, brutality, savagery, atrocity, bestiality, animality, viciousness, ferocity, violence, vandalism, sadism, monstrousness, terrorism, heinousness, fiendishness, bloodthirstiness, bloodlust **3 callousness**, unfeelingness, unnaturalness, hardness, hardheartedness, heartlessness, obduracy, stonyheartedness, coldness, cold-heartedness, cold-bloodedness, gloating, unholy joy, *Schadenfreude*, harshness, roughness, severity, ruthlessness, sternness **4 bitterness**, tartness, acrimony, asperity, resentment, acerbity, sourness, sharpness, vengefulness, mordacity, acidity, causticity, spite, rancour, gall, spleen, bile, virulence, venom, vitriol, vindictiveness, grudge, beastliness, waspishness **5 intolerance**, persecution, intimidation, victimization, tyrannization, bullying, harassment **6 inconsiderateness**, insensitivity, thoughtlessness, heedlessness, unmindfulness, unhelpfulness, unobligingness, unkindness, unfriendliness, ungraciousness, uncharitableness **7 act of malevolence**, harm, disservice, mischief, crime, threat, menace, intimidation, blackmail, foul play, atrocity, outrage, bloodshed, torture, slaughter, murder, killing, massacre, homicide, genocide, fraticide, patricide, matricide, infanticide, abuse, hurt, assault, rape

ADJECTIVES 8 malevolent, ill-willed, ill-natured, ill-disposed, evil, malignant, pernicious, wicked, hating, hateful, malicious, malefic, baleful, intolerant, persecuting, oppressive, tyrannical, intimidatory, menacing, harassing **9 cruel**, inhumane, subhuman, dehumanized, atrocious, outrageous, barbaric, brutal, savage, bestial, vicious, ferocious, violent, sadistic, monstrous, terrorful, heinous, bloodthirsty, cannibalistic, murderous, fiendish, devilish, satanic, demoniac, diabolical, hellish **10 callous**, unfeeling, unnatural, obdurate, hard, hard-hearted, heartless, cold, cold-hearted, cold-blooded, steely, stony, flinty, harsh, rough, severe, stern, grim, dour, gruff, rugged, tough **11 merciless**, pitiless, ruthless **12 hostile**, truculent, antagonistic, mean, nasty, spiteful, rancorous, splenetic, virulent, venomous, poisonous, baneful, vitriolic, vindictive, beastly, snide, waspish, viperish, bitter, tart, acrimonious, resentful, acerbic, sour, astringent, mordant, sarcastic, acidic, acrid, caustic, sharp, cutting, biting **13 inconsiderate**, thoughtless, insensitive, uncaring, unconcerned, unfeeling, unresponsive, unheedful, unmindful, unhelpful, unobliging, unaccommodating, unsympathetic, unkind, unfriendly, sullen, ungracious, inhospitable, unchristian

VERBS 14 be malevolent, hate, loathe **15 kill**, murder, slaughter, massacre **16 torment**, attack, harm, hurt, injure, abuse, rape, molest, maltreat, beat, tyrannize, oppress, persecute, intimidate, bully, harass, victimize, terrorize, torture, menace, hound, harry, threaten, frighten, scare, demand **17 be pitiless**, be merciless

446 Mammals

NOUNS 1 mammal, warm-blooded animal, homoiotherm **2 egg-laying mammal**, prototherian, monotreme, platypus **3 pouched mammal**, metatherian, marsupial **4 placental mammal**, eutherian **5 insect-eating mammal**, shrews, moles, etc.), anteater, scaly anteater, pangolin, pholidote, spiny anteater, echidna, ant bear, aardvark **6 flying mammal**, chiropteran **7 flesh-eating mammal**, carnivore, canine, wolves, foxes, jackals, etc.), otters, badgers, etc.), civets, etc.), *or* hyaenas), feline **8 dog**, bitch, whelp, pup, puppy, mongrel, lurcher, cur, tyke, pariah dog, pi-dog, hound, gundog, watchdog, tracker dog, sniffer dog, guide dog, sheepdog, show dog, toy dog, Fido, **9 cat**, wild cat, big cat, mouser, ratter, tom, gib, queen, grimalkin **10 marine mammal**, dolphins, porpoises), phocids, sealions, walrus), sea cow **11 gnawing mammal**, rodent, squirrels, chipmunks, etc.), rats, mice, lemmings, gerbils, voles, etc.), cavies, etc.), leporids, rabbits **12 toothless mammal**, sloths **13 pachyderm**, subungulate, Jumbo, mastodon, mammoth), rhinoceros, hippopotamus **14 hoofed mammal**, ungulate, ungulant, tapirs, rhinoceroses), artiodactyl, hogs, swine), hippopotamus, ruminant, cud-chewer, llamas, etc.), giraffe, okapi, bovid, antelopes, gazelles, goats, ovines, sheep **15 primate**, lorises, bushbabies, tarsiers, etc.), anthropoids, monkeys, howlers, marmosets, tamarins, etc.), baboons, etc.), apes, great apes, orangutan, chimpanzee, gorilla), *Homo sapiens*, human, human being), primatology **16 mammologist**, primatologist

ADJECTIVES 17 mammalian, warm-blooded, homoiothermic, prototherian, monotrematous, metatherian, marsupialian, eutherian **18 insectivorous**, anteating, pholidote, tubulidentate, edentate **19 chiropteran**, dermopteran, winged **20 carnivorous**, unguiculate, canine, doggy, foxy, vulpine, lupine, ursine, weaselly, musteline, viverrine, feline, leonine **21 cetacean**, cetaceous, pinnipedian **22 rodent-like**, rodentian, gnawing, murine, ratty, mousy **23 rabbit-like**, rabbity, lagomorphic **24 pachydermatous**, subungulate, proboscidean, elephantine **25 ungulate**, unguligrade, cloven-hoofed, perissodactyl, equine, horsy, asinine, mulish, artiodactylous, piggy, porcine, swinish, ruminant, camelid, cervid, cervine, bovid, bovine, bullish, taurine, ovine, caprine, hircine, cavicorn **26 primate**, primatial, prosimian, anthropoid, simian

VERBS 27 give birth, drop, farrow, lamb, foal, calve **28 lactate**, milk, nurse, suckle **29 graze**, ruminate

447 Management

VERBS 1 manage, administer, organize, orchestrate, mastermind, govern, rule, regulate, control, supervise, superintend, motivate, direct, lead, oversee, manipulate, manoeuvre, influence, handle, conduct, run, minister, prescribe, caretake, invigilate, nurse, look after, police, legislate **2 direct**, command, lead, head, boss, pioneer, precede, dictate, hold power, have responsibility, preside, chair, captain, skipper, pilot, cox, steer, navigate, indicate, advise, counsel, shepherd, guide, conduct, escort, accompany, channel, canalize, funnel, route, train, introduce

NOUNS 3 management, administration, organization, orchestration, control, conduct, motivation, manipulation, running, handling, managership, stewardship, proctorship, agency, commission, power, authority, supervision, superintendence, overview, surveillance, care, charge, patronage, protection, tact, judgment, decision-making, skill, policy, housekeeping, housewifery, husbandry, economics, statesmanship, statecraft, government, regimen, regulation, legislation, department, ministry, cabinet, bureaucracy, civil service, secretariat, government office **4 directorship**, responsibility, command, control, dictatorship, leadership, premiership, chairmanship, captaincy, superiority, guidance, steering, pilotage, steersmanship **5 guide**, controls, reins, helm, rudder, wheel, tiller, joystick, pole star, lodestar, needle, compass, binnacle, automatic pilot, direction-finding, beam, radar, lighthouse, foghorn, buoy **6 governing body**, administration, quango, committee, cabinet, council, board, directorate, management, executive, employers, bosses **7 council**, round table, board room, court, tribunal, presidium, consistory, vestry, cabinet, panel, board, commission, assembly, conference, conventicle, congregation, ecclesia, conclave, convocation, synod, convention, congress, meeting, summit, durbar, diet, moot, folkmoot, comitia, zemstvo, soviet, genro, hearing, audience, sitting **8 leader**, governor, Messiah, Mahdi, ayatollah, guru, maharajah, spearhead, team captain, shepherd, teamster, pacemaker, compere, ringmaster, high priest, conductor, precentor, drum major, ringleader, demagogue, rabble-rouser, agitator, captain, condottiere, autocrat

9 manager, manageress, VIP, kingpin, administrator, executive, executor, doer, statesman, politician, procurator, housekeeper, housewife, househusband, chatelaine, steward, bailiff, agent, superintendent, supervisor, inspector, overseer, foreman, ganger, gaffer, charge hand, warden, matron, sister, protector, proctor, chief whip, custodian, caretaker, curator **10 official**, officer, tin god, marshal, steward, representative, senator, peer, civil servant, apparatchik, vizier, secretary, minister, secretary-general, bureaucrat, Eurocrat, mandarin, magistrate, commissioner, prefect, intendant, consul, proconsul, counsellor, praetor, quaestor, aedile, ambassador, envoy, alderman, mayor, councillor

ADJECTIVES 11 managerial, administrative, executive, organizational, directorial, leading, hegemonic, directional, guiding, steering, navigational, governing, controlling, political, official, bureaucratic, governmental, presidential, gubernatorial, legislative, judicial, authoritative, officious, dictatorial, despotic, tyrannical, supervisory, nomothetic, high-level, top-level **12 parliamentary**, congressional, senatorial, legislative, deliberative, unicameral, bicameral, conciliar, convocational, ecclesiastical, synodal

448 Market

NOUNS 1 market, mart, street market, bazaar, flea market, flower market, auction room, saleroom, corn exchange, wheat pit, custom house, horse fair **2 fair**, world fair, international fair, trade fair, show, motor show, boat show, exhibition, exposition **3 seller's market**, buyer's market, bear market, bull market, black market **4 free market**, open market, Common Market, single market **5 stock market**, Stock Exchange, securities market, commodity exchange, bourse, The City, bucket shop **6 marketplace**, forum **7 emporium**, arcade, shopping mall, pedestrian precinct, shopping centre, trading centre, entrepot, depot, warehouse, wharf **8 store**, shop, retail outlet, department store, chain store, multiple store, boutique, bargain basement, corner shop, supermarket, superstore, hypermarket, concern, firm, establishment, trading company **9 stall**, booth, stand, newsstand, kiosk, barrow, vending machine, counter **10 bazaar**, bring-and-buy sale, rummage sale

449 Marriage

• *I married beneath me – all women do.* Nancy Astor.

• *But if they cannot contain, let them marry: for it is better to marry than to burn.* Bible: I Corinthians.

• *Marriage has many pains, but celibacy has no pleasures.* Samuel Johnson.

• *Marriage is like life in this – that it is a field of battle, and not a bed of roses.* Robert Louis Stevenson.

NOUNS 1 marriage, matrimony, wedlock, conjugality, union, match, alliance, conjugal bliss, nuptial bond, wedded bliss, marriage bed **2 alliance**, merger, union, link, connection, consolidation, association, amalgamation, partnership, tieup **3 types of marriage**, monogamy, polygamy, Mormonism, polygyny, polyandry, bigamy, deuterogamy, trigamy, remarriage, morganatic marriage, love match, levirate, trial marriage, mixed marriage, intermarriage, miscegenation, exogamy, endogamy, misalliance, mesalliance, free love, arranged marriage **4 marriageability**, nubility, ripeness, good match, suitable match, eligible party **5 wedding**, wedding ceremony, white wedding, church wedding, nuptial mass, marriage vows, nuptials, hymenal rites, betrothal, spousal, civil wedding **6 bridal party**, bride, bridesmaid, attendant, flower girl, bridegroom, groom, best man, usher **7 spouse**, bride, blushing bride, bridegroom, groom, soul mate, helpmate, helpmeet **8 married couple**, bridal pair, newlyweds, honeymooners **9 married man**, husband, househusband, consort, benedick, monogamist, monogynist, old man, cuckold, bigamist, polygamist **10 married woman**, wife, housewife, lady, good lady, old lady, matron, common-law wife, concubine, better half **11 partner**, cohabitant, live-in lover **12 matchmaker**, marriage broker, go-between, mediator, marriage bureau, dating agency

VERBS 13 marry, wed, elope, cohabit, honeymoon, commit bigamy **14 join in marriage**, give away **15 matchmake**, match **16 live together**, cohabit **17 merge**, unite, ally, link, connect, consolidate

ADJECTIVES 18 matrimonial, marital, conjugal, connubial, nuptial, hymeneal, spousal, premarital, concubinal, matronly, wifely, bridal **19 married**, wedded, united, espoused, partnered, joined, paired, coupled, mated, newlywed, matched, one **20 marriageable**, nubile, eligible, suitable, betrothed, engaged, promised, affianced, plighted **21 monogamous**, bigamous, digamous, polygamous, polygynous, polyandrous

450 Master

NOUNS 1 master, mistress, lord, overlord, liege, nobleman, aristocrat, lady, dame, husband, wife, sir, madam, matron, mother superior, housemother, patriarch, matriarch, dowager, elder, landowner, squire, landlord, landlady, proprietor, governor, sahib, bwana **2 sovereign**, monarch, king, Rex, queen, Regina, queen mother, queen regent, prince, crown prince, prince regent, princess, crown princess, emperor, Caesar, empress, rajah, rani, Kaiser, Kaiserin, tsar, tsarina, Pharaoh, shah, khan, mikado, Mogul, maharajah, nabob, sultan **3 leader**, president, prime minister, premier, chancellor, minister, cabinet member, governor general, high commissioner, pasha, suzerain, viceroy, proconsul, consul, mayor, Lord Mayor, Lady Mayor, mayoress, judge, magistrate, sheriff, constable, marshal, justice, official, chief whip, officer, functionary, dignitary, ruler, potentate, protector, chief, chieftain, headman, sheik, rajah **4 absolute ruler**, autocrat, tyrant, dictator, despot, satrap, warlord, shogun, oppressor, captor, martinet, Big Brother, tin god, petty tyrant **5 company leader**, executive, director, chair, chairman, chairwoman, chairperson, manager, controller, tycoon

ADJECTIVES 6 masterful, magistral,

lordly, noble, aristocratic, magisterial, majestic, matronly, patriarchal, matriarchal, divine, royal, principal, main, major, great, parliamentary, autocratic, authoritarian, dominating, domineering, coercive, imperious, dictatorial, despotic, oppressive, executive, managerial, capitalistic, plutocratic, oligarchic, papal, pontifical, cardinal, rabbic, rabbinical, commanding **7 excellent**, expert, specialist, professional, scholarly, intellectual, masterly, skilful, adept, proficient, first-rate, supreme, consummate, competent, good at

VERBS 8 master, rule, lead, govern, dictate, oppress, conquer, vanquish, defeat, beat, overpower, overcome, crush, quell, subdue, subjugate, dominate, control, command, direct, manage, head **9 learn**, understand, comprehend, apprehend, grasp, acquire

451 Materials

NOUNS 1 materials, raw materials, resources, the essentials, the basics, elements, components, constituents, stuff, substance, matter, staple, stock, grain, grist, meat, fuel, mineral, metal, clay, soil, sand, glass, plastic, polythene, polystyrene, acrylic, nylon, polyester, polyurethane, latex, cellulose, fibreglass, carbon fibre, rope, yarn, fibre, fabric, cloth, textile, hide, parchment, vellum, wood, timber, board, beam, plank, lath **2 building material**, building block, breeze block, stone, marble, masonry, shingle, tile, slate, thatch, paving stone, flagstone, cobble, compo, composition, cement, concrete, hard core, gravel, asphalt **3 paper**, stationery, sheet, quire, ream, foolscap, writing paper, notepaper, typing paper, computer paper, wrapping paper, toilet paper, rag paper, rice paper, greaseproof paper, newsprint, cardboard, card, pasteboard, cartridge paper, Bible paper, tissue paper, tracing paper, crepe paper, cellophane

452 Material World

NOUNS 1 material world, real world, nature, materiality, existence, corporeity, corporality, bodiliness, substantiality, physical being, concreteness, tangibility, palpability, solidity, density, weight **2 materialization**, embodiment, incarnation, corporation, epiphany, manifestation, reincarnation, metempsychosis, realization, positivism, materialism, empiricism, scientism, unspirituality, worldliness **3 materialist**, Marxist, realist, humanist, positivist, chemist, physicist, atomist **4 matter**, material, materiality, stuff, mass, fabric, body, frame, structure, substance, corpus, plasma, protoplasm, cells, organism, element, principle, origin, factor, component, constituent, mineral, monad, element, isotope, atom, molecule, elementary particle, electron, neutron, meson, proton, quark, nucleus, nucleon, photon, quantum, ion **5 object**, body, person, thing, something, commodity, article, item, artefact **6 natural science**, biology, chemistry, geophysics, physics, mechanics, thermodynamics, electromagnetism

ADJECTIVES 7 material, tangible, substantial, sensible, real, natural, massy, solid, massive, concrete, palpable, ponderable, weighty, physical, empirical, spatiotemporal, objective, impersonal, clinical, incarnate, embodied, somatic, corporal, bodily, fleshly, carnal, reincarnated, realized, materialized, worldly, earthly

VERBS 8 be material, exist, substantialize, reify, objectify, externalize, make real, corporealize, embody, incarnate

453 Mathematics

- *Let no one ignorant of mathematics enter here.* Plato.
- *Numbers constitute the only universal language.* Nathaniel West.

NOUNS 1 mathematics, pure mathematics, arithmetic, algebra, calculus, geometry, trigonometry, numerical analysis, systems analysis, statistics, mathematical logic, metamathematics, numeracy, calculation, computation, reckoning, numeration, enumeration, quantification, numbering, counting, figuring, quantifying, mental arithmetic, measurement, count, census, tally, score, numbers, figures, sums, formula, solution, result **2 mathematician**, arithmetician, algebraist, geometrician, numerical analyst, systems analyst **3 natural number**, cardinal, ordinal, finite number, infinite number, transfinite number **4 number system**, counting system, decimal system, binary system, octal notation, hexadecimal notation, duodecimal notation, base, radix point, decimal point, significant digits, significant figures, fixed-point notation **5 mathematical symbol**, plus sign, minus sign, multiplication sign, division sign, equals sign, radical sign, integral sign, implication sign, operator **6 addition**, summation, sum, aggregate, total, addend **7 subtraction**, difference, subtrahend **8 multiplication**, product, multiplier, multiplicand, multiple, factor, power, exponent, index, surd, factorial, factorization, exponentiation **9 division**, long division, divisibility, quotient, ratio, proportion, percentage, reciprocal, inverse, dividend, divisor, remainder, fraction, decimal, truncation, rounding up **10 other mathematical terms**, logarithm, sequence, series, set, matrix, binomial expression, binomial, polynomial, coefficient, equation, algorithm, fractal, function, mapping, transformation, calculus, differentiation **11 graph**, chart, plot, bar graph, histogram, pie chart, scatter diagram, scattergram, axis, scale, origin **12 geometry**, plane geometry, solid geometry, coordinate geometry, analytic geometry, algebraic geometry, projective geometry, differential geometry, spherical geometry, Euclidean geometry **13 trigonometry**, plane trigonometry, spherical trigonometry, triangulation, sine rule, cosine rule **14 statistics**, descriptive statistics, statistical inference, statistical analysis, probability theory, vital statistics, parametric statistics **15 statistical methods**, population, sample, random sample, stochastic process, frequency distribution, probability distribution, parameter, average, mean, median, mode, weighting, standard deviation, range, correlation **16 mathematical logic**, formal logic, propositional calculus, logical proposition, statement, premise, assertion, denial, logical formula, logical connective, operator, negation, conjunction, disjunction, alternation, conditional, relationship, truth value, logical value

ADJECTIVES 17 mathematical, algebraic, topological **18 numerical**, positive, negative, even, odd, integral, whole, digital, fractional, decimal, denary, binary **19 numerable**, enumerable, denumerable, countable, quantifiable, measurable, mensurable, calculable, computable, soluble, insoluble, decidable **20 pictorial**, diagrammatic, graphic **21 logical**, deductive, inductive, inferential, equivalent, consistent, compatible, necessary, sufficient, contingent, conditional, tautological, contradictory

454 Maxim

NOUNS 1 maxim, saying, proverb, adage, aphorism, apophthegm, saw, gnome, oracle, mot, witticism, epigram, epigraph, motto, slogan, catchphrase, catchword, watchword, byword, epithet, tag, moral, axiom, truth, truism, banality, cliché, platitude, commonplace, bromide, precept, order, dictum, formula, mantra, theorem, rule, law

ADJECTIVES 2 proverbial, aphoristic, gnomic, epigrammatic, axiomatic, banal, clichéd, platitudinous, commonplace, trite, hackneyed, stock, stereotyped, sententious, moralistic, preceptive, witty, pithy

VERBS 3 aphorize, epigrammatize, proverb, moralize, pronounce, utter, theorize, formulate, observe

455 Meaning

NOUNS 1 meaning, signification, sense, message, idea, denotation, substance, essence, spirit, sum, gist, pith, core, contents, text, matter, topic, value, drift, tenor, purport, import, implication, connotation, colouring, effect, force, relevance, bearing, scope, context, meaningfulness, expression, diction, style, semantics, semasiology, sematology, semiotics **2 significance**, seriousness, importance, import, substance **3 comprehension**, clarity, plainness, explicitness, univocal, monosemy, unambiguity, double meaning, multivocal, polysemy, ambiguity **4 type of meaning**, denotation, plainness, literality, connotation, interpretation, explanation, definition, reference, application, construction, context, intention, intelligibility, derivation, etymology, usage, practice, jargon, idiom, equivalence, synonym, identity, opposite, antonym, semantic shift, metaphor, trope, latency, nonsense **5 point**, purpose, aim, object, end, idea, plan, design, intention, intent, value

ADJECTIVES 6 meaningful, etymological, denotative, comprehensible, intelligible, unambiguous, univocal, monosemous, clear, plain, lucid, perspicuous, literal, express, explicit, pointed, declaratory, affirmative, indicative, repeated, tautological, identical, similar, synonymous, equivalent, paraphrastic, tantamount, connotative, implied, implicit, inferred, tacit, suggestive, unclear, obscure, confused, technical, professional, special, contrary, opposite, antonymous, homonymous, extended, transferred, ambiguous, multivocal, polysemous, equivocal, symbolic, figurative, metaphorical, allegorical, idiomatic, significative, importing, purporting, evocative, expressive, interpretative, telling, eloquent, allusive, meaningless, nonsensical **7 significant**, consequential, serious, important, weighty, substantial, pithy, meaty **8 semantic**, semasiological, semiotic, linguistic, philological, verbal **9 meant**, implied, intended, deliberate, designed, planned

VERBS 10 mean, signify, communicate, denote, declare, assert, affirm, express, inform, tell, connote, imply, indicate, symbolize, represent, betoken, designate, import, purport, intend, point to, spell, convey, tell of, evidence, contemplate, allude to, refer to, hint at, suggest, intimate, rephrase, paraphrase, repeat, tautologize, coincide, accord, contradict **11 infer**, deduce **12 intend**, aim, purpose, plan, design, destine, predestine, cause, result in, bring about, entail, involve, portend

456 Meanness

ADJECTIVES 1 mean, miserly, parsimonious, ungenerous, grudging, tight, tightfisted, close, near, money-grubbing, niggardly, penurious, penny-pinching, scrimping, cheeseparing, mingy **2 unpleasant**, nasty, unkind, hurtful, spiteful, petty, small-minded, despicable, base, shabby, sordid

NOUNS 3 parsimony, niggardliness, miserliness, ungenerousness, tightness, tightfistedness, closefistedness, cheeseparing, stinginess **4 unpleasantness**, nastiness, hurtfulness, pettiness, spite, baseness, beastliness, shabbiness, lowliness **5 miser**, niggard, skinflint, hoarder, money-grubber, Scrooge

VERBS 6 hoard, save up, save, stint, scrimp, skimp **7 grudge**, begrudge

457 Means

NOUNS 1 means, way, manner, mode, steps, course, the wherewithal, the basics, power, capacity, ability, capability, trump card, ace, tool, instrument, vehicle, medium, agency, conveniences, facilities, appliances, tools, technology, knowledge, technique, knack, skill, process, approach, resort, recourse, expedient, device, contrivance, makeshift, substitute, remedy, cure, last resort, alternative **2 supplies**, provisions, stock, equipment, machinery, munitions, ammunition **3 human resources**, workforce, manpower, personnel, staff **4 financial resources**, funds, wealth, money, substance, liquidity, cash, capital, assets, premises, property, investments, revenue, income, receipts, credits, overdraft, creditworthiness, backing, support, sponsorship **5 reserves**, store, backup, emergency funds, nest egg

VERBS 6 find means, enable, facilitate, find, supply, furnish, provide, equip, prepare, staff, finance, fund, promote, sponsor, float, subsidize, plan, contrive

458 Measurement

NOUNS 1 measurement, mensuration, measure, metage, quantification, gauging, calibration, calculation, computation, metrology, assessment, valuation, rating, evaluation, appraisal, estimate, approximation, determination, survey, triangulation, geodesy, topography, cartography **2 measurability**, mensurability **3 size**, magnitude, height, altitude, depth, length, distance, range, scope, breadth, width, volume, capacity, weight, quantity, amount, dosage, degree, extent, value, coordinates, latitude, longitude, azimuth **4 measuring system**, metric system, imperial system, apothecaries' measure, troy weight **5 measuring instrument**, measuring rod, yardstick, foot rule, feeler gauge, plumb line, chain, ruler, tape measure, scale, vernier, dividers, callipers, set square, protractor, quadrant, sextant, octant, astrolabe, log, echo sounder, dipstick, waterline

VERBS 6 measure, admeasure, quantify, meter, gauge, calibrate, grade, graduate, calculate, assess, value, cost, rate, evaluate, appraise, estimate, determine, survey, triangulate, plumb, sound, fathom, probe, assay, weigh, time, size up **7 measure out**, weigh out, dole out, share

ADJECTIVES 8 metrical, metric, micrometric, volumetric, photometric, barometric, tachometric, optometric, psychometric, linear, cubic, mensural, mensurational, quantitative, metrological, geodetic, topographic **9 measured**, quantified, metered, gauged, calibrated, graduated, reckoned, assessed, valued, rated, estimated, determined, surveyed, triangulated, plotted **10 measurable**, mensurable, quantifiable, meterable, gaugeable, calculable, computable, assessable, appraisable

459 Mediation

VERBS 1 mediate, negotiate, arbitrate, referee, umpire, judge, officiate, reconcile, conciliate, pacify, propitiate, moderate, intercede, intervene, interpose

NOUNS 2 mediation, negotiation, arbitration, give-and-take, coming-together, conciliation, reconciliation, diplomacy, statesmanship, judgment, umpirage, pacification, propitiation, moderation, intervention, interposition, intercession, stepping-in, troubleshooting, good offices **3 mediator**, intermediary, intercessor, negotiator, arbiter, referee, umpire, judge, diplomat, statesman, pacifier, propitiator, peacemaker, dove, appeaser, conciliator, moderator, troubleshooter, middleman, go-between, liaison, matchmaker, pander, adviser, counsellor **4 representative**, rep, delegate, spokesperson, mouthpiece, agent, publicist, press agent, ombudsman, attorney, accountant, consultant, adviser, counsellor, pleader, propitiator **5 conference**, parley

ADJECTIVES 6 mediatory, arbitral, diplomatic, intercessory, pacificatory, propitiatory

460 Medicine

• *The art of medicine is generally a question of time.* Ovid.

NOUNS 1 medicine, medical practice, medical profession, medical ethics, Hippocratic oath, medical jurisprudence, allopathic medicine, conventional medicine, internal medicine, tropical medicine, industrial medicine, occupational medicine, community medicine, public-health medicine, preventive medicine, medical care, health care, general practice, private medicine **2 natural medicine**, traditional medicine, folk medicine, faith healing, holistic medicine, alternative medicine, complementary medicine, supplementary medicine, fringe medicine, herbalism, homeopathy, naturopathy, osteopathy, chiropractic, acupuncture, acupressure, shiatsu, aromatherapy, reflexology **3 medical specialty**, anaesthetics, anaesthesiology, gynaecology, obstetrics, paediatrics, teratology, embryology, geriatrics, gerontology, nostology, orthopaedics, rheumatology, osteology, gastroenterology, nephrology, urology, venereology, genitourinary medicine, dermatology, neurology, ophthalmology, otology, nose, and throat), otorhinolaryngology, otolaryngology, nuclear medicine, cardiology, oncology, radiology, haematology, serology, immunology, endocrinology, biochemistry, medical genetics, eugenics, bacteriology, microbiology, virology, parasitology, toxicology, epidemiology, posology, nosology, aetiology, symptomatology, semeiology, pathology, forensic medicine, biomedicine **4 dentistry**, exodontics, endodontics, orthodontics, prosthodontics, periodontics, periodontology, fillings, crowning, capping, scaling, polishing, extraction **5 veterinary medicine**, animal welfare **6 health care**, health education, community medicine, public-health medicine, preventive medicine, prophylaxis, immunization, inoculation, vaccination, fluoridation, nutrition, dietetics, hygiene, genetic counselling, midwifery, chiropody, podiatry, call-out, home visit, case history, medical, physical, internal examination, second-opinion, referral, prognosis **7 diagnosis**, diagnostics, prognosis, test, screening, sample, biopsy, puncture, amniocentesis, fetoscopy, radiography, diagnostic radiology, barium meal, barium enema, radiograph, X-ray, arteriography, angiogram, lymphogram, venogram, mammothermography, mammogram, pyelogram, scanning, ultrasound scan, tomogram, CT scan, PET scan, endoscopy, bronchoscopy, laparoscopy, gastroscopy, colposcopy, ureteroscopy, cystoscopy, stethoscope, ophthalmoscope, auriscope, otoscope, endoscope, fibrescope, fetoscope, bronchoscope, gastroscope, laparoscope, colposcope, ureteroscope, cystoscope **8 treatment**, therapy, therapeutics, nursing, medical intervention, allopathy, medication, prescription, naturopathy, homeopathy, herbalism, chemotherapy, immunotherapy, radiotherapy, therapeutic radiology, gene therapy, dialysis, surgery, physiotherapy, orthontics, osteopathy, chiropractic, speech therapy, occupational therapy, rehabilitation **9 surgery**, general surgery, heart surgery, open-heart surgery, bypass surgery, brain surgery, neurosurgery, plastic surgery, dental surgery, psychosurgery, major surgery, minor surgery, keyhole surgery, laser surgery, surgical operation, operation, premedication, sedation, induction, anaesthesia, acupuncture, incision, section, resection, division, excision, amputation, advancement, transplantation, grafting, transfusion, perfusion **10 hospital**, general hospital, teaching hospital, community hospital, cottage hospital, NHS hospital, private hospital, infirmary, sanitorium, nursing home, convalescent home, rest home, hospice, ward, operating theatre, ICU), dispensary, clinic, polyclinic, out-patient clinic, health centre, surgery **11 doctor**, physician, surgeon, medical practitioner, family doctor, locum, medical student, hospital doctor, intern, resident, houseman, house physician, house surgeon, registrar, consultant, health officer **12 healer**, therapist, faith healer, acupuncturist, homeopath, naturopath, aromatherapist, reflexologist, osteopath, chiropractor, bonesetter, herbalist **13 medical specialist**, specialist, consultant, clinician, diagnostician, heart surgeon, brain surgeon, neurosurgeon **14 dentist**, dental surgeon, oral surgeon, exodontist, endodontist, orthodondist, prosthodontist, periodontist, periodontologist **15 veterinarian**, veterinary **16 nurse**, sister, matron, school nurse, day nurse, night nurse, district nurse, health visitor, midwife, Florence Nightingale **17 paramedic**, radiographer, physiotherapist, occupational therapist, speech therapist, dietician, nutritionist, chiropodist, hygienist, dental hygienist, nurse, midwife, carer, ambulanceman, stretcher-bearer, dresser, medical auxiliary, orderly, dental technician **18 patient**, in-patient, out-patient, case

VERBS 19 practise medicine, hold surgery, examine, refer, diagnose, prognosticate, immunize, inoculate, vaccinate, test for, X-ray, scan, treat, doctor, prescribe, medicate, administer, inject, minister to, nurse, tend, cure, heal **20 practise surgery**, sedate, anaesthetize, operate, induce, incise, excise, amputate, transfuse, perfuse, suture, dialyse **21 practise dentistry**, descale, polish, fill, stop

ADJECTIVES 22 medical, iatric, Hippocratic, clinical, allopathic, homeopathic, surgical, osteopathic, gynaecological, obstetric, paediatric, geriatric, neurological, dermatological, urological, ophthalmological, cardiac, radiological, epidemiological, forensic, pathological **23 dental**, oral, orthodontic, exodontic, endodontic, prosthodontic, periodontic **24 diagnostic**, symptomatological, symptomatic, prognostic **25 therapeutic**, medicinal, preventive, prophylactic

461 Melody

NOUNS 1 melody, tune, air, song, aria, strain, measure, theme, subject, motif, leitmotif, line, cantus, canto, refrain, reprise, descant, chorus **2 song**, chanson, aubade, serenade, lullaby, berceuse, barcarolle, round, madrigal, glee, lay, roundelay, lilt, shanty, yodel, lyric, calypso, spiritual, chant, plainchant, cantide, chorale, carol, hymn, psalm, anthem **3 melodiousness**, musicality, euphony, harmoniousness, chime, concord, consonance **4 harmonics**, unison, homophony, monophony, monody, counterpoint, polyphony, heterophony, cantus firmus, tonality, resolution, cadence, fauxbourdon, faburden, continuo, syncopation, timing, rhythm, tempo, beat, phrasing, passage, figure, se-

quence, orchestration, instrumentation, arrangement, passacaglia
ADJECTIVES 5 melodious, musical, tuneful, lyrical, canorous, lilting, singable, catchy, tripping, soft, sweet, dulcet, velvety, mellow, smooth, sweet-sounding, honeyed, mellifluous, Orphean, silvery, golden-toned, fine-toned, true, well-pitched, clear, chiming, full-toned, resonant, full, rich, euphonious **6 harmonious**, concordant, consonant, agreeing, unanimous, attuned, homophonic, monophonic, monodic, polyphonic, synchronous, syncopated, corresponding, assonant
VERBS 7 harmonize, accord, chime in, synchronize, attune, tune, agree, conform, correspond, rhyme **8 set to music**, melodize, harmonize, symphonize, orchestrate, syncopate, score **9 sing**, vocalize, lilt, warble, trill

462 Memory

- *Memories are hunting horns whose sound dies on the wind.* Guillaume Apollinaire.
- *Old men forget; yet all shall be forgot,/ But he'll remember, with advantages,/ What feats he did that day.* William Shakespeare.

NOUNS 1 memory, recollection, remembrance, recall, retention, memorization, reminiscence, anamnesis, retrospection, reflection, hindsight, evocation, nostalgia, recognition **2 retrospect**, review, flashback, *déjà vu*, history, memoirs, autobiography **3 memento**, souvenir, token, keepsake, memorabilia, trophy, relic, commemoration, memorial, monument, statue, plaque **4 reminder**, memorandum, memo, note, diary, album, scrapbook, record, mnemonic, cue **5 day to remember**, memory, centenary, bicentenary, tercentenary, anniversary, fame **6 artificial memory**, computer memory
ADJECTIVES 7 memorable, unforgettable, notable, noteworthy, remembered, unforgotten, indelible, haunting, evocative, reminiscent, nostalgic, reminding **8 remembering**, retrospective **9 memorized**, unforgotten **10 memorial**, commemorative
VERBS 11 memorize, learn, remember **12 remember**, recall, recollect, conjure up, recognize, identify, review, retrace, recapture, hark back, reminisce **13 remind**, prompt, brush up, recapitulate, review **14 commemorate**, memorialize, remember, honour, toast, observe **15 be remembered**, make history

463 Meteorology and Climatology

NOUNS 1 meteorology, aerology, weather forecasting, micrometeorology, macrometeorology, atmospheric physics, hydrometeorology, hyetography, nephology, nephanalysis, anemology **2 meteorologist**, climatologist, weather forecaster, weatherman, weatherwoman **3 weather**, pattern, conditions, the elements, weather lore, Groundhog Day, dog days, halcyon days, blackthorn winter **4 weather forecast**, outlook, shipping forecast, general synopsis, hurricane warning, tornado watch, weather map, isobar, isotherm, Meteorological Office, air pressure, air temperature, dewpoint, humidity, air density, wind speed, wind-chill factor, anemogram, barometer, aneroid barometer, barograph, weatherglass, thermometer, wind gauge, windsock, wind cone, wind sleeve, drogue, weather vane, weathercock, wind rose, rain gauge, weather radar **5 atmosphere**, air, troposphere, stratosphere, ionosphere, ozone layer, ozonosphere, exosphere, tropopause, stratopause, atmospheric dust, pollution, atmospheric circulation, air current, airflow, air stream, jetstream, thermal, downdraught, updraught, front, cold front, warm front, occlusion **6 weather system**, pressure system, frontal system, depression, cyclone, warm sector, anticyclone, trough **7 wind**, breeze, zephyr, sea breeze, gale, storm, hurricane, tornado, typhoon, scud, squall, wind storm, dust storm, sandstorm **8 wind strength**, wind force, wind speed, Beaufort scale, windiness, gustiness, breeziness, high wind, blow, blast **9 wind direction**, north wind, east wind, south wind, west wind, prevailing wind, head wind, crosswind, tail wind, following wind, favourable wind, wind shift, backing, veering, wind vortex, eddy, waterspout, whirlwind, dust devil **10 wind system**, trade winds, doldrums, horse latitudes, roaring forties, antitrade winds **11 cloud**, cirrus, cirrocumulus, altostratus, cirrostratus, altocumulus, nimbostratus, stratocumulus, stratus, cumulus, cumulonimbus, rain cloud, nimbus, scud, storm cloud, thundercloud, anvil cloud, dark cloud, noctilucent cloud, cloud cover, cloudiness, overcast sky **12 thunderstorm**, thunder, thunderclap, lightning, lightning flash, track, fork lightning, sheet lightning, ball lightning, thunderbolt, electric storm **13 sun**, sunshine, clear sky, cloudless sky, blue sky, sunlight, halo, corona, parhelion, anthelion, heat, heatwave, Indian summer, muggy spell, dryness, drought **14 precipitation**, dew, rain, rainfall, snowfall, raindrop, hailstone, snowflake, ice crystal, hydrometeor, rainwater, drizzle, shower, flurry, scattered showers, April showers, thundery shower, rainstorm, torrential rain, driving rain, deluge, downpour, cloudburst, spate, raininess, showeriness, pluviosity, wetness, flood, acid rain **15 rainbow**, double rainbow, fogbow **16 hail**, soft hail, hailstorm, sleet **17 snow**, snow storm, blizzard, driven snow, whiteout, snow cover, snowdrift, wet snow, powdery snow, granular snow, spindrift, consolidated snow, melt, slush **18 coldness**, cold snap, cold wave **19 fog**, ground fog, coastal fog, fog bank, freezing fog, smog, mist, brume, haze, fogginess, haziness **20 frost**, hoar frost, rime **21 climate**, local climate, microclimate, regional climate, macroclimate, maritime climate, continental climate, mountain climate, desert climate, tundra climate, tropical climate, subtropical climate, temperate climate, moderate climate, cool climate, polar climate, climatic zone, tropics, subtropics, temperate zone, continental zone, subpolar zone, polar zone **22 climatic change**, ice age, glaciation, interglaciation, postglaciation, global warming

ADJECTIVES 23 meteorologic, meteorological, synoptic, elemental, climatic **24 frontal**, cyclonic **25 fine**, fair, bright, sunny, dry, calm, clear, cloudless, mild, settled, fresh, bracing, brisk, crisp **26 windy**, breezy, blowy, gusty, blustery, squally, biting, freezing, bitter, icy, gale-force, northerly, boreal **27 stormy**, inclement, tempestuous **28 cloudy**, overcast, overclouded, dull, gloomy, grey, cirrose, cirriform, cumuliform, cumulous, stratous, stratiform, cumulonimbiform **29 warm**, mild, moderate, temperate, balmy, muggy, damp, close, sweltering, blistering **30 rainy**, pluvial, showery, wet, drizzly **31 cool**, chilly, nippy, frosty, icy, snowy, slushy, sleety **32 foggy**, fogbound, smoggy, misty

VERBS 33 forecast, predict **34 blow**, stir, sigh, sough, whisper, murmur, whistle, moan, gust, buffet, bluster **35 rain**, precipitate, shower, drizzle, pour, pelt, teem **36 snow**, hail, ice over, freeze, thaw **37 fog**, befog

464 Middle

NOUNS 1 middle, centre, epicentre, midst, midpoint **2 core**, nucleus, heart, hub, focus, pivot, fulcrum, bull's-eye, kernel, marrow, inside, interior, heartland, midst, focal point, keystone, lynchpin **3 median**, mean, golden mean, balance, par, average, medium, happy medium **4 midline**, equator, the Line, diameter, bisection, midsection, waistline **5 middle distance**, equidistance, midfield, midcourse, midstream, halfway, moiety **6 middle ground**, no-man's-land, grey area, compromise, mediation **7 middle age**, mid-life crisis **8 middle class**, bourgeoisie, professional class, white-collar class, merchant class, suburbia, burgherdom **9 middleman**, broker, distributor, intermediary, third party, interventionist, intercessor, counsellor, ombudsman, negotiator, spokesperson, mouthpiece, go-between, mediator, arbitrator, moderator, umpire, referee, medium, messenger

ADJECTIVES 10 middle, mid, central, medial, middlemost **11 midway**, halfway, equidistant, mezzanine, midstream, equatorial **12 core**, nuclear, focal, pivotal, inner, inside **13 median**, medial, mesial, mean, average, medium **14 mediatory**, intermediary, interim, neutral, moderate, middle-of-the-road **15 middling**, average, mediocre, ordinary, indifferent, undistinguished

VERBS 16 place in the middle, centre, focus, pivot, balance, interpose, sandwich **17 average**, bisect, halve, divide fifty-fifty **18 stand in the middle**, straddle **19 mediate**, arbitrate, umpire, referee, intervene, intercede, compromise, negotiate, bargain, meet halfway

465 Middle Way

NOUNS 1 middle way, mid-way, midpoint, centre, diameter, radius, nondeviation, straight line, short cut, beeline, short circuit, midcourse, median, medium, happy medium, average **2 middle of the road**, neutrality, noncommital, impartiality, compromise, moderation, balance, half measures, lukewarmness, mutuality

ADJECTIVES 3 middle, central, equidistant, midway, halfway, medial, intermediate, lukewarm, half-and-half, even, fifty-fifty, neutral, moderate, middle-of-the-road, unextreme, noncommital, detached,

indifferent, independent, nonpartisan, nonaligned, impartial, irresolute **4 undeviating**, direct
VERBS 5 be in the middle, hold straight **6 be halfway**, compromise, equalize, equivocate

466 Military Affairs

• *War is the continuation of politics by other means.* Karl von Clausewitz.
NOUNS 1 military affairs, military strategy, warcraft, arms, siegecraft, military tactics, logistics, campaign, strategic objectives, mobilization, military service, recruiting, conscription, impressment, operations, rank, base, camp, barracks **2 the military**, national defence, the services, army, navy, air force, marines, special forces, regular forces, mercenary forces, volunteer army, irregulars, reserves, Territorial Army, Home Guard, Senior Service, militia **3 military training**, military academy **4 military organization**, evacuation service, battle group, column, rank, file, detail, detachment, task force, squad, section, platoon, company, troop, battery, battalion, regiment, brigade, division, air division, submarine division, army corps, medical corps, dental corps, nurse corps, drum corps, bugle corps, quartermaster corps, transportation corps, field army, flight, squadron, wing, fleet, task group, flotilla **5 military staff**, general staff, Defence Council, commander, commanding officer, junior officer, platoon commander, company commander, battalion commander, regimental commander, brigade commander, cavalry commander, artillery commander, general officer, flag officer, senior commander, divisional commander **6 military law**, court marshal **7 militarism**, military tradition, military salute, military music, military honours
ADJECTIVES 8 military, martial, militant, naval, soldierly, gladiatorial, strategic, tactical, offensive, defensive, pre-emptive, aggressive, pugnacious, combative, bellicose, warlike **9 enlisted**, conscripted, drafted, commissioned, noncommissioned, regular, irregular, reserve
VERBS 10 enlist, join up, recruit, conscript, draft

467 Misanthropy

NOUNS 1 misanthropy, misandry, misogyny, cynicism, unsociability, antisociability, selfishness, egotism, inhumanity **2 misanthrope**, misandrist, misogynist, male chauvinist, antifeminist, sexist loner, solitary, unsocial person, cynic, egotist
ADJECTIVES 3 misanthropic, antisocial, unsociable, inhuman, cynical, egotistic, selfish, misandrous, man-hating, woman-hating
VERBS 4 become a misanthrope (*or* **misanthropist**), distrust people

468 Misinterpretation

VERBS 1 misinterpret, misunderstand, misapprehend, mistranslate, misread, misconstrue, misconceive, misjudge, misdiagnose, mistake, err, blunder, misspell, misrepresent, pervert, distort, wrench, twist, misquote, equivocate, read into, add, omit, suppress, subtract, falsify, garble, exaggerate, inflate, overestimate, underestimate, traduce, travesty, par-

ody, caricature, burlesque, ridicule, defame
NOUNS 2 misinterpretation, misunderstanding, misapprehension, mistranslation, misreading, misconstruction, misapplication, misdiagnosis, misconception, misjudgment, miscomputation, mistake, error, blunder, solecism, misspelling, misteaching, misrepresentation, false impression, lying, perversion, distortion, wrenching, twisting, manipulation, misquotation, equivocalness, circumlocution, word-play, catachresis, addition, omission, suppression, subtraction, falsification, garbling, overestimation, underestimation, exaggeration, inflation, traducement, travesty, parody, caricature, burlesque, ridiculing, defamation
ADJECTIVES 3 misinterpreted, misunderstood, mistranslated, misread, misconstrued, misconceived, mistaken, wrong, misspelt, solecistic, catachrestic, misquoted, garbled, falsified, distorted, exaggerated, inflated, misrepresented

469 Misjudgment

NOUNS 1 misjudgment, miscalculation, misconception, misconstruction, misinterpretation, misunderstanding, cross purposes, inexactness, underestimation, overestimation, undervaluation, overvaluation, false reading, distortion, deception, fallacy, fallibility, gullibility, self-deception **2 mistake**, error, blunder **3 injustice**, mistrial, partiality, partisanship, one-sidedness, predilection, predisposition, favouritism, nepotism, intolerance, discrimination, unfairness, inequality, unlawfulness, bias, prejudice, chauvinism, sectarianism, provincialism, parochialism, insularity, xenophobia, racism, apartheid, anti-Semitism, sexism, ageism, homophobia, bigotry, fanaticism, narrow-mindedness, tunnel vision, narrow mind **4 prejudgment**, preconception, fixation, obsession, predetermination
ADJECTIVES 5 misjudging, mistaken, wrong, muddled, fallible, gullible, misguided, misled, deluded **6 unjust**, unfair, discriminatory, prejudicial, partial, partisan, subjective, one-sided, predisposed, preferential, intolerant, biased, prejudiced, jaundiced, warped, twisted, chauvinistic, sectarian, provincial, parochial, insular, xenophobic, racist, colour-prejudiced, anti-Semitic, sexist, ageist, class-prejudiced, homophobic, snobbish, bigoted, fanatical, narrow-minded, hidebound, pedantic, unimaginative, prejudged, preconceived **7 misjudged**, misunderstood, misconstrued, misinterpreted, out, wrong, mistaken, ill-timed
VERBS 8 misjudge, miscalculate, misreckon, misinterpret, misconstrue, misunderstand, misconceive, misread, mistake, twist, distort, miss, trip, slip, stumble, blunder, bungle **9 be unjust**, discriminate, take sides, prejudge **10 bias**, prejudice, jaundice, warp

470 Misrepresentation

NOUNS 1 misrepresentation, distortion, deformation, twist, dissimiliarity, perversion, falsification, lie, fib, falsehood, exaggeration, grotesquerie, colouring, overemphasis, overdramatization, caricature, travesty, parody, burlesque, guy, flattering, nonrealism, daubing, botch **2 misinformation**, disinformation, misteaching, misevaluation, misinterpretation, garbling

VERBS 3 misrepresent, distort, deform, twist, pervert, falsify, slant, lie, exaggerate, colour, overemphasize, overdramatize, caricature, parody, travesty, burlesque, guy, flatter, overembellish, daub **4 misinform**, disinform, misteach, misevaluate, misinterpret, garble

ADJECTIVES 5 misrepresented, biased, slanted, unrepresentative, distorted, deformed, twisted, perverted, false, untrue, wrong, incorrect, inaccurate, dissimilar, unlike, unfair, unjust, exaggerated, caricatured, parodied, grotesque, flattering **6 misinformed**, mistaught, misinterpreted, garbled

471 Misuse

VERBS 1 misuse, abuse, misemploy, misdirect, divert, misappropriate, expropriate, embezzle, defraud, violate, desecrate, defile, profane, prostitute, pervert, distort, pollute, spoil, ill-use, ill-treat, mistreat, molest, harm, injure, manhandle, beat, batter, attack, force, strain, exploit, oppress, overwork, overtax, fatigue, impair, damage, misgovern, misrule, mismanage, maladminister, mishandle, bungle, waste, misapply, misjudge

NOUNS 2 misuse, abuse, misemployment, manipulation, misdirection, diversion, misappropriation, embezzlement, peculation, fraud, violation, desecration, profanation, defilement, impiety, prostitution, perversion, distortion, pollution, mistreatment, molestation, ill-treatment, ill-use, violence, force, outrage, assault, injury, harm, evil, exploitation, oppression, misrule, mismanagement, maladministration, malpractice, mishandling, bungling, malapropism, solecism, barbarism, overuse, extravagance, waste

ADJECTIVES 3 misused, abused, misemployed, misdirected, diverted, misappropriated, violated, desecrated, defiled, perverted, distorted, polluted, spoilt, unclean, ill-treated, beaten, battered, exploited, used, oppressed, mishandled, bungled **4 abusive**, violent, harmful, injurious, forceful, offensive, damaging, evil, exploitative, oppressive, fraudulent, extravagant, wasteful, barbarous, solecistic, outrageous

472 Mixture

NOUNS 1 mixture, mingling, stirring, shaking, blending, harmonization, association, combination, integration, syncretism, eclecticism, fusion, merger, union, amalgamation, conglomeration, composition, miscibility, infusion, suffusion, transfusion, instillation, infiltration, pervasion, permeation, saturation, penetration, impregnation, contamination, pollution, contagion, adulteration, involvement, entanglement, confusion, disorder, jumble, muddle, scramble, chaos, entropy, randomness, heterogeneity, hybridization, mongrelism, cross-breeding, miscegenation, intermarriage, syngamy **2 mixed thing**, blend, mélange, composition, harmony, association, synthesis, marriage, combination, compound, alloy, amalgam, fusion, infusion, solution, cocktail, punch, brew, linctus, potion, concoction, confection, potpourri, pastiche, stew, soup, broth, goulash, hash, ragout **3 miscellany**, medley, anthology, collection, thesaurus, variety, patchwork, mosaic, variegation, dappling, speckling, motley, job lot, hotchpotch, hash, mess, farrago, gallimaufry, potpourri, mishmash, linsey-woolsey, ragbag, jumble, lucky dip, tombola, conglomeration, muddle, tangle, imbroglio, confusion, kaleidoscope, phantasmagoria, babel, clatter, clamour, pandemonium, menagerie, zoo, circus, assortment, oddments

VERBS 4 mix, admix, stir, shake, knead, pound, pulverize, mash, brew, infuse, instil, imbue, impregnate, tinge, dye, colour, speckle, dapple, variegate, suffuse, combine, integrate, fuse, compound, alloy, amalgamate, merge, blend, harmonize, mingle, intersperse, interlard, interleave, interlay, intertwine, interweave, interlace, sprinkle, dilute, adulterate, temper, spice, season, fortify, lace, spike, pep up, doctor, meddle with, tamper with, spoil, mar, debase, contaminate, cross-fertilize, crossbreed, hybridize **5 mix up**, muddle, scramble, jumble, shuffle, confuse, bewilder, puzzle, confound **6 become mixed**, blend, integrate, penetrate, permeate, pervade, stain, infiltrate, infect, pollute, contaminate, intermarry **7 be mixed up**, misunderstand, puzzle over

ADJECTIVES 8 mixed, interracial, interfaith, mingled, interspersed, interlaced, interwoven, intertwined, miscible, soluble, stirred, shaken, blended, harmonized, combined, integrated, syncretic, eclectic, fused, mashed, alloyed, merged, amalgamated, half-and-half, tempered, sophisticated, adulterated, diluted, involved in, complicated, tangled, unsorted, disordered, jumbled, confused, chaotic, topsy-turvy, miscellaneous, random, patchy, heterogeneous, hybrid, mongrel, cross-bred, crossed, miscegenetic, interbred, intermarried, multiracial, multicultural, kaleidoscopic, variegated, dappled, speckled, mottled, motley, tinged, dyed, coloured **9 mixed-up**, muddled, jumbled, scrambled, confused, bewildered, puzzled, confounded

473 Moderation

•*Moderation is a fatal thing, Lady Hunstanton. Nothing succeeds like excess.* Oscar Wilde.

NOUNS 1 moderation, reasonableness, restraint, check, control, equanimity, composure, sang-froid, self-possession, sedateness, sobriety, coolness, calmness, quietness, nonviolence, temperance, steadiness, impartiality, neutrality, fairness, justness, average, happy medium, adjustment, modulation, regulation, compromise, mitigation, relaxation, remission, alleviation, assuagement, mollification, tranquillization, abatement, reduction, diminution **2 moderator**, controller, calming influence, restraining hand, peacemaker, mediator, arbitrator, judge, referee, umpire, chair person, cushion, buffer, restraint, brake, wet blanket, sedative, soporific, soothing influence, palliative, lenitive, analgesic, anaesthetic

VERBS 3 be moderate, sober up, settle down, disarm, remit, relent, ease off **4 moderate**, correct, adjust, modulate, regulate, mediate, judge, arbitrate, chair, preside, referee, umpire, curb, tame, check, restrict, constrain, limit, repress, restrain, chasten, govern, control, calm, temper, mollify, soften, cushion, dampen, subdue, sedate, tranquillize, anaesthetize, still, quieten, hush, lull, rock, sweeten, dulcify, mitigate, palliate, extenuate, weaken, obtund, blunt, dull, assuage, ease, soothe, relieve, alleviate, lighten, neutralize, smooth over, appease, pacify, allay, abate, play down, censor, tone down, euphemize

ADJECTIVES 5 moderate, medium, equable, balanced, steady, modest, judicious, just, fair, nonviolent, harmless, gentle, mild, weak, poor, middling, mediocre, indifferent, average, unexceptional, limited, restricted, sensible, rational, reasonable, restrained, controlled, chastened, subdued, quiet, untroubled, peaceful, tranquil, low-key, temperate, sober, calm, cool **6 politically moderate**, neutral, liberal, tolerant, centre, non-extreme, non-radical, non-reactionary, mugwumpish, non-committal **7 moderating**, lenitive, soothing, nonirritant, alleviative, assuaging, easing, pain-killing, analgesic, anodyne, calming, sedative, tranquillizing, narcotic, hypnotic, mesmeric, soporific, smooth, soft, bland, emollient, demulcent, lubricating, comforting

474 Modesty

• *Be modest! It is the kind of pride least likely to offend.* Jules Renard.

NOUNS 1 modesty, meekness, humility, unpretentiousness, unassumingness, unostentatious, unobtrusiveness **2 blushing**, flushing, colouring, reddening **3 bashfulness**, coyness, prudishness, demureness, shamefacedness, skittishness, chastity **4 shyness**, timidity, diffidence, self-consciousness, retiring, disposition, timorousness, embarrassment **5 self-deprecation**, self-effacement, distrust, self-doubt **6 reserve**, restraint, reticence, constraint

ADJECTIVES 7 modest, meek, humble, unpretentious, unpretending, unassuming, unostentatious, unobtrusive, unboastful, unimposing, unimpressive **8 blushing**, flushed, red, ruddy, reddening, crimsoning, nervous, awkward, shamefaced **9 bashful**, coy, prudish, shockable, demure, chaste, pure, shamefaced, confused, chaste **10 shy**, timid, diffident, self-conscious, retiring, timorous, embarrassed, frightened, mouselike, shrinking, unimportant, inarticulate **11 self-deprecating**, self-effacing, self-doubting, unambitious, deprecating **12 reserved**, restrained, reticent, constrained, backward, retiring, reluctant, unseen

VERBS 13 be modest, deprecate oneself **14 escape notice**, avoid, hang back, hesitate **15 be self-conscious**, blush, flush, crimson, colour up

475 Moisture

NOUNS 1 moisture, dampness, wetness, wateriness, sogginess, soddenness **2 mistiness**, fogginess, cloud, rain, pluviosity, showeriness, scotch mist, drizzle **3 humidity**, dankness, mugginess, stickiness, clamminess, closeness, humidification, dew point **4 seepage**, percolation, permeation, rising damp **5 sprinkle**, spraying, sparge, asperge, hosing, splash, spatter, splatter **6 dew**, dewdrops, evening damp, fog drip, false dew **7 bogginess**, swampiness, marshiness, muddiness **8 marsh**, swamp, fen, bog, quagmire, flood plain, quicksand, mud, slime, ooze, mire, wet

ADJECTIVES 9 moist, damp, wet, soggy, sodden, humid, clammy, sticky, muggy, close, dank, tacky **10 misty**, foggy, cloudy, watery, rainy, showery, drizzling, mizzly, dewy **11 marshy**, swampy, boggy, fenny, soggy, oozy, squashy, squelchy, splashy, sludgy, slushy, muddy, sodden, waterlogged **12 seeping**, dripping, percolating, splashed, spattered, weeping, tearful, dribbling, drivelling, drooling

VERBS 13 moisten, dampen, wet **14 sprinkle**, spatter, spray, hose, splash **15 be moist**, be damp, be soggy, squelch, drizzle **16 seep**, drip, percolate, leak, ooze, trickle, weep, sweat, perspire, exude, bleed, salivate, dribble

476 Money

• *Money is like muck, not good except it be spread.* Francis Bacon.

• *A feast is made for laughter, and wine maketh merry: but money answereth all things.* Bible: Ecclesiastes.

NOUNS 1 money, legal tender, specie, coinage, monetary unit, currency, fluctuating currency, hard currency, soft currency, sterling, gold, silver, bullion, coin, paper money, cowrie **2 cash**, hard cash, petty cash, ready money, pelf, mammon **3 fortune**, wealth, riches, millions, billions, crores **4 change**, small change, coins, silver, pin money, allowance, pocket money, spending money, centime, sou, paisa, piastre **5 funds**, cash supplies, monies, treasure, purse, liquid assets, wherewithal, means, ready money, capital, reserves, balances, finances, exchequer, cash flow, remittance **6 British money**, decimal coinage, penny, two pence, tuppence, five pence, ten pence, twenty pence, fifty pence, pound coin, farthing, halfpenny, ha'penny, thrupenny bit, sixpence, shilling, half-crown, half-a-crown, crown, guinea, sovereign, noble **7 national coins**, franc, Deutschmark, guilder, krona, markka, drachma, lira, peseta, escudo, peso, cruzado, rupee, rouble, yuan, yen, won, kip, dinar, zloty, lek, riyal, dirham, rand, inti **8 ancient coins**, shekel, talent, denarius, obolus, soldo, ducat, sou, bezant **9 numismatics**, numismatology **10 paper money**, note, banknote, draft, money order, postal order, cheque, traveller's cheque, Eurocheque, certificate, debenture, promissory note, IOU, coupon, scrip, bond **11 false money**, counterfeit money, forgery, kite, snide, clipped coinage, obsolete coinage, devalued currency, rubber cheque, monopoly money **12 bullion**, gold bar, ingot **13 treasurer**, cashier, teller, payer, bursar, almoner, purser, bookkeeper, accountant, banker, financier, minter, coiner, forger **14 treasury**, public purse, exchequer, counting house, custom house, bursary, bank, building society, coffer, treasure chest, depository, strongroom, strongbox, safe, safe-deposit box, cash box, money box, moneybag, piggy bank, money belt, pocket, wallet, change purse **15 till**, cash register, cash desk

ADJECTIVES 16 monetary, pecuniary, financial, fiscal, numismatic, chrysological, budgetary, coined, stamped, minted, nummular, nummary, fiduciary, devalued, depreciated, withdrawn, demonetized, decimal
VERBS 17 monetize, mint, coin, print, stamp, issue, circulate, counterfeit **18 demonetize**, call in, debase, clip, devalue **19 bank**, invest, save, deposit, draw, withdraw, cash, encash

477 Morality

• *No morality can be founded on authority, even if the authority were divine.* A. J. Ayer.
NOUNS 1 morality, morals, ethics, principles, standards, ideals, beliefs, scruples, behaviour, conduct, ethos, attitudes, customs, mores, habits **2 good morals**, integrity, propriety, probity, decency, goodness, virtue, honour, honesty, nobility, rectitude, uprightness, righteousness, right, conscience, justice, fairness, spirituality, piousness **3 moral purity**, faultlessness, perfection, sinlessness, sainthood, immaculacy, innocence, modesty, bashfulness, coyness, pudency, shame, chastity, abstinence, continence, celibacy, Encratism, temperance, coldness, frigidity, virginity **4 self-righteousness**, narrow-mindedness, mealy-mouthedness, prudery, Grundyism, priggishness, primness, smugness, sanctimony, pietism, puritanism, gravity, seriousness, sternness, censorship, expurgation, bowdlerization, euphemism, genteelism, affectation, shockability, squeamishness **5 moralist**, puritan, Victorian, prig, prude, prohibitionist, teetotaller, censor **6 moral**, lesson, teaching, message, point, precept, homily, maxim, apophthegm, adage, proverb, saying, saw
ADJECTIVES 7 moral, ethical, principled, high-minded, good, decent, honourable, honest, noble, upright, righteous, virtuous, right-minded, right, proper, just, fair, scrupulous **8 pure**, faultless, perfect, sinless, immaculate, spotless, purified, refined, snowy, white, innocent, modest, bashful, blushing, coy, shy, chaste, undefiled, unfallen, virgin, vestal, maidenly, untouched, unwedded, celibate, continent, temperate, Platonic, sublimated, sexless, cold **9 moralistic**, self-righteous, narrow-minded, mealy-mouthed, prudish, priggish, prim, old-maidish, smug, sanctimonious, holier-than-thou, pietistic, pious, puritan, Victorian, strait-laced, grave, serious, severe, stern, censorious, edifying, clean, publishable, quotable, mentionable, expurgated, bowdlerized, euphemistic, genteel, affected
VERBS 10 be moral, abstain, wait **11 moralize**, sermonize, preach, pontificate, lecture

478 Motion

NOUNS 1 motion, movement, migration, mobility, motility, locomotion, walking, perambulation, pedestrianism, going, running, rushing, marching, motivity, actuation, kinetics, dynamics, kinesis, kinematics, kenesiatrics, kinesipathy **2 momentum**, propulsion, impulsion, mobilization, motivation, actuation, impetus, stir, restlessness, action, activity, agitation, bustle, course, passage, set, trend, stream, flow, flux, flight, current, rush, run, drift, transit, traffic, transport, travel, riding **3 motion towards**, advance, approach, arrival, progress, headway, evolution **4 backward motion**, regression, backing, backflowing, refluence, reflux, retreat, withdrawal, departure, exit, egress, sternway **5 circuition**, circumnavigation, rotation, oscillation, fluctuation, vibration, gyration, agitation **6 descending motion**, descent, sinking **7 ascending motion**, ascent, rising, soaring, mounting **8 rapid motion**, speed **9 slow motion**, slowness **10 regular movement**, rhythm, precession, following **11 bodily movement**, exercise, athletics, gymnastics, aerobics, gesticulation, wave, gesture, thumbs up **12 gait**, walk, carriage, bearing, tread, pace, step, stride, stroll, saunter, tramp, stamp, run, lope, jog, trot, amble, dance step, hop, skip, jump, leap, waddle, swagger, shuffle, creep, stalk, strut, goosestep, march, scamper, scramble

VERBS 13 be in motion, move, stir, budge, go, flow, drift, stream, progress, advance, develop, evolve, proceed, wade through, back, regress, retrogress, subside, ebb, wane, deviate, soar, mount, rise, ascend, climb, descend, sink, plunge, oscillate, gyrate, rotate, spin, whirl, shift **14 set in motion**, move, actuate, push, nudge, shove, drive, hustle, motivate, pull, tug, draw, haul, propel, impel, throw, mobilize, send, dispatch, scatter, disperse, gather, transfer, transport, convey, transpose **15 walk**, march, stride, tramp, lope, tread, trip, amble, jog, stroll, saunter, shuffle, waddle, dance, leap, toddle, patter, potter, strut, stagger, mince, stalk, run, rush, dash, dart, roll, coast, trundle, travel, roam, wander, drift, dodge, duck, weave

ADJECTIVES 16 moving, motive, motor, motile, motional, mobile, motivational, locomotive, automotive, self-propelled, shifting, impelling, propelling, driving, travelling, riding, running, rushing, flowing, streaming, flying, transitional, fleeting, mercurial, restless, active, agitated, bustling, scurrying, stirring, wandering, drifting, nomadic, peripatetic, ambulant, erratic **17 directional**, advancing, progressive, backward, regressive, retrogressive, backtracking, refluent, downward, sinking, plunging, descending, subsiding, upward, ascending, rising, soaring, mounting, climbing, rapid, speedy, slow, toddling, pottering, regular, recurring, rhythmic, periodic, uniform, continuous, circuitous, rotary, centripetal, centrifugal, axial, radial, oscillating, fluctuating, vibrating, agitating, irregular, sideward, oblique, angular, random, Brownian, gyratory

479 Motionlessness

NOUNS 1 motionlessness, immobility, stillness, inactivity, fixity, rigidity, stiffness, standstill, stop, halt, pause, lock, stability, equilibrium, poise, balance, stasis, steadiness, inertness, dormancy, passiveness, apathy, latency, torpor, indifference, indolence, lotus-eating, languor, stagnancy, vegetation, coma, deathliness, deadliness, trance, catalepsy, numbness, suspension, cessation, stagnation, deadlock, stalemate, truce, lull, suspense, abeyance, stoppage, embargo, freeze **2 repose**, rest, sleep, slumber, insensibility, death, quiescence, silence, quietness, placidity, tranquillity, serenity, peace, composure, contemplation, satori, nirvana, ataraxia, calmness, imperturbability, stillness, hush, lull, windlessness, doldrums, horse latitudes, anticyclone **3 resting place**, refuge, shelter, journey's end, home, haven, quarters, bivouac, bed, pillow, hammock, grave, tomb, mausoleum, cemetery, graveyard

ADJECTIVES 4 motionless, immobile, still, inactive, unmoving, immotive, static, stationary, stagnant, standing, steady, poised, balanced, immovable, fixed, stiff, stuck, paralysed, petrified, transfixed, sedentary, stock-still, spellbound, frozen, becalmed **5 sedentary**, stay-at-home, housebound, home-loving, domesticated, supine, bedridden, disabled, idle, unemployed, inert, dormant, passive, latent, languid, apathetic, indifferent, indolent, phlegmatic, sluggish, vegetating, unaroused, suspended, abeyant, sleeping, slumbering, smouldering, groggy, heavy, leaden, dull, flat, slack, tame, dead, lifeless, catatonic **6 quiescent**, silent, still, hushed, insensible, soundless, placid, tranquil, calm, serene, peaceful, restful, composed, contemplative, smooth, unruffled, untroubled, unperturbed, unagitated, unhurried, unstirring, stolid, stoic, impassive, inexcitable, imperturbable, pacific, halcyon, undisturbed, sequestered

VERBS 7 be motionless, stand still, freeze, remain, abide, stay, sit, remain seated, perch, land, alight, mark time, wait, tread water, coast, cease, stop, halt, decelerate, settle down, pause, tarry, relax, stagnate, vegetate, idle, hang fire, sleep, slumber **8 make motionless**, immobilize, suspend, stalemate, lock, jam, catch, stick, lodge, embargo, prohibit, freeze, soothe, lull, tranquillize

480 Motive

NOUNS 1 motive, cause, reason, rationale, grounds, excuse, pretext, motivation, driving force, lodestar, ideal, intention, objective, design, purpose, aim, goal, hope, desire, ambition, impetus, stimulation, impulse, compulsion, inspiration, calling, vocation **2 inducement**, influence, encouragement, invitation, incentive, provocation, enticement, lure, attraction, charm, fascination, bewitchment, magnetism, seductiveness, blandishment, cajolery, coaxing, flattering, teasing, wheedling, pleading, advocacy, advice, persuasion, propaganda, agitprop, pressure, lobbying, solicitation, advertising, sales talk, patter **3 stimulus**, fillip, tonic, sop, prod, goad **4 negative stimulus**, threat, castigation, big stick **5 positive stimulus**, flattery, charm, profit, money, payment, benefits, rise, bonus, hand-out, gift, donation, gratuity, tip **6 suggestibility**, susceptibility, receptivity, impressibility, tractability, malleability, adaptability, docility

VERBS 7 be motivated, succumb, submit, concede, give in **8 motivate**, start, initiate, begin, instigate, induce, prompt, actuate, move, cause, bring on, influence, persuade, convince, suggest, recommend, advocate, advise, counsel, talk into, win over, enlist, recruit, interest, intrigue, prevail upon, attract, captivate, coax, cajole, flatter, energize, galvanize, electrify, encourage, inspire, arouse, exhort, stimulate, excite, challenge, provoke, spur on, hustle, incline **9 manipulate**, play on, lobby, prejudice, bias, predetermine, predispose, mislead, insinuate, tempt, entice, seduce, lure, hypnotize, force, compel, nag, drive, push, bully, browbeat, prod, goad, inveigle, incite

ADJECTIVES 10 motivational, influential, directional, incentive, attractive, magnetic, persuasive, hortatory, provocative, incitive, instigative, inflammatory, hypnotic, mesmeric, irresistible, suggestive, influencing, convincing, compelling, encouraging, challenging, provoking, stimulating, electrifying, inciting, instigating, energizing, kinetic, galvanizing, inflaming, rousing, insinuating, teasing, tantalizing, alluring, tempting, inviting **11 motivated**, persuaded, moved, influenced, induced, prompted, impelled, caused, directed, encouraged, exhorted, challenged, urged, egged on, spurred on, pressured, lobbied, prodded, goaded, provoked, stimulated, electrified, energized, animated, galvanized, inspired, inflamed, incited, roused, charmed, enticed, lured, attracted, seduced, bewitched, coaxed, flattered, spellbound, hypnotized **12 suggestible**, susceptible, receptive, impressible, tractable, malleable, adaptable, docile, compliant

481 Mountains

NOUNS 1 mountain, mount, alp, range, chain, sierra, cordillera, massif, highlands, heights, precipice, summit, peak, tor, crag, pinnacle, crest, ridge, saddle, spur, hill, hillock, hummock, downs, hilltop, fell, monticule, foothill, climb, mountaineering, alpinism **2 orology**, orometer, orologist **3 mountaineer**, mountain climber, rock climber, alpinist, mountain-dweller, hill-dweller, abominable snowman, yeti, Bigfoot, Sasquatch **4 major mountains and ranges**, Himalayas, Alps, Pyrenees, Caucasus, Andes Mountains, Everest, K2, Annapurna, Matterhorn, Mont Blanc, Eiger, Ararat, Kilimanjaro, Mount Logan, Mount Cook, Mount Olympus

ADJECTIVES 5 mountainous, alpine, Himalayan, Olympian, altitudinous, elevated, lofty, topmost, cloud-capped, snow-capped, snow-clad, highland, hilly, upland **6 orogenic**, orographic, orogenetic

VERBS 7 climb a mountain, mountaineer

482 Multitude

NOUNS 1 multiplicity, multitudinousness, numerousness, multifoldness, countlessness, innumerability **2 multitude**, many, lots, millions, billions, trillions **3 profuseness**, rifeness, abundance **4 throng**, multitude, mass, mob, crowd, congregation, horde, host, army, troop, legion, fleet, high turnout, rout, ruck, jam, clutter, press, crush, swarm, flock, flight, cloud, hail, bevy, covey, shoal, hive, colony, nest, brood, pack, bunch, drove, array, galaxy

ADJECTIVES 5 multitudinous, numerous, legion, multiple, multifold, multifarious **6 many**, considerable **7 numberless**, innumerable, countless, incalculable, myriad, immeasurable, uncounted, untold, infinite, endless, limitless, boundless **8 ample**, abundant, profuse, rife, plentiful, copious, bumper **9 crowded**, thronged, mobbed, congested, massed, packed, jam-packed, crushed, cluttered

VERBS 10 crowd, throng, mob, mass, congregate, pack, jam, press, crush, swarm, teem, crawl, pullulate, hum, buzz, bristle, seethe, mill, troop, flock, pour, stream, flood, brim, overflow **11 overcrowd**, overpopulate, overman, overstaff, outnumber, overrun, infest, swamp

483 Music

- *Music has charms to soothe a savage breast.* William Congreve.
- *Music is the arithmetic of sounds as optics is the geometry of light.* Claude Debussy.
- *If music be the food of love, play on,/ Give me excess of it, that, surfeiting,/ The appetite may sicken and so die.* William Shakespeare.

NOUNS 1 music, harmony, melody, musicality, tunefulness, melodiousness, musicalness **2 music making**, playing, performance, concert, recital, prom, show, improvisation, orchestration, instrumentation **3 classical music**, romantic music, impressionist music, twelve-tone music, musique concrète, minimalist music, chamber music, contrapuntal music, choral music, operatic music, organ music, symphonic music, orchestral music, madrigal **4 sacred music**, church music, hymn, psalm, anthem, oratorio, mass, requiem, cantata, spiritual, gospel, hymnody, psalmody **5 campanology**, bell ringing, change ringing, peal, handbell **6 dance music**, ballet music, disco **7 jazz**, modern jazz, third-stream jazz, cool jazz, acid jazz, fusion, blue note, blues, trad, Dixieland, syncopation, ragtime, swing, jive, doowop, bebop, Afro-Cuban, bop **8 popular music**, pop, easy listening, hit, charts, top twenty, Karaoke **9 rock**, hard rock, heavy metal, punk rock, new wave, indie, ska, rap, ragamuffin, ragga, reggae, soul, jazz-funk, hip-hop, grunge **10 world music**, soul, ska, reggae, ragga, bhangra, kwela, mbaqanga, township jazz, marabi, son, salsa, merengue, zouk, qawwali, macumba, marabenta, soca **11 folk music**, folksong, folk rock, border ballad, country music, hillbilly music, bluegrass **12 Tin Pan Alley**, Nashville **13 melody**, tune, air, aria, strain, song, line, descant, harmony, concord, concert, attunement, chime, synchronization, unison, euphony, homophony, monody, resolution, cadence, theme, subject **14 harmonics**, melodics, rhythmics, musicology **15 musical note**, note, pitch, keys, keyboard, sharp, flat, accidental, natural, tone, semitone, keynote, overtone, harmonic, tonic, supertonic, mediant, subdominant, dominant, submediant, subtonic, interval, major interval, diatessaron, diapason, gamut, scale, chord, arpeggio, grace, ornament, appoggiatura, acciaccatura, mordent, turn, shake, trill, tremolo, vibrato **16 notation**, sheet music, score, tonic sol-fa, solfeggio, solmization, time signature, key signature, clef, bar, stave, line, space, brace, rest, pause, interval, breve, semibreve, minim, crotchet, quaver, semiquaver, demisemiquaver **17 tempo**, time, beat, rhythm, metre, timing, syncopation, upbeat, downbeat **18 singer**, songster, vocalist **19 musician**, player, instrumentalist, performer, artiste, soloist, virtuoso, bard, minstrel, troubadour, busker, composer, orchestrator, librettist, lyricist, balladeer, psalmist, musical director, MD, conductor, maestro, kappelmeister, choir master, chorus master, bandmaster, repetiteur, syncopator, jazzman, **20 musical group**, orchestra, chamber group, duo, trio, quartet, quintet, sextet, septet, octet, nonet, ensemble, band

ADJECTIVES 21 musical, musicophile, musicianly **22 harmonic**, tuneful, in tune, tonal, symphonious, synchronous, homophonic, harmonious, melodious, mellifluous, dulcet, singable **23 composed**, orchestrated **24 instrumental**, vocal, choral, operatic, liturgical, hymnal, psalmic, minimalist, contrapuntal, bass, baritone, alto, tenor, soprano **25 jazz**, syncopated, avant-garde, cool, traditional, trad, Dixieland, swinging

VERBS 26 harmonize, melodize, attune, assonate **27 compose**, orchestrate, instrumentate, score, adapt, arrange, transcribe **28 play**, perform, render, interpret, improvise, swing **29 sound**, blow, toot, whistle, lip, tongue, trumpet, bow, fiddle, pluck, strum, pick, twang **30 sing**, vocalize, croon, carol, warble, quaver **31 conduct**, direct

484 Mutedness

ADJECTIVES 1 faint-sounding, subdued, hushed, muted, low, quiet, soft, gentle, piano, pianissimo, indistinct, unclear, distant, weak, whispered, murmured, muttered, mumbled, inaudible **2 nonresonant**, deadened, dulled, damped, muted, muffled, stifled, smothered, silenced, dull, heavy

NOUNS 3 mutedness, faintness, lowness, softness, indistinctness **4 faint sound**, undertone, bated breath, mumbling, susurration, rustling, crackle, whining **5 dull sound**, thud, clunk, thump, bump, plump, plunk

VERBS 6 mute, lower, subdue, dampen, soft-pedal, deaden, dull, muffle, stifle, hush, quieten, soften, still **7 sound faint**, murmur, mutter, mumble, whisper, breathe, susurrate, rustle, crackle, sigh, moan, whine, hum, croon, drone **8 be nonresonant**, thud, clunk, thump, plump, plunk, plonk, plop

485 Naivety

ADJECTIVES 1 naive, naïf, artless, simple, simple-minded, ingenuous, guileless, childlike, uncontrived, unstudied, plain, homespun, unskilled, natural, primitive, ignorant, Arcadian, young, innocent, green, immature, inexperienced, trusting, gullible, uninhibited, unaffected, spontaneous, candid, frank, open, straightforward, undesigning, truthful, veracious, true, honest, sincere, honourable, aboveboard, blunt, outspoken, transparent, matter-of-fact, down-to-earth, literal-minded, modest, shy, inarticulate, unpretentious, Philistine

NOUNS 2 naivety, artlessness, simplicity, simple-mindedness, ingenuousness, guilelessness, youth, innocence, greenness, immaturity, inexperience, unworldliness, unsophistication, callowness, credulity, gullibility, plainness, unaffectedness, naturalness, ignorance, primitiveness, savagery, candour, frankness, openness, straightforwardness, bluntness, matter-of-factness, outspokenness, veracity, truth, honesty, probity, sincerity, modesty, unpretentiousness, Philistinism, imperfection, uncouthness, vulgarity, crudity **3 naive person**, lamb, child, youth, innocent, beginner, novice, greenhorn, simpleton, fool, simple soul, Philistine, provincial, rustic

VERBS 4 be naive, trust

486 Narrowness

ADJECTIVES 1 narrow, slender, thin, close, tight, strait, clinging, cramped, pinched, compressed, contracted, pent, pent-up, close-fitting, figure-hugging, limited, restricted, straitened, confined, constricted, circumscribed **2 fine**, fine-spun, threadlike, hairlike, filamentous, filiform, spindle-shaped, bacilliform, spidery, wispy, scanty, tenuous, exiguous, delicate **3 tapered**, tapering, convergent, attenuated, attenuate, pointed, peaked, conical, cone-shaped

NOUNS 4 narrowness, slenderness, thinness, closeness, tightness, straitness, limitation, restriction, confinement, constriction, circumspection **5 narrow place**, confined space, small gap, tight squeeze, chink, crack, narrows, strait, straits, channel, tunnel, passage, corridor, bottleneck, ravine, gully, ditch, isthmus, peninsula **6 fineness**, spideriness, wispiness, tenuity, exiguity **7 narrow thing**, neck, waist, fingers, strip, band, stripe, taper, spindle, stick, rod, pipe, tube, wire, thread, strand, hair, filament, splinter, wisp, streak, line, knife-edge, razor's edge, point, peak, spire, cone, wedge, narrow gauge **8 narrowing**, shrinking, tapering, taper, convergence, contraction, stricture

VERBS 9 narrow, tighten, cramp, pinch, compress, contract, limit, restrict, straiten, confine, constrict, circumscribe, taper, converge, attenuate

VERBS 10 narrowly, tightly, closely, nearly, only just

487 Nearness

NOUNS 1 nearness, closeness, proximity, propinquity, immediacy, intimacy, inseparability, handiness, convenience, accessibility, approximation, approach, convergence, juncture, collision course, conjunction, syzygy, appulse, perigee **2 short distance**, no distance, short cut, step, stone's throw, spitting distance, striking distance, earshot, close range, close quarters, brink, verge, hair's-breadth, finger's-breadth, inch, millimetre, ace, near miss **3 near place**, vicinity, vicinage, neighbourhood, locality, precinct, environs, surroundings, purlieus, confines, approaches, foreground, front **4 neighbour**, next-door neighbour

ADJECTIVES 5 near, nigh, close, proximate, proximal, side-by-side, shoulder-to-shoulder, cheek-by-jowl, hand-in-hand, arm-in-arm, elbow-to-elbow, bumper-to-bumper, intimate, inseparable, neck-and-neck, close-run, nearby, local, home, neighbouring, vicinal, next-door, next, adjoining, contiguous, immediate, nearest, closest, to hand, at hand, handy, convenient, accessible, nearer, closer, approximate, approximating, nearing, approaching, converging

488 Necessity

- *Teach thy necessity to reason thus:/ There is no virtue like necessity.* William Shakespeare.
- *Necessity knows no law.* Publilius Syrus.

NOUNS 1 necessity, essential, fundamental, must, necessary, prerequisite, imperative, precondition, requisite, requirement, want, need, desideratum **2 indispensability**, indispensableness, essentialness **3 lack of choice**, obligation, constraint, duty, compulsion, coercion, no choice, no alternative, no option **4 need**, poverty, penury, want, hardship, indigence, privation **5 inevitability**, certainty, unavoidability, inexorability, ineluctability, one's lot, destiny, fate, nemesis, doom, karma **6 necessitarianism**, determinism, fatalism, predetermination, predestination, force majeure **7 involuntariness**, compulsion, instinctiveness, reflex, reflex action, Pavlovian reaction

ADJECTIVES 8 necessary, essential, required, requisite, indispensable, fundamental, needed, imperative, urgent **9 obligatory**, compulsory, mandatory, binding **10 needy**, needful, necessitous, poor, destitute, indigent, poverty-striken **11 inevitable**, certain, inescapable, unavoidable, ordained, preordained, inexorable, ineluctable, fated, doomed, karmic, predestined, destined, necessitarian **12 involuntary**, compulsory, impulsive, automatic, instinctive, intuitive, mechanical

VERBS 13 necessitate, require, need, want, demand, call for, entail, involve **14 compel**, force, coerce, impel, mandate, oblige, impose, dictate **15 be compelled**, be cornered **16 preordain**, ordain, predetermine, predestine, destine, fate **17 make a virtue of necessity**

489 Negation

NOUNS 1 negation, abnegation, negative, negativism, negative attitude, pessimism, defeatism, despondence, noncorroboration, no **2 rejection**, refusal, denial, disavowal, disallowance, prohibition, invalidation, disclaimer, nonacceptance, declining, veto, nonbelief, disbelief, atheism, unbelief, agnosticism, apostasy, nonobservance, disobedience, recusance, recusancy, disownment, repudiation, renunciation, disclamation, dissociation **3 rebuttal**, refutation, rejoinder, retortion, retort, challenge, objection, demurral, demur, defiance, obstruction, deprecation, dissent, doubtfulness, questioning, protest, denial, contradiction, contravention, contrary assertion, disagreement, impugnation, disaffirmation, antithesis, reverse, opposite, contrary, contrariness, countering, contesting **4 renunciation**, abrogation, recantation, repudiation, abjuration, forswearing, swearing-off, relinquishment, revocation, repeal, rescindment, retraction, cancellation, nullification, annul-

ment, countermand **5 nonexistence**, nothingness, nothing, nullity, nonentity, void, vacuity
VERBS 6 be negative, be pessimistic, negate, abnegate, not corroborate, say no, reject, refuse, deny, not admit, disavow, disallow, prohibit, make impossible, invalidate, decline, refuse consent, veto, disbelieve, practise atheism, be agnostic, not observe, disobey, disown, repudiate, renunciate, disclaim **7 rebut**, refute, rejoin, retort, challenge, object, demur, defy, obstruct, deprecate, dissent, doubt, express doubts, question, refuse credence, protest, deny, emphatically deny, contradict, controvert, contravene, disagree, impugn, disaffirm, reverse, be opposite, counter, contest, disprove, cross, cross-appeal **8 renounce**, abrogate, recant, repudiate, abjure, forswear, swear off, relinquish, revoke, repeal, rescind, retract, cancel, nullify, annul, countermand, invalidate, apostasize, tergiversate **9 be nothing**, not exist
ADJECTIVES 10 negative, pessimistic, defeatist, despondent, abnegative, atheistic, agnostic, recusant, doubtful, protestant, defiant, contrary, obstructive, contradictive, contradictory, repudiative, renunciative, renunciatory, abrogative, revocatory, abjuratory, deprecative **11 rejected**, refused, denied, refuted, rebutted, disobeyed, disavowed, disallowed, prohibited, obstructed, contravened, invalidated, declined, vetoed, disbelieved, disowned, disclaimed, relinquished, renounced, negated, deprecated, repudiated, repealed, rescinded, retracted, reversed, recanted, cancelled, nullified, annulled, countermanded, challenged, questioned, contested **12 rebutting**, refuting, rejecting, prohibiting, refusing, denying, forswearing, rejoining, retorting, objecting, opposing, obstructing, deprecating, dissenting, doubting, questioning, challenging, contradicting, countering, disagreeing, impugning **13 nonexistent**, unexisting, vacant

490 Negligence

NOUNS 1 negligence, carelessness, inattention, thoughtlessness, unmindfulness, nonchalance, unconcern, oblivion, insouciance, disregard, neglectfulness, dereliction, forgetfulness, heedlessness **2 indifference**, informality, casualness, inexactitude, unscrupulousness, superficiality, shallowness, off-handedness, slackness, shoddiness, laziness, untidiness, messiness, slovenliness, sloppiness
ADJECTIVES 3 negligent, neglectful, careless, inattentive, thoughtless, unmindful, nonchalant, unconcerned, uncaring, oblivious, insouciant, disregardful, forgetful, heedless **4 indifferent**, informal, casual, lackadaisical, inexact, unscrupulous, superficial, shallow, off-handed, procrastinating, avoiding, delaying, slack, lax, half-done, slipshod, slapdash, incomplete, shoddy, lazy, untidy, dirty, messy
VERBS 5 be neglectful, neglect, disregard, ignore, forget, not heed, procrastinate, avoid, delay, leave undone

491 Negotiation

NOUNS 1 negotiation, mediation, arbitration, conciliation, compromise, exchange, discussions, bargaining, bartering, horse trading, trade-off, haggling, wrangling, making terms, treaty-making, diplomacy **2 basis for negotiations**, contract, terms, conditions, offer, provision, article, requirement, qualification, clause, proviso, stipulation, concession, reservation, strings **3 discussion**, round-table discussion, conference, bargaining session, debate, high-level talks, summit, cabinet meeting

VERBS 4 negotiate, mediate, arbitrate, seek agreement, seek accord, settle, conciliate, cooperate, compromise, exchange views, discuss, communicate, bargain, barter, horse trade, trade off, trade, haggle, wrangle, make terms, make conditions, stipulate, make concessions, add strings, use diplomacy, confer, hold talks, deliberate, do business **5 make conditions**, impose conditions, make proposals, make demands **6 act as a go-between**, broker, matchmake

ADJECTIVES 7 negotiated, mediated, arbitrated, negotiable, practicable, practical, feasible, workable, pragmatic, transferable, conveyable, exchangeable, trade-off, conditional, provisional, provisory, stipulatory, concessionary, conciliatory, compromising, collective, haggling, wrangling, treaty-making

492 Newness

NOUNS 1 newness, recentness, contemporaneity, topicality, currency, up-to-dateness, new production, mint condition, modernism, innovation, invention, originality, unfamiliarity, newfangledness, gimmickry, novelty, neology **2 trendiness**, high fashion, modernism, New Wave, New Look, New Age **3 immaturity**, inexperience, youth, virginity, dewiness, callowness, greenness, rawness, naivety, ingenuousness, innocence, freshness **4 beginning**, birth, start, inception, commencement, inauguration, initiation, generating, opening, auspication, grand opening, house-warming, unveiling, launching, maiden voyage, first night **5 fresh start**, new start, clean slate, renewal, regeneration, renovation, restoration, refurbishment, rejuvenation, repainting, resurrection, revival, revivification, remake, change, reconstruction, reorganization, updating, new look, new leaf **6 avant-garde**, advance guard, vanguard, van, fashionable set, in-group, in-set, in-crowd, jet set, beautiful people, young generation **7 new thing**, trend **8 new arrival**, newborn baby, newcomer, beginner, fledgling, amateur, novice, tyro, greenhorn, new recruit, new member, freshman, fresher, new convert, neophyte, new boy, new broom, debutante, latecomer, upstart, parvenu, nouveau riche

ADJECTIVES 9 new, brand new, newly, recent, contemporary, topical, current, up-to-date, modern, futuristic, ultramodern, postmodern, innovative, revolutionary, inventive, advanced, original, first, latest, most recent, state-of-the-art, newly produced, just out, new-made, oven-fresh, mint condition, trendy, gimmicky, neological **10 unfamiliar**, unknown, unheard of, unprecedented, unused, untried, untested, newfangled, novel, nontraditional **11 immature**, inexperienced, budding, aspiring, upstart, parvenu, nouveau riche, amateurish, amateur, novice, apprentice, embryonic, inchoate, newborn, youthful, virginal, dewy, callow, green, raw, naive, ingenuous, innocent, fresh **12 inaugurated**, initiated, opened, unveiled, launched **13 renewed**, renovated, restored, refurbished, regenerated, rejuvenated, refreshed, freshened up, touched up, repainted, resurrected, revived, revivified, remade, changed, reconstructed, redesigned, modernized, new-look **14 avant-garde**, advanced, trendy

VERBS 15 become new, begin again, start anew, renew oneself, start afresh **16 be trendy**, go modern, innovate, invent **17 begin**, commence, generate, inaugurate, initiate, open, unveil, launch **18 make new**, renew, renovate, restore, refresh, freshen up, touch up, refurbish, rejuvenate, regenerate, repaint, resurrect, revive, remake, change, reconstruct, rebuild, redesign, modernize, update

493 News

NOUNS 1 news, breaking news, hard news, straight news, facts, information, intelligence, current affairs, journalism **2 news event**, eyewitness account, press conference **3 reporting**, reportage, news gathering, coverage, newscasting, sportscasting, newspapering, investigative reporting, analytical journalism, scoop, exclusive **4 journalist**, reporter, cub reporter, newspaperman, newsman, news hound, newscaster, sportscaster, freelance writer, foreign correspondent, gossip columnist, critic, chequebook journalism, hack, scandalmonger, muckraker, leader writer, editor, anchorman, newsreader, news commentator, press secretary, press officer **5 mass communication**, mass media, news organization, news outlet, news media, print media, electronic media, press, quality press, tabloid press, popular press, yellow press, gutter press, newspaper, broadsheet, heavy, scandal sheet, special edition, extra, newsmagazine **6 radio news**, television news, newscast, sportscast, documentary **7 press agency**, news agency, news service, wire service, syndicate, Reuters, Press Association **8 newsroom**, press room, news desk, sports desk, press office **9 news story**, news item, running story, feature story, editorial, leader, column, gossip column, news programme, news update, news flash, news bulletin, scoop, exclusive, extra, press release, press notice, handout, hard news **10 copy**, feature copy, subbed copy **11 headline**, head, by-line, banner head

VERBS 12 report, broadcast, transmit, cover, document, disclose, break, issue, dispatch, scoop, publish, publicize, circulate, interview, write, freelance, edit

ADJECTIVES 13 journalistic, reportorial, reportable, editorial, newsworthy, newsy

494 Night-time

NOUNS 1 evening, eve, early evening, vespers, sunset, sundown, lighting-up time, dusk, twilight, nightfall, day's end, moonrise, moonset, darkfall, eventide **2 night**, nighttime, bedtime, darktime, darkness **3 midnight**, 12 midnight, 12 o'clock, 2400 hours, night watch **4**

evening thing, sunset, evening star, Venus, Hesperus, evening news, evening class, evening primrose, rush hour, afternoon tea, dogwatch **5 night thing**, owl, night shift, night school, nightlife, nightclub, dinner, sleep

ADJECTIVES **6 evening**, afternoon, postmeridian, vesperine, twilight, dusky, crepuscular, nocturnal, dark

495 Nonadhesion

NOUNS **1 nonadhesion**, noncohesion, noncoherence, incoherence, noncombination, separation, immiscibility, nonuniformity, disorder, confusion, chaos, entropy, looseness, bagginess, floppiness, wateriness, runniness, liquid, fluidity, slipperiness, frangibility, fragileness, crumbliness, friability **2 aloofness**, privacy, discreteness, separateness, independence, freedom, isolation, seclusion, solitude **3 individualist**, nonconformist, dissenter, free spirit, independent, bohemian, maverick, eccentric, separatist, isolationist, hermit, ascetic, anchorite, monk

VERBS **4 unstick**, unglue, peel off, pull off, pull apart, detach, unfasten, unpin, undo, free, loose, separate, knock off, shake off, unseat **5 come unstuck**, come off, fall off, drop off, peel off, come undone, liquefy, melt, thaw, run, become runny, come adrift, totter, tumble, dangle, flap, flop, wave **6 be aloof**, stay alone, seek privacy, separate from, seek solitude

ADJECTIVES **7 nonadhesive**, nonadhering, noncohesive, immiscible, decomposed, broken up, frangible, fragile, noncoherent, incoherent, nonstick, dry, smooth, slippery, unconsolidated, loose, undone, friable, crumbly, free, wide-ranging, lax, slack, relaxed, loose-fitting, baggy, flapping, flopping, floppy, dangling, hanging, peeling off, pulling off, pendulous, waving, flying, streaming, running, runny, watery, liquid **8 aloof**, private, discrete, separate, independent, free, isolated, unassimilated, secluded, solitary

496 Noncompletion

NOUNS **1 noncompletion**, incompleteness, nonfulfilment, nonachievement, nonaccomplishment, failure, draw, tie, stalemate, deadlock, noncontinuation, non sequitur, procrastination, delay, shortfall, half measures, omission, missing link, never-ending story, lack, imperfection, superficiality, rough sketch, perfunctoriness, desultoriness, neglect, negligence, oversight, loose ends, rough edges, underdevelopment, immaturity, skimpiness, scantiness, scrappiness **2 never-ending task**, Penelope's web **3 quitter**, defeatist, idler, slacker, daydreamer, shirker, procrastinator

ADJECTIVES **4 uncompleted**, undone, unfinished, unperformed, unprocessed, unfulfilled, unconsummated, unrealized, unattained, unachieved, unaccomplished, unexecuted, never-ending, incomplete, imperfect, fragmentary, missing, short, truncated, neglected, unelaborated, perfunctory, inattentive, neglectful, desultory, procrastinating, delaying, superficial, half-finished, half-baked, underdone, underdeveloped, immature, unripe, lacking, skimpy, scanty, scrappy

VERBS 5 not complete, not finish, leave undone, leave unfinished, not fulfil, not achieve, not accomplish, not finalize, half finish, half do, half begin, lack, sketch out, skimp, scrimp, scrape by, give up, procrastinate, delay **6 drop out**, fall out

497 Nonconformity

NOUNS 1 nonconformity, unconformity, disaccord, disagreement, inconsistency, incongruity, incompatibility, disparity, contrast, difference **2 dissent**, nonconcurrence, disagreement, dissidence, noncompliance, infringement, infraction, nonobservance, disobedience, recalcitrance, contrariety, contumely, protest, recusance, revolt, rebellion **3 nonconformism**, unorthodoxy, heterodoxy, heresy, iconoclasm, schism, revisionism, deviationism, unconventionality, unconventional behaviour, eccentricity, Bohemianism **4 unusualness**, uncommonness, exceptionality, extraordinariness, uniqueness, rareness, rarity, individuality, singularity, originality, oddity, queerness, curiosity, peculiarity, strangeness, bizarreness, outlandishness, weirdness, freakishness, quirkiness, grotesqueness **5 idiosyncrasy**, quirk, peculiar trait, peculiarity, mannerism **6 deviation**, deviance, aberration, vagary, abnormality, anomaly, unnaturalness, mutation, perversion, variant, exception **7 nonconformist**, nonconformer, maverick, unconventionalist, Bohemian, free spirit, dropout, hippie, beatnik, independent, freethinker, outsider **8 dissenter**, dissident, protester, radical, revolutionary, zealot, fanatic, crank, iconoclast, schismatic, apostate, heretic, recusant, rebel, anarchist, renegade, young Turk **9 hermit**, loner, lone wolf, solitary, solitudinarian, solitaire, eremite, anchorite, marabout, ascetic, stylite, recluse, isolationist **10 eccentric**, character, natural, original, oddity

ADJECTIVES 11 nonconforming, unconformable, inconsistent, incongruous, incompatible, contrasting **12 nonconformist**, unorthodox, heterodox, heretical, iconoclastic, schismatic, schismatical, dissident, dissenting, dissentient, contumacious, recusant, radical, revolutionary, rebellious, anarchic, renegade, uncompliant, unsubmissive, recalcitrant, contrary **13 unconventional**, maverick, independent, freethinking, Bohemian, fringe, beat, hippie, wandering, nomadic **14 eccentric**, offbeat, idiosyncratic, quirky, individual, singular, original, rare, unusual, exotic, unique, exceptional, far-out, way-out, odd, queer, curious, peculiar, strange, bizarre, outlandish, weird, freakish, grotesque **15 irregular**, nonstandard, not done, misplaced **16 solitary**, standoffish, unsociable, antisocial, lone, reclusive, isolated **17 abnormal**, anomalous, unnatural, deviant, aberrant

VERBS 18 not conform, dissent, protest, rebel, revolt **19 be independent**, break away, break step, break bounds, drop out

498 Nonexistence

NOUNS 1 nonexistence, nonbeing, nonentity, unbeing, nonsubsistence, nonoccurrence **2 nothingness**, nullity, nihility, nothing, nil, nought, zero, love, naught **3 negativeness**, negativity, negation, denial **4 emptiness**, vacuity, vacancy, vacuum, void, limbo, blank, hole, gap, break, lacuna, interval **5 nonreality**, imagination, fantasy **6 absence**, none, no-one **7 not any**, nil **8 extinction**, obliteration, annihilation, obsolescence

ADJECTIVES 9 nonexistent, absent, missing, minus, negative, null, void, vacant, empty, blank, devoid **10 unreal**, imaginary, illusory, fanciful **11 no more**, extinct, died out, vanished, dead, passed away, all over, defunct, obsolete, past, finished, ended, annihilated, obliterated

VERBS 12 cease to exist, vanish, disappear, end, dissolve, evaporate, die, expire, pass away, die out, peter out **13 cause not to exist**, annihilate, destroy, exterminate, eradicate, wipe out, stamp out, extinguish, snuff out, kill, murder, abort, cancel, invalidate, annul, negate, end

499 Nonmaterial World

NOUNS 1 nonmaterial world, metaphysical world, other world, heaven, heavenly kingdom, Elysium, Valhalla, Olympus, hell, underworld, Hades, eternity, eternal life, afterlife, perpetuity **2 unworldliness**, otherworldliness, unearthliness, spirituality, religion, immateriality, unreality, incorporeity, insubstantiality, intangibility, disembodiment, disincarnation, dematerialization, impalpability, imponderability, shadowiness **3 spiritual world**, the occult, spiritualism, supernaturalism, animism, astral plane, spirit, ghost, phantom **4 parapsychology**, psychokinesis, precognition, clairvoyance, telepathy **5 idealism**, transcendentalism, Platonism, Neo-Platonism, Hegelianism **6 internal world**, nonexternality, subjectivity, solipsism, selfhood, consciousness, the conscious, myself, me, yours truly, self, ego, superego, subconscious, the unconscious, id, psyche, spirit, soul

ADJECTIVES 7 nonmaterial, nonphysical, metaphysical, imaginary, illusory, ethereal, heavenly, eternal, perpetual, unworldly, otherworldly, other, unearthly, transcendent, extramundane, spiritual, celestial, religious, higher, immaterial, unreal, incorporeal, insubstantial, intangible, airy, without mass, disincarnated, disembodied, dematerializing, impalpable, imponderable, shadowy **8 parapsychological**, extrasensory, supersensible, precognitive, clairvoyant, telepathic, psychokinetic, occult, spiritual, supernatural, animist, astral **9 idealistic**, Platonic, Neo-Platonic, Hegelian **10 internal**, nonexternal, subjective, personal, solipsist, conscious, subconscious, unconscious, psychoanalytic

VERBS 11 enter a nonmaterial world, spiritualize, dematerialize, immaterialize, disembody, disincarnate

500 Nonobservance

NOUNS 1 nonobservance, nonadherence, nonconformity, disconformity, noncompliance, noncooperation, rejection, indifference, inattention, avoidance, disregard, obliviousness, oversight, forgetfulness, carelessness, remissness, negligence, neglect, thoughtlessness, slight, casualness, procrastination, laxity, informality, superficiality, perfunctoriness, repudiation, disdain, discourtesy, bad faith **2 nonperformance**, nonpractice, noncompletion, nonfulfilment, omission, failure, default, shortcoming, insufficiency **3 disregard of orders**, noncompliance, insubordination, disobedience, disrespect, disloyalty, dissidence, mutinousness, mutiny, defection, desertion

501 Nonsense

NOUNS 1 nonsense, rubbish, trash, balderdash, rot, twaddle, drivel, gibberish, gobbledygook, absurdity, senselessness, bombast, empty talk, bunkum, amphigory, nonsense verse **2 solecism**, malapropism, spoonerism, wellerism, howler, witticism, epigram, riddle, pun, joke **3 tomfoolery**, horseplay, antics, capers, high jinks, silliness, silly season, vagary, whimsicality, banter, buffoonery, drollery, clowning, burlesque, farce, scrape, prank

ADJECTIVES 4 nonsensical, foolish, silly, absurd, meaningless, senseless, idiotic, mad, crazy, ridiculous, ludicrous, asinine, anserine, preposterous, fanciful, imaginative, fatuous, funny, jocular, humorous, droll, waggish, comic, merry

VERBS 5 talk nonsense, rave, rant, gabble, garble, blarney, rhapsodize, romance, joke, pun, quip **6 fool**, fool around, clown, lark about, skylark

502 Nonuse

ADJECTIVES 1 unused, inoperational, absent, unusable, unemployable, useless, impractical, unapplied, undisposed of, in hand, in reserve, reserved, preserved, idle, fallow, untried, in abeyance, suspended, deferred, pigeonholed **2 new**, clean, fresh, unopened, virgin, unexploited, untapped, undeveloped, untrodden, untouched **3 not wanted**, unrequired, unneeded, unnecessary, unsold, unbought, remaindered, remaining, left-over, superfluous, redundant, otiose, vacant, free, dispensed with, waived, shunned, unemployed, laid off, redundant, superannuated, retired, idle **4 disused**, derelict, abandoned, discarded, cast-off, jettisoned, scrapped, laid up, mothballed, decommissioned, frozen, rusting, in limbo, neglected, done with, used up, run down, worn out, retired, supplanted, superseded, superannuated, discontinued

VERBS 5 not use, not utilize, not touch, leave alone, abstain, forbear, avoid, dispense with, overlook, neglect, waste, keep, spare, save, reserve, store, decline, refuse **6 stop using**, disuse, ban, stop, cease, leave, lay up, mothball, decommission, freeze, dismantle, set aside, store away, stockpile, hang up, discard, dump, ditch, scrap, jettison, throw away, slough, cast off, relinquish, suspend, withdraw, cancel, abrogate, drop, supersede **7 stop work**, quit, resign, retire, be dismissed, discharge, lay off, pay off

NOUNS 8 nonuse, abeyance, suspension, abstinence, forbearance, avoidance, neglect, unemployment, redundancy, reserve **9 newness**, cleanness, blankness, purity, freshness, virginity **10 disuse**, desuetude, dereliction, abandonment, rejection, limbo, inactivity, idleness, disposal, scrapping, dismissal, discharge, resignation, retirement

503 Notch

NOUNS 1 notch, indentation, nick, nock, hack, cut, incision, incisure, dent, groove, cleft, slit, split, gash, gouge, tooth, score, kerf, serration, serrulation, crenel **2 notched thing**, arrow, leaf, shell, scallop, Vandyke collar, jack-o'-lantern, saw blade, pinking shears, cog, dogtooth, zigzag **3 rung**, peg, notch, step

ADJECTIVES 4 notched, notchy, indented, crenate, cut, slit, split, toothed, cogged, dentate, scalloped, pinked, jagged, incisural, saw-toothed, serrated

VERBS 5 notch, indent, nick, nock, cog, hack, cut, incise, dent, slit, split, gash, gouge, score, kerf, serrate, pink **6 notch up**, score, achieve, accomplish, add to

504 Number

NOUNS 1 number, numeral, no., figure, digit, cipher, character, decimal, symbol, sign, constant, variable, notation, Arabic numeral, Roman numeral, decimal system **2 mathematical result**, sum, summation, total, running total, score, reckoning, tally, bill, aggregate, whole, amount, quantity, difference, residual, remainder, product **3 ratio**, proportion, percentage, percent, fraction, numerator, denominator **4 power**, exponent, index, root, square root, cube root, surd, logarithm, log, mantissa

ADJECTIVES 5 numerical, numeric, numerary, numerative, numerate, digital **6 odd**, impair, even, pair, cardinal, ordinal, imaginary, real, rational, irrational, arithmetical, geometrical, algorithmic, digital, round, whole, prime, positive **7 fractional**, decimal, exponential, logarithmic, logometric, differential, integral, surd, radical, finite

VERBS 8 number, enumerate, count, tell, tally, reckon, notch up, tot up, sum up **9 total**, come to, make, equal, amount to

505 Obedience

NOUNS 1 obedience, compliance, complaisance, acquiescence, deference, obsequiousness, dutifulness, goodness, observance, conformity, willingness, readiness, nonresistance, meekness, submissiveness, passivity, yielding, docility, subservience, servility, slavishness, tractability, pliance **2 loyalty**, fidelity, fealty, allegiance, service, faithfulness, devotion, constancy, comity, steadfastness **3 obeisance**, homage, worship, reverence, kneeling, humility, respect, courtesy, bow, curtsy, genuflection, obsequy, salaam, prostration

VERBS 4 obey, comply, acquiesce, consent, assent, defer to, yield to, conform, discharge, submit, yield, bear allegiance, serve, wait upon **5 show obeisance to**, pay homage, worship, kneel, show respect, pay tribute, bow, curtsy, bend, stoop, genuflect, salaam, prostrate oneself, grovel

ADJECTIVES 6 obedient, compliant, complaisant, acquiescent, deferential, obsequious, dutiful, conforming, law-abiding, willing, meek, submissive, passive, yielding, docile, resigned, disciplined, biddable, subservient, servile, slavish, tractable, amenable, pliant, manageable, malleable, tame

7 loyal, faithful, devoted, dedicated to, constant, steadfast, staunch, true, sycophantic **8 obeisant**, worshipping, reverential, kneeling, humble

506 Obliqueness

NOUNS 1 obliqueness, deviation, divergence, skewness, deflection, indirection, transverseness, crookedness, convolution, digression, meandering, twist, turn, bias, swerve, zigzag, inclination, curvature, slope, slant, cant, bank, slide, camber, pitch, tip, tilt, list **2 oblique line**, diagonal, slash, solidus, separatrix, stroke, virgule, bevelled edge, rakish angle, rhomboid, hairpin curve, dogleg, slide **3 deviousness**, circumlocution, periphrasis, circuitousness, indirection, furtiveness, backhandedness, evasion, equivocation, prevarication, hedging, deception, distortion, euphemism, dissemblance

ADJECTIVES 4 oblique, deviating, divergent, skewed, diagonal, deflected, indirect, sidelong, transverse, sideways, crooked, convoluted, digressive, meandering, tangent, bevelled, twisted, turning, bending, zigzag, inclining, sloping, slanting, pitched, tilting, leaning, listing, off-course **5 devious**, circumlocutory, periphrastic, circuitous, roundabout, indirect, sidelong, furtive, backhand, evasive, equivocal, hedging, deceptive, distorted, euphemistic, dissembling

VERBS 6 be oblique, transect, deviate, diverge, skew, deflect, crook, digress, meander, twist, turn, veer, bend, swerve, zigzag, incline, camber, curve, slope, slant, cant, bank, pitch, tip, tilt, lean **7 deviate**, circumlocute, evade, equivocate, prevaricate, hedge, deceive

507 Obliteration

VERBS 1 obliterate, erase, expunge, eliminate, delete, remove, efface, deface, overprint, paint over, scribble out, cover up, conceal, scratch out, score out, strike out, cross out, rule out, rub out, sponge off, wash off, wipe out, blot out, black out, white out, cancel, annul, abrogate, blue-pencil, censor, destroy, eradicate, extirpate, annihilate, demolish, raze, liquidate, exterminate, purge, vaporize, bury **2 forget**, block out

NOUNS 3 obliteration, erasure, expunction, elimination, deletion, dele, removal, effacement, defacement, writing over, printing over, painting over, illegibility, covering up, concealment, crossing out, rubbing out, cancellation, annulment, abrogation, cessation, editing, censorship, destruction, eradication, extirpation, annihilation, demolition, liquidation, extermination, purge, interment, burial **4 eraser**, rubber, correction fluid, paint-stripper, sponge **5 forgetfulness**, amnesia, absentmindedness, mental block

ADJECTIVES 6 obliterated, erased, expunged, eliminated, deleted, effaced, concealed, crossed out, rubbed out, vaporized, liquidated, extirpated, cancelled, edited, censored, destroyed, eradicated, annihilated, demolished, exterminated, buried

508 Oblivion

NOUNS 1 oblivion, abstractedness, detachment, ataraxia, withdrawal, absorption, introspection, depersonalization, catatonia, senselessness, insensibility, unconsciousness, coma, stupor, narcosis, trance, rapture, ecstasy **2 blankness**, vacancy, vacuity, absentmindedness, forgetfulness, amnesia, mental block **3 poor memory**, hazy recollection **4 unthinkingness**, thoughtlessness, unmindfulness, heedlessness, inattention, disregard, neglect, carelessness, selfishness, ingratitude **5 death**, annihilation, obliteration **6 amnesty**, pardon

ADJECTIVES 7 oblivious, abstracted, detached, withdrawn, introspective, distracted, preoccupied, blind, deaf, unaware, depersonalized, catatonic, senseless, insensible, unconscious, rapturous, ecstatic, hypnotic **8 blank**, vacant, vacuous, empty-headed, absentminded, forgetful, amnesic, Lethean **9 unthinking**, thoughtless, unmindful, heedless, inattentive, disregarding, neglectful, careless, selfish, ungrateful **10 forgotten**, unmemorable, past

VERBS 11 be forgotten, be lost **12 forget**, miss, overlook **13 be forgetful**, dry

509 Obscurity

NOUNS 1 obscurity, obfuscation, unintelligibility, incomprehensibility, opacity, cloudiness, obsidian, fogginess, difficulty, Johnsonese, purple prose, tortuousness, convolution, complexity, gobbledegook, confusion, muddle, indistinctness, vagueness, imprecision, inexactness, inaccuracy, indefiniteness, abstraction, indirectness, allusion, ambiguity, equivocalness, convolution, enigma, abstruseness, profundity, depth, overcompression, verbiage

ADJECTIVES 2 obscure, unclear, obfuscatory, unintelligible, incomprehensible, opaque, cloudy, foggy, fuzzy, murky, obsidian, difficult, Johnsonian, ornamental, purple, tortuous, convoluted, involved, complex, confused, gnostic, muddled, indistinct, vague, uncertain, imprecise, inexact, inaccurate, indefinite, abstract, indirect, allusive, ambiguous, Cimmerian, cabalistic, equivocal, shapeless, amorphous, mysterious, enigmatic, cryptic, abstruse, esoteric, arcane, recondite, profound, overcompressed, elliptical, diffuse

VERBS 3 make obscure, obfuscate, complicate, confound, muddy, confuse

510 Observance

NOUNS 1 observance, compliance, recognition, following, heeding, regard, caring, keeping, acknowledgment, attention to, vigilance, diligence, conscientiousness, conformity, accordance, regularity, dependability, reliability, accuracy, attachment, faithfulness, fidelity, loyalty, obedience, duty **2 religious observance**, ritual, ceremony, rite, liturgy, service **3 performance**, practice, procedure, convention, custom, usage, routine, discharge, execution, acquittal, fulfilment

VERBS 4 observe, comply with, recognize, adhere to, stick to, cling to, heed, regard, care, keep, follow, abide by, acknowledge, attend to, conform to **5 observe religious ceremony**, officiate, celebrate mass **6 perform**, practise, execute, acquit, carry out, fulfil, meet

ADJECTIVES 7 observant, heeding, watchful, regarding, attentive, careful of, conscientious, diligent, meticulous, scrupulous, fastidious, punctual, literal, pedantic, exact, accurate, reliable, responsible, dependable, dutiful, constant, compliant, conforming, obedient, adhering to, faithful, devout, religious, orthodox, traditional, conventional, loyal

511 Obstinacy

ADJECTIVES 1 obstinate, stubborn, obdurate, headstrong, pig-headed, mulish, pertinacious, wilful, self-willed, awkward **2 refractory**, recalcitrant, wayward, arbitrary, perverse, contrary, contumacious, disobedient, unruly, restive, unmanageable, intractable, uncontrollable, ungovernable, unpersuadable, incorrigible, irrepressible, stiff-necked, hard-mouthed, indocile, cross-grained, crotchety **3 unyielding**, firm, determined, resolute, dogged, tenacious, persevering, stiff, wooden, rigid, adamant, inelastic, inflexible, unbending, obdurate, case-hardened, uncompromising, intransigent, unmoved, uninfluenced, unrelenting, immovable, irreversible, persistent, incurable, chronic, dour, grim, inexorable, unappeasable, implacable, merciless **4 set**, habituated, hidebound, conservative, obscurantist, reactionary, blimpish, unteachable, impervious, blind, deaf, opinionated, dogmatic, hard-line, pedantic, obsessed

NOUNS 5 obstinacy, stubbornness, obduracy, adamantine, bull-headedness, pig-headedness, mulishness, pertinaciousness, self-will, perversity, contumacy, disobedience, resistance, intractability, incorrigibility, stiff neck, wrongheadedness, cussedness, dourness **6 determination**, will, single-mindedness, resolution, grimness, doggedness, tenacity, perseverance, inelasticity, inflexibility, woodenness, toughness, hardness, intransigence, immovability, hard line, irreversibility **7 opinionatedness**, dogmatism, rigorism, intolerance, prejudice, bias, bigotry, zealotry, fanaticism, obsession, blindness, closed mind, narrowmindedness, illiberality, obscurantism

VERBS 8 be obstinate, persist, persevere, not budge, sit tight, stay put, stand firm, insist

512 Occultism

- *All argument is against it; but all belief is for it.* Samuel Johnson.
- *There are more things in Heaven and Earth, Horatio/ Than are dreamt of in your philosophy.* William Shakespeare.

NOUNS 1 occultism, esotericism, supernaturalism, mysticism, shamanism, spiritism, animism, Rosicrucianism, hermeticism, cabbalism, voodooism, witchcraft, magic, transcendentalism, psychic research, metapsychism, parapsychology, psychosophy, theosophy, anthroposophy, scientology, pseudopsychology, spiritualism, mediumism, poltergeistism, mesmerism, hypnotism, alchemy, astrology, prophecy, fortune telling, telepathy, telergy, mind reading, faith healing, astral projection, telekinesis, psychokinesis, fork bending, telaesthesia, teleportation, levitation, pyramidology, ufology, phrenology, Kirlian photography, psychorrhagy, psychography, spirit writing, trance speaking **2 the occult**, the paranormal, supernature, spirit world, astral plane, esoterica, occultness, unearthliness, otherworldiness, spirituality, eeriness, ghostliness **3 witchcraft**, witchery, Wicca, coven, Hallowe'en, witching hour, sorcery, wizardry, necromancy, spellcraft, enchantment, bedevilment, possession, voodooism, voodoo, hoodoo, wanga, jujuism, obi, doiism, magianism, totemism, fetishism, vampirism, magic, theurgy, thaumaturgy, natural magic, sympathetic magic, white magic, chaos magic, black magic, black art **4 witch**, witch doctor, wangateur, medicine man, isangoma, mundunugu, shaman, sorcerer, sorceress, magician, mage, magus, Merlin, necromancer, wizard, warlock, lamia, enchanter, enchantress, spellbinder, siren, mermaid **5 spell**, charm, philtre, rune, wanga, evil eye, hex, jinx, conjuration, incantation, hocus pocus, mumbo jumbo, abracadabra, paternoster, open sesame, abraxas, glossolalia **6 talisman**, mascot, amulet, periapt, fetish, totem, juju, obi, mojo, tiki, relic, emblem, mandala, ankh, scarab, crucifix, four-leaf clover, rabbit's foot, garlic, silver bullet, bell, familiar spirit, black cat, magic circle, magic carpet, wishbone, wishing well **7 spirit**, soul, geist, atman, psyche, the unconscious, the subconscious, id, ego, superego, third eye, astral body, linga sharira **8 psychic power**, sixth sense, intuition, feyness, second sight, psi faculty, third eye, precognition, premonition, clairvoyance, clairaudience, clairsentience, insight, foresight, crystal vision, psychometry, telepathy, telekinesis, metapsychosis **9 divination**, prophecy, soothsaying, clairvoyance, prediction, precognition, fortune-telling, tea-leaf reading, Tarot-reading, dowsing, water-divining, hydromancy, radiaesthesia, augury, sortilege, haruspicy, ichthyomancy, ophiomancy, pythonism, mantology, palmistry, chiromancy, chirognomy, crystal-gazing, astrology, sideromancy, astrodiagnosis, astromancy, numerology, arithmomancy, logomancy, dream interpretation, oneiromancy, I Ching, psephomancy, capromancy, pyromancy, metereomancy, geomancy, hieromancy, theomancy, necromancy **10 psychic phenomenon**, déjà vu, telepathic dream, premonition, maya, trance, dharana, dhyana, samadhi, hypnosis, séance, ectoplasm, exteriorized protoplasm, aura, emanation, biofeedback, cosmic vibration, synchronicity, crop circle, UFO sighting **11 ghost**, spirit, ghoul, phantom, apparition, manifestation, materialization, poltergeist, shade, manes, lemures, spectre, phantasm, wraith, presence, undead, vampire, zombie, fetch, demon, jinni, fairy, fay, sylph, genius, elf, pixie, alfar, brownie, gnome, dwarf, troll, trow, kobold, orc, werewolf, werecat, goblin, imp, sprite, hobgoblin, leprechaun, changeling, cluricaune, gremlin, alien, Martian **12 occultist**, psychic, esoteric, mystic, druid, druidess, houngan, mind reader, telekinetic, fork bender, transcendentalist, spiritualist, spiritist, medium, ecstatic, faith healer, psychometer, parapsychologist, pyramidologist, ufologist, adept, mahatma, yogi, fakir, exorcist **13 diviner**, psychic, clairvoyant, clairaudient, clairsentient, seer, prophet, soothsayer, augur, auspex, haruspex, astrologer, fortune teller, crystal gazer, palmreader, wise woman, sibyl, pythoness

ADJECTIVES 14 occult, cryptic, paranormal, supersensible, superphysical, supernatural, hermetic, symbolic, latent, covert, enigmatic, arcane, esoteric, obscure, secret, mysterious, encoded, cabbalistic **15 witchlike**, wizardly, necromantic, druidic, shamanic, talismanic, Circean, magical, enchanting, charming, spellbinding, entrancing, fascinating, incantational, hypnotic, voodooistic, totemistic, fetishistic, diabolic, demonic, undead, vampiric **16 psychic**, subconscious, transcendental, cosmic, telepathic, telekinetic, psychokinetic, telergic, telaesthetic, radiaesthetic, extrasensory, spiritualistic, mediumistic, psychosensory, parapsychological **17 divinatory**, prophetic, clairvoyant, clairaudient, clairsentient, premonitory, precognitive, augural, haruspical, sibylline, oracular **18 spiritual**, immaterial, incorporeal, intangible, disembodied, ethereal, airy, elemental, ghostly, spectral, shadowy, phantasmal, unearthly, otherworldly, astral, alien, extraterrestrial, extramundane, supramundane, transmundane, unworldly, eerie, weird, eldritch, uncanny **19 bewitched**, enchanted, spellbound, entranced, fascinated, hypnotized, mesmerized, hag-ridden, obsessed, possessed, bedevilled, cursed, hexed, jinxed

VERBS 20 occult, obscure, mystify, encode, spiritualize, dematerialize, immaterialize **21 bewitch**, enchant, charm, mesmerize, hypnotize, spellbind, hex, jinx, curse, sorcerize, theurgize, thaumaturgize, shamanize, diabolize, demonize, bedevil **22 conjure**, invoke, evoke **23 divine**, prophesy, soothsay, predict, forecast, foretell, foresee, intuit **24 experience psychic phenomena**, hallucinate, transfer thoughts, read minds, bend forks, astral-project

513 Offer

NOUNS 1 offer, proffer, proposal, invitation, proposition, bid **2 tentative offer**, suggestion, presentation, submission, feeler, advance, overture, motion, chance, opening **3 business offer**, merger, bid, buyout, ultimatum, firm price, asking price **4 illegal offer**, bribe, slush fund **5 offering**, sacrifice, martyrdom, gift, present, dedication, consecration, oblation, offertory, collection, incense, contribution, donation, subscription, propitiation, conciliation, appeasement, expiation, self-immolation

VERBS 6 offer, proffer, propose, bid, approach, submit, suggest, advance, hold out, advertise, auction, lure, bait, spur, goad, persuade, induce **7 offer to buy**, bid, negotiate **8 volunteer**, provide, present, give, furnish, lend **9 offer one's life**, sacrifice oneself **10 be a candidate**, solicit votes **11 offer reparation**, atone, make amends, apologize, propitiate, conciliate, appease, pacify, expiate **12 offer wor-**

ship, celebrate mass, minister, officiate **13 make an offering**, dedicate, consecrate, burn incense, contribute
ADJECTIVES **14 offered**, inviting, propositional, sale-price, persuasive, advertised, illegal, bribed, cheap, reduced, requested, available, on hire **15 voluntary**, unprompted, unforced, charity, unpaid, philanthropic, humanitarian **16 sacrificial**, martyred, consecrated, oblatory, contributory, donated, propitiatory

514 Oiliness

NOUNS **1 oiliness**, unctuousness, greasiness, lubricity, fatness, pinguidity, richness, creaminess, butteriness, sebaceousness, adiposis, soapiness **2 smoothness**, slickness, slipperiness **3 lubrication**, oiling **4 anointment**, unction, inunctum, chrism **5 lubricant**, antifriction, black lead, plumbago, graphite, glycerine, silicone, wax, grease, mucilage, mucus, spit, synovia, saliva, soap, lather, grease gun, oilcan **6 ointment**, unguent, salve, balm, lotion, cream, pomade, brilliantine, hair oil, spikenard, nard, lanolin, embrocation, liniment, emollient, soothing syrup, lenitive, demulcent, eyewash **7 oil**, grease, ester **8 fat**, adeps, adipocere, ester, tallow, lanolin, blubber, sebum, ceresin, wax, soap, soapflakes, soap powder, suet, lard, butter, margarine, cream **9 petroleum**, fossil oil, fuel oil, crude, petrol, two-star, four-star, unleaded, white gas, kerosene, paraffin, diesel oil **10 resin**, rosin, resinoid, resina, oleoresin, tar, bitumen, asphalt, varnish, japan, gum acaroides
ADJECTIVES **11 oily**, unctuous, unguinous, greasy, oleic, oleaginous, fat, fleshy, adipose, pinguid, blubbery, tallowy, suety, lardy, rich, creamy, buttery, butyric, milky, paraffinic, mucoid, waxy, sebaceous, cereous, soapy, saponaceous, smooth, slick, slippery, slithery **12 unguent**, chrismal, chrismatory **13 lubricant**, lenitive, emollient, soothing **14 resinous**, rosiny, bituminous, pitchy, tarry, asphaltic, varnished, japanned, myrrhy, masticic **15 basted**, greased **16 lubricated**, well-oiled, well-greased, smooth-running
VERBS **17 oil**, grease, lubricate, oleaginize, wax, soap, lather, moisten, smooth **18 anoint**, salve, unguent, embrocate, dress, smear, daub, slick, pomade, spread, baste, butter, butter up, cream, lard, glycerolate

515 Oldness

NOUNS **1 oldness**, elderliness, age, mellowness, venerableness, maturity, seniority, dotage, senility, decrepitude **2 old people**, the elderly, elders, grandparents, ancestors, forebears, senior citizens, pensioners **3 antiquity**, primitiveness, ancientness, rust, decay, olden days, distant past **4 antiquarianism**, classicism, medievalism, archaism **5 old thing**, archaism, antique, Victoriana, heirloom, museum piece, artefact, relic, Stonehenge, listed building, fossil **6 tradition**, custom, common law, folklore, legend **7 ancient people**, prehistoric man, humanoid, protohuman, apeman, hominid **8 prehistoric animal**, woolly mammoth, mastodon, sabre-toothed tiger, dinosaur, brontosaurus, tyrannosaurus, ichthyosaurus, pterodactyl, ammonite **9 antiquarian**, classicist, medievalist, archaeologist **10 staleness**, sourness, rottenness, overripeness

ADJECTIVES 11 old, elderly, aged, venerable, veteran, senior, patriarchal, mature, mellow, ripe, grey-haired, white-haired, grizzled, hoary, decrepit, senile, senescent **12 olden**, antiquarian, antique, ancient, timeworn, archaic, outdated, moth-eaten, musty, crumbling, mouldering, stale, time-honoured, rooted, established, traditional, age-old, ancestral, immemorial, antediluvian, adamic, old-world, prewar, venerable, vintage **13 former**, previous, prior, erstwhile, one-time, sometime, quondam, retired **14 historic**, heroic, Helladic, Hellenic, classical, Roman, Ottoman, Byzantine, medieval, Saxon, Norman, feudal, Gothic **15 primal**, primordial, primitive, primeval, early, antediluvian, prelapsarian, Precambrian, glacial, prehistoric

VERBS 16 be old, go back **17 grow old**, age, decline, deteriorate, fade, burn out, decay, rot, spoil, wither, moulder, decompose, rust, crumble

516 One

NOUNS 1 one, unity, unit, integer, ace, entity, singleton, single, monad, atom, point, item, article, module, individual, person, persona **2 item**, detail, bit, piece **3 oneness**, singleness, wholeness, integrality, unity, union, undividedness, solidarity, indissolubility, coherence **4 singularity**, individuality, uniqueness, specialness, particularity, identity **5 aloneness**, solitude, isolation, apartness, separateness, isolationism, unilateralism, detachment, aloofness, insularity, privacy, seclusion, loneliness **6 singleness**, celibacy, divorce, separation, widowhood **7 single person**, single, bachelor, spinster, maiden aunt, divorcee, widow **8 loner**, lone wolf, only child, solitary, hermit, eremite, anchorite, marabout, stylite, ascetic, recluse, isolationist **9 soloist**, one-man band, monologist **10 single thing**, unicycle, uniped, monocle, monohull, singleton, solitaire, patience, single ticket, single file, single cream

ADJECTIVES 11 one, single, solo, mono, monadic, atomic, individual, solitary, sole **12 one-sided**, unilateral, uniplanar, one-way, unidirectional, one-size, one-piece, unisex, unicellular, unipolar, unicameral, monolingual **13 whole**, entire, complete, integral, unified, united, joined, undivided, indivisible, inseparable, indissoluble, solid **14 singular**, individual, special, particular, distinct, unique, only-begotten, one-off **15 solo**, one-man, one-woman, independent, single-handed, alone, unaided, unassisted, unaccompanied **16 alone**, solitary, isolated, apart, separate, isolationist, unilateralist, detached, aloof, insular, withdrawn, reclusive, lonely, friendless, deserted, abandoned **17 single**, unmarried, divorced, separated, widowed

VERBS 18 be one, stand alone, go solo, withdraw **19 become one**, unite, unify, integrate, cohere, merge, combine, fuse, join **20 single out**, pick out, isolate

517 Opaqueness

ADJECTIVES 1 opaque, nontransparent, nontranslucent, dense, thick, solid, impenetrable, impermeable, impervious, light-tight, dark, black, windowless, blank, covered **2 shady**, obscure, dark, murky, dirty, grimy, dusty, dull, lustreless, matt, muddy, turbid, cloudy, milky, fuzzy, blurred, vague, dim, hazy, smoky, foggy, misty, clouded, obfuscated, opaline, frosted, smoked, filmy **3 mirror-like**, reflecting **4 inscrutable**, baffling, mystifying, cryptic, enigmatic, arcane, recondite, unclear, ambiguous, indefinite, unknowable, unfathomable **5 unintelligent**, dim, stupid, dense, thick, dull, obtuse

NOUNS 6 opaqueness, filminess, density, thickness, solidity, impenetrability, impermeability, imperviousness, darkness, blackness, murkiness, dirtiness, dullness, muddiness, turbidity, cloudiness, milkiness, fuzziness, dimness, haziness, fogginess, obfuscation, reflection **7 opaque thing**, brick wall, muddy water, haze, mist, film, steam, smoke, cloud, fog, peasouper, blizzard, sandstorm, smokescreen, frosted glass, screen, curtain, blind **8 obscurity**, inscrutability, abstruseness, ambiguity, unclearness, unintelligibility **9 stupidity**, thick-headedness, dull-wittedness

VERBS 10 be opaque, cloud over, steam up, mist, fog **11 make opaque**, thicken, muddy, stir up, cloud, darken, dim, frost, smoke, devitrify, screen, cover, coat, obfuscate **12 obscure**, mystify, puzzle

518 Opening

NOUNS 1 opening, gap, hole, hollow, cavity, aperture, orifice, gape, duct, passage, space, interval, slot, split, crack, crevice, chasm, pass, fault, break, fracture, rupture, cut, tear, cleft, fissure, perforation, piercing, pricking, puncture **2 opener**, key, passkey, password, open sesame, tin-opener, bottle-opener, drill, reamer, awl, needle, pin, bodkin, punch, auger, bit, probe, pick, axe, saw, trephine, trepan, lance, lancet, bayonet **3 body orifice**, pore, sweat gland, aural cavity, ear, nostril, anus, cloaca, urethra, vagina, mouth **4 hole**, keyhole, peephole, knothole, eyehole, eyelet, buttonhole, porthole, borehole, blowhole, airhole, shaft, well, mine, excavation, cavern, cave **5 porous thing**, sponge, sieve, colander, teabag, honeycomb, screen, mosquito net, nylon stockings, lattice, grate, grille **6 passageway**, gangway, hallway, corridor, aisle, entrance, exit, doorway, postern, pass, gorge, window, arch, gate, porch, portal, manhole, tunnel, mousehole, rabbithole, conduit, funnel, hose, sewer, drain, pipe, pipeline, windpipe, artery, vein, colon, alimentary canal, ureter, sperm duct, stoma, vent, flue **7 open space**, clearing, meadow, beach, desert, court, yard, glade **8 openness**, frankness, bluntness, explicitness, candour, honesty, sincerity, artlessness, ingenuousness **9 opportunity**, open door, toehold, foothold, chance, possibility, occasion, vacancy, position **10 beginning**, start, commencement, initiation, inception, dawn, birth, inauguration

ADJECTIVES 11 open, wide-open, unclosed, uncovered, unfolded, exposed, visible, ajar, split, torn, cracked, creviced, cleft, fissured, breached, gaping **12 opened up**, unblocked, unlocked, unbarred, unfastened, unsealed, uncovered, uncorked, unobstructed, patent, clear, evident, obvious, manifest, unimpeded, unhindered, unrestricted, accessible, open-door, available, vacant, unenclosed, unprotected, extended, bare **13 holed**, perforated, porous, permeated, sievelike, cribriform, honeycombed, spongy, leaky, injected, penetrated, probed, pierced, pricked, punctured, lanced, bayoneted, stabbed, slashed, gashed, shot, bored, hollowed, drilled, burrowed, tunnelled, sunk, excavated, cavernous, spacial **14 open**, frank, blunt, explicit, plain, candid, unreserved, open-hearted, open-faced, honest, sincere, ingenuous, naive **15 beginning**, commencing, dawning, initial, inceptive, inaugural, introductory, first

VERBS 16 open, uncover, unwrap, unfold, expose, disclose, reveal, show, leave ajar, split, tear, crack, cleave, breach, hack, hew, cut, saw, break, fracture, rupture, gape, erupt **17 open up**, unblock, unlock, unbolt, unbar, unlatch, unfasten, unseal, uncover, uncork, clear, free, access, extend **18 hole**, perforate, permeate, honeycomb, fissure, slot, trephine, trepan, inject, penetrate, probe, pierce, prick, puncture, lance, bayonet, knife, stab, slash, gash, shoot, bore, hollow, drill, burrow, tunnel **19 provide passage for**, drain, pipe, funnel, vent, sieve **20 begin**, start, commence, initiate, dawn, inaugurate

519 Operation

NOUNS 1 operation, implementation, execution, action, performance, exercise, treatment, work, course, procedure, agency, measure, process, movement, motion, power, force, stress, strain, swing **2 joint operation**, cooperation, coordination, interaction, takeover, merger **3 business**, office, production, undertaking, venture, matter, cause, affair, task, work, job, position **4 management**, responsibility, effectiveness, efficiency, direction, handling, manipulation, manoeuvring, maintenance

VERBS 5 be operational, operate, work, go, run, act, play, do, idle, tick over, serve, perform **6 activate**, actuate, make happen, effectuate, influence, stimulate, motivate, wind up, plug in, turn on, switch on, set going, start up **7 take action**, use, handle, deal with, manage, manipulate, manoeuvre, wield, process, treat, employ, implement, execute, move, power, drive, cause, work upon, maintain, service

ADJECTIVES 8 operational, functional, going, working, usable, running **9 workable**, operable, doable, manageable, manipulatable, manoeuvrable, negotiable, practicable, useful **10 operative**, in force, relevant, significant, important, crucial, critical, key, influential, efficacious

520 Oppositeness

• *Doublethink means the power of holding two contradictory beliefs in one's mind simultaneously, and accepting both of them.* Geoge Orwell.

NOUNS 1 oppositeness, contraposition, opposure, antithesis, contrariety, contradiction, contrariness, confrontment, contrast, reverse, inversion, obverse, converse, back, rear, polarity, counterpole, poles apart, antipodes **2 opposites**, contraries, antipodes **3 opposition**, resistance, obstruction, hindrance, confrontation, disapproval, antagonism, hostility, defiance, contention, impugnation, conflict, disagreement, argument, antipathy, enmity, inimicality, animosity

ADJECTIVES 4 opposite, other, contrapositive, antipodal, contrary, contrariwise, contrasting, reverse, inverse, obverse, converse, confronting, oncoming, face-to-face, eyeball-to-eyeball **5 opposing**, resistant, obstructive, hindering, confrontational, disapproving, antipathetic, antagonistic, hostile, defiant, contentious

521 Opposition

NOUNS 1 opposition, hostility, antagonism, antipathy, dislike, hate, aversion, repugnance, disapproval, disapprobation, unfriendliness **2 objection**, complaint, fuss, clamour, demurral, remonstration, expostulation, protest, dissent, dissidence, controversy, disputation, disagreement, argument, contradiction, contravention, challenge, impugnation, rebuttal, refutation, controversion, denial, refusal, rejection **3 conflict**, friction, disaccord, dissension, crosscurrent, collision, clashing, confrontation, strife, discord, rivalry, vying, competition, emulation, contention, fighting, battle, war, attack, defence, bad blood **4 uncooperativeness**, unhelpfulness, negativeness, unwillingness, nonacceptance, dissociation, obstructiveness, prevention **5 contrariness**, perverseness, oppugnancy, stubbornness, obstinacy, disobedience, fractiousness, refractoriness, recalcitrance **6 contrariety**, disagreement, difference, discrepancy, inconsistency, disparity, contrast, contradistinction, antithesis, polarity **7 countermeasure**, counterargument, counterproposal, countercheck, countermove, counterattack

VERBS 8 oppose, stand against, traverse, fight against **9 be contrary**, go against, militate against, counter **10 be against**, discountenance, disapprove of, disagree with, object to, not tolerate, reject, dislike **11 object**, complain, demur, gripe, grouse, moan, take exception, protest, remonstrate, expostulate, deprecate, dissent, assail, criticize, disagree, take issue, dispute, oppugn, contradict, contravene, rebut, refute, negate, deny, controvert, gainsay, counter, retaliate, defend, defy, challenge, impugn, combat **12 confront**, face, breast, stem, conflict, clash, grapple with, contend, vie with, rival, emulate **13 withstand**, resist, obstruct, hinder, check, block, bar, defy, disobey **14 counteract**, antagonize, countervail, act against, countercheck, counterattack, countermine, frustrate, cross, thwart, foil, prevent, counterbalance

ADJECTIVES 15 oppositional, opposing, hostile, antagonistic, inimical, unfriendly, unfavourable, unpropitious, adverse, contrary, counteractive, cross, averse, disapproving, alien **16 discordant**, disagreeing, contentious, dissentient, dissident, different, conflicting, clashing, adversarial, confronting, head-on, challenging, defiant, rival, competitive, competing, contending, at odds **17 contrary**, opposite, reverse, inconsistent, incompatible, contradictory, repugnant, antithetical, adversative, irreconcilable **18 uncooperative**, unhelpful, negative, unwilling, obstructive, contrary, perverse, oppugnant, stubborn, obstinate, disobedient, fractious, refractory, recalcitrant

522 Orangeness

ADJECTIVES 1 orange, reddish-yellow, ochreous, amber, saffron, apricot, peach, golden, old-gold, or, carroty, Titian, ginger, tan, bronze, brassy

NOUNS 2 orangeness, ochre, raw sienna, cadmium orange, henna **3 orange thing**, orange, marmalade, orangeade, orange juice, tangerine, mandarin, clementine, satsuma, peach, apricot, nectarine, carrot, pumpkin, marigold, sunflower, saffron, goldfish, amber, brass, copper, sand **4 figurative orange thing**, orange blossom, orangewood, orangery, orange pekoe, orange stick

523 Orbital Motion

NOUNS 1 orbital motion, wheeling, rounding, circling, circularity, rotation, turning, spiralling, gyre, helix, coil, ellipse, revolution, circulation, circumnavigation, circumambulation, circumflexion **2 circuitousness**, circulation, roundaboutness, indirection, meandering, deviance, digression, circumlocution, excursion, circumbendibus, turning, cornering **3 orbit**, cycle, circle, wheel, circuit, ambit, round trip, lap, loop, walk, turn, rounds, beat **4 orbiting body**, satellite, moon, planet, sun, star, asteroid, Sputnik **5 ringroad**, orbital, bypass

VERBS 6 orbit, circuit, revolve, turn, circulate, spiral, gyre, wheel **7 ring**, circle, compass, surround, skirt, gird, girdle, loop, bend, curve, flank, lap, circumvent, circumambulate, circummigrate **8 detour**, deviate, bypass, digress

ADJECTIVES 9 orbital, rotatory, revolutionary, circuitous, circulatory, turning, roundabout, indirect, oblique, meandering, deviating, circumnavigable, circumambient **10 circular**, round, O-shaped, wheel-shaped, curved, spiral, helical, elliptical, cyclical, gyratory, coiled **11 orbiting**, wheeling, circling, spiralling, turning

524 Order

• *A place for everything, and everything in its place.* Samuel Smiles.

NOUNS 1 order, organization, formalization, arrangement, array, disposition, layout, pattern, composition, formation, structure, set-up, distribution, line-up, prioritization, system, scheme **2 grouping**, categorization, classification, codification, specification, pigeonholing, cataloguing, indexing, listing **3 hierarchy**, pecking order, series, sequence, gradation, progression, alphabetical order **4 position**, place, class, grade, category, degree, rank, status **5 orderliness**, tidiness, neatness, cleanness, smoothness, straightness **6 methodicalness**, meticulousness, punctiliousness, accuracy, straightness, systematization **7 method**, system, discipline, organization, routine, custom, habit, rule, pattern, plan, scheme, structure, coherence, coordination, uniformity, regularity, symmetry **8 harmony**, concord, stability, quiet, peace, calm, tranquillity, stillness **9 discipline**, control

ADJECTIVES 10 ordered, organized, formalized, arranged, arrayed, disposed, composed, structured, schematic, systematic, symmetrical, balanced **11 grouped**, categorized, classified, codified, specified, pigeonholed, indexed, catalogued **12 hierarchical**, serial, sequential, gradational, progressive, alphabetical, numerical, graded **13 orderly**, tidy, neat, clean, smooth, straight, correct, trim, spruce, dapper, smart, sleek, slick, groomed, kempt **14 well-ordered**, well-organized, methodical, meticulous, punctilious, systematic, scientific, businesslike, formal, accurate, straight, regular **15 habitual**, routine, usual, regular **16 harmonious**, concordant, stable, steady, quiet, peaceful, calm **17 disciplined**, controlled, restrained, law-abiding, peaceable, docile, obedient, well-behaved

VERBS 18 order, arrange, array, dispose, lay out, organize, marshal, manage, compose, form, structure, set up, align **19 systematize**, methodize, rationalize, standardize, sort out, sift, group, categorize, classify, catalogue, codify, index, pigeonhole, rank, grade, place, position, tabulate **20 harmonize**, stabilize, regularize, regulate, synchronize **21 tidy**, neaten, clean, smooth, straighten, correct, smarten up, spruce up **22 pacify**, calm, cool down, discipline, control, govern **23 be in order**, work, function **24 line up**, fall in

525 Originality

•*All good things which exist are the fruits of originality.* John Stuart Mill.

NOUNS 1 originality, creativity, creation, nonimitation, dissimilarity, genuineness, authenticity, inventiveness, innovation, initiation, imagination, individuality, independence, idiosyncrasy, eccentricity, novelty, newness, uniqueness, freshness, precedence **2 original**, autograph, holograph, signature, manuscript, first edition, source, model, paradigm, blueprint, pattern, mould, prototype, archetype, test case

ADJECTIVES 3 original, creative, inventive, imaginative, innovative, first, pioneering, seminal, prototypal **4 novel**, unique, different, personal, individual, one-off, unparalleled, unprecedented, unheard-of, off-beat, sui generis, inimitable, incomparable, new, fresh, avant-garde, revolutionary, transcendent **5 authentic**, genuine, real, bona fide, verified, true, natural, sincere, unadulterated, uncopied, patented

VERBS 6 originate, invent, innovate, create, devise, design, imagine, dream up, conceive, generate, pioneer, start, initiate, begin

526 Ornament

NOUNS 1 ornament, adornment, decoration, garnish, trimming, embellishment, colour, flourish, embroidery, frills, arrangement, floridness, floweriness, arabesques, purple passages, preciosity, euphuism, rhetoric, figurativeness, metaphor, simile, trope, alliteration, assonance, hyperbaton **2 affectation**, pomposity, pretension, ostentation, showiness, false front, magniloquence, grandiloquence, loftiness, eloquence, rhetoric, orotundity, vigour, extravagance, overstatement, exaggeration, hyperbole, turgidity, flatulence, boasting, bombast, rant, fustian, rodomontade, Johnsonese, diffuseness, circumlocution

ADJECTIVES 3 ornate, elaborate, fancy, decorated, adorned, garnished, trimmed, embellished, beautified, gilded, coloured, rich, luxuriant, florid, flowery, precious, euphuistic, euphemistic, extravagant, overstated, exaggerated, hyperbolic, affected, pompous, pretentious, ostentatious, flamboyant, showy, meretricious, frothy, fussy, overloaded, stiff, stilted, pedantic, ponderous, Latinate, sesquipedalian, Johnsonian, diffuse, circumlocutory, convoluted, tortuous, rhetorical, declamatory, oratorical, eloquent, grandiloquent, magniloquent, lofty, high-flown, loud, brassy, ringing, ranting, orotund, high-pitched, grandiose, stately, bombastic, fustian, inflated, tumid, turgid, antithetical, alliterative

VERBS 4 ornament, adorn, decorate, garnish, trim, deck, festoon, embellish, beautify, enhance, grace, embroider, enrich, gild, overlay, overload, euphuize, euphemize, elaborate, overstate, ring, sing, boast

527 Oscillation

NOUNS 1 oscillation, fluctuation, alternation, pendulation, libration, nutation, reciprocation, periodicity, frequency **2 vibration**, resonance, pulsation, rhythm, tempo, pulse, throb, beat, heartbeat, throbbing, staccato, rat-a-tat, rataplan, drumming, flickering, shaking, quivering, shivering, palpitation, flutter, tremor, agitation, pitter-patter **3 vacillation**, wavering, equivocation, indecision, hesitation, irresolution **4 rock**, roll, reel, lurch, careen, pitch, shake, dance, swing, sway, waggle, waver, undulation, brandishing, flourishing, shaking **5 oscillator**, bob, pendulum, vibrator, metronome, swing, teeterboard, rocker, rocking chair, seesaw

VERBS 6 oscillate, fluctuate, alternate, vary, swing, sway, pendulate, nutate, reciprocate, seesaw, teeter, shuttle, wibble-wobble **7 vibrate**, resonate, pulsate, beat, drum, tick, throb, flutter, agitate, shake, quiver, rattle, shiver, flicker, tremble, palpitate, pant **8 vacillate**, waver, hesitate, fluctuate **9 rock**, roll, reel, lurch, careen, pitch, shake, dance, stagger, totter, tumble, swing, sway, swag, waggle, waddle, wave, waver, dangle, nod, flutter, bob **10 wave**, undulate, brandish, flourish, shake, wield, float, fly, flutter

ADJECTIVES 11 oscillating, swinging, fluctuating, alternating, reciprocal, back-and-forth, to-and-fro, up-and-down, seesaw, harmonic, libratory **12 vibrating**, resonant, pulsating, beating, throbbing, staccato, rhythmic, flickering, quivering, shivering, shaking, agitating **13 vacillating**, wavering, hesitant **14 rocking**, rolling, reeling, lurching, careening, pitching, shaking, dancing, tossing, staggering **15 waving**, undulating, sinusoidal, shaking, tremulous, seismic, succussive

528 Outline

NOUNS 1 outline, plan, summary, synopsis, abstract, epitome, précis, notes, bare essentials, frame, profile, projection, ground plan, layout, blueprint, representation, limning, emblem, sample, survey, contour, illustration, etching, engraving, delineation, depiction, chart, graph, diagram, portrayal, picture, thumbnail sketch, tracing, skeleton, bare bones, reduction, abridgement, digest, condensation, contraction **2 shadow**, silhouette, shape, form, relief, profile, contour, figure **3 edge**, horizon, skyline, coastline, perimeter, border, fringe, flange, margin, circumference, surround, rim **4 map**, town plan, Mercator projection, Peters' projection, globe

VERBS 5 outline, plan, sketch out, rough out, summarize, abstract, epitomize, précis, note, frame, profile, project, blueprint, picture, portray, sketch, limn, represent, sample, survey, illustrate, etch, engrave, delineate, depict, chart, graph, diagram, trace, reduce, abridge, digest, condense

ADJECTIVES 6 outlined, summarized, brief, impressionistic, representative, emblematic, sample, random, descriptive, delineative, depictive, thumbnail, skeletal, abridged, abbreviated, circumscriptive, projectional

529 Overestimation

NOUNS 1 overestimation, overvaluation, overrating, miscalculation, rashness, overoptimism, idealism, conceit, hubris, arrogance, egomania, exaggeration, overstatement, hyperbole, hype, megalomania **2 overestimate**, pipe dream, fool's paradise, Utopia

VERBS 3 overestimate, overvalue, overrate, overprize, overprice, overcharge, misjudge, miscalculate, exaggerate, overstate, hype, overpraise

ADJECTIVES 4 overestimating, overconfident, rash, overoptimistic, overenthusiastic, hubristic **5 overestimated**, overvalued, overrated, overpriced, dear, expensive, misjudged

530 Overstepping

VERBS 1 overstep, overrun, overpass, overgrow, overgo, overreach, leapfrog, overspread, overflow, irrupt, flood, spill over **2 cross**, cross over **3 exceed**, surpass, outdo, outclass, excel, transcend, surmount, rise above, outrival, outbid, outmanoeuvre, outflank, outstrip, outdistance, outride, outrun, overtake, shoot ahead, lap, leave standing, race **4 exaggerate**, overdo, superabound, overrate, overestimate, strain, stretch, overbid, overact, overplay **5 transgress**, trespass, infringe, encroach, entrench, impinge, violate, breach, usurp, squat, poach, make inroads, barge in, intrude, invade, overrun

NOUNS 6 overstepping, overrunning, overtaking, overgrowth, inundation, overflowing, irruption **7 crossing**, transcursion, transilience, transcendence, leap-frog, jump, excursion **8 transgression**, trespass, incursion, infringement, infraction, encroachment, intrusion, invasion, infestation, violation, breach, usurpation **9 excessiveness**, exaggeration, overacting, overplaying, overestimation, overrating, arrogation, hyperbole, excess, overfulfilment, surplus, redundance, overindulgence, intemperance **10 expansionism**, overextension, ribbon development

ADJECTIVES **11 overrun**, overspread, overgrown, overflowing, brimming, flooding, inundated, infested, beset, teeming, swarming, plagued, encroaching, trespassing, intrusive **12 excessive**, unwarranted, overreaching, undue, uncalled-for, exorbitant **13 exaggerated**, overdone, pretentious, affected, hyperbolic, overrated, overindulgent, overambitious, strained, far-fetched, grandiose, grandiloquent **14 surpassing**, overextended **15 out of reach**, unreachable, far away, cut off, secluded, forbidden

531 Pacification

NOUNS **1 pacification**, peacemaking, irenics, nonviolence, ahimsa, satyagraha, conciliation, propitiation, appeasement, mollification, moderation, reconciliation, détente, rapprochement, accommodation, adjustment, agreement, compromise, mediation, arbitration, convention, entente, understanding, treaty, nonaggression pact, truce, lull, cessation, armistice, cease-fire, moratorium, test ban **2 peace offering**, irenicon, olive branch, friendliness, white flag, peace pipe, calumet, wergild, blood money, compensation, reparation, atonement, restitution, amnesty, pardon, mercy, forgiveness

VERBS **3 pacify**, avoid war, conciliate, propitiate, disarm, reconcile, placate, appease, satisfy, content, allay, ease, alleviate, soothe, tranquillize, mollify, assuage, quell, subdue, smooth over, compose, restore, heal, harmonize, accommodate, mediate **4 make peace**, stop fighting, compromise, meet halfway, agree, disarm, suspend hostilities

ADJECTIVES **5 pacificatory**, conciliatory, placatory, propitiatory, appeasing, irenic, dove-like, friendly, disarming, satisfying, calming, soothing, emollient, lenitive, mediatory, negotiated, pacifiable, satisfied

532 Painting and Sculpture

• *A picture has been said to be something between a thing and a thought.* Samuel Palmer.

NOUNS **1 art**, the arts, fine arts, applied arts, plastic art, graphic arts, decorative arts, design, industrial design, industrial art, commercial art, kinetic art, calligraphy, batik, screen printing, embroidery, tapestry, wood carving, metalwork, enamelling, mosiacs, ceramics, stained glass, photography, lithography **2 artistry**, art, skill, flair, technique, composition, golden section, perspective, foreshortening, draughtsmanship, brushwork, painterliness, talent, mastery, invention, taste, virtu, connoisseurship, craftsmanship, artisanship **3 work of art**, masterpiece, old master, picture, likeness, image, illustration, painting, miniature, tableau, illumination, reproduction, plate, print, photogravure, woodcut, aquatint, poster, picture postcard, montage, photomontage, collage, brass rubbing, frottage, painting, canvas, daub, fresco, mural, icon, altarpiece, cave painting, action painting, finger painting, oil painting, aquarelle, wash, impasto, encaustic, grisaille, drawing, delineation, sketch, draft, outline, study, vignette, silhouette, doodle, scribble, graffito, caricature, cartoon, comic, animation, silverpoint drawing, diagram **4 art subject**, portrait, nude, landscape, seascape, cloudscape, townscape, scene, prospect, panorama, pastoral, nocturne, interior, historical painting, battle painting, genre painting, conversation piece, still-life, flower painting **5 artist's materials**, pen, pencil, ink, chalk, charcoal, crayon, pastel, paintbrush, palette, palette knife, spatula, mahlstick, spraygun, airbrush, paintbox, oils, watercolours, acrylics, gouache, gesso, tempera, distempes, ground, medium, solvent, siccative, fixative, size, varnish, paper, sketchbook, easel, stretcher, drawing frame, camera obscura, camera lucida **6 sculpture**, plastic art, modelling, carving, relief, intaglio, anaglyptics, cameo, medallion, medal, embossing, engraving. etching, chalcography, zincography, xylography, lignography, linocut, lithograph, cerography, glyptography, chasing, aquatint, mezzotint, plate, chasing, pointing, stonecutting, statuary, statue, statuette, figure, figurine, bust, head, torso, group, caryatid, earth art, mobile, stabile, marble, bronze, terracotta, whittling, scrimshaw, petroglyph, maquette, moulding, ceroplastics, casting **7 sculptor's materials**, mallet, chisel, burin, graver, style, modelling tool, point, spatula, drill, punch, pointing machine, welding torch, cutting torch, soldering iron, armature, modelling clay, wax, plaster, marble, granite, bronze, terracotta **8 artist**, designer, craftsman, artisan, painter, colourist, dauber, aquarellist, pastellist, portraitist, sign painter, pavement artist, drawer, draughtsman, sketcher, delineator, illustrator, copyist, illuminator, miniaturist, cartoonist, caricaturist, animator, doodler, enameller, old master, modern master **9 sculptor**, carver, statuary, monumental mason, figurist, modeller, moulder, caster, engraver, etcher, aquatinter, chaser, lapidary

VERBS 10 paint, colour, colourize, tint, coat, brush, tone, overpaint, underpaint, scumble, wash, shade, daub, illuminate, ink in **11 draw**, sketch, draft, pencil, chalk, limn, outline, doodle, cartoon, caricature, depict, copy, trace, stencil, silhouette, hatch **12 sculpt**, carve, cut, chisel, chip, whittle, shape, cast, model, mould **13 engrave**, grave, incise, etch, chase, scrape, bite, impress, emboss, aquatint **14 design**, lay out, compose, arrange

ADJECTIVES 15 pictorial, graphic, calligraphic, linear, optical, illusionist, photographic, iconic **16 sculptural**, marmoreal, monumental, graven, moulded, plastic, glyptic, anaglyptic, ceroplastic **17 artistic**, painterly, decorative, picturesque **18 realist**, naturalist, photorealist, verist, socialist realist, regionalist, precisionist, purist, classical, neoclassical, romantic, neoromantic, impressionist, neoimpressionist, postimpressionist, pointillist, divisionist, minimalist, primitive, naive, Fauvist, vorticist, concrete, constructivist, cubist, expressionist, neoexpressionist, figurative, symbolist, Dadaist, abstract, eclectic, mannerist, postmodernist, rayonist, Orphistic, suprematist, synchronic, synthetic, analytic, Renaissance, Baroque, rococo, Gothic, Hellenistic, Etruscan, Celtic

533 Parallelism

NOUNS 1 parallelism, equidistance, concentricity, coextension, collimation, nonconvergence, nondivergence, correlation, correspondence, balance, alignment, equality, uniformity **2 parallel thing**, parallelogram, parallelepiped, parallel bars, railway tracks

ADJECTIVES 3 parallel, equidistant, concentric, coextensive, nonconvergent, nondivergent **4 correlated**, correspondent, balanced, aligned, equal

VERBS 5 parallel, run abreast, coextend **6 correlate**, correspond, balance, align

534 Part

NOUNS 1 part, fragment, particle, portion, proportion, majority, minority, fraction, half, moiety, third, quarter, eighth, tenth, tithe, percentage, aliquot, divisor, factor, quotient, dividend, share, quota, remainder, balance, surplus, element, faction, class, category, group, family, genus, species, phylum, division, segment, sector, arc, curve, semicircle, hemisphere, partition, compartment, department, ward, community, parish **2 particular**, detail, item, article, chapter, episode, instalment, fascicule, part, number, issue, edition, canto, verse, section, paragraph, sentence, clause, phrase, word, page, folio, sheet, leaf, volume, passage, quotation, citation, sound bite, gobbet, extract, text, deposit, tranche, advance, foretaste, preview, appetizer, sample **3 stage**, phase, leg, lap, round **4 component**, constituent, ingredient, element, particle, molecule, member, appendage, organ, limb, wing, flipper, fin **5 largest part**, bulk, mass, majority, lion's share, bare essentials, gist, summary **6 branch**, offshoot, ramification, petal, tendril, leaf, leaflet, shoot, scion, sucker, sprig, limb, spur, twig, stem, stalk **7 piece**, bit, segment, patch, insertion, addition, swatch, scrap, off-cut, rag, shred, wisp, speck, morsel, bite, crumb, sliver, splinter, snippet, chip, slice, tranche, wedge, finger, rasher, cutlet, chunk, hunk, lump, slab, bar, clod, sod, shard, flake, scale, drop, portion, helping **8 bits and pieces**, miscellanea, oddments, bin ends, shavings, clippings, parings, peelings, leavings, detritus, moraine, debris, rags **9 participation**, role, character, duty

VERBS 10 part, divide, share, apportion, cut up, dissect, segment, sectionalize, compartmentalize, partition, separate, split, bisect, sever, fragment

ADJECTIVES 11 partial, broken, fragmented, in smithereens, brashy, crumbly, incomplete, limbless, headless, imperfect, inadequate, insufficient, scrappy, bitty, piecemeal, unfinished, fractional, aliquot, proportional, partitive, segmental, sectional, compartmental, departmental, divided, molecular, atomic, elemental, sliced, diced, minced, ground

535 Party

NOUNS 1 party, group, body, band, company, set, bunch, gang, cabol, alliance, federation, mob, outfit, troupe, force, side, league, ring, camp, crew, team, squad, corps, troop, coterie, clique, cadre, circle, committee, council, congregation, sect, denomination, church, fellowship, fraternity, brotherhood, guild, trade union, society, order, association, partnership, institution, establishment, enterprise, foundation, corporation, conglomerate, syndicate, consortium, cartel, monopoly **2 society**, community, race, tribe, clan, family, class **3 political grouping**, the right, the left, democracy, federalism, republicanism, liberalism, socialism, communism, coalition, alliance, federation, union, league, confederation, cell, bloc, caucus, junta, splinter group, offshoot, faction, grass-roots movement, fringe group, cabal **4 partisanship**, partiality, factionalism, sectionalism, clannishness, cliquishness, exclusiveness, sectarianism, separatism **5 member**, initiate, belonger, affiliate, insider, cardholder, card-carrier, associate, fellow **6 political party member**, politician, Green, activist, party worker, loyalist, stalwart, right-winger, liberal, moderate, independent, hardliner, left-winger, radical, socialist, communist, sectarian, comrade **7 social gathering**, event, get-together, gala, reception, shindig, ceilidh, soirée, beanfeast, wedding breakfast

ADJECTIVES 8 leagued, cliquish, clubbish, inner-circle, exclusive, congregational, sectarian, denominational, communal, fraternal, brotherly, sisterly, cooperative, institutional, corporate, incorporated, syndicated, consortial **9 societal**, racial, tribal, clannish, familial, federal **10 political**, politicized, party-minded, partisan, bipartisan, affiliated, associated, right-wing, true-blue, left-wing, leftist, popular, middle-of-the-road, liberal, independent, nonpartisan, green, radical, socialistic, communistic, factional, sectional, sectarian, separatist, particular **11 social**, hospitable, congenial, gala

VERBS 12 be in league with, group together, club together, fraternize, unionize, associate with, incorporate, syndicate, federate, collaborate **13 be a member**, subscribe to, join, sign up, enlist, enrol, initiate, belong to **14 be a party member**, align oneself, side with, sign on **15 politicize**, democratize, federalize, liberalize, socialize, communize, ally, federate **16 host**, have company, invite, entertain, regale **17 socialize**, gather

536 Passage

NOUNS 1 passage, passing through, movement, transit, transmission, transference, transduction, transfusion, crossing, traversing, transcursion, journey, voyage, trip, perambulation, patrol, round **2 passing along**, walking, driving, riding, flying, progress, thoroughfare, road, route, course, track, path, orbit, circulation, parking, layby, diversion **3 passage into**, entrance, entry, ingress, penetration, intervention, infiltration, transudation, permeation, percolation **4 access**, approach, road, path, footpath, stepping stones, pass, channel **5 crossing point**, intersection, junction, crossroads, roundabout, clover leaf, flyover, bridge, pontoon, viaduct, underpass, tunnel, ford, traffic lights, Belisha beacon, island, central reservation, frontier post **6 passport**, visa, pass, safe conduct, ID, clearance, papers

VERBS 7 pass, flash by, overtake, skirt **8 proceed**, go, move along, travel, journey, voyage, circulate, patrol **9 enter**, penetrate, infiltrate, permeate, percolate, osmose **10 cross**, traverse, transit, negotiate, ford, step over, bridge, straddle, bestride, span, overfly, traject, transmit, transport

ADJECTIVES 11 passing, overtaking, moving, proceeding, transferring, transducing, crossing, traversing **12 penetrating**, infiltrating, transudating, permeating, percolating

537 Past Time

- *Even God cannot change the past.* Agathon.
- *Study the past, if you would divine the future.* Confucius.
- *The past is a foreign country: they do things differently there.* L. P. Hartley.

NOUNS 1 past time, yesterday, prehistory, history, ancient times, antiquity, time immemorial, bygone days, olden days **2 retrospection**, remembrance, reminiscence, review, reprise **3 geological period**, geological epoch, Precambrian era, Palaeozoic era, Mesozoic era, Cenozoic era, Tertiary period, Quaternary period **4 prehistoric age**, Stone Age, Palaeolithic period, Mesolithic period, Neolithic period, Chalcolithic period, Bronze Age **5 historical period**, heroic age, Classical Age, Dark Ages, Middle Ages, Renaissance, *ancien régime*, Industrial Revolution **6 people of the past**, cave-dweller, caveman, Neanderthal man, the ancients, Egyptians, Babylonians, Ethiopians, ancient Greeks, ancient Romans, Huns, Incas, Aztecs, Picts, Vandals, Goths, Saxons, Angles, Maori, Aborigines **7 thing of the past**, museum piece, antique, relic, remains, vestiges, fossil, monument, ancient ruin, artefact, megalith, dolmen, cromlech, menhir, Stonehenge, pyramid **8 antiquarianism**, classicism, medievalism, archaeology, palaeontology, palaeoanthropology, palaeogeography, palaeethnology **9 fossilization**, petrification, fossil, ammonite, trilobite, dinosaur, mammoth, amber, coal, peat, oil **10 genealogy**, lineage, pedigree

VERBS 11 be past, be over **12 pass**, finish, end, elapse, expire, become extinct **13 look back**, remember, reminisce, review, reprise, regress, antiquarianize, archaize, hark back **14 excavate**, exhume

ADJECTIVES 15 past, historical, old, prehistoric, protohistoric, ancient, early, elder, primitive, primal **16 over**, gone, gone forever, bygone, finished, exhausted, ended, done, spent, completed, irrecoverable **17 antiquarian**, ancestral, antecedent, preceding, foregoing, outdated, outworn, outmoded, old hat, anachronistic, antiquated, fossilized, old-fashioned, obsolete, passé, stale **18 former**, late, quondam, sometime, obsolescent, retired, emeritus, superannuated **19 retrospective**, retroactive, diachronic, remembering

538 Payment

NOUNS 1 payment, disbursement, remittance, expenditure, outlay, defrayment, payoff, discharge, quittance, release, satisfaction, liquidation, clearance, settlement, receivables, receipt, ready cash, money, deposit, earnest, handsel, instalment, premium, standing order, direct debit, subscription, tribute, donation, contribution, offering, appeal **2 repayment**, reimbursement, refund, compensation, recompense, indemnity, restitution, payment-in-lieu, substitution **3 pay**, remuneration, salary, stipend, emolument, honorarium, fee, commission, royalty, advance, payroll, payout, pay packet, income, earnings, reward, tip, gratuity, pension, annuity, payoff **4 grant**, grant-in-aid, subsidy, subvention, donation, contribution, subscription, tribute, damages, indemnity, penalty, tax, ransom

VERBS 5 pay, disburse, remit, expend, spend, subscribe, trade **6 pay off**, discharge, satisfy, redeem, meet, liquidate, clear, settle **7 defray**, stand, treat, give, donate, contribute, fund **8 pay one's way**, share expenses **9 pay back**, repay, reimburse, refund, compensate, recompense, indemnify **10 remunerate**, distribute, reward, tip **11 be profitable**, benefit **12 retaliate**, avenge oneself, reciprocate **13 atone**, make amends

ADJECTIVES 14 paying, disbursing, expending **15 paid**, liquidated, debt-free, cleared, settled **16 payable**, due, owed, remittable, refundable **17 profitable**, worthwhile, advantageous, lucrative, remunerative, rewarding **18 receiving pay**, earning, salaried, wage-earning, hired, prepaid **19 paying in return**, compensatory

539 Peace

• *Give peace in our time, O Lord.* The Book of Common Prayer.

NOUNS 1 peace, peacetime, quiet life, no hassle, quiescence, rest, stillness, harmony, concord, palmy days, golden times, Pax Romana, truce, cessation, armistice, ceasefire, surrender, demobilization, coexistence, neutrality, nonalignment, noninvolvment, indifference, nonintervention, avoidance, nonaggression, amity, friendship, pacifism, nonviolence, ahimsa, disarmament, peace movement, irenics, peace pipe, calumet, nonaggression pact, disarmament treaty **2 symbol of peace**, dove, lamb, olive branch, white flag, peace sign, V-sign, peace pipe, Christ, angel, broken arrow **3 pacifist**, peacemaker, dove, neutral, civilian, noncombatant, conscientious objector

VERBS 4 be at peace, observe neutrality **5 make peace**, pacify, mediate

ADJECTIVES 6 peaceful, quiet, tranquil, serene, still, calm, halcyon, piping, palmy, golden, harmonious, peacelike, dovelike, innocent, mild, easy-going, good-natured, agreeable, tolerant, peaceable, law-abiding, nonaggressive, pacifist, nonviolent, passive, civilian, neutral, nonaligned, conciliatory

540 Penitence

NOUNS 1 penitence, repentance, contrition, remorsefulness, self-reproach, regretfulness, sorriness, shamefulness, scruples, qualms, soul-searching, compunction, guilt, hair shirt, guilty conscience, pangs, confession, recantation, apology, reformation **2 type of penance**, atonement, reparation, mortification, breast-beating, flagellation, prostration

VERBS 3 be penitent, repent, feel remorse, blame oneself, regret, feel sorry, apologize, show compunction, blame oneself, recant **4 do penance**, atone, make amends, scourge oneself, prostrate oneself

ADJECTIVES 5 penitent, repentant, contrite, remorseful, regretful, lamenting, sorry, apologetic, sorrowful, rueful, ashamed, self-condemning, compunctious, guilty, conscience-stricken, confessing, reformed, converted **6 penitential**, atoning

541 Perfection

• *Perfection has one grave defect; it is apt to be dull.* W. Somerset Maugham.

ADJECTIVES 1 perfect, finished, completed, fulfilled, polished, ripened, ready, matured, exact, just right, ideal, best, flawless, faultless, impeccable, infallible, indefectible, correct, precise, accurate, spot on, irreproachable, immaculate, unstained, spotless, blemish-free, uncontaminated, pure, blameless, exemplary, innocent, impeccant, saintly, sound, unbroken, uncracked, undamaged, unmarred, unspoiled, unscathed, unscarred, airtight, watertight, intact, whole, entire, absolute, utter, total, excellent, sublime, superb, dazzling, brilliant, masterly, expert, proficient, skilled, consummate, supreme, transcendent, unsurpassable, unequalled, unmatched, unrivalled, peerless, top, number-one, archetypal, classical **2 perfectionist**, purist, pedantic, precise, punctilious, meticulous, fastidious, scrupulous, particular, exacting

NOUNS 3 perfection, perfectness, finish, completion, consummation, polish, ripeness, readiness, maturity, exactness, idealness, flawlessness, faultlessness, impeccability, infallibility, indefectability, correctness, preciseness, accuracy, irreproachability, immaculacy, spotlessness, purity, blamelessness, guiltlessness, innocence, impeccancy, soundness, wholeness, completeness, excellence, brilliance, mint condition, mastery, expertise, skill, transcendence, quintessence, peak, zenith, acme, summit, pinnacle, capstone, pattern, standard, archetype, paragon, ultimate, extreme, last word, crowning achievement, masterpiece **4 perfectionist**, purist, pedant, stickler, expert, master

VERBS 5 perfect, finish, complete, fulfil, realize, accomplish, achieve, execute, ripen, mature, consummate, correct, rectify, improve, ameliorate, elaborate, polish, refine **6 be perfect**

542 Performing Arts

NOUNS 1 drama, the theatre, the stage, amateur dramatics, dramaticism, theatricals, histrionics, Thespian art, fringe theatre, repertory, alternative theatre, street theatre **2 play**, show, work, piece, vehicle, script, text, lines, libretto, prompt book, monodrama, duodrama, two-hander, dialogue, skit, sketch, playlet, charade, curtain-raiser, double bill, dramatic cycle, farce, pantomime, mime, dumbshow, masque, melodrama, heroic drama, sociodrama, psychodrama, kitchen-sink drama, docudrama, community drama, improvisation, happening, radio play, teleplay, screenplay, scenario, serial **3 musical drama**, opera, operetta, musical, rock opera, ballet **4 show business**, entertainment industry, vaudeville, variety, burlesque, music hall, West End **5 dramaturgy**, dramatic art, stagecraft, theatre craft, theatrical convention, dramatic convention, dramatic irony, alienation effect, plot, subplot, characterization, story, dialogue, monologue, soliloquy, staging, choreography, action, sensationalism, spectacle **6 tragedy**, tragic drama, high tragedy, Greek tragedy, Renaissance tragedy, Shakespearean tragedy, revenge tragedy, domestic tragedy, romantic tragedy, melodrama **7 comedy**, high comedy, low comedy, situation comedy, sex comedy, black comedy, satirical comedy, farce, knockabout, stand-up comedy, slapstick, burlesque, high camp, alternative comedy, satyr play, Restoration comedy **8 theatrical performance**, performance, show, production, presentation, exhibition, bill, premiere, preview, first night, gala night, debut, farewell performance, command performance, benefit, matinée, sell-out, full house, hit **9 theatre**, venue, playhouse, hall, hippodrome, auditorium, arena, amphitheatre, stadium, circus, odeon, outdoor theatre, theatre-in-the-round, music hall, opera house, concert hall, cinema, movie theatre, picture house, nightclub, booth, showboat, big top, pavilion **10 stage**, the boards, acting area, proscenium, bridge, apron, trap, stage left, stage right, upstage, downstage, centrestage, frontstage, orchestra pit, podium, rostrum, soapbox, wings, backstage, dressing room, greenroom, stage door, flies, gridiron, lightboard, switchboard, sounddesk **11 auditorium**, seating, stalls, pit, front rows, box, royal box, circle, dress circle, balcony, gallery, mezzanine, standing room, foyer **12 stage set**, scenery, prop, costume, makeup, greasepaint, decor, flat, cyclorama, drop curtain, backdrop, backcloth, gauze, transparency, drape, safety curtain, footlights, floodlight, spotlight, houselights, colour wheel, gelatin, iris diaphragm, projector, stroboscope **13 acting**, playacting, playing, role-playing, impersonation, personation, portrayal, representation, characterization, interpretation, projection, mimicry, character acting, method acting, the Method, improvisation, overacting, barnstorming, stage whisper, aside, entrance, exit, cue, stage presence, showmanship, star quality **14 role**, part, character, title role, leading role, protagonist, antagonist, supporting character, minor role, bit part, walk-on part, straight man, cameo, vignette, chorus, stock character, juvenile lead, love interest, breeches part, fool, stage villain, stage drunk, principal boy, principal girl **15 actor**, actress, play-actor, player, Thespian, trouper, tragedian, comedian, improviser, film star, superstar, matinée idol, understudy, stand-in, extra, spear-carrier, diva, prima donna, narrator **16 cast**, characters, chorus, ensemble, company, outfit **17 dramatist**, dramaturge, playwright, scenarist, screen writer, script writer, librettist, choreographer **18 producer**, director, auteur, stage manager, impresario, exhibitor, promoter, showman, ringmaster, theatrical agent, playbroker, patron **19 stagehand**, stage crew, sound man, lighting man, scene painter, scene shifter, flyman, dresser, wardrobe mistress, make-up artist, callboy, prompter, front-of-house staff **20 entertainer**, artiste, performer, quick-change artiste, drag artiste, impersonator, impressionist, mimic, ventriloquist, conjuror, magician, mountebank, hypnotist, escapologist, mindreader, memory artist, comic, stand-up comic, minstrel, troubadour, busker, chorus girl, chorus boy, presenter **21 dancer**, ballerina, coryphée, figurant, Terpsichorean, erotic dancer **22 circus performer**, tightrope walker, ropewalker, high-wire artist, equilibrist, trapeze artist, tumbler, acrobat, contortionist, juggler, strongman, stuntman, human cannonball, fire-eater, snake charmer, lion tamer, bareback rider, ringmaster

VERBS 23 act, perform, enact, play, playact, mime **24 overact**, send up, overplay, upstage, barnstorm, improvize **25 underact**, fluff

ADJECTIVES 26 dramatic, dramaturgic, melodramatic, spectacular, theatrical, mimetic, musical, operatic, choral, balletic, choreographic, Terpsichorean, histrionic, Thespian, stagy, protagonistic **27 tragic**, tragi-comic, comic, farcical

543 Period

NOUNS 1 period, interval, span, time, timespan, term, stretch, space, fit, spell, break **2 time period**, era, aeon, age, generation, epoch, millennium, chiliad, century, decade, decennium, quinquennium, year, quarter, month, fortnight, week, day, hour, minute, second, moment, instant, millisecond, microsecond **3 geological period**, era, epoch, eon **4 period of activity**, stint, spell, phase, turn, watch, session, shift, working day, man-hour, school term, academic year, semester, tenure, fiscal year, sentence, bout **5 recurrent period**, series, season, cycle, iteration, menstrual cycle, biorhythm, circadian rhythm, biological clock **6 periodicity**, recurrence, return, repetition **7 periodical**, magazine, journal, newsletter, bulletin, weekly

ADJECTIVES 8 periodical, regular, repetitive, iterative, returning, recurrent, quinquennial, millennial, cyclic, seasonal, yearly, annual, biennial, monthly, weekly **9 periodic**, intermittent, sporadic, discontinuous

VERBS 10 be periodical, recur, reappear, repeat, iterate, reiterate **11 make periodical**, regulate

544 Permanence

NOUNS 1 permanence, continuance, continuity, everlastingness, perpetuity, establishment, entrenchment, persistence, perseverance, dependability, steadfastness, reliability, endurance, abidance, durability, survival, subsistence, conservation, preservation, environmentalism, indestructibility, imperishability, immortality, eternity, changelessness, constancy, immutability, finality, fixedness, firmness, solidity, steadiness, stability, immobility **2 conservatism**, rightism, stubbornness **3 conservationist**, environmentalist

VERBS 4 be permanent, last, continue, persist, persevere, stand fast, resist change, endure, abide, survive, subsist, outlive, last forever, set in **5 make permanent**, perpetuate, conserve, preserve, sustain, keep, immortalize, fix, finalize, establish, stabilize

ADJECTIVES 6 permanent, lasting, unchanging, everlasting, perpetual, persistent, persevering, continuing, constant, changeless, invariable, unalterable, immutable, unfailing, dependable, reliable, steadfast, sustained, perennial, evergreen, abiding, enduring, surviving, subsisting, durable, stable, fixed, established, entrenched, longstanding, indestructible, conserved, preserved, imperishable, unbreakable, inviolable, immortal, undying, eternal, firm, solid, steady, rock-steady, immovable, rigid, static **7 conservative**, traditional, right-wing, true-blue, reactionary, obstinate, stubborn, old-fashioned, unprogressive

545 Permission

NOUNS 1 permission, authorization, leave, approval, consent, approbation, blessing, benevolence, clearance, authority, legality, law, mandate, sanction, endorsement, confirmation, ratification, verification, corroboration, validation, tolerance, dispensation, exemption, nonliability, connivance, acquiescence, concession, licence, free hand, carte blanche, blank cheque, indulgence, leniency, permissiveness, laissez-faire attitude, promiscuity **2 permit**, grant, warrant, charter, patent, certificate, credentials, diploma, testimonial, recommendation, reference, seal, signature endorsement, voucher, ticket, docket, chit, licence, release, waiver, imprimatur, green card, pass, passport, visa, password, leave, furlough, vacation, sabbatical

VERBS 3 permit, allow, let, make possible, authorize, approve, clear, sanction, endorse, confirm, ratify, verify, corroborate, validate, tolerate, exempt, connive, acquiesce, countenance, license, legitimize, legalize, enable, empower, facilitate, consent, bless, give dispensation **4 be permissive**, be lax, indulge, spoil, favour **5 be permitted**, have authorization **6 ask permission**, request

ADJECTIVES 7 permitted, allowed, authorized, warranted, sanctioned, licensed, legal, lawful, licit, decriminalized, chartered, patent, above board, legitimate, acceptable, worthwhile, approved, passed, unconditional **8 permitting**, permissive, admissible, allowing, printable, tolerant, lenient, indulgent, loose, lax, overindulgent, irresolute

546 Perseverance

NOUNS 1 perseverance, persistence, doggedness, determination, resolution, tenacity, pertinacity, stubbornness, obstinacy, insistence, patience **2 commitment**, single-mindedness, concentration, attention, application, sedulity, assiduity, industriousness, tirelessness, indefatigability, effort **3 constancy**, steadfastness, fidelity, staunchness, maintenance, continuance, ceaselessness, diligence, permanence, iteration **4 stamina**, endurance, staying power, fortitude, strength, courage, true grit, backbone

VERBS 5 persevere, persist, repeat, iterate, plod, slog away **6 maintain**, sustain, keep up, continue **7 hold out**, stand firm, not budge, hang on **8 endure**, survive, remain

ADJECTIVES 9 persevering, persistent, tenacious, sedulous, assiduous, dogged, determined, resolute, stubborn, obstinate, enduring, staunch, faithful, diligent, surviving, patient, plodding, slogging away, industrious **10 steady**, unfaltering, unwavering, unflagging, undrooping, unwearied, untiring, indefatigable, vigilant, unfailing, unremitting, constant, continual, unceasing, renewed, iterated, reiterated **11 indomitable**, undefeated, unconquerable, unbeaten, undaunted, undiscouraged, undeterred

547 Persuasion

NOUNS 1 persuasion, influence, inducement, pressure, insistence, prompting, lobbying, sales pitch **2 flattery**, cajolery, coaxing, teasing, wheedling, blandishment, honeyed words, urging, incitement, encouragement, pleading, advocacy, solicitation, invitation, temptation **3 incentive**, lure, allurement, seduction, attraction, bewitchment, carrot, siren song, winning ways, fascination, charm, sex appeal, charisma **4 exhortation**, rallying cry, clarion call **5 propaganda**, promotion, publicity, advertising, pamphleteering, consciousness-raising, agitprop, indoctrination, hard selling **6 advertising**, sales promotion, direct mail, soft sell, hard sell, publicity **7 persuadability**, docility, tractability, willingness, pliancy, pliability, softness, susceptibility, credulity, suggestibility, impressibility **8 incentive**, inducement, stimulus, fillip, nudge, threat, prod, slap, spur, goad, whip, rod, big stick **9 enticement**, lure, trap, decoy, bait, greased palm **10 bribe**, kickback, backhander **11 motive**, reason, cause, rationale, justification, grounds, motivation, driving force, impetus, mainspring, causation, intention, objective, aim, goal, aspiration, ambition, ideal, guiding principle, vocation, conscience

VERBS 12 persuade, influence, advise, counsel, induce, pressure, lobby, insist, move, motivate, incline, dispose, prompt, instigate, cause, convince, win over, prevail upon, urge, impel, push into, intimidate, browbeat, coerce, compel, force, convert, indoctrinate, brainwash, procure, enlist, engage, coax, wheedle, cajole, sweet-talk, blandish, conciliate, appease **13 tempt**, allure, entice, seduce, tantalize, tease, inveigle, ensnare, coax, wheedle, pander to **14 bribe**, tip, reward, suborn, corrupt **15 be persuaded**, yield, succumb, submit, concede, agree, consent

ADJECTIVES 16 persuasive, influential, impressive, convincing, cogent, hortatory, didactic, protreptic, directive, compelling, forceful, effective, winning, inducing, incentive, motivating, encouraging, stimulating, challenging, rousing, provocative, teasing, tantalizing, tempting, alluring, attractive, inviting, magnetic, fascinating, bewitching, hypnotic, mesmeric, charismatic, irresistible **17 persuadable**, credulous, receptive, tractable, docile, inspired, motivated, incited, spurred on, encouraged, egged on

548 Pharmacology

NOUNS 1 pharmacology, pharmacy, pharmaceutics, pharmacodynamics, pharmacokinetics, pharmocognosy, chemotherapy, posology **2 pharmacologist**, pharmacist, pharmaceutist, chemist **3 drug**, medicine, medication, preparation, potion, dose, draught, tonic, healing agent, ethical drug, prescription drug, over-the-counter drug, premedication, wonder drug, panacea, cure-all, catholicon, elixir, placebo, tolerance, side effect **4 prescription**, formula, dose, course, essence, vehicle, excipient, galenical, confection **5 pill**, tablet, capsule, cachet, lozenge, pastille, dragee, troche, powder **6 ointment**, salve, cream, balm, balsam, lotion, ungent, embrocation, paint, poultice, fomentation, unction, oil, liniment, emollient, demulcent, abirritant **7 drops**, guttae **8 pessary**, suppository **9 inhalant**, spray, atomizer, nebulizer **10 linctus**, gargle, mouthwash, wash, eyebath, undine **11 injection**, intramuscular injection, intravenous injection, venoclysis, intubation, drip, implant, pellet, transdermal injection, patch, epidural, inhalation

ADJECTIVES 12 pharmacological, pharmacodynamic, pharmacokinetic

VERBS 13 administer, inject, inoculate, instil, infuse, perfuse, apply, anoint, insert, implant, take in, inhale

549 Philanthropy

NOUNS 1 philanthropy, humanitarianism, humaneness, welfarism, benevolence, charity, altruism, dedication, helpfulness, kindness, compassion, brotherly love, goodwill, grace, beneficence, unselfishness, generosity, openhandedness, munificence **2 public spiritedness**, social conscience, citizenship, civism, utilitarianism, Benthamism, humanitarianism, socialism, communism **3 philanthropist**, benefactor, humanitarian, idealist, altruist, visionary, utopian, utilitarian, Benthamite, internationalist, welfare worker, social worker, almoner, volunteer, aid worker, missionary, helping hand, Good Samaritan **4 welfare state**, social welfare, social services, poor relief, assistance, benefit **5 charity**, aid, good works, relief, gift, hand-out, donation, fund, flag day, charity event, fund raiser, telethon

ADJECTIVES 6 philanthropic, humanitarian, benevolent, beneficent, humane, charitable, altruistic, aid-giving, alms-giving, generous, munificent, kind, compassionate, gracious, big-hearted, public spirited, idealistic, enlightened, reforming, visionary, liberal, utilitarian

VERBS 7 be charitable, do good, help

550 Philosophy

- *Do not all charms fly/ At the mere touch of cold philosophy.* John Keats.
- *Philosophy is not a theory but an activity.* Ludwig Wittgenstein.

NOUNS 1 philosophy, viewpoint, outlook, attitude, opinion, doctrine, thought, judgment, principle, thesis, conjecture, speculation, hypothesis, concept, explanation, rationalization **2 philosophical system**, belief system, value system, ethos, morals, moral code, ideology, world view, creed, position **3 detachment**, stoicism, self-control, self-restraint, dispassion, coolness, calmness, level-headedness, reasonableness, commonsense, rationality, objectivity, equanimity, tolerance, balance, thoughtfulness, serenity **4 philosophical investigation**, examination, introspection, analysis, challenge, questioning, elenchus, speculation, deliberation, conceptual thought, intuition, abstract thought, deduction, induction, inference, calculation **5 philosophical argument**, discussion, dialogue, symposium, conversation, colloquy, debate, dialectic, syllogism, thesis, antithesis, synthesis, interlocution, argument, logomachy, polemic, eristic, rhetoric **6 branch of philosophy**, logic, moral philosophy, ethics, metaethics, medical ethics, legal ethics, axiology, deontology, political philosophy, metaphysics, ontology, epistemology, gnosiology, phenomenology, teleology, cosmology, aesthetics, semantics, semiotics **7 philosopher**, thinker, academic, logician, dialectician, sophist, syllogist, metaphysician, cosmologist, moralist, theorist, speculator, hypothesizer, hypothecator, surmiser, investigator, researcher, analyst, inquirer, searcher, dreamer, idealist, ideologue, visionary, doctrinarian **8 sage**, wise man, savant, academic, intellectual, highbrow, pundit, counsellor, mentor

ADJECTIVES 9 of philosophy, theoretical, philosophical, notional, abstract, esoteric, ideological, moral, ethical, normative, prescriptive, nomothetic, descriptive, conceptual, ideal, visionary, metaphysical, hypothetical, conjectural, speculative, impractical **10 rational**, reasonable, logical, objective, impartial, sound, plausible, pragmatic, commonsensical, realistic, lucid, well-reasoned **11 thoughtful**, attentive, meditative, cogitative, contemplative, reflective, speculative, pensive, introspective **12 detached**, unemotional, imperturbable, unruffled, unconcerned, dispassionate, cool, calm, collected, composed, level-headed, equanimous, tolerant, self-controlled, stoical, patient, serene **13 learned**, wise, academic, intellectual, erudite, scholarly, profound

VERBS 14 philosophize, think about, speculate, suppose, hypothesize, surmise, consider, conceptualize, contemplate, cogitate, excogitate, ratiocinate, ruminate, reflect, deliberate, ponder, muse, wonder, challenge, analyse, examine, explore, look into, scrutinize, investigate, question, query, inquire, search, soul-search, introspect, brood, dream, idealize **15 rationalize**, reason, think through, syllogize, interpret, construe, deduce, infer, evaluate, realize, comprehend, grasp, define, expound, explain, elucidate, clarify, illuminate, demonstrate, show, illustrate, exemplify, justify **16 discuss philosophically**, debate, exchange ideas, comment on, criticize, argue, logomachize, polemicize, contend, contest, dispute, dissent, refute, answer, respond, negate

551 Photography

NOUNS 1 photography, colour photography, black-and-white photography, aerial photography, astrophotography, underwater photography, wildlife photography, fashion photography, portraiture, photojournalism, time-lapse photography, telephotography, macrophotography, microphotography, flash photography, infrared photography, cinematography, stereophotography, holography, phototopography **2 photoreproduction**, photocopying, Xerography, photogrammetry, photogravure, photolithography, photointaglio, photocopy **3 photograph**, photo, snapshot, take, daguerreotype, transparency, slide, radiograph, X-ray, shadowgraph, portrait, close-up, long shot, pin-up, rogues' gallery, photobiography, studio photograph, multiple image, action sequence, photomontage, photomural, stereoscopic image, hologram, microphotograph, microcopy, microfilm **4 film**, photographic plate, photographic paper, bromide paper, roll film, panchromatic film, chromogenic film, cine film, Super-8, X-ray film, infrared film, graininess, film speed, sensitivity, photosensitivity, ISO rating, ASA number, DIN number, DX code, hypersensitization, photographic density, opacity, characteristic curve, dynamic range, reciprocity failure, saturation level, fog level, flare, overexposure, underexposure **5 emulsion**, silver halide, gelatin, backing **6 development**, processing, printing, enlargement, darkroom, enlarger, developer, stop bath, fixing solution, hypo, frame, negative, print, diapositive, sepia, lanternslide, slide projector, overhead projector, screen **7 camera**, twin-lens reflex, large-format camera, box Brownie, automatic camera, compact camera, disc camera, plate camera, camera obscura, cine camera, pinhole camera, videocamera, TV camera, security camera

VERBS 8 photograph, shoot, focus, stop down, open up, zoom in, pan, expose, develop, process, print, enlarge, blow up, reduce

ADJECTIVES 9 photographic, photogenic

552 Physical Pain

NOUNS 1 pain, hurt, soreness, suffering, malaise, affliction, misery, discomfort, distress, irritation, tenderness, sore spot, inflammation, pinprick, twinge, pangs, smarting, throes, cramp, spasm, stitch, throbbing, agony, convulsion, anguish, ordeal, hell, martyrdom, passion, purgatory, lancination, stab, torment, punishment, flogging **2 painful condition**, headache, migraine, toothache, earache, laryngitis, ulcer, hunger pains, indigestion, heartburn, pyrosis, dyspepsia, stomachache, colic, grips, hernia, rupture, backache, lumbago, sciatica, rheumatism, arthritis, myalgia, neuralgia, angina, dysmenorrhoea, period pains, labour pains **3 injury**, wound, lesion, trauma, scratch, scrape, graze, abrasion, bruise, contusion, bump, hit, sprain, burn, scald, cut, stab, puncture, jab, tear, slash, gash, laceration, bite, fracture, mauling, savaging, bloody nose **4 pain-relief**, analgesia

ADJECTIVES 5 painful, sore, hurting, distressing, chronic, acute, stinging, tingling, smarting, cramping, lancinating, aching, tender, raw, throbbing, biting, gnawing, gripping, stabbing, shooting, grinding, splitting, pounding, agonizing, purgatorial, excruciating, racking, harrowing, burning, searing, scalding, traumatic, extreme **6 injured**, wounded, bruised, grazed, cut, punctured, scraped, sprained, lacerated, torn, fractured, broken **7 feeling pain**, suffering, hurting, distressed, sore, aching, in agony, wincing, writhing, tormented, tortured, afflicted, martyred, raw, black-and-blue, bleeding, blistered **8 inflicting pain**, painful, hurtful, torturing, tormenting, brutal

VERBS 9 feel pain, suffer, hurt, ache, agonize, be afflicted, smart, wince, flinch, twitch, chafe, writhe **10 be painful**, hurt, sting, tingle, smart, cramp, ache, throb, bite, gnaw, grip, stab, shoot, grind, pound, burn **11 inflict pain**, hurt, injure, wound, hit, scratch, scrape, graze, prick, pinch, nip, tweak, sting, bruise, contuse, bump, sprain, burn, scald, jab, cut, tear, slash, gash, draw blood, puncture, impale, fracture, punish, shoot, maul, mangle, savage, bite, claw, knife, stab, beat, batter, smash, flog, thrash, traumatize, excruciate, wring, harrow, torment, torture, rack, martyr **12 express pain**, cry, sob, wail, moan, gasp, whimper, groan, squeal, squawk, yelp, scream, shriek, screech, howl

553 Physical Pleasure

NOUNS 1 physical pleasure, well-being, ease, contentment, comfort, enjoyment, conviviality, fun, zest, happiness, felicity, delight, bliss, euphoria, indulgence, luxury, sensuousness, loveliness, tastiness, sweetness, fragrance, self-indulgence, profligacy, gourmandising, epicureanism, sensualism, hedonism, dissipation, carnality, voluptuousness, eroticism, titillation, satisfaction, gratification, orgasm, climax, masturbation **2 good time**, happy hour, fun time **3 pleasurable things**, comforter, amenity, cushion, comfort blanket, featherbed, treat, spread, jamboree, splurge, sweetmeats, ambrosia, nectar, creature comforts, wall-to-wall carpeting, free lunch, luxury goods, revelry, carnival, spree, orgy, love-in, aphrodisiac, love-potion **4 idealized pleasure**, easy street

ADJECTIVES 5 pleasant, comfortable, easeful, restful, relaxing, soothing, comforting, warm, congenial, agreeable, likable, nice, pleasing, satisfying, gratifying, refreshing, enjoyable, convivial, delectable, charming, delightful, idyllic, Elysian, paradisiacal, luscious, opulent, luxuriant, exquisite, sumptuous, de luxe, lush, welcome, inviting, snug, cosy, soft, cuddly, heart-warming, lovable, blissful, palatable, delicious, mouth-watering, ambrosial, sweet, succulent, juicy, perfumed, euphonious, dulcet, titillating, seductive, sensual, erotic, carnal **6 pleased**, relaxed, comfortable, warm, cosy, content, happy, at ease, delighted, sensual, profligate, voluptuous, licentious, hedonistic, fun-loving, wanton, sybaritic, excited, titillated, gratified, satisfied, mollycoddled, cosseted, pampered

VERBS 7 feel pleasure, enjoy, relish, revel in, delight in, enjoy oneself, have fun, make merry, bask, indulge oneself, gormandize, splurge, luxuriate, wallow, purr, nestle **8 give pleasure**, please, cheer, gladden, delight, charm, gratify, indulge, entertain, amuse, treat, regale, cuddle, hug, fondle, pet, stimulate, arouse, tickle, titillate, thrill, excite, satisfy **9 comfort**, ease, relieve, slake, alleviate, appease, salve, soothe, soften, sympathize with, refresh, cuddle, warm, mother, pet, coddle, cosset, pamper

554 Physics

NOUNS 1 physics, exact science, natural science, natural philosophy **2 classical physics**, classical mechanics, Newtonian mechanics, dynamics, statics, kinematics, hydrodynamics, aerodynamics, acoustics, ultrasonics, optics, heat, thermodynamics, electricity, magnetism, electroacoustics, electrodynamics, electromagnetism **3 modern physics**, quantum theory, quantum mechanics, wave mechanics, matrix mechanics, quantum statistics, statistical mechanics, atomic physics, nuclear physics, particle physics, statistical physics, spectroscopy, solid-state physics, crystallography, low-temperature physics, cryogenics, plasma physics, magnetohydrodynamics, radiation physics **4 experimental physics**, theoretical physics, pure physics, applied physics, medical physics, geophysics, astrophysics, cosmology, physical chemistry **5 theory**, quantum theory **6 law**, uncertainty principle **7 atom**, atomic structure, nucleus, proton, neutron, nucleon, binding energy, electron, electron configuration, electron shell **8 ion**, cation, anion, charge number **9 radioactivity**, decay, radioisotope, radionuclide, half-life, dose equivalent, cosmic rays, radiometric dating, radiocarbon dating, radiography, radiology **10 nuclear fission**, fission, chain reaction, atom smashing, fusion, nuclear engineering **11 elementary particle**, fundamental particle, subatomic particle, particle, lepton, electron, muon, tauon, neutrino, quark, quark flavour, quark colour, hadron, baryon, meson, proton, neutron, nucleon, pion, pi meson, kaon, K meson, fermion, boson, antiparticle, antiproton, antineutron, positron, antielectron **12 quantum**, quantum number, charge, spin, isospin, parity, strangeness, charm, beauty, up, down

ADJECTIVES 13 physical, classical, mechanical, dynamic, static, kinetic, kinematic, hydrodynamic, aerodynamic, ultrasonic, subsonic, optical, thermal, calorific, thermodynamic, cryogenic, electrical, magnetic, electrodynamic, atomic, crystallographic, spectroscopic, spectrometric, quantum

VERBS 14 physically, mechanically, dynamically, statically, kinetically, kinematically, hydrodynamically, aerodynamically, acoustically, ultrasonically, subsonically, thermodynamically, cryogenically, crystallographically, spectroscopically, spectrometrically

555 Piquancy

NOUNS 1 piquancy, pungency, strong flavour, spiciness, sting, tanginess, smokiness, tartness, bite, kick, sourness, bitterness, gaminess, raciness, poignancy, aroma, zest **2 seasoning**, flavouring, condiment, salt, pepper, garnish, dressing, mayonnaise, French dressing, vinaigrette, marinade, relish, sauce, ketchup, chutney, pickle, gherkin, onion, garlic, curry **3 stimulation**, titillation, liveliness, spirit, zest, archness, harshness

ADJECTIVES 4 piquant, pungent, aromatic, flavourful, appetizing, stinging, biting, hot, peppery, seasoned, spiced, herby, savoury, tangy, tart, sharp, sour, bitter, minty, highly seasoned, spicy, salty, strong, smoky, cured, kippered, pickled, soused, gamy **5 stimulating**, interesting, intriguing, titillating, exciting, lively, restorative, medicinal, provocative, spirited, arch

VERBS 6 season, flavour, salt, pepper, marinate, souse, smoke, kipper, cure, dry, pickle **7 be piquant**, sting, bite, goad, interest, stimulate, revive, restore, titillate, intrigue, excite

556 Pitilessness

NOUNS 1 pitilessness, unsympatheticness, uncompassionateness, intolerance, unfeelingness, mercilessness, inclemency, ruthlessness, hardheartedness, heartlessness, hardness, flintiness, callousness, inhumanity, cruelty, severity, remorselessness, unforgivingness, revengefulness **2 inflexibility**, implacability, unyieldingness, intractability

ADJECTIVES 3 pitiless, unpitying, unfeeling, unmoved, unresponsive, impassive, uncaring, obdurate, unsympathetic, heartless, hardhearted, cold, coldhearted, stonyhearted, hard, harsh, severe, flinty, tough, callous, ruthless, cruel, soulless, brutal, cold-blooded, sadistic, barbarous, remorseless, vengeful, vindictive **4 inflexible**, unbending, unrelenting, inexorable, implacable

VERBS 5 be pitiless, lack compassion

557 Pity

NOUNS 1 pity, sympathy, commiseration, condolence, feeling, empathy, understanding, compassion, mercifulness, charity, humanity, kindness, benevolence, tenderness, gentleness, caring, softheartedness, warmheartedness, tenderheartedness **2 condolence**, sympathy, shared grief, mourning, sorrow, comfort, balm, consolation, commiseration, remorse, compunction, regret, lament, wake **3 mercy**, compassion, grace, favour, quarter, forgiveness, mercifulness, forbearance, long-suffering, second chance, clemency, leniency, reprieve, relief, mitigation, pardon **4 misfortune**, disappointment

ADJECTIVES 5 pitying, sympathetic, comforting, consoling, commiserative, condolent, understanding, compassionate, caring, tenderhearted, gentle, kind, kindhearted, softhearted, warmhearted, benevolent, gracious, generous, clement, yielding, lenient, forbearant, charitable, humane, merciful **6 pitiful**, heart-rending, heart-breaking, pathetic, sad, distressing, grievous, touching, moving, tear-jerking

VERBS 7 pity, feel for, sympathize with, empathize with, show understanding **8 sorrow**, grieve, lament, condole with, commiserate, offer comfort, console, soothe, weep for **9 show mercy**, forgive, pardon, absolve, reprieve, spare, forbear, relent, unbend, relax, give quarter **10 excite pity**, thaw, soften, move, touch, affect, reach, grieve **11 ask for mercy**, plead with

558 Plan

NOUNS 1 plan, scheme, design, programme, project, proposal, proposition, suggestion, motion, amendment, resolution, intention, budget, schedule, timetable **2 policy**, procedure, system, strategy, emergency procedure, tactics, forethought, foresight, statesmanship, diplomacy, operational research, management review, way, approach, address, attack, steps, measures, countermeasures, actions, reactions, counteractions, coup, coup d'état, scenario, forecast, prediction, brochure, prospectus, manifesto, platform, ticket, mandate, formula **3 expedient plan**, contrivance, resource, last resort, *pis aller*, eleventh-hour rescue, winning card, trump card, antidote, remedy, answer, loophole, way out, technicality, device, gimmick, trick, stratagem, artifice, ruse, ploy, shift, fiddle, swindle, masterstroke, inspiration, brainwave, bright idea, notion, invention, improvisation **4 plot**, scheme, intrigue, web, cabal, conspiracy, inside job, insider dealing, racket, game, manipulation, machination, string pulling, put-up job, secrecy **5 map**, atlas, scale drawing, blueprint, layout, diagram **6 outline**, summary, skeleton, rough, sketch, model, pattern, pilot scheme, prototype, draft, proof **7 planning**, scheming, contrivance, organization, order, systematization, rationalization, centralization, headquarters, base

VERBS 8 plan, scheme, design, contrive, organize, systematize, methodize, rationalize, centralize, order, programme, propose, suggest, resolve, intend, project, aim **9 plan out**, draw up, draft, frame, shape, form, work out, sketch, design, schedule, timetable, adjust, revise, redo, recast **10 invent**, create, concoct, hatch, formulate, think up, hit upon, discover, contrive, devise **11 plan ahead**, prepare, arrange, prearrange, predetermine, calculate, budget, forecast, predict, foresee, envisage **12 plot**, scheme, conspire, intrigue, machinate, cabal, concoct, brew, hatch, undermine, countermine, trap, ensnare, work against

ADJECTIVES 13 planned, intended, intentional, rational, meant, premeditated, contrived, designed, organized, schematic, systematic, orderly, methodical, worked out, prepared, strategic, tactical, under discussion, under consideration, in draft, in proof **14 planning**, scheming, cunning, contriving, resourceful, ingenious, purposeful, involved, in deep, intriguing, plotting

559 Plants

NOUNS 1 plants, flora, vegetation, growth, herbage, verdure **2 plant**, seedling, herb, flower, wild flower, weed, cultivated plant, garden plant, house plant, pot plant, hothouse plant, cereal, vegetable, medicinal herb, wort, cactus, xerophyte, hydrophyte, air plant, epiphyte, parasite, ephemeral, annual, biennial, perennial, tree, sapling, shrub, bush, evergreen, climber, twiner, vine **3 plant science(s)**, botany, phytology, plant taxonomy, phytography, phytochemistry, phytogenesis, phytosociology, phytogeography, phytopathology, palaeobotany, palynology, ethnobotany, pteridology, bryology, mycology, phycology, algology, lichenology, dendrology, economic botany, arboriculture, silviculture, horticulture, forestry, pomology, crop husbandry **4 herbarium**, botanic garden

ADJECTIVES 5 plantlike, vegetable, vegetal, vegetative, herbal, herbaceous, grassy, leafy, verdant, overgrown **6 of plants**, ephemeral, annual, biennial, perennial, bulbous, cormous, tuberous, woody, deciduous, evergreen, leafy, foliate, succulent, xerophytic, aquatic, hydrophytic, epiphytic, parasitic, saprophytic, insectivorous, carnivorous **7 botanical**, botanic

VERBS 8 vegetate, grow, germinate, root, sprout, shoot, bud, gemmate, unfold, leaf, flower, flourish, burgeon, overgrow, overrun, dehisce **9 be dormant**, abscise, wilt

560 Pleasantness

ADJECTIVES 1 pleasant, pleasing, nice, enjoyable, pleasurable, agreeable, acceptable, gratifying, satisfying, tasteful, inviting, welcome, charming, appealing, sweet, lovely, delightful, idyllic, heavenly, divine, sublime **2 likable**, amiable, affable, friendly, cordial, compatible, congenial, engaging, good-natured, easygoing, amusing, bright, sunny, attractive, kindly, courteous, polite, well-mannered, chivalrous **3 comfortable**, soothing, relaxing, restful, dulcet, mellow, emollient, easy, cosy **4 tasty**, palatable, appetizing, tempting, savoury, flavourful, mouthwatering, delicious, delectable, luscious, juicy **5 pleasure-loving**, hedonistic, epicurean, gourmet, gourmand

NOUNS 6 pleasantness, pleasurableness, niceness, agreeableness, charm, appeal, loveliness, delightfulness, heaven **7 pleasure**, enjoyment, satisfaction, ease, comfort, luxury, creature comforts, self-indulgence, hedonism, epicureanism, voluptuousness, entertainment, amusement **8 amiability**, affability, friendliness, cordiality, compatibility, congeniality, attractiveness, kindliness, courtesy, chivalry, politeness **9 tastiness**, palatability, deliciousness, delectability **10 pleasant thing**, treat, delicacy, luxury, holiday, honeymoon, pleasantry, compliment, praise, tribute

VERBS 11 give pleasure, please, gratify, satisfy, comfort, soothe, agree with, charm **12 like**, appreciate, delight in, enjoy

561 Plurality

NOUNS 1 plurality, many, several, some, a number, a handful **2 multiplicity**, numerousness, multitudinousness, multifariousness, variety, diversity, compositeness, multiformity, many-sidedness, polygon, polyhedron, multilateralism, polygamy, polygyny, polyandry, polytheism, pluralism **3 majority**, more, greatest number, most, greater part, bulk, mass, preponderance **4 multiplication**, proliferation, increase, multiple, product, multiplier

ADJECTIVES 5 plural, multiple, many, several, some, upwards of, more, most, majority, numerous **6 various**, divers, sundry, multifarious, multiform, composite, multilateral, polygonal, many-sided, multifaceted, versatile, multipurpose, multirole, polymorphous, multinational, multiracial, multilingual **7 multiplicative**, multiplied, multiple, manifold, multifold

VERBS 8 pluralize, multiply, proliferate, propagate, increase

562 Possession

NOUNS 1 possession, ownership, proprietorship, enjoyment, proprietary rights, lordship, dominion, sovereignty, holding, grasp, grip, retention, claiming, taking, appropriation, control, occupation, landowning, custody, title, lease, freehold, tenure, tenancy, monopolization, engrossment, forestalment, sublease, squatter's right, claim, heirship, heritage **2 legal terms**, pre-emption, prescription, fee simple, seisin, uti possidetis **3 medieval ownership**, villeinage, socage, burgage, frankalmoign, fee, fief **4 possession**, property, freehold, estate, plantation, colony, dependency, protectorate, dominion, personal effects, belongings, accoutrements, appurtenances, stuff

VERBS 5 possess, own, command, buy, hold, enjoy, occupy, dwell in, monopolize, forestall, engross, tie up, rent, let

ADJECTIVES 6 possessing, possessory, owning, landowning, landed, property-owning, having, holding, enjoying, proprietorial, occupying, squatting, exclusive, unshared **7 possessed**, owned, held, belonging to, on hand, in store, exclusive

563 Possibility

- *The grand Perhaps!* Robert Browning.
- *Your If is the only peace-maker; much virtue in If.* William Shakespeare.

NOUNS 1 possibility, potential, plausibility, likelihood, prospect, chance, odds, promise, opportunity, virtuality, eventuality **2 possibleness**, conceivability, credibility, feasibility, viableness, practicability, workability, operability, accessibility, admissibility, flexibility, approachability, availability, aptitude, ability, capacity **3 strong possibility**, good chance, sporting chance, opening, luck, sure bet, evens **4 remote possibility**, faint hope, slim chance, poor prospect

ADJECTIVES 5 possible, potential, conceivable, imaginable, thinkable, credible, believable, feasible, admissible, viable, tenable, reasonable, practical, doable, workable, performable, operable, achievable, attainable, realizable, likely, accessible, approachable, reachable, available, flexible, able **6 potential**, possible, promising, undeveloped, future, prospective, eventual

VERBS 7 make possible, enable, empower, permit, allow, gamble **8 be possible**, could be

564 Poverty

• *There's no scandal like rags, nor any crime so shameful as poverty.* George Farquhar.

ADJECTIVES 1 poor, impecunious, penniless, moneyless, penurious, poverty-stricken, lowpaid, underprivileged, deprived, needy, indigent, wanting, straitened, hand-to-mouth, destitute **2 insolvent**, in debt, owing, bankrupt, ruined, impoverished, pauperized, broken, dispossessed, stripped **3 beggarly**, mendicant, homeless, hungry, starving, barefoot, in rags, tatty, threadbare, shabby, scruffy, mean, seedy, squalid, dirty, slummy **4 inadequate**, insufficient, deficient, lacking, scarce, meagre

NOUNS 5 poverty, poorness, impecuniousness, pennilessness, penury, impoverishment, pauperism, deprivation, privation, hardship, need, necessitousness, indigence, want, lack, distress, difficulties, dire straits, reduced circumstances, hand-to-mouth existence, destitution, low pay, slender means, subsistence level, breadline **6 insolvency**, debt, indebtedness, dependence, unsoundness, bankruptcy, ruin, financial embarrassment, dispossession, disinheritance, hard times, depression, recession, slump, belt-tightening, empty purse, bare cupboard **7 beggary**, mendicancy, homelessness, hunger, fasting, famine, raggedness, tatters, shabbiness, scruffiness, meanness, seediness, squalor, dilapidation, slum, workhouse **8 renunciation of wealth**, asceticism **9 inadequacy**, insufficiency, deficiency, lack, shortage, dearth, scarcity, paucity, meagreness, scantness **10 pauper**, indigent, down-and-out, bankrupt, insolvent, beggar, mendicant, lazar, poor relation, vagrant, bag lady, tramp, homeless person, squatter **11 the poor**, the needy, the have-nots, the underprivileged, the disadvantaged, Third World, poor white

VERBS 12 be poor, need, want, lack **13 lose one's money**, go bankrupt **14 impoverish**, beggar, pauperize, ruin, bankrupt, dispossess, disinherit, disendow, deprive, strip

565 Powderiness

NOUNS 1 powderiness, pulverulence, dustiness, chalkiness, flouriness, efflorescence **2 crumbliness**, flakiness, friability, pulverableness, brittleness **3 graininess**, granularity, mealiness, branniness, grittiness, sandiness, sabulosity **4 pulverization**, powdering, milling, multure, frosting, grinding, trituration, crushing, mashing, smashing, beating, pounding, contusion, grating, shredding, crumbling, flaking, levigation, granulation, comminution, erosion, abrasion, attrition, brecciation, fragmentation, sharding, atomization, micronization, disintegration, attenuation, decomposition **5 powder**, dust, dirt, chalk, efflorescence, pounce, face powder, attritus, dustball, fluff, pussies, kittens, slut's wool, lint, soot, ash, sawdust, coaldust, fallout, smog, cosmic dust, dust cloud, dust storm **6 crumb**, flake, dandruff, scurf, filings, raspings, snowflake, fragment **7 grain**, granule, speck

ADJECTIVES 8 powdery, dusty, pulverulent, scobiform, dirty, sooty, chalky, calcareous **9 mealy**, branny, floury, farinaceous **10 grainy**, gritty, granular, sandy, sabulous, arenaceous, gravelly, shingly, pebbly, brecciated **11 pulverized**, powdered, ground, granulated, disintegrated, crushed, grated, shredded, sifted, pestled, comminuted, triturated, levigated **12 crumbly**, friable, crisp, flaky, scaly **13 pulverizable**, triturable

VERBS 14 powder, dust, flour, sand, sprinkle, scatter **15 pulverize**, powder, comminute, triturate, levigate, bray, pestle, disintegrate, fragment, shard, brecciate, atomize **16 crumble**, chip **17 grind**, granulate, grain, mill, flour **18 grate**, shred, abrade, rub down, scrape, rasp **19 beat**, pound, bray, smash, mash, hammer, bruise, knead, crush, squash, crunch, kibble **20 come** (*or* **fall**) **to dust**, disintegrate, break up, granulate, decompose **21 weather**, erode

566 Power

- *Power tends to corrupt, and absolute power corrupts absolutely. Great men are almost always bad men... There is no worse heresy than that the office sanctifies the holder of it.* Lord Acton.
- *Power is the ultimate aphrodisiac.* Henry Kissinger.
- *The balance of power.* Robert Walpole.

NOUNS 1 power, potency, forcefulness, might, greatness, omnipotence, government, authority, sovereignty, hegemony, control, sway, superiority, ascendancy, prevalence, predominance, influence, persuasion, charisma, mana, magic, endurance, stamina, force, virility, muscle, strength, effort, exertion **2 ability**, potentiality, capability, competence, effectuality, efficiency, efficacy, proficiency, capacity, faculty, property, virtue, attribute, endowment, gift, flair, native wit, talent, skill, qualification, aptitude, fitness, scope, range, reach, compass **3 vitality**, dynamism, vigour, energy, vivacity, animation, verve, liveliness, drive **4 energy**, work, heat, horsepower, manpower, force, pressure, traction, thrust

VERBS 5 be powerful, be able, govern, manage, control, dominate, compel, force, endeavour, stress, strain, ascend, prevail, predominate, influence, have charisma, qualify, have drive **6 give power**, empower, enable, authorize, endow, give teeth, arm, strengthen, energize, animate, electrify, charge, transistorize, magnetize, plug in, switch on, turn on, charge up **7 generate power**, fuel, pump, radiate, heat, cool, light

ADJECTIVES 8 powerful, potent, mighty, virile, strong, great, prevailing, prevalent, predominant, superior, influential, omnipotent, almighty, empowered, endowed, authoritative, sovereign, hegemonic, plenipotentiary, competent, capable, fit, able, gifted, talented, qualified, equal to, up to, effectual, efficient, proficient, forceful, compelling, charismatic, compulsive **9 operative**, working, switched on, armed, in force, valid **10 full of energy**, dynamic, vigorous, lively, vivacious, animated, spirited, attractive, drawing, pulling, impelling, propulsive, moving, locomotive, kinetic, driven, automated, on line, pro-active, on stream **11 charged**, high-tension, magnetic, polarized, mechanized, electric **12 powered**, electrical, atomic, nuclear, thermonuclear, geothermal, hydroelectric, wave-powered, solar

567 Powerlessness

NOUNS 1 powerlessness, ineffectiveness, inefficiency, impotence, inability, incapacity, incompetence, emptiness, barrenness, sterility, futility, uselessness, inutility, incapability, ineptitude, unfitness, disqualification, invalidation, decrepitude, frailty, fragility, power vacuum, energy depletion, neutralization, disarmament **2 futile effort**, dead letter, empty threats, bluster, impotent fury **3 helplessness**, defencelessness, vulnerability, harmlessness, innocence, weakness, softness **4 disability**, invalidity, weakness, mental handicap, physical disability, sexual impotence, sterility, infertility, prostration, exhaustion, tiredness, fatigue, collapse, breakdown, faint, swoon, unconsciousness, coma, catatonia, narcosis, stroke, heart attack, apoplexy, paralysis, hemiplegia, paraplegia, quadriplegia, tetraplegia, atrophy, ataxia, incontinence

VERBS 5 be powerless, be impotent, stand defenceless, not work, not operate, fail, do nothing, look on, stand by, faint **6 remove power from**, invalidate, incapacitate, disable, disqualify, abrogate, disarm, demilitarize, neutralize, weaken, emaciate, debilitate, sap, undermine, consume, exhaust **7 overpower**, disarm, prostrate, bowl over, wind, knock out, numb, paralyse, cripple, maim, hamstring, stifle, smother, suffocate, strangle, deaden, muzzle, silence, deflate **8 make impotent**, sterilize, vasectomize, castrate, geld, spay, neuter, emasculate, evirate, effeminize, unman, unnerve

ADJECTIVES 9 powerless, unable, incapable, unauthorized, invalid, illegal, disfranchised, inoperative, unemployed, switched off, suspended, deactivated, in abeyance, mothballed, broken down, deposed, disqualified, unfit, inept, good-for-nothing, unworkable, worthless, useless, ineffective, inefficient **10 unprotected**, undefended, unguarded, defenceless, ill-equipped, unarmed, unfortified, exposed, pregnable, untenable, dependent, subject, vulnerable, harmless, innocent **11 impotent**, weak, feeble, frail, debilitated, etiolated, tired, fatigued, exhausted, used up, decrepit, senile, paraplegic, paralytic, unconscious, comatose, catatonic, drugged, insensible, incapacitated, disabled, paralysed, crippled, incontinent, prostrate, supine, irresolute, spineless, unnerved, demoralized, shell-shocked, helpless, drifting, rudderless **12 unsexed**, sterilized, barren, infertile, vasectomized, emasculated, castrated, gelded, neutered, spayed, caponized, unmanned

568 Precedence

NOUNS 1 precedence, antecedence, going before, anteriority, anteposition **2 priority**, primacy, supremacy, dominion, pre-eminence, superiority, seniority, prerogative, privilege, forefront, vanguard, pole position, the lead, urgency, importance **3 preparation**, groundwork, foundation, development, exploration, pioneering, innovation, avant-gardism, breakthrough, discovery **4 precedent**, antecedent, lead, example, standard, prototype, model, pattern, paradigm, yardstick **5 preface**, foreword, proem, prologue, frontispiece, introduction, opening, preliminaries, prelude, overture, curtain raiser, apéritif, appetizer **6 preview**, trailer, taster, premonition, omen **7 prefix**, prefixion **8 precursor**, forerunner, herald, harbinger, messenger, announcer, leader, vanguard, scout, pilot, explorer, pathfinder, trailblazer, avant-garde, pioneer, frontiersman, founding father, trendsetter, innovator, inventor **9 predecessor**, forebear, forefather, ancestor, firstborn

ADJECTIVES 10 preceding, antecedent, anterior, precessional, leading, first, earliest **11 prior**, former, ex, late, erstwhile, one-time, previous, last, earlier, foregoing, abovementioned, aforementioned, aforenamed **12 primary**, senior, superior, supreme, pre-eminent, leading, first, foremost, headmost, chief **13 precursory**, preliminary, initial, introductory, elementary, basic, inaugural, baptismal, prefatory **14 preparatory**, foundational, developmental, leading, guiding, piloting, exploratory, reconnoitring, founding, discovering, innovatory, avant-garde, pioneering

VERBS 15 precede, antecede, predate, lead, guide, pilot, indicate, spearhead **16 take precedence**, outrank, be superior, have priority **17 give priority**, put first **18 forerun**, pioneer, explore, reconnoitre, discover, invent, found, inaugurate, initiate, innovate, influence **19 forecast**, foretell, presage, introduce, herald, usher in, ring in

569 Predetermination

VERBS 1 predetermine, destine, predestine, appoint, foreordain, preordain, decree **2 premeditate**, preconceive, plan, preset, prearrange

ADJECTIVES 3 predetermined, destined, predestined, fated, doomed, appointed, foreordained, preordained **4 deliberate**, intentional, willed, premeditated, prepense, planned, preplanned, considered, measured, weighed, calculated, designed, prearranged, preset, pre-established, fixed, set, controlled, studied, advised, devised, contrived, packed, primed

NOUNS 5 predetermination, predestination, foreordination, preordination, destiny, fate, doom, lot, karma, kismet, will **6 premeditation**, predeliberation, resolve, project, plan, intention, prearrangement, preparation, agenda, plot, packed jury, primed witness, preconceived opinion, foregone conclusion

570 Prediction

NOUNS 1 prediction, forecast, foretelling, forewarning, prophecy, apocalypse, revelation, prognosis, presentiment, premonition, hunch, feeling, foreboding, foresight, presage, prefiguration, expectation, prospect, horoscope **2 divination**, clairvoyance, augury, soothsaying, astrology, horoscopy, haruspicy, vaticination, fortune-telling, palmistry, chiromancy, crystal-gazing, reading cards, cartomancy, I Ching, casting lots, sortilege, bibliomancy, oneiromancy, hydromancy, pyromancy, geomancy, necromancy, occultism, dowsing, discovery, guesswork **3 plan**, programme, prospectus, schedule, itinerary, almanac, preview, announcement, notice, publication, warning, danger signal, hint, suggestion **4 model**, test design **5 omen**, sign, indication, portent, presage, augury, auspice, prognostication, syndrome, symptom, caution, warning, harbinger, precursor, forerunner, herald, messenger, prefigurement, foretoken, type, ominousness **6 good-luck sign**, talisman, mascot, horseshoe, four-leaf clover, rabbit's foot, shooting star, amber, bloodstone, lodestone **7 bad-luck sign**, broken mirror, spilt salt, peacock feather, owl **8 oracle**, sage, prophet, doom merchant, Cassandra, seer, visionary, vaticinator, soothsayer, clairvoyant, telepathist, medium, occultist, pythoness, sorcerer, witch, warlock, Delphic oracle, Pythian oracle, sibyl **9 forecaster**, consultant, meteorologist, tipster, speculator, futurologist, diviner, dowser, astrologer, fortune-teller, palmist, crystal-gazer, augur, auspex **10 cards**, tarot cards, runes, dice, lot, tripod, crystal ball, mirror, tea leaves

VERBS 11 predict, foresee, forecast, foretell, prophesy, reveal, guess, speculate, prognosticate, vaticinate, forebode, augur, presage, portend, foreshow, herald, harbinger, indicate, signify, betoken, represent, typify, hint, suggest, announce, notify, advertise, warn, lower, menace, threaten, promise **12 divine**, soothsay, interpret dreams, vaticinate

ADJECTIVES 13 predicting, foretelling, forewarning, presentient, prescient, foreseeing, clairvoyant, fortune-telling, weather-wise, prophetic, oracular, mantic, vatic, fatidic, apocalyptic, sibylline, premonitory, foreboding, cautionary, heralding, prefiguring, precursory **14 predicted**, foretold, forecast **15 presageful**, portentous, significant, fateful, augural, auspicial, haruspical, propitious, promising, fortunate, favourable, ominous

571 Preparation

VERBS 1 prepare, get ready, take steps, pioneer, bridge, make contact **2 do the groundwork**, found, establish, predispose, incline, begin, research, document, outline, draft, sketch, blueprint, plan, organize, plot, contrive, concert, prearrange, predetermine **3 be prepared**, forearm, guard against, insure, take precautions, save, anticipate **4 prepare for action**, make ready, mobilize, make operational, commission, fix, adjust, focus, tune, wind, gear up, arrange, array, order, assemble, stow, tee up, prime, cock, stoke up **5 equip**, fit, furnish, provide, supply, rig out, arm, crew **6 brief**, inform, instruct, teach, educate, train, coach, groom, drill, exercise **7 develop**, mature, mellow, ripen, force, bring on, cook, hatch, incubate, breed, grow, cultivate, nurse, nurture, raise, produce, concoct, elaborate **8 prepare oneself**, get ready, train, exercise, rehearse, practise, limber up

NOUNS 9 preparation, getting ready, taking steps, pioneering, mobilization, tuning, priming, loading, cocking, planning, organization, prearrangement, consultation, forethought, anticipation, foresight, promotion, inauguration, flotation **10 preparations**, preliminaries, measures, steps, trial run, experiment, practice, rehearsal, study, spadework, groundwork, foundation, basis, framework, sketch, draft, rough, outline, plan, blueprint, prototype, pilot scheme, arrangement, savings, reserves **11 fitting out**, provisioning, furnishing, supply, appointment, commission, equipment, kit, gear, outfit, marshalling, array, armament **12 briefing**, instruction, education, training, drill, exercise, practice, apprenticeship, novitiate **13 development**, maturation, ripening, seasoning, hardening, inurement, acclimatization, brewing, gestation, hatching, incubation, nursing, nurture, cultivation, tillage, sowing, planting, flowering, fruition, production **14 preparedness**, readiness, maturity, ripeness, mellowness, puberty, fitness

ADJECTIVES 15 preparatory, preliminary, introductory, basic, elementary, provisional, stopgap, makeshift **16 developing**, maturing, cooking, stewing, brewing, marinating, brooding, hatching, incubating, in progress, afoot, forthcoming, impending, under consideration, mooted, planned **17 prepared**, ready, alert, vigilant, mobilized, standing by, all set, teed up, keyed up, spoiling for, trained, qualified, experienced, practised, well-rehearsed, organized, tuned, primed, briefed, instructed, tutored, forewarned, forearmed, in harness, armed, equipped, furnished, well-appointed, groomed, accoutred **18 in hand**, operational **19 developed**, matured, ripened, mellow, seasoned, weathered, hardened, veteran, adult, full-grown, fledged, blooming, fruiting, well-done, elaborate, wrought, laboured, completed **20 ready-made**, cut-and-dried, ready-to-wear, prefabricated, processed, convenience, oven-ready, ready-to-cook

572 Presence

NOUNS 1 presence, existence, being, manifestation, reality, actuality, materialness, solidity **2 omnipresence**, ubiquitousness, pervasiveness, permeation, diffusion, attendance, appearance, frequenting, visiting, participation, accompaniment, companionship, society **3 residence**, occupancy, inhabitance **4 availability**, plenty, sufficiency, accessibility, readiness, handiness, convenience, proximity, nearness, immediacy, propinquity, vicinity **5 ghostly presence**, ghost, apparition, manifestation, spectre

ADJECTIVES 6 present, existent, extant, real, actual, material, solid, manifest, omnipresent, ubiquitous, infinite, everywhere, pervasive, diffusive, penetrating, permeating, suffusive, ghostly, spectral **7 attendant**, participating, watching, witnessed, associated, accompanying, concomitant, companionable, sociable, regular **8 resident**, in occupation, live-in, in-house **9 available**, plenty, sufficient, accessible, at hand, on, on tap, ready, handy, convenient, near, close

VERBS 10 be present, be, exist, occur, live, breathe, pervade, permeate, penetrate, suffuse, diffuse, imbue, impregnate, fill, soak, saturate, infiltrate, overrun, overswarm, appear, materialize **11 attend**, participate, take part, stand by, spectate, witness, see, watch, observe, view, visit, appear, turn up, report, frequent **12 reside**, occupy, inhabit

573 Present Time

NOUNS 1 present time, this moment, this instant, today **2 the present day**, this time, contemporary life **3 actuality**, happening, existence **4 up-to-dateness**, modernity

VERBS 5 be present, exist, be

ADJECTIVES 6 present, current, existent, extant, topical, actual, contemporary, modern, fashionable, up-to-date **7 occasional**, temporary, provisional, interim, passing **8 available**, at hand, ready, here, there, in attendance, nearby, close by

574 Preservation

NOUNS 1 preservation, protection, safekeeping, perpetuation, continuation, prolongation, conservation, permanence, ecology, green movement, conservation area, nature reserve, reservation, park, saving, salvation, redemption, deliverance, retention, maintenance, support, provision, frugality, economy, insulation, storage, refrigeration, boiling, pickling, marination, curing, smoking, dehydration, desiccation, canning, tinning, processing, packaging, irradiation, sterilization, hygiene, quarantine, upkeep, service, valeting, cleansing, painting, varnishing, waterproofing, embalming, mummification **2 preserver**, formaldehyde, alcohol, camphor, mothball, amber, plastic, salt, brine, spice, pickle, marinade, aspic, ice, refrigerator, vacuum flask, jar, bottle, can, tin, paint, varnish, creosote, lifeline, life belt, safety device, seat belt, air bag, gas mask, incubator, respirator, iron lung, charm, amulet, mascot, talisman **3 preserved thing**, listed building, protected species, mummy, fossil, frozen food, vacuum-packed food, long-life milk, dehydrated food, processed food, canned food, tinned food, preserves, jam, marmalade, conserve

VERBS 4 preserve, protect, guard, perpetuate, continue, prolong, uphold, defend, conserve, freeze, refrigerate, irradiate, pickle, salt, souse, marinate, cure, smoke, kipper, dehydrate, dry, bottle, can, tin, process, season, paint, varnish, whitewash, creosote, waterproof, embalm, mummify, stuff, maintain, service, support, bolster, sustain, supply, safeguard, keep, store, save, nurse, mother, tend, cherish, treasure, grasp, hug, hide

ADJECTIVES 5 preserving, conserving, protecting, prophylactic, preventive, salubrious, hygienic, redemptive, energy-saving, ecological, environment-friendly, conservational **6 preserved**, kept, alive, fresh, undecayed, intact, whole, perfect, dehydrated, desiccated, dried, frozen, pickled, marinated, salted, corned, soused, smoked, cured, canned, tinned, potted, bottled, mummified, embalmed, stuffed, mothballed, stored, conserved, protected, saved

575 Price

NOUNS 1 price, cost, charge, quotation, estimate, amount, figure, price cut, price war, tariff, cheapness **2 value**, worth, valuation, assessment, premium, prize, bounty **3 fee**, rate, ceiling, floor, commission, cut, refresher, charge, demand, dues, subscription, surcharge, supplement, extra, service charge, corkage, fare, hire, rental, overcharge, price-fixing **4 bill**, invoice, reckoning **5 cost**, outlay, costs, expenses, expenditure **6 business costs**, overheads, office supplies, postage, utilities, wages, damages, transport charges, freightage, wharfage, lighterage **7 tax**, taxes, dues, capital levy, death duty, estate duty, rates, community charge, Peter's pence, tithe, tenths, octroi, surtax, supertax, cess, Inland Revenue, National Insurance, deduction, personal allowance, rating, assessment, appraisement, valorization, rateable value **8 levy**, duty, impost, toll, excise, customs, tariff, charge, fine, penalty, imposition, exaction, aid, benevolence, tribute, blackmail **9 historical taxes**, Danegeld, stamp tax, salt tax, gabelle, window tax

VERBS 10 price, value, evaluate, appraise, rate **11 charge**, ask, demand, exact, levy, tax **12 cost**, amount to

ADJECTIVES 13 priced, valued, rated, assessed **14 chargeable**, rateable, taxable, dutiable

576 Pride

• *Pride goeth before destruction, and an haughty spirit before a fall.* Bible: Proverbs.

NOUNS 1 pride, proudness, self-confidence, self-esteem, self-importance, self-regard, self-respect, honour, courage **2 unapproachability**, disdain, obstinacy, stiff-neckedness, touchiness, self-sufficiency **3 conceit**, vanity, arrogance, insolence, haughtiness, self-admiration, overconfidence, pretension, egotism, affectation, uppitiness, self-praise, snobbery, vainglory, overambitiousness **4 prestige**, dignity, reputation, augustness, style **5 stateliness**, loftiness, proud bearing, nobility, condescension **6 majesty**, grandeur, venerability, sedateness, lordliness, princeliness, solemnity **7 fulfilment**, satisfaction **8 worthiness**, sobriety **9 ostentation**, display **10 boastfulness**, swank, side, big-headedness, puffed-out chest, bumptiousness **11 prejudice**, contempt, class distinction, racial hatred, Paki-bashing, sexism, ageism, xenophobia, social discrimination, feminism, white supremacy, segregation, apartheid **12 object of pride**, favourite

ADJECTIVES 13 proud, self-important, self-confident, self-esteeming, self-regarding, spirited, courageous, house-proud, supercilious, hoity-toity, high-hatted **14 unapproachable**, disdainful, obstinate, starchy, erect, stiff-necked, prickly, touchy, independent, self-sufficient, hardened, unbending, distant, aloof **15 oppressive**, overweening, overbearing **16 conceited**, vain, arrogant, pompous, insolent, brazen, unblushing, unabashed, condescending, haughty, self-admiring, affected, uppity, self-praising, snobbish, vainglorious, purse-proud, strutting, conceited, nose-in-the-air, snooty **17 prestigious**, dignified, august, high-flying, stylish, commanding, patronizing, impressive **18 stately**, lofty, condescending, aristocratic, noble, majestic, imposing, grand, venerable, sedate, solemn, grave, sombre, worthy, august, pompous, high-and-mighty, high-nosed, regal, lordly, princely, royal, kingly, queenly, statuesque, elevated, imperious, authoritative **19 fulfilled**, satisfied **20 ostentatious**, showy, plumed, crested, fine, grand, fashionable **21 boastful**, puffed up, inflated, big-headed, ungracious, strutting, swaggering, swanky, cocky, bumptious, self-glorifying **22 prejudiced**, contemptuous, class conscious, despising, undemocratic, xenophobic, racially prejudiced, anti-semitic, sexist

VERBS 23 be proud, have pride **24 be proud of**, glory in **25 be too proud**, be vain **26 be ostentatious**, show off, swank, swagger **27 disdain**, despise, condescend, patronize, pull rank **28 feel pride**, preen oneself, congratulate oneself, boast, hug oneself **29 make proud**, gratify, elate **30 save face**

577 Priority

NOUNS 1 priority, precedence, preexistence, antecedence, previousness **2 greater importance**, seniority, supremacy, superiority, lead, pre-eminence, first class, first place, first division **3 matter of priority**, first concern **4 claim to priority**, prerogative, privilege, primogeniture **5 gift of priority**, advantage, head start **6 foretaste**, preview, prerelease, trailer, presage, presentiment, prediction, precursor, herald, forerunner, prequel, preface, foreword, introduction

VERBS 7 be before, precede, anticipate, foreshadow, antedate, antecede, forerun, take precedence, lead, head **8 do before**, pre-empt, anticipate, forestall, precede, preface, introduce, preview, prepare beforehand, prefabricate

ADJECTIVES 9 prior, previous, former, earlier, first, leading, forward, foremost, first-class, first-division, avant garde, advanced, primal

578 Prison

NOUNS 1 prison, jail, lockup, compound, pound, dungeon, oubliette, prison camp, concentration camp, labourcamp, Gulag, halfway house, reformatory, detention centre, borstal, community home, approved school **2 the inside (Inf)**, prison **3 prison cell**, cage **4 prison sentence**, life **5 prisoner**, hostage, captive, convict, inmate **6 prison officer**, warder, guard, keeper, custodian, jailer **7 imprisonment**, confinement, internment, captivity

ADJECTIVES 8 imprisoned, captive, on remand, in detention, confined, interned, incarcerated

VERBS 9 imprison, jail, confine, intern, incarcerate, impound, lock up, put away

579 Probability

NOUNS 1 probability, likelihood, chance, odds, liability, proneness, predictability, prospect, forecast, outlook, expectation, presumption, anticipation, prognosis **2 tendency**, propensity, trend, drift, tenor, tone, swing, bearing **3 plausibility**, probability, possibility, reasonability, credibility **4 chance**, strong possibility, best bet, fair expectation **5 probability theory**, mathematical probability, statistical probability, empirical probability, probability distribution

ADJECTIVES 6 probable, likely, expected, undoubted, indubitable, unquestionable, apparent, ostensible, evident, presumable, predictive, prone, liable, apt, anticipated, prospective, tending **7 plausible**, probable, possible, reasonable, credible

VERBS 8 be probable, seem likely, promise **9 make probable**, make likely **10 think likely**, expect, anticipate, presume, suppose, daresay, predict, prognosticate, foresee, look for, count on, reckon

580 Probity

NOUNS 1 probity, honourableness, goodness, integrity, respectability, decency, incorruptibility, principles, ethics, morality, high ideals, high-mindedness, uprightness, nobleness, good character, repute, trustworthiness, reliability, dependability, honesty, truthfulness, candidness, frankness, openness, veracity, plainness, straightforwardness, sincerity, scrupulousness, fastidiousness, carefulness, conscientiousness, meticulousness, soundness, impartiality, fairness, equity, justice, clean hands, clear conscience, good faith, faithfulness, fidelity, constancy, steadfastness, trueness, loyalty, devotion **2 purity**, sanctity, faith, virtue, virginity, innocence, righteousness, godliness, holiness

ADJECTIVES 3 honourable, respectable, decent, good, reputable, incorruptible, high-minded, principled, fastidious, ethical, moral, upright, upstanding, noble, trustworthy, sure, reliable, dependable, responsible, dutiful, honest, true, truthful, candid, frank, open, above board, law-abiding, veracious, plain, straightforward, sincere, undeceitful, scrupulous, careful, meticulous, conscientious, sound, impartial, fair, straight, equitable, bona fide, just, faithful, constant, steadfast, loyal, true-blue, devoted, chivalrous, gentlemanly **4 pure**, undefiled, sanctified, saintly, pious, religious, godly, virtuous, virginal

VERBS 5 be honourable, behave well, fear God, act morally, deal fairly, shoot straight

581 Production

NOUNS 1 production, making, preparation, creation, invention, innovation, origination, inspiration, discovery, doing, productivity, output, throughput, turnout, effort, endeavour, attempt, try, undertaking, project, enterprise, performance, execution, accomplishment, achievement, art, writing, composition, musicianship, authorship, literary work, cogitation, conception, formulation, concoction, brewing, moulding, forming, shaping, casting, technology, skill, handiwork, craftsmanship, design, planning, organization **2 manufacture**, making, fabrication, construction, building, engineering, tectonics, architecture, erection, establishment, business, industry, processing, treatment, machining, assembly, conveyor belt, assembly line, workshop, factory, technology, ecodevelopment, industrialization, mass production, automation, high technology, computerization, robotics, development, growth, agriculture, growing, market gardening, farming, stockbreeding **3 product**, manufacture, artefact, article, item, thing, object, creation, creature, result, consequence, effect, outcome, issue, output, turnout, extract, essence, decoction, concoction, confection, compound, end-product, by-product, spin-off, offshoot, waste product, slag, leavings **4 mental product**, brainchild, brainwave, fiction **5 work of art**, production, performance, work, composition, piece, opus, sonata, symphony, concerto, ballet, opera, literary work, book, pamphlet, article, poem, story, novella, novel, play, sketch, film **6 great work**, magnum opus, masterwork, masterpiece **7 produce**, goods, merchandise, wares, commodity, pottery, china, stoneware, ironware, kitchenware, hardware, brown goods, fabric, cloth, textile, drapery, white goods, hosiery, animal products, meat, dairy products, milk, eggs, skin, fur, leather, fruit, crop, harvest, vintage, yield, interest, return, dividend, revenue, income, offspring, egg **8 construction**, structure, building, edifice, pile, dome, tower, skyscraper, church, cathedral, temple, mausoleum, tomb, cenotaph, monument, pyramid, ziggurat, acropolis, Colosseum, theatre, hospital, college, school, hall, habitation, house, mansion, palace, castle, fort, folly, stonework

VERBS 9 produce, make, create, originate, invent, innovate, fabricate, engineer, manufacture, output, mine, quarry, extract, exploit, process, industrialize, mechanize, automate, computerize, mass-produce, synthesize, blend, combine, cobble together, assemble, build, construct, erect, establish, found, institute, structure, arrange, stage, direct, cause, beget, bear, spawn, generate, engender, breed, hatch, sow, grow, farm, cultivate, raise, rear, educate, train, develop, evolve, cogitate, imagine, conceive, plan, devise, formulate, achieve, accomplish, implement, execute, effect, yield, supply, provide, furnish, present, show, reveal, unfold, uncover, find, discover, write, compose, shape, mould, fashion, design, spin, weave, sew, carve, sculpt, forge, cast, coin, mint, mill, machine, prefabricate, multiply, reproduce, propagate

ADJECTIVES 10 productive, creative, innovative, inventive, original, formative, structural, constructive, architectonic, manufacturing, industrial, developed, mechanized, automated, computerized, robotic, postindustrial, developing, agricultural, fertile, fruitful, fecund, prolific, rich, profitable, remunerative, lucrative, paying, high-yielding, interest-bearing **11 produced**, created, man-made, synthetic, artificial, manufactured, processed, ready-made, machine-made, mass-produced, handmade, homemade, homespun, tailor-made, architect-designed, custom-built, invented, imagined, devised, worked out, discovered, begotten, bred, hatched, sown, grown, raised

582 Prominence

NOUNS 1 prominence, eminence, distinction, importance, salience, mark, repute, esteem, prestige, kudos, cachet, glory, position, impressiveness, exaltedness **2 projection**, spit, headland, promontory, cape, ness, point, peninsula, jetty, pier, mountain, peak, fortification, overhang, outcrop, shelf, ledge **3 protuberance**, bump, swelling, protrusion, face, forehead, brow, proboscis, trunk, antenna, beak **4 conspicuousness**, obviousness, distinctness

ADJECTIVES 5 protuberant, protrudent, swelling, sticking out, proud, jutting out, bumpy **6 eminent**, prominent, distinctive, important, salient, reputable, esteemed, glorious, impressive, exalted **7 conspicuous**, distinct, well defined, unblurred, clear-cut

VERBS 8 protrude, swell, stick out, stand out, poke out, project, jut out, overhang **9 be prominent**, have distinction

583 Promise

NOUNS 1 promise, commitment, pledge, vow, oath, one's word, testimony, swearing, deposition, adjuration, affidavit, affirmation, assurance, profession, promise-making, gentleman's agreement, covenant, bond, handshake, compact, contract, intention, engagement **2 guarantee**, security, warranty, promissory note, contract, insurance premium, IOU, voucher, pawn ticket **3 potential**, possibilities, capacity, capability, ability, hope, good omen **4 promised land**, Canaan, Israel, El Dorado, Utopia, Erewhon, Shangri-la, Elysian Fields, eternal life, the millennium

VERBS 5 promise, pledge, confirm, assure, proffer, affirm, vow, commit oneself, swear, testify, pledge oneself, undertake to, covenant, contract, exchange vows **6 guarantee**, warrant, certify, assure, answer for, vouch for, commit oneself, take on, accept responsibility, secure, insure, underwrite **7 be auspicious**, augur well **8 show potential**, have possibilities, hope, improve, develop, evolve **9 promise oneself**, contemplate, desire

ADJECTIVES 10 promised, pledged, bound, committed, testimonial, sworn, on oath, adjuratory, votive, affirmative, assured, professed, engaged, betrothed **11 guaranteeing**, authenticating, certified, assured, attested, certain, warranted, underwritten, signed, securing, pledging, committed, bound, obligated, promissory **12 auspicious**, propitious, promising, encouraging, hopeful, potential, possible, likely, fortunate, favourable, optimistic, good, bright, fair, golden, rosy **13 future**, eventual, destined, fated, potential, prospective, probable, possible, anticipated

584 Property

NOUNS 1 property, possession, realty, freehold, leasehold, estate, title, right, copyright, patent, receipt, claim, rent-roll, domain, building, benefice, living, small holding, homestead, farm, cottage, bungalow, house, ranch, hacienda, chalet, villa, manor, mansion, flat, apartment, tenement, penthouse, plantation, castle, land, acreage, tract, grounds, lot, plot, parcel, allotment, common, territory, dependency **2 legal terms**, personalty, domain, demesne, chose, messuage, tenement, tenure, hereditament, fee simple, fee tail, mortmain, dead hand, immovables, movables, jointure, entail, remainder, reversion **3 historic property terms**, toft, allodium, feu, frankalmoign, fee, fiefdom, feudality, villeinage, socage, burgage, copyhold, seigneury **4 possessions**, personal effects, belongings, gear, stuff, things, worldly goods, trappings, temporalities, paraphernalia, accoutrements, appurtenances, accessories, appendages, impedimenta, luggage **5 personal estate**, circumstances, state, assets, resources, collateral, valuables, wealth, inheritance, legacy, heirloom, funds, income, capital, revenue, means, substance, securities, portfolio, tangibles, intangibles, stock, merchandise, wares, goods, contents **6 marriage settlement**, dowry, bride price, dot, marriage portion, allotment, allowance, pin money

ADJECTIVES 7 propertied, proprietary, possessing, freehold, leasehold, copyhold, movable, immovable, real, allotted, territorial, landed, praedial, manorial, seignorial, feudal, feodal, allodial, patrimonial, hereditary, testamentary, limited, assessed, collateral, secured, tangible, intangible, fixed, frozen, liquid, net, endowed, dowered, established

VERBS 8 own property, possess, have resources, inherit, endow, dower, bless with, bequeath, grant

585 Propulsion

NOUNS 1 propulsion, impulsion, pulsion, propelling, drive, momentum, thrust, impetus, push, shove, butt, bunt, shunt, kick **2 throwing**, projection, trajection, jaculation, flinging, slinging, pelting, precipitation, pitching, casting, hurling, lobbing **3 ejection**, expulsion, ejector seat **4 throw**, toss, pitch, cast, bowl, fling, sling, swipe, shy, hurl, chuck, chunk, lob, heave, flip, knock, put, pass, kick, punt, dribble, throw-in, yorker, stroke, drive, fastball, curve, sinker, slider, knuckleball, spitball, spitter, service, return, volley, smash, rally, kill, slice **5 shooting**, gunnery, ballistics, artillery, firing, musketry, trapshooting, skeet, archery **6 shot**, discharge, gunshot, volley, fusillade, salvo, bombardment, cannonade, tattoo, spray, ejection, detonation, bowshot **7 missile**, projectile, weapon, shot, grapeshot, ball, pellet, bullet, slug, shell, mortar, cannonball, torpedo, rocket, trajectile, ejector, ejectamenta, arrow, dart, shaft, bolt, slingstone

ADJECTIVES 8 propulsive, propellant, pulsive, motive, driving, shoving **9 projectile**, trajectile, jaculatory, ejective, ballistic, missile

VERBS 10 propel, push, shove, thrust, impel, launch, move, traject, project, jaculate, drive, kick, pedal, row, pole, treadle **11 move forward**, advance, sweep, hustle, drive, butt, bunt **12 roll**, bowl, trundle **13 throw**, toss, pitch, cast, hurl, fling, sling, lob, heave, shy, york, catapult, pelt, lapidate, stone, shower, snowball, jerk, flip, snap, pass, serve, return, volley, slice, smash, put, dart, lance **14 push**, shove, send flying, shoulder, ease along, pitchfork **15 eject**, expel **16 bat**, slam, slog, drive, loft, cut, pull, glance, shank, slice **17 kick**, dribble, punt **18 shoot**, discharge, explode, fire, loose off, volley, bombard, cannonade, detonate, let fly, gun, pistol, strike, hit, fell, blast **19 riddle**, pepper **20 blow up**, fulminate **21 snipe**, pick off, pot, potshot **22 load**, prime, charge, cock **23 start**, launch, set going, kick off, bully off

586 Prosperity

NOUNS 1 prosperity, well-being, welfare, wealth, success, fame, fortune, luxury, comfort, ease, thriving, security, plenty, affluence, boom, bull market, prestige, glory **2 good fortune**, luck, winning streak, bonanza, auspiciousness, favour, blessings **3 time of plenty**, good times, golden age, halcyon days, palmy days, salad days, heyday, honeymoon period, holiday, summer

VERBS 4 be prosperous, prosper, do well, succeed, make good, progress, advance, arrive, go far, thrive, flourish, blossom, profit **5 be fortunate**, be lucky **6 be auspicious**, bode well, promise well, augur well, favour

ADJECTIVES 7 prosperous, successful, thriving, flourishing, booming, well-to-do, well-off, rising, upwardly mobile, profiteering, famous, affluent, rich, opulent, wealthy, luxurious, fat, comfortable, cosy, at ease, bullish, fortunate, lucky, palmy, halcyon, golden, rosy, blissful, blessed, favourable, promising

587 Protest

NOUNS 1 protest, opposition, objection, dissent, dissatisfaction, disagreement, disapproval, disapprobation, negation, negativity, contravention, hostility, discontent, recalcitrance, refractoriness, challenge, refutation, noncooperation, noncompliance, disobedience, anger, defiance, recusance, mutiny, nonpayment, expostulation, deprecation, intercession, counteraction, warning, complaint, clamour, outcry, denial, contradiction, repudiation, disclaimer, renunciation **2 disorder**, agitation, lawlessness, anarchy, insurgency, sedition, treason, rioting, rebellion, revolt, mutiny, insurrection, uprising, coup d'état, putsch, terrorism, war, assassination, regicide **3 gesture of protest**, strike, go-slow, boycott, picketing, demonstration, sit-in, work-in, raised fist, slow handclap, boo, hiss, whistle, catcall, jeer, howl, raspberry **4 protester**, objector, complainer, grumbler, bellyacher, moaner, troublemaker, agitator, malcontent, rabble-rouser, dissident, dissenter, critic, separatist, sectarian, dropout, nonconformist, hippie, rebel, demonstrator, striker, scab, blackleg, tub-thumper, suffragette **5 seditionist**, anarchist, nihilist, spy, revolutionary, urban guerrilla, partisan

VERBS 6 protest, oppose, object, dissent, resist, disagree with, disapprove of, deprecate, detract, contravene, challenge, disobey, defy, mutiny, expostulate, intercede, counteract, warn, complain, clamour, say no, deny, contradict, repudiate, disclaim, renounce **7 complain**, groan, grumble, grouse, whine, gripe, bellyache, moan, rant, boo, hiss, tut-tut, whistle, catcall, jeer **8 cause mischief**, strike, go slow, boycott, picket, agitate against, demonstrate against, riot, rebel, revolt, mutiny, terrorize

ADJECTIVES 9 protesting, opposing, dissenting, dissatisfied, disapproving, negative, negating, hostile, critical, discontent, malcontent, unconsenting, deprecatory, recalcitrant, refractory, challenging, noncooperative, noncompliant, nonconformist, disobedient, angry, contrary, defiant, recusant, counteractive, denying, contradictive, repudiated, clamourous, hissing, booing **10 law-breaking**, lawless, insubordinate, insurgent, mutinous, seditious, treasonous, riotous, rebellious, revolutionary, anarchist, nihilist, terrorist, guerrilla

588 Provision

NOUNS 1 provision, supplying, furnishing, equipping, logistics, fitting out, purveying, catering, service, delivery, distribution, self-service, takeaway, procuring, pandering, feeding, entertainment, clothing, accommodation, maintenance, support, assistance, subsidy, subvention, equipment, stock, feed, pipeline, source, commissariat, victualling, supplies, stores, reserves, rations, iron rations, helping, portion, share, reinforcement, replenishment, refill, topping-up, plenitude, yield, produce, product, return, increase, gain, conservation, economy, budgeting, preparation, precaution, measure **2 provisions**, food, provender, sustenance, victuals, comestibles **3 provider**, supplier, donor, giver, creditor, lender, bursar, purser, treasurer, waiter, waitress, steward, butler, quartermaster, storekeeper, victualler, sutler, drysalter, grocer, greengrocer, baker, poulterer, fishmonger, butcher, vintner, milkman, wholesaler, retailer, middleman, shopkeeper, wet nurse, feeder, procurer **4 caterer**, purveyor, hotelier, restauranteur, maître d'hôtel, innkeeper, host, publican, licensee, alewife, landlord, housekeeper, housewife, cook, chef

VERBS 5 provision, supply, provide, furnish, equip, purvey, cater, afford, offer, lend, contribute, give, endow, present, find, arm, man, staff, fit out, kit out, fix up, prepare, make ready, keep supplied, yield, produce, bring in, fly in, pump in, procure, pander, pimp, service, sell, distribute, deliver, hand out, serve, dish up, victual, feed, cook for, clothe, accommodate, board, put up, maintain, keep, support, stock, budget, store, stockpile, hoard, bunker, forage, fuel, tap, draw on, milk, extract, export, import **6 replenish**, resupply, reinforce, fill, refill, fill up, top up, restock, revictual, refuel, reload, make good

ADJECTIVES 7 provisioning, supplying, providing, furnishing, equipping, catering, commissarial, self-service, takeaway, sufficing, sufficient, available, in stock **8 provisional**, supplied, provided, furnished, equipped, all found, all-in, well-appointed, catered, offered, given, staffed, prepared, ready

589 Psychology and Psychiatry

NOUNS 1 psychology, abnormal psychology, psychoanalysis, apperceptionism, associationism, animal psychology, ethology, behavioural psychology, behaviourism, clinical psychology, child psychology, criminal psychology, educational psychology, experimental psychology, Gestaltism, configurationism, group psychology, metapsychology, neuropsychology, psychobiochemistry, psychobiology, psychodynamics, psychogenesis, psychognosis, psychography, psycholinguistics, psychologism, psychometry, psychopathology, psychopharmacology, psychophysics, psychophysiology, psychosociology, psychotechnology, psychological warfare, psychosexuality, reactology, reflexology, orgone theory **2 psychiatry**, medicopsychology, prophylactic psychiatry, psychodiagnostics, psychodiagnosis, antipsychiatry, neuropsychiatry, orthopsychiatry, psychogeriatrics, psychological medicine, psychosocial medicine **3 psychiatric treatment**, psychiatric care, psychotropic drug, psychosurgery, leucotomy, prefrontal leucotomy, psychoanalysis, psychoanalytic method, the couch, assertiveness training, psychotherapy, behaviour therapy, autosuggestion, biofeedback, aversion therapy, desensitization, conditioning, counselling, group psychotherapy, group dynamics, family therapy, consciousness raising, sensitivity training, marriage guidance, logotherapy, mind cure, occupational therapy, regression therapy, drama therapy, psychocatharsis, role playing, sex therapy, suggestionism, hypnotherapy, autohypnosis, narcotherapy **4 psychometrics**, psychometry, intelligence testing, psychological screening, psychography, lie detector, polygraph **5 disordered personality**, neurotic, neuropath, psychoneurotic, sociopath, escapist, paranoid personality, schizoid personality, dual personality, multiple personality, split personality, schizothyme, schizothymic personality, cyclothyme, cycloid personality, psychopath, psychotic **6 psychological disorder**, neurosis, psychosis, psychoneurosis, phobia, shell shock, psychopathia martialis, breakdown, nervous breakdown, mental breakdown, schizophrenia, dementia praecox, hebephrenia, catatonia, cyclothymia **7 psychologist**, psychologue, clinician, psychiatrist, psychotherapist, psychoanalyst, analyst, psychopathologist, psychotechnologist, psychobiologist, psychochemist, psychophysiologist, psychophysicist, psychographer, psychosociologist, hypnotherapist, narcotherapist, dramatherapist, behaviour therapist **8 psychiatrist**, neuropsychiatrist, psychogeriatrician **9 psychiatric hospital**, mental hospital

ADJECTIVES 10 psychological, psychiatric, neuropsychiatric, psychotherapeutic, psychoanalytical, psychodiagnostic, psychometric, psychopathological, psychosocial, psychosomatic, psychophysical, psychobiological, psychoneurological, psychosexual, psychogenic, psychogenetic, psychotechnical, psychogeriatric **11 psychologically disturbed**, neurotic, disturbed, nervous, traumatized, emotional, schizoid, sociopathic, psychopathic, psychotic, hypochondriacal, paranoid, dissociated **12 subconscious**, subliminal, unconscious, repressed, suppressed, inhibited, restrained

VERBS 13 psychologize, psychoanalyse, analyse

590 Publication

NOUNS 1 publication, publishing, dissemination, circulation, ventilation, divulgence, disclosure, promulgation, broadcasting, loudspeaker, loud hailer, broadcast, announcement, declaration, proclamation, pronouncement, statement, speech, sermon, notification, public notice, report, communiqué, bulletin, manifesto, pronunciamento, edict, decree, encyclical, ukase, ban, rumour, hearsay, gossip **2 mass media**, communication, telecommunication, television, radio, broadcasting, narrowcasting, cablecasting **3 journalism**, the press, fourth estate, Fleet Street, tabloid press, popular press, gutter press, reporting **4 newspaper**, paper, freesheet, giveaway, daily, broadsheet, tabloid, sheet, edition, extra, supplement **5 journal**, periodical, review, gazette, magazine, newsmagazine, comic, serial, series, daily, weekly, fortnightly, monthly, quarterly, seasonal, annual, organ, trade paper, newsletter, news-sheet **6 publicity**, limelight, spotlight, coverage, public eye, fame, notoriety, infamy, common knowledge, openness, manifestation, publicness, currency **7 publicizer**, publicist, promoter, propagandist, publicity agent, press agent, image-maker, advertiser, hidden persuader, copywriter, PR person, announcer, messenger, proclaimer, crier, herald, barker, spieler, tout, pamphleteer **8 newspaper man**, newswoman, press baron, journalist, reporter, correspondent, investigative journalist, chequebook journalist, columnist, agony aunt, freelancer, stringer, press photographer, critic, editor

VERBS 9 make public, inform, divulge, reveal, disclose, expose, ventilate, air, communicate, broadcast, transmit, relay, telecast, televise, radio, narrowcast, disseminate, diffuse, propagate, promulgate, release, circulate, mention, gossip, retail **10 proclaim**, publish, announce, notify, pronounce, declare, declaim, herald, trumpet, blast, blazon, cry, thunder **11 publish**, report, cover, write up, serialize, syndicate, edit, copyedit, subedit, typeset, set, print, issue, scoop, put out, distribute **12 publicize**, advertise, request, bill, placard, pamphleteer, propagandize, promote, boost, sell, push, feature, highlight, spotlight, pinpoint, emphasize, headline, splash, make famous, make someone, extol, glorify, rave about, overrate, puff **13 be published**, come out, circulate **14 become famous**, achieve fame, make it **15 be sold**, sell well

ADJECTIVES 16 published, printed, circulating, current, open, public, revealed, disclosed, exposed, announced, declared, proclaimed, ventilated, aired, communicated, disseminated, distributed, circularized, broadcast **17 well-known**, celebrated, renowned, famous, popular, infamous, notorious, flagrant, blatant, glaring, sensational **18 publishing**, declaratory

591 Punishment

- *There is no peace, saith the Lord, unto the wicked.* Bible: Isaiah.
- *Love is a boy, by poets styl'd,/ Then spare the rod, and spoil the child.* Samuel Butler.
- *My object all sublime/ I shall achieve in time –/ To let the punishment fit the crime –/ The punishment fit the crime.* W. S. Gilbert.

VERBS 1 punish, discipline, chastise, chasten, correct, castigate, admonish, reprimand, reprove, rebuke, chide, scold, tell off, dust down, hurt, afflict, inflict, visit, impose, persecute, victimize, shame, pillory, keelhaul, picket, spread-eagle, imprison, lock up, demote, degrade, unfrock, suspend, expel, send down, cashier, drum out, ban, proscribe, banish, exile, deport, ostracize, blackball, outlaw, confiscate, sequestrate, deprive, forfeit, fine, amerce, mulct **2 penalize**, condemn, sentence, exact retribution, settle, fix, retaliate, settle with, pay back **3 hit**, strike, smack, slap, lambaste, paddle, slipper, cuff, clout, drub, trounce, belt, strap, leather, wallop, welt, cane, birch, switch, whack, thwack, thrash, flog, whip, horsewhip, lash, scourge, flay, flail, flagellate, bastinado, cudgel **4 torture**, torment, thumbscrew, rack, press, mutilate, kneecap, persecute **5 execute**, condemn, kill, lynch, electrocute, hang, gibbet, gas, shoot, guillotine, behead, decapitate, decollate, strangle, garrotte, bowstring, burn, flay alive, stone, lapidate, dismember, impale, crucify, purge, massacre, decimate, slaughter **6 be punished**, suffer

NOUNS 7 punishment, penalization, discipline, chastisement, chastening, chiding, correction, lesson, castigation, admonition, reprimand, reproof, rebuke, scolding, telling off, dusting down, persecution, victimization, example, shame, ducking, keelhauling, detention, house arrest, imprisonment, incarceration, confinement, internment, prison sentence, penal servitude, hard labour, chain gang, labour camp, penal colony, Gulag, transportation, galleys, demotion, downgrading, unfrocking, suspension, expulsion, banishment, deportation, ostracism, blackballing, outlawing, proscription, confiscation, sequestration, escheat, deprivation, expropriation, forfeit, fining, amercement, mulct, deodand **8 penalty**, official punishment, condemnation, sentence, liability, legal obligation, dueness, damages, costs, compensation, restoration, restitution, payment **9 retribution**, Nemesis, just deserts, justice, doomsday, judgment, reckoning, retaliation, reprisal, requital, repayment **10 affliction**, visitation, imposition, trial, task, dose, bitter pill, hard lines, adversity, suffering, damage, loss **11 penance**, atonement, self-mortification, asceticism, hara-kiri, seppuki **12 corporal punishment**, hitting, striking, spanking, smacking, slapping, paddling, drubbing, trouncing, beating, caning, birching, thrashing, flogging, whipping, horsewhipping, scourging, flagellation, hit, spank, smack, blow, buffet, cuff, clout, stroke, stripe, torture, third degree, racking, strappado **13 capital punishment**, execution, legalized killing, death penalty, traitor's death, electrocution, hanging, poison, injection, shooting, guillotining, beheading, decapitation, decollation, strangulation, garrotte, stoning, lapidation, impalement, crucifixion, flaying alive, auto-da-fe, drowning, noyade, massacre, purge, genocide, the Holocaust, Final Solution, slaughter, martyrdom **14 instrument of punishment**, pillory, stocks, ducking stool, dunce's cap, hairbrush, belt, strap, thong, quirt, lash, whip, horsewhip, cowhide, knout, scourge, cat-o'-nine-tails, whipping post, ruler, ferule, stick, birch, switch, cane, rod, cudgel, cosh, club, rubber hose, bicycle chain, sandbag, chain, irons, bilboes, fetters, cell **15 instrument of torture**, rack, thumbscrew, iron boot, pilliwinks, triangle, wheel, treadmill, Iron Maiden, Scavenger's Daughter, torture chamber **16 instrument of execution**, electric chair, noose, halter, scaffold, gallows, gibbet, gas chamber, hemlock, poison, lethal injection, bullet, firing squad, axe, block, guillotine, garrotte, bowstring, cross, stake **17 penology**, penal code

ADJECTIVES 18 punitive, punishing, penalizing, capital, corporal, disciplinary, corrective, instructive, castigatory, admonitory, vindictive, retributive, revengeful **19 punished**, disciplined, castigated, imprisoned, fined, beaten, tortured **20 punishing**, hard, arduous, strenuous, exhausting, gruelling, laborious, back-breaking, demanding, taxing, torturous **21 punishable**, liable, amerceable

592 Purchase

VERBS 1 purchase, buy, get, obtain, procure, acquire, order, teleshop, afford, snap up, hoard, monopolize, buy out, bargain, barter, bid, offer, invest in, bull, stag **2 shop**, market, spend, expend **3 buy back**, repurchase, redeem **4 buy off**, bribe, square, suborn, corrupt **5 defray**, pay for

NOUNS 6 purchase, buy, acquisition, purchases, shopping, bargain **7 purchasing**, buying, deferred payment, hire purchase, the HP, the never-never, tick, takeover, greenmail, pre-emption, cornering, forestalling, bid, offer **8 shopping**, shopping spree, catalogue buying, teleshopping, spending, expenditure **9 repurchase**, redemption **10 bribery**, subornment **11 custom**, patronage **12 purchaser**, buyer, customer, patron, client, clientele, consumer, shopper, emptor, teleshopper, spender, credit-card holder, bargain-hunter, haggler, investor, speculator, bull, stag, vendee, transferee, consignee, offerer, bidder, taker, acceptor, hoarder, pre-emptor, redeemer

ADJECTIVES 13 bought, purchased, charged, emptional, ransomed, redeemed, bribed **14 buying**, purchasing, shopping, marketing, teleshopping, cash-and-carry, cut-price, bidding, bargaining, haggling, investing, speculative, bullish, pre-emptive

593 Purity

NOUNS 1 purity, cleanness, freshness, clearness, clarity, spotlessness, immaculacy, stainlessness, sinlessness, innocence, faultlessness, flawlessness, perfection, morality, high-mindedness, moral rectitude, virtue, decency, honesty, honour, integrity, piety, virginity, chastity, delicacy, propriety, good taste, simplicity, modesty, pudency, primness, priggishness, prudery, censorship, bowdlerization, expurgation, euphemism, coyness, sanctimoniousness, Puritanism, Grundyism **2 purification**, cleansing, washing, lustration, Asperges, purgation, flushing, dialysis, purging, clearance, riddance, expulsion, elimination, ventilation, airing, fumigation, deodorization, antisepsis, disinfection, sterilization, decontamination, disinfestation, delousing **3 purifier**, cleansing agent, soda, carbolic acid, detergent, washing powder, soapflakes, soap, shampoo, mouthwash, gargle, toothpaste, dentifrice, lotion, hand cream, cold cream, disinfectant, deodorant, air-freshener, filter **4 purgative**, cathartic, enema, diuretic, nauseant, emetic, laxative, aperient **5 pure person**, saint, virgin, maid, virgo intacta, vestal virgin, spinster, old maid, monk, nun, Puritan, Quaker, paragon **6 prude**, prig, Victorian, moral guardian **7 purebred**, thoroughbred **8 simplicity**, homogeneity, uniformity, oneness, absoluteness, bedrock

VERBS 9 be pure, have integrity, have virtue, resist temptation **10 purify**, clean, purge, wash, lave, lustrate, freshen, fumigate, deodorize, edulcorate, ventilate, desalinate, decontaminate, disinfect, chlorinate, pasteurize, sanitize, sterilize, refine, sublimate, distil, strain, filter, percolate, leach, lixiviate, sift, sieve, winnow, depurate, clarify, clear, skim, scum, despumate, rack, decarbonize, decoke, elutriate, flush, dialyse, catheterize, drain, flush out, censor, expurgate, blue-pencil **11 simplify**, unify, unscramble, unravel, sort out, weed out, eliminate, expel, eject

ADJECTIVES 12 morally pure, virtuous, righteous, decent, moral, chaste, virginal, faithful, high-minded, unerring, perfect, noble, spotless, sinless, innocent, uncorrupt, honourable, angelic, modest, prudish, prim, priggish, coy, euphemistic, Christian, sanctimonious, Puritanical **13 pure**, cleansed, spotless, stainless, unblemished, immaculate, unsullied, untarnished, unspoilt, unpolluted, uncontaminated, unadulterated, undiluted, neat, unflavoured, unfragranced, unspiced, unseasoned, uncoloured, untinged, clear, refined, blank, purebred, thoroughbred **14 purified**, cleansed, spick-and-span, shining, polished, scrubbed, snow-white, dainty, nice, deodorized, disinfected, aseptic, antiseptic, sterilized, sterile **15 purifying**, cleansing, purificatory, lustral, hygienic, sterilizing, germicidal, sanitary, disinfectant, detergent, purging **16 simple**, one, single, homogeneous, unified, monolithic, uniform, undifferentiated, indivisible, elemental, entire, unadulterated, undefiled, unalloyed, uncompounded, unblended, mere, sheer, utter, irreducible, basic, fundamental, elementary, intrinsic, unmixed, unmingled, no frills, unravelled, disentangled, intelligible **17 direct**, unsophisticated, simplistic, homespun, unqualified, unmitigated, wholehearted, single-minded, downright, sincere, unpretentious, honest, honourable, unaffected, undisguised

594 Purpleness

NOUNS 1 purpleness, purplishness, imperial purple, bishop's purple, mourning colour **2 purple pigment**, Tyrian purple, gentian violet, Parma violet, cobalt violet, methyl violet, mauveine, amaranth, permanent magenta, Windsor violet, Thalo purple **3 purple things**, lavender, lilac, violet, heather, foxglove, hyancinth, heliotrope, plum, damson, aubergine, beetroot, purple martin, purple emperor **4 figurative purple thing**, purple prose, purple patch **5 lividness**, lividity

ADJECTIVES 6 purple, purplish, purply, lavender, lilac, mauve, purple-red, fuchsia, magenta, maroon, plum-coloured, damson-coloured, puce, amaranthine, hyacinthine, heliotrope, violet, violaceous, amethystine, purpure, aubergine, mulberry, purple-blue **7 livid**, black-and-blue **8 furious**, livid

VERBS 9 empurple, bruise

595 Pursuit

NOUNS 1 pursuit, pursuing, seeking, search, quest, hunting, tracking, trailing, stalking, spooring, chasing, following, dogging, shadowing, manhunt, dragnet, persecution, witch-hunt, kangaroo court, hounding, persistence, perseverance, prosecution, execution **2 chase**, pursuit, run, paper chase, steeplechase, race, hunt, hounding, casting, tally-ho, beat, drive, battue, beating, shooting, gunning, blood sport, fox hunt, stag hunt, pheasant shoot, grouse shoot, duck shoot, turkey shoot, big-game hunt, safari hunt, pigsticking, deer stalking, hawking, falconry, fowling, fishing, angling, whaling, beagling, coursing, ratting, trapping, ferreting, rabbiting, lamping **3 hunting and fishing equipment**, fishing rod, casting rod, bait, fly, fishing net, keepnet, dragnet, gun, rifle, shotgun, fowling-piece **4 activity**, work, business, occupation, career, leisure pursuit, hobby, pastime, interest **5 pursuer**, seeker, searcher, researcher, quester, chaser, follower, dogger, shadow **6 hunter**, tracker, trailer, stalker, huntsman, huntress, Nimrod, Diana, whipper-in, beater, hounds, pack, gun dog, marksman, shot, gun, big-game hunter, poacher, guddler, trapper, ratcatcher, fowler, falconer, hawker, fisherman, piscator, angler, shrimper, oysterman, trawlerman, whaler, headhunter, cannibal, man-eater, mouser, hawk **7 the hunted**, prey, quarry, game, victim, fugitive, escapee, deserter, missing person

VERBS 8 pursue, seek, search for, hunt for, quest after, fish for, dig for, persecute, oppress, harass, harry, chivy **9 follow**, track, trail, stalk, spoor, prowl after, sneak after, dog, shadow, sleuth, scent out, sniff out **10 chase**, run after, whoop, halloo, hark, run down, ride down, rush at, charge at, tilt at, leap at, jump at, grab away **11 hunt**, shoot, bag, fish, fly-fish, angle, trawl, whale, shrimp, catch, net, hook, guddle, trap, ensnare, stalk, fowl, hawk, course, start game, start up, beat, flush, lay traps, set snares **12 aim at**, steer for, woo, court, mob, swarm over **13 follow up**, persist, persevere, press on **14 carry on**, continue, practise, conduct, prosecute, execute

ADJECTIVES 15 pursuing, seeking, searching, questing, following, chasing **16 hunting**, shooting, fishing **17 pursued**, sought, followed, chased, hounded, hunted

596 Qualification

NOUNS 1 qualification, eligibility, suitability, suitedness, acceptability, appropriateness, propriety, fitness, preparedness, readiness, adequacy, sufficiency, efficacy, appositeness, relevance, applicability, aptness, ability, capability, worthiness, deservedness, meritedness, dueness, entitlement, competence, efficiency, proficiency, potentiality **2 ability**, facility, faculty, capability, capacity, quality, mastery, attribute, tendency, endowment, talent, skill, genius, flair, gift, bent **3 qualifications**, authorization, permit, licence, documentation, certification, diploma, degree, licentiate, baccalaureate, examinations, skills, expertise, experience, record, background, history, references, credentials, testimonial **4 permission**, authorization, empowerment, enablement, investment, endowment **5 modification**, qualification, adjustment, adaptation, alteration, change, variation, modulation, coordination, regulation, attunement, improvement, reconciliation, palliation, mitigation, softening **6 specification**, qualification, definition, determination, limitation, restriction, circumscription, bounding, confinement, control, check, demarcation, delimitation, prescription, proscription, mandate, bounds **7 condition**, qualification, grounds, reservation, parameter, stipulation, obligation, requisite, prerequisite, provision

ADJECTIVES 8 qualified, capable, able, eligible, suitable, suited, well-adapted, acceptable, appropriate, fit, prepared, ready, apt, worthy, deserved, merited, competent, efficient, professional, businesslike, proficient, equipped, endowed, talented, gifted, masterful, expert, skilled, experienced, practised **9 authorized**, certified, empowered, enabled, permitted, licensed, entitled, allowed **10 modified**, adjusted, adapted, altered, changed, varied, variational, modulated, coordinated, conditioned, regulated, attuned, improved, reconciled, palliative, mitigatory, softened **11 conditional**, qualificatory, reserved, stipulatory, parametric, obligatory, requisitional, provisional, provisory, specified, defined, mandatory, determined, limiting, restricted, circumscribed, contingent, bound, confined, controlled, checked, curbed, demarcated, delimited

VERBS 12 qualify, permit, authorize, empower, enable, invest, endow, equip, license, certify, pass **13 be qualified**, suit, fit, suffice, apply, deserve, merit **14 modify**, qualify, adjust, adapt, alter, change, vary, colour, modulate, coordinate, regulate, attune, improve, reconcile, temper, palliate, tone down, mitigate, moderate, soften, allow, extenuate **15 specify**, qualify, frame, define, determine, limit, restrain, restrict, circumscribe, bind, confine, control, check, demarcate, delimit, prescribe, proscribe, stipulate, reserve

597 Quantity

NOUNS 1 quantity, amount, measurement, extent, dimension, proportions, size, space, area, magnitude, multitude, amplitude, length, width, breadth, thickness, thinness, height, altitude, depth, deepness, capacity, volume, weight, mass, matter, substance, body, bulk, gravity, heaviness **2 certain amount**, portion, piece, share, lot, load, batch, bunch, pack, packet, parcel, part, mess, limit, stint, quota, quorum, dosage, ration, quantum, mass, mountain, lake, chunk, hunk, majority, increase, addition, extension, more, most, some, few, pittance, dribble, fraction, minority, decrease, subtraction, less **3 total**, whole, all, entirety, aggregate, sum, count **4 numbers**, integers, variable, plurality, zero, infinity

ADJECTIVES 5 quantitative, measured, weighed, counted, sized, ample, high, deep, long, wide, massive, voluminous, thick, thin, heavy, light, bunched, packed, sparse, mountainous, increased, added, extended, greater, majority, most, many, any, about, approximate, plural, infinite, all, total, whole, entire, enough, small, some, certain, limited, rationed, finite, few, smaller, least, numbered, fractional

598 Question

NOUNS 1 question, query, doubt, uncertainty, reservation, problem, difficulty, confusion, puzzle, challenge, objection, issue, point, proposition, request, entreaty **2 questioning**, inquiry, querying, interrogation, interpellation, cross-examination, inquisition, challenge, argument, investigation, analysis, inspection, scrutiny, survey, review, study, probe, inquest, research, poll, search **3 questionnaire**, question paper, quiz, examination, test, poll, census, checklist, trial, catechism, hearing, audition **4 difficult question**, controversy, moot point, catch, knotty problem, poser, stumper, mystery, mind boggler, brainteaser, conundrum, riddle, enigma, dilemma, crux, crisis, Hobson's choice **5 easy question**, formality, trivia quiz **6 uncertainty**, questioning, doubt, scepticism, Pyrrhonism, agnosticism, misgiving, mistrust, distrust, hesitation **7 questionableness**, dubiousness, doubtfulness, implausibility, unlikelihood, improbability, uncertainty, risk, unreliability, untrustworthiness, deceptiveness, deceitfulness **8 curiosity**, inquisitiveness, inquiring mind, insatiable curiosity, wonder, puzzlement, soul-searching, probing **9 question mark**, query, interrogation mark

ADJECTIVES 10 questioning, requesting, pleading, inquiring, interrogative, curious, inquisitive, elenctic, investigative, examining, fact-finding, knowledge-seeking, exploratory, analytic, interpellant, probing, searching, researching, questing, prying, introspective, wondering **11 problematic**, difficult, confusing, puzzling, challenging, quizzical, tricky, sticky, knotty, tough, mysterious, riddling, enigmatic, crucial, examinational **12 questionable**, doubtful, uncertain, moot, at issue, debatable, controversial, borderline, arguable, disputable, equivocal, suspicious, dubious, implausible, unlikely, improbable, chancy, risky, unreliable, unverifiable, untrustworthy, deceptive, ambiguous, shady **13 sceptical**, doubting, Pyrrhonist, agnostic, distrustful, journalistic, scientific, criminal, philosophical, legal, experimental, conjectural, guessing **14 questioned**, asked, interrogated, cross-examined, quizzed, examined, analysed, researched, challenged, investigated, inspected, scrutinized, reviewed, surveyed, studied, probed, polled

VERBS 15 question, inquire, ask, quiz, query, plead, entreat, request, appeal, interpellate, examine, test, try, check, catechize, hear, interview, sound out, investigate, analyse, inspect, scrutinize, survey, scan, review, study, fact-find, probe, research, poll, canvass, search, wonder, introspect, pry, hunt, pursue, seek **16 interrogate**, question, examine, cross-question, cross-examine, torture **17 be questioned**, be interrogated **18 doubt**, question, have misgivings, mistrust, distrust, suspect, disbelieve, moot, propose, debate, discuss, dispute, contest, impugn, refute, confute, disagree, dissent, object, hesitate, conjecture, guess, risk **19 confuse**, challenge, puzzle, pose, boggle, mystify, stump, trick **20 pop the question**, propose, get engaged,

599 Rail Transport

NOUNS 1 railway, main-line railway, light railway, tramway, cog railway, rack railway, inclined railway, cablecar, funicular, monorail, telpher, elevated railway, underground, tube, metro **2 track**, main line, branch line, spur, loop, siding, lay by, cutting, embankment, gradient, level crossing, signal, lights, semaphore, signal box, water tower **3 rail**, metals, narrow gauge, standard gauge, broad gauge, roadbed, permanent way, ballast, sleeper, fishplate, frog, points, crossover, turntable **4 locomotive**, engine, diesel locomotive, diesel-electric, electric locomotive, steam locomotive, iron horse, tank engine, shunter **5 rolling stock**, car, carriage, railcar, dining car, sleeper, luggage van, guard's van, mailcoach, Pullman, freight car, gondola, low-loader, hoppercar **6 train**, passenger train, express, slow train, stopping train, milk train, mail train, night mail, freight train, goods train, double header, twin bill, bogie, coupling, drawbar, draw gear **7 railway station**, terminus, railhead, halt, platform, bay, booking office, waiting room, left-luggage office, barrier, depot, shed **8 railway worker**, railwayman, engine driver, motorman, fireman, guard, inspector, platelayer, lengthman, pointsman, signalman, station manager

600 Raising

VERBS 1 raise, erect, build, put up, lift, levitate, uplift, hoist, heist, hike, hoick, heft, heave, lever, jack up, prop up, shoulder, boost, uphold, support, buoy up, help up **2 send up**, lob, loft, flight, sky, shoot up, propel, blow up, swell, increase **3 promote**, heighten, aid, perk up, elevate, enshrine, exalt, enhance, apotheosize, lionize, deify, beatify, canonize, sublimate, chair, shoulder **4 gather up**, pick up, pluck up, take up, haul up, drag up, dredge up **5 arise**, rise, rear, stand up

NOUNS 6 raising, elevation, lifting, erection, escalation, rearing, uplift, levitation, hoist, heave, upheaval, sublevation, upthrow, upcast, upthrust, ascent **7 lift**, boost, upswinging, upgrading, aid, promotion, exaltation, apotheosis, god-making, deification, canonization, beatification, enshrinement, assumption **8 height**, eminence, sublimity

ADJECTIVES 9 raised, lifted, upraised,

elevated, levitated, erected, set up, escalated, upreared, uplifted, upcast, upbuoyed, attolent, supportive, upstanding, vertical, hoisted, heaved, mounted, lobbed, thrown, blown up **10 exalted**, eminent, prominent, promoted, upgraded, lofty, sublime, high-flown, elevated, enshrined, deified, canonized, lionized

601 Rashness

NOUNS 1 rashness, recklessness, hastiness, impetuousness, precipitancy, imprudence, improvidence, indiscretion, inattention, negligence, carelessness, heedlessness, regardlessness, incautiousness, inconsideration, unwariness, irresponsibility, wildness, impulsiveness, capriciousness, frivolity, levity, flippancy, foolhardiness, folly, daring, audacity, temerity, presumption, overconfidence, impatience, hotheadedness, excitability, desperation, adventurousness, brinkmanship **2 rash move**, risk

ADJECTIVES 3 rash, reckless, hasty, impetuous, precipitate, headlong, breakneck, imprudent, improvident, injudicious, indiscreet, inconsiderate, thoughtless, ill-considered, inattentive, negligent, slapdash, hit-and-miss, careless, heedless, regardless, incautious, uncircumspect, unwary, irresponsible, wild, impulsive, capricious, frivolous, flippant, couldn't-careless, devil-may-care, free-and-easy, happy-go-lucky, foolhardy, foolish, harebrained, hotheaded, madcap, daredevil, death-defying, danger-loving, risk-taking, adventurous, daring, bold, audacious, overconfident, impatient

VERBS 4 be rash, rush into, gamble, take risks

602 Reality

• *Human kind/ Cannot bear very much reality.* T. S. Eliot.

NOUNS 1 reality, objective existence, actuality, occurrence, presence, entelechy, materiality, corporeality, substance, matter, thing, solidity, substantiality, tangibility, substantivity, validity, fact, factuality, historicity **2 real world**, universe, cosmos, physical world, natural world **3 realism**, naturalism, authenticity, pragmatism, verisimilitude, documentary, cinema vérité **4 realist**, pragmatist **5 realities**, basics

ADJECTIVES 6 real, actual, occurring, existing, entelechial, true, factual, valid, historical, material, corporeal, tangible, solid **7 realistic**, natural, lifelike, truthful, authentic, genuine, faithful **8 practical**, realistic, pragmatic, expedient, sensible, matter-of-fact, no-nonsense, no-frills, down-to-earth, businesslike, hard-headed, level-headed, sound, functional, utilitarian, useable, serviceable, workable **9 realizable**, achievable, attainable, practicable, plausible, feasible, possible

VERBS 10 be real, exist, occur, loom large **11 make real**, actualize, materialize, factualize, realize, reify **12 establish reality**, validate, authenticate, verify, prove, demonstrate, establish, ascertain, substantiate, corroborate, confirm, attest, uphold, certify, sustain, reinforce

603 Rear

NOUNS 1 rear, behind, background, hinterland, backstage, back door,

postern, tradesman's entrance, afterpart, wake, train, tail end, heel, coda, endpiece, back matter, colophon, afterword, verso, afterpiece, epilogue, afterthought, continuation, appendix, supplement, suffix, stern, poop deck **2 rear end**, end, rump, behind, stern, bottom, anus, posterior, backside, buttocks, back, fundament, hindquarters, haunches, hunkers, tail **3 rearing up**, rising up
ADJECTIVES 4 rear, back, hind, hindermost, postern, posterior, mizzen, dorsal, lumbar, tail, end, continued, supplemental, anal, caudal, latter **5 bred**, well-bred
VERBS 6 be in the rear, trail, tag along, lag behind, follow **7 rear up**, rise up, lean backwards **8 nurture**, raise, breed, stock, incubate, fatten up

604 Reason

NOUNS 1 reason, mind, intellect, rationality, intelligence, understanding, perception, judgment, wisdom, sense **2 reasoning**, rationalizing, rationality, logic, ratiocination, generalization, inference, deduction, induction, syllogism **3 debate**, polemics, dialectics, apologetics, argumentation, dissent, dispute, disputation **4 explanation**, cause, motive, grounds, premise, pretext, theory, basis, assumption, justification, defence, speculation, hypothesis
ADJECTIVES 5 reasoning, reasonable, rational, thinking, intellectual, intelligent, understanding, perceptive, knowledgeable, judgmental, wise, sensible **6 rational**, logical, ratiocinative, analytical, inferential, deductive, inductive, *a priori*, *a posteriori* **7 argumentative**, dissenting, disputing, litigious, polemic **8 causal**, theoretical, assumptive, valid, explanatory, justified
VERBS 9 reason, rationalize, analyse, think, logicalize, understand, perceive, judge, ratiocinate, generalize, synthesize, infer, deduce **10 be reasonable**, show wisdom **11 debate**, argue, dissent, dispute **12 premise**, theorize, postulate, philosophize, assume, explain, justify

605 Receipt

NOUNS 1 receipt, voucher, counterfoil **2 money received**, receipts, gate money, revenue, proceeds, royalties, incomings, credits, profits, turnover, interest, gain, bonus, premium, tax, rates, dues, duty, customs, tariff, import levy **3 income**, privy purse, emolument, earnings, remuneration, salary, wages, pay, fees, pension, annuity, tontine, grant, allowance, spending money, bursary, scholarship, fellowship, maintenance, aliment **4 legacy**, inheritance, dower, bequest, heritage, birthright **5 winnings**, prize, draw, raffle, lottery
ADJECTIVES 6 received, paid, credited, gained, gotten, accepted, taken, receipted, acknowledged, inherited, bequeathed, hereditary, patrimonial, bursarial, granted, salaried, waged
VERBS 7 receive, get, gain, take, acquire, accept, admit, receipt, acknowledge, mark paid, earn, gross, net, inherit, accrue, pay

606 Receiving

NOUNS 1 receiving, recipience, getting, taking, acceptance, acquisition, collection, receivership, inheritance, heritage, patrimony, legacy, bequest, birthright, heirship, succession, primogeniture, hereditament **2 something received**, gift, token, tribute, prize, trophy, earnings, profits, income, salary, pay, revenue, proceeds, receipts, returns, gate money, takings, credits, dividend, bursary, stipend, scholarship, fellowship, maintenance, annuity, tontine, fringe benefit, winnings, ill-gotten gains, allowance, pin money, pocket money, alimony, pension, compensation, bonus, commission **3 acknowledgment of payment**, bill, voucher, ticket, counterfoil **4 reception**, admitting, admission, greeting, welcoming, entertaining, baptism, christening, confirmation, initiation, debut, lobby, living room, drawing room **5 recipient**, receiver, acceptor, buyer, purchaser, customer, acquirer, obtainer, procurer, holder, payee, endorsee, consignee, trustee, allottee, lessee, licensee, earner, pensioner, annuitant, dependent, scholarship winner, exhibitioner, fellow, winner, prize-winner, message-receiver, addressee, reader, listener, viewer, spectator, audience, charity case, beggar, sufferer, scapegoat, victim **6 beneficiary**, heir, heiress, inheritor, inheritress, successor **7 collector**, customs officer, exciseman, bailiff, confiscator, sequestrator, official receiver **8 receiver**, radio receiver, radar receiver, telephone receiver, headset

VERBS 9 receive, get, take, accept, acquire, gain, collect, obtain, secure, come by, earn, gross, net, clear, bring in, take home, pocket, inherit, succeed to, come into, take over, acknowledge, receipt **10 receive someone**, admit, greet, welcome, usher in, entertain, host, baptize

ADJECTIVES 11 receiving, recipient, taking, accepting, wage-earning, salaried, paid, compensated, pensioned, awarded, rewarded, given **12 receptive**, welcoming, open-minded **13 received**, accepted, taken, acquired, gained, collected, secured, inherited, admitted, heard, read, seen, acknowledged, welcomed, entertained, baptized, christened **14 receivable**, takable, gettable, collectable, compensatory, pensionary

607 Reciprocity

NOUNS 1 interchange, reciprocation, interplay, interaction, compromise, exchange, balance, justice, bartering, swap, trade-off, alternation, compensation, retaliation, return, retort, reaction, requital, counteraction **2 interconnection**, interrelationship, interdependence, mutuality, symbiosis, cooperation, partnership, sharing, opposite number, complement, counterpart **3 correlation**, correspondence, similarity, parallelism, comparability, analogy, analogue, allegory, equivalence, symmetry, proportionality, pattern, tally

ADJECTIVES 4 reciprocal, interacting, interchangeable, interplaying, give-and-take, compromising, exchanged, changed, bartered, swapped, trade-off, alternative, balancing, seesaw, compensatory, retaliatory, reacting, recoiling, requited **5 interconnected**, interrelated, interlocking, interlinked, interdependent, mutual, symbiotic, cooperative, two-way, bilateral, complementary **6 correlative**, correspondent, comparable, analogous, allegorical, parallel, proportional, patterned, matching, equivalent

VERBS 7 reciprocate, interchange, interplay, interact, compromise, exchange, change, counterchange, barter, swap, trade off, alternate, compensate, balance, seesaw, take turns, retaliate, react, counteract, counterstrike, recoil, requite, return **8 interrelate**, interconnect, interlock, interlink, interdepend, interassociate, neutralize, cooperate, partner, pair, twin, participate, share **9 correlate**, correspond, identify with, parallel, compare, proportion, tally, answer, match

608 Recoil

VERBS 1 recoil, rebound, cannon, ricochet, boomerang, kick back, backfire, backlash, spring back, bounce back, bound back, uncoil, return, swing back, revert, reflect, mirror, reverberate, resound, echo **2 respond**, react, counteract, reply, retort, rebuff, answer, riposte, retaliate, flinch, shrink, wince, cringe, blink, blench, quail, draw back, pull back, recoil, retreat, avoid, evade, sidestep, duck, shy, dodge, swerve, sheer off **3 get a response**, hit home

NOUNS 4 recoil, rebound, bounce, bound, spring, elasticity, resilience, reflex, kickback, bounceback, ricochet, boomerang, cannon, oscillation, return, reflux, refluence, backfire, echo, reflection, reverberation, repercussion, reversion, backlash **5 reflector**, mirror, sounding board, echo chamber, springboard, trampoline **6 response**, reaction, reply, retort, riposte, rebuff, repercussion, conditioned reflex, retroaction, retreat, recoil, fall-back, pullout, evasion, avoidance, sidestepping, duck, shy, dodge, side step, flinch, wince

ADJECTIVES 7 recoiling, rebounding, resilient, springy, bouncing, bounding, elastic, resonant, vibrating, reverberative, reflective, repercussive **8 reactive**, reacting, responsive, retortive, antiphonal, reflex, knee-jerk, reactionary, retroactive

609 Record

NOUNS 1 record, recording, documentation, document, form, papers, chronicle, history, annals, archives, account, narrative, memoir, autobiography, biography, case history, obituary, resumé, correspondence, memorabilia, cutting, photograph, picture, snapshot, portrait, sketch, representation, list, inventory, file, dossier, portfolio, official publication, Hansard, government papers, transactions, minutes, report, memo, reminder, note, entry, item, return, invoice, bill, statement, receipt, voucher, docket, counterfoil, stub, tally, scoresheet **2 certificate**, credential, charter, authorization, passport, diploma, muniments, deed, title, document, ticket, warranty, testimonial, affidavit, deposition **3 notes**, annotations, marginalia, adversaria, jottings **4 inscription**, signature, autograph, initials, legend **5 copy**, photocopy **6 record book**, notebook, scrapbook, album, minute book, register, rollbook, directory, logbook, diary, journal, calendar, cartulary, tablet, table, notepad, jotter, ledger, cashbook, chequebook, catalogue, index, card, microfilm, microfiche, microcard, tape, disk, database **7 recording**, record, single, pressing, cassette, tape, film **8 registration**, registry, record-keeping, recording, writing, printing, inscribing, engraving, epigraphy, enrolment, enlistment, empanelment, booking, reservation, entry, bookkeeping, accounts, filing, indexing, cataloguing **9 recording instrument**, photocopier, camera, camcorder, tape recorder, cassette recorder, wiretap, answering machine, dictaphone, cash register, seismograph, speedometer, gauge, black box **10 monument**, memorial, column, pillar, tomb, mausoleum, pyramid, shrine, statue, bust, plaque, tablet, slab, gravestone, tombstone, monolith, obelisk, megalith, dolmen, menhir, cromlech, cairn, barrow, earthwork, mound, testimonial, cup, trophy, prize, ribbon, medal, decoration, memento **11 vestige**, trace, track, trail, piste, scent, spoor, mark, footprint, fingermark, tyremark, tidemark, stain

VERBS 12 record, document, chronicle, log, inscribe, register, enrol, file, index, catalogue, tabulate, list, empanel, copy, photocopy, print, input, tape, videotape, film, photograph, represent, relate, narrate, recount **13 inscribe**, transcribe, write, take minutes, note, take down, jot, engrave, cut, incise, etch **14 register**, enter, docket, enrol, enlist, empanel, book, reserve, list, itemize, tabulate

ADJECTIVES 15 recorded, documented, chronicled, logged, noted, inscribed, written down, on paper, printed, entered, registered, enrolled, filed, indexed, listed, copied, photographed, photocopied, input, taped, videotaped, filmed

610 Redness

ADJECTIVES 1 red, pink, coral, shell-pink, flesh-coloured, peach-coloured, salmon-pink, shocking pink, damask, carnation, rosy, roseate, cherry, cerise, blood-red, carmine, crimson, scarlet, Turkey red, vermilion, vermeil, gules, brick-red, pillarbox red, flame-coloured, ruby, wine-coloured, beetroot-red, fuchsia, cyclamen, magenta, maroon, oxblood, rust-coloured, rufous **2 red-faced**, red-cheeked, rosy-cheeked, glowing, blooming, flushing, blushing, ruddy, sanguine, rubicund, florid, blowzy, rouged, reddened, flushed, sunburnt, hectic, feverish, fiery **3 red-haired**, ginger-haired, carroty, sandy, Titian, auburn **4 bloody**, blood-stained, bloodshot

NOUNS 5 redness, reddening, rubescence, rubefaction, rufescence, blush, flush, scarlet fever, glow, warmth, rosiness, bloom, ruddiness, floridness **6 red pigment**, cadmium red, cadmium scarlet, Windsor red, Grumbacher red, Thalo red, Indian red, murex, cochineal, carmine, kermes, dragon's blood, cinnabar, vermilion, red lead, ruddle, rose madder, alizarin, crimson lake, Venetian red, rosaniline, solferino, red ochre, henna, rouge, blusher, lipstick **7 red thing**, ruby, garnet, carnelian, fire, flame, sunset, dawn, rust, brick, blood, gore, rose, geranium, carnation, poppy, cherry, strawberry, raspberry, redcurrant, plum, peach, tomato, beetroot, red clover, redwood, cardinal, robin redbreast, redwing, red deer, red fox, red salmon, red admiral, red meat, claret, port, burgundy, Mars, red giant, red dwarf, red card, red ink, red light, fire engine, pillarbox, red cheeks, rosy cheeks, apple cheeks, cherry lips, strawberry mark, red hair **8 figurative red thing**, red carpet, red herring, red-letter day, red tape, red alert, red-light district, red-hot mama, Red Cross, Red Crescent, Red Sea

VERBS 9 redden, flush, blush, glow, colour, crimson, rubefy, ruddle, rouge, raddle

611 Refinement

NOUNS 1 elegance, style, grace, taste, distinction, dignity, quality, polish, finish, culture, civility, good breeding, correctness, delicacy, beauty, courtesy, decency, seemliness, decorum, urbanity, propriety, sophistication, gracious living **2 subletly**, distinction **3 etiquette**, custom

ADJECTIVES 4 refined, elegant, graceful, tasteful, dignified, polished, delicate, well-finished, well-bred, urbane, well-mannered, well-spoken, courteous, distingué, ladylike, gentlemanly, genteel, civilized, cosmopolitan, sophisticated, discriminating, fastidious, sensitive, artistic, aesthetic, appreciative

VERBS 5 refine, purify

612 Refreshment

VERBS 1 refresh, freshen, tidy, spruce up, clean, air, ventilate, aerate, fan, shade, cool, chill, refrigerate, brace, stimulate, exhilarate, invigorate, enliven, vitalize, animate, strengthen, fortify, restore, renew, recruit, recreate, resuscitate, revive, reanimate, reinvigorate, revitalize, rejuvenate, renovate, repair, ease, relieve, dispel, feed **2 be refreshed**, respire, come to, perk up, be restored, recover, recuperate, revive, renew oneself, cool off

ADJECTIVES 3 refreshing, bracing, stimulating, exhilarating, invigorating, fortifying, revitalizing, fresh, cool, cold, comforting, relieving, recreative, reviving, restorative **4 refreshed**, cool, braced, stimulated, exhilarated, invigorated, enlivened, fortified, revitalized, recovered, revived, restored

NOUNS 5 refreshment, freshness, tidiness, cleanness, ventilation, aeration, respiration, shade, coolness, refrigeration, stimulation, exhilaration, invigoration, vitalization, animation, perking up, restoration, renewal, recruitment, recreation, recovery, recuperation, resuscitation, revival, reanimation, reinvigoration, revitalization, rejuvenation, renovation, repair, ease, relief, rest **6 refresher**, reviver, restorative, stimulant, tonic, air, breeze, oxygen, shower, rest, repose, break, vacation, holiday, recess, leave **7 refreshments**, refection, food, drink

613 Refuge

NOUNS 1 refuge, sanctuary, asylum, retreat, traffic island, pedestrian crossing, resort, recourse, foxhole, dugout, pit, bolt hole, trench, blockhouse, air-raid shelter, Anderson shelter, burrow, hide-out, priest hole, cache, lap, bed, hearth, home, sanctum, chamber, monastery, nunnery, cloister, cell, hermitage, ivory tower, sanctum sanctorum, temple, ark, acropolis, citadel, rampart, bulwark, parapet, battlement, fortification, bastion, stronghold, fortress, keep, ward, rock, pillar, mainstay, buttress, prop **2 shelter**, cover, roof, lee, windbreak, hedge, wall, fence, camp, stockade, enclosure, raincoat, umbrella, tarpaulin, shield, screen, fireguard, mudguard, bumper, awning, shutter, blind, curtain, shade, sun block, sunshade, parasol, eyeshade, sunhat, topee, goggles, haven, harbour, port, quay, ghat, marina, dock, safe house, padded cell, asylum, sheltered housing, almshouse, orphanage, hospice, charity, social security **3 animal shelter**, kennels, cattery, hole, burrow, den, lair, earth, covert, warren, lodge, snake pit, nest, eyrie, fold, pen, sheepfold, pound, sty, barn, stall, stable, byre, coop

VERBS 4 shelter, seek sanctuary, seek asylum, retreat

614 Refusal

NOUNS 1 refusal, thumbs down, rejection, denial, repulsion, negation, red light, noncompliance, resistance, retention, recalcitrance, unwillingness, noncooperation, nonacceptance, denigration, strike, lock-out, nonpayment **2 dissent**, dissidence, veto, disagreement, opposition, objection, discordance, refutation, repudiation, rebuttal, rebuff, contradiction, confutation, renunciation, confrontation, demonstration, civil disobedience, controversy, prohibition, counterorder, interdiction, ban **3 abnegation**, relinquishment, self-restraint, self-sacrifice

VERBS 4 refuse, reject, deny, say no, repulse, repel, negate, resist, retain, not cooperate, denigrate, decline, turn down, avoid, turn away, shrink from, flinch at, jib at, strike, lock out, default **5 dissent**, disagree, oppose, disallow, reject, repudiate, rebuff, spurn, snub, object, refute, rebut, contradict, confute, nullify, renunciate, confront, withstand, vote against, veto, prohibit, forbid, interdict, embargo **6 refuse oneself**, deny oneself, renounce, forebear, demur, abstain

ADJECTIVES 7 refused, uncooperative, unconsenting, uncompliant, resistant, negative, recalcitrant, unwilling, nonaccepting, turned down, turned away, thrown out, ejected, excluded, withheld, retained, strike-bound **8 dissenting**, disagreeing, repudiating, demurring, opposing, adversarial, protesting, objecting to, discordant, refuting, denying, disallowed, not permitted, not granted, contradictory, contrary, contravening, confutative, renunciative, rejecting, rebuffed, revoking, confrontational, controversial, prohibitionary, prohibited, interdictive, banned **9 abnegating**, relinquishing, self-sacrificing

615 Refutation

NOUNS 1 refutation, disproof, disproval, invalidation, negation, naysaying, nullification, annulment, disaffirmation, disconfirmation, confounding, discrediting, abrogation, disallowal, dismissal, reversal, undermining, subversion, overthrow, destruction **2 denial**, rebuttal, contradiction, confutation, contravention, contention, negation, disaffirmation, rejection, repudiation, renunciation, abnegation, recantation, recusance, withdrawal, reversal, disclaimer, disavowal, disownment **3 countercharge**, counteraccusation, counterclaim, counterstatement, counterblast, counteraction, comeback, counter-argument, rebuttal, rejoinder, reply, answer, response, retort, riposte, retaliation, objection, defence **4 refutability**, confutability, disprovability, defeasibility, weakness

ADJECTIVES 5 refutable, confutable, disprovable, defeasible, weak, faulty, flawed, unfounded, groundless, unsound, objectionable **6 refuting**, confuting, confounding, contradictory, counteractive, retaliatory, answering, responding, contravening, rebutting, repudiating, renouncing, abnegating, disclaiming, disowning, discrediting, exploding, disproving, negating, invalidating

VERBS 7 refute, confute, confound, disprove, invalidate, nullify, annul, negate, disallow, forbid, dismiss, abrogate, dispose of, disconfirm, discredit, expose, show up, belie, deflate, undermine, overturn, overthrow, defeat, outsmart, outwit, demolish, destroy, explode, crush, squash, quash, floor, silence **8 deny**, contradict, gainsay, naysay, argue against, question, dispute, oppose, controvert, contravene, disaffirm, reject, repudiate, renounce, abnegate, recant, reverse, withdraw, disclaim, disavow, disown **9 countercharge**, counterclaim, counterblast, rebut, parry, retaliate, answer, reply, rejoin, respond

616 Region

NOUNS 1 region, area, territory, terrain, zone, belt, section, sector, place, space, ground, geographical unit, landmass, continent, peninsula, island **2 geographical region**, zone, longitude, meridian, latitude, parallel, equator, tropics, subtropics, horse latitudes **3 regional boundary**, bounds, pale, confines, marches, shore, territorial waters, continental shelf, exclusion zone **4 territorial division**, political entity, nation, state, power, superpower, territory, country, republic, kingdom, realm, domain, principality, sultanate, dominion, protectorate, mandate, possession, colony, dependency, commonwealth **5 state**, territory, province, region, country, shire, metropolitan district, division, district, canton, duchy, borough, ward, riding, bailiwick, hundred, wapentake, soke, constituency, electorate, precinct, diocese, bishopric **6 regions**, highlands, lowlands, borders, march, corridor, countryside, green belt, hinterland, heartland, back-country, provinces, outback, bush, brush, backwoods, backwater, outpost, wilderness, virgin territory **7 regions of the world**, Old World, New World, Occident, Orient, Middle East, Far East, Antipodes, Third World **8 urban area**, built-up area, city, metropolitan area, megalopolis, metropolis, city centre, precinct, uptown, downtown, ghetto **9 settlement**, village, hamlet, town, municipality, suburbs **10 locality**, neighbourhood, vicinity, area, haunt, circuit, beat, round, orbit, walk **11 sphere**, field, arena, province, ambit, theatre, territory, pale, jurisdiction, scope, realm, domain, bailiwick, interest, line, discipline, forte **12 regionalism**, provincialism, parochialism

ADJECTIVES 13 regional, areal, spatial, geographical, topographic, territorial, zonal, longitudinal, latitudinal, highland, lowland, peninsular, insular, tropical, subtropical, continental, eastern, western, northern, southern, Occidental, Oriental **14 national**, provincial, sectional, divisional, municipal, urban, metropolitan, suburban, rural, colonial, dependent, republican, democratic **15 local**, next-door, neighbouring, nearby, provincial, parochial, diocesan, back-country, back-woods, small-town, uptown, downtown

617 Regularity

NOUNS 1 regularity, frequency, recurrence, periodicity, repetition, return, serialization, timing, phasing, pattern, symmetry, alternation, reciprocity, wave motion, oscillation, undulation, swing, rhythm, tempo, measure, beat, pulsation, throb **2 cycle**, return, revolution, rotation, orbital motion, life cycle, biorhythm, circadian rhythm, menstruation, period, routine, round, beat, orbit, circuit, lap, shift, relay, turn, go **3 anniversary**, commemoration, centenary, sesquicentennial, bicentenary, tricentenary **4 orderliness**, regularity, balance, uniformity, evenness, steadiness, levelness, flatness, ordinariness, continuity, constance, consistency, normality, regulation, rule, order, law, custom, tradition **5 regular thing**, pendulum, metronome, metre, rhythm, beat, tempo, drumbeat, heartbeat, pulse, breathing, shuttle service, comet, tide, serial, annual vacation

VERBS 6 be regular, recur, repeat, succeed, intermit, reciprocate, alternate, tick, throb, pulse, undulate, oscillate, swing, sway, ply, commute, shuttle **7 be cyclic**, cycle, circle, orbit, return, turn, spin, revolve, rotate, menstruate **8 commemorate**, celebrate **9 make regular**, balance, regulate, time, adjust, order, rule, normalize, rationalize, systematize, steady, serialize

ADJECTIVES 10 regular, frequent, periodic, recurrent, repeating, repetitive, tidal, reciprocal, alternating, to-and-fro, oscillatory, revolving, returning, timed, isochronal, phasic, serial, rhythmic, measured, swinging, steady, stable, clockwork, beating, ticking, throbbing, pulsating, undulating, constant, even, symmetrical, consistent, level, flat **11 cyclic**, circular, orbital, revolving, rotational, routine, hourly, daily, diurnal, quotidian, nightly, tertian, weekly, hebdomadary, fortnightly, monthly, seasonal, biannual, annual, perennial, bissextile, biennial, Metonic cycle, biorhythmic, menstrual **12 anniversary**, commemorative, annual, yearly, centenary, sesquicentennial, bicentenary, tricentenary, Metonic, millennial **13 orderly**, regular, balanced, uniform, even, steady, level, flat, ordinary, everyday, typical, routine, continual, constant, methodical, metrical, consistent, normal, legal

618 Rejection

VERBS 1 reject, decline, refuse, rebuff, repulse, repel, spurn, disallow, return, ignore, disregard, vote against **2 discard**, throw away, scrap, ditch, set aside, renounce, abandon, eliminate, eject, jettison, expel, dismiss, oust, depose **3 exclude**, except, exempt, blackball, cold-shoulder, slight, snub, brush off, freeze out, not want, sniff at, scorn, disdain, mock, deride, laugh at **4 revoke**, cancel, abrogate, negate, repudiate, apostatize, recant, deny

NOUNS 5 rejection, declining, nonacceptance, refusal, disapproval, slight, snub, rebuff, repulse, spurn, kick, brush-off, cold shoulder, exclusion, exception, exemption **6 discarding**, disuse, abandonment, elimination, ejection, expulsion, dismissal, unemployment, redundancy, defeat **7 abrogation**, cancellation, negation, abnegation, repudiation, apostasy, recantation, denial **8 rejected thing**, reject, discard

ADJECTIVES 9 rejected, declined, turned down, unselected, ineligible, unqualified, unsuitable, unacceptable, unrequited, returned, unusable, unwanted, discarded, disused, thrown away, cast out, dismissed, redundant

619 Rejoicing

NOUNS 1 rejoicing, celebrating, jubilation, exultation, triumph, happiness, joyfulness, delight, jolliness, merriment, roistering, festivities, celebration, holiday, festival, anniversary, jubilee, party, revel, feast, street party, banquet **2 fanfare**, salute, applause, ovation, cry, shout, yell, cheer, hurrah, huzzah, hosanna, hallelujah, hymn, praise, glory, thanksgiving **3 laughter**, giggling, tittering, hilarity, laugh, titter, chortle

VERBS 4 rejoice, celebrate, jubilate, exult, triumph, glory, make merry, roister, revel, carouse, feast **5 fête**, lionize, praise, honour **6 dance**, skip, frolic, rollick, clap, applaud, cry, shout, yell, cheer, give thanks **7 laugh**, titter

ADJECTIVES 8 rejoicing, celebratory, jubilant, exultant, triumphant, glorious, ecstatic, euphoric, happy, joyful, cheery, merry, jolly, revelling, applauding **9 laughing**, giggling, tittering, laughable, comic

620 Relatedness

NOUNS 1 relatedness, relationship, relevance, pertinence, germaneness, bearing, appositeness, connectedness, affinity, friendship, propinquity, kinship, bond, tie, rapport, consanguinity, partnership, link, tie-up, involvement, implication, merger, association, affiliation, alliance, linkage, liaison, interconnection, mutuality, combination, correspondence, agreement, similarity, parallel, comparison, cross-reference, analogy, correlation, homology, addition, adjunct, attachment, appendix **2 interrelatedness**, similarity, equality, comparability, homology, correlation, reciprocity, interdependence, cross-reference, citation, complementarity, interconnection, association, mutuality, relativity, proportionality, interlocking, interlinkage, interalliance, interassociation, covariation, interaction, interplaying, interworking, intercourse, intercommunication, interweaving, intertwining, interlacing, interpenetration, interchanging, engagement, intermeshing, alternation, seesaw, relativeness, ratio, proportion, scale **3 relative position**, rank, class, classification, order, degree, echelon, rating

ADJECTIVES **4 related**, relevant, pertinent, germane, apposite, connected, associated, affiliated, allied, linked, bonded, kindred, cognate, agnate, akin to, consanguineous, wedded, bound, joined, tied, twinned, paired, involved, implicated, merged, combined, added, attached **5 interrelated**, correlated, reciprocal, interdependent, complementary, interconnected, associated, mutual, relative, proportional, interlocked, interlinked, interallied, interassociated, interwoven, intertwined, interchanged, interacting, interworking, engaged, intermeshed, cross-referred, corresponding, agreed, similar, parallel, comparable, analogous, equal, homologous, relational, commensurate **6 ranked**, classed, classified, ordered

VERBS **7 relate to**, apply to, bear upon, pertain, appertain, affect, interest, refer to, touch upon, associate, connect, juxtapose, bracket, couple, tie up, reconcile, contrast, cross-refer, answer to, liaise with, deal with **8 be proportionate to**, correspond to, correlate, compare, interconnect, interlock, interpenetrate, interlink, interassociate, interact, interplay, interwork, balance, liken, parallel, equalize, proportion, symmetrize, match, equate, accord, fit **9 have a relative position**, rank

621 Relief

NOUNS **1 ease**, solace, comfort, consolation, alleviation, reassurance, relaxation, mollification, appeasement, mitigation, assuagement, abatement, remission, respite, lull, palliation, anaesthetization, tranquillization **2 aid**, assistance, help, succour, support, rescue, deliverance, liberation, release, emancipation, salvation **3 reliever**, comforter, consoler, mollifier, remedy, cure, balm, palliative, anodyne, analgesic, painkiller, anaesthetic, tranquillizer, sedative, opiate, soporific, hypnotic **4 charity**, alms, benefaction, gift, donation, aid **5 helper**, auxiliary, deputy, assistant, helpmate, helpmeet, aide, paramedic, girl Friday, understudy, substitute, replacement, stand-in, locum, reserve, stop-gap, backup, supporter **6 profile**, silhouette, delineation, outline, form, contour, elevation, embossment, projection, relievo

ADJECTIVES **7 relieved**, calmed, restored, refreshed, eased, comforted, soothed, consoled, reassured, mollified, appeased, relaxed, sedated, assuaged **8 relieving**, helping, refreshing, restorative, comforting, consoling, reassuring, relaxing, easing, calming, soothing, balsamic, curative, remedial, assuaging, palliative

VERBS **9 relieve**, ease, solace, comfort, pacify, soothe, calm, quiet, console, alleviate, reassure, allay, mollify, appease, mitigate, moderate, temper, assuage, abate, diminish, lessen, soften, relax, palliate, tranquillize, sedate **10 save**, rescue, reprieve, deliver, liberate, emancipate **11 assist**, help, aid, deputize for, substitute for, understudy for, replace **12 relieve from duty**, dismiss, fire **13 relieve oneself**, urinate **14 take away**, confiscate, disencumber, sequestrate, commandeer, dispossess, snatch, steal

622 Religion

- *Man is by his constitution a religious animal.* Edmund Burke.
- *Religion...is the opium of the people.* Karl Marx.

NOUNS 1 religion, faith, belief-system, creed, dogma, doctrine, persuasion, superstition, denomination, church, movement, order, sect, cult, faction, chapter, **2 religiousness**, piety, sanctimony, puja, reverence, observance, strictness, faithfulness, ritualism, deism, theism, mysticism, spirituality, chohan, Kavannah, self-sacrifice, humility, devotion, zeal, fervour, religiosity, overpiety, preachiness, churchiness, unctuousness, Bible-bashing, bibliolatry, fundamentalism, salvationism, fanaticism, witch-hunting, heresy-hunting **3 religious person**, saint, bodhissatva, marabout, martyr, pilgrim, hajji, mystic, charismatic, holyman, sadhu, sannyasi, bhikshu, fakir, believer, worshipper, convert, neophyte, catechumen, devotee, disciple **4 religionist**, zealot, iconoclast, formalist, precisian, preacher, pulpiteer, sermonizer, salvationist, evangelist, TV evangelist, televangelist, fundamentalist, fanatic, crusader, ghazi **5 monk**, nun, prior, prioress, abbot, abbess, monastic, sister, brother, kalogeros, trapa, talapoin, bo-san, shonin, bhikku, bhikkunis, bonze, fakir, dervish, caloyer, cenobite, friar, pilgrim, stylite, pillarist, hermit, anchorite, ascetic **6 priest**, priestess, pope, pontif, chief rabbi, hakam, Grand Lama, Kalif, hierophant, Arch Druid, Arch Druidess, Brahman, guru, pundit, cardinal, bishop, archbishop, patriarch, clergyman, clergywoman, ecclesiastic, cleric, minister, ministress, pastor, pastoress, deacon, deaconess, ordinand, dean, canon, monsignor, parson, vicar, rector, curate, chaplain, rabbi, kohen, mullah, imam, ayatollah, qadi, dhammaduta, zen-ji, lama, poonghie, witch-doctor, churchwarden, almoner, verger, beadle, sexton, hazzan, muezzin, mukdam, maftir **7 priesthood**, hierocracy, ecclesiasticism, clericalism, sacerdotalism, Brahminism, the ministry, pastorate, the Church, the clergy, the cloth, holy orders, ordination, investiture, rabbinate, pontificate, papacy, popedom, cardinalship, primacy, prelature, abbacy, bishopric, episcopate, deanship, curacy, rectorship, vicarship, pastorship, deaconship, chaplaincy, diocese, see, archdiocese, province **8 theology**, divinity, theological metaphysics, patristics, natural theology, physicotheology, ontotheology, feminist theology, liberation theology, hierology, hagiology, soteriology, Christology, Mariology, angelology, Buddhology, eschatology, secularism, ecclesiology, doctrinism, rationalism

ADJECTIVES 9 religious, pious, devout, holy, godly, saintly, seraphic, cherubic, transcendent, spiritual, mystic, other-worldly, churchgoing, practising, strict, faithful, orthodox, reverent, worshipful, prayerful, reverential, God-fearing, theopathic, humble, self-sacrificing, monastic, anchoretic, ascetic, ardent, unctuous, zealous, overreligious, priest-ridden, formalistic, Pharisaic, ritualistic, churchy, holier-than-thou, self-righteous, sanctimonious, fervent, preachy, canting, Bible-worshipping, fundamentalist, evangelical, crusading, militant, missionary, fanatical, witch-hunting **10 priestly**, sacerdotal, clerical, ministerial, churchly, pastoral, canonical, papal, pontifical, episcopal, rabbinic, prelatic, presbyteral, hierophantic, druidic, hierocratic, parochial **11 theological**, religious, divine, patristic, physicotheological, ontotheological, hierological, hagiological, soteriological, Christological, eschatological, doctrinal, ecclesiological, canonical

VERBS 12 be religious, get religion, meet God, recant, repent, turn, convert, be converted, be saved, believe, have faith, revere, observe, worship, adore, obey, devote oneself, prostrate oneself, humble oneself **13 preach**, sermonize, proselytize, evangelize, convert, convince, baptize, Christianize, Islamize, Judaize, depaganize, crusade, witch-hunt, heresy-hunt **14 ordain**, consecrate, read in, invest, frock, anoint

623 Relinquishment

VERBS 1 relinquish, surrender, drop, unclench, release, loose, resign, abdicate, yield, waive, forgo, cede, transfer, hand over, assign, forfeit, lose, renounce, abnegate, recant, tergiversate, forswear, abstain, avoid, shed, slough, cast off, divest, doff, repudiate, discard, tear up, shred, jettison, scrap **2 withdraw**, decline, scratch, retire, abdicate, resign, stand down, submit, depart, leave, quit, vacate, evacuate, abandon, forsake, desert, AWOL, play truant, strike, down tools, stop, walk out, secede, divide, schismatize, change sides, apostatize, jilt, postpone, shelve, table, invalidate, annul, void, cancel

NOUNS 3 relinquishment, surrender, resignation, retirement, abdication, yielding, waiving, forgoing, transfer, cession, forfeit, abnegation, renunciation, recantation, abandonment, desertion, going, departure, leaving, evacuation, dereliction, defection, absence, truancy, withdrawal, secession, schism, strike, abstinence, avoidance, disuse, discontinuance, desuetude, cancellation, abolition, annulment, abrogation

ADJECTIVES 4 relinquished, surrendered, dropped, waived, forgone, scrapped, jettisoned, castaway, forsaken, apostatical, abandoned, derelict, deserted, stranded, jilted, cancelled, void, invalid, discontinued **5 apathetic**, indifferent, noncommittal, resigned, retired, withdrawn, aloof

624 Remainder

NOUNS 1 remainder, rest, relic, remnant, frustum, piece, chunk, shard, shell, husk, stump, rump, stub, plug, dottle, butt, fag end, scrag end, body, torso, corpse, bones, fossil, fragments, bits, debris, wreckage, ruins, record, vestige, trace, track, trail, footprint, afterglow, memorabilia, souvenir, reminder, survival, aftereffect **2 residue**, deposit, sediment, silt, precipitate, alluvium, moraine, loess, detritus, residual, leftovers, grounds, dregs, lees, dross, scum, slag, ashes, scoria, sludge, bilge, powder, sawdust, shavings, filings, crumbs, husks, chaff, stubble, sweepings, peelings, slough, scurf, clippings, trimmings, remnants, castoffs, offcuts, scraps, lumber, jumble, junk, rubbish, refuse, litter, dirt, waste **3 difference**, discrepancy, surplus, margin, carry-over, credit, profit, excess, loss, deficit **4 surplus**, excess, overgrowth, abundance, redundancy, pleonasm, surfeit, superfluity, overload, glut, leftovers, extras, spares, bonus **5 estate**, effects, hereditament, acquest, bequest

VERBS 6 be left, remain, survive, result, continue, subsist, stay **7 leave**, owe, deposit, bequeath, exclude, reject, abandon, discard, cast off

ADJECTIVES 8 remaining, residual, resultant, left, hereditary, patrimonial, vestigial, precipitated, deposited, sedimentary, surviving, bereft, widowed, orphaned, abandoned, discarded, rejected **9 surplus**, net, unused, outcast, left over, unwanted, outstanding, owed, carried over, extra, spare, excess, overabundant, overloaded, redundant, superfluous

625 Remedy

- *Well, now, there's a remedy for everything except death.* Miguel de Cervantes.
- *Extreme remedies are most appropriate for extreme diseases.* Hippocrates.

NOUNS 1 remedy, cure, antidote, help, aid, succour, relief, moderator, corrective, amendment, redress, amends, restitution, expiation, atonement, recuperation, recovery, specific, answer, solution, prescription, recipe, formula, nostrum, panacea, heal-all, cure-all, catholicon, elixir **2 medicine**, remedy, pharmaceutical, drug, physic, materia medica, pharmacopoeia, pharmacognosy, galenical, herb, simple, balm, balsam, medication, placebo, pill, bolus, tablet, tabloid, capsule, lozenge, pastille, draught, dose, drench, drip, injection, shot, infusion, potion, elixir, decoction, preparation, mixture, powder, electuary, linctus **3 prophylactic**, preventive, contraception, sanitation, quarantine, isolation, hygiene, prophylaxis, immunization, inoculation, vaccination, antisepsis, disinfection, sterilization, disinfectant, bactericide, germicide, insecticide **4 antidote**, countermeasure, antitoxin, counterpoison, counterirritant, antihistamine, antibody, antiserum, mithridate, theriac, antipyretic, febrifuge, quinine, vermifuge, anthelmintic, antigen, interferon, antibiotic, immunosuppressant, antispasmodic, anticonvulsant, anticoagulant **5 analgesic**, painkiller, anodyne, nepenthe, palliative, balm, salve, demulcent, analgesia, anaesthesia, acupuncture **6 purgative**, cathartic, laxative, aperient, diuretic, expectorant, emetic, nauseant, antacid, carminative, digestive, douche **7 tonic**, restorative, roborant, cordial, reviver, refresher **8 therapy**, therapeutics, treatment, nursing, first aid, aftercare, course, cure **9 hospital**, infirmary, sanatorium, dispensary, clinic, convalescent home, rest home, hospice, asylum, lazaretto

ADJECTIVES 10 remedial, corrective, therapeutic, medicinal, analeptic, curative, first-aid, restorative, helpful, beneficial, healing, curing, hygienic, sanitary, salubrious, salutiferous, panacean, all-healing, soothing, paregoric, balsamic, demulcent, emollient, palliative, lenitive, anodyne, analgesic, narcotic, hypnotic, anaesthetic, insensible, peptic, digestive, purging, cleansing, cathartic, emetic, vomitory, laxative, antidotal, counteracting, theriacal, prophylactic, preventive, disinfectant, antiseptic, antipyretic, febrifugal, tonic, sttimulative, dietetic, alimentary **11 medical**, pathological, Aesculapian, Hippocratic, Galenic, allopathic, homeopathic, herbal, surgical, anaplastic, rhinoplastic, orthopaedic, orthotic, vulnerary, traumatic, obstetric, gynaecological, paediatric, geriatric, clinical

VERBS 12 remedy, correct, restore, fix, mend, help, aid, succour, treat, heal, cure, palliate, alleviate, soothe, demulce, neutralize, relicvc **13 doctor**, practise medicine, treat, prescribe, advise, attend, minister to, tend, nurse, revive, hospitalize, physic, medicate, drench, dose, purge, inject, dress, bind, bandage, plaster, staunch, poultice, foment, set, drug, dope, anaesthetize, operate, amputate, trepan, trephine, curette, cauterize, bleed, phlebotomize, transfuse, perfuse, massage, manipulate, draw, extract, pull, stop, fill, crown, immunize, vaccinate, inoculate, sterilize, pasteurize, antisepticize

626 Repair

VERBS 1 repair, mend, patch up, fix, put right, rectify, correct, reactivate, remedy, amend, edit, emend, adjust, overhaul, service, maintain, cobble, retread, reface, cover, thatch, reline, splice, bind, tie up, darn, patch, reupholster, stop, fill, plug, plaster, seal, paper over, caulk, reassemble, cannibalize **2 refurbish**, renovate, redecorate, recondition, revamp, refit, restore, renew, remodel, refashion, reform, touch up, freshen up, improve, upgrade, modernize **3 restore**, return, replace, retrocede, repatriate, put back, restitute, atone, recall, reappoint, reinstall, re-establish, reinstitute, reintroduce, relaunch, rehabilitate, reconstitute, reformulate, reprogramme, reinforce, reconstruct, reform, reorganize, reorient, rebuild, remake, redo, service, overhaul, valet, reintegrate, replant, reclaim, reforest, recycle, reprocess, revalidate, revive, rally, strengthen, replenish, restock, reassemble, reconvene, redeem, ransom, rescue, save, salvage, deliver **4 be restored**, recover, revive, rally, get well, bounce back, convalesce, recuperate, survive, reawaken, be reborn, reappear **5 revive**, revitalize, resuscitate, regenerate, reawaken, resurrect, reanimate, rekindle, reinvigorate, restore vitality, rejuvenate, refresh **6 cure**, heal, nurse, treat, medicate, detoxify, doctor, operate, bandage, set, cicatrize **7 resort**, go, head for, leave for

NOUNS 8 repair, reparation, mending, patching up, fixing, rectification, correction, reactivation, remedy, amendment, editing, emendation, maintenance, servicing, overhauling, tuning, adjustment, renovation, restoration, renewal, reconditioning, reintegration, reassembling, mend, darn, patching, cobbling, soling, resurfacing, splicing, binding, reinforcement, refit, new look **9 restoration**, returning, replacement, retrocession, repatriation, restitution, redress, amends, reparation, atonement, retrieval, recovery, recall, reinvestment, reinstitution, reinstallation, rehabilitation, replanting, reafforestation, reclamation, gentrification, recycling, reprocessing, salvage, redemption, rescue, salvation, deliverance, re-establishment, reconstitution, rebuilding, reformation, reprogramming, reconstruction, reorganization, readjustment, reorientation, remodelling, reconversion, reaction, counteraction, resumption, derestriction, recruitment, reinforcement, strengthening, replenishment **10 revival**, recovery, renewal, revivification, revitalization, reawakening, resurgence, recurrence, comeback, rally, refreshment, recruitment, boom, prosperity, reactivation, reanimation, resuscitation, respiration, rejuvenation, second spring, Indian summer, rebirth, renaissance, palingenesis, regeneration, resurrection, reappearance, revivalism **11 recuperation**, convalescence, recovery, healing, mending, cure, rallying, upturn, cicatrization, closing, scab formation, remedy, moderation, easing, relief, psychotherapy

ADJECTIVES 12 repaired, mended, patched up, fixed, right, correct, restored, reconditioned, renovated, redecorated, remade, rebuilt, reconstructed, reconstituted, refurbished, re-equipped, refitted, redone, rectified, reinforced, improved, like new, renewed, reborn, redeemed, saved, resuscitated, revived, renascent, resurgent, phoenix-like, reclaimed, recovered **13 repairable**, restorable, mendable, rectifiable, recoverable, retrievable, redeemable, curable, operable, treatable **14 cured**, healed, healthy, better **15 restorative**, reparative, analeptic, reviving, recuperative, curative, sanative, healing, medicated

627 Repeated Sound

NOUNS 1 drumming, thrumming, roll, rumbling, grumbling, booming, reverberation, echo, vibration, pulsation, palpitation, throbbing, pounding, pulse, beating, tattoo **2 humming**, whirring, buzzing, hum, purr, drone, mutter, murmur **3 rattle**, clatter, chatter, babble, clack **4 knocking**, knock-knock, rat-a-tat, rub-a-dub, pitter-patter, ticktock **5 ringing**, pinging, pip, chiming, pealing, carillon **6 musical repetition**, rhythm, trill, tremolo, vibrato, refrain, burden, chorus, canon **7 repeated word**, reiteration, restatement, anaphora, epistrophe, catchword, buzzword, cliché, truism, slogan

VERBS 8 drum, thrum, roll, rumble, grumble, boom, reverberate, resound, resonate, echo, vibrate, pulse, throb, pound, beat **9 hum**, whirr, buzz, purr, drone, mutter, murmur **10 rattle**, clatter, clack, chatter, babble, sputter **11 knock**, tap, ticktock, patter **12 ring**, ping, clang, chime, peal, toll **13 trill**, quaver, warble **14 repeat**, reiterate

ADJECTIVES 15 drumming, rolling, thrumming, reverberant, resonant, throbbing, pounding, beating, loud, insistent, persistent, incessant **16 humming**, whirring, buzzing, droning, monotonous, repetitive **17 rattling**, clattering, chattering, sputtering, clicking, ticking **18 pealing**, chiming

628 Repetition

NOUNS 1 repetition, repeating, rehearsal, practising, recital, duplication, reproduction, replication, recurrence, imitation, copying, plagiarism, echo, echolalia, reecho, ditto, anaphora **2 iteration**, reiteration, repeating, relating, recounting, retelling, recapitulation, review, résumé, summary, peroration, restatement, tautology, redundancy, padding, filling, quotation **3 repetitiveness**, repetition, monotony, tedium, uniformity, regularity, invariability, familiarity, daily grind, humdrum, rut, routine, habit, cliché **4 return**, reappearance, comeback, renewal, reprise, recurrence, rebirth, reincarnation, renaissance, revival, restoration, recycling **5 repeat**, repetition, encore, curtain call, rerun, reshowing, replay, return match, repeat order, second helping, reprint, offprint, reissue, new edition **6 reverberation**, echo, resonance, vibration, oscillation, rhythm, beat, pulse, throb, drumming, hammering, rhyme, alliteration **7 replica**, double, duplicate, copy, photocopy **8 creature of habit**, copycat, parrot, mimic

ADJECTIVES 9 repeated, duplicated, doubled, reproduced, replicated, echoed, mirrored, imitative, parrotlike **10 iterated**, reiterated, retold, twice-told, recounted, related, restated, quoted **11 reprinted**, reissued, remade, replayed, reshown, revived, restored, renewed, reborn, reincarnated, reheated, recycled **12 repetitious**, duplicative, reproductive, doubling, echoing, iterative, reiterant, tautological, redundant, otiose, pleonastic, recapitulative, harping, stuck-in-a-groove, wordy **13 monotonous**, tedious, boring, uniform, invariable, changeless, monotone, singsong, familiar, habitual, humdrum, mundane, routine, stale, clichéd, hackneyed **14 recurrent**, regular, periodic, cyclical, returning, recurring, reappearing, ubiquitous, haunting, continual, continuous, constant, incessant, ceaseless **15 reverberatory**, resonant, vibrational, oscillatory, rhythmical, beating, pulsating, throbbing, drumming, hammering, chiming, chanting, rhyming

VERBS 16 repeat, redo, rehearse, practise, duplicate, double, reproduce, replicate, plagiarize, copy, echo, mirror, parrot, imitate **17 iterate**, reiterate, repeat, relate, recite, recount, retell, recapitulate, perorate, review, resume, summarize, restate, reemphasize, quote, cite **18 harp**, plug, labour, churn out, trot out, din into **19 return to**, go back, relapse, regress, revert, remember **20 renew**, resume, restart, revive, restore, recycle, reprocess, reheat, reprint, reissue, rerun, replay **21 be repeated**, recur, return, reappear **22 resound**, reverberate, echo, vibrate, oscillate, beat, pulse, throb, drum, thrum, hammer, pound

629 Representation

• *Taxation without representation is tyranny.* James Otis.

NOUNS 1 representation, depiction, delineation, portrayal, rendering, embodiment, personification, incarnation, realization, typification, epitome, quintessence, type, figuration, symbolization, indication, manifestation, evocation, presentation, imitation, exemplar, impersonation, impression, similarity, semblance, likeness, realism, lookalike, spitting image, double, doppelgänger, copy, duplicate, facsimile, replica, reflection, outline, description, writing, pictogram, hieroglyphics, runes, notation **2 reproduction**, photograph, carbon copy, photocopy, print, graphics, etching, engraving, lithograph, collotype, blueprint, diagram, chart, graph, plan, draft, sketch, cartoon, caricature, picture, illustration, tracing, drawing, artwork, painting, watercolour, portrait, illumination **3 acting**, portraying, playing, impersonating, posing, characterizing, performing, enactment, role-playing, mimicry, charade, mime **4 image**, symbol, likeness, visual, photograph, duplicate, idea, thought, after-image, reflection, projection, hologram, silhouette, icon, idol, effigy, gargoyle, sculpture, statue, statuette, bust, figure, figurine, waxwork, model, replica, manikin, tailor's dummy, doll, golliwog, soft toy, puppet, marionette, fantoccini, snowman, gingerbread man, scarecrow, guy, robot **5 map**, town plan, road map, sketch map, elevation, Mercator's projection, chart, cartogram, statistics, atlas, globe, star map, map-making **6 representative**, example, sample, specimen, cross-section, agent, agency, proxy, substitute, replacement, stand-in, deputy, delegate, ambassador

VERBS 7 represent, depict, delineate, portray, render, embody, personify, incarnate, realize, typify, symbolize, epitomize, manifest, evoke, present, imitate, impersonate, resemble, copy, duplicate, reproduce, reflect, mirror, image, catch, capture, register, record, photograph, film, snap, shoot, scan, X-ray, process, print, enlarge **8 act**, portray, present, dramatize, play, role-play, characterize, perform, enact, impersonate, pose as, mimic, mime, masquerade **9 paint**, draw, sketch, caricature, picture, illustrate, draft, plan, diagram, design, outline, describe, trace, shape, form, mould, carve, sculpt, cast, cut, engrave, etch, print, plot, map, chart **10 stand for**, mean, denote, exemplify, show, pass for, replace

ADJECTIVES 11 representational, depictive, delineatory, portraying, symbolic, emblematic, figurative, typical, quintessential, archetypal, characteristic, exemplary, evocative, descriptive, illustrative, graphic, pictorial, hieroglyphic, reflecting, similar, like, imitative, iconic, diagrammatic, vivid, realistic, naturalistic, true-to-life, impressionistic, abstract, nonrepresentational, surrealistic, artistic

630 Reproduction

NOUNS 1 reproduction, multiplication, proliferation, repetition, replication, duplication, copying, photocopying, printing, offset lithography, publishing, reconstruction, renovation, renewal, restoration, revival, resuscitation, reanimation, regeneration, resurrection, resurgence, reincarnation, rebirth **2 print**, reprint, offprint, photocopy, copy, duplicate, facsimile, edition, clone **3 propaga-**

tion, generation, procreation, sex, sexual intercourse, copulation, coition, breeding, spawning, eugenics, genesis, biogenesis, abiogenesis, autogenesis, parthenogenesis, virgin birth, fertilization, impregnation, pollination, fecundation, test-tube baby, conception, germination, pregnancy, gestation, incubation, hatching, birth, parturition, nativity, natality, fructification, fruition, florescence **4 development**, growth, adolescence, puberty, adulthood, parenthood, parentage, paternity **5 propagator**, pollinator, fertilizer, cultivator, procreator, begetter, parent, sire **6 progeny**, offspring, child, baby **7 obstetrics**, midwifery, childbirth, confinement, labour, accouchement, contractions, epidural, waters, delivery, Caesarian, embryo, fetus, caul, umbilical cord, placenta, afterbirth, amniocentesis, obstetrician, gynaecologist, midwife, pregnant woman, mother-to-be, primigravida, unigravida, multigravida, gooseberry bush **8 organs of reproduction**, genitalia, pudenda, privates, vulva, clitoris, labia, vagina, uterus, womb, cervix, ovary, Fallopian tubes, ovipositor, ovum, egg, penis, phallus, male member, foreskin, testicles, testes, scrotum, prostate, vas deferens, semen, sperm, seed, pollen, stigma, style, gynoecium

VERBS 9 reproduce, repeat, echo, duplicate, replicate, clone, copy, photocopy, mass-produce, print, reprint, turn out **10 reproduce oneself**, conceive, fall, carry, give birth **11 have young**, spawn, hatch, drop, foal, lamb, farrow, pup, whelp, calve, cub, kitten, litter, germinate, sprout, bloom, flower, fruit **12 multiply**, burgeon, proliferate **13 propagate**, generate, produce, procreate, breed, beget, spawn, engender, father, sire, impregnate, fertilize, fecundate, inseminate, pollinate, hatch, incubate, raise, rear, bud, graft **14 have sex**, make love

ADJECTIVES 15 reproduced, printed, duplicated, copied, repeated, renewed, re-created, reborn, renascent, resurgent, resurrectional **16 reproductive**, generative, procreative, originative, seminal, spermatic, germinal, genetic, sexual, genital, vulvar, clitoral, vaginal, cervical, ovarian, penile, phallic, scrotal, in season, on heat, pregnant, impregnated, fertilized, fecundated, breeding, broody, enceinte, gravid, expecting, parturient, in labour, antenatal, perinatal, postnatal, puerperal, obstetric, viviparous

631 Reptiles and Amphibians

NOUNS 1 reptile, reptilian, cold-blooded animal **2 lizard**, saurian, lacertilian, iguana, chameleon, gecko, skink, monitor, glass snake, Komodo dragon, basilisk, legless lizard, slow worm, rhynocephalian **3 snake**, serpent, ophidian, constrictor, boa, python, anaconda, viper, adder, grass snake, asp, cobra, mamba, rattlesnake, basilisk **4 chelonian**, chelonid, tortoise, turtle **5 crocodilian**, crocodile, alligator **6 extinct reptile**, dinosaur, ornithischian, ornithopod, saurischian, sauropod, ichthyopterygian, ichthyosaur, sauropterygian, plesiosaur, nothosaur, mosasaur, pterosaur, therapsid **7 amphibian**, frog, bullfrog, toad, newt, salamander, batrachian, caecilian, apodan, tailed amphibian, urodele, caudate, salientian, anuran, **8 young amphibian**, frogspawn, tadpole, polliwog, froglet, toadlet, axolotl, neoteny **9 herpetology**, ophiology, reptile house, reptilarium **10 herpetologist**, ophiologist

ADJECTIVES 11 reptilian, reptiliform, cold-blooded, poikilothermic, lizardlike, saurian, lacertilian, turtlelike, chelonian, crocodilian, scaly **12 snakelike**, snaky, serpentine, serpentiform, ophidian, ophiomorphic, colubrine, colubriform, anguine **13 amphibian**, batrachian, apodan, salamandrian, newtlike, caudate, neotenous, froggy, toadish

VERBS 14 live as a reptile, creep, crawl, glide, twist **15 live as an amphibian**, creep, crawl, hop

632 Repulsion

VERBS 1 repel, drive away, head off, repulse, turn back, reject, rebuff, snub, cold-shoulder, slight, cut, spurn **2 eject**, expel, send packing **3 fend off**, deflect, ward off, head off **4 be repulsive**, disgust, revolt, sicken, nauseate, repel, upset

NOUNS 5 repulsion, repellence, ugliness, repulsiveness, recoil, polarization, disaffinity, diamagnetism **6 repulse**, rebuff, dismissal, snub, cot, cold shoulder, spurning, refusal, rejection, ejection **7 deflection**, defence, foil, counterstroke, parry

ADJECTIVES 8 repulsive, repellent, repugnant, offensive, noisome, off-putting, antipathetic, ugly, abhorrent, obnoxious, disgusting, nauseating, sickening, foul, loathsome, horrible, appalling, hideous **9 abducent**, centrifugal, repelling **10 defensive**, resistant

633 Repute

NOUNS 1 estimation, reputation, report, reference, regard, esteem, favour, cachet, approval, approbation, distinction, eminence, mark

ADJECTIVES 2 reputable, creditworthy, respected, honoured, emeritus, popular, distinguished, eminent, approved, renowned, famous, fabled **3 reputed**, alleged

VERBS 4 have repute, be famous

634 Request

NOUNS 1 request, asking, entreaty, importunity, pressure, persuasion, insistence, urgency, imploring, soliciting, accosting, invitation, application, appeal, bid, cry, desire, favour, wish, want, petition, round robin, invocation, incantation, prayer, supplication, adjuration, begging, beseeching, pestering, solicitation, suggestion, proposition, approach, offer, requirement, claim **2 demand**, requisition, order, indent, summons, call, notice, claim, injunction, dunning, command, ultimatum, threat, blackmail, exaction **3 solicitation**, chain letter, mendicancy, begging, cadging, busking, fund-raising, appealing, canvassing, charity events, benefit concert

VERBS 4 request, want, ask for, entreat, pressure, insist, urge, implore, solicit, accost, hustle, invite, apply for, appeal, bid, cry, desire, wish, petition, invoke, incant, pray for, supplicate, adjure, beg, beseech, cajole, coax, pester, tout, hawk, suggest, persuade, proposition, propose, move, approach, offer, apply, require, claim, court **5 demand**, requisition, order, indent, summon, call, claim, invoice, charge, bill, levy, tax, dun, command, threaten, blackmail, exact **6 solicit money**, beg, cadge, busk, raise funds

ADJECTIVES 7 requesting, asking, insistent, urgent, inviting, desired, petitioned, round-robin, invocational, incantational, adjuratory, entreating, beseeching, propositional, proposable, offered, required, courting **8 demanding**, claiming, requisitionary, injunctive, forcible, threatening, blackmailing **9 begging**, cadging, mendicant

635 Requirement

NOUNS 1 requirement, essential, necessity, a must, desideratum, needs, necessaries, order, indent, requisition, stipulation, specification, requisite, proviso, standards, request, ultimatum, injunction **2 need**, want, lack, insufficiency, shortage, shortfall, slippage, gap, lacuna, demand, call, seller's market, consumption, input, intake, debt **3 needfulness**, occasion, necessity, essentiality, indispensability, desirability, want, pinch, poverty, breadline, predicament, urgency, exigency, emergency, crisis, vitalness, obligation

ADJECTIVES 4 required, essential, necessary, needed, vital, indispensable, compulsory, obligatory, requisite, prerequisite, demanded, ordered, requested, desired, wanted, on call, earmarked, reserved, booked, lacking, missing **5 necessitous**, needy, poor, pinched, penniless, bankrupt, destitute, lacking, needing, craving, longing for, hungry, starving, deprived **6 demanding**, calling for, imperative, urgent, exigent, exacting, pressing

VERBS 7 require, need, want, lack **8 miss**, long for, desire, crave, clamour for, claim **9 find necessary**, must have, use, consume **10 necessitate**, involve, oblige, compel, demand, request, stipulate, dictate, order, requisition, indent, reserve, book, earmark

636 Resentment; Anger

NOUNS 1 resentment, bitterness, rancour, rankling, acrimony, spleen, gall, acidity, heart-burning, soreness, grudge, malice, jealousy, envy, displeasure, dissatisfaction, disapproval, disapprobation, ill humour, animosity, irritation, vexation, discontent, annoyance, aggravation, exasperation, pique, peevishness **2 offence**, umbrage, hurt, indignity, insult, affront, wrong **3 cause of offence**, provocation, last straw, sore point, tender spot, dangerous subject, pinprick **4 anger**, wrath, rage, fury, passion, ire, choler, aggression, belligerence, bellicosity, crossness, snappishness, sullenness, heat, vehemence, violence, outburst, temper tantrum, convulsion, storm, scene, ferment, fret, explosion, shouting **5 quarrel**, argument, tiff, fight **6 sign of anger**, black look, frown, scowl, glower, glare, growl, snarl, bark

VERBS 7 resent, feel offended, feel insulted, feel piqued, feel sore, feel discontented, bear malice, find intolerable, suffer, feel, smart under **8 offend**, provoke, vex, annoy, aggravate, goad, sting, exasperate, irritate, antagonize, incense, arouse, inflame, nettle, fret, insult, affront, outrage, grieve, wound, chafe, pique, huff, rile, rankle, ruffle, work up, bother, harass, pester, tease, bait, pinprick, torment, goad, sting **9 be offended**, feel hurt, feel pique, mind, take umbrage **10 be angry**, rage, rave, rant, bluster, fulminate, burn, fume, seethe, simmer, smoke, smoulder, boil, glower, glare, frown, scowl, lour, look daggers, snarl, growl, snap, fret, chafe, storm, breathe fire, quarrel, fight, raise Cain, raise hell, go berserk **11 become angry**, explode, colour, ignite, kindle, lose control, bridle **12 vent one's anger**, snap at **13 make angry**, aggravate, huff, put out, enrage, infuriate, madden, ulcerate

ADJECTIVES 14 resentful, offended, insulted, affronted, hurt, pained, put-out, indignant, reproachful, bitter, virulent, acrimonious, sharp, acid, splenetic, acerbic, caustic, irritated, vexed, wrought-up, discontented, disapproving, displeased, provoked, riled, worked-up, annoyed, aggravated, exasperated, piqued, peeved, nettled, stung, sore, grudging, malicious, jealous, envious, bileful, spiteful, ill-humoured **15 angry**, irate, ireful, cross, aggressive, belligerent, bellicose, wrathful, furious, infuriated, choleric, indignant, livid, enraged, raging, incensed, fuming, boiling, burning, smouldering, sulphurous, huffed, beside oneself, frenzied, foaming, rabid, berserk, hopping mad, stuttering, gnashing, growling, snapping, dangerous, violent, fierce, savage

637 Resignation

NOUNS 1 resignation, relinquishment, departure, withdrawal, renouncement, renunciation, surrender, quitting, retirement, abdication **2 stoicism**, sanguinity, phlegm, indifference **3 resignedness**, acceptance

VERBS 4 resign, quit, stand down, stand aside, abdicate, abandon, desert, leave, depart, withdraw, vacate, drop, give up, forgo, renunciate, surrender **5 resign oneself**, accept

ADJECTIVES 6 resigning, abdicating, retiring, past, former, one-time, sometime, late, emeritus, pensioned off, forced out, outgoing **7 resigned**, accepting, acquiescent, stoical, sanguine

638 Resistance

NOUNS 1 resistance, refusal, unwillingness, noncooperation, opposition, objection, challenge, stand, brave front, strike, walkout, deprecation, protest, dissent, defiance, repulse, repellence, rebuff, reluctance, renitency **2 obstinacy**, intractability, refractoriness, recalcitrance, stubbornness, obduracy, firmness, hardness, toughness, callousness, stiffness, starchiness, rigidity, inflexibility **3 resistance movement**, self-defence, withstanding, civil disobedience, mutiny, uprising, insurgence, insurrection, revolution, revolt, guerrilla warfare **4 desisting**, denial, self-restraint, refusal, refraining, abstaining

VERBS 5 resist, withstand, endure, stand against, refuse, strike, walk out, not cooperate, oppose, object to, confront, contend with, obstruct, hinder, challenge, deprecate, protest, dissent, defy, repulse, repel **6 be obstinate**, stand firm **7 revolt**, mutiny, rise up, fight off **8 desist**, deny oneself, restrain from, refrain from, abstain from

ADJECTIVES **9 resistant**, renitent, withstanding, reluctant, refusing, striking, unwilling, noncooperative, opposing, objecting, challenging, deprecative, protesting, dissenting, defiant, rebuffing, repulsing, repellent, obstructive **10 obstinate**, intractable, refractory, recalcitrant, callous, hard, rigid, firm, tough, stiff, starchy, stubborn, obdurate, inflexible, unbending, unyielding, unmalleable, die-hard, hardline, traditional **11 resisting**, unsubmissive, undefeated, unsubdued, unbowed, unquelled, unbeatable, invincible, bulletproof, self-defensive, revolutionary, rebellious, mutinous, insurgent, reactionary, terrorist **12 desisting**, denying, refraining, abstaining

639 Resolution

ADJECTIVES **1 resolute**, resolved, determined, decided, decisive, deliberate, single-minded, concentrated, purposeful, intent **2 tenacious**, persevering, persistent, dogged, zealous, thorough, all-consuming, earnest, serious, insistent, pressing, urgent, driving, forceful, energetic, vigorous, hard-hitting, desperate, all out, wholehearted, committed, devoted, dedicated, tireless **3 strong-willed**, uncompromising, unbending, inflexible, unyielding, intransigent, adamant, obstinate, stubborn, relentless, ruthless, merciless, inexorable, implacable, stern, grim, hard, cast-iron **4 undaunted**, heroic, game, unfearing, unshaken, unshrinking, unflinching, unwavering, unhesitant, steadfast, indomitable, unconquered, unbeaten, steeled **5 steady**, constant, firm, solid, immovable, unchangeable, staunch, reliable, dependable

VERBS **6 be resolute**, mean business **7 resolve**, decide, determine, purpose, intend, will, fix, settle, seal, conclude **8 brace oneself**, dare **9 undertake**, set to, tackle, commit oneself, devote oneself **10 insist**, urge, press, stand firm, stay put **11 persist**, persevere, soldier on

NOUNS **12 resolution**, resolve, determination, doggedness, decidedness, decisiveness, purposefulness **13 concentration**, seriousness, single-mindedness, commitment, devotion, dedication, earnestness, zeal, ardour, eagerness, drive, vigour, energy **14 tenacity**, persistence, perseverance, stubbornness, obstinacy, relentlessness, ruthlessness, inexorability, implacability, sternness, pitilessness, hardness, steeliness, inflexibility, insistence, pressure **15 will**, intent, self-control, self-restraint, self-possession, steadiness, constancy, firmness, stability, staunchness, reliability **16 fortitude**, spirit, grit, backbone, mettle, daring, dauntlessness, courage, pluck, dash, aplomb, élan, moral fibre, clenched teeth

640 Resonance

NOUNS **1 resonance**, reverberation, resounding, rebounding, hollowness, echo, reflection, recurrence, vibration, whirring, humming, buzzing **2 ringing**, tintinnabulation, campanology, peal, toll, knell, chime, tinkle, jingle, chink, clink, ping, ting-a-ling, clang, sounding brass, blare, flourish, fanfare **3**

deepness, lowness, profundity, booming, thundering, sonorousness, plangency, bass, basso profondo, baritone **4 sources of resonance**, tube, tunnel, bell, chimes, clapper, gong, triangle, trumpet **5 resonator**, sounding board

ADJECTIVES 6 resonant, reverberating, reboant, stentorian, resounding, rebounding, hollow, echoing, vibrating, pulsating, carrying, lingering, persisting, humming, whirring **7 ringing**, tintinnabular, pealing, tolling, sounding, chiming, tinkling, jingling, pinging, clanging **8 deep**, low, sepulchral, sonorous, vibrant, booming, thundering, full, rich, plangent, mellow, melodious, rounded

VERBS 9 resonate, reverberate, resound, rebound, boom, echo, recur, vibrate, whir, hum, buzz **10 ring**, tintinnabulate, peal, toll, sound, knell, chime, tinkle, jingle, jangle, chink, clink, ping, twang, clang, blare, trumpet

641 Respect

• *Let them hate, so long as they fear.* Lucius Accius.

NOUNS 1 respect, regard, esteem, consideration, attention, honour, favour, approbation, approval, appreciation, repute, recognition, prestige **2 admiration**, adoration, adulation, worship, idolization, veneration, awe, reverence, homage, fealty, obeisance **3 respectfulness**, deference, humbleness, humility, devotion, loyalty, courtesy, comity **4 mark of respect**, salute, nod, bow, scrape, stooping, curtsy, bob, genuflection, kneeling, prostration, salaam, kowtow **5 presenting arms**, flypast, red carpet **6 greeting**, welcome, salutation, obeisance **7 respects**, regards, greetings, salutations, compliments

ADJECTIVES 8 respectful, regardful, considerate, attentive, honorific, ceremonious **9 showing respect**, deferential, courteous, polite, gracious, dutiful, obeisant, humble, submitting, compliant, obsequious, servile, ingratiating, fawning **10 reverent**, venerative, admiring, adoring, worshipping, adulatory, deifying, idolizing **11 in a respectful stance**, standing, prostrate, saluting, bare-headed, forelock-tugging, nodding, bending, bowing, curtseying, bobbing **12 respected**, esteemed, honoured, revered, reverenced, admired, appreciated, valued, prized, time-honoured **13 respectable**, reputable, upright, worthy, venerable, estimable, praiseworthy **14 awe-inspiring**, imposing, impressive, important, authoritative, august

VERBS 15 respect, regard, esteem, rank high, value, admire, prize, treasure, favour **16 revere**, venerate, honour, admire, adore, cherish, worship, lionize, hero-worship, idolize, deify **17 praise**, exalt, extol, acclaim, glorify **18 show respect**, defer to, heed, obey, consider, do homage **19 take off one's hat to**, rise, stand, nod, bow, bend, stoop, salaam, curtsy, bob, genuflect, kneel, prostrate oneself, make obeisance, grovel **20 salute**, present arms, greet, welcome **21 command respect**, impose, impress, rank high

642 Restraint

NOUNS 1 restraint, constraint, suppression, repression, strictness, coercion, hindrance, impediment, obstacle, retardation, deceleration, stopping, prevention, control, curb, check, veto, ban, bar, blackball, prohibition, restriction, injunction, interdict, D-notice, discipline, punishment, authority, duress, pressure, censorship, quelling, quashing, smothering, stifling, throttling, crushing, smashing, crackdown, limitation, stipulation, requirement, limitations, retrenchment, constriction, squeeze, curtailment, circumscription, exclusivity, copyright, charmed circle, demarcation **2 economic restraint**, rationing, pay freeze, price control, credit squeeze, rate-capping, restrictive practice, monopoly, cartel, closed shop, intervention, protectionism, mercantilism, tariff wall **3 self-restraint**, self-control, self-discipline, temperance, continence, abstinence, abstemiousness, asceticism, spartanism, moderation, inhibition, introversion, formality, reserve, modesty, shyness, quietness, embarrassment **4 detention**, quarantine, blockade, siege, guarding, custodianship, custody, impoundment, curfew, remand, arrest, sentence, incarceration, imprisonment, internment, confinement, captivity, kidnapping, bondage, slavery **5 means of restraint**, diet, fast, ban, veto, damper, governor, drag, cramp, clamp, gag, muzzle, leash, lead, tether, reins, bridle, harness, yoke, corset, straitjacket, fetters, bonds, chains, shackles, handcuffs, manacles, trammels, bilboes

VERBS 6 restrain, constrain, suppress, repress, oppress, coerce, hinder, impede, bottle up, retard, slow, stop, veto, blackball, brake, prevent, pull back, control, curb, check, ban, bar, prohibit, restrict, drag, interdict, regulate, discipline, police, patrol, punish, pressure, censor, subdue, crack down, quell, quash, smother, stifle, throttle, crush, smash, stipulate, limit, retrench, constrict, squeeze, cut, curtail, demarcate, circumsribe, hem in, box in, localize, copyright, exclude **7 economize**, ration, control prices, freeze pay, squeeze credit, cap rates, monopolize, intervene **8 restrain oneself**, control oneself, deny oneself, hold back, diet, slim, fast, keep calm, say nothing **9 detain**, quarantine, blockade, besiege, starve out, guard, protect, impound, remand, refuse bail, arrest, apprehend, seize, sentence, incarcerate, imprison, intern, confine, kidnap **10 gag**, muzzle, silence, interdict, leash, tether, hobble, rein in, harness, collar, yoke, girdle, straitjacket, fetter, bind, tie up, chain, shackle

ADJECTIVES 11 restraining, constrained, suppressive, oppressive, strict, coercive, slow, preventive, under control, prohibitive, conditional, restrictive, tied down, in check, injunctive, interdictive, severe, disciplined, punished, authoritative, pressurized, censored, banned, stifling, limiting, required, constrictive, narrow, cramped, circumscriptive, exclusive, copyrighted, rationed, frozen, rate-capped, monopolistic, interventional, protective **12 self-restrained**, self-controlled, self-disciplined, dieting, fasting, temperate, continent, abstinent, abstemious, ascetic, spartan, moderate, inhibiting, introversive, formal, reserved, quiet, modest, shy, embarrassing, pent up **13 detained**, quarantined, shut-in, housebound, snowbound, fogbound, besieged, custodial, arrested, sentenced, incarcerated, imprisoned, in custody, on remand, confined, captive, kidnapped, enslaved, gagged

643 Retaliation

NOUNS 1 retaliation, reprisal, revenge, vengeance, redress, just deserts, dueness, justice, retribution, reparation, repayment, Nemesis, punishment, backlash, boomerang, counterstroke, counterblast, counterplot, counteraction, counter suit, comeback, riposte, retort, rejoinder, reciprocation

VERBS 2 retaliate, recoup, repay, punish, counter, riposte, parry, be quits, reciprocate, avenge, retort, answer, counter charge, react, boomerang, recoil, round on, hit back, resist **3 serve one right**, restitute

ADJECTIVES 4 retaliatory, in self-defence, retaliative, retributive, punitive, recriminatory, reciprocal, revengeful, vindictive

644 Retention

NOUNS 1 retention, retainment, grabbing, prehension, adhesion, stickiness, viscidity, hanging on, clinging on, tenaciousness, persistence, handhold, foothold, toehold, clutch, clamp, clinch, clench, grasp, hug, embrace, clasp, cuddle, squeeze, compression, seizure, grip, stranglehold, headlock **2 detention**, suppression, repression, containment, envelopment, enclosing, imprisoning, bottling up, plug, stop, stopper, cork, locking in, saving, cherishing, maintenance **3 tools for gripping**, pliers, wrench, spanner, tongs, tweezers, pincers, nippers, vice, clamp, grip, forceps, grapnel, grappling iron, hook, anchor, fastening, stapler, glue, gum, paste, adhesive, clasp, clip, paperclip, fingers, fist, hand, paw, claw, talon, fingernails, teeth, fangs, tentacle, tendril **4 wall**, bulwark, embankment, abutment, buttress, fence **5 retentiveness**, constipation, remembrance, recall

VERBS 6 retain, keep, buttonhole, cleave to, grab, stick to, agglutinate, staple, glue, gum, paste, cling on, show tenaciousness, clutch, clamp, clinch, clench, grasp, hug, embrace, grapple, clasp, cuddle, squeeze, compress, seize, grip, throttle, strangle **7 detain**, suppress, repress, restrain, imprison, catch, steady, support, contain, envelop, enclose, keep in, hold in, wall in, fence in, bottle up, plug, stop, cork, clog, constipate, lock in, retain, withhold, save, maintain, preserve **8 remember**, recall

ADJECTIVES 9 retentive, retaining, tenacious, cohesive, adhesive, costive, constipated, clogged, indissoluble, firm, sticky, gluey, gummy, prehensile, tight-fisted, parsimonious, grasping, gripping, clinging, clasping, vicelike, strangling, throttling **10 retained**, stuck firm, fast, held, bound, glued, gummed, grasped, gripped, clasped, clutched, pinioned, pinned, stapled, strangled, detained, imprisoned, penned, walled in, fenced in, contained, circumscribed, saved, withheld

645 Reversion

NOUNS 1 reversion, return, regression, recession, retrogression, withdrawal, apostasy, retraction, recantation, repentance, retreat, retirement, retroversion, retroflexion, retrospection, reaction, retroaction, counteraction, backfire, ricochet, recoil, boomerang effect, backlash, counter-revolution, counter-reformation, about-turn, U-turn, volte-face, atavism, recidivism, backsliding **2 restoration**, reconversion, reinstatement, transfer, restitution, compensation, revival, resumption, recommencement, recovery, retrieval, recycling, retaliation **3 turning point**, crisis **4 return**, swing, shuttling, commuting **5 reply**, retort, answer, response, feedback

VERBS 6 reverse, turn, return, revert, regress, recede, retrogress, recidivate, withdraw, retract, retreat, retire, recant, renege, backslide, relapse, archaize, react, counteract, backfire, ricochet, recoil **7 restore**, reconvert, revive, resume, compensate, reinstate, restart, recommence, undo, unmake, remake, start afresh, recover, retrieve, recycle **8 return**, swing back, rebound, recoil, kick back, shuttle **9 reply**, retort, answer, respond, confute, refute

ADJECTIVES 10 regressive, recessive, reversionary, retroverse, retrograde, restitutive, compensatory, retrospective, reflexive, reactive, retroactive, atavistic **11 reversed**, regressed, retracted, recanted, retreated, retired, reverted, reacted, recoiled, backfired, returned, restored, reinstated, revived, resumed, recovered, retrieved, recycled, replied, retorted, answered, responded **12 reversible**, returnable, restorable, recoverable, retrievable

646 Reward

NOUNS 1 reward, remuneration, recompense, deserts, justice, guerdon, satisfaction, recognition, credit, acknowledgment, thanks, gratitude, favour, tribute, acclaim, acclamation, bouquet, praise, honours, decoration, title, honorary degree **2 prize**, award, crown, trophy, cup, pot, shield, certificate, medal, wooden spoon, prize money, jackpot, kitty, Nobel Prize, Booker Prize **3 grant**, aid, assistance, subsidy, subvention, fellowship, scholarship, stipend, exhibition, bursary **4 reward for service**, remuneration, fee, retainer, honorarium, emolument, payment, payoff, pension, pay, wages, salary, redundancy money, income, earnings, wage scale, increment, commission, bonus, incentive, inducement, enticement, offer, bait, lure, perquisite **5 turnover**, return, gain, profit, profit margin **6 compensation**, indemnification, satisfaction, consideration, solatium, damages, requital, retaliation, reparation, amends **7 bounty**, premium, gift, gratuity, tip **8 secret money**, slush fund, blackmail

VERBS 9 reward, remunerate, recompense, guerdon, satisfy, recognize, credit, acknowledge, thank, pay tribute, acclaim, praise, award, present, honour **10 grant**, aid, assist **11 pay**, remunerate, give, tip, bribe, repay, retaliate, settle up, compensate, indemnify, requite, make reparation, make amends **12 be rewarded 13 get paid 14 gain**, reap

ADJECTIVES 15 rewarding, satisfying,

paying, profitable, money-making, lucrative, remunerative **16 rewarded**, recognized, credited, acknowledged, acclaimed **17 compensatory**, indemnificatory, reparatory, retributive **18 giving**, generous, open-handed

647 Ridiculousness

NOUNS 1 ludicrousness, daftness, absurdity, laughableness, pricelessness, foolishness, comicality, drollery, eccentricity, clowning, buffoonery, whimsicality, zaniness, bizarreness, bathos, folly, senselessness **2 slapstick comedy**, farce, burlesque **3 object of ridicule**, idiot, fool, clown, eccentric **4 joke**, malapropism, spoonerism, drollery, clowning

ADJECTIVES 5 ridiculous, preposterous, daft, laughable, priceless, absurd, asinine, foolish, funny, comical, clownish, droll, eccentric, bizarre, zany, humourous, witty, comic, farcical, slapstick, clownish, hilarious, risible, fatuous, burlesque

648 Right

NOUNS 1 fairness, justice, equity, impartiality, equality, even handedness **2 correctness**, accurateness, authenticity, validity, legitimacy, truth, genuineness, veracity **3 properness**, correctness, honesty, decency, propriety, seemliness, probity, integrity, honour **4 righteousness**, virtue, uprightness, integrity, rectitude, uprightness, probity **5 righting wrong**, reform, rectification **6 right**, entitlement, due, desert

ADJECTIVES 7 right, fair, just, equitable, equal, impartial, fair-minded, open-minded, square, unbiased, disinterested, even-handed, objective, neutral **8 correct**, accurate, true, authentic, genuine, valid, legitimate, veracious, unerring, precise **9 in the right**, justified, excusable, forgivable, unimpeachable, unchallengeable, rightful, deserved, due **10 moral**, moralistic, ethical, high-principled, righteous, virtuous, godly, clean, pure, honest, honourable, truthful, upright, upstanding, straight **11 right-minded**, decent, law-abiding, sporting **12 all right**, fine, fit, well

VERBS 13 be right, be justified, deserve **14 be fair**, arbitrate **15 put right**, rectify, redress, reform, mend, fix, repair

649 Ritual

NOUNS 1 ritual, procedure, custom, habit, convention, routine, formality, ceremony, formula, religious observance, rite, liturgy **2 rite of worship**, honour, reverence, veneration, adoration, glorification, exaltation, praise, thanksgiving, blessing, hymn-singing, psalm-singing, confession, astiamnu, penitence, offering, almsgiving, chalukah, potlatch, sacrifice, asvamedha, muda, supplication, prayer **3 public worship**, prayer meeting, abodah, musaph, church service, minchah, maarib, memorial service, yahrzeit, azan **4 hymn**, hymning, psalm-singing, chant, niggun, kontakion, kanon, plainsong, mantra, Rigveda, Samaveda, anthem, cherubicon, carol, exultet, doxology, antiphon, response, paean, gospel song, Homeric hymn, Vedic hymn, maoz tzur, nusach, yigdal **5 prayer**, orison, devotion, impetration, petition, request, invocation, epidesis, nembutsu, gayatri, allocution, intercession, geullah, anamnesis, vigils, comprecation, supplication, intention, rogation, eulogia, blessing, motzi, kol nidre, benediction, nishmat, grace, rosary, Hail Mary, Ave Maria, Kyrie Eleison, mantra, alenu, dharani, om **6 religious manual**, prayer book, breviary, missal, farse, lectionary, pontifical, ordinal, canon, rubric, machzor, siddur **7 place of worship**, church, kirk, mission, meetinghouse, chapel, conventicle, chantry, abbey, cathedral, minster, basilica, oratory, temple, tabernacle, synagogue, shul, mosque, masjid, wat, pantheon, ziggurat, pagoda, shrine **8 church**, nave, chancel, choir, sanctuary, altar, pulpit, lectern, pew, stall, confessional, cloister, aisle, clerestory, triforium, font, rood screen, crypt, presbytery, sacristy **9 shrine**, sanctuary, reliquary, tabernacle, dagoba, cella, naos, stupa, tope, marae **10 sacred object**, relic, ark, Torah scrolls, aron-ha-kodesh, phylactery, asterisk, crucifix, black stone, Bo tree, icon, holy water, asperger, incense, rosary beads, beadroll, prayer-wheel, prayermat, prayer shawl, tallith, candle, menorah, bugia, Holy Grail, chalice, juju, totem, talisman, charm, amulet, fetish, totem pole **11 holy day**, holiday, feast, feast day, fast day, religious festival, festival, fiesta, festivity **12 worshipper**, venerator, follower, communicant, celebrant, fold, flock, sheep, congregation

VERBS 13 perform rites, ritualize, observe, celebrate, commune, oblate, confess, receive absolution, minister, officiate, anoint, bless, baptize, christen, sprinkle, absolve, denounce, excommunicate, exorcise **14 offer worship**, honour, revere, venerate, adore, glorify, exalt, extol, magnify, laud, praise, celebrate, give thanks, kneel, genuflect, bow, stoop, cross oneself **15 pray**, request, invoke, impetrate, petition, rogate, supplicate, implore, beseech, give thanks

ADJECTIVES 16 ritualistic, ceremonial, festive, impetrational, petitionary, invocational, supplicatory, liturgical, hymnological, hymnographical, comminatory, laudational, doxological, sacramental, sacral, oblational, libational, chrismal, sacrificial, nuptial, matrimonial, penitential, funereal, baptismal, symbolic, eucharistic, transubstantial, totemistic, fetishistic **17 worshipping**, reverent, devout, pious, observant, religious, devotional, prayerful, dutiful, solemn

650 Rivers

NOUNS 1 river, meandering river, navigable river, freshet, watercourse, waterway, canal, stream, streamlet, rivulet, millstream, rillet, brook, bourn, runnel, rill, beck, brooklet, creek, wadi, tributary, confluence, branch, feeder, affluent, distributary, fork, effluent, anabranch, river system **2 channel**, midchannel, midstream, sandbank, meander, embankment, headstream, riverhead, fountainhead, backwater, waterfall, cataract, cascade, force, rapids, chute, shoot, nappe, spillway, overflow, sluiceway, bore, mouth, delta, river crossing, ford, bridge **3 river flow**, millstream, millrace, course, current, under-

current, undertow, eddy, whirlpool, vortex, maelstrom, Charybdis, flux, drift, ripple, wash, wake, crosscurrent, counterflow, backflow, ebb, reflux, backwash, torrent, washout, flush
VERBS 4 flow, meander, race, braid, run, course, channel, pour, stream, babble, bubble, gurgle, trill, trickle, eddy, ripple, flood, overflow, cascase, fall, flow back **5 cause to flow**, irrigate **6 stop the flow**, stem, staunch
ADJECTIVES 7 fluvial, fluviomarine, fluent, effluent, profluent, affluent, confluent, convergent, streaming, running, coursing, meandering, serpentine, ripply, racing, torrential, vortical, inundant, falling, ebbing **8 flooded**, deluged, inundated, swamped **9 hydrologic(al)**, fluvioterrestrial

651 Road Transport

NOUNS 1 road, route, highway, main road, trunk road, A road, clearway, motorway, toll road, side road, B road, single track, farm track **2 carriageway**, lane, dual carriageway, hard shoulder, corner, S-bend, hairpin bend, chicane, camber, intersection, T-junction, crossroads, box junction, roundabout, slip road, feeder road, filter, one-way system, traffic lights, pedestrian crossing, zebra crossing, panda crossing, pelican crossing **3 personal transport**, walking, shanks's pony, moving pavement, travelator, lift **4 litter**, stretcher, pallet, bier, sedan, horse litter **5 handcart**, cart, pushcart, handbarrow, wheelbarrow, push car, trolley **6 baby carriage**, pram, perambulator, baby walker, baby buggy, pushchair, stroller **7 animal transport**, horse, pack animal, pack horse, mule train, pony express, draught animal, carthorse, draught horse, carriage, dray **8 sled**, sledge, sleigh, toboggan, luge, snowboard, bobsled, jumper, drag, dray, dogsled, troika, motorized sled, snowmobile, bombardier, Sno-Cat, Skimobile **9 bicycle**, bike, cycle, push-bike, roadster, sit-up-and-beg, minibike, trailbike, mountain bike, chopper, hobbyhorse, velocipede, boneshaker, penny-farthing, tandem, tricycle, trike, unicycle, bicycle rickshaw **10 motorcycle**, motorbike, bike, scooter, moped, autocycle, sidecar, autorickshaw **11 bicycle part**, frame, fork, crossbar, wheel, spoke, brake, brake block, crank, pedal, rat trap, toeclip, bicycle chain, chainguard, gear, clanger, derailleur, handlebars, saddle, saddlebag, pannier, kickstand, mudguard, mud flap, bicycle pump **12 cyclist**, bicyclist, motorcyclist **13 car**, motorcar, automobile, auto, runabout, saloon, hatchback, coupé, estate, shooting brake, sports car, convertible **14 police car**, patrol car, squad car, panda car, police van **15 cab**, taxi, taxicab, minicab, hackney cab **16 bus**, omnibus, single decker, double decker, coach, charabanc **17 truck**, lorry, wagon, cart, transporter, articulated vehicle, juggernaut, tractor, trailer **18 miscellaneous motoring terms**, autocade, aquaplaning, automobilia, brakefade, bump start, car alarm, carnet, carsickness, crash barrier, double declutch, double parking, driving licence, endorsement, garage, gas, grab, green card, gritter, handbrake turn, hard standing, hit-and-run accident, hitch-hiker, hot-wiring, immobilizer, jack, joyride, knock-for-knock, lighting-up time, lock, logbook, mileage, misfiring, MOT, motorcade, nearside, no-claims bonus, offside, oversteer, overtaking, parking meter, pile up, piston slap, pit, registration number, road-holding, road test, shimmy, shunt, sideslip, skid, speed trap, stall, tail-spin, tax disc, test drive, three-point turn, tow, traction, trade plate, traffic jam, turning circle, underseal

652 Rotation

NOUNS 1 rotation, revolution, volution, orbit, cycle, full circle, circulation, turbination, circumference, circumrotation, circumnutation, circumvolution, gyration, spin, dizziness, giddiness **2 turning**, whirling, swirling, twirling, spinning, pivoting, pirouetting, wheeling, whir, reeling, centrifugation, rolling, bowling, trolling, trundling, volutation, spiral, twisting, torsion **3 reel**, pirouette, turn, roll, whirl, wheel, swirl, twirl, spin, dance, whirlabout **4 vortex**, whirl, whirlwind, maelstrom, charybdis, cyclone, tornado, whirlpool, eddy, swirl, surge, gurge **5 axle**, axis, shaft, spindle, axlebar, axle-true, axlebox, journal, hotbox, swivel, pivot, gudgeon, trunnion, pole, radiant, fulcrum, pin, pintle, hinge, hingle, rowlock, oarlock, hub, nave, distaff, mandrel, gimbal, bearing, ball bearing, bushing, jewel **6 rotator**, wheel, cartwheel, gearwheel, gear, cog, pinwheel, flywheel, charka, spinning jenny, Ixion's wheel, spinning top, humming top, bobbin, spindle, spool, drill, Archimedes' screw, rotor, circular saw, gyro, gyroscope, autogyro, spin-dryer, centrifuge, ultracentrifuge, impeller, turbine, propeller, prop, screw, airscrew, winder, capstan, extractor fan, turntable, gramophone record, disc, windmill, treadmill, spit, turnspit, whisk, egg beater, food processor, revolving door **7 science of rotation**, gyrostatics

VERBS 8 rotate, revolve, spin, turn, orbit, circle, circulate, circuit, twirl, pirouette, gyre, gyrate, swing, waltz, circumnutate, circumvolve, swing round, spin round, whirl, wheel, pivot, swivel **9 roll**, wind, roll up, fold, scroll, furl, reel, spin, twist, screw, crank, yarn, wamble, roll along, bowl, trundle, troll **10 swirl**, eddy, whirlpool, surge, gurge, seethe, mill around, stir, roil, moil, mix, flounder, wallow, welter

ADJECTIVES 11 rotating, revolving, gyrating, turning, orbiting, swivelling, pivoting, whirling, spinning, swirling, twirling, reeling, wheeling, rolling, trolling **12 rotary**, orbital, pivotal, trochilic, circumrotatory, circumgyratory, gyratory, centrifugal, centripetal, circling, cyclic, circulatory, torsional, vortical, cyclonic, turbinated, vertiginous, dizzy, giddy

653 Roughness

ADJECTIVES 1 rough, rough-hewn, roughcast, unsmooth, textured, rippled, undulatory, wrinkled, crinkled, crinkly, crumpled, rugose, uneven, corrugated, nonuniform, irregular, ruffled, muricate, inequal, rugged, ragged **2 coarse**, rough-grained, cross-grained, grainy, granulated, gravelly, stony, rocky, craggy, scraggly, snaggy, nodose, lumpy, slubbed, hispid, villous, spiny, nubby, studded, knobby, knobbly, knotted, gnarled, knurled, bouclé, shattered, broken, jagged, sharp, serrated, ridged, rough-edged, deckle-edged, corrugated, grated, tweed, potholed, furrowed, rutty, pitted, pockmarked, pimply, scabby, encrusted, scaly, warty, blistered, cracked **3 barbed**, prickly, scratchy, notched, hacked, hairy, unshorn, hirsute, shockheaded, bushy, woolly, flocculent, lanate, furry, matted, curly, frizzy, fuzzy, shaggy, bristly, barbellate, setiform, setose, strigose, hispid, unkempt, unshaven, stubbled, bearded **4 bumpy**, jolting, agitated, turbulent, choppy **5 unfinished**, incomplete, unpolished, unrefined, shapeless, rudimentary, preliminary, cursory, crude, raw, rough-and-ready, sketchy

NOUNS 6 roughness, unsmoothness, wrinkliness, rugosity, unevenness, corrugation, nonuniformity, irregularity, inequality, joltiness, bumpiness, ruggedness, raggedness, granulation, coarseness, cragginess, scraggliness, nodosity, lumpiness, turbulence, choppiness, hispidity, bristliness, horripilation, villosity, spininess, nubbiness, scaliness, scabrousness, hairiness, shagginess, knobbliness, scratchiness, brokenness, jaggedness, serration, saw edge **7 rough thing**, roughcast, sandpaper, glasspaper, emery paper, file, corrugated iron, washboard, grater, steel wool, scrubbing brush, nailbrush, sackcloth, homespun, tweed, linsey-woolsey, corduroy, knot, kink, bouclé, acne, goose flesh, barbed wire, broken glass, splinter, burr, bristle, awn, thistle, prickle, barb, thorn, scale, scab, shag, stubble, five-o'clock shadow, braid, dreadlocks, beard, moustache **8 rough ground**, canyon, mountain, sierra, dirt track, sheeptrack, furrow, rut, crack, undergrowth **9 broken water**, ripple, tidal wave, tsunami, choppy sea, air pocket, hurricane, tornado **10 rough idea**, rough, mock-up, draft, preliminary sketch, unfinished piece, crudeness, incompleteness, shapelessness, rudiment, cursoriness, sketchiness

VERBS 11 be rough, lack uniformity, ripple, crack, chap, have acne, horripilate, bristle, prickle, scale, bump, jolt **12 make rough**, roughcast, rough-hew, ruffle, wrinkle, crease, fold, crinkle, crumple, rumple, corrugate, granulate, coarsen, stud, emboss, break, crack, hack, serrate, crenate, notch, engrail, indent, mill, sandpaper, grate, knot, kink, tousle, tangle, gnarl, pothole **13 be unfinished**, approximate, sketch, draft

654 Roundness

NOUNS 1 roundness, rotundity, orbicularity, sphericity, globosity, gibbousness, convexity **2 round body**, shapeliness, pear shape, fatness, corpulence, obesity, fleshiness, stoutness, plumpness, portliness, paunchiness podginess, tubbiness, chubbiness, pot-belly **3 round thing**, circle, circuit, orbit, sphere, globe, orb, egg, spheroid, hemisphere, ball, bubble, balloon, marble, pellet, bead, pill, pea, bulb, globule **4 cylinder**, roller, rod, rung, tube, cigar, pipe, stalk, trunk, bole, column **5 cone**, cor-

net, horn, trumpet **6 round**, turn, bowl, lap, circuit, chukker, orbit, ambit, circumambulation, circumnavigation, groove **7 round**, part-song **8 round**, live ammunition
ADJECTIVES 9 round, rotund, orbicular, gibbous, spherical, globose, convex, egg-shaped, ovoid, cylindrical, tubular, conical, bell-shaped, bulbous, spherelike **10 well-rounded**, pear-shaped, shapely, fleshy, fat, overweight, obese, corpulent, stout, plump, portly, paunchy, podgy, tubby, chubby
VERBS 11 make round, roll, smooth, turn, balloon out, coil up, roll up, ball, round off **12 move round**, orbit, circle, circulate, circumambulate

655 Rule

- *The exception proves the rule.* Saying.
- *The golden rule is that there are no golden rules.* George Bernard Shaw.

NOUNS 1 rule, regulation, law, directive, injunction, statute, bylaw, order, prescription, decree, edict, ukase, fiat, commandment, act, covenant, ordinance **2 canon**, code, rulebook, constitution, charter **3 rule** (*or* **law**) **of nature**, sod's law, Murphy's law, Parkinson's law, natural law **4 guide**, direction, instruction, prescription, precept, principle, tenet, keynote, axiom, maxim, canon, norm, standard, criterion **5 precedent**, forerunner, example, model, pattern, prototype **6 custom**, habit, convention, tradition, wont, praxis, way, method, system, practice, procedure, routine, drill, rut, groove, policy **7 uniformity**, constancy, consistency, regularity **8 authority**, command, direction, management, administration, influence, control, sway, dominion, domination, power, supremacy, mastery
ADJECTIVES 9 legal, statutory, mandatory, compulsory, obligatory, de rigueur, regulatory, injunctive, prescriptive, procedural, administrative **10 customary**, habitual, accustomed, wonted, conventional, traditional, regulation, standard, routine, usual, normal, typical, copybook, regulated, methodical, systematic **11 uniform**, constant, consistent, regular **12 ruling**, authoritative, commanding, influential, controlling, powerful, dominant, supreme, masterful
VERBS 13 rule, ordain, decree, prescribe, lay down, decide, determine, adjudicate, judge, deem, find, resolve, settle, pronounce, declare **14 regulate**, standardize, normalize, systematize, organize **15 be the rule**, hold sway, prevail **16 direct**, guide, steer, control, regulate, lead, administer, manage, run, superintend, supervise, oversee, govern, dominate, command **17 obey orders**,

656 Safety

NOUNS 1 safety, security, protection, invulnerability, impregnability, immunity, harmlessness, avoidance, welfare, guarantee, warranty, certainty, assurance, confidence, faith, rescue **2 protection**, safeguard, precaution, vetting, surveillance, passport, pass, permit, escort, convoy, guard, defence, bulwark, bastion, moat, ditch, palisade, stockade, haven, sanctuary, asylum, refuge, shelter, orphanage, care, keeping, custody, charge, safekeeping, grasp, grip, embrace, ward, patronage, support, aid, sponsorship, auspices, aegis, tutelage, protectorate, guardianship, wardship, custodianship, surrogacy, anchor, shield, breastplate, panoply, armour, deterrent, weapon, hygiene, immunization, vaccination, inoculation, prophylaxis, contraception, quarantine, isolation, segregation, seclusion, insurance, surety, buffer, cushion, screen, cover, umbrella, shelter, savings, collateral, provision **3 protector**, guardian, mentor, tutor, patron, benefactor, champion, chaperon, governess, duenna, nurse, nanny, baby-sitter, child-minder, companion, keeper, defender, preserver, shepherd, coastguard, lifeguard, lifesaver, bodyguard, minder, doorman, vigilante, conservator, custodian, curator, warden, warder, watcher, surveillant, lookout, watchman, guard, sentry, sentinel, garrison, picket, vanguard, militia, gamekeeper, forester, firewatcher, fireman, police, detective, patrolman, sheriff, watchdog, Cerberus **4 safety device**, protection, precautions, alarm, guardrail, railing, mail, chainmail, armour, toughened glass, deterrent, respirator, mask, ear muffs, bolt, deadlock, lightning conductor, fuse, earth, fire alarm, safety helmet, seat belt, escape hatch, parachute, lifeboat, life buoy, lifeline, lead, reins, brake, fetter, bar, lock, key, stopper, ballast, breakwater, groyne, embankment, seawall, harbour, lighthouse, lightship

ADJECTIVES 5 safe, secure, protected, guarded, defended, assured, sure, certain, sound, snug, spared, preserved, intact, undamaged, unharmed, uninjured, unhurt, unscathed, garrisoned, well-defended, insured, covered, immunized, vaccinated, inoculated, disinfected, salubrious, hygienic, in harbour, clear, unaccused, unthreatened, unmolested, unexposed, sheltered, shielded, screened, patronized, imprisoned, reliable, dependable, trustworthy, guaranteed, warranted, benign, innocent, tame, harmless, innocuous, unthreatening, risk-free, unhazardous, nonflammable, nontoxic, unpolluted, edible, drinkable **6 invulnerable**, immune, impregnable, sacrosanct, inexpugnable, unassailable, unattackable, ungettable, unbreakable, unchallengeable, defensible, tenable, strong, proof, foolproof, fail-safe, mothproof, childproof, weatherproof, waterproof, showerproof, leakproof, rustproof, fireproof, shatterproof, bulletproof, bombproof, armoured, steel-clad, panoplied, snug, tight, seaworthy, airworthy, shrink-wrapped, vacuum-packed, freeze-dried **7 tutelary**, protective, custodial, guardian, surrogate, shepherdlike, watchful, vigilant, keeping, guarding, protecting, preserving, prophylactic, antiseptic

VERBS 8 be safe, protect oneself, take precautions, demand assurances, survive, escape, take refuge, hide, lie low **9 protect**, safeguard, defend, spare, support, champion, vouch for, shield, harbour, rescue, deliver, patronize, keep, conserve, preserve, store, hide, conceal, house, shelter, imprison, ward, care for, mind, mother, nurse, tend, foster, cherish, monitor, chaperon, immunize, inoculate, vaccinate, pasteurize, fluorinate, disinfect, sanitize, assure, promise, guarantee, cushion, buffer, ensconce, enfold, embrace, envelop, enclose, insulate, cover, shade, screen, secure, fortify, strengthen, entrench, armour, convoy, escort, shepherd, flank

657 Sale

VERBS 1 sell, vend, transfer, convey, market, merchandise, deal, trade, barter, exchange, unload, dump, hawk, peddle, push, promote, canvass, solicit, tout, auction, wholesale, retail, handle, carry, stock, realize, encash, gain, lose, undercut, reduce **2 be sold**, change hands

NOUNS 3 selling, vending, disposal, transfer, conveyance, transaction, deal, marketing, merchandising, distribution, promotion, advertisement, traffic, trade, dealing, barter, exchange, trafficking, peddling, canvassing, soliciting, auction, wholesale, retail, simony, monopoly **4 sale**, sell-out, summer sale, clearance, closing-down sale, jumble sale, garage sale, carboot sale, bazaar **5 sales**, boom, recession **6 salesmanship**, service, pitch, sales patter, spiel, hard sell **7 market**, product testing, marketability, salability **8 merchandise**, product, article, vendible, line, range, repertoire, store, best-seller, loss-leader, staple, commodity, stock, supplies, wares, goods, durables, perishables, sundries, freight, load **9 seller**, vendor, consignor, transferor, bear **10 salesman**, shop assistant, shopwalker, representative, rep, agent **11 pedlar**, rag-and-bone man, hawker, tinker, Gypsy, traveller, huckster, colporteur, costermonger, barrow boy, market trader **12 wholesaler**, marketer, merchandiser, merchant, businessman, entrepreneur, speculator, operator, monopolist, oligopolist, importer, exporter, dealer, middleman, broker, jobber, financier, banker, moneylender, cambist, procurer, trafficker **13 retailer**, middleman, regrater, shopkeeper, storekeeper, dealer, merchant, tradesman, monger, florist, milliner, tailor, mercer, haberdasher, grocer, greengrocer, provisioner, butcher, baker

ADJECTIVES 14 saleable, vendible, marketable, merchantable **15 sold**, in demand

658 Sameness

NOUNS 1 sameness, selfsameness, uniformity, identicalness, isotrophy, indistinguishability, oneness, unity, solidarity, mergence, coalescence, assimilation, agreement, repetition, redundancy, tautology, verbatim, homoousia **2 equivalence**, correspondence, concordance, accordance, harmony, agreement, congruence, equipollence, interchangeability, reciprocation, representation, similarity, homoiousia, parallelism, coincidence, synchronicity, synonymousness, homogeneity, homonym, homograph, homophone, analogy, analogue, simile, metaphor, reflection **3 lookalike**, double, doppelgänger, alter ego, ka, ba, twin, homophyly, reflection, pair, match, suit, portrait **4 duplicate**, triplicate, imitation, copy, photocopy, microcopy, facsimile, photograph, print, offprint, reproduction, impression, hologram, replica, representation, model, mould, stamp **5 equality**, parity, symmetry, balance, equilibration, equiponderance, impartiality, justice, par, tie, draw, deuce, stalemate, deadlock **6 regularity**, routine, constancy, changelessness, smoothness, evenness, levelness, equilibrium, homeostasis, homogeneity, consistency, invariability, uniformity, standardization, conformity, monotonousness, repetition, flatness, treadmill

VERBS 7 be the same, be identical, correspond, agree, harmonize, merge, coalesce, coincide, match, tally, answer, interchange, reciprocate, imitate, shadow, reflect, repeat **8 make the same**, unify, unite, join, merge, homogenize, coalesce, assimilate, synthesize, synchronize, consubstantiate, parallel, equate, pair, twin, symmetrize, balance, smooth, level, flatten, even up, stereotype, standardize, regulate, phase, mass-produce, automate **9 duplicate**, triplicate, copy, imitate, ape, photocopy, fax, photograph, shoot, enlarge, print, reproduce, replicate, mould **10 be equal**, match, balance, equiponderate, equilibrate, stalemate, deadlock, break even **11 be regular**, repeat, iterate, persist, drag on, harp on, hum, drone

ADJECTIVES 12 same, selfsame, identical, isotrophic, indistinguishable, undifferentiated, repetitious, unvarying, repeated, redundant, verbatim, united, solid, one, homogeneous, merging, absorbed, coalescent, assimilated, agreed, consubstantial **13 equivalent**, corresponding, concordant, accordant, harmonious, agreeing, congruent, equipollent, interchangeable, reciprocal, representative, parallel, similar, homoiousian, coincidental, synchronous, synonymous, homogeneous, homographic, homonymic, homophonic, analogous, reflective **14 lookalike**, twin, homophyllic, matching, like, paired **15 duplicate**, triplicate, copied, faxed, photographic, reprinted, offprinted, reproduced, holographic, replicated, moulded **16 equal**, coequal, symmetrical, balanced, equiponderant, equidistant, level, impartial, par, tied, drawn, love-all, stalemated, deadlocked, neck-and-neck **17 regular**, clockwork, routine, hourly, daily, weekly, monthly, yearly, annual, constant, smooth, steady, even, level, changeless, homeostatic, homogenous, consistent, unvariable, unaltered, invariant, unchanging, undeviating, undiversified, uniform, flat, standardized, conforming, mundane, repetitive, monotonous

659 Same Time

NOUNS 1 same time, simultaneity, contemporaneousness, coevality, accompaniment, coexistence, concomitance, concurrence **2 present time**, today **3 synchronism**, isochronism **4 equal race**, dead heat, tie **5 contemporary**, coeval, compeer, friend, classmate, brother, sister

VERBS 6 be simultaneous, coexist, accompany, concur, coincide **7 synchronize**, chorus **8 run equally**, tie

ADJECTIVES 9 simultaneous, coeval, contemporary, coexistent, coeternal, concomitant, coincident, concurrent, photo-finish, accompanying **10 synchronized**, isochronal, timed, phased, in time **11 equal**, level

660 Sanity

NOUNS 1 sanity, stability, normality **2 rationality**, reasonableness, intelligibility, lucidity, coherence, common sense, wits **3 sane person**, Mr Normal

ADJECTIVES 4 sane, normal **5 rational**, reasonable, coherent, intelligible, lucid, clear-headed, balanced, level-headed, stable, steady, sound, sensible

VERBS 6 be sane, ratiocinate

661 Satisfaction

NOUNS 1 satisfaction, fulfilment, gratification, thankfulness, contentedness, serenity, equanimity, happiness, pleasure, enjoyment, comfort, ease, satiation, smugness **2 reparation**, recompense, compensation, atonement, amends, apology, indemnity, expiation, reconciliation, appeasement **3 satisfactoriness**, sufficiency

ADJECTIVES 4 satisfied, fulfilled, gratified, thankful, content, serene, uncomplaining, undemanding, secure, safe, happy, pleased, satiated, full, comfortable, smug **5 satisfying**, fulfilling, gratifying, pleasing, pacifying, comforting, satiating, filling **6 satisfactory**, sufficient, enough, adequate, acceptable, passable

VERBS 7 be satisfied, delight in **8 satisfy**, gratify, fulfil, content, please, indulge, satiate, sate, fill, quench **9 comfort**, pacify, placate, lull, appease, reassure, assure, convince **10 suffice**, serve, do, answer **11 recompense**, compensate, atone, make amends, apologize, indemnify, expiate, reconcile

662 Seas

NOUNS 1 sea, ocean, seven seas, the deep, high seas, ocean blue, main, the billow, brine, ocean floor **2 tide**, tidal current, tidal flow, riptide, high water, spring tide, equinoctial tide, ebb tide, rising tide, flood, low water, neap tide, thalassometer **3 wave**, billow, swell, surge, heave, undulation, waviness, wavelet, ripple, spume, foam, froth, surf, breaker, roller, white horses, choppy sea, eagre, tidal wave, tsunami **4 oceanography**, thalassography, hydrography, bathymetry

ADJECTIVES 5 oceanic, nautical, tidal, briny, billowing, swelling, surging, breaking, rolling, choppy, turbulent, marine, maritime, ocean-going, seaworthy, seafaring, submarine, subaquatic, thalassic, pelagic, estuarine, littoral, sublittoral, intertidal, abyssal **6 oceanographic(al)**

VERBS 7 billow, swell, surge, undulate, ripple, foam, froth

663 Season

NOUNS 1 season, period, spell, term **2 spring**, springtime, vernal season, seedtime, Easter, budtime **3 summer**, summertime, summertide, Whitsuntide, midsummer, Midsummer Day, dog days, haymaking, Indian summer **4 autumn**, harvest, harvest moon, hunter's moon **5 winter**, wintertime, midwinter, Christmas, the Season

VERBS 6 spend the season, summer, winter, overwinter **7 season**, harden, anneal, inure, discipline, toughen, mature, acclimatize **8 mitigate**, temper, leaven

ADJECTIVES 9 seasonal, equinoctial **10 spring**, vernal, flowery, sappy, juicy **11 summer**, aestival **12 autumn**, golden **13 winter**, hibernal, midwinter, hiemal **14 seasonable**, appropriate, suitable, convenient, timely, well-timed, welcome, providential **15 seasoned**, hardened, toughened, matured, inured **16 mitigated**, tempered, leavened, mollified **17 in season**, in heat, oestrous

664 Secrecy

- *Stolen waters are sweet, and bread eaten in secret is pleasant.* Bible: Proverbs.
- *O fie miss, you must not kiss and tell.* William Congreve.

NOUNS 1 secrecy, silence, privacy, confidentiality, classified information, censorship, blackout, suppression, misinformation, concealment **2 secretiveness**, stealth, furtiveness, clandestineness, shiftiness, covertness, espionage, counterintelligence, spy, mole, intrigue, plot, conspiracy **3 mystification**, mystery, enigma, puzzle, problem, poser, intricacy, complexity **4 brain-teaser**, brain-twister, charade, Chinese puzzle, tangram, maze, labyrinth, crossword, anagram, acrostic, riddle, conundrum, rebus, cipher, code, cryptogram, coder, decoder **5 anonymity**, Unknown Warrior, invisible man, code name, X, Anon., stage name, pen name

ADJECTIVES 6 secret, private, privy, intimate, confidential, closed, secluded, sealed, isolated, unrevealed, undisclosed, undivulged, unspoken, untold, top-secret, classified, restricted, censored, suppressed **7 secretive**, silent, close, reticent, surreptitious, stealthy, furtive, sly, clandestine, covert, undercover, underhand, conspirational **8 mysterious**, enigmatic, inscrutable, unknowable, esoteric, cabbalistic, arcane, occult, abstruse, mystifying, confusing, bewildering, puzzling, perplexing, unresolved, unintelligible, problematic, complex, intricate, labyrinthine, difficult, knotty, cryptic, hidden, concealed, camouflaged, disguised, incognito

VERBS 9 keep secret, conceal, hide, withhold, suppress, gag, whitewash, censor, seal, ban, restrict, classify, keep mum, hush up **10 mystify**, puzzle, baffle, perplex, bewilder, confuse **11 make mysterious**, obscure, obfuscate

665 Secretion

NOUNS 1 secretion, exudation, emission, transudation, excretion, discharge, release, voidance, ejection, emanation, securnment, lactation, lacrimation, crying, weeping, guttation, salivation, sweating **2 secreted substance**, secretion, hormone, chalone, digestive juice, bile, gall, mucus, phlegm, sputum, saliva, tears, rheum, semen, milk, colostrum, sweat, sebum, musk, pheromone, honeydew, nectar, latex, resin, tannin **3 gland**, nectary, laticifer, hydathode

ADJECTIVES 4 secretory, exudative, transudatory, emissive, excretory, emanative, glandular, merocrine, eccrine, apocrine, holocrine, secreting, lactating, lactiferous, lacrimatory, crying, weeping, sebaceous, sebiferous, sweating, sudatory **5 of a secretion**, glandular, hormonal, endocrine, adrenal, ovarian, testicular, seminal, pineal, pituitary, placental, luteal, thyroidal, exocrine, eccrine, lacrimal, mammary, lacteal, mucous, mucoid, sudoral, sebaceous, salivary, parotid, sialoid, gastric, pyloric, pancreatic **6 inducing secretion**, lactogenic, sialogogic, lacrimatory, sudatory

VERBS 7 secrete, exude, transude, produce, emit, excrete, discharge, release, liberate, void, eject, emanate, secern, produce, lactate, lacrimate, cry, weep, salivate

666 Security

NOUNS 1 protection, safety, invulnerability, impregnability, immunity, asylum, sanctuary, shelter, refuge, cover, mainstay, anchor, support, hope, defence, safeguard, shield, deterrent, reliance, faith, confidence, courage, insurance **2 promise**, pledge, word, assurance, insurance, credit, honour, recognizance, warrant, guarantee, underwriting, certificate, bond, coupon, passport, visa, permit, authority, authorization, share, debenture, mortgage, deed, insurance policy, will, collateral, indemnity, covenant, receipt, IOU, counterfoil, stub, ticket, docket, acquittance, quittance, authentication, verification, endorsement, stamp, seal **3 safe**, lockbox

ADJECTIVES 4 secure, safe, sure, protective, sheltered, invulnerable, impregnable, immune, safeguarded, shielded **5 guaranteed**, warranted, certified, authenticated, assured, certain, reliant, unshaken, gilt-edged, covered, insured, mortgaged, guaranteed, covenanted, pledged, promised **6 accomplished**, done, won **7 fast**, fixed, sound, steadfast, stable, steady

VERBS 8 secure, protect, police, patrol, guard, shelter, safekeep, lock away, anchor, support, defend, safeguard **9 promise**, pledge, assure, insure, warrant, guarantee, stand surety, stand bail, vouch for, endorse, seal, stamp, countersign, indemnify, underwrite **10 certify**, authenticate, cover, insure, mortgage, pledge, promise **11 secure one's objective**, accomplish, win, succeed **12 make fast**, fortify, stabilize, steady, strengthen, fix to, nail down, screw down **13 reserve**, book

667 Selection

VERBS 1 select, choose, decide, determine, plump for, opt, accept, adopt, coopt **2 prefer**, like best, favour, fancy, incline, lean, tend **3 side with**, back, support, endorse, embrace, espouse, take sides **4 pick**, single out, pass, approve, recommend, propose, nominate, second, appoint, commission, designate, delegate, detail, highlight, preselect, earmark, reserve, distinguish, identify, separate, isolate, abstract, excerpt, cull, anthologize, glean, winnow, sift, skim

NOUNS 5 selection, choice, decision, determination, judgment, discretion, discrimination, eclecticism, finickiness, fastidiousness, adoption, cooption, nomination, appointment, commission, designation, pick, variety, range **6 preference**, predilection, partiality, inclination, leaning, tendency, prejudice, bias, favouritism, taste, liking, favour, fancy, preferability **7 choice**, option, alternative, dilemma, Hobson's choice **8 chosen thing**, pick, selection, assortment, gleanings, excerpts

ADJECTIVES 9 selecting, choosing, deciding, decisive, eclectic, optional, discretional, volitional, exercising choice, selective, particular, discriminating, discerning, showing preference, preferential **10 chosen**, selected, picked, sorted, assorted, seeded, well-chosen, worth choosing, select, choice, A-1, recherché, hand-picked, elite, elect, designate, elected, returned, adopted, deselected, on approval, preferable, better, desirable, advisable, preferred, special, favourite, fancy, pet, God's own **11 elective**, electoral, voting, enfranchised, vote-catching, electioneering

668 Self-Indulgence

NOUNS 1 self-indulgence, self-gratification, hedonism, sybaritism, epicureanism, luxury, sensuality, voluptuousness **2 dissipation**, dissoluteness, licentiousness, debauchery, profligacy, carousal, orgy **3 overindulgence**, immoderation, uncontrol, unrestraint, abandon, indiscipline, inordinateness, overdoing, excess, incontinence, concupiscence, intemperance, drunkenness, crapulence, addiction, overeating, greed, gluttony, gourmandizing, extravagance, wastefulness **4 self-absorption**, self-obsession, self-devotion, self-worship, self-love, narcissism, vanity, self-centredness

ADJECTIVES 5 self-indulgent, self-gratifying, pleasure-seeking, hedonistic, sybaritic, epicurean, sensual, voluptuous **6 dissipated**, dissolute, riotous, fast-living, high-living, free-living, licentious, debauched **7 overindulgent**, immoderate, uncontrolled, unrestrained, undisciplined, abandoned, inordinate, excessive, incontinent, concupiscent, intemperate, drunk, crapulent, addicted, greedy, gluttonous, gourmandizing, extravagant, wasteful **8 self-absorbed**, self-obsessed, self-devoted, self-worshipping, self-loving, narcissistic, vain, self-centred

VERBS 9 indulge oneself, luxuriate in **10 overindulge**, overdo, waste, squander, dissipate, gorge

669 Selfishness

NOUNS 1 selfishness, self-interest, self-pity, self-preservation, self-indulgence, self-serving, self-seeking, possessiveness, covetousness, jealousy, envy, avarice, acquisitiveness, mundaneness, materialism, greed, ambition, careerism, opportunism, individualism, stinginess, miserliness, niggardliness, meanness **2 egoism**, ego, conceit, vanity, self-love, narcissism, self-centredness

ADJECTIVES 3 selfish, self-indulgent, self-interested, self-seeking, possessive, covetous, jealous, envious, avaricious, acquisitive, materialistic, ambitious, greedy, monopolistic, opportunistic, individualistic, ungenerous, uncharitable, stingy, miserly, niggardly, mean, mean-spirited, parsimonious **4 egoistic**, conceited, vain, narcissistic, self-loving, self-absorbed

VERBS 5 be selfish, indulge oneself, have ambition, covet, envy, acquire, monopolize, possess **6 be egoistic**, love oneself

670 Self-Restraint

NOUNS 1 self-restraint, self-control, self-discipline, self-denial, self-abnegation, constraint, restriction, repression, avoidance, eschewal, forbearance, renunciation, relinquishment, refrainment, abstaining, abstemiousness, ascesis, celibacy, chastity, purity, continence, temperance, soberness, teetotalism, prohibition, dieting, vegetarianism, veganism, fasting, asceticism, Spartanism, frugality, parsimony, economy, plainness **2 moderation**, prudence, reasonableness, happy medium **3 calmness**, composure

VERBS 4 be self-restrained, refrain, abstain, repress, retard, avoid, eschew, forbear, renounce, relinquish, forgo, ban, curb, brake, veto, temper, diet, starve, fast **5 moderate**, circumscribe **6 be calm**, lack emotion

ADJECTIVES 7 self-restrained, self-controlled, self-disciplined, self-denying, restrictive, strict, repressive, prohibited, renunciative, relinquished, restrained, refraining, forbearing, abstaining, abstemious, celibate, continent, chaste, pure, temperate, sober, teetotal, dieting, fasting, Lenten, ascetic, plain, frugal, economical, parsimonious, stinting, sparing, costive **8 moderate**, prudent, reasonable, measured, circumscribed, confined **9 calm**, composed

671 Semiliquid

NOUNS 1 semiliquid, semifluid, emulsion, emulsoid, colloid, paste **2 semiliquidity**, semifluidity, erassitude, spissitude, viscosity, viscidity **3 muddiness**, slushiness, sloppiness, ooziness, miriness, turbidity **4 pulpiness**, sponginess, doughiness, pastiness, pithiness, squashiness, stodginess, sogginess, mushiness, flabbiness, creaminess, juiciness, succulence, fleshiness, sappiness **5 pulping**, pulpification, blending, steeping, maceration, mastication **6 thickening**, coagulation, curdling, clotting, gelation, inspissation, incrassation, emulsification **7 soup**, stew, gravy, gruel, porridge, slops **8 pulp**, purée, pap, mush, stodge, squash, dough, bonnyclabber, curd, paste, mousse, fool, pudding, pith, junket, jelly, gel, gelatin, agar, aspic, jam, treacle, syrup, rob **9 mucus**, mucilage, phlegm, pituita, clot, grume, gore, pus, glue, size, gluten, albumen **10 mud**, slush, muck, sludge, slop, ooze, slime, mire, swill, silt, sediment, grounds, dirt, dregs, lees, puddle, mudhole, chughole **11 pulper**, macerator, blender, masher, pulp engine, food processor, thickener

ADJECTIVES 12 semiliquid, semifluid, emulsive, colloidal, sticky, pasty, slimy, incrassate, inspissate, viscous **13 muddy**, slushy, sludgy, squelchy, sloppy, oozy, miry, turbid, dirty, waterlogged, marshy, silty **14 pulpy**, spongy, doughy, squashy, stodgy, soggy, mushy, flabby, creamy, soupy, starchy **15 juicy**, succulent, fleshy, sappy, overripe, runny, watery, milky **16 thick**, thickened, coagulated, curdled, clotted **17 gelatinous**, jelly-like, treacly **18 mucilaginous**, gluey, glutinous

VERBS 19 pulp, purée, mash **20 thicken**, curdle, clot, churn, congeal, emulsify, inspissate, incrassate **21 gelatinize**, gelatinify

672 Sensation

NOUNS 1 sensation, feeling, awareness, sentience, perception, experience, impression, sensum, response, reaction, receptivity, consciousness, emotion, sentiment, sight, hearing, touch, taste, smell, sixth sense, ESP, telepathy, clairvoyance, agitation, excitement **2 ability to sense**, sensitivity, feelings, susceptibility, irritability, tenderness, thin skin, vulnerability, hyperaesthesia, prickliness, ticklishness, touchiness, delicacy, sensuousness, warm-bloodedness, over-sensitivity **3 stimulus**, goad, prick, stimulant, heightener, thrill, throb, prickle, tingle, frisson, fluttering, buzz, kick, tickle, itch, horripilation, gooseflesh, formication

ADJECTIVES 4 sensible, sensitive, aware, sentient, feeling **5 conscious**, awake, sleepless **6 susceptible**, impressionable, perceptive, responsive, over-sensitive, allergic, thin-skinned, delicate, tender, touchy, irritable, tetchy, jumpy, excited, temperamental, agitated, irritated, thrilled, stirred, hyperactive, hot-blooded, carnal, epicurean, sensuous **7 sensate**, perceptible, tactile, palpable, tangible, audible, visible **8 exciting**, sensational, titillating, thrilling, stimulating, keen, breath-taking, impressive, stirring, emotive, poignant, striking, electric, hair-raising, itchy, prickly, tingly **9 sensory**, nervous

VERBS 10 sense, respond, react, tingle, prickle, tickle, itch, be irritated, have goose-pimples, horripilate, detect, feel, perceive, see, hear, touch, taste, smell, realize **11 awake**, regain consciousness **12 arouse sensation**, wake, enliven, activate, stir, disturb, agitate, impress, invigorate, quicken, animate, stimulate, titillate, whet, galvanize, thrill, excite

673 Sensitivity

ADJECTIVES 1 sensitive, impressionable, suggestible, impressible, susceptible, affectible, receptive, responsive, perceptive, sentient, feeling, delicate, aware, empathetic, sympathetic, compassionate, caring, tender, soft-hearted, emotional **2 oversensitive**, touchy, irritable, irascible, thin-skinned, highly strung, temperamental, nervy **3 sore**, painful, raw, tender, allergic, sensitized, ticklish, itchy **4 accurate**, precise

NOUNS 5 sensitiveness, sensibility, impressionability, suggestibility, impressibility, susceptibility, affectibility, receptivity, responsiveness, awareness, delicacy, tenderness, empathy, sympathy, commiseration, compassion, pity **6 oversensitivity**, touchiness, irritability, irascibility, raw feelings **7 soreness**, rawness, tenderness, ticklishness, allergy, itchiness **8 accuracy**, precision

VERBS 9 be sensitive, feel for, pity, sympathize

674 Separation

NOUNS 1 separation, disconnection, disunion, discontinuity, disjunction, dislocation, separability, disintegration, breakage, breakup, dispersion, scattering, dissolution, decomposition, breakdown, dissection, analysis, resolution, disruption, fragmentation, shattering, splitting, fission, separating, parting, severance, uncoupling, divorce, divergence, spreading, deviation, split, schism, detachment, unfastening, loosening **2 setting apart**, ejection, expulsion, exception, exemption, rejection, boycott, avoidance, exclusion, selection, choice, division, severance, discrimination, apartheid, segregation, zoning, compartment, no-go area, ghetto, cage, prison, isolation, loneliness, seclusion, quarantine, conservation, preservation, reservation, deprivation, expropriation, removal, withdrawal, resignation, retirement, nonattachment, nonalignment **3 separateness**, immiscibility, severalty, separatism, nationalism, isolationism, difference, dichotomy, division, segmentation, partition, cutting, scission, section, break, tear, laceration, rip, rent, fissure, split, gap, breach, rift, crack, cleft, chasm, cleavage, slit, slot, gash, incision, hole, rupture, opening, ladder, abscission, decapitation, amputation, castration, curtailment, retrenchment **4 disunity**, disagreement, dissension, opposition, hostility **5 separator**, dividing line, caesura, comma, slash, solidus, dash, hyphen, partition, diaeresis, umlaut **6 boundary**, fence, hedge, wall, ha-ha, screen, curtain, limit, frontier **7 separates**, coordinates

VERBS 8 separate, part, sever, break, fracture, chip, crack, rupture, snap, disunite, dissociate, divorce, unhitch, uncouple, disconnect, unplug, disengage, displace, wrench, dislocate, detach, unseat, throw, untie, unfasten, undo, unbutton, unclasp, unzip, unlock, unbind, unfetter, disentangle, unravel, unpick, ladder, loosen, slacken, relax, liberate, release, eject, expel, dispel, scatter, disband, demobilize, disperse, disintegrate, break up, cannibalize, slit, split, rive, cleave, rend, tear, rip, lacerate, hack, hew, cut, chop, stab, slash, gash, saw, slice, shred, mince, mash, grind, crunch, bite, carve up, disassemble, dismantle, dissolve, decompose, decay, degrade, blow up, smash, shatter, shiver, splinter, crumble, pulverize **9 set apart**, store, conserve, preserve, reserve, select, sort, distinguish, differentiate, discern, discriminate, exclude, except, boycott, ban, bar, blacklist, banish, ostracize, isolate, insulate, remove, detract, subtract, deduct, strip, denude, peel, pare, flake, skin, flay, shear, clip, pluck, decapitate, amputate, curtail, dock, lop **10 divide**, sectionalize, segment, fragment, fractionalize, factorize, analyse, anatomize, dissect, bisect, halve, apportion, dismember, quarter, partition, compartmentalize, circumscribe, segregate, sequester, seclude, quarantine, maroon, estrange, alienate **11 disagree**, dissent **12 diverge**, depart, scatter, disperse, deviate, bifurcate, part, escape, quit, leave, relinquish **13 come between**, divide

ADJECTIVES 14 separate, disunited, disjointed, disjunctive, dislocated, divorced, disconnected, unplugged, unstuck, untied, undone, unzipped, loosened, liberated, released, expelled, ejected, unfettered, unchained, free, discontinuous, partitioned, bipartite, multipartite, dichotomous, dividing, halved, quartered, dismembered, disembowelled, cut, torn, severed **15 apart**, asunder, broken, shattered, split, schizoid, rent, riven, cloven, cleft, dispersed, scattered, fugitive, divergent **16 unjoined**, unfastened, adrift, detached, nonaligned, neutral, discrete, distinct, differentiated, separative, excluded, excepted, exempt, abstracted, withdrawn, uninvolved, unmixed, immiscible, unassimilated, unrelated, alien, foreign, external, extrinsic, self-sufficient, insular, isolated, secluded, lonely, alone, left, abandoned, rejected, selective **17 disagreeable**, unharmonious, dissenting, hostile, adverse, opposite, antipathetic **18 separable**, severable, partiable, divisible, fissionable, scissile, tearable, dissolvable, discernible, distinguishable

675 Sequence

NOUNS 1 sequence, succession, consecutiveness, progression, procession, serialization **2 series**, chain, string, train, line, run, course, cycle, rotation **3 continuity**, extension, prolongation, protraction, follow-through, segue **4 sequel**, continuation, series, saga **5 consequence**, sequel, effect, result, product, outcome **6 aftermath**, afterglow, aftertaste, legacy, byproduct, spin-off, fallout **7 afterthought**, second thoughts **8 addition**, insert, supplement, adjunct, addendum, codicil, appendix, conclusion, afterword, refrain, chorus, coda, postlude, subscript, suffixation, subjunction **9 conclusion**, end, finish, completion, termination, last words, parting shot **10 rear**, back, posterior, tail, train, trail, wake

ADJECTIVES 11 sequential, succeeding, successional, following, serial, consecutive, sequacious, continuous **12 alternating**, every other, antiphonal **13 next**, near, later, latter **14 consequent**, resulting, ensuing **15 additional**, supplementary, appendant, suffixed, postpositive, postpositional **16 rear**, back, last, end, posterior

VERBS 17 follow in sequence, segue **18 succeed**, inherit, supersede, supplant, usurp, substitute, replace **19 follow close**, trail **20 result**, ensue, arise, spring, emanate, issue, flow **21 bring up the rear**, lag, dawdle

676 Seriousness

ADJECTIVES 1 solemn, grave, serious, thoughtful, pensive, sedate, staid, sober, stern, severe, unsmiling, straight-faced, grim, poker-faced, stony-faced, deadpan, humourless, sombre, dour, sullen, glum, long-faced **2 earnest**, sincere, genuine, resolute, determined, purposeful, intent, dedicated, committed, eager **3 important**, significant, serious, weighty, momentous, crucial, vital, life-and-death, critical, dangerous

NOUNS 4 solemnity, gravity, gravitas, thoughtfulness, staidness, sternness, severity, grimness, humourlessness, dourness, sullenness **5 earnestness**, sincerity, resolution, determination, dedication, commitment, eagerness **6 importance**, significance, consequence, weightiness, momentousness, moment

VERBS 7 be serious, frown, glare

677 Servant

NOUNS 1 servant, help, retainer, domestic, worker, farmhand, labourer, handyman, employee, assistant, subordinate, subaltern, attendant, orderly, factotum, follower, henchman, liegeman, menial, underling, hireling, inferior, minion, flunky, lackey **2 attendant**, usher, maitre d'hotel, maid, valet, butler, batman, hostess, waiter, waitress, steward, sommelier, stewardess, potboy, page, porter, caddie, caretaker, concierge **3 personal attendant**, companion, confidante, nurse, nursemaid, au pair, governess, nanny, chaperon, driver, chauffeur, batman, bodyguard, henchman, tutor, barber, hairdresser, masseur **4 office assistant**, secretary, clerk, man Friday, tea lady, messenger, runner, courier, employee **5 domestic servant**, domestic, steward, housekeeper, chamberlain, butler, major-domo, cook, maid, maidservant, housemaid, parlourmaid, chambermaid, nursemaid, nannie, au pair, house boy, handmaiden, lady-in-waiting, gentleman's gentleman, manservant, dishwasher, daily help, charwoman, chauffeur, driver, gardener, footman, stableboy, groom **6 slave**, serf, slave-girl, bondservant, thrall

VERBS 7 serve, work for, help, tend, look after, minister to, assist, clean for, accompany, follow, oblige

ADJECTIVES 8 serving, attending, helping, ministering, aiding, obedient, menial, subject, servile

678 Servility

NOUNS 1 servility, slavishness, deference, compliance, pliancy, subservience, menialness, abjectness, submission, slavery, serfdom, helotism **2 sycophancy**, obsequiousness, fawning, grovelling, toadying, sponging, parasitism, cringing, bootlicking, backscratching, time-serving, obeisance, prostration, mealymouthing, crawling, bowing-and-scraping, ingratiation, truckling **3 sycophant**, toady, time-server, creep, crawler, bootlicker, groveller, suck, mealymouth, yes-man, smoothie, lapdog, poodle, creature, cat's paw, dupe, stooge, doormat, instrument, puppet, minion, lackie, slave **4 adherent**, hanger-on, follower, appendage, satellite, dangler, dependent, shadow, collaborator

ADJECTIVES 5 servile, slavish, deferential, compliant, subservient, menial, abject, submissive **6 sycophantic**, obsequious, flattering, fawning, grovelling, toadying, sponging, parasitic, cringing, footlicking, bootlicking, backscratching, apple-polishing, handshaking, time-serving, obeisant, prostrate, mealymouthed, crawling, ingratiating, truckling, soft-soaping, smarmy, whining, free-loading, cringing, cowering, snivelling, leechlike, beggarly, hangdog, kowtowing, bowing, scraping, crawling, sneaking, creepy, unctuous, soapy

VERBS 7 be servile, swallow insults **8 fawn**, toady, flatter, truckle, crawl, grovel, curry favour, bootlick, lickspittle, creep to, spaniel **9 knuckle under**, cower, cringe, crouch, kneel, stoop, prostrate oneself, defer to, bow, kowtow, bend, bob **10 pander to**, cater for, serve, stooge for, squire, comply **11 beg**, wheedle **12 conform**, comply **13 sponge**, parasitize

679 Severity

NOUNS 1 severity, strictness, fastidiousness, pedantry, meticulousness, stringency, sternness, ruggedness, toughness, harshness, hardness, intolerance, uncharitableness, rigorousness, fundamentalism, rigidity, formality, orthodoxy, firmness, restraint, inflexibility, stubbornness, obstinacy, bigotry, regimentation, discipline, clampdown, authority, power, inclemency, asperity, callousness, pitilessness, inhumanity, cruelty **2 suppression**, oppression, repression, subjugation, subjection, persecution, coercion, harassment, victimization, extortion, exploitation, inquisition, censorship, expurgation, absolutism, authoritarianism, autocracy, totalitarianism, militarism, dictatorship, despotism, tyranny, Fascism, Nazism, iron hand, jackboot **3 unadornment**, plainness, simplicity, austerity, asceticism, restraint, self-denial, self-mortification, asceticism, Spartanism

VERBS 4 be severe, restrain, regiment, discipline, chastise, punish, intimidate, frighten, squeeze, crush, bully, bait **5 suppress**, oppress, repress, subjugate, subject, persecute, coerce, harass, abuse, misgovern, misrule, mishandle, victimize, extort, exploit, enslave, censor, expurgate, tyrannize, torment, terrorize **6 be unadorned**, show self-restraint

ADJECTIVES 7 severe, strict, rigorous, harsh, hard, uncompromising, unbending, stubborn, obstinate, stern, rigid, firm, inflexible, uncharitable, Draconian, exacting, pedantic, formal, orthodox, fundamental, fastidious, stringent, censorious, regimented, disciplined, rugged, tough, hardhearted, intolerant, inquisitorial, bigoted, inclement, callous, pitiless, merciless, unsparing, unforgiving, inhumane, cruel, brutal, coercive, oppressive, repressive, exploitative, undemocratic, militaristic, authoritarian, totalitarian, despotic, dictatorial, autocratic, Fascist, tyrannical, domineering, dominating **8 suppressed**, oppressed, repressed, subjugated, persecuted, coerced, harassed, censored, expurgated, exploited, victimized, tyrannized, tortured **9 unadorned**, plain, simple, purist, restrained, self-restrained, austere, ascetic, spartan, prudish

680 Shallowness

ADJECTIVES 1 shallow, shoal, reefy **2 superficial**, surface, one-dimensional, cursory, hasty, slight, light, skin-deep, thin, flat, trivial, trifling, lightweight, unimportant, petty, meaningless, empty, flimsy, frivolous, foolish

NOUNS 3 shallowness, shoaliness, superficiality, triviality, cursoriness, slightness, lightness, surface, sprinkling **4 shallow thing**, skin, cuticle, veneer, film, shallows, shoal, ford, low tide, puddle, pool, wetlands, swamp, shelf, reef, bank, sandbank, sand bar, flats, pool, puddle, scratch, graze

VERBS 5 be shallow, skim, touch, scrape **6 make shallow**, shoal

681 Shapelessness

NOUNS 1 shapelessness, formlessness, featurelessness, amorphousness, undevelopment, incompleteness, rawness, obscurity, vagueness, obscureness, unclearness, fuzziness, blurriness, haziness, mistiness, fogginess **2 shapeless thing**, blob

VERBS 3 make shapeless, deform, distort, misshape, twist, bend, obscure, blur **4 disorder**, cause chaos, muddle

ADJECTIVES 5 shapeless, formless,

amorphous, unfinished, undefined, indefinite, undeveloped, incomplete, raw, uncut, vague, obscure, unclear, shadowed, fuzzy, blurred, hazy, misty

682 Sharpness

ADJECTIVES 1 sharp, pointed, needle-like, acicular, mucronate, acuminate, spearlike, lanceolate, lance-shaped, hastate, arrow-like, sagittal, unblunted, tapered, tapering, fastigiate, pyramidal, convergent, spindle-shaped, fusiform **2 spiked**, star-shaped, stellate, barbed, spiny, acanthoid, prickly, pricky, bristly, hispid, awned, stinging, thorny, brambly, briery **3 sharp-edged**, honed, razor-edged, knife-edged, cultrate, keen-edged, double-edged, cutting, swordlike, ensiform **4 toothed**, fanged, tusked, horned, corniculate, cornute, odontoid, dentiform, denticulate, cusped, muricate, serrated, notched, emarginate, comblike, pectinate, snagged, craggy
NOUNS 5 sharpness, pointedness, acumination, mucronation, spininess, thorniness, bristliness, prickliness, denticulation, dentition **6 sharp point**, cusp, vertex, prong, tine, sting, dent, notch, cutting edge, knife edge
VERBS 7 be sharp, peak, converge, acuminate, spiculate, bristle, prickle, prick, stick, pierce, sting, cut, needle, gore, bite **8 make sharp**, hone, file, sandpaper, grind, oilstone, strop, strap, whet, taper, edge, point, notch, serrate

683 Shortfall

VERBS 1 fall short, miss, want, lack, require, need, lose, lag **2 fail**, disappoint **3 fall through**, slump **4 miss**, miscarry, go astray
NOUNS 5 shortfall, insufficiency, shortage, famine, dearth, scarcity, lack, loss, deficit, want, need, requirement, incompleteness, perfunctoriness, cursoriness **6 shortcoming**, inadequacy, minus, fault, imperfection, inferiority, blemish, defect, deficiency, default, defalcation, decline, slump
ADJECTIVES 7 short, deficient, needy, wanting, lacking, scarce, missing, amiss, minus, inadequate, insufficient, unreached, unfulfilled, unfinished, incomplete, half-done **8 defective**, broken, faulty, poor, disappointing, blemished, shop-soiled, imperfect, inadequate, perfunctory, cursory, substandard, inferior

684 Shortness

NOUNS 1 shortness, diminutiveness, littleness, stubbiness, stumpiness, stockiness, dumpiness, squatness, stuntedness, lowness, snubness, transience, briefness, brevity, skimpiness, scantiness, curtness, terseness, conciseness, succinctness **2 shortening**, abbreviation, abridgement, compression, capsulization, encapsulation, epitomization, elision, aphaeresis, syncope, apocope, foreshortening, cutting, truncation, curtailment, retrenchment, reduction, cut, docking, clipping, trimming, pruning, mowing, shearing, shaving **3 shortened version**, synopsis, summary, précis, résumé, conspectus, compendium, abbreviation, digest, abridgement, abstract, capsule, outline, epitome **4 short thing**, short cut, shorts,

miniskirt, crew cut **5 abruptness**, curtness, brusqueness, gruffness
ADJECTIVES 6 short, diminutive, little, stubby, stumpy, thickset, stocky, dumpy, squat, stunted, low, snub, retroussé, pug-nosed, transient, brief, skimpy, scanty, curt, terse, concise, succinct, synoptic, summary **7 shortened**, abbreviated, abridged, condensed, compressed, digested, abstracted, capsulized, encapsulated, epitomized, elliptical, elided, foreshortened, cut, sawn-off, truncated, curtailed, curtal, docked, bobbed, clipped, trimmed, cropped, pruned, mown, sheared, shorn, shaved, polled **8 abrupt**, curt, brusque, gruff, rude
VERBS 9 shorten, abbreviate, abridge, condense, compress, digest, abstract, capsulize, encapsulate, epitomize, summarize, elide, telescope, foreshorten, truncate, cut short, curtail, retrench, reduce, dock, bob, clip, trim, crop, reap, prune, lop, mow, shear, shave, poll, decapitate, axe, slash, stunt, skimp, take up **10 short-cut**, cut across

685 Showiness

NOUNS 1 showiness, ostentation, demonstrativeness, pretension **2 airs**, loftiness **3 dramatics**, histrionics, theatre, sensationalism **4 flashiness**, gaudiness, loudness, extravagance, bombast, flamboyance, panache, dash, splash, splurge, garishness, glitter, tinsel, tawdriness, meretriciousness, colourfulness, dazzle **5 pomposity**, pontification, stuffiness, self-importance, grandiloquence, turgidity **6 blatancy**, flagrancy, shamlessness, brazenness, luridness, extravagance, sensationalism, obtrusiveness, crudeness, self-importance **7 pomp**, majesty, pageantry, parade, circumstance, state, pride, formality, solemnity, stiffness **8 bravado**, machismo, heroics, back-slapping **9 grandeur**, splendour, magnificence, gorgeousness, resplendence, brilliance, glory, sumptuousness, lavishness, luxuriousness, elegance, elaborateness, luxury, ritziness, poshness, plushness **10 exhibitionism**, vanity, boasting, flaunting, swaggering, strutting, swashbuckling, peacockry **11 ritual**, drill, smartness, protocol, form **12 magniloquence**, flourish **13 ceremonial**, function, procession, march-past, review, fly-past **14 show**, display, demonstration, manifestation, exhibition, parade, étalage, pageant, fête, gala, tournament, tattoo, spectacle, tableau, display, stunt, fireworks, carnival, play, act, scene, concert, opera, ballet
ADJECTIVES 15 showy, ostentatious, demonstrative, pretentious, shameless **16 lofty**, high-and-mighty, deluded **17 dramatic**, histrionic, theatrical, sensational, daring, stagey **18 flashy**, gaudy, loud, extravagant, flamboyant, exhibitionist, bombastic, garish, frilly, glittering, tinselly, tawdry, meretricious, colourful, dazzling, painted, foppish, rakish **19 pompous**, stuffy, self-important, grandiloquent, bombastic, turgid, pontificating, windy **20 blatant**, flagrant, shameless, brazen, lurid, extravagant, sensational, obtrusive, vulgar, crude, public, screaming **21 majestic**, stately, royal, proud, formal, solemn, stiff, starchy, dignified, grand, fine, cer-

emonious **22 brave**, heroic, macho, dashing **23 grand**, awe-inspiring, imposing, splendid, spectacular, scenic, magnificent, gorgeous, resplendent, brilliant, glorious, sumptuous, lavish, luxurious, elegant, elaborate, luxuriant, expensive **24 vain**, swaggering, swashbuckling **25 ritualistic**, smart, correct, formal, ceremonial, stickling

VERBS 26 show, exhibit, display, demonstrate, manifest, parade, present, perform, act, window-dress, stage-manage, march, promenade, sport **27 flourish**, brandish, wave, emblazon, proclaim, vaunt **28 show off**, flaunt oneself, prance, promenade, peacock, strut, swagger **29 put on airs**, pontificate, exaggerate **30 put on a show**, glitter, dazzle

686 Side

NOUNS 1 side, laterality, edge, hillside, flank, starboard, port, ribs, hip, cheek, jowl, temple, jaw, sideboards **2 surface**, facing **3 side direction**, windward side, right-hand side, left-hand side, lee side, far side, near side **4 aspect**, feature, facet, element, bright side, funny side, dark side **5 team**, group, circle

ADJECTIVES 6 side, sidelong, oblique, lateral, flanking, skirting, facing, right, left, far, near, two-sided, many-sided, multifaceted, bilateral

VERBS 7 be alongside, edge, flank, skirt **8 move sideways**, sidestep, sidle, avoid **9 side with**, support, back

687 Sign

NOUNS 1 sign, symbol, meaning, connotation, representation, signal, indicator, signature, autograph, fingerprint, signpost, banner, poster, placard, emblem, eagle, swastika, cross, crescent, mandala, talisman, mojo, image, token, evidence, omen, brand, trademark, hallmark, imprint, track, trail, traces, scent, clue, cue, key, lead, marker, symptom, syndrome, shibboleth, password, cipher, code, hieroglyphics, rune, equal sign **2 symbolism**, semiotics, symptomatology, iconology **3 gesture**, signing, dactylology, ticktack, kinesics, demeanour, look, twinkle, glance, smile, blush, ogle, leer, wink, tic, twitch, frown, scowl, pout, moue, grimace, laugh, cheer, hiss, sigh, moan, hoot, boo, whistle, catcall, clenched fist, V-sign, pointing, wave, clapping, applause, touch, handshake, grip, hug, nudge, push, shove, slap **4 signal**, message, pips, heliograph, semaphore, smoke signal, red flag, green light, red light, beacon, SOS, rocket, flare, horn, hooter, foghorn, whistle, fire alarm, siren, alarm bell, bleep, bell, knell **5 indicator**, guide, index, gauge, thermometer, barometer, speedometer, mileometer, cynosure, pointer, finger, arm, needle, arrow, cursor, timekeeper, stopwatch, blinker, winker, compass, radar, weathercock, windsock, signpost, roadsign, milestone, landmark, earthwork, cairn, monument, lighthouse, buoy, lodestar, Pole Star, watermark, tidemark **6 word**, catchword, slogan, watchword, shibboleth, call, cry, shout, hail, proclamation, publication, announcement, invitation, summons, command, fanfare, sennet, reveille, charge, advance, rally, tattoo, retreat, drumbeat, SOS **7 punctuation**, point, full stop, period, comma, colon, semicolon, quotation mark, inverted comma, exclamation mark, question mark, query, interrobang, apostrophe, parentheses, brackets, braces, hyphen, dash, en rule, em rule, blank, ellipsis, swung dash, asterisk, dagger, obelus, solidus, stroke, virgule, caret, accent, circumflex, breve, umlaut, tilde, cedilla, hacek, hamse, dieresis, diacritic, macron, indention, paragraph

VERBS 8 use signs, sign, autograph, initial, countersign, signal, gesture, indicate, point to, signpost, mark, direct, guide, blaze, demarcate, delineate, fingerprint **9 signify**, represent, symbolize, mean, denote, connote, imply, indicate, suggest, intimate, symptomize, characterize, typify, betoken, disclose, reveal, signalize, emphasize, highlight **10 gesture**, motion, gesticulate, mime, mimic, imitate, sign, beckon, gaze, glance, ogle, leer, wink, frown, scowl, pout, moue, grimace, snap, bite, twinkle, smile, laugh, hiss, sigh, moan, hoot, boo, whistle, wave, point, clap, applaud, salute, greet, hug, nudge, pat, stroke, caress, jog, push, shove, poke, prod, slap, stamp, stomp, kick **11 signal**, semaphore, wigwag, communicate, publish, inform, announce, declare, herald, hail, proclaim, call, cry, shout, summon, command, warn, alert, honk **12 punctuate**, abbreviate, accent, indent, parenthesize, underline, italicize, underscore, stress, dot, dash, hyphenate

ADJECTIVES 13 signifying, indicative, significative, identifying, directional, pointing, connotative, denotative, signalizing, disclosing, revealing, explanatory, betraying, telltale, signalling, symbolic, semiotic, symptomatic, diagnostic, expressive, implicative, demonstrative, meaningful, suggestive, evidential, representative, nominal, diagrammatic, typical, characteristic, individual, special, interpretive, prophetic, presageful **14 gestural**, gesticulative, dactylographic, signing, thumbing, looking, glancing, smiling, winking, grimacing, laughing, sighing, moaning, whistling, clapping, patting, pushing, slapping **15 signalling**, telegraphic, flashing, warning, summoning, ringing, bleeping, shouting, hailing, proclaiming, publishing, announcing, inviting

688 Silence

- *Thou still unravish'd bride of quietness, / Thou foster-child of silence and slow time.* John Keats.
- *Whereof one cannot speak, thereon one must remain silent.* Ludwig Wittgenstein.

VERBS 1 be silent, keep quiet **2 silence**, quieten, hush, still, lull, quell, subdue, mute, stifle, smother, muffle, muzzle

ADJECTIVES 3 silent, quiet, inaudible, noiseless, soundless, taciturn, mute, mum, tight-lipped, dumb, voiceless, aphonic, aphasic, speechless, dumbfounded, wordless, hushed, still, calm, peaceful, quiescent, soft, faint, muted, soundproof, unspoken, tacit, solemn

NOUNS 4 silence, quiet, inaudibility, noiselessness, soundlessness, taciturnity, muteness, dumbness, voicelessness, aphonia, laryngitis, speechlessness, wordlessness, hush, stillness, lull, rest, calm, peace, quietude, softness, faintness, mutedness

689 Similarity

NOUNS 1 similarity, sameness, resemblance, synonymy, homonymy, likeness, similitude, affinity, kinship, seeming, analogy, correspondence, equivalence, comparability, parallel, uniformity, conformity, parity, equality, proportionality, accordance, agreement, nearness, approximation, closeness, suchlike, duplication, similation, imitation, semblance, assimilation, simile, metaphor, parable, allegory, portrayal, copying, aping **2 copy**, photocopy, stencil, duplicate, Mimeograph, reproduction, imitation, twin, clone, trend, style, fashion **3 copier**, photocopier, duplicator, stenciller, press, printer, camera, VCR **4 counterpart**, equivalent, correspondent, pendant, reciprocal, coordinate, twin, copy, clone, doppelgänger, image, double, lookalike, reflection, shadow, understudy, other, fellow, mate

ADJECTIVES 5 similar, same, synonymous, symmetrical, akin, like, alike, resembling, allied, connected, related, matching, corresponding, analogous, equivalent, comparable, commensurable, parallel, identical, approximate, near, close, quasi, connatural, homogeneous, assonant, alliterative, rhyming, favouring **6 simulated**, artificial, false, imitation, cultured, ersatz, synthetic, aped, mimicked, imitated, mocked, phoney, counterfeit, copied, duplicated, replicated **7 lifelike**, realistic, photographic, exact, faithful, graphic, vivid

VERBS 8 be similar, resemble, correspond, coincide, agree, accord, tally, compare, favour, suggest, evoke, seem like, reflect, mirror, echo, match **9 make similar**, equalize, homogenize, assimilate, compare **10 imitate**, emulate, copy, reproduce, duplicate, Xerox, fax, clone, simulate, camouflage, portray, ape, mimic, counterfeit, replicate

690 Simplicity

- *O holy simplicity!* John Huss.
- *Our life is frittered away by detail...Simplify, simplify.* Henry David Thoreau.

ADJECTIVES 1 simple, plain, basic, ordinary, common, everyday, workaday, homy, homespun, humble, lowly, austere, severe, Spartan, spare, ascetic, stark, bald, bare, naked, classic, neat, uncluttered, clear, clean, pure, unadulterated, uncomplicated, unpretentious, unaffected, unassuming, modest, chaste, unsensational, restrained, sober, serious, dry, stodgy, tedious, boring, humdrum, mundane, usual, vernacular, matter-of-fact, prosaic, quotidian, mundane, unimaginative, uninspired, unpoetical **2 unadorned**, unembellished, undecorated, unornamented, untrimmed, ungarnished, unpainted, uncoloured **3 natural**, artless, simple-hearted, candid, frank, blunt, open, guileless, ingenuous, honest, veracious, direct, straightforward, plain-speaking, forthright, unpretentious, unaffected, unassuming

NOUNS 4 simplicity, plainness, ordinariness, commonness, homeyness, humbleness, lowliness, austerity, severity, spareness, asceticism, starkness, baldness, bareness, nakedness, neatness, clarity, cleanness, purity, unpretentiousness, modesty, chastity, restraint, soberness, seriousness, dryness, stodginess, tediousness, boredom, usualness, matter-of-factness, mundaneness, idiom, vernacular, prose, plain English **5 unadornment**, unembellishment **6 naturalness**, artlessness, candidness, frankness, bluntness, openness, honesty, veracity, directness, straightforwardness, unpretentiousness

VERBS 7 be simple, simplify

691 Situation

NOUNS 1 situation, position, orientation, direction, bearings, latitude, longitude, aspect, side, frontage, altitude, topography, geography, location, site, setting, place, spot, point, seat, venue, scene **2 circumstances**, setting, background, footing, basis, standing, standpoint, position, place, context, factor, contingency, condition, juncture, case, state, status quo, climate, atmosphere, scene **3 difficult circumstances**, plight, predicament, fix, jam **4 employment**, post, position, job, service, station, office, place, livelihood **5 rank**, sphere, status, standing, station

ADJECTIVES 6 situated, positioned, located, set, placed, sited, seated, stationed, orientated, pointed, appointed, employed, posted **7 situational**, directional, topographical, geographical **8 circumstantial**, contextual, contingent, grounded, based, climatic, atmospheric, surrounding

VERBS 9 be situated, be located, lie, stand, rest **10 situate**, place, position, locate, site, put, install, stand, fix, set, station, post, deploy

692 Size

NOUNS 1 size, magnitude, amplitude, gauge, scale, extent, scope, range, reach, limit, expanse, spread, coverage, area, length, breadth, width, height, depth, radius, diameter, calibre, scantling, girth, circumference, mass, bulk, volume, capacity, cubature, content, room, space, accommodation, stowage, tonnage, displacement, burden **2 bigness**, largeness, greatness, sizableness, ampleness, generousness, voluminousness, bagginess, capaciousness, spaciousness, roominess, hugeness, enormity, immenseness, massiveness, grandness, prodigiousness, tallness, bulkiness, unwieldiness, cumbersomeness, broadness, wideness, comprehensiveness, expansiveness, extensiveness **3 large scale**, outsize, oversize **4 gigantism**, giantism, hypertrophy, hyperplasia, acromegaly **5 fatness**, obesity, overweight, corpulence, portliness, rotundity, roundness, endomorphy, grossness, fleshiness, flabbiness, bloatedness, puffiness, fullness, plumpness, paunchiness, buxomness, bustiness, plumpishness, podginess, tubbiness, chubbiness, adiposity **6 squatness**, dumpiness, stockiness, squareness, burliness, brawniness, beefiness, meatiness, chunkiness, heaviness, heftiness, hulkiness **7 mass**, lump, chunk, hunk, block, clump, cluster, wad, heap, mountain, clod, cake **8 fat**, cellulite, potbelly **9 big thing**, giant, monster, whale, dinosaur, mam-

moth, mastodon, elephant, hippopotamus, leviathan, behemoth
ADJECTIVES 10 medium, average, standard **11 big**, large, great, full-grown, full-blown, full-scale, large-scale, considerable, substantial, bumper, ample, generous, voluminous, baggy, capacious, spacious, roomy, huge, enormous, immense, massive, gigantic, colossal, titanic, monstrous, mammoth, monster, Gargantuan, towering, monumental, grand, imposing, epic, tremendous, stupendous, prodigious, megalithic, macroscopic, astronomical, bulky, mighty, broad, comprehensive, expansive, extensive, vast, limitless **12 fat**, obese, overweight, endomorphic, gross, fleshy, flabby, bloated, puffy, swollen, distended, full, plump, podgy, tubby, chubby, bonny, adipose, stout, corpulent, portly, rotund, round, roly-poly, well-fed, overfed, squab, dumpy, full-faced, chubby-cheeked, double-chinned, pot-bellied, paunchy, buxom, busty, bosomy, full-bosomed, well-endowed, top-heavy **13 stocky**, stout, thickset, heavyset, squat, square, well-built, burly, strapping, lusty, brawny, beefy, meaty, heavy, chunky, hefty, hulking, lumbering
VERBS 14 measure, gauge, size, grade, group, rank, sort, match, graduate, adjust, proportion **15 be big**, bulk, loom

693 Skill

NOUNS 1 skill, ability, proficiency, competence, efficiency, faculty, capability, capacity, adroitness, dexterity, handiness, deftness, adeptness, address, ease, facility, grace, style, versatility, adaptability, flexibility, touch, control, mastery, virtuosity, excellence, prowess, expertise, professionalism, forte, strength, speciality, métier, accomplishment, attainment, acquirement, experience, knowledge, technique, craftsmanship, art, delicacy, execution, perfection, ingenuity, resourcefulness, craft, cleverness, sharpness, sophistication, sagacity, finesse, tact, discretion, discrimination, gimmick, contrivance, trick, stratagem, tactics **2 aptitude**, talent, innate ability, propensity, inclination, tendency, bent, faculty, endowment, gift, flair, knack, genius, aptness, fitness **3 masterpiece**, creation, jewel, masterwork, magnum opus, coup, exploit, feat, act, deed, brilliance, bravura, trump, clincher, collector's piece, classic **4 expert**, professional, practitioner, specialist, authority, doyen, pundit
ADJECTIVES 5 skilful, able, proficient, competent, efficient, talented, gifted, excellent, superb, topnotch, topflight, apt, adroit, dexterous, deft, adept, slick, agile, sure-footed, nimble, green-fingered, clever, quick-witted, shrewd, cunning, smart, intelligent, diplomatic, wise, versatile, adaptable, ingenious, resourceful, panurgic, sound, masterful, magisterial **6 gifted**, talented, endowed **7 expert**, experienced, tried, seasoned, veteran, versed in, instructed, trained, practised, well-prepared, qualified, specialized, proficient, competent, efficient, professional **8 well-made**, well-crafted, professional, workmanlike, shipshape,

finished, stylish, elegant, artistic, Daedalian
VERBS 9 be skilful, excel, shine, exploit **10 be expert**, demonstrate

694 Slowness

VERBS 1 move slowly, amble, saunter, stroll, laze, creep, crawl, inch along, trickle, ooze, drip, idle, shuffle along, toddle along, scuff, mince, trudge, shamble, plod along, limp, hobble **2 hesitate**, drawl, pause, falter, flag, dawdle, linger, loiter, tarry, hover, delay, lag **3 slow down**, ease off, slacken off, relax, moderate, decelerate, retard, delay, detain, impede, arrest, obstruct, hinder, stay, check, curb, rein in, brake
ADJECTIVES 4 slow, ambling, strolling, sauntering, lumbering, snail-paced, faltering, flagging, creeping, crawling, dragging, waddling, slouching, shuffling, plodding, clumsy, limping, halting, hobbling, shambling, tottering **5 unhurried**, leisurely, sluggish, languorous, lethargic, inert, slack, slothful, languid, lazy, indolent, sluggardly, listless, idle, apathetic, phlegmatic, methodical, patient, deliberate, circumspect, gradual, Fabian, meticulous, restrained, easy, moderate, gentle, relaxed **6 hesitant**, tentative, softly-softly, cautious, reluctant, lagging, dawdling, drawling **7 delayed**, detained, checked, arrested, obstructed, impeded, retarded, restrained, slack, backward, behind, late, hysteretic, dilatory, lingering
NOUNS 8 slowness, leisureliness, unhurriedness, sluggishness, languor, lethargy, inertia, slackness, sloth, laziness, indolence, inertness, lentitude, dilatoriness, methodicalness, patience, deliberation, circumspection, gradualism, Fabianism, meticulousness **9 deceleration**, brake, curb, restraint, friction, retardation, slackening **10 slow motion**, walk, amble, stroll, saunter, dawdle, piaffer, dragging, lumbering, creeping, crawl, trudge, waddle, slouch, shuffle, plod, limp, hobble, shamble, trot **11 lingering**, lagging, dawdling **12 hesitation**, tentativeness, caution, reluctance, drawling, tardiness, procrastination, unwillingness, delay, hold-up, work-to-rule, detention, setback, check, arrest, obstruction **13 slow thing**, funeral march, fugue **14 slow creature**, sloth, tortoise

695 Smoothness

ADJECTIVES 1 smooth, streamlined, frictionless, even, flush, sleek, bald, clean-shaven, hairless, glabrous, smooth-haired, combed, brushed, groomed, silken, satiny, velvety, smooth-skinned, peach-like, fleecy, woolly, soft **2 uniform**, even, regular, horizontal, plane, level, harrowed, rolled, steam-rolled, flattened, blunt, curved, rounded, waterworn, flat, ironed, unwrinkled, uncrumpled, unruffled **3 soothing**, peaceful, still, quiet, calm, dead **4 polished**, varnished, burnished, waxed, enamelled, lacquered, glazed, glacé, gleaming, shiny, glossy, glassy, mirror-like, slippery, skiddy, slithery, buttery, lubricated, oily, greasy **5 smooth-mannered**, well-mannered, suave, sophisticated, urbane, glib, slick, sleek, sycophantic
NOUNS 6 smoothness, evenness, flushness, uniformity, regularity,

horizontality, levelness, flatness, peacefulness, stillness, calmness, serenity, calm, quiescence, levigation, sleekness, silkiness, satininess, velvetiness, fleeciness, softness, shininess, lustre, finish, glossiness, glassiness, slipperiness, slitheriness, unctuousness, lubrication

VERBS 7 smooth, streamline, plane, even, level, harrow, mow, rake, flatten, comb, rub, roll, press, iron, mangle, shave, sand, levigate, starch, buff, polish, glaze, glacé, butter, wax, varnish, paint, coat, pave, lubricate, oil **8 go smoothly**, glide, skate, roll, ski, float, bowl along, slip, slide, skid, coast **9 smooth over**, soothe, calm, appease, pacify, allay, ameliorate, assuage, mitigate, alleviate, charm

696 Sobriety

ADJECTIVES 1 sober, clear-headed, abstinent, abstemious, temperate **2 nonalcoholic**, alcohol-free

VERBS 3 be sober, abstain **4 give up alcohol**, sign the pledge **5 sober up**, detoxify

NOUNS 6 sobriety, abstinence, abstemiousness, temperance, teetotalism

697 Sociability

NOUNS 1 sociability, socialness, affability, amicability, amiability, friendliness, neighbourliness, kindness, gregariousness, warmth, geniality, cordiality, conviviality, enjoyment, joviality, jollity, revelry, festivity, merriment, gaiety, cheer, hospitality, companionability, compatibility, clubbishness, fraternization, participation, membership, cooperation, conversation, intercourse, communicativeness, communion, association, consociation, affiliation, familiarity, intimacy **2 social ambition**, social climbing, status-seeking, popularity, *savoir-vivre*, refinement, breeding, courtesy, affability **3 meeting**, appointment, engagement, rendezvous, assignation, date, social, gathering, tête-à-tête, soirée, coffee, tea, reception, entertainment, reunion, visiting, interview, calling, frequentation **4 meeting place**, stadium, public hall, restaurant, salon, drawing room **5 party**, entertainment, festivity, feast, banquet, dinner, at-home, house-warming, barn-raising, ball, masquerade, smoker, debut, presentation, dance, disco, barbecue **6 human society**, humanity, mankind, humankind, community, commune, public, social class, elite, gentry, nobility, aristocracy, caste, peer group, family **7 good company**, comradeship, friendship, fellowship, fraternity, camaraderie, togetherness, bonhomie, cordiality **8 welcome**, warmth, greeting, handshake, embrace, kiss

VERBS 9 be sociable, entertain, invite, host, hug, embrace, preside, participate, mixer, share, toast, drink to, pledge, gate-crash **10 visit**, see, unbend, relax, sojourn, stay **11 fraternize**, hobnob, introduce oneself **12 welcome**, greet

ADJECTIVES 13 sociable, affable, social-minded, communal, collective, common, public, civic, companionable, amicable, amiable, affable, clubbish, communicative, friendly, courteous, civil, urbane, easy-going, free-and-easy, party-minded, cordial, genial, witty, amusing, charming, charismatic, extrovert, gregarious, outgoing, hearty, lively, hail-fellow-well-met, convivial, jolly, jovial, merry, cheerful, smiling, welcoming, warm, affectionate, hospitable, neighbourly **14 popular**, beloved, liked, sought after, welcome, entertained **15 festive**, carnival-like, entertaining, fun

698 Sociology

- *Man was formed for society.* William Blackstone.
- *No man is an island, entire of itself; every man is a piece of the Continent, a part of the main.* John Donne.
- *Man is a social animal.* Benedict Spinoza.

NOUNS 1 sociology, social science, behavioural science, social anthropology, sociobiology, political behaviour, social psychology, macrosociology, social morphology, comparative sociology, human ecology **2 sociological research**, social survey, demographic research, community study, sociometric technique, sociological model **3 society**, community, community relations, social heterogeneity, homogeneity, collectivity, rural society, folk society, ruralism, rural-urban migration, urban environment, urbanization, suburbanization **4 social services**, social security, welfare state, social work **5 sociologist**, social scientist, sociobiologist, social psychologist

ADJECTIVES 6 sociological, societal, social, socioeconomic, behavioural, interactive, communal, community-wide, educational

VERBS 7 socialize, interact, organize, urbanize, industrialize

699 Softness

ADJECTIVES 1 soft, nonrigid, flaccid, limp, rubbery, flabby, floppy, flimsy, unstrung, relaxed, slack, lax, loose, sprung **2 pliant**, giving, yielding, melting, flexible, bendable, stretchable, elastic, lithe, willowy, supple, lissom, loose-limbed, springy, acrobatic, athletic, plastic, extensile, ductile, tractile, adaptable, malleable, mouldable, shapable, impressible, waxy, doughy, pasty **3 smooth**, satiny, silky, velvety, plush, downy, feathery, fluffy, flossy, woolly, fleecy, flocculent **4 compressible**, squeezable, padded, foam-filled, pneumatic, pillowed, podgy, pudgy, spongy, mashy, soggy, squashy, squishy, squelchy, juicy, overripe, pulpy, pithy, medullary, muddy, boggy, marshy, mossy **5 softhearted**, warm-hearted, sympathetic, compassionate, gentle, tender, kind, delicate, mild, easygoing, relaxed, lenient, lax, complaisant **6 impressionable**, susceptible, sensitive, formable, nonresistive, easing, mollifying, appeasing

NOUNS 7 softness, pliability, flexibility, bendability, give, suppleness, limberness, litheness, nonrigidity, springiness, elasticity, plasticity, ductility, tensileness, tractability, malleability, impressibility, rubberiness, extendibility, extensibility, looseness, slackness, flaccidity, flabbiness, floppiness **8 smoothness**, downiness, fluffiness, furriness, woolliness, flocculence, flossiness, featheriness, silkiness, velvetiness, satininess **9 compressibility**, sponginess, pulpiness, doughiness, semiliquidity, sogginess, marshiness, bogginess, squashiness **10 soft thing**, feather,

feather bed, eiderdown, pillow, cushion, sofa, padding, upholstery, wadding, foam, fluff, puff, fur, cotton wool, fleece, silk, satin, velvet, velveteen, plush, down, thistledown, kapok, paste, dough, putty, wax, soap, butter, pulp, mousse, mud, marsh, bog **11 gentleness**, tenderness, delicacy, mellowness, mildness, kindness, sensitiveness, easiness, leniency, laxity, mollification, mollifying, appeasement, compliance

VERBS 12 soften, unstiffen, sag, flop, relax, slacken, loosen, bend, unbend, spring, mould, shape, impress, wax, pad, cushion, plump, fluff, featherbed, tenderize, mellow, mature, ripen, oil, grease, lubricate, knead, massage, mash, whip, pulp, squash, pulverize, chew, macerate, steep, drench, melt **13 ease**, relax, unwind, mellow, temper, lessen, mitigate, demulce, assuage, soothe, subdue, mollify, massage **14 yield**, give, relent, appease, comply, obey

700 Soliloquy

NOUNS 1 soliloquy, monologue, monody, monodrama

VERBS 2 soliloquize, monologize, think aloud **3 monopolize the conversation**, do all the talking

ADJECTIVES 4 soliloquizing, monologic, apostrophic, monodramatic, soloistic, thinking aloud

701 Sophistry

NOUNS 1 sophistry, casuistry, philosophism, jesuitry, illogicality, fallaciousness, speciousness, invalidity, untenableness, unsoundness, irrationality, inconsistency, circularity, equivocation, subterfuge, sleight, distortion, misapplication, solecism **2 sophism**, paralogism, pseudosyllogism, solecism, paradox, antilogy, fallacy, dodge, trick, ruse, shuffle, quibble, quip, quirk, cavil, contrivance, stratagem, subterfuge, scheme, misinformation, propaganda, hogwash **3 cunning**, sophistication, craftiness, artfulness, artifice, slyness, foxiness, slipperiness, shiftiness, trickiness, sneakiness, insidiousness, machination, manipulation, demagoguery, mystification **4 quibbling**, captiousness, hairsplitting, nit-picking, cavilling, subtlety, paltering, prevarication, hedging, shuffling **5 hypocrisy**, deceit, duplicity, pretence, humbug, double-dealing, insincerity, disingenuousness, guile, evasion, mendacity, fakery, chicanery, quackery, charlatanism, mountebankery

ADJECTIVES 6 sophistic, rhetorical, logic-chopping, paralogistic, pseudosyllogistic, specious, fallacious, spurious, faulty, flawed, inconsistent, circular, equivocal, erroneous, illogical, paradoxical, contradictory, unreasonable, irrational, unfounded, baseless, groundless, invalid, untenable, unsound, distorted, misapplied, contrived, tortuous, misleading, spurious, inconsequential, dubious, fictitious, illusory, superficial, empty **7 cunning**, sophisticated, crafty, artful, sly, foxy, sneaky, shifty, dodgy, tricky, insidious, underhand, perfidious, evasive, elusive, manipulating, demagogic, mystifying **8 quibbling**, cavilling, captious, hair-splitting, nit-picking, shuffling, hedging, equivocal, prevaricating **9 hypocritical**, deceptive, pretended, feigning, dissembling, dissimulating, double-dealing, unreliable, insincere, disingenuous, fraudulent, dishonest, lying, mendacious, false, bogus, sham, counterfeit, fake

VERBS 10 practise sophistry, misapply, misconstrue, misrepresent, misquote, falsify, distort, strain, warp, slant, twist, gloss, whitewash, embroider, disguise, camouflage, mask, juggle, rig, contrive, scheme, manipulate, machinate, propagandize, misinform, mislead, mystify **11 deceive**, dissimulate, dissemble, pretend, feign, bluff, masquerade, lie, fake, dodge, trick, elude, evade, charm, sweet-talk, double-deal **12 quibble**, cavil, split hairs, nit-pick, palter, hedge, shuffle, pettifog, equivocate

702 Sorrow

- *Adieu tristesse/ Bonjour tristesse/ Tu es inscrite dans les lignes du plafond./* (Farewell sadness/ Good day sadness/ You are written in the lines of the ceiling). Paul Éluard.
- *If you have tears, prepare to shed them now.* William Shakespeare.
- *'Tis held that sorrow makes us wise.* Alfred, Lord Tennyson.

NOUNS 1 sorrow, sadness, regret, unhappiness, heartache, downheartedness, heavyheartedness, wretchedness, misery, desolation, heartbreak, suffering, distress, anguish, languishment, agony, pain, torment, woe, grief, dolour **2 depression**, melancholy, malaise, droopiness, dreariness, joylessness, cheerlessness, lowness, dejection, despondency, gloom, the doldrums, dispiritedness

ADJECTIVES 3 sad, unhappy, sorrowful, crestfallen, downhearted, heavyhearted, distressed, miserable, wretched, forlorn, languishing, tormented, woebegone, tearful, doleful, dolorous, mournful, pining, heartbroken, disconsolate, inconsolable, desolate, grief-stricken **4 depressed**, melancholic, downcast, low, droopy, dreary, joyless, dejected, dispirited, despondent, atrabilious, lugubrious, grey, lacklustre, listless, gloomy, morose, glum, dismal, long-faced, moody, moping **5 distressing**, depressing, dispiriting, sorry, lamentable, heartbreaking, harrowing, painful

VERBS 6 grieve, sadden, languish, pine, mourn, sigh, lament, cry, weep, sob, moan, howl, wail **7 despair**, despond, lose heart, droop, mope, wilt, flag, brood **8 depress**, dishearten

703 Sourness

NOUNS 1 sourness, tartness, bitterness, sharpness, dryness, acerbity, acidity, astringency, acidulousness, vinegariness, unripeness **2 unpalatability**, bitterness, gall, acridity, bile, staleness, rancidness, mould, rottenness, unwholesomeness, rankness, brackishness **3 spleen**, rancour, bile, crabbedness, moroseness, sullenness

ADJECTIVES 4 acid, sharp, sour, tangy, tart, pungent, acerbic, acidulous, lemony, vinegary, unripe, green, immature, unsweetened, dry, acrid, biting **5 unpalatable**, unappetizing, uninviting, unsavoury, unpleasant, disagreeable, nasty, disgusting, foul-tasting, nauseating, uneatable, inedible, dank, brackish, undrinkable, corked, harsh, stale, rough, rancid, mouldy, rotten, high, bad, off, curdled, fermented, unwholesome, contaminated, poisonous **6 splenetic**, rancorous, bilious, sarcastic, harsh, crabbed, bitter, morose

VERBS 7 sour, acidify, sharpen, curdle, spoil, turn, ferment, go bad **8 disgust**, nauseate

704 Space

- *That's one small step for man, one giant leap for mankind.* Neil Armstrong.
- *I am a passenger on the spaceship, Earth.* Richard Buckminster Fuller.

NOUNS 1 space, expanse, extent, measure, size, length, breadth, width, height, depth, surface, area, diameter, circumference, tract, volume **2 empty space**, emptiness, void, nothingness, infinity, sky, heavens **3 geographical space**, region, clearing, glade, expanse, stretch, tract, reach, hinterland, grassland, prairie, steppe, veld, plain, upland, moorland, wilderness, waste **4 spaciousness**, roominess, extensiveness, expansiveness, capaciousness, voluminousness, vastness **5 reserved space**, room, accommodation, capacity, stowage, storage, seating, berthage **6 available space**, room, latitude, leeway, scope, swing, play, margin, clearance, windage, amplitude, headroom, seaway **7 range**, reach, coverage, scope, compass, radius, sweep, stretch, grasp, sphere, field, area, gamut, spectrum **8 intervening space**, distance, interval, gap, remove, break, hiatus, lacuna, blank, pause, interruption, intermission, lapse, while, duration, span, spell, stretch, period **9 fourth dimension**, space-time

ADJECTIVES 10 spatial, dimensional, proportional, two-dimensional, surface, radial, superficial, flat, cubic, volumetric, stereoscopic, space-time **11 extensive**, regional, widespread, far-reaching, wide-ranging, far-flung, global, worldwide, interstellar, intergalactic, universal, boundless, infinite, unconfined, uncircumscribed **12 spacious**, roomy, airy, lofty, capacious, voluminous, commodious, cavernous, sizeable, ample, vast, great, immense, enormous, outsized, expansive, extended, long, broad, wide, deep

705 Sparseness

ADJECTIVES 1 sparse, thin, empty, vacuous, void, scarce, rare, tenuous, delicate, fine, wispy, light, windy, airy, gaseous, vaporous, volatilizable, ethereal, buoyant, insubstantial, immaterial, slight, flimsy, incorporeal, uncompressed, uncompact, compressible, spongy **2 rarefied**, expansive, extensive, extending, attenuated, dilative, etherealized, thinning, diluted, weak, adulterated

NOUNS 3 sparseness, thinness, emptiness, vacuity, voidness, scarcity, rarity, tenuity, delicacy, fineness, wispiness, lightness, windiness, airiness, gaseousness, volatility, ethereality, buoyancy, insubstantiality, immateriality, slightness, flimsiness, incorporeality, compressibility, sponginess **4 rarefaction**, expansion, extension, attenuation, dilation, etherealization, thinning, dilution

VERBS 5 make sparse, thin, rarefy, gasify, vaporize, volatilize, empty, exhaust, attenuate, etherealize, dilute, water down, cut

706 Speech

• *Let your speech be alway with grace, seasoned with salt, that ye may know how ye ought to answer every man.* Bible: Colossians.

• *But words once spoke can never be recall'd.* Earl of Roscommon.

NOUNS **1 faculty of speech**, language, talking, speaking, dialogue, conversation, colloquy, discourse, tongue, langue, parole, vocabulary, vernacular, idiom, dialect, patois, parlance, slang, cant, jargon, patter, chat **2 power of speech**, articulateness, eloquence, fluency, grandiloquence, magniloquence, orotundity, talkativeness, volubility, loquacity, prolixity, logorrhoea, verbosity, verbiage, wordiness, verbal diarrhoea **3 articulation**, diction, elocution, enunciation, vocalization, utterance, timbre, intonation, pitch, inflection, stress, pronunciation, accent, brogue, twang, burr, trill, drawl, nasality, stridor, lisping, stammer, stutter, speech impediment, mispronunciation, cacoepy, ventriloquism, sign language, meaningful looks **4 utterance**, vocalization, expression, locution, phoneme, remark, comment, dictum, statement, declaration, pronouncement, interjection, exclamation, ejaculation, gasp, mutter, murmur, whisper, aside, response, address, greeting **5 speech**, oration, address, panegyric, eulogy, encomium, valedictory, obsequies, reading, recital, broadcast, sermon, exhortation, homily, harangue, mouthful, earful, tirade, diatribe, invective, obloquy, lecture, dissertation, peroration **6 art of public speaking**, oratory, rhetoric, speechifying, tub-thumping, declamation

VERBS **7 speak**, talk, say, utter, declare, proclaim, state, tell, relate, recite, quote, cite, enunciate, voice, express, verbalize, blurt out, interject, exclaim, ejaculate, interrupt, respond **8 speak loudly**, shout, yell, cry, bawl, roar, boom, thunder, trumpet, blare, scream, shriek, screech **9 speak in a particular way**, whisper, murmur, mutter, mumble, gasp, warble, coo, chant, cackle, crow, bark, yelp, growl, snap, snarl, squeak, whine, sob, wail, drawl **10 speak to**, address, lecture, sermonize, hold forth, orate, speechify, perorate, rant, tub-thump

ADJECTIVES **11 speech**, oral, verbal, lingual, linguistic, vocal, spoken, voiced, vocalized, pronounced **12 phonetic**, phonic, tonic, tonal, nasal, twangy, throaty, guttural **13 speaking**, articulate, fluent, talkative, loquacious, voluble, outspoken **14 eloquent**, silver-tongued, smooth-talking, rhetorical, grandiloquent, magniloquent, tub-thumping, ranting

707 Sport

NOUNS **1 sport**, game, contest, match, event, meeting, bout, round, set, tournament, knockout, league, division, indoor sport, outdoor sport, participator sport, spectator sport, contact sport **2 sportsground**, venue, stadium, field, track, ground, course, links, court, ring, arena, green **3 sportsman** (*or* **sportswoman**), player, contender, defender, challenger, opponent, athlete

ADJECTIVES **4 sporting**, competitive,

agonistic, sportive, sporty, athletic
VERBS 5 participate, take part, compete, join in

708 Stability

NOUNS 1 stability, steadiness, steadfastness, rootedness, fixedness, solidity, soundness, secureness, strength, durability, permanence, consistency, reliability, constancy, rest, quietude, calm, immobilization, hardening, stiffening, firmness, inflexibility, homeostasis, balance, equality, stasis, immutability, unchangeableness, changelessness, invariability, irreversibility, indestructibility **2 determination**, resolution, resolve, nerve, iron will, inflexibility, toughness, hardness, steeliness, obstinacy, stubbornness, obduracy, aplomb **3 stabilizer**, keel, centreboard, fin, aerofoil, spoiler, counterbalance, counterweight, ballast, support, prop, buttress, beam, crossbeam, joist
VERBS 4 be stable, stick fast, hold, adhere, stand, stay put, harden, stiffen, stabilize, settle down, stay, take root **5 make stable**, steady, transfix, freeze, balance, equalize, fix, establish, confirm, validate, ratify, ensure, secure, found, erect, support, buttress, engrave, stamp, print, stereotype, set, bind, root, entrench, tie **6 show determination**, persist, persevere, stand firm
ADJECTIVES 7 stable, steady, steadfast, solid, sound, firm, stiff, secure, strong, durable, permanent, consistent, reliable, constant, dependable, predictable, unchangeable, unvarying, inalterable, irrevocable, irreversible, restful, quiet, calm, immobile, immovable, aground, well-founded, frozen, hard, inflexible, unshakable, incontrovertible, indisputable, indefeasible, homeostatic, equal, immutable, invariable, incommutable, intransmutable, indissoluble, imperishable, inextinguishable, invulnerable, indestructible, ineradicable, indelible, evergreen, enduring, perpetual **8 stabilized**, unchanged, unaltered, settled, transfixed, stereotyped, anchored, moored, tethered, tied, chained, grounded, stranded, rooted, established, ingrained, entrenched, engraved **9 determined**, resolute, resolved, certain, sure, iron-willed, inflexible, unwavering, tough, hard, steely, obstinate, stubborn

709 State

NOUNS 1 state, condition, situation, circumstances, lot, fettle, form, order, repair, estate, position, role, status, standing, rank, place, posture, footing, class, echelon, category, structure, aspect, guise, shape, phase, light, mode, manner, way, style, lifestyle, fashion, complexion, appearance, tone, modality, modus vivendi, modus operandi, trend, stamp, fit, mould **2 predicament**, problem, dilemma, plight, trouble **3 state of affairs**, the way of the world **4 state of mind**, mood, humour, disposition, temper, temperament, attitude, vein, morale, fettle **5 physical state**, shape, trim
VERBS 6 be in a state of, stand, lie, sit, fare, manage **7 be in a predicament**, have difficulties
ADJECTIVES 8 in a state of, conditional, modal, ranking, placed, situated, classed, high-spirited, good-

humoured, low-spirited, bad-humoured, temperamental, stylish

710 Stealing

NOUNS 1 stealing, thieving, theft, larceny, taking, pilfering, filching, purloining, robbing, ram-raiding, mugging, purse-snatching, pickpocketing, burglary, housebreaking, safe-cracking, hijacking, skyjacking, piracy, cattle raiding, shoplifting, kleptomania, light-fingeredness, poaching, borrowing **2 kidnapping**, abduction, shanghaiing, impressment **3 theft**, autotheft, robbery, burglary, break-in, hold-up **4 stolen goods**, spoils, contraband, pillage, booty, loot, plunder, prize, pickings, stealings **5 plundering**, pillaging, raiding, foraging, foray, looting, sacking, ransacking, privateering, bucaneering, brigandism, banditry, outlawry, freebooting, despoliation, spoliation, depredation, grave-robbing, ravaging, raping **6 illegal borrowing**, misappropriation, plagiarism, cheating, piracy, bootlegging, copying, imitating **7 dishonesty**, cheating, deception, graft, embezzlement, fraud, forgery, counterfeiting, extortion

VERBS 8 steal, thieve, pilfer, filch, appropriate, purloin, rob, borrow, ram-raid, mug, pickpocket, burglarize, housebreak, hijack, skyjack, shoplift, poach **9 kidnap**, abduct, shanghai, impress **10 plunder**, pillage, raid, forage, loot, sack, ransack, freeboot, despoil, spoliate, depredate, ravage, rape **11 infringe**, plagiarize, cheat, pirate, bootleg, copy **12 act dishonest**, defraud, deceive, bilk, dupe, embezzle

ADJECTIVES 13 stolen, purloined, pilfered, thieving, burglarious, brigandish, kleptomaniac, larcenous, ill-gotten, kidnapped, hijacked, skyjacking, poaching, predatory, buccannering, privateering, piratelike, raiding, plunderous, looting, pillaging, spolitory, marauding, foraging, ravaging **14 fraudulent**, dishonest, cheating, deceptive, infringed, pirated, plagiarized, misappropriated, unauthorized

711 Stench

NOUNS 1 stench, stink, malodour, smelliness, fetidness, mephitis, miasma, gas, effluvium, reek, exhalation, osmidrosis, sweatiness, fug, staleness, mustiness, frowstiness

ADJECTIVES 2 stinking, smelly, reeking, noisome, offensive, malodorous, foul-smelling, mephitic, miasmic, overpowering, unwholesome, sweaty, unwashed, fetid, frowsty, frowzy, musty, unventilated, fusty, fuggy, stale, rank, olid, graveolent, gassy, asphyxiating, sulphurous **3 putrid**, putrescent, decaying, rotting, rotten, decomposed, high, off, gamy, rancid

VERBS 4 stink, smell, reek, have halitosis

712 Store

NOUNS 1 store, accumulation, hoard, mass, heap, load, stack, stockpile, buildup, backlog, reservoir, bundle, bagful, packet, bucketful, amount, quantity, crop, harvest, vintage, mow, haystack, stock, stock-in-trade, merchanidse, property, assets, capital, holding, investment, fund, reserves, savings, deposit, treasure, cache, hiding-place, trousseau, provision, pool, kitty **2 resource**, deposits, quarry, mine, gold-mine, coalmine, coalface, seam, stringer, lode, pipe, vein, gasfield, oilfield, oil well, gusher, fountain, fount, spring, source, strike **3 supply**, stream, tap, pipeline, cornucopia, abundance, plenty, repertoire, range, collection **4 storage**, stowage, gathering, garnering, accumulation, conservation, preservation, silage, bottling, protection, stabling, warehousing, space, room, accommodation, boxroom, loft, attic, hold, bunker, basement, cellar, storeship, storehouse, storeroom, stockroom, warehouse, shed, stable, garage, depository, depot, entrepot, dock, wharf, magazine, arsenal, armoury, gunroom, treasury, exchequer, strongroom, vault, coffer, moneybox, moneybag, till, strongbox, safe, bank, memory, hive, honeycomb, granary, garner, barn, silo, reservoir, cistern, tank, gasometer, battery, dump, tip, landfill, sump, drain, cesspool, pantry, larder, buttery, stillroom, chamber, cupboard, cabinet, shelf, drawer, refrigerator, freezer, portmanteau, suitcase, holdall, chest, trunk, box **5 collection**, accumulation, set, archives, inventory, record, file, folder, bundle, portfolio, archive, repository, museum, gallery, library, yearbook, diary, almanac, encyclopedia, dictionary, thesaurus, zoo, menagerie, aquarium, waxworks

VERBS 6 store, amass, accumulate, heap, stack, load, stow, pack, bundle, mothball, stable, warehouse, garner, gather, harvest, reap, mow, pick, glean, stock, bulk-buy, board, stockpile, increase, augment, bunker, provision, supply, fill, fuel, refill, refuel, replenish, save, keep, retain, file, bottle, pickle, conserve, preserve, leave, reserve, fund, bank, deposit, invest, treasure, hive, bury, hide, conceal, secrete, cache

ADJECTIVES 7 stored, amassed, accumulated, heaped, abundant, plentiful, stacked, loaded, hoarded, held, saved, unused, unspent, unexpended, banked, funded, invested, available, spare, supernumerary, preserved, conserved

713 Straightness

ADJECTIVES 1 straight, linear, rectilinear, perpendicular, horizontal, vertical, true, right, plumb, rigid, uncurled, unbent **2 straightforward**, simple, direct, plain, clear **3 continuous**, uninterrupted **4 traditional**, conventional, conservative, moderate, old-fashioned, cautious **5 honourable**, straightforward, candid, plain, frank, open, overt, manifest, direct, unambiguous, truthful

NOUNS 6 straightness, directness, linearity, rectilinearity **7 straight line**, beeline, plumbline, perpendicular, row **8 directness**, plainness, truth, honesty, straightforwardness, simplicity, clarity, fairness, scrupulousness

VERBS 9 straighten, unravel, iron out, flatten out, uncurl, unbend, unroll, unfurl, untangle, unfold, disentangle, uncoil, untwist, unscramble **10 be straight**, talk plainly

714 Strength

NOUNS 1 strength, power, potency, might, force, athleticism, assertiveness, aggressiveness, bellicosity, virility, manliness, musculature, sinews, brawn, burliness, greatness, superiority, effectuality, firmness, steadfastness, determination, stability, durability, survivability, stamina, resourcefulness, resolution, stoutheartedness, backbone, courage, pluck, grit, nerve, bravery, toughness, tenacity, resilience, resistance, fortification, protection, impregnability, impenetrability, inviolability **2 healthiness**, soundness, fitness, vitality, liveliness, energy, enthusiasm, zeal, compulsion, vehemence, vim, vigour, youth, acuity, keenness **3 intensity**, concentration, depth, emphasis, stress, urgency, rashness, cogency, weight, pressure **4 strengthening**, toughening, tempering, reinforcing, hardening, stiffening, fortifying, protecting, invigorating, restoring, refreshing, reviving

VERBS 5 be strong, overwhelm, overpower, outmatch, overmaster, rally, recover, revive, convalesce, hold out **6 strengthen**, confirm, underline, underscore, emphasize, stress, reinforce, fortify, protect, entrench, buttress, sustain, support, brace, toughen, harden, temper, energize, animate, quicken, enliven, invigorate, boost, revive, reinvigorate

ADJECTIVES 7 physically strong, powerful, athletic, muscular, sinewy, burly, brawny, virile, manly, Herculean, amazonian, strapping, healthy, robust, sound, fit, hardy, lusty, feisty, vigorous, sturdy, tough, stalwart **8 potent**, forceful, powerful, mighty, redoubtable, formidable, great, high-powered, overwhelming, superior, compelling, convincing, persuasive, effective, cogent, telling, trenchant, weighty, clear-cut, distinct, unmistakable, marked, urgent, pressing, severe, intense, vehement, extreme, drastic, Draconian, thoroughgoing, well-founded, firm, staunch, fervent **9 strong in spirit**, firm, steadfast, determined, resolute, stouthearted, courageous, plucky, resilient, resourceful, acute, keen, dedicated, enthusiastic, energetic, zealous, eager, tough, tenacious, unyielding, brave, assertive, aggressive, bellicose **10 strong to the senses**, striking, bold, daring, stark, brilliant, bright, dazzling, glaring, loud, strong-smelling, strong-tasting, biting, mordant, sharp, pungent, piquant, spicy, hot, concentrated, undiluted, pure, neat, intoxicating **11 strengthened**, toughened, reinforced, fortified, well-armed, well-protected, protective, hard-wearing, heavy-duty, well-built, stout, substantial, durable, tough, resistant, restored, revived

715 Structure

NOUNS 1 structure, arrangement, organization, plan, pattern, tectonics, architecture **2 fabric**, build, texture, tissue, warp, weft, weave, content, substance, materials, work **3 form**, formation, morphology, shape, mould, architecture, physique, build, setup, make-up, fashion, fabrication, conformation, configuration, format, composition, constitution, creation, body **4 framework**, bodywork, skeleton, latticework, scaffold, rack, shell, chassis, cadre, doorframe, casement **5 structuring**, formation, making, shaping, creation, building, production, forging, patterning **6 construction**, building, edifice, construct, erection, elevation, establishment, house, skyscraper, tower, pyramid, pile, prefabrication, superstructure, complex, works, infrastructure **7 skeleton**, exoskeleton, carapace, endoskeleton, bone, horn, cartilage, keratin, ossicle, ossification, osteoblast, chrondroblast, tendon **8 science of structure**, adenography, adenology, anatomy, angiography, angiology, anthropotomy, histology, morphology, myology, neurology, organology, osteography, osteology, promorphology, splanchnography, splanchnology, zootomy, geomorphology **9 artistic structure**, structuralism, post-structuralism, constructionism, deconstructionism, composition, choreography, design, balance, unity, rhythm

ADJECTIVES 10 structural, constructional, organizational, superstructural, substructural, infrastructural, textural, architectural, tectonic **11 organic**, organismal, organological **12 skeletal**, bony, osteal, osseous, ossiferous

VERBS 13 structure, organize, plan, pattern, arrange, prepare, design, draw up **14 shape**, form, formulate, evolve, raise, make, manufacture, fashion, fabricate, elaborate, mould, frame, compose, create **15 construct**, build, erect, devise, concoct **16 assemble**, put together

716 Style

• *Style is the man himself.* Comte de Buffon.

NOUNS 1 style, fashion, mode, manner, way, technique, approach, tone, tenor, idiom, vein, strain, quality, character, mannerism, speciality, peculiarity, affectation **2 stylishness**, elegance, grace, charm, flair, panache, élan, chic **3 inelegance**, plainness, affectation, overelaboration, heavy-handedness, lumpishness **4 literary style**, diction, phrasing, wording, phraseology, idiolect, vocabulary, language, oratory **5 stylist**, rhetorician, orator

ADJECTIVES 6 styled, phrased, worded, expressed **7 stylish**, elegant, graceful, chic, sophisticated **8 inelegant**, common, vernacular, heavy-handed, clumsy, plain, dowdy, dumpy

VERBS 9 style, state, put, express, phrase, word, formulate, frame, couch

717 Subjection

NOUNS 1 subjection, subjugation, inferiority, subordination, juniority, dependence, symbiosis, wardship, tutelage, apprenticeship, obedience, subservience, servitude, servility, service, employment, allegiance, disenfranchisement, defeat, captivity, constraint, indentureship, bondage, enslavement, slavery, peonage, feudalism, vassalage, thraldom, serfdom **2 domination**, mastery, overpowering, overcoming, discipline, restraint, control, conquest, conquering, suppression, oppression, repression, intimidation, colonialism **3 subordinate**, inferior, assistant, helper, apprentice, student, learner, servant, right-hand man, secretary, employee, conscript, substitute, underling, minion, tool, lackey, flunkey, sycophant **4 dependent**, child, orphan, junior, protege, charge, ward, hanger-on, follower

VERBS 5 subject, subjugate, subdue, lower, humble, subordinate, humiliate, regiment, tame, kick around, browbeat, henpeck, exploit, trample on, tutor, apprentice, employ, disenfranchise, indenture **6 defeat**, vanquish, capture, constrain, dominate, overpower, overcome, master, discipline, restrain, control, conquer, suppress, oppress, repress, intimidate **7 be subject to**, depend on, grovel, obey

ADJECTIVES 8 subject, subjecting, subjugated, browbeaten, henpecked, inferior, lower, substitute, subordinate, junior, dependent, apprenticed, subservient, obedient, servile, employed, employable, captive, in harness, unfree, compulsory, involuntary, indentured, enslaving **9 dominating**, overpowering, overcoming, controlling, conquering, suppressive, oppressive, repressive, intimidating

718 Submission

NOUNS 1 submission, appeasement, deference, obedience, tameness, succumbing, subservience, slavishness, servitude, collaboration, acquiescence, compliance, consent, concession, assent, agreeing, nonresistance, passivity, resignation, fatalism, supineness, lethargy, apathy, inactivity, surrender, yielding, capitulation, surrender, cession, abandonment, relinquishment, abdication, resignation, deference, homage, bow, curtsy, humility, kneeling, genuflection, kowtow, prostration, grovelling

VERBS 2 submit, yield, obey, give in, defer to, bow to, accept, resign oneself, appease, acquiesce, comply, consent, assent, relent, abide, overlook, ignore, disregard, allow, grant, concede, withdraw, retreat, retire, step aside, pass up, capitulate, surrender, give way, relinquish, abdicate, resign **3 succumb**, knuckle under, collapse, sag, wilt, tire, faint, drop, submit, do homage, bow, curtsy, apologize, eat dirt, endure, stomach, suffer, bend, kneel, kowtow, toady, crouch, cringe, crawl

ADJECTIVES 4 submitting, surrendering, quiet, meek, humble, tame, docile, unresisting, law-abiding, peaceful, subservient, servile, menial, lowly, abject, obedient, slavish, unconcerned, fatalistic, resigned, subdued, acquiescent, concessionary, assenting, pliant, accommodating, malleable, biddable, tractable, amenable, agreeable, soft, weak-kneed, bending, crouching, crawling, cringing, prostrate, boot-licking, sycophantic, toadying

719 Substitution

NOUNS 1 substitution, change, exchange, commutation, alternation, switch, swap, shuffle, representation, replacement, deputing, vicariousness, supplanting, supersession, surrogation, equivalence, alternative, expedient, compromise, stopgap, compensation **2 substitute thing**, symbol, representation, synonym, doublet, metaphor, analogy, transplant, prosthesis, pacemaker, succedaneum, bandage, remount

VERBS 3 be a substitute, relieve, succeed, supplant, supersede, oust, displace, replace, ghost write, represent, act for, double for, imitate, fill in, stand in, understudy, deputize, cover for, take over, foster **4 take a substitute**, exchange, commute, compromise, count as, treat as **5 give a substitute**, exchange, switch, swap, shuffle, interchange, compensate for, symbolize

ADJECTIVES 6 substitute, alternate, acting, deputy, proxy, reserve, replacement, equivalent, lookalike, soundalike, surrogate, second, additional, stopgap, makeshift, temporary **7 substituted**, exchanged, switched, swapped, replaced, deputized, supplanted

720 Subtraction

NOUNS 1 subtraction, deduction, minus, discounting, detraction, devaluation, diminution, decrease, cut, retrenchment, shrinkage, decimation, discount, offset, exception, abstraction, exclusion, withdrawal, elimination, expulsion, ejection, extraction, precipitation, sedimentation, removal, alleviation, relief, erosion, corrosion, deletion, erasure, obliteration, eradication, editing, bowdlerization, expurgation, extirpation, chopping, lopping, mutilation, amputation, decapitation, severance, excision, circumcision, docking, curtailment, condensation, abridgment, abbreviation, shortening, castration **2 subtracted item**, decrement, subtrahend, minuend, allowance, remission, discount, refund, rebate, cut, limitation, restriction, drawback, shortfall, loss

VERBS 3 subtract, deduct, detract from, devalue, diminish, decrease, condense, abbreviate, abridge, decimate, cut, discount, allow, offset, leave out, take out, except, abstract, exclude, omit, eliminate, withdraw, expel, eject, remove, unload, alleviate, relieve, shift, drain, empty, void, file down, corrode, erode, rub out, cross out, cancel, delete, erase, obliterate, cull, eradicate, thin out, weed, uproot, extirpate, rip out, extract, precipitate, pick out, hand-pick, censor, blue-pencil, bowdlerize, expurgate, garble **4 take off**, sever, cut off, amputate, behead, decapitate, excise, lop, prune, dock, curtail, shorten, circumcise, castrate, geld, caponize, emasculate, unman, spay, uncover, strip, doff, denude, divest, skin, peel

ADJECTIVES 5 subtracted, removed, deducted, excepted, abstracted, withdrawn, extracted, excluded, expelled, ejected, eliminated, eradicated, deleted, erased **6 subtractive**, reductive, extirpative, deductive, abstract, removable **7 reduced**, decreased, minus, curtailed, mutilated, headless, decapitated, docked, chopped, lopped, severed, limbless, shortened, condensed, abridged, abbreviated, cut-price, discounted, devalued, diminished, lessened, decimated, eroded

721 Success

- *Sweet Smell of Success.* Ernest Lehman.
- *The world continues to offer glittering prizes to those who have stout hearts and sharp swords.* F. E. Smith.
- *There are no gains without pains.* Adlai Stevenson.

NOUNS 1 success, achievement, accomplishment, attainment, feat, sensation, breakthrough, mastery, ascendancy, fame, stardom, celebrity, name, happiness, thriving, plenty, luxury, prosperity, fortune, wealth, riches, affluence, luck **2 victory**, triumph, conquest, win, beating, whipping, thrashing, hiding, trouncing, knockout, overrunning **3 successful thing**, best seller, chart-topper, blockbuster, checkmate, hit, bull's-eye, grand slam

VERBS 4 be successful, prosper, thrive, flourish, flower, blossom, accomplish, effect, achieve, compass, pass, qualify, graduate, get on, advance, progress, arrive **5 overcome obstacles**, manage, prevail, persevere, escape, surmount **6 be effective**, work, go, do, answer, pay dividends **7 be victorious**, conquer, win, beat, defeat, vanquish, prevail, quell, subdue, crush, capture, subject, suppress, subjugate, checkmate **8 defeat heavily**, rout, romp home, wipe out, break, bankrupt, destroy, thrash, whip, trounce, overwhelm, crush, drub, whitewash **9 overmaster**, beat, overpower, overcome, overthrow, overturn, override, outclass, outplay, trump, outflank **10 succeed to**, inherit

ADJECTIVES 11 successful, winning, wealthy, prosperous, fruitful, thriving, flourishing, favourable, famous, efficacious, effective, masterly, best-selling, chart-topping, best-ever, lucky, fortunate, never-failing, surefire, surefooted, certain, rising **12 rewarding**, profitable, lucrative, paying, gainful, remunerative, advantageous **13 victorious**, winning, triumphant, prizewinning, the best, world-beating, undefeated, unbeaten, unbowed, unvanquished, invincible

722 Succession

NOUNS 1 succession, sequence, order, arrangement, cycle, rota, list, turn, hierarchy, pecking order, Buggins's turn, queue, tailback, series, run, chain, train, retinue, entourage, suite, wake, following, subsequence, procession, progression, flow, flux, continuation, course **2 descent**, lineage, family tree, tribe **3 subordination**, inferiority, second place, second class, second eleven **4 accession**, takeover, inauguration, assumption, taking over, transfer, changeover, elevation, promotion **5 successor**, descendant, inheritor, heir, heiress, beneficiary, replacement, substitute, new broom **6 subordinate**, inferior, assistant, subaltern **7 follower**, hanger-on, sycophant, dependant, upstart, no-hoper **8 sequel**, continuation, development, follow-up, conclusion, end, result, dénouement, consequence, outcome, upshot, aftermath, postlude, coda

VERBS 9 succeed, follow, come after, result from, ensue **10 follow in office**, accede to, succeed, take over

ADJECTIVES 11 succeeding, successional, following, next, proximate, close, near, sequential, consecutive, ordered, arranged, second, another, every, alternate, subsequent, consequent, ensuing, pursuant, late, latter **12 subordinate**, inferior

723 Sudden Sound

NOUNS 1 bang, slam, wham, whack, thump, thud, blast, report, discharge, explosion, burst, volley, round, salvo, shot, detonation, blowout, backfire, boom, peal, thunderclap, crash **2 crack**, crepi-

tation, sizzling, spitting, click, snap, slap, smack, clap, tap, rap, rat-tat-tat, knock, pop, plop **3 belch**, hiccup
VERBS 4 bang, slam, wham, blast, discharge, burst, explode, blow up, detonate, backfire, boom, thunder, resound, echo, rumble, peal, crash **5 crack**, crepitate, sizzle, fizzle, spit, effervesce, click, clunk, clatter, rattle, snap, clap, rap, tap, slap, smack, pop, plop, plonk **6 belch**, hiccup
ADJECTIVES 7 banging, crashing, slamming, bursting, exploding, booming, thundering, ear-splitting **8 crackling**, crepitant, sizzling, spitting, clicking, rattling

724 Sufficiency

ADJECTIVES 1 sufficient, enough, adequate, satisfactory, acceptable, sufficing, self-sufficient, complete, competent, equal to, fitting, suitable, satisfying, contenting, measured, commensurate, hand-to-mouth, makeshift **2 plentiful**, ample, superfluous, redundant, openhanded, generous, bountiful, lavish, liberal, extravagant, prodigal, wholesale, unsparing, unmeasured, endless, inexhaustible, bottomless, great, luxuriant, riotous, lush, rank, fat, fertile, prolific, profuse, abundant, copious, overflowing, superabundant, rich, opulent **3 filled**, full, chock-a-block, flush, replete, sated, stuffed, glutted, bloated, satisfied, contented, well-provided, well-provisioned, well-stocked, well-furnished, teeming, crawling
VERBS 4 suffice, satisfy, content, do, answer, quench, work, serve, qualify, reach, pass muster, meet requirements, stand, support, fulfil, fill, refill, replenish, sate, overeat, gorge **5 be plentiful**, proliferate, teem, swarm, bristle with, crawl with, exuberate, riot, luxuriate, flow, stream, shower, brim, overflow **6 have enough**, afford
NOUNS 7 sufficiency, enough, adequacy, satisfaction, quorum, qualification, requirement, pass, assets, competence, autarky, self-sufficiency, minimum, acceptability, contentment, fulfilment, completion, repletion, one's fill, bellyful **8 plenty**, cornucopia, abundance, proliferation, profusion, outpouring, shower, flood, spate, stream, lots, galore, fullness, copiousness, amplitude, plenitude, affluence, riches, wealth, feast, banquet, orgy, riot, prodigality, extravagance, luxury, fertility, fecundity, productivity, prolificacy, luxuriance, lushness, superabundance, glut, superfluity

725 Sullenness

NOUNS 1 sullenness, sulkiness, surliness, glumness, moroseness, moodiness, mopiness, melancholy, atrabiliousness, dejection, grumpishness, whininess, unsociability, sourness, grimness **2 sign of sullenness**, long face, pout, sigh, moan, the blues, the sulks, the sullens, the pouts **3 irritableness**, irascibility, discontent, dissatisfaction, petulance, temperament, ill temper, touchiness, peevishness, grumpiness, gruffness, crossness, crankiness, cussedness, spitefulness, spleen, liver **4 sign of irritableness**, scowl, frown, grimace, lour, glower, glare, black look, growl, snarl
ADJECTIVES 5 sullen, sulky, surly, serious, pouting, melancholy, atra-

bilious, moody, morose, glum, grim, stern, dour, sour, gloomy, sombre, dismal, dark, black, dejected, depressed, cheerless, ill-humoured, ill-natured, blue **6 irritable**, irascible, disagreeable, discontented, dissatisfied, smouldering, temperamental, bad-tempered, surly, resentful, churlish, touchy, tetchy, testy, acid, tart, vinegary, grumpy, quarrelsome, cantankerous, curmudgeonly, dyspeptic, bitter, peevish, petulant, shrewish, vixenish, cross, abrupt, brusque, gruff, frowning, unsmiling, louring, glowering, scowling, grumbling, grousing, snarling **7 overcast**, cloudy, louring
VERBS 8 be sullen, sulk, mope, brood, fret, pout, whine, whinge **9 make sullen**, deject, depress **10 be irritable**, glare, lour, glower, smoulder, frown, scowl, grimace, growl, grouch, snarl, snap, spit, grumble, mutter, complain, grouse **11 make irritable**, irritate, annoy, acerbate, embitter, envenom

726 Summary

NOUNS 1 summary, synopsis, précis, résumé, digest, epitome, abstract, review, recapitulation, gist, drift, conspectus, survey, bird's-eye view, overview, rundown, sketch **2 outline**, skeleton, plan, blueprint, syllabus, prospectus, brochure, abridgment, abbreviation, shortening, diminution, contraction, truncation, pruning, compression, apheresis, apocope, syncope **3 compendium**, anthology, compilation, corpus, chrestomathy, miscellany, album, scrapbook, ephemera, cuttings, extracts, excerpts **4 summariness**, briefness, brevity, shortness, terseness, brusqueness, conciseness, pithiness, succinctness, compactness, pointedness
ADJECTIVES 5 summary, brief, short, curt, brusque, terse, concise, pithy, compendious, succinct, compact, pointed, epigrammatic, laconic **6 shortened**, abbreviated, abridged, summarized, synopsized, clipped, pruned, docked, truncated, cut, contracted, compacted
VERBS 7 summarize, précis, synopsize, condense, digest, epitomize, encapsulate, reduce, shorten, abbreviate, abridge, contract, pot, truncate, outline, sketch, sum up, resume, recapitulate, abstract **8 compile**, consolidate, anthologize, excerpt

727 Summit

NOUNS 1 summit, top, peak, pinnacle, acme, zenith, meridian, pole, apogee, climax, culmination, maximum, limit, apex, vertex, cusp, point, tip, extremity, crest, brow, ridge, pitch, exosphere, sky, heaven **2 head**, crown, cap, topknot, pinhead, heading, headpiece, crownpiece, masthead, topmast, topgallant, topsail, spire **3 architectural summit**, capital, chapiter, necking, gorgerin, abacus, architrave, epistyle, taenia, entablature, cornice, cymatium, finial, fastigium, headstone, keystone, quoin, capstone, copestone, gable, pediment, frontispiece, tympanum, lintel, frieze, ceiling, roof, ridgepole, penthouse, stairhead **4 top layer**, topping, icing, frosting, superstratum, topsoil, topside
ADJECTIVES 5 top, tiptop, uppermost, highest, ultimate, maximum, consummate, climactic, culminating,

crowning, meridian, polar, head, leading, chief, capital, supreme, paramount, summital, zenithal, apical **6 topped**, capped, crowned, tipped, crested, headed, covered, roofed

VERBS 7 top, cap, crown, head, lead, peak, culminate, climax, surmount, overarch, cover, roof

728 Superiority

NOUNS 1 superiority, precedence, eminence, preeminence, primacy, greatness, preponderance, predominance, prepotence, transcendence, prestige, ascendency, loftiness, altitude, sublimity, priority, seniority, influence, leverage, say, effectiveness, excellence, quality, perfection, virtuosity, inimitability, incomparability, majority, supremacy, paramountcy, prominence, success, domination, privilege, right **2 leadership**, authority, jurisdiction, power, authorization, rule, sway, control, hegemony, sovereignty, kingship, imperium, dominion, lordship, command, generalship, captaincy, directorship, management, prime ministership, presidency, premiership, headship, mastership **3 advantage**, odds, points, handicap, edge, lead, head start, upper hand, vantage point, favour, lion's share, seeded position **4 summit**, top, height, high ground, acme, zenith, pinnacle, peak, climax **5 superior**, master, prophet, leader, chief, executive, manager, head, superintendent, foreman, commander, general, captain, ruler, king, emperor, sheik, sultan, prime minister, president, premier, governor, mayor, archbishop, cardinal, pope, rabbi, imam, elder, senior, principal, fugleman, headmaster, headmistress **6 paragon**, genius, prodigy, nonpareil, virtuoso, prima donna, diva, expert, specialist, laureate, high-flier, mastermind, superman, superwoman, champion, victor, superstar, celebrity, prizewinner

VERBS 7 be superior, excel, exceed, predominate, transcend, prevail, better, surpass, win, triumph, defeat, overcome, best, beat, tower above, peak, culminate, climax, pass, outdistance, top, trump, overstep, override, overleap, overtop, overlook, overshadow, eclipse, extinguish, batter, thrash, trounce **8 outdo**, outplay, outrank, outvie, outbid, outshine, outstrip, outwit, outgo, outtrump, outrace, outpace, outmarch, outrun, outride, outjump, outdistance, outreach, outperform **9 lead**, head, direct, manage, run, front, spearhead, captain

ADJECTIVES 11 superior, greater, better, finer, higher, over, super, above, surpassing, eclipsing, overtopping, arch, exceeding, leading, outclassing, ahead, above average, ascendent, preferred, favourite **12 dominant**, dictatorial, magisterial, authoritative, ruling, overriding, governing, ordering, imperial, sovereign **13 best**, greatest, supreme, superlative, crowning, cardinal, capital, matchless, peerless, unparalleled, unrivalled, unequalled, unapproachable, unsurpassed, inimitable, incomparable, unique, unbeatable, invincible, perfect, highest, maximal, utmost, topmost, tiptop, prime, dominant, preponderant, hegemonic, prevailing, paramount, foremost, main, chief, principal, central, focal, first, record, top-ranking, champion, gold-medal, victorious, winning, triumphant, world-beating, record-holding, A1, number-one, pre-eminent, supernormal, immortal, ultimate **14 excellent**, major, first-rate, first-class, top-flight, prestigious, master, superb, prominent, eminent, important, distinguished, singular, outstanding, star

729 Support

NOUNS 1 support, buttress, abutment, reinforcement, underpinning **2 supporting part**, mainstay, prop, fulcrum, brace, buttress, abutment, bulwark, rampart, wall, embankment, mounting, scaffolding, framework, skeleton, backbone, transom, chassis, underframe, undercarriage, underpinning, underlay, bracket, strut, pier, girder, rafter, beam, crossbar, lintel, balustrade, pilaster, column, post, pillar, caryatid, shaft, stem, pile, foundation, cornerstone, keystone, bedrock, basement, groundwork, substructure, pedestal, base, stand, tripod, table, mantelpiece **3 body support**, sling, bandage, splint, crutch, cane, stick, walker, staff **4 rest**, headrest, footrest, footstool, chair, saddle, sofa, couch, ottoman, davenport, bed, cradle, crib, mattress, pillow **5 supporting garment**, girdle, corset, brassiere **6 moral support**, encouragement, furtherance, backing, advocacy, championship, protection, friendship, sympathy, empathy, aid, abetment, help, succour, assistance, cooperation, corroboration, collaboration, approval, endorsement, intercession **7 financial support**, provision, sponsorship, backing, patronage, sustenance, maintenance, subsistence, contribution, grant, allowance, stipend, pension, subsidy

ADJECTIVES 8 supportive, retaining, foundational, ground, basal, upholding, sustaining, maintaining, helpful, encouraging, kindly, sympathetic, empathetic, understanding, reassuring, cooperative, corroborative, collaborative, benevolent, patronal, well-disposed, favourable, contributory, stipendiary, advocatory, preferential, intercessional, auxiliary, subsidiary, ancillary, substitute, discipular, attending **9 supportable**, bearable, tolerable, endurable, sufferable, acceptable, manageable

VERBS 10 support, bear, carry, hold up, prop, back up, shore up, buttress, reinforce, strengthen, bolster, brace, abut, bulwark, rampart, wall, embank, scaffold, frame, underpin, bracket **11 bear**, tolerate, endure, stomach, brook, abide, countenance, suffer, submit to **12 support financially**, finance, pay for, fund, back, subsidize, sponsor, patronize, underwrite, maintain, keep, pension, contribute **13 give moral support**, stand by, back up, encourage, strengthen, buoy up, carry, back, champion, uphold, defend, assist, aid, further, forward, abet, help, succour, sustain, foster, cooperate, corroborate, collaborate, propose, second, favour, praise, honour, endorse

730 Supposition

NOUNS 1 supposition, assumption, presumption, notion, idea, fancy, conceit, ideality, pretence, affectation, presupposition, condition, stipulation, conditions, proposal, offer, submission, argument, postulation, premise, theory, hypothesis, explanation, tentative explanation, model, theorem, topic, thesis, position, stand, attitude, orientation, standpoint, opinion **2 basis of supposition**, hint, clue, data, datum, evidence, deduction, induction, inference, suspicion, sneaking suspicion, hunch, inkling, intimation, instinct, intuition, thought, thinking, supposability, conjecturability, probability **3 conjecture**, speculation, suspicion, guess, surmise, gamble, try, shot, gambling, guessing, intuition

VERBS 4 suppose, assume, presume, imagine, pretend, fancy, dream, think, conceive, opine, divine, suspect, intuit, infer, deduce, conclude, surmise, conjecture, guess, guesstimate, believe, understand, gather, presuppose, presurmise, premise, posit, postulate, assert, affirm, predicate, take it, reason, speculate, hypothesize, theorize, let, sketch, draft, outline, plan **5 propound**, propose, suggest, offer, moot, move, request, submit, argue, put forward, advance, advise, outline, adumbrate, allude, hint, persuade, urge

ADJECTIVES 6 suppositional, assumptive, presumptive, notional, conjectural, guessing, intuitive, propositional, hypothetical, theoretical, postulatory, putative, unverified, moot, armchair, speculative, gratuitous, suggestive, hinting, allusive, stimulating, thought-provoking **7 supposed**, assumed, presumed, premised, postulated, surmised, conjectured, guessed, hypothesized, understood, taken, proposed, suggested, mooted, topical, given, granted, assented, suppositive, putative, inferred, deduced, pretended, alleged, reputed, so-called, titular, quasi, unreal, abstract, fanciful, imagined, fabled, untrue, supposable, assumable, presumable, surmisable **8 meant**, intended, designed, expected

731 Surprise

NOUNS 1 surprise, unexpectedness, unpredictability, unpreparedness, unreadiness, miscalculation, misjudgment **2 amazement**, wonder, astonishment, astoundment, stupefaction, incredulity, disconcertment, disappointment **3 shock**, horror, surprisal, start, jump, fright, turn, jolt, blow, thunderbolt, bombshell **4 surprising thing**, wonder, the unexpected, serendipity, treat, windfall, twist, reversal

ADJECTIVES 5 surprised, unprepared, unsuspecting, unaware, startled, ambushed **6 amazed**, awed, marvelling, admiring, impressed, astonished, astounded, stupefied, stunned, speechless, struck dumb, dumbfounded, thunderstruck, staggered, shocked, disconcerted **7 surprising**, unexpected, unanticipated, unforeseen, unpredictable, sudden, unannounced, amazing, astounding, astonishing, staggering, shocking, serendipitous, unusual, unprecedented, abnormal, freakish

VERBS 8 surprise, take unawares, discover, startle, jolt, frighten, take aback **9 ambush**, capture, ensnare, trap, pounce on **10 amaze**, astonish, astound, dumbfound, stupefy, stagger, boggle, stun, shock, disconcert, disappoint, electrify **11 be surprised**, start

732 Surroundings

NOUNS 1 surroundings, environment, environs, area, neighbourhood, confines, locale, background, backdrop, setting, arena, stage, scene, outskirts, outposts, perimeter, periphery, precincts, vicinity, suburb **2 encirclement**, envelopment, enfoldment, encompassment **3 atmosphere**, ambience, milieu, aura, feeling, tone, overtone

ADJECTIVES 4 surrounding, environmental, neighbourhood, background, outlying, perimetric, peripheral **5 surrounded**, encircled, enveloped, wrapped, enfolded, encompassed, girded, circumscribed, circumambient, roundabout, hemmed-in **6 atmospheric**, ambient

VERBS 7 surround, environ, outlie, encircle, circle, envelop, enfold, encompass, surround, enclose, contain, edge

733 Suspension

NOUNS 1 suspension, hanging, dangling, pendency, pendulousness, pensileness, hang, swing, dangle, drape, droop **2 projection**, overhang, overlie **3 hanger**, suspender, hook, peg, nail, knob, clothesline, clotheshorse, braces, gallows, gibbet **4 interruption**, pause, postponement, suspension, deferment, adjournment, moratorium, cooling-off period, shelving, tabling, delay, procrastination, stopping, withholding, stay, discontinuance

ADJECTIVES 5 suspended, hanging, dangling, swinging, sagging, pendulous, pendent **6 projecting**, overhanging, jutting, sticking out **7 interrupted**, postponed, delayed, suspended, deferred, adjourned, shelved, tabled, withheld, stopped, stayed, discontinued, abeyant

VERBS 8 suspend, hang, hook up, put up, drape, hang down, dangle, swing, droop **9 project**, overhang, overlie, jut, beetle **10 interrupt**, postpone, suspend, defer, adjourn, shelve, table, delay, procrastinate, pause, withhold, stop, discontinue

734 Sweetness

NOUNS 1 sweetness, sugariness, syrupiness, cloying, sickliness, saccharinity, fragrance, pleasantness, melodiousness, freshness **2 sweetener**, sugar, sucrose, glucose, fructose, dextrose, lactose, syrup, treacle, molasses, saccharine, aspartame, cyclamate, honey, honeydew, jam, jelly, preserve, conserve, marmalade, nectar, delicacies, sweetmeats, glacé fruit **3 dessert**, pudding, sweet, cake, gateau, pie, pastry, patisserie **4 confectionery**, sweets, bonbon, chocolate, toffee, fudge, lollipop, liquorice, peppermint

ADJECTIVES 5 sweet, saccharine, cloying, sickly, honeyed, sugared, treacly, syrupy, ambrosial, nectared, candied, crystallized, glazed, iced, bittersweet **6 pleasant**, fresh, smooth

VERBS 7 sweeten, sugar, sugar-coat, honey, ice, glaze

735 Swiftness

ADJECTIVES 1 swift, fast, quick, rapid, fleet, speedy, high-velocity, darting, dashing, snappy, round, smart, expeditious, hustling, hurrying, hasty, double-quick, rapid-fire, alacritous, prompt, sudden, early, immediate, instantaneous, express, meteoric, jet-propelled, supersonic, hypersonic, ultrasonic, electric, high-geared, streamlined, running, runaway, charging, racing, galloping, cantering, light-footed, nimble, agile, winged, flying, hurtling, whirling, rattling, headlong, tempestuous, pelting, breakneck, precipitate, expeditious, darting, flashing **2 mentally quick**, quick-witted, bright, lively, brisk, vigorous, mercurial, quicksilver, reckless **3 accelerating**, quickening, speeding-up, getaway, overtaking

VERBS 4 be swift, speed, run, lope, race, chase, hurtle, bowl along, sweep along, scoot, scamper, scuttle, scurry, rush, dash, whisk, skirr, charge, stampede, gallop, canter, trot, expedite, precipitate, hasten, hurry, career, careen, fly, wing, thunder along, rattle along, streak, flit, zoom, zip, whizz, hustle, expedite, lunge, spring, bound, leap, pounce, swoop, dive **5 accelerate**, quicken, speed up, spurt, sprint, gather momentum, dash off, dart off, tear off, bolt, spring, dash, scamper, leave standing, overtake, overhaul, pass, lap, outdistance, outrun, outstrip, outclass **6 hurry someone up**, hasten, urge on, drive

NOUNS 7 speed, velocity, speediness, swiftness, quickness, fastness, fleetness, promptness, rapidity, celerity, briskness, rattling pace, speeding, driving, racing, bowling along, dispatch, expedition, precipitation, hastiness, hurry, flurry, instantaneity, agility, nimbleness, rashness, career, full pelt, utmost speed, full speed, breakneck speed, knot, Mach number, tachometer, speedometer, mileometer, accelerometer, cyclometer, gauge, anemometer **8 acceleration**, quickening, speed-up, spurt, burst, thrust, drive, impetus, impulse, jump, spring, bound, pounce, leap, swoop, swoosh, vroom, zip, zoom, dive, getaway, rush, dash, scamper, run, sprint, canter, gallop, tantivy, overtaking, passing **9 quickness of mind**, quick-wittedness, alacrity, mental agility

736 Symmetry

NOUNS 1 symmetry, uniformity, balance, proportion, harmony, rhyme, chiasmus, counterbalance, equality, equilibrium, equipose, congruence, correspondence, parallelism, correlation, coordinateness, interrelation, interconnectedness, interdependence, interaction **2 symmetry operation**, reflection, rotation, inversion **3 evenness**, regularity, conformity, consistency, uniformity, eurhythmy, harmony

ADJECTIVES 4 symmetrical, uniform, balanced, proportional, harmonious, counterbalanced, equal, equilateral, even-sided, isosceles, congruent, correspondent, correlational, coordinate, interdependent, interacting, reciprocal, enantiomorphic **5 even**, even-sided, regular, consistent, uniform, eurhythmic

VERBS 6 symmetrize, make uniform, balance, proportion, harmonize, counterbalance, equalize, equilibrate, correlate, coordinate, even, regularize

737 Taciturnity

ADJECTIVES 1 taciturn, quiet, reserved, reticent, withdrawn, shy, uncommunicative, unforthcoming, diffident, reserved, tight-lipped, antisocial, unsociable, sullen **2 silent**, mute, dumb, voiceless, speechless **3 sparing with words**, laconic, monosyllabic, guarded, cautious, secretive, uninformative, vague, evasive, brusque, short, curt

NOUNS 4 taciturnity, quietness, reticence, reserve, diffidence, shyness, uncommunicativeness, shortness, brevity, brusqueness, curtness, gruffness, sullenness, evasiveness **5 silence**, muteness, dumbness, voicelessness, speechlessness **6 guarded speech**, laconism, conciseness

VERBS 7 be taciturn, stay silent, keep quiet **8 lapse into silence**, pipe down, dry up

738 Taking

NOUNS 1 taking, capture, seizure, obtaining, snatching, grabbing, clutching, grasping, avarice, greed, rapacity, consumption, employment, engagement, possession, inheritance, rape, ravishment, violation, deflowerment, takeover, buy-out, merger, appropriation, plagiarism, arrogation, annexation, colonization, subjection, subjugation, subduing, conquering, confiscation, nationalization, assumption, requisition, indention, acquisition, usurpation, coup, getting, profit-taking, winning, cadging **2 taking back**, recovery, retrieval, recoupment, regaining, recapturing, reclaiming, taxing, levying, foreclosing, eviction, seizure, confiscation, dispossession, distraint, repossession, expropriation, disinheritance, deprivation, divestment, annexation, impounding, sequestration, withdrawing, retracting, recanting, backtracking **3 taking away**, removal, eradication, deletion, erasure, subtraction, extraction, deduction, cut, asset-stripping, borrowing, plagiarism, imitation, purloining, stealing, thieving, theft, raiding, plundering, pillaging, marauding, sacking, looting, despoiling, grabbing, capturing, arresting, apprehending, abduction, slavery, kidnapping, hijacking, skyjacking, piracy, extorting, swindle, embezzlement, blackmail, deception **4 taking in**, hospitality, access, shelter, sanctuary **5 takings**, catch, tax, levy, pickings, revenue, receipts, proceeds, turnover, earnings, winnings, savings, spoils, booty, plunder **6 taker**, usurper, bag-snatcher, cadger, sequestrator, receiver, expropriator, asset-stripper, plagiarist, bootlegger, raider, pillager, marauder, looter, abductor, embezzler, robber, mugger, rapist, kidnapper, hijacker, extortionist, blackmailer, racketeer, leech, parasite, predator

VERBS 7 take, capture, seize, obtain, snatch, grab, grasp, accept, consume, employ, engage, inherit, possess, squat, rape, ravish, violate, deflower, takeover, merge, appropriate, plagiarize, annex, colonize, conquor, subject, subjugate, earmark, confiscate, nationalize, communalize, requisition, indent, acquire, usurp, win **8 take back**, recover, retrieve, recoup, recapture, regain, reclaim, tax, levy, foreclose, evict, seize, confiscate, dispossess, repossess, distrain, expropriate, disinherit, deprive, divest, annex, impound **9 withdraw a statement**, retract, recant **10 take away**, remove, eradicate, delete, erase, subtract, extract, deduct, cut, mine, tap, milk, borrow, plagiarize, imitate, purloin, steal, thieve, pilfer, shoplift, raid, plunder, pillage, sack, loot, despoil, grab, capture, trap, arrest, apprehend, abduct, kidnap, enslave, shanghai, hijack, skyjack, extort, swindle, embezzle, fleece, blackmail, dupe, outwit **11 be hospitable**, take in

ADJECTIVES 12 taking, avaricious, greedy, grasping, rapacious, predatory, possessive, acquisitive, acquiring, inheriting, assaulted, raped, appropriated, requisitionary, acquisitional, retrievable, tax-raising, expropriatory, confiscatory, commandeering, annexed, deductive, asset-stripped, plundered, extortionate, deceptive

739 Talkativeness

NOUNS 1 talkativeness, loquacity, volubility, garrulousness, verbosity, wordiness, prolixity, logorrhoea, logomania, verbal diarrhoea, long-windedness, fluency, glibness, multiloquence, eloquence **2 effusiveness**, gushiness, candour, openness, frankness, communicativeness **3 talk**, chat, babble, gabble, jabber, rap, prattle, prating, palaver, gab, blab, gossip, tittle-tattle, waffle

ADJECTIVES 4 talkative, loquacious, voluble, garrulous, verbose, wordy, prolix, long-winded, chattering, babbling, gabbling, jabbering, jibbering, fluent, glib, multiloquent **5 effusive**, gushing, expansive, candid, frank, communicative, sociable, chatty, conversational, gossipy, tattling, prattling

VERBS 6 be talkative, chat, chatter, babble, gabble, jabber, gibber, prate, gab, natter, gas, prattle, rattle on, ramble on, blab, blabber **7 talk too much**, expatiate, gush, spout, hold forth, drone on **8 outtalk**, shout down, bamboozle

740 Taste

• *Taste is the feminine of genius.* Edward Fitzgerald.

NOUNS 1 taste, palate, sapidity, deliciousness, palatability **2 taste of life**, experience, liking, preference, inclination, predilection, refinement, discrimination, elegance, cultivation, vulgarity, enjoyment, success, disappointment **3 appetizer**, starter, hors d'oeuvre, apéritif, delicacy, dainty, titbit, sample, drop, morsel, mouthful, nibble, nip, sampling **4 flavour**, gusto, relish, savour, richness, sweetness, saltiness, sourness, bitterness

ADJECTIVES 5 tasty, palatable, delicious, edible, esculent, comestible, sapid, savoury, appetizing, inviting, relishable, delectable, dainty, epicurean, flavourful, ambrosial, potable, drinkable, toothsome, mouthwatering, succulent, sharp, unpleasant, unpalatable, acid, spicy, sweet, sour, tart, bitter, pungent **6 tasteful**, cultivated, refined, discriminating

VERBS 7 taste, try, sample, eat, nibble, drink, test, experience, savour, degust, smack, enjoy, appreciate **8 make taste**, enhance, flavour, dress, garnish

741 Tastelessness

NOUNS 1 tastelessness, blandness, mildness, insipidity, plainness, unsavouriness, tameness, dullness, vapidness, weakness, thinness, feebleness, adulteration, dilution **2 dilution**, watering down, staleness, flatness, banality, triteness, lifelessness, dryness, aridity, monotony, boredom, jejuneness, dissatisfaction **3 bad taste**, inelegance, insensitivity, raciness, coarseness, crudeness, crassness, tackiness, tawdriness, gaucheness, vulgarity

ADJECTIVES 4 tasteless, bland, mild, insipid, plain, tame, dull, rapid, weak, thin, feeble, flat, stale, dry, arid, humdrum, monotonous, nondescript, unexciting, uninviting, lifeless, flavourless, unsalted, unseasoned, watered down, diluted, adulterated, unappetizing, banal, trite, uninspired, boring, jejune, unsatisfying, indifferent **5 coarse**, tasteless, inelegant, insensitive, undiscriminating, racy, tacky, tawdry, gauche, gaudy, vulgar, crude, crass

VERBS 6 be tasteless, lose interest, show indifference, bore **7 dilute**, water down, thin, weaken **8 have bad taste**, lack refinement

742 Tendency

NOUNS 1 tendency, tenor, drift, trend, course, current, stream, fashion, taste, turn, cast, climate, influence **2 attitude**, disposition, proclivity, susceptibility, affinity, attraction, liability, probability, proneness, bent, inclination, gravitation, leaning, bias, prejudice, partiality, weakness, readiness, preparedness, propensity, predilection, liking, penchant, humour, mood, vein, grain, strain, tincture, tone, quality, character, genius **3 aptitude**, ability, talent

VERBS 4 tend, incline, lean, be disposed, prepare, approach, affect, contribute, redound, influence, turn to, point to, lead to, conduce to

ADJECTIVES 5 tending to, trending, leading, inclining, leaning, intending, working towards, aiming at, pointing to, conducive to, calculated, prejudiced, partial, biased, tendentious, probable, likely, liable to, apt to, prone to

743 Texture

NOUNS 1 texture, surface, finish, feel, touch, sensation, structure, constitution **2 grain**, denier, smoothness, fineness, refinement, softness, delicacy, daintiness, filminess, gossameriness, fluffiness, downiness, fuzziness, peachiness, satininess, silkiness, roughness, graininess, granulation, grittiness **3 nap**, pile, shag, nub, knub, protuberance, indentation, pit **4 weave**, web, network **5 textile**, fabric, cloth, stuff, staple, material **6 fibre**, yarn, thread, string

ADJECTIVES 7 textural, woven **8 rough**, coarse, grained, granular, gritty, ribbed, twilled, tweedy, woolly, hairy, fibrous, homespun, hodden **9 smooth**, fine, fine-grained, fine-woven, close-woven, refined, satiny, silky **10 delicate**, dainty, filmy, gossamery, finespun, thinspun, subtle, fine-drawn **11 fluffy**, downy, fuzzy

VERBS 12 coarsen, roughen, granulate, grain, gnarl **13 smooth**, flatten, iron out **14 go against the grain**, rumple

744 Thickness

ADJECTIVES 1 thick, broad, wide, deep, massive, substantial, bulky, ample, chunky, heavy, stout, buxom, endomorphic, fat, corpulent, obese, overweight, well-fed, plump, portly, round, rotund, flabby, chubby, podgy, tubby, pot-bellied, solid, padded, swollen, incrassate, stocky, sturdy, thickset, barrel-chested, bull-necked, thick-lipped, thick-stemmed, thick-skinned **2 dense**, full-bodied, semiliquid, viscous, condensed, congealed, coagulated, clotted, thickened, intensified, boiled-down, reduced, crowded, abundant, packed, swarming, teeming, jammed, chock-a-block **3 thick-witted**, slow-witted, dull, dense, stupid, obtuse, dim **4 thick-skinned**, callous, insensitive

NOUNS 5 thickness, breadth, width, depth, mass, massiveness, bulk, bulkiness, chunkiness, heaviness, stoutness, buxomness, fatness, corpulence, obesity, plumpness, portliness, roundness, rotundity, flabbiness, chubbiness, podginess, tubbiness, potbelly, fat, blubber, padding, solidity, body, fullness, viscosity, density **6 denseness**, viscosity, condensation, congealment, coagulation, thickening, intensity, abundance, impenetrability

VERBS 7 thicken, congeal, condense, coagulate, clot, reduce, gel, set, solidify, harden, intensify, compress, crowd **8 fatten**, coarsen, thicken, fill out

745 Thinness

ADJECTIVES 1 thin, slender, slim, svelte, gracile, sylphlike, willowy, twiggy, slight, small-framed, leptosomic, ectomorphic, narrow-waisted, wasp-waisted, flat-chested, girlish, boyish, spindle-legged, thin-faced, hatchet-faced, lantern-jawed, lean, spare, wiry, bony, rangy, lanky, gawky, underweight, skinny, scrawny, scraggy, puny **2 emaciated**, malnourished, undernourished, underfed, starved, anorexic, wizened, shrivelled, withered, wasted, peaked, tabescent, marasmic, gaunt, haggard, hollow-cheeked, sunken-eyed, drawn, pinched, cadaverous, corpselike, skeletal, frail, wraithlike **3 slimming**, dieting, reducing, slenderizing, weight-watching **4 fine**, delicate, light, insubstantial, flimsy, sheer, diaphanous, gossamer, gauzy, lacy, papery **5 thinned**, diluted, watered-down, watery, runny, weak, rarefied, attenuated, flattened **6 scant**, sparse

NOUNS 7 thinness, slenderness, slimness, gracility, willowiness, twigginess, slightness, leanness, spareness, wiriness, boniness, ranginess, lankiness, gawkiness, skinniness, scrawniness, scragginess, puniness **8 emaciation**, malnutrition, starvation, anorexia nervosa, wasting, atrophy, tabescence, tabes, marasmus, gauntness, haggardness, cadaverousness, boniness **9 diet**, slimming, weight-watching, calorie-counting **10 fineness**, delicacy, lightness, insubstantiality, flimsiness, sheerness, diaphanousness, gauziness, laciness, paperiness, gossamer, gauze, muslin, lace, paper, tissue, wafer, lath, slat, shaving **11 thinning**, dilution, wateriness, runniness, weakness, rarefaction, attenuation, meagreness, paucity, scantiness, sparseness **12 thinner**, diluter

VERBS 13 become thin, slim, slenderize, reduce, diet **14 be emaciated**, starve, undereat **15 make thin**, thin down, thin out, dilute, water down, weaken, rarefy, attenuate, flatten

746 Thought

NOUNS 1 thought, thinking, cognition, reasoning, cogitation, mental process, thought process, cerebration, deduction, ratiocination **2 intellectual exercise**, deep thinking, headwork, brainwork **3 thoughtfulness**, concentration, contemplation, reflection, consideration, speculation, retrospection, pensiveness, reverie, brown study, introspection, musing, daydreaming **4 deliberation**, pondering, abstractedness **5 creative thought**, inventiveness, originality **6 idea**, thought, notion, concept, belief, premise, theory, hypothesis, conjecture, fancy, supposition, surmise, intuition, inkling, conclusion, principle, precept, attitude **7 thinker**, philosopher, professor, academic, intellectual, highbrow, genius, scholar, student

ADJECTIVES 8 thoughtful, thinking, reasoning, mental, intellectual, cognitive, cerebral, ruminative, philosophical **9 concentrating**, contemplative, pensive, reflective **10 speculative**, introspective, meditative, profound, deliberative, pondered, musing, inventive, dreamy, notional, conceptual, fanciful, theoretical, conjectural **11 reasoning**, intelligent, rational, logical, intellectual, philosophical, professorial, scholarly

VERBS 12 think, reason, cogitate, ruminate, ponder, consider, meditate, cerebrate, ratiocinate, ideate, speculate **13 concentrate**, contemplate, mull over, reflect **14 have second thoughts**, rethink **15 think about**, deliberate **16 have an idea**, premise, theorize, conjecture, hypothesize, deduce, infer, speculate, suppose, surmise, conclude, originate **17 philosophize**, intellectualize

747 Three

NOUNS 1 three, trey, trio, threesome, triad, trinity, trine, triune, triple, treble **2 trident**, tripod, trivet, tricorn, triangle, trihedron, three-wheeler, tricycle, trimaran, three-decker, three-hander, triumvirate, trihebdomadary, troika, triennial, triennium, trimester, trinomial, trilogy, triptych, trimeter, tristich, triplet, trefoil **3 threeness**, triality, trimorphism, triplicity, tripleness, trebleness **4 triplication**, tripling **5 trisection**, tripartition, trichotomy **6 third**, tierce, third party, third person, Third World, third age

ADJECTIVES 7 three, triple, triplex, triadic, trinal, trine, triform, trimorphic, ternary, trinary, triune, treble, triplicate, threefold, trifold, cubed, third **8 three-sided**, triangular, trigonal, trilateral, trihedral, deltoid, fan-shaped, three-pointed, three-pronged, trident, tridentate, tricorn, three-leaved, trifoliate, three-legged, tripedal, tripodic, three-ply, three-way, tridimensional, trilingual, trimetric, triennial **9 trisected**, tripartite, three-part, trichotomous

VERBS 10 triple, triplicate, treble **11 trisect**, trichotomize

748 Thrift

• *I knew once a very covetous, sordid fellow, who used to say, 'Take care of the pence, for the pounds will take care of themselves.'* Earl of Chesterfield.

NOUNS 1 thrift, economy, carefulness,

prudence, frugality, austerity **2 act of thrift**, economy drive, retrenchment, cutback
ADJECTIVES 3 thrifty, economical, conserving, saving, labour-saving, time-saving, money-saving, canny, careful, prudent, economizing, sparing, frugal, spartan, austere, meagre
VERBS 4 be thrifty, make do, budget, conserve **5 save**, economize, retrench, cut down, cut costs, cut corners

749 Thrive

VERBS1 prosper, do well, succeed, advance, flourish, get on, bloom
ADJECTIVES 2 thriving, successful, prosperous, flourishing, bloomy **3 wealthy**, rich

750 Time

- *O aching time! O moments big as years!* John Keats.
- *Come what come may, / Time and the hour runs through the roughest day.* William Shakespeare.
- *But meanwhile it is flying, irretrievable time is flying.* Virgil.

NOUNS 1 time, space-time, time warp, time travel, time machine, timeslip, chronon **2 duration**, continuation, extent, span, lifespan, course, stretch, space, spell, period, stint, reign, office, tenure, tenancy **3 term**, semester, quarter, cycle, season, year, month, fortnight, week, day, hour, minute, second, aeon, millennium, century, decade, olympiad, era, epoch **4 indefinite period**, age, aeon, ages, days, heyday, palmy days **5 interval**, interlude, lull, break, breather, respite, pause, interim, interregnum, meantime, breathing space **6 time measurement**, chronology **7 chronometry**, horology, time-keeping, watchmaking **8 date**, day, Calends, Nones, Ides, birthday, anniversary, occasion, red-letter day, moment, instant, juncture, point, zero hour **9 musical time**, rhythm, metre, beat, tempo, polyrhythm, pulse, syncopation **10 timer**, counter, timepiece, clock, watch, chronometer, horologe, chronograph, calendar
VERBS 11 pass, elapse, roll on, flow, continue, drag, fly **12 time**, clock, monitor, record, count, judge, set, schedule, timetable, mark time **13 spend**, while away, squander, fritter
ADJECTIVES 14 temporal, time-based, time-related **15 lasting through time**, long-lasting, chronic, constant, eternal, perpetual, everlasting, immemorial, time-honoured, horological, pending **16 periodic**, cyclic, repetitive, annual, yearly, biannual, biennial, monthly, weekly, daily **17 occasional**, sporadic, intermittent **18 between times**, interim, intermediate, intercalary, intercalated, intervallic, interwar, interglacial **19 of known date**, dated, chronological, chronometric, chronographic, chronogrammatic

751 Timekeeping

NOUNS 1 timekeeping, timing, dating, scheduling, timetabling **2 timetable**, calendar, schedule, diary, journal, programme, course, curriculum **3 chronology**, chronography, dendrochronology, radiocarbon dating, thermoluminescence, calendar, era, epoch, date, date line, time zone, clock time, local time, civil time, astronomical time, solar time, sidereal time, hour, summer time, 12-hour clock, 24-hour clock **4 horology**, clockmaking **5 timekeeper**, timepiece, horologe **6 clock**, grandfather clock, carriage clock, travelling clock, alarm clock, repeater, cuckoo clock, water clock, clepsydra, speaking clock, atomic clock, biological clock, escapement **7 watch**, wristwatch, digital watch, pocket watch, fob, turnip, hunter, half-hunter **8 face**, clockface, watchface, dial, hands, gnomon **9 hourglass**, sandglass, egg timer, sundial, chronograph **10 signal**, hooter, siren, four-minute warning, gong, bell, minute-gun, starting gun

VERBS 11 keep time, clock, time, monitor, schedule, timetable, slate **12 chronologize**, calendar, date, record, chronicle **13 measure time**, mark time, beat time, keep time

ADJECTIVES 14 timekeeping, horological, chronometric, chronographic, chronologic, annalistic, diaristic, calendrical

752 Timelessness

NOUNS 1 timelessness, eternity **2 agelessness**, datelessness, immortality, deathlessness **3 immutability**, permanence, perpetuity

VERBS 4 perpetuate, immortalize, eternalize, memorialize

ADJECTIVES 5 timeless, eternal, ageless, dateless, immortal, undying, lasting, everlasting, continuous, perpetual **6 changeless**, permanent, immutable, imperishable

753 Timeliness

NOUNS 1 timeliness, opportuneness, providence, suitability, convenience, appropriateness, propitiousness, auspiciousness, favourableness, aptness, fitness, readiness, ripeness **2 opportunity**, golden opportunity, chance, luck, opening, lucky break, elbow room, clear field, scope **3 critical time**, crisis, nexus, pinch, rub, crux

VERBS 4 be timely, suit the occasion **5 take the opportunity**, profit by

ADJECTIVES 6 timely, opportune, seasonable, providential, propitious, auspicious, appropriate, apropos, suitable, suited, befitting, convenient, heaven-sent, welcome, favourable, fortunate, lucky, happy **7 critical**, crucial, decisive, momentous, pivotal **8 in time**, punctual, well-timed, well-judged, eleventh-hour

754 Title

NOUNS 1 right, birthright, honour, knighthood, glorification, celebrity, renown, name, note, fame, glory, station, order, lionization, handle, dedication, commeration, conservation, sanctification, enthronement, knighting, ennoblement, exalting, canonization **2 entitlement**, due, expectation, obligation **3 honours**, accolade, favour, award, medal

ADJECTIVES 4 entitled, worthy, deserving, meritorious, renowned, celebrated, sung, famous, fabled **5 worshipful**, honoured, right honourable, reverent, princely

VERBS 6 be entitled to, earn, deserve

755 Tool

NOUNS 1 tool, implement, instrument, utensil, apparatus, appliance, machine, device, contraption, gadget, contrivance, screwdriver, hammer, drill, perforator, punch, wrench, spanner, pliers, pincers, tweezers, nippers, chisel, axe, knife, saw, rope, cable, peg, nail, tack, screw, nut, bolt, hanger, hook, prop, lever, jemmy, crowbar, jack, pivot, grip, lug, handle, shaft, tiller, helm, rudder, pulley, sheave, wheel, switch, stopcock, trigger, pedal, pole, weapon, arms **2 garden tool**, spade, shovel, trowel, fork, sickle, scythe, rake, hoe, mattock, clough, dibber, riddle, roller, secateurs, shears **3 machine**, machinery, mechanism, works, clockwork, wheelwork, part, component, spring, cam, gear, clutch, synchromesh, motor, engine, turbine, generator, dynamo, servomotor, robot, automaton **4 mechanics**, engineering, electronics, hydrodynamics, hydromechanics, hydraulics, cybernetics, automation, computerization, robotics, technics, technology, high tech, low tech **5 equipment**, tools, utensils, furniture, appointments, fittings, fixtures, trappings, kit, gear, tackle, paraphernalia

ADJECTIVES 6 mechanical, motorized, technological, hydraulic, electronic, powered, power-driven, labour-saving, robotic, automatic, automated

VERBS 7 use tools, hammer, screw, ram, drill, punch, wrench, chisel, chop, saw, nail, tack, hook, lever, crowbar, shovel, rake, hoe, riddle

756 Topic

NOUNS 1 topic, subject, contents, text, matter, theme, plot, angle, interest, concern, point, motif, leitmotiv, programme, statement, message, argument, thesis, theorem, proposition, supposition, keynote, essence, idea, gist, drift, pith, meat, basis, foundation **2 issue**, concern, focus, question, topic, problem, moot point, case, point, item, motion **3 matter of interest**, events, news, happenings, rumour, gossip, story, affair, business **4 sphere**, domain, business, concern, area, branch, course **5 educational topic**, subject, course, project

ADJECTIVES 6 topical, current, present, immediate, contemporary, up-to-date, up-to-the-minute **7 focused**, subjective, angled, pointed, founded, based, supposed, proposed, programmed, thematic, central **8 problematic**, moot, undecided, questioned, challenged, curious, interesting, thought-provoking **9 local**, familiar, domestic, nearby

VERBS 10 focus on, concentrate on, centre on, contain, include, state, argue, propose **11 raise the point**, point out, deal with, discuss, debate, contend, question

757 Touch

NOUNS 1 touch, feeling, tactile, sensation, impression, aesthesia, sensitivity, tactility, tangibility, solidity, concreteness, reality, palpability, texture, consistency, feel **2 touching**, handling, fingering, palpating, manipulating, massaging, stroking, rubbing, fondling, holding, grasping, gripping, clutching, osteopothy, chiropractic, fondling **3 contiguity**, convergence, confluence, conjunction, meeting, joining, node, connection, nexus, meeting-place, meeting-point, joint, junction, intersection, overlap

ADJECTIVES 4 touchable, palpable, tangible, solid, concrete, material, real, substantial, perceptible, attainable, handy, reachable, getable, sensory, tactual, tactile, sensuous, touch-sensitive, sensitive **5 touching**, adjacent, adjoining, meeting, contiguous, bordering, abutting, intersecting, glancing, colliding, crashing, overlapping, interfacing, connecting, hand-in-hand **6 handed**, right-handed, dextral, left-handed, sinistral, ambidextrous, light-handed, neat, delicate, heavy-handed, clumsy, manual, hand-operated, touch-operated, hands-on, able

VERBS 7 touch, contact, feel, finger, handle, palpate, manipulate, manoeuvre, massage, rub, nuzzle, knead, caress, kiss, stroke, fumble, fondle, maul, paw, grope, graze, skim, shave, brush, flick, tickle, nip, pinch, stick, tweak, twitch, pull, pluck, hit, pat, tap, dab, knock, slap, bat, punch, kick, press, jab, poke, prod, nudge, elbow, tinker with, toy with, fiddle with, buttonhole, seize, catch, hold, grab, snatch, clutch, grasp **8 abut**, adjoin, border, verge on, contact, meet, touch, reach, converge, interface, join, connect, overlap, attach, couple, splice, conjoin, impinge, brush, skim, graze, glance, kiss, collide, impact, bump, clash, crash, crunch, intersect **9 be touched by**, feel, be sensitive, tingle

758 Toughness

ADJECTIVES 1 tough, strong, rugged, solid, sturdy, resistant, resisting, durable, hard-wearing, lasting, infrangible, untearable, unbreakable, shatterproof, shockproof, chip-proof, fractureproof, bulletproof, bombproof, fireproof **2 toughened**, case-hardened, tanned, hardened, tempered, annealed, vulcanized **3 hard**, rigid, stiff, nonelastic, unsprung, leathery, coriaceous, firm, clinging, cohesive, viscid, chewy, fibrous, woody, ligneous, gristly, cartilaginous, rubbery, overdone, hard-boiled, inedible **4 powerful**, athletic, muscular, brawny, burly, sinewy, strapping, weather-beaten, lean, wiry, stringy, robust, enduring, untiring, unflagging, indefatigable, tenacious, resilient, hardy, stalwart, rough, brutal, vicious **5 mentally tough**, resolved, single-minded, unyielding, stubborn, obstinate, obdurate, inflexible, hardhearted, stern, unfeeling, callous, cynical

NOUNS 6 toughness, strength, ruggedness, solidness, sturdiness, resistance, durability, survivability, lastingness, infrangibility, unbreakableness, hardness, rigidness, stiffness, firmness, cohesiveness, viscidity, leatheriness, stringiness, rubberiness, chewiness, inedibility **7 physical strength**, muscularity, brawn, leanness, wiriness, stringiness, vitality, vigorousness, stamina, robustness, stalwartness, tenacity, endurance, resilience, hardiness, brutality, viciousness **8 mental toughness**, resolve, single-mindedness, unyieldingness, stubbornness, obstinacy, obdurateness, inflexibility, hardheartedness, sternness, unfeelingness

VERBS 9 be tough, resist, last, survive, endure, toughen, harden, stiffen, cling **10 make tough**, strengthen, harden, tan, mercerize, vulcanize, temper, anneal, case-harden, shatterproof, bulletproof

759 Traction

NOUNS 1 traction, pulling, draught,

drawing, heaving, tugging, retractiveness, towage, haulage **2 pull**, tug, tow, heave, draw, draught, haul, lug, drag, strain, trawl **3 jerk**, yank, twitch, tweak, pluck, wrench, snatch, hitch, start, bob, flip, flick, jiggle, jolt **4 friction**, drag, grip, purchase **5 magnetism**, attraction, drawing power **6 towline**, drawer, puller, tower, hauler, dragnet, windlass, tugboat, tractor **7 magnet**, magnetizer

ADJECTIVES 8 tractional, pulling, drawing, hauling, tugging, towing, attracting **9 retractive**, ductile **10 magnetic**, attractive

VERBS 11 pull, haul, draw, heave, tow, hale, lug, tug, trail, train, trice, warp **12 drag**, trawl, dredge, winch, lift, tug, draggle, snake, troll, rake **13 pull at**, tug, yank, jerk, tweak, twitch, pluck, snatch, wrench, hitch, flip, flick, jig, jolt **14 draw in**, retract, withdraw **15 pull towards**, attract

760 Trade

VERBS 1 trade, exchange, barter, truck, swap, transact, deal, merchandise, market, sell, peddle, push, promote, traffic, smuggle, racketeer, profiteer, nationalize, privatize, commercialize, intervene, float **2 speculate**, venture, risk, gamble, invest, operate, bull, bear **3 bargain**, negotiate, deal, haggle, chaffer, huckster, higgle, dicker, offer, tender, bid, outbid, overbid, underbid, gazump, gazunder, stickle, charge, take

NOUNS 4 trade, commerce, business, exchange, trade-off, barter, truck, swap, transaction, deal, trading, dealing, merchandising, trafficking, factorage, factorship, brokerage, agiotage, arbitrage, stock-jobbing, share-pushing, profit-making, traffic, prostitution, smuggling, black market, racketeering **5 business**, venture, undertaking, enterprise, industry, profession, vocation, calling, craft, métier, job **6 company**, firm, concern **7 speculation**, gambling, investment **8 bargaining**, negotiation, haggling, higgling, horse-trading, tender, offer, bid, takeover, merger, greenmail, bargain, deal, agreement, contract **9 trader**, businessman, merchant, dealer, wholesaler, retailer, vendor, seller, purchaser, exporter, importer, distributor, broker, jobber, speculator, horse-trader, profiteer

ADJECTIVES 10 mercantile, trading, exchanging, swapping, commercialistic, capitalist, wholesale, retail, exchangeable, marketable, merchantable **11 commercial**, economic, monetary, financial **12 profitable**, profit-making, risky **13 unprofitable**, charitable, non-profit-making, loss-making, unremunerative **14 professional**, vocational, occupational **15 contractual**, tendered, negotiated **16 corporate**, limited, public, nationalized, private

761 Transfer

NOUNS 1 transfer, translocation, transmittal, transposition, metathesis, transposal, transplacement, metempsychosis, transplantation, removal, relocation, moving, displacement, delocalization, deportation, expulsion, extradition, relegation, shift, transition, interchange, trade, exchange, barter **2 transportation**, conveyance, transshipment, dispatch, sending, posting, export, import, transit, bridge, passage, vection, carriage, delivery, handover, haulage, cartage, carry, portage, waft, truckage, waggonage, lighterage, freightage, expressage, airlift **3 transmission**, conduction, convection, osmosis, transpiration, throughput, diapedesis, transduction, transfusion, perfusion, decantation, dispersal, contagion, infection, contamination, communication, contact, dissemination, spread, diffusion, metastasis **4 translation**, transcription, transumption, transliteration, copying, photocopying **5 means of transport**, conveyance, car, vehicle, truck, lorry, juggernaut, bus, taxi, tram, carriage, van, train, freighter, bicycle, conveyor belt, escalator, lift, sledge

VERBS 6 transfer, transmit, translocate, transpose, metathesize, transplant, consign, conduct, convect, radiate, transpire, transfuse, diffuse, perfuse, spread, disseminate, disperse, metastasize, infect, decant, siphon, channel, exchange, barter **7 transport**, take, convey, freight, dispatch, send, remit, consign, transmit, forward, expedite, ship, carry, deliver, hand over, haul, heave, pack, tote, lug, manhandle, push, lift, airlift, truck, bus, ship **8 post**, airmail, forward, fax **9 bring back**, fetch, get, bring, procure, obtain, retrieve, chase, disperse, bequeath, commit, assign, entrust, pass on, deport, expel **10 take away**, manhandle, side, relegate, remove, relocate, displace, ladle, shovel, dig, shift **11 translate**, transcribe, transliterate, copy

ADJECTIVES 12 transferable, transmittable, transmissible, communicable, contagious, infectious, transfusable, importable, shifting, conveyable, mailable, consignable, conductive, exchangeable, negotiable, removable, portable, transportable, transposable, carriageable, roadworthy

762 Transfer of Property

NOUNS 1 transfer of property, transmission, deeding, conveyancing, consignment, delivery, handover, changeover, lease, let, rental, hire-purchase, buying, sale, trade, trade-off, barter, conversion, exchange, interchange, nationalization, privatization, takeover, substitution, delegation, devolution, settlement, vesting, conferment, assignment, disposal, gift, dowry, bequeathal, heritability, succession

VERBS 2 transfer property, convey, deliver, deed, lease, lend, let, rent, hire, buy, sell, trade, barter, convert, exchange, interchange, nationalize, privatize, consign, cede, substitute, delegate, devolve, settle, vest, confer, assign, dispose, bequeath **3 be transferred**, change hands

ADJECTIVES 4 transferring, exchangeable, negotiable, conveyed, made over, assigned, consignable, devisable, bequeathing

763 Transience

- *Faith, Sir, we are here to-day, and gone tomorrow.* Aphra Behn.
- *They are not long, the days of wine and roses.* Ernest Dowson.
- *Ships that pass in the night, and speak each other in passing* Henry Wadsworth Longfellow.

NOUNS 1 transience, transitoriness, impermanence, momentariness, suddenness, quickness, brevity, ephemerality, instability, evanescence **2 transient thing**, passing fashion, shooting star, meteor **3 short duration**, moment

VERBS 4 be transient, pass, flit, fly, be fleeting, melt away, decay, rot, fade, evanesce, evaporate, vanish, disappear **5 make transient**, curtail

ADJECTIVES 6 transient, fleeting, flying, fugitive, quick, ephemeral, perishable, unstable, brief, short, shortlived, evanescent, volatile, disappearing, fading, decaying, passing, transitory, meteoric, momentary **7 impermanent**, temporary, one-off, single-use, throwaway, biodegradable, nondurable, brittle

764 Transparency

ADJECTIVES 1 transparent, clear, limpid, pellucid, colourless, crystalline, glassy, vitreous, hyaline, transpicuous, dioptric, refractive, nonreflective, watery, liquid, clarified, pure **2 translucent**, see-through, revealing, diaphanous, lucent, gauzy, open-textured, sheer, thin, flimsy, filmy, fine, insubstantial **3 semitransparent**, translucent, milky, pearly, misty, smoky, tinted, stained, frosted, opalescent **4 easily seen through**, open, guileless, ingenuous, direct, forthright, straightforward, frank, candid, open-hearted, undisguised, evident, obvious, patent, manifest, plain

NOUNS 5 transparency, clarity, clearness, limpidity, pellucidity, colourlessness, glassiness, vitreousness, crystallinity, wateriness, purity, cleanness **6 translucency**, diaphanousness, gauziness, sheerness, thinness, flimsiness, filminess, fineness, insubstantiality **7 semitransparency**, translucency, milkiness, pearliness, mistiness, smokiness **8 glass**, crystal, bulletproof glass, reinforced glass, stained glass, fibreglass, window pane, windshield **9 openness**, apparentness, obviousness, plainness, lucidity, guilelessness, ingenuousness, straightforwardness, forthrightness

VERBS 10 be transparent, reveal, shine through, crystallize, liquefy **11 make transparent**, crystallize, purify, clarify, refine, brighten, cleanse, open

765 Transport

NOUNS 1 transport, commuting, carriage, haulage, portage, shipment, transshipment, cartage, distribution, forwarding, sending, loading, offloading, containerization, palletization, road, rail, air **2 thing transported**, cargo, freight, goods, load, payload, consignment, shipment, contents, mail, luggage, baggage

VERBS 3 transport, haul, portage, ship, cart, convey, consign, carry, distribute, deliver, forward, dispatch, export, send, move, remove, load, transship, bus, fly

ADJECTIVES 4 transportable, movable, portable, roadworthy, airworthy, seaworthy, door-to-door, commercial, shipped, freight, private, forwarded, loaded, unloaded, bussed, commuting, passenger, express, short-range, long-range, supersonic, waterborne, towed, navigated, inland, ocean-going, merchant, piped

766 Trap

NOUNS 1 trap, pitfall, pit, snare, gin,

springe, trapdoor, danger, hazard, catch, snag, catch-22, obstacle, firetrap, minefield, trick, deception, ruse, subterfuge, artifice, stratagem, surprise, ambush, quagmire, quicksand, marsh, sandbank, shoal, breakers, shallows, coral reef, rock, chasm, abyss, crevasse, precipice, rapids, crosscurrent, undertow, vortex, maelstrom, whirlpool, tidal wave, flash flood, storm, squall, gale, hurricane, tornado, cyclone, volcano, earthquake
VERBS 2 trap, entrap, snare, net, catch, surprise, ambush, trick, deceive

767 Trees

NOUNS 1 tree, shrub, bush, sapling, conifer, deciduous tree, broadleaf, tree fern, shade tree, timber tree, tropical hardwood, Christmas tree, fruiter, bonsai tree, dwarf tree, hedgerow tree, standard, maiden, pollard, coppice **2 timber**, wood, cordwood, log, pole, flitch, faggot, brushwood, firewood, pulpwood, sapwood, alburum, wetwood, heartwood, duramen, trunkwood, branchwood, bark, cork, tree-ring dating **3 trees**, tree line, timber line, forest, rainforest, jungle, virgin forest, coniferous forest, taiga, woodland, woods, chaparral, brush, bocage, wood, copse, spinney, coppice, thicket, bower, arbour, undergrowth, leaf mould, beech mast, brake, covert, bosket, plantation, stand, wood lot, tree farm, arboretum, pinetum, pinery, tree nursery, orchard **4 forestry**, tree farming, agroforestry, afforestation, reforestation, deforestation, conservation, dendrology, arboriculture, silviculture, treen, treenware **5 forester**, forest manager, ranger, verderer, woodlander, woodcutter, lumberjack, timberman, woodsman, logger, tapper, tree surgeon, arboriculturist, arborist
ADJECTIVES 6 treelike, arboreal, arboraceous, arborescent, dendritic, dendroid, dendriform, palmate, palmaceous, branching, slender, willowy, shrubby, bushy, gnarled, coniferous, evergreen, piny **7 woody**, ligneous, ligniform, hard-grained, soft-grained, wooden, treen, oaken, beechen **8 wooded**, forested, forestal, timbered, afforested, reafforested, tree-covered, arboreous, woodland, sylvan, sylvatic, sylvestral, bosky, copsy **9 arboricultural**, silvicultural
VERBS 10 manage trees, thin, prune, grub, lop, top, pollard, coppice, tap, fell

768 Trophy

NOUNS 1 trophy, award, reward, prize, medal, medallion, plate, cup, blue ribbon, statuette, wreath, chaplet, garland, palm, laurels, crown, spurs, garter, decoration, citation **2 spoils**, booty, loot, plunder, pillage, winnings **3 memento**, souvenir, keepsake

769 Truth

- *The truth that makes men free is for the most part the truth which men prefer not to hear.* Herbert Sebastian Agar.
- *And ye shall know the truth, and the truth shall make you free.* Bible: John.

NOUNS 1 truth, fact, verity, rightness, unerroneousness, unmistakenness, unfalseness, unfallaciousness, unspeciousness, unspuriousness **2 reality**, actuality, existence, substance **3 the truth**, facts, the case, God's truth, gospel, Holy Writ **4 truism**, axiom, maxim, aphorism, platitude, proverb, precept, principle **5 truthfulness**, frankness, veracity, honesty, objectivity, probity, candour, sincerity, openness, forthrightness, straightforwardness, directness, bluntness, plainness, baldness, outspokenness, ingenuousness, naivety, artlessness, guilelessness, simpleness, unaffectedness **6 authenticity**, realness, genuineness, officialness, originality, inimitability, uniqueness, purity, unadulteration, validity, legitimacy, rightfulness, soundness, solidity, unquestionability, unqualifiedness, unrefutability, unconfutability **7 confirmation**, determination, ascertainment, authentication, verification, validation, certification, demonstration, establishment, attestation, substantiality, corroboration, proof, facts, logic, evidence **8 accuracy**, perfection, preciseness, exactness, meticulousness, detail, definition, fastidiousness, correctness, rightness, aptness, rigour, faultlessness, absoluteness, flawlessness, particularization, punctiliousness, micrometry, documentation, squaring, setting, truing, trimming, delicateness, refinement, fineness, niceness, subtleness, faithfulness **9 uniformity**, regularity, constancy, straightness, unchangeableness **10 literalness**, denotation **11 pedantry**, strictness, rigidity, severity, rigour, literal-mindedness, closeness, authority, cogency, weight, force, legality, lawfulness **12 true to life**, lifelikeness, verisimilitude, realism, representationalism **13 faithfulness**, loyalty, fidelity

ADJECTIVES **14 true**, veritable, veracious, factual, right, unmistaken, unfictitious, honest-to-goodness, honest-to-God, gospel, Biblical **15 existing**, real, actual, substantial **16 truistic**, intrinsic, primary, axiomatic, aphoristic, platitudinous, proverbial, preceptive **17 truthful**, frank, veracious, honest, veridical, undisguised, unexaggerated, objective, unbiased, candid, sincere, open, openhearted, forthright, straightforward, direct, blunt, unflattering, plain, bald, outspoken, ingenuous, naive, artless, guileless, simple, unpretending, unpretentious, unassuming, unaffected **18 authentic**, real, genuine, official, original, inimitable, unique, pure, unadulterated, sterling, hall-marked, valid, bona fide, legitimate, rightful, sound, solid, substantial, undoubted, unquestionable, unqualified, unrefuted, unconfuted, undenied **19 proved**, authenticated, ascertained, verified, validated, certified, demonstrated, confirmed, determined, established, attested, substantiated **20 accurate**, precise, exact, perfect, word-perfect, definitive, meticulous, pinpoint, detailed, particularized, defined, microscopic, correct, right, apt, rigorous, faultless, absolute, flawless, punctilious, mathematical, scientific, documented, fine, squared, trued, set, trimmed, delicate, refined, nice, subtle, faithful **21 uniform**, regular, constant, straight, undeviating, unchanging **22 literal**, denotative, verbatim, textual, word-for-word **23 pedantic**, strict, rigid, severe, rigorous, literal-minded, close, authoritative, cogent, weighty, forceful, legal, lawful **24 lifelike**, verisimilar, realistic, veracious, unmistaken, naturalistic **25 faithful**, loyal

VERBS 26 be true, hold good **27 bring into existence**, actualize **28 be truthful**, show sincerity **29 prove (to be) true**, confirm, determine, ascertain, authenticate, verify, validate, certify, demonstrate, establish, attest, substantiate **30 be accurate**, perfect, pinpoint, detail, define, correct, particularize, document, adjust, square, true, set, trim, refine, regularize **31 be literal**, be actual **32 seem lifelike**, ring true, carry conviction **33 render**, represent

770 Two

NOUNS 1 two, deuce, pair, couple, brace, duet, duo, twosome, dyad, square **2 double**, doublet, couplet, distich, duet, two-hander, diptych, double-decker, tandem, two-seater, two-wheeler, two-piece, duplex, bivalve, biped, bipod, binoculars **3 duality**, doubleness, duplexity, bilingualism, bisexuality, ambidexterity, ambiguity, double meaning, double entendre, dual personality, duplicity, two-facedness, double-crossing, double-sidedness **4 doubling**, pairing, twinning, gemination, cloning, duplication **5 twin**, double, lookalike, doppelgänger, clone, duplicate, copy, carbon-copy **6 halving**, dichotomy, bisection, bipartition, bifurcation **7 half**, fifty percent, moiety, hemisphere, semicircle

ADJECTIVES 8 two, dual, double, duple, duplex, binary, dyadic, twofold, bifold, paired, coupled, twinned, matched, mated, doubled, squared, two abreast, second **9 two-sided**, double-sided, two-way, dual-purpose, two-ply, two-storey, two-dimensional, biennial, biannual, biform, bipartite, bifurcate, bipedal, binocular, bifocal, bilateral, bicameral, bilingual, ambidextrous **10 double-edged**, double-barrelled, ambiguous, ironic, ambivalent, duplicitous, two-faced, hypocritical, double-crossing **11 double**, twin, duplicate, geminate, repeat, second, duplicated, geminated, copied, repeated **12 half**, halved, bisected, dichotomous, bifurcated, cloven

VERBS 13 pair, couple, bracket, double-harness, twin, match, mate, matchmake **14 double**, square, duplicate, replicate, clone, twin, geminate, copy, mirror, echo **15 halve**, bisect, transect, cleave, sunder, dichotomize **16 go halves**, go fifty-fifty **17 have it both ways**,

771 Ugliness

NOUNS 1 hideousness, unsightliness, repulsiveness, gracelessness, homeliness, plainness, deformity, contortedness, mutilation, defacement **2 eyesore**, carbuncle

ADJECTIVES 3 ugly, hideous, repulsive, graceless, plain, homely, unsightly, unseemly, unshapely, deformed, contorted, mutilated, defaced, disfigured, unlovely, unprepossessing, ill-favoured, monstrous, misshapen, misbegotten, gruesome, wan, grisly, graceless, inelegant, unaesthetic, unbecoming, unattractive, indelicate, uncouth, ungainly, distasteful

VERBS 4 make ugly, disfigure, deface, distort, deform, mutilate, blemish, mask, misshape, impair

772 Unaccustomedness

ADJECTIVES 1 unaccustomed, unused, nonobservant, unfamiliar, unwonted, unhabituated, untaught, untrained, uneducated, inexperienced, innocent, naive, new, fresh, raw, callow, green, rusty, unskilful, unseasoned, immature, undomesticated, untamed, unbroken **2 not customary**, nonprevalent, unwonted, unpractised, unnecessary, unfashionable, bad form, tactless, gauche, vulgar, antiquated, old-fashioned, old hat, stale, defunct, outgrown, discarded, disused, unconventional, nonconformist, untraditional, unprecedented, avant-garde, original, experimental, odd, strange

NOUNS 3 unaccustomedness, disusage, discontinuance, inexperience, unfamiliarity, unskilfulness, deterioration, staleness, rustiness

VERBS 4 be unaccustomed, slip, lapse **5 disaccustom**, cure, reform

773 Uncertainty

ADJECTIVES 1 uncertain, unsure, unknown, doubtful, dubious, speculative, conjectural, hypothetical, provisional, disputable, contestable, controversial, moot, questionable, suspicious, distrustful, unbelieving, sceptical, agnostic **2 irresolute**, indecisive, vacillating, wavering, hesitant, faltering, undecided, unsettled **3 confused**, bewildered, disconcerted, worried, perplexed, nonplussed, confounded, baffled, puzzled, discomposed, embarrassed, shy, timid, difficult, enigmatic, problematic **4 indemonstrable**, unverifiable, unprovable, unconfirmable, unlikely, improbable **5 uncertified**, undocumented, unchecked, uncorroborated, unverified, unauthenticated, unsigned, unratified, unascertained, unofficial **6 indeterminate**, indefinite, vague, unclear, undefined, borderline, ambiguous, equivocal, indistinct, obscure, inaccurate, inexact, imprecise, broad, general **7 unreliable**, fallible, undependable, untrustworthy, treacherous, dishonest, perfidious, insecure, transient, unsound, unstable, unsteady, inconsistent, shaky, precarious, risky, hazardous, dangerous, perilous, eccentric, erratic, irregular **8 capricious**, whimsical, fickle, irresponsible, skittish, volatile, mercurial, fitful, changeable, fluctuating, wavering, inconstant

NOUNS 9 uncertainty, unsureness, doubtfulness, dubiousness, disputability, contestability, controvertibility, questionableness, guesswork **10 suspicion**, conjecture, distrust, caution, doubt, disbelief, incredulity, denial, rejection, scepticism, agnosticism **11 irresoluteness**, indecision, unsettledness, vacillation, wavering, hesitation, ambivalence **12 confusion**, bewilderment, disconcertion, confoundment, perplexity, bafflement, puzzlement, predicament, quandary, embarrassment **13 indemonstrability**, unverifiability, unprovability, unconfirmability, unlikelihood **14 indeterminacy**, indefiniteness, vagueness, unclearness, ambiguity, equivocalness, indistinctness, obscurity, inaccuracy, inexactness, imprecision, broadness, generality **15 unreliability**, fallibility, untrustworthiness, treacherousness, insecurity, transience, infirmity, insubstantiality, unsoundness, instability, unsteadiness, inconsistency, precariousness, eccentricity, irregularity, unpredictability, risk **16 capriciousness**, whimsicality, fickleness, volatility, fitfulness, changeableness, mutability, fluidity, fluctuation, wavering, inconstancy, variability

VERBS 17 be uncertain, doubt, question, moot, distrust, disbelieve, suspect, speculate, conjecture, dispute, contest **18 hesitate**, vacillate, dither, waver, falter, equivocate **19 make uncertain**, obscure, mystify, baffle, faze, confound, confuse, perplex, disturb, disconcert, embarrass, worry, bewilder, flummox, non-plus, puzzle **20 change**, mutate, fluctuate, vary, move **21 risk**, chance, gamble, hazard, venture

774 Uncovering

NOUNS 1 uncovering, opening, bareness, nakedness, nudity, naturism, exposure, exhibitionism, flashing **2 undressing**, dishabille, unclothing, disrobement, striptease, stripping **3 nakedness**, nudity **4 shedding**, moulting, shaving, scalping, depilation, exfoliation, excoriation, flaying, skinning, exuviation **5 baldness**, hairlessness

ADJECTIVES 6 uncovered, opened, exposed, bare, naked, nude, divested, undressed, unclothed **7 shed**, moulted, shaven, scalped, flayed **8 bald**, hairless

VERBS 9 uncover, open, bare, expose, exhibit, divest, undress, disrobe, undo, peel off, tear off, strip **10 shed**, moult, slough off, recede **11 remove**, pluck, shave, scalp, depilate, tonsure, exfoliate, excoriate, flay, skin

775 Underestimation

NOUNS 1 underestimation, undervaluation, underrating, misjudgment, miscalculation, minimization, deprecation, depreciation, detraction, understatement, litotes, self-effacement, humility, modesty, affectation, pessimism

VERBS 2 underestimate, undervalue, underrate, misprize, misjudge, miscalculate, minimize, understate, pooh-pooh, belittle, disparage, underpraise, underprice

ADJECTIVES 3 underestimating, deprecating, detracting, disparaging, scornful, minimizing, conservative, moderate, pessimistic, defeatist, modest **4 underestimated**, undervalued, underrated, misjudged, miscalculated

776 Understatement

NOUNS 1 understatement, underemphasis, conservativeness, minimization, underestimation, unobtrusiveness, unsubstantiality **2 detraction**, belittlement **3 subtlety**, delicacy, restraint, elegance, refinement, finesse, discrimination **4 simplicity**, plainness, clinicalness, modesty, bareness, austerity, starkness, unelaborateness, minimalism, beauty unadorned, unpretentiousness, unostentatiousness **5 reserve**, reticence, restraint, constraint, diffidence, modesty **6 suggestion**, trace, touch, dash, smattering, sprinkling, tinge, taste, jot, iota, suspicion, inkling **7 imperceptibility**, inconspicuousness, unimpressiveness, faintness, shadowiness **8 insipidness**, pallidness, blandness, tastelessness, vapidity, wateriness **9 down-playing**, dilution, diminishment, curtailment, moderation, restraint, con-

straint, disregard, deprecation **10 deflation**, puncturing
ADJECTIVES 11 understated, underemphasized, conservative, minimized, underestimated, unobtrusive, unsubstantial, undervalued **12 subtle**, delicate, restrained, elegant, refined, tasteful, discriminating, fastidious **13 simple**, plain, modest, bare, austere, stark, clinical, unelaborate, unpretentious, unostentatious, unadorned, unaffected **14 reserved**, reticent, restrained, constrained, diffident, modest, quiet, subdued, retiring, unassuming **15 imperceptible**, inconspicuous, unimpressive, faint, shadowy, vague **16 insipid**, pallid, bland, diluted, watered-down, tasteless, half-hearted **17 deflated**, punctured, depreciated, cut-down **18 downplayed**, toned-down, moderated, de-emphasized, watered-down, reduced, diminished, curtailed, restrained, constrained
VERBS 19 understate, underemphasize, underreckon, minimize, underplay, underestimate, undervalue **20 detract from**, underpraise, belittle, deflate, puncture **21 play down**, underplay, moderate, de-emphasize, deprecate, dilute, reduce, diminish, curtail, restrain

777 Undertaking

VERBS 1 undertake, do, tackle, confront, try, attempt, endeavour, start, launch, initiate, begin, assume, direct, manage, execute, volunteer, agree, promise, contract, pledge, vow, engage, pioneer, venture
NOUNS 2 undertaking, engagement, venture, affair, business, occupation, job, task, assignment, project, enterprise, campaign, mission, pilgrimage, operation, exercise, programme, plan, design, quest, adventure, search, inquiry, speculation, gambling, try, attempt, struggle, effort, endeavour, work **3 contract**, agreement, promise, pledge, vow, assurance, guarantee, obligation, engagement **4 volunteer**, adventurer, speculator, innovator, pioneer
ADJECTIVES 5 undertaken, done, executed, incurred, assumed, self-imposed, assigned, promised **6 enterprising**, resourceful, innovative, pioneering, adventurous, speculative, daring, courageous, go-ahead, progressive, opportunist, ambitious, responsible **7 overambitious**, rash

778 Undress

NOUNS 1 undress, uncovering, disrobing, divestment, denuding, stripping, baring, nudism, naturism, gymnosophy, revealing, exposing, toplessness, striptease, exhibitionism **2 nudity**, nakedness **3 dishabille** (*or* **deshabille**), informality, nightwear, pyjamas, bathrobe, kimono, underwear, swimwear, miniskirt, shorts, G-string, jockstrap, décolletage, rags **4 baldness**, hairlessness, alopecia, calvities **5 peeling**, shedding, moulting, decortication, excoriation, desquamation, exfoliation, abscission, ecdysis **6 depilation**, alopecia, denuder, electrolysis, wax, razor, shaving, plucking, shearing, haircut **7 nude**, naturist, stripper, stripteaser, ecdysiast
ADJECTIVES 8 undressed, unclothed, uncovered, unclad, bared, nude, naked, stripped, strip-searched, disrobed, unattired, undraped, ungarbed, naturistic **9 in dishabille**,

underdressed, half-dressed, bareheaded, hatless, topless, décolleté, low-cut, off-the-shoulder, strapless, miniskirted, tattered, threadbare, ragged **10 exposed**, divested, unveiled, denuded, bare, topless, discalced, pornographic, X-rated **11 peeling**, shedding, sloughy, exuvial, exfoliatory, leafless, desquamative, ecdysial, moulting, unfledged, unfeathered **12 hairless**, bald, thin, tonsured, clean-shaven, smooth

VERBS 13 undress, unclothe, uncover, disrobe, unveil, divest, doff, remove, drop, undo, unbutton, unzip, unhook, unlace, untie, change, strip, bare, expose, disclose, reveal **14 make nude**, denude, strip, disrobe, strip-search, unwrap, fleece, shear, shave, pluck, deplume, peel, pare, flay, abrade **15 peel**, shed, slough, moult, scale, flake, decorticate, excoriate, desquamate

779 Uniformity

NOUNS 1 uniformity, similarity, evenness, consistency, sameness, homogeneity, symmetry, steadiness, steadfastness, stability, permanence, inevitability, persistence, levelness, smoothness, constancy, continuousness, regularity, routine, habit **2 conformity**, equality, correspondence, identicalness, regimentation, standardization, normalization, uniformity, plainness, blankness, automation, orderliness, method, computerization, pattern, stereotype, cliché, copy **3 agreement**, accord, equanimity, consensus, unison, unity **4 monotony**, repetition, invariability, identicalness, sameness, routine, dullness, drabness, tediousness, humdrumness, boredom, greyness, droning, groove, rut, drill, singsong, ding-dong

ADJECTIVES 5 uniform, identical, even, consistent, same, alike, homogeneous, constant, continuous, regular, inevitable, unchanging, unvarying, permanent, steady, steadfast, stable, persistent, equal, level, smooth, continuing, unruffled, unbroken, immutable **6 conforming**, equal, correspondent, standard, normalized, uniform, mechanical, identical, regimented, mass-produced, ready-to-wear, off-the-peg, undifferentiated, monolithic, plain, faceless, characterless, featureless, blank, bland, normal, automatic, orderly, aligned, computerized, stereotyped **7 agreeing**, equanimous, united, solid **8 monotonous**, repetitious, invariable, identical, same, methodical, routine, dull, drab, humdrum, tedious, unrelieved, boring

VERBS 9 be uniform, homogenize, equalize, regulate, regularize, stabilize, steady, persist, continue, smooth, balance **10 conform**, regiment, standardize, normalize, harmonize, align, drill, grade, size, homogenize, automate, mass-produce, order, computerize, pattern, stereotype, typecast, mould, copy **11 agree**, unite **12 be monotonous**, repeat, persist

780 Unimportance

ADJECTIVES 1 unimportant, insignificant, immaterial, circumstantial, irrelevant, ineffectual, uninfluential, forgettable, inconsequential, insubstantial, inessential, unnecessary, dispensable, expendable, small, little, negligible, forgivable, venial, nondescript **2 obscure**, disregarded, overlooked, neglected, contemptible, good-for-nothing, wretched, paltry, pitiful, pathetic, impoverished, lowly, humble, scruffy, shabby, weak, powerless, impotent **3 secondary**, minor, incidental, by-side, subsidiary, peripheral **4 trivial**, petty, trifling, nugatory, piffling, piddling, pettifogging, frivolous, puerile, childish, featherbrained, foolish, insubstantial, superficial, shallow, small, tiny, token, nominal, small-time, light-weight, cheap, twopenny-halfpenny, inferior, bad, poor, shoddy, jerry-built, tawdry, rubbishy, trashy, pulp, worthless, second-rate, mediocre

NOUNS 5 unimportance, insignificance, immateriality, unrelatedness, irrelevance, inconsequence, inessentiality, dispensability, expendability, insubstantiality, nothingness, nullity, vacancy, emptiness **6 obscurity**, contemptibility, wretchedness, paltriness, meanness, weakness, powerlessness **7 triviality**, pettiness, frivolousness, flippancy, superficiality, shallowness, smallness, cheapness, inferiority, worthlessness, uselessness, inutility **8 trifle**, inessential, triviality, technicality, detail, minutiae, trivia, mere nothing, bagatelle, whit, jot, iota, drop, chaff, gossamer, fraction, doit, fleabite, pinprick, jest, joke, peccadillo, sideshow **9 bauble**, toy, trinket, novelty, gewgaw, knick-knack, bric-a-brac, trumpery, frippery **10 nonentity**, nobody, figurehead, mediocrity, lightweight, subordinate

VERBS 11 be unimportant, not matter **12 think unimportant**, disregard, overlook, underrate, underestimate **13 make unimportant**, trivialize, belittle, degrade, denigrate, demote, relegate, humiliate, disparage

781 Unintelligibility

ADJECTIVES 1 unintelligible, incomprehensible, meaningless, unclear, obscure, esoteric, inconceivable, inexplicable, unaccountable, gibbering, incoherent, rambling, inarticulate, undiscoverable, unfathomable, inapprehensible, impenetrable, inscrutable, blank, deadpan, impassive, inaudible, muted, garbled, undecipherable, illegible, undiscernible, invisible, hidden, private, arcane, cryptic, mysterious, enigmatic, esoteric, gnostic, sphinxlike, oracular, profound, occult, mystic, transcendental, inexpressible, unpronounceable, unutterable, ineffable, incommunicable **2 unexplained**, unsolvable, unresolved **3 unrecognizable**, incognizable, indistinguishable, unidentifiable, indistinct, undefined, hidden, indefinite **4 difficult**, confusing, puzzling, baffling, perplexing, complex, complicated, recondite, abstruse, elusive, amorphous, obscure, enigmatic, inscrutable, mysterious, nebulous, vague, unclear, ambiguous, equivocal **5 strange**, odd, weird, abnormal, unexpected, bizarre, quaint **6 confused**, puzzled, baffled, perplexed, mystified, wondering, bewildered, flummoxed, stumped

VERBS 7 be unintelligible, defy comprehension, gibber, ramble, babble, doodle, scrawl, puzzle, baffle, perplex, mystify, bewilder, flummox, confound, stump **8 make un-**

intelligible, scribble, scrawl, scramble, garble, encode, encipher, obscure, complicate **9 find unintelligible**, misjudge, misunderstand, puzzle **10 be unexplained**, remain unsolved

NOUNS 11 unintelligibility, incomprehensibility, inapprehensibility, meaninglessness, nonsense, unclearness, obscurity, uncertainty, ambiguity, equivocalness, esotericism, difficulty, perplexity, bafflement, confusion, mystification, impenetrability, inscrutability, inconceivability, inexplicability, unaccountability, secrecy, babbling, mumbling, stuttering, stammering, blankness, impassivity, inaudibility, faintness, muteness, illegibility, unreadability, mystery, profoundness, mysticism, transcendentalism, ineffability **12 puzzle**, problem, conundrum, secret, code, cipher, gibberish, scrawl, scribble, mystery, enigma

782 Union

NOUNS 1 union, joining, junction, concurrence, confluence, convergence, meeting, rendezvous, liaison, concrescence, coalescence, fusion, synthesis, merger, combination, cohesion, tenacity, agglutination, concretion, consolidation, solidification, coagulation, compaction, closeness, nearness, touching, contact, contiguity, compactness, association, collection, congress, concourse, gathering, assembly, crowd, alliance, coalition, bond, link, concatenation, hyphenation, connection, inosculation, network, communication, exchange, intercourse, trade, commerce **2 agreement**, accord, unity, concurrence, unanimity, solidarity, harmony, peace, concord **3 unification**, assemblage, collection, jointing, articulation, structure, organization, composition, knitting, weaving, suture, tightening, contraction, ligation, knotting **4 sexual union**, mating, coupling, copulation, intercourse, coition, fornication, intimacy, procreation, propagation, reproduction, pairing, wedlock **5 joint**, join, hyphen, conjunction, copula, junction, knot, hitch, splice, node, link, seam, suture, bond, weld, hasp, catch, hook, fastening, clasp, hinge, bracket, ginglymus, ankle, wrist, knee **6 point of union**, junction, rendezvous, focus, intersection

VERBS 7 unite, join, link, hyphenate, couple, pair, match, marry, bracket, assemble, collect, gather, mobilize, combine, mix, mass, accumulate, merge, consolidate, associate, incorporate, unify, include, comprise, embrace, pack, compact, compress, condense, concentrate, narrow, constrict, tauten, truss, converge, meet, coalesce, cohere, adhere, interlock, engage, grip, grapple, clinch, accompany **8 agree**, unite **9 link**, attach, annex, affix, suffix, prefix, stick, tape, staple, pin, clip, nail, bolt, screw, rivet, connect, thread, concatenate, contact, network, interconnect, span, straddle, bridge, communicate, yoke, harness, leash, tie, splice, knot, lash, hitch, entwine, braid, twist, interlace, truss, tether, fetter, handcuff, shackle, bind, gird, swaddle, swathe, wrap, clasp, clinch, grip, dovetail, fit, clamp, lock, engage, wed, join, weld, solder, fuse, cement, glue, weave, sew, suture, stitch, fasten **10 make**

love, marry, wed, cohabit, enjoy, possess, bed, couple, copulate, mate, pair, serve, cover

ADJECTIVES **11 united**, joined, connected, accompanied, partnered, betrothed, promised, engaged, married, wedded, intimate, involved, inextricable, inseparable, intricate, indivisible, associated, symbiotic, incorporated, cooperative, merged, unified, conjoint, composite, combined, coalescent, collected, cohesive, adhesive, concretive, assembled, articulated, seamed, stitched, sewn, patched **12 agreeable**, agreed, united, unanimous, solid, harmonious, peaceful **13 conjunctive**, adjunctive, connective, copulative, coagulating, solidifying, condensing, possessive, copulatory, venereal **14 tied**, bound, knotted, lashed, hitched, yoked, spliced, stitched, interwoven, plaited, secured, fastened, attached, adhering, cohesive, glued, secure, wedged

783 Unpleasantness

ADJECTIVES **1 unpleasant**, displeasing, disagreeable, unacceptable, rebarbative, uncomfortable, painful, discomfiting, discordant, unharmonious, trying, annoying, irksome, invidious, unwelcome, disliked, distasteful, unpalatable, unsavoury, nasty, horrible, hateful, horrid, disgusting, offensive, odious, repulsive, loathsome, revolting, sickening **2 objectionable**, awkward, unattractive, ungracious, discomforting, impolite, uncivil, discourteous, unchivalrous, unkind, uncouth, impertinent, rude, boorish, mean, cantankerous, obnoxious, quarrelsome, crabbed, aggressive **3 unpalatable**, unappetizing, inedible, acid, bitter, sour, rancid, off **4 painful**, sore, tender, aching

NOUNS **5 unpleasantness**, disagreeableness, pain, discomfort, affront, offence, umbrage, distastefulness, unpalatability, nastiness, offensiveness **6 objectionability**, awkwardness, unattractiveness, ungraciousness, impoliteness, incivility, discourtesy, unkindness, impertinence, rudeness, boorishness, meanness, cantankerousness, aggressiveness **7 dissension**, disagreement, disharmony, friction, disunity, discord, aggravation, antagonism **8 quarrel**, argument, squabble, scuffle, wrangle, brawl, altercation, row, conflict, strife, chastisement, vendetta **9 pest**, nuisance, boor, oaf, lout

VERBS **10 displease**, discomfort, embarrass, enrage, offend, repel, appal, disgust, revolt, horrify, sicken **11 quarrel**, disagree, dissent, argue, nag, insult, offend, squabble, wrangle, scrap, bicker, fight **12 be painful**, hurt, ache, throb

784 Unreality

NOUNS **1 unreality**, nonexistence, unactuality, subjectivity, unsubstantiality, intangibility, impalpability, incorporeality, ethereality **2 illusion**, fantasy, chimera, phantasmagoria, fancy, figment, pipe dream, daydream, nightmare, hallucination, mirage, Fata Morgana, will-o'-the-wisp, jack-o'-lantern, ignis fatuus, ghost, spectre, spirit, wraith, shade **3 delusion**, fallacy, self-deception, trompe l'oeil **4 theorization**, hypothesis, assumption, speculation, conjecture, guesswork, fiction, idealism **5 artificial-**

ity, imitation, simulation, shadow, image, fake
ADJECTIVES 6 unreal, nonexistent, incorporeal, intangible, impalpable, insubstantial, ethereal, elusive, fleeting, obscure, nebulous, tenuous, vague, flimsy, indeterminate, indefinite, undefined, blurred, shadowy, ghostly, spectral **7 illusory**, imaginary, subjective, fantastic, dreamlike, chimerical, phantasmagorical, fanciful, hallucinatory, figmental, visional **8 theoretical**, hypothetical, abstract, ideal, speculative, assumed, putative, mythical, fanciful, imaginary, fictional, made-up **9 unrealistic**, idealistic, utopian, visionary **10 not the real thing**, artificial, synthetic, manmade, simulated, imitation, mock, pretend, dummy, sham, fake, false, spurious, specious, phony, bogus, counterfeit, so-called
VERBS 11 imagine, fantasize, conjure up, daydream **12 theorize**, hypothesize, conceptualize, conjecture **13 idealize**, romanticize **14 delude**, deceive, mislead, misrepresent, belie, distort, pervert, twist, embellish **15 fabricate**, manufacture, simulate, imitate, invent

785 Unrelatedness

NOUNS 1 unrelatedness, irrelevance, pointlessness, inappositeness, extraneousness, randomness, arbitrariness, illogicality, inapplicability, inaptitude, inappropriateness, unconnectedness, difference, heterogeneity, disconnection, disassociation, disjuncture, foreignness, separateness, independence, nonconformity, singularity, unilateralism, neutrality, individuality, rootlessness, divorce, insularity, isolation **2 distortion**, disparity, imbalance, asymmetry, disproportion, dissimilarity **3 misconnection**, misrelation, misalliance
ADJECTIVES 4 unrelated, irrelevant, inapposite, inapplicable, inapt, inappropriate, unconnected, separate, unilateral, disassociated, extraneous, heterogenous, independent, singular, unallied, unaffiliated, detached, reclusive, discrete, segregated, uninvolved, divorced, foreign, alien, exotic, free **5 illogical**, improbable, impractical, immaterial, incommensurable, nonessential, extrinsic, aleatoric, random, arbitrary, incidental, remote, far-fetched, distant, out-of-the-way, strained, laboured **6 distorted**, disproportionate, imbalanced, asymmetrical, dissimilar, unequal, discordant **7 misconnected**, unrelated
VERBS 8 be unrelated, digress, ramble **9 be unconcerned**, disown

786 Unsociability

NOUNS 1 unsociability, ungregariousness, unclubbability, uncongeniality, incompatibility, unfriendliness, unhappiness, sullenness, moroseness, taciturnity, reticence, uncommunicativeness, standoffishness, haughtiness, reserve, aloofness, remoteness, detachment, indifference, apartness, reclusiveness, coolness, frigidity, iciness, frostiness, inhospitality, unreceptiveness, ungraciousness, discourtesy, avoidance, withdrawal, privacy, domesticity, seclusiveness, self-containment, retirement, singleness, celibacy, unapproachability, inaccessibility, exclusivity **2 shyness**, bashfulness, timidity, diffidence, modesty, introversion, anthropophobia **3 sep-**

aration, seclusion, isolation, solitariness, loneliness, exclusion, retreat, rejection, exile, banishment, deportation, expulsion, segregation, apartheid, blacklist, blackball, ostracism, boycott, quarantine, concealment, purdah **4 solitary place**, retreat, sanctuary, sanctum, den, study, cloister, cell, ivory tower, secret garden, backwater, desert island **5 outsider**, foreigner, exile, refugee, outcast, pariah, leper, flotsam, outlaw

ADJECTIVES 6 unsociable, ungregarious, uncompanionable, uncongenial, uncommunicative, reclusive, reticent, sullen, morose, private, autistic, unforthcoming, unapproachable, withdrawn, domestic, seclusive, retiring, standoffish, aloof, haughty, remote, removed, distant, detached, indifferent, inaccessible, self-contained, forbidding, discourteous, impolite, ungracious, rude, disrespectful, unfriendly, cool, icy **7 shy**, bashful, timid, taciturn, silent **8 lonely**, solitary, isolated, secluded, stay-at-home, unpopular, friendless, boycotted, shunned, frozen-out, outlawed, desolate, forlorn, uninvited, deserted, avoided, rejected, ostracized, exiled, banished, expelled, displaced, confined, concealed, single, celibate, divorced **9 secluded**, private, isolated, quiet, remote, deserted, desolate, hidden, cloistered

VERBS 10 be unsocial, stand aloof, retire **11 ignore**, avoid, exclude, shun, ban, segregate, blacklist, blackball, repel, snub, rebuff, isolate, ostracize, reject, ban, boycott, prohibit, outlaw, displace, exile, banish, deport, expel, disbar, conceal, confine, quarantine, seclude, sequester

787 Untimeliness

NOUNS 1 untimeliness, inopportuneness, inauspiciousness, unpropitiousness, unfavourableness, unseasonableness, ominousness, immaturity, unripeness, prematurity, earliness, lateness, unpunctuality, inexpedience, inappropriateness, unsuitableness, awkwardness, inconvenience, intrusion, interruption, disturbance **2 anachronism**, chronological error, misdating, parachronism **3 lost chance**, misfortune, mischance, misjudgment, mistake, error, blunder **4 mishap**, misadventure, contretemps, accident, disaster

VERBS 5 take untimely action, mistime, misjudge, intrude, disturb, disrupt, interrupt **6 lose one's chance**, miss out **7 be busy**, be occupied **8 make a mistake**, err, misjudge, blunder **9 have a mishap**, suffer injury

ADJECTIVES 10 untimely, mistimed, inopportune, inauspicious, unpropitious, unfavourable, unseasonable, ill-starred, ominous, premature, early, late, unpunctual, inexpedient, inappropriate, unsuited, inapt, unbefitting, inconvenient, intrusive, interrupting, disturbing **11 anachronistic**, misdated, parachronistic **12 busy**, engaged **13 mistaken**, erroneous, erring, misjudging, blundering **14 accidental**, unlucky, unfortunate, infelicitous, disastrous

788 Untruth

NOUNS 1 untruth, falsehood, prevarication, libel, slander, perjury, fallaciousness, inaccuracy, erroneousness, inexactness, distortion, concoction, fabrication, fiction, faction, perversion, overestimation, exaggeration, overstatement, underestimation, understatement, misrepresentation, misconstruction, misstatement, misinformation **2 unrealness**, phoniness, bogusness, spuriousness, forgery, counterfeitness, unauthenticity, artificiality, syntheticness, invention, myth **3 lying**, untruthfulness, fibbing, fabrication, falsification, mendaceousness, pseudology, perfidy, libel, slander **4 lie**, fib, fable, story, tall tale, fantasy **5 half-truth**, half-lie, near-truth, equivocation, misinterpretation **6 nonsense**, moonshine **7 duplicity**, double-dealing, equivocalness, irony, ambidexterity, Judas kiss **8 pretence**, deception, concealment, evasion, pretext, subterfuge, shift, ambiguity, ambivalence, show, insincerity, meretriciousness, uncandidness, make-believe, unfrankness, excuse, feigning, imposture, bluff, speciousness, hollowness, affectation, artificiality, sham, flummery, tokenism, posture, impersonating, attitudinizing, cheating **9 hypocrisy**, delusion, dissembling, insincerity, disingenuousness, artifice, play-acting, representation, window-dressing, varnish, mealy-mouthedness, flattery **10 dishonesty**, falseness, duplicity, deceitfulness, treachery, faithlessness, mendaciousness, improbity, fraud, cozenage, forgery, put-up job, racket, dodge, cheat, swindle, Machiavellianism **11 liar**, fibber, phoney, perjurer, prevaricator, pseudologist **12 cheat**, fraud, counterfeiter, swindler, imposter, impersonator, pretender, humbug, fake, shark, phoney, sham, quack, mountebank, charlatan, poser

ADJECTIVES 13 untrue, false, libelous, slanderous, perjurious, fallacious, erroneous, fictionalized, imagined, distorted, concocted, fabricated, dreamed-up, misrepresented, inaccurate, nonsensical, distorted, perverted, exaggerated **14 unreal**, fake, bogus, phoney, sham, false, spurious, forged, counterfeit, inauthentic, artificial, invented, make-believe **15 lying**, untruthful, fibbing, fabricating, prevaricating, mendacious, perfidious, falsifying, propagandizing, libelling, slandering, perjuring, storytelling, equivocating, evasive, shifty **16 misinformed**, misled, deceived, duped, outsmarted, fooled, cheated **17 duplicitous**, deceiving, dissembling, double-dealing, equivocal, backhanded, tongue-in-cheek, ambidextrous **18 pretentious**, deceptive, showy, hypocritical, insincere, meretricious, pretending, posing, posturing, play-acting, dissembling, feigning, bluffing, unnatural, false, phoney, hollow, affected, sanctimonious, mealy-mouthed, artificial, false-faced, tokenistic **19 dishonest**, false, duplicitous, deceitful, treacherous, mendacious, insincere, disingenuous, Machiavellian, cunning, sly, wily, cheating, defrauding, swindling, impersonating, pretending, shamming, humbug, fraudulent **20 unfaithful**, faithless, promiscuous, adulterous, fickle, deceitful, false

VERBS 21 lie, fib, fabricate, fictionalize, romanticize, imagine, palter, prevaricate, distort, pervert, concoct, misrepresent, misstate, libel, slander, perjure, falsify, rumour, gossip, misinterpret **22 make unreal**, fake, falsify, forge, counterfeit, fabricate, invent **23 talk nonsense**, talk hogwash **24 pretend**, deceive, conceal, show, feign, bluff, posture, pose, attitudinize, humbug, delude, dissemble, play-act, imitate, impersonate, represent, evade, shift, shuffle, affect **25 be dishonest**, falsify, deceive, hoax, sham, cheat, fraud, cozen, counterfeit, forge

789 Unwillingness

ADJECTIVES 1 unwilling, disinclined, indisposed, loath, reluctant, demurring **2 refusing**, unconsenting, unreconciled, unconvinced, dissenting, adverse, opposed, opting out **3 cautious**, wary, chary, hesitant, shy, bashful, modest, shrinking, unenthusiastic, half-hearted, lukewarm, unhelpful, uncooperative **4 procrastinating**, postponing, delaying, sluggish, lazy, neglectful, negligent **5 reluctant**, resistant, protesting, sulky, dissenting

VERBS 6 be unwilling, resist, reject, disagree, dissent, protest **7 refuse**, recoil, blench, flinch, fight, shrink from, duck, jib, shirk, elude **8 hold back**, postpone, delay, demur, procrastinate, shelve, hesitate **9 not cooperate**, dissent, obstruct, dissociate oneself, abstain, opt out **10 grudge**, sulk

NOUNS 11 unwillingness, loathness, reluctance, disinclination, indisposition, dislike, disagreement, demur, objection **12 opposition**, resistance, renitency, recalcitrance, filibuster, balking, refusal, rejection, opt-out, rebuff, noncooperation **13 dissociation**, abstention, unenthusiasm, half-heartedness, apathy, indifference, faintheartedness, backwardness, slowness, hesitation, wariness, scruple, qualm, doubt, repugnance, abhorrence, recoil, aversion, shrinking, shyness, bashfulness **14 disobedience**, nonobservance, noncompliance, indocility, refractoriness, fractiousness, the sulks, sullenness, perfunctoriness, undependability, unreliability **15 delay**, shelving, postponement, procrastination, laziness

790 Use

VERBS 1 use, utilize, employ, exercise, practise, adopt, try, administer, allot, exhaust, spend, expend, absorb, consume, waste, squander, handle, finger, trouch, tread, work, drive, manipulate, manoeuvre, operate, wield, ply, brandish, treat, overwork, tax, task, fatigue, mould **2 frequent**, shop at **3 exploit**, maximize, milk, drain, extract, convert, reuse, recycle, reclaim, play on, befool, abuse **4 resort to**, fall back on **5 dispose of**, control, command, assign, allot, allocate, apportion, requisition, deploy, motivate, enjoy, possess, consume

NOUNS 6 use, utilization, exploitation, employment, exercise, practice, operation, disposal, enjoyment, usufruct, possession, conversion, application, deployment, resort, recourse, control, management, treatment, handling, carefulness, ill-treatment, misuse, abuse, depreciation, dilapidation, exhaustion, consumption, waste, reuse, recycling, reclamation, usefulness, advantage, benefit, good, profit, service, practicality, convertibility, applicability, utility,

function, purpose, point, avail, functioning, power, wont, habit
ADJECTIVES 7 used, utilized, employed, exercised, occupied, exhausted, consumed, spent, worn, threadbare, shabby, down-at-heel, dilapidated, second-hand, preowned, cast-off, reused, recycled, reclaimed, dog-eared, well-worn, shopsoiled, beaten, hackneyed, stale, pragmatic, practical, utilitarian, everyday, ordinary, convenient, makeshift, provisional, exploited, subservient **8 usable**, utilizable, employable, exploitable, convertible, applicable, available, functioning, working, useful, profitable, advantageous, consumable, disposable

791 Usefulness

ADJECTIVES 1 useful, handy, helpful, utilitarian, pragmatic, practical, applied, functional, commodious, convenient, advisable, sensible, suitable, expedient, applicable, versatile, multipurpose, adaptable, disposable, throwaway, available, operative **2 usable**, serviceable, reusable, recyclable, employable, workable, valid **3 instrumental**, subsidiary, subservient, able, competent, efficacious, effective, powerful, conducive, tending, adequate **4 profitable**, remunerative, lucrative, paying, gainful, productive, fruitful, beneficial, advantageous, salutary, edifying, worthwhile
NOUNS 5 usefulness, purpose, point, utility, handiness, helpfulness, aid, service, avail, practicality, application, functionalism, commodity, convenience, suitability, expediency, applicability, versatility, adaptability, readiness, availability **6 usability**, serviceability, employability, workability, value, worth, merit, good, virtue, function **7 instrumentality**, ability, competence, efficacy, power, potency, clout, influence, adequacy **8 benefit**, advantage, gain, profit, return
VERBS 9 be useful, help, aid, advance, promote, avail, serve, function, work, operate, suffice **10 benefit**, advantage, do good, bring results, profit, gain **11 find useful**, utilize, employ

792 Uselessness

ADJECTIVES 1 useless, inutile, futile, unhelpful, unfit, unapt, unsuitable, inapplicable, inconvenient, inexpedient, impractical, unworkable, nonfunctional, ornamental, redundant, superflous, excessive, unnecessary, unwanted, expendable, dispensable, disposable, throwaway, unusable, unserviceable, unemployable, unqualified, unskilled, unable, incompetent, inept, inefficient, feckless, impotent, powerless, inadequate, nonfunctioning, inoperative, spent, effete, invalid, void, null, abrogated, obsolete, outmoded, old-fashioned, antiquated, worthless, valueless, rubbishy, trashy **2 futile**, purposeless, pointless, Sisyphean, hopeless, in vain, idle, unavailing, abortive, unsuccessful, profitless, loss-making, uneconomic, unproductive, fruitless, barren, wasted, squandered, time-wasting
NOUNS 3 uselessness, inutility, futility, unhelpfulness, disservice, unfitness, unaptness, unsuitability, inapplicability, inconvenience, inexpedience, impracticality, unworkability, redundancy, superfluousness, expendability, dispensability, disposability, unem-

ployability, unskilfulness, inability, incompetence, ineptitude, inefficiency, fecklessness, impotence, powerlessness, inadequacy, effeteness, worthlessness **4 futility**, purposelessness, pointlessness, hopelessness, vanity, idleness, failure, profitlessness, bootlessness, unproductiveness, fruitlessness, barrenness, sterility, waste **5 waste of effort**, false scent, red herring, wild-goose chase, fool's errand, half measures, tinkering **6 refuse**, rubbish, junk, litter, scrap, throwaway, disposable, castoff, reject, leftovers, lumber, stuff, spoilage, wastage, bilge, sweepings, shavings, bits, crumbs, debris, muck, dirt, dross, compost, rubbish dump, tip, sump, drain, cesspool

VERBS 7 be useless, hinder, achieve nothing **8 make useless**, disqualify, disable, render unfit, unman, disarm, cripple, lame, dismantle, disassemble, undo, decommission, lay up, deactivate, sabotage, obstruct, abrogate, devalue, cheapen, impair, deface, pollute, contaminate, destroy, obliterate, sterilize, castrate, emasculate, exhaust, use up **9 waste effort**, leave unfinished,

793 Vacillation

ADJECTIVES 1 vacillating, wavering, irresolute, unresolved, undecided, uncommitted, equivocal, tergiversating, undetermined, indecisive, unsure, uncertain, hesitating, dithering, stalling, evasive, shifty **2 changeable**, variable, unstable, inconstant, temperamental, mercurial, fickle, whimsical, capricious, restless, irresponsible, giddy, flighty, feather-brained, superficial, unfaithful **3 timid**, tremulous, nervy, jumpy, jittery, panicky, faint-hearted, cowardly, squeamish, weak, pusillanimous, spineless, insipid **4 unsteady**, unreliable, teetering, tottering, apathetic, indifferent, suggestible, impressionable, flexible, pliant

VERBS 5 vacillate, waver, fluctuate, oscillate, seesaw, wobble, teeter, sway, dither, stall, equivocate, tergiversate, quibble, palter **6 hesitate**, back away, balk, shy, jib, shirk, evade **7 be irresolute**, delay, procrastinate **8 balance**, discuss, debate **9 change sides**, apostatize, be unfaithful, commit adultery **10 compromise**, yield

NOUNS 11 vacillation, irresolution, indecision, uncertainty, equivocation, tergiversation, doubt, hesitation, nonperseverance **12 inconstancy**, fluctuation, changeableness, variability, fickleness, whimsicality, capriciousness, irresponsibility **13 timidity**, tremulousness, nervousness, jumpiness, jitteryness, faint-heartedness, cowardice, squeamishness, weakness, pusillanimity **14 apathy**, indifference, half-heartedness, listlessness, impressibility, suggestibility, pliancy, passivity, inertness

794 Vanity

NOUNS 1 vanity, vainness, immodesty, overproudness, insubstantiality, conceit, self-importance, big-headedness **2 self-satisfaction**, self-congratulation, smugness, complacency **3 cockiness**, perkiness, bumptiousness, pertness, aggressiveness, obtrusiveness, self-confidence, swank **4 self-admiration**, self-esteem, self-worship, self-endearment, narcissism **5 self-interest**, egotism, self-centredness, me-ism **6 boastfulness**, pride, conceit, arrogance, side, showing off

ADJECTIVES 7 vain, immodest, overproud, insubstantial, conceited, self-important, stuck-up, snooty, big-headed **8 self-satisfied**, complacent, contented **9 self-admiring**, narcissistic, smug, supercilious **10 cocky**, perky, pert, bumptious, pompous, aggressive, self-confident, swanky, pretentious, affected **11 self-interested**, selfish, egocentric, solipsistic **12 boastful**, proud, arrogant, exhibitionistic, ostentatious, self-opinionated, stuck-up, peacockish, know-it-all, dogmatic, opinionated, puffed up, blatant, swaggering, pompous, pretentious **13 opinionated**, dogmatic

VERBS 14 be vain, swagger **15 show off**, boast, swank, strut **16 be affected**, dress up, doll up **17 make conceited**, inflate

795 Variegation

NOUNS 1 variegation, variety, difference, diversification, dichroism, polychromatism, motley, spectrum, rainbow effect, iridescence, opalescence, pearliness, chatoyancy **2 check**, chequer, plaid, tartan, mosaic, patchwork, inlay, damascine, marquetry, parquetry **3 striping**, striation, band, bar, line, streak, marbling, crack, craze, crackle **4 maculation**, mottling, dappling, brindling, stippling, pointillism, freckling, spottiness, patchiness, speckle, dot, macula, foxing, pimple

ADJECTIVES 5 variegated, bicolour, dichroic, trichoic, polychromatic, multicoloured, pied, varicoloured, many-hued, motley, kaleidoscopic, spectral, prismatic, colourful, florid, ornamental, embroidered **6 iridescent**, opalescent, nacreous, pearly, semitransparent, shot, pavonine, moiré, watered **7 checked**, chequered, plaid, tartan, tortoiseshell, inlaid, tessellated, patched, piebald, pinto, skewbald **8 striped**, striate, banded, barred, lined, streaked, marbled, veined, jaspé, reticulate, panelled **9 mottled**, dappled, brindled, tabby, grizzled, pepper-and-salt, roan, spotted, maculate, dotted, studded, peppered, sprinkled, powdered, dusted, cloudy, blemished, fly-spotted, speckled, freckled, spotty

VERBS 10 variegate, diversify, pattern, chequer, check, patch, spangle, damascene, inlay, enamel, tessellate, mottle, dapple, brindle, stipple, grizzle, spot, maculate, stud, pepper, sprinkle, powder, dust, speckle, freckle, stripe, striate, band, bar, streak, marble, vein, craze, crack, cloud, stain, blot

796 Verification

VERBS 1 verify, validate, confirm, ratify, authenticate, certify, record, document, assure, guarantee, warrant, second, support, sign, endorse, vindicate, ensure, check **2 prove**, demonstrate, illustrate, clarify, show, evince, corroborate, sustain, support, substantiate, determine, ascertain, establish **3 testify**, attest, affirm, state, assert, avow, aver

NOUNS 4 verification, validation, confirmation, ratification, authentication, certification, documentation, attestation, affirmation, avouchment, avowal, averment, assurance, surety, double check,

crosscheck **5 proof**, demonstration, illustration, clarification, corroboration, support, substantiation, circumstantiation, determination, ascertainment **6 evidence**, confirmation, statement, credential, testimonial, reference, recommendation, seal, signature, documentation, passport
ADJECTIVES 7 verifiable, certifiable, documented, authentic, recorded, seconded, proved **8 verificatory**, demonstrative, illustrative, evidential, determining, validating, assuring, establishing, confirming, testificatory, ratificatory, prima facie, corroborative, supportive, substantial, circumstantial, probative, collative **9 verified**, validated, confirmed, ratified, authenticated, certified, documented, attested, affirmed, avouched, avowed, averred, assured, sure, certain

797 Verticality

NOUNS 1 verticality, uprightness, erectness, straightness, perpendicularity, squareness, sheerness, precipitousness, steepness, fall **2 making vertical**, upending, standing up, straightening, rearing, rising, elevating, building **3 plumb line**, square
VERBS 4 be vertical, be upstanding **5 make vertical**, erect, build, elevate, raise, stick up, cock up, prick up, set up, upend, straighten, plumb **6 fall vertically**, plummet
ADJECTIVES 7 vertical, upright, erect, upended, standing, straight, plumb, sheer, precipitous **8 unbowed**, rampant, rearing, upraised, cocked up **9 perpendicular**, orthogonal, right-angled, square

798 Veto

NOUNS 1 veto, ban, embargo, injunction, interdiction, counterorder, check, curfew, thumbs down, suspension, cancellation, denial, rejection, refusal, rebuff, abrogation, annulment, repealing, restriction, circumscription, exclusion, ostracism, prohibition, taboo, repression, suppression, prevention, restraint, obstruction, impediment, obstacle, disallowance, abolition, temperance, unpermissibility, illicitness, crackdown **2 censorship**, proscription, deletion, blue pencil, restricted information
VERBS 3 veto, ban, embargo, interdict, counterorder, contermand, check, turn down, withhold permission, deny, suspend, cancel, reject, refuse, rebuff, abrogate, annul, repeal, revoke, restrict, circumscribe, exclude, ostracize, blackball, debar, forbid, prohibit, disallow, prevent, obstruct, impede, inhibit, abolish, outlaw, criminalize **4 censor**, proscribe, delete, blue-pencil, classify secret, make taboo, restrict, stop, repress, suppress, restrain, stifle, cancel
ADJECTIVES 5 vetoed, banned, embargoed, contraband, injunctive, interdictive, suspended, cancelled, denied, rejected, refused, blackballed, restrictive, forbidden, impermissible, unauthorized, circumscriptive, exclusive, prohibited, barred, taboo, repressive, suppressive, preventive, obstructive, inhibited, illicit **6 censored**, proscriptive, deleted, blue-pencilled, blacked out, unprintable, unmentionable, unsayable, classified, top-secret

799 Vindication

NOUNS 1 vindication, exoneration, exculpation, absolution, remission, acquittal, discharge, dismissal, release, pardon, clearance, purging, reinstatement, restitution, restoration **2 defence**, rebuttal, refutation, rejoinder, retort, recrimination, counterargument, plea, justification, explanation, grounds, truth, reason, excuse, alibi, cause, extenuating circumstances, mitigation, palliation, qualification **3 cover-up**, whitewash **4 revenge**, vengeance, reprisal, requital, retribution

VERBS 5 vindicate, exonerate, exculpate, absolve, remit, excuse, pardon, clear, acquit, discharge, dismiss, release, liberate, free, purge, reinstate, restore, rehabilitate **6 justify**, defend, rebut, refute, rejoin, retort, recriminate, argue, plead, attest to, warrant, explain, prove, demonstrate, corroborate, substantiate, alibi, champion, uphold, extenuate, mitigate, palliate, soften, ease **7 cover up**, whitewash **8 avenge**, revenge

ADJECTIVES 9 vindicatory, exculpatory, exonerative, justifying, defensive, argumentative, refuting, rejoining, retorting, rebutting, explanatory, excusatory, supportive, corroborative, apologetic, extenuating, mitigative, qualifying, palliative, remissive **10 innocent**, acquitted, dismissed, discharged, released, pardoned, cleared, restored **11 vindicable**, justifiable, defensible, arguable, refutable, rebuttable, warrantable, admissible, allowable, reasonable, explainable, excusable, pardonable, remissible, forgivable, condonable, venial, exemptible **12 vindictive**, vengeful, requiting, retributive, unforgiving, spiteful, venomous, malicious

800 Violence

NOUNS 1 violence, ferocity, vehemence, excess, severity, virulence, intensity, power, force, strength, vigour, bluster, roughness, harshness, fierceness, aggression, wildness, fury, frenzy, passion, agitation, turbulence, impetuosity, forcefulness, might, energy, boisterousness, destructiveness **2 physical violence**, torture, strong-arm tactics, thuggery, hooliganism, vandalism, terrorism, brute force, bestiality, savagery, barbarity, bloodlust, bloodthirstiness, slaughter, homicide, murder, rape **3 instance of violence**, onrush, assault, charge, sortie, attack, outburst, commotion, disturbance, tumult, brouhaha, riot, uproar, roughhouse, fracas, clash, wrench, dislocation, shock, outrage, atrocity, murder, bloodbath, throe, paroxysm, convulsion, spasm, tremor, earthquake, cataclysm, eruption, explosion, flare-up

ADJECTIVES 4 violent, ferocious, vehement, excessive, outrageous, severe, virulent, intense, extreme, acute, unmitigated, blustering, bluff, rough, harsh, fierce, aggressive, tyrannical, heavy-handed, forceful, powerful, vigorous, energetic, wild, furious, angry, fuming, frenzied, frantic, frenetic, hysterical, kicking, struggling, thrashing, maddened, crazed, enraged, berserk, intemperate, unrestrained, uncontrollable, ungovernable, unruly, untamed, raging, rabid, irrepressible, ebullient, fiery, impassioned, ardent, fervent, eruptive, bursting, convulsive, catastrophic, cataclysmic, devastating, explosive, boiling, agitated, turbulent, tumultuous, tempestuous, stormy, riotous, uproarious, boisterous, rampant, roaring, murderous, barbarous, savage, brutal, bestial, cruel, vicious, bloodthirsty, ravening, hotheaded, headstrong, bellicose

VERBS 5 be violent, run riot, run amok, hurtle, hurl oneself, crash in, burst in, surge forward, charge, stampede, riot, roughhouse, rage, storm, bluster, roar, see red, go berserk **6 use violence**, force, strike, hit, mug, beat up, assault, abuse, violate, rape, ravish, torture, ill-treat, break, smash, destroy, strain, pull, wrench, twist, sprain, dislocate, fracture, break in, burst in, shock **7 make violent**, jolt, goad, whip up, incite, inflame, foment, exacerbate, aggravate, whet, sharpen, irritate, exasperate, anger, infuriate

801 Virtue

• *Virtue is like a rich stone, best plain set.* Francis Bacon.

NOUNS 1 virtue, righteousness, probity, goodness, moral rectitude, morality, spirituality, saintliness, sanctity, godliness, holiness, perfection, nobleness, magnanimity, philanthropy, benevolence, generosity, altruism, unselfishness, disinterestedness, idealism, uprightness, stainlessness, innocence, honour, integrity, decency **2 virtues**, morals, mores, ethics, principles, ideals, faith, hope, charity, love, prudence, justice, temperance, soberness, self-control, character, chastity, purity, virginity, fortitude, honesty, duty, obedience, grace **3 worth**, excellence, credit

ADJECTIVES 4 virtuous, righteous, good, Christian, moral, spiritual, saintly, angelic, sanctified, godly, holy, perfect, unerring, noble, magnanimous, philanthropic, benevolent, generous, altruistic, unselfish, disinterested, idealistic, upright, irreproachable, impeccable, guiltless, blameless, stainless, spotless, immaculate, uncorrupt, innocent, honourable, decent, chivalrous **5 ethical**, high-principled, faithful, charitable, loving, prudent, just, honest, dutiful, obedient, temperate, sober, self-controlled, chaste, pure **6 worthy**, commendable, excellent

VERBS 7 be virtuous, be good

802 Viscosity

NOUNS 1 viscosity, viscidity, viscousness, thickening, spissitude, inspissation, incrassation, stickiness, tackiness, glueyness, adhesiveness, glutinousness, gumminess, syrupiness, treacliness, mucilaginousness, gelatinousness, jellylikeness, colloidality, doughiness, pastiness, clamminess, ropiness, stringiness, toughness **2 adhesive**, glue, mastic, wax, beeswax, gum, chicle, resin, paste, size, birdlime **3 paste**, size, glair **4 emulsion**, collodion **5 mucus**, phlegm, albumen, pus **6 gelatin**, jelly, syrup, honey, treacle **7 slime**, goo

ADJECTIVES 8 viscous, viscid, inspissate, incrassate, sticky, tacky, adhesive, gluey, waxy, glutinous, colloidal, emulsive, gumbo, gummy, thick, stodgy, heavy, mucilaginous, clammy, ropy, stringy **9 gelatinous**, jelly-like, syrupy, treacly

VERBS 10 stick, glue, gum, paste **11 thicken**, jellify

803 Visibility

ADJECTIVES 1 visible, viewable, observable, distinguishable, discernible, perceptible, perceivable, discoverable, detectable, noticeable, conspicuous, clear, open, overt, plain, evident, manifest, obvious, patent, unconcealed, exposed, apparent, distinct, identifiable, recognizable, unmistakeable, public, available, present, concrete, material, tangible, palpable, external, outward, superficial **2 clear**, plain, bright, signposted, distinct, defined, sharp, high-definition, open, exposed, uncovered, showy, vivid, brilliant, spectacular, eye-catching, remarkable, outstanding, striking, prominent, stark, lucid, visual, highlighted, spotlighted

NOUNS 3 visibility, range, eyeshot, horizon, skyline, observability, discernibility, perceptibility, perceivability, detectability, identifiability, recognizability, distinctness, conspicuousness, overtness, evidence, presence, tangibility **4 clarity**, clearness, plainness, brightness, brilliance, definition, focus, sharpness, exposure, prominence, starkness, obviousness, blatancy, showiness **5 manifestation**, display, demonstration, exposition, exhibition, show

VERBS 6 be visible, be seen, show, stand out **7 appear**, materialize, crop up **8 make visible**, focus, show, reveal, disclose, demonstrate, manifest, display, exhibit, indicate, uncover, expose, illuminate, unmask, spotlight

804 Vision

NOUNS 1 vision, seeing, sight, eyesight, scotopia, long sight **2 eye**, orb, eyeball, sclera, cornea, iris, pupil, lens, aqueous humour, vitreous humour, retina, cone, rod, blind spot, optic nerve, conjunctiva **3 observation**, examination, scanning, inspection, supervision, perusal, scrutiny, scan, study, survey, watchfulness, surveillance, espionage, peering, prying, voyeurism **4 visualization**, consideration, contemplation, imagination, insight, prevision, anticipation, foresight, planning, perception, discernment, awareness, understanding **5 imagination**, daydreaming, stargazing, pipedream, clairvoyance, crystal-gazing, scrying, illusion, mirage, hallucination, will-o'-the-wisp, fata morgana, chimera, figment, apparition, semblance, phantom, spectre, wraith, ghost **6 look**, glance, glimpse, peep, peek, squint, gaze, stare, gape, grimace, glare, glower, scowl, evil eye, leer, ogle, old-fashioned look, glad eye, roving eye **7 view**, sight, aspect, vista, panorama, prospect, outlook, scene, landscape, show, spectacle, pageant, tableau, exhibition, performance, painting, drawing, photograph, film, eyesore **8 reflection**, image, likeness, representation, mirror, looking glass, reflector, cat's eye, speculum, camera, telephoto lens **9 viewpoint**, perspective, scope, range, eyeshot, bird's-eye view, peephole, window, windscreen, squint, belvedere, mirador, gazebo, watch tower, bridge, crow's nest, observatory, planetarium, theatre, cinema, stadium, amphitheatre, arena **10 visual aid**, eyeglass, glasses, frames, lenses, bifocals, monocle, lorgnette, pince-nez, eyeshade, sunglasses, goggles, magnifying glass, loupe, microreader, opera glasses, binoculars

VERBS 11 see, sight, glimpse, espy, notice, witness, spot, perceive, discern, distinguish, descry, recognize, discover, sightsee **12 look**, regard, eye, grimace, ogle **13 inspect**, examine, view, reconnoitre, scrutinize, study, pore over, survey, scan, peruse **14 watch**, observe, monitor, oversee, invigilate **15 visualize**, picture, imagine, consider, contemplate, anticipate, foresee, plan, perceive **16 imagine**, fancy, conjure up, daydream, stargaze, crystal-gaze, scry, foresee **17 make visible**, reveal, reflect, mirror, show, display, exhibit, demonstrate, point out, uncover, unmask **18 be visible**, appear, emerge

ADJECTIVES 19 visual, optical, ophthalmic, ocular, binocular, mirror-like, reflecting, two-dimensional, telescopic, microscopic, stereoscopic, three-dimensional, panoramic, scenic, visional, illusionary **20 seeing**, sighted, sharp-eyed, eagle-eyed, hawk-eyed, staring, glaring, goggle-eyed, pop-eyed, noticing, watching, looking, observant, watchful, vigilant, aware, perceptive, clear-sighted, far-sighted, perspicacious, discerning, imaginative **21 bespectacled**, long-sighted **22 visible**, perceivable, perceptible, discernible, detectable, recognizable, apparent, observable, distinct, clear-cut, evident, manifest, plain, obvious, patent, conspicuous, noticeable, eye-catching

805 Voicelessness

NOUNS 1 voicelessness, aphonia **2 inarticulation**, hoarseness, huskiness, croakiness, raucousness **3 speech defect**, aphasia, dysphasia, dysphemia, stammer, stutter, paraphasia, lallation, babbling, lisping **4 whispering**, murmur, mumble, undertone, aside, mutter, surd, sigh **5 mutism**, deaf-mutism, dumbness, speechlessness, taciturnity, reticence **6 voiceless speech**, sign language, gesture, gesticulation **7 mute**, damper

ADJECTIVES 8 voiceless, aphonic, dysphonic, surd, silent **9 low-voiced**, whispering, inaudible, muted, muttering, murmuring, mumbling, muffled, faint, low, breaking, cracked, hoarse, husky **10 speechless**, inarticulate, mute, dumb, tongue-tied, taciturn, reticent, silent, silenced, gagged, choked, dumbfounded **11 inarticulate**, unintelligible, aphasic, dysphasic, dysphemic, stammering, stuttering, paraphasic, babbling, lisping, sibilant

VERBS 12 be voiceless, be silent **13 have difficulty speaking**, stammer, stutter, babble, lisp, hiss, sign **14 strike dumb**, dumbfound, muffle, mute, deaden, silence, hush, gag, suppress, cut short **15 speak in a low voice**, whisper, mutter, mumble

806 Vulgarity

NOUNS 1 tastelessness, bad taste, coarseness, gaudiness **2 tawdriness**, shoddiness **3 grossness**, impropriety, unseemliness, ill-breeding, commonness, incivility, incorrectness, bad manners, boorishness **4 inelegance**, uncouthness

ADJECTIVES 5 vulgar, coarse, gross,

cheap, ill-bred, infra dig, inelegant, ungentlemanly, unladylike, unfeminine, plebeian, loud, showy, meretricious, ostentatious, garish, day-glo, gandy, tawdry **6 discourteous**, boorish, uncouth, unseemly, unrefined, gauche, awkward, disorderly, unpolished, tasteless, unfashionable, uncultured, barbarian, parvenu **7 ribald**, bawdy, rabelaisian, provocative, immoral, blue, unmentionable, unquotable, unprintable, filthy, obscene, smutty, barbarius, lewd

VERBS 8 vulgarize, coarsen, cheapen, commercialize

807 War

• *C'est magnifique, mais ce n'est pas la guerre.* / (It is magnificent, but it is not war.) Pierre Bosquet.

• *More than an end to war, we want an end to the beginnings of all wars.* Franklin D. Roosevelt.

• *Cry 'Havoc!' and let slip the dogs of war.* William Shakespeare.

NOUNS 1 war, warfare, conflict, intervention, arms, the sword, polemic, quarrel, sabre-rattling, psychological warfare, intimidation, cold war, phoney war, trade war, Cod war, civil war, revolt, revolution, class war, crusade, jihad, world war, Armageddon, blitzkrieg, blitz, atomic war, nuclear war **2 glory of war**, chivalry, drums, bugle, trumpet, battle cry, war cry **3 god of war**, Mars, Ares, Odin, Wotan, Bellona, Athena, Eris, Fea, Indra, Karttikeya **4 belligerency**, militancy, hostilities **5 bellicosity**, pugnacity, combativeness, aggressiveness, hawkishness, Ramboism, sabre-rattling, militancy, expansionism, patriotism, jingoism **6 art of war**, warcraft, siegecraft, castrametation, fortification, generalship, soldiership, seamanship, airmanship, march, ballistics, gunnery, logistics, battle plan, manoeuvres, tactics, strategy **7 war measures**, arming, rally, call-up, mobilization, recruitment, conscription, national service, enlisting, volunteering, rationing, blackout, censorship, propaganda **8 warfare**, war, warpath, battles, skirmishes, sieges, bloodshed, violence, fighting, campaigning, soldiering, bombing, blockading, besieging, investment, enclosure, chemical warfare, germ warfare, nuclear warfare, sanctions, attrition, psychological warfare, attack, defence, Star Wars, blitzkrieg, blitz, trench warfare, jungle warfare, bush-fighting, guerrilla warfare, sniping, campaign, expedition, mission, operation, invasion, incursion, raid, command, password **9 battle**, armed conflict, action, fight, scrap, skirmish, brush, collision, clash, shoot-out, offensive, blitz, attack, defence, stand, engagement **10 battleground**, killing field, combat zone, front line

VERBS 11 go to war, open hostilities, fight, rise, rebel, revolt, overthrow, arm, militarize, mobilize, rally, recruit, conscript, commission, enlist, enrol **12 be at war**, campaign, soldier, invade, attack, raid, ambush, defend, counterattack, manoeuvre, march, blockade, beleaguer, besiege, invest, surround, slaughter, slay, kill, ravage, rape, burn, scorch, destroy **13 battle**, contest, dispute, resist, stand, charge, engage, confront, skirmish, contend, combat

ADJECTIVES 14 warring, fighting, battling, campaigning, belligerent, aggressive, bellicose, militant, mobilized, called-up, conscripted, armed, uniformed, arrayed, embattled, attacking, defending **15 warlike**, militaristic, bellicose, hawkish, unpacific, Ramboesque, aggressive, belligerent, pugnacious, combative, gung-ho, war-loving, warmongering, bloodthirsty, battle-hungry, war-fevered, fierce, tough **16 military**, mercenary, martial, veteran, battle-scarred, shell-shocked, knightly, chivalrous, soldierly, naval, operational

808 Warning

NOUNS 1 warning, caution, caveat, example, advice, counsel, lesson, notification, information, intelligence, news, tip, tip-off, wink, pinch, nudge, hint, announcement, publication, ultimatum, admonition, reprimand, deterrent, dissuasion, protest, expostulation, forewarning, foreboding, premonition, omen, portent, prediction, augury, gathering storm, conscience, muttering, sign, symptom, indication, signal, death knell, menace, danger **2 danger signal**, alarm, beacon, light, shout, bell, whistle, horn, siren, blast, honk, toot, ring, klaxon, tocsin, alert, tattoo, trumpet-call, war-whoop, flare, SOS, mayday, start, tremor, paleness **3 false alarm**, scare, hoax, bugbear, bugaboo, bogey, nightmare

VERBS 4 warn, caution, advise, counsel, tip, wink, pinch, nudge, hint, notify, inform, apprise, alert, forewarn, prepare, predict, augur, remind, admonish, reprove, lour, menace, threaten, dissuade, remonstrate **5 be warned**, beware **6 raise the alarm**, honk, toot, toll, knell, alert, arouse, scare, startle, frighten, alarm, cry

ADJECTIVES 7 warning, cautionary, exemplary, advisable, counsellable, instructive, informative, notifying, hinting, monitory, admonitory, protesting, symptomatic, prognostic, predicting, premonitory, boding, foreboding, ill-omened, ominous, presageful, menacing, minatory, threatening, deterrent, dissuasive **8 warned**, cautioned, advised, counselled, cautious, wary, forewarned

INTERJECTIONS 9 look out!, beware!, careful!, watch out!, watch it!

809 Waste

VERBS 1 waste, squander, lavish, splurge, dissipate, scatter, disperse, slop, spill, overwork, overcrop, impoverish, misuse, abuse, misapply, consume, devour, swallow, expend, exhaust, deplete, drain, empty, wear, erode, gnaw, damage, impair, pollute, emaciate, wither, wilt, shrivel, decay, decline, leak, melt away, burn, gut **2 lay waste**, devastate, ravage, ruin, destroy, demolish, sabotage, vandalize, loot, plunder, sack, raze, despoil, pillage, kill

NOUNS 3 waste, squandering, extravagance, overspending, economy, thriftlessness, improvidence, prodigality, lavishness, splurge, spree, spending, outlay, expenditure, dissipation, dispersion, spillage, overwork, misuse, abuse, misapplication, consumption, exhaustion, depletion, erosion, damage, emaciation, atrophy, decay, decline, decrease, drainage, ebb, outflow, loss, melting, liquefac-

tion, evaporation, vaporization, deterioration, overproduction **4 destruction**, vandalism, arson, sabotage, havoc, devastation, wreck, ruin, looting **5 waste product**, litter, refuse, rubbish, garbage
ADJECTIVES 6 wasteful, extravagant, unnecessary, uneconomic, improvident, thriftless, prodigal, lavish, spendthrift, time-consuming **7 waste**, superfluous, unwanted, unused, leftover, useless

810 Water

NOUNS 1 water, H_2O, Adam's ale, Adam's wine, hydrol, fluid, liquid, moisture, distilled water, hard water, soft water, drinking water, tap water, soda water, limewater, rain water, running water, spring, fountain, well water, hydrothermal water, fresh water, salt water, brine, meltwater, ice, standing water, lavender water, rose water, holy water, hydromancy **2 wateriness**, wetness, dampness, moistness, raininess, dewiness, steam, condensation, haze, mist, fog **3 hydrotherapeutics**, hydropathy, hydrotherapy, irrigation **4 watering**, irrigation, wetting, hosing down, sprinkling, spraying, squirting, spargefaction, aspergation, splashing, spattering, swashing, affusion, soaking, drenching, sousing, drowning, inundation, immersion, steeping, imbruement, ducking, saturation, percolation, leaching **5 sprinkler**, watering can, sparger, sprayer, aspergillum, sprinkler, aerosol, atomizer, vaporizer, water pistol **6 irrigator**, well, oasis, conduit, hydrant, hosepipe, tap, standpipe, pump, shadoof, Persian wheel **7 hydrography**, hydrology, hydrometry, hygrometry, hydraulics, hydrodynamics, hydromechanics, hydrokinetics, hydrostatics
ADJECTIVES 8 watery, aqueous, aquatic, hydrous, hydrated, hydraulic, hydrodynamic, hydrometric **9 diluted**, saturated **10 wet**, soaked, drenched, sodden, wringing, sopping, soused, waterlogged, streaming, dripping, awash, soggy, bathed, steeped, flooded, awash, swamped, drowned, submerged, dipped, ducked **11 wetting**, watering, moistening, damping, humectant
VERBS 12 water, moisten, sprinkle, irrigate, hydrate, wet, soak, drench, douse, souse, drown, immerse, submerse, imbrue, permeate, percolate, leach, lixiviate, flood, inundate, saturate, waterlog, deluge, swamp, submerge, pour on, flow on, duck, dunk **13 dilute**, water down **14 sprinkle**, spray, sparge, asperge, mist, atomize, shower, scatter, splash, splatter, spatter, bespatter, clash, paddle, slop **15 hose**, syringe, squirt, inject, douche, sponge, wash

811 Water Transport

NOUNS 1 water travel, shipping, boating, sailing, rowing, seafaring, cruising, voyaging, passage, crossing, inland navigation, navigation **2 waterway**, seaway, ocean track, steamer route, ferry crossing, river, lake **3 vessel**, ship, boat, craft, rowboat, skull, sailboat, pleasure boat, yacht, steamship, liner, ferry, canal boat, narrow boat, barge, merchant ship, freighter, tanker, fishing boat, trawler, drifter, whaler **4 navigation**, astronavigation, compass reading, pilotage, helmsmanship, seamanship, steering, dead reckoning, plotting, sextant, quadrant, log, gyrocompass, astrocompass, needle, card, compass card, binnacle, chronometer, chart, ephemeris, bearings, buoy, lighthouse, radio-beacon station, goniometer, radar, sonar, navigational satellite, helm, wheel, tiller **5 nautical person**, naval officer, admiral, sailor, seaman, coastguardsman, marine, seafarer, mariner, ship's master, quartermaster, captain, skipper, navigator, pilot, helmsman, steersman, wheelman, circumnavigator, ship's steward, boatswain, bosun's mate, coxswain, shipmate, deckhand, leadsman, foretopman, reefer, cabin boy, fisherman, whaler, old salt, sea dog, pirate, privateer, buccaneer, argonaut, sea god, Neptune, Poseidon, marine scientist, shipbuilder **6 boatman**, waterman, yachtsman, canoeist, paddler, rower, oarsman, sculler, galley slave, punter, gondolier

VERBS 7 navigate, circumnavigate, plot, chart, steer, set sail, spread canvas, launch, cast off, weigh anchor, scud, luff, pay off, veer, back, crab, tack, gybe, yaw, race, land, make port, drop anchor, moor, tie up, dock **8 capsize**, overturn, list, heel over, keel over, careen

ADJECTIVES 9 nautical, naval, marine, seafaring, seaworthy, seaborne, afloat, waterborne, sailorly, able-bodied, amphibious, amphibian, seasick, natatory **10 navigational**, navigating, navigable

812 Way

NOUNS 1 way, mode, manner, means, form, method, system, technique, procedure, process, proceeding, order, practice, skill, conduct, algorithm, approach, tack, tactics, routine, operation, fashion, style, tone, guise, progress **2 route**, itinerary, course, track, trail, direction, line, march, beat, road, run, trajectory, orbit, lane, detour, bypass, circumlocution, circumference, circuit, access, approach, doorway, door, entrance, adit, drive, path, hallway, vestibule, corridor, gangway, gangplank, passage, aisle, staircase **3 road**, thoroughfare, artery, motorway, *autoroute*, ring road, clearway, overpass, causeway, underpass, flyover, junction, crossroads, intersection, roundabout, byway, street, drive, avenue, boulevard, crescent, circus, close, place, court, row, terrace, lane, alley, cul de sac, dead end **4 path**, footpath, pavement, by-path, towpath, track, trail, rut **5 arcade**, colonnade, gallery, portico, aisle, cloister, triforium, nave, loggia, promenade, esplanade **6 tunnel**, underpass, subway, underground **7 bridge**, span, viaduct, aqueduct, overpass, overcrossing, footbridge, overbridge, drawbridge, stepping-stones **8 railway**, railroad, track, line, tramline, underground, tube, metro, junction, level crossing, embankment, cutting, siding, stop, station, platform, signal box, rails, points, sleeper, tracks, roadbed **9 channel**, canal, conduit, aisle, alley, lane, inlet, exit, outlet, gulf, culvert, strait, sound, dike, ditch, sewer, waterway, watercourse, river, estuary, delta, stream **10 cableway**, wireway **11 flight path**, airlane, skyway, runway, taxiway, blastoff, trajectory, orbit

VERBS 12 find one's way, enter, approach, detour, bypass
ADJECTIVES 13 accessible, through, connecting, communicating, linked, bridged, flyover, spanned, arched, main, arterial, trunk, paved, cobbled, skid-proof, signposted, signalled, well-lit, floodlit, well-used, busy, crowded, beaten

813 Weakness

NOUNS 1 weakness, feebleness, impotence, enfeeblement, softness, limpness, flaccidity, floppiness, slackness, looseness, dilapidation, impairment, damage, decay, rust, wear, deactivation, neutralization, adulteration, dilution, instability, fragility, delicateness, delicacy, puniness, smallness, helplessness, innocence, harmlessness, vulnerability, defencelessness, defect **2 indecisiveness**, irresolution, hesitance, doubtfulness, pusillanimity, ineffectuality, slowness, sheepishness, spinelessness, nervelessness, nervousness, timorousness **3 poor health**, sickliness, debility, frailty, infirmity, weakliness, faintness, paleness, anaemia, asthenia, thinness, anorexia, senility, caducity, decrepitude, dizziness, giddiness, vertigo, shakiness, lameness, blindness, deafness, enervation, deflation, depletion, dissipation, impoverishment, burnout, failure, waning, flagging, weariness, exhaustion, fatigue **4 weakling**, dupe, victim, milksop, namby-pamby, hypochondriac, invalid, kitten, infant, baby **5 weak thing**, reed, cobweb, gossamer, thread, sandcastle, paper, matchstick, glass, china
VERBS 6 be weak, weaken, sicken, faint, languish, flag, fail, fall, droop, flop, wilt, fade, decline, dwindle, crumble, wear, yield, sag, break, split, shake, tremble, totter, teeter, stagger, dodder, limp **7 weaken**, enfeeble, debilitate, unnerve, rattle, alarm, shake, slacken, deflate, diminish, reduce, decimate, extenuate, thin, lessen, deplete, drain, impoverish, starve, deprive, rob, sap, undermine, impair, damage, invalidate, spoil, mar, disarm, disable, strain, sprain, lame, maim, cripple, hurt, harm, injure, wound, strip, denude, expose, adulterate, dilute, soften
ADJECTIVES 8 weak, impotent, powerless, feeble, soft, limp, flaccid, floppy, drooping, sagging, slack, relaxed, gimcrack, shoddy, rickety, wobbly, creaky, seedy, brittle, fragile, delicate, puny, ineffectual, helpless, defenceless **9 dilapidated**, broken-down, weather-beaten, worn, rotten, decayed, rusted, withered, diminished, depleted, drained **10 ill**, sickly, faint, pale, pallid, bloodless, anaemic, asthenic, groggy, languid, feeble, weakly, wasted, thin, skinny, emaciated, skin-and-bone, anorexic, frail, decrepit, infirm, crippled, lame, hobbling, shaky, feeble-minded **11 weakened**, debilitated, enervated, dissipated, sapped, wearied, exhausted, fatigued, tired, weary, failed **12 weak-willed**, indecisive, irresolute, wavering, dithering, pusillanimous, vacillating, hesitant, half-hearted, nervous, timid, cowardly, sheepish, effete, mealy-mouthed, spineless, lily-livered, chicken-hearted, namby-pamby, limp-wristed **13 insufficient**, inadequate, insubstantial, inconclusive, invalid, unconvincing, unsatisfactory, lacking, want-

ing, deficient, flimsy, slight, small, thin, light, shallow, hollow, substandard, poor, pathetic, below par, imperceptible, inaudible, invisible, faint, low, distant, muffled, tasteless

814 Wealth

ADJECTIVES 1 wealthy, rich, affluent, well-off, well-paid, prosperous, well-to-do, moneyed, propertied, well-situated, well-endowed **2 solvent**, sound, solid **3 opulent**, luxurious, lavish, sumptuous, palatial, splendid, first-class, de luxe, expensive, diamond-studded, gilded **4 lush**, fat, fertile, fecund, productive, prolific, abundant, plentiful
NOUNS 5 wealth, richness, affluence, prosperity, fortune, resources, capital, assets, means, income, gain, profit, moneymaking, savings, investments, estate, money, property, possessions **6 money**, riches, filthy lucre, mammon, pelf **7 opulence**, luxury, lavishness, sumptuousness, comfort, ease, plenty, abundance, profusion, superfluity, bounty, cornucopia **8 solvency**, soundness, solidity, substance, credit-worthiness, independence **9 plutocracy**, timocracy
VERBS 10 be rich, enjoy **11 get rich**, prosper, inherit **12 seek riches**, chase fame and fortune **13 make rich**, bequeath, endow

815 Weapon

NOUNS 1 weapon, arm, deterrent, deadly weapon, defensive weapon, offensive weapon, conventional weapon, nuclear weapon, secret weapon, death ray, laser, natural weapon, teeth, fist, claws **2 arms**, weaponry, munitions, armaments, rocketry, missilery, gunnery, musketry **3 arms race**, arms traffic, arms trade **4 arsenal**, armoury, arms depot, ammunition ship, ammunition dump, gun room, gun rack, magazine, powder keg, caisson, bullet-pouch, cartridge belt, bandolier, quiver, scabbard, sheath **5 missile weapon**, missile, ballistic missile, guided missile, Cruise missile, Scud, antimissile missile, Patriot, torpedo, Polaris, Trident, antitank weapon, bazooka, rocket-launcher, rocket, shell, flare, shrapnell, whiz-bang, V-1, V-2, bullet **6 historical missile weapon**, javelin, harpoon, dart, bola, lasso, boomerang, catapult, throwstick, arrow, poisoned arrow, shaft, bolt, quarrel, barb, stone, fléchette, longbow, crossbow, arbalest, ballista, mangonel, trebuchet, sling, blowpipe, ball **7 blunt weapon**, club, bludgeon, truncheon, cudgel, cosh, mace, battering ram, warhammer, staff, sandbag, knuckle-duster, bicycle chain **8 sharp weapon**, lance, jerid, harpoon, gaff, pike, assegai, partisan, bill, halberd, axe, tomahawk, hatchet, chopper, gisarme, sword, cutlass, claymore, hanger, sabre, scimitar, yataghan, falchion, blade, bilbo, Toledo, rapier, foil, épée, bayonet, dagger, poniard, dirk, skean, sgian-dhu, stylet, stiletto, machete, matchet, kukri, kris, parang, panga, knife, bowie knife **9 firearm**, gun, revolver, pistol, piece, automatic, semiautomatic, repeater, rifle, shotgun, smoothbore, rifled bore, calibre, carbine, breechloader **10 historical gun**, arquebus, hackbut, matchlock, flintlock, fusil, musket, Brown Bess, Blunderbuss, muzzleloader, chassepot, needle-gun, petronel, pistolet **11 guns**, ordnance, cannonry, artillery, galloping guns, battery, field gun, rifle, siege gun, heavy gun, heavy metal, howitzer, trench-mortar, mine-thrower, trench gun, anti-aircraft gun, Bofers gun, bazooka, machine gun, pom-pom, Bren gun, Sten gun, submachine gun, subgun, uzi, kalashnikov, AK-47, gat, flamethrower, guncarriage, limber, caisson **12 historical guns**, bombard, falconet, swivel, basilisk, petard, carronade, culverin, mortar, canon royal, seventy-four, Big Bertha, Gatling gun, mitrailleuse, Maxim gun, Lewis gun **13 ammunition**, round, buckshot, bullet, projectile, missile, slug, pellet, shell, shrapnel, flak, ack-ack, wad, cartouche, cartridge, dud, blank, grapeshot **14 explosive**, gunpowder, propellant, saltpetre, dynamite, gelignite, nitroglycerine, lyddite, melinite, cordite, gun cotton, plastic explosive, semtex, cap, detonator, fuse, priming, charge, warhead **15 bomb**, shell, grenade, Molotov cocktail, megaton bomb, atom bomb, nuclear bomb, hydrogen bomb, neutron bomb, cluster bomb, fragmentation bomb, nailbomb, firebomb, napalm bomb, mine, letter bomb, carbomb, booby trap, depth charge, torpedo, tin fish, V-1, doodlebug, V-2

816 Whiteness

ADJECTIVES 1 white, pure-white, snow-white, lily-white, milky, lactescent, whitish, albescent, off-white, pearly, ivory, alabaster, marble, chalky, creamy, magnolia, ecru, unbleached, undyed, greige, silver, argent, fair-skinned, albinotic **2 whitened**, bleached, blanched, decolorized, faded, colourless, achromatic, semitransparent, whitewashed, snow-capped, hoary, frosty, foaming, spumy **3 white-haired**, fair, flaxen-haired, tow-headed, Nordic, canescent, hoary, grizzled **4 pale**, pallid, sallow, waxen, ashen, livid **5 pure**, chaste, virginal, clean

NOUNS 6 whiteness, snowiness, milkiness, lactescence, albescence, pearliness, chalkiness, creaminess, silveriness, fairness, greyness, canescence, hoariness, colourlessness, achromatism, etiolation, paleness, sallowness, albinism **7 purity**, chastity, cleanness **8 light**, luminosity

VERBS 9 whiten, bleach, blanch, blanco, pipeclay, whitewash, calcimine, wash, clean, pale, blench, fade, decolorize, etiolate, frost

817 Whole

NOUNS 1 whole, wholeness, totality, integrality, integrity, fullness, completeness, indivisibility, oneness, unity, universality, generality, holism, comprehensiveness, inclusiveness **2 whole thing**, entity, integer, unit, entirety, Gestalt, totality, sum, summation, total, aggregate, corpus, complex, ensemble, system, world, globe, universe, cosmos, macrocosm **3 whole situation**, panorama, overview, survey, conspectus, synopsis, world view, circuit, lap **4 all**, everything, everybody **5 unit**, family, ensemble, set, series, pack, kit

ADJECTIVES 6 whole, integral, total, holistic, general, universal, complete, full, integrated, unified, all, every, any, each, individual, single, one, all-inclusive, comprehensive, gross, all-embracing, across-the-board, global, worldwide **7 uncut**, entire, unabridged, unexpurgated, undivided, undiminished, unbroken, intact, unharmed, undamaged, unimpaired, unspoiled, unadulterated, uncontaminated, untouched, inviolate, virgin, pure, faultless, flawless **8 sound**, able-bodied, strong, fit, well

VERBS 9 be whole, unite, unify, integrate, total, sum up, amount to, number, comprise, embrace **10 complete**, fulfill, succeed, accomplish, culminate, climax, round off, end

818 Wickedness

NOUNS 1 wickedness, badness, sinfulness, sin, evil, cruelty, brutality, wrong, improbity, iniquity, flagitiousness, unrighteousness, wrongdoing, evildoing, misbehaviour, disrepute, recidivism, backsliding, deterioration, naughtiness, disobedience, dishonesty, peccability, transgression, trespass, delinquency, criminality, corruption, vitiation, shamelessness, vileness, baseness, heinousness, viciousness, hellishness, malevolence, villainy, knavery, roguery, enormity, inhumanity, infamy, flagrancy, outrage, abomination **2 vice**, immorality, amorality, unvirtuousness, impurity, indecency, lust, vulgarity, carnality, debauchery, degeneracy, profligacy, depravity, turpitude, degradation **3 venial sin**, fatal flaw, imperfection, shortcoming, failing, frailty, foible, weakness, laxity, infirmity, fault, defect, demerit, deficiency, indecorum, impropriety, indiscretion, unseemliness **4 religious sin**, impiety, ungodliness, blasphemy, sacrilege, desecration, profaneness, idolatry, devilry, devil worship, Satanism, diabolism, witchcraft **5 criminality**, guilt, foul play, illegality, lawbreaking, crime, misdemeanour, shoplifting, delinquency, felony, robbery, rape

ADJECTIVES 6 wicked, bad, sinful, evil, wrong, erring, iniquitous, nefarious, flagitious, unrighteous, misbehaving, improper, disreputable, disgraceful, fallen, knavish, roguish, rascally, slipping, sliding, recidivous, deteriorating, naughty, disobedient, dishonest, transgressing, trespassing, delinquent, criminal, corrupt, rotten, shameless, unprincipled, worthless, unscrupulous, conscienceless, despicable, reprehensible, vile, base, foul, beastly, heinous, vicious, cruel, brutal, hellish, maleficent, malevolent, hard-hearted, callous, villainous, miscreant, inhuman, infamous, flagrant, outrageous, abominable, atrocious, irredeemable, unforgivable, unpardonable, irremissible, inexpiable **7 immoral**, vicious, unvirtuous, ruined, scarlet, unchaste, impure, indecent, obscene, gross, shocking, outrageous, lustful, vulgar, carnal, debauched, degenerate, profligate, depraved, degraded, perverse **8 venial**, vulnerable, imperfect, failing, frail, infirm, feeble, weak, lax, human, defective, deficient, indecorous, indiscreet, unseemly, flagrant **9 impious**, irreligious, ungodly, blasphemous, sacrilegious, profane, accursed, damned, reprobate, infernal, devilish, diabolical, satanic, fiendish **10 criminal**, offensive, culpable, accusable, blameworthy, guilty, foul, illegal, unlawful, lawbreaking

VERBS 11 be wicked, err, slip, stumble, stray, misbehave, sin, transgress, trespass, offend, shock, disgrace oneself, lapse **12 make wicked**, mislead, tempt, pervert, corrupt, distort, demoralize, brutalize, seduce, shame

819 Will

NOUNS 1 will, volition, conation, willing, intention, intent, purpose, wish, desire, pleasure, fancy, choice, option, preference, inclination, disposition **2 willpower**, determination, steadfastness, resoluteness, tenacity, single-mindedness **3 wilfulness**, self-will, waywardness, obstinacy, obduracy, doggedness, intransigence, pigheadedness, stubbornness **4 free will**, independence, self-determination, autonomy **5 will**, testament, codicil, inheritance, estate

ADJECTIVES 6 willed, volitional, intentional, deliberate, willing, disposed **7 iron-willed**, determined, purposeful, steadfast, resolute, adamant, unyielding, tenacious, single-minded **8 wilful**, self-willed, headstrong, wayward, stubborn, dogged, obstinate, obdurate, intransigent, pigheaded, bullheaded **9 autocratic**, authoritarian, arbitrary **10 free**, independent, autonomous, self-determined

VERBS 11 wish, will, want **12 choose**, decide, select, opt for **13 intend**, determine, purpose, plan, cause **14 follow one's own will**, please oneself **15 impose one's will**, dominate, command, demand, order, ordain, decree, trample over, bulldoze, bully **16 bequeath**, will, leave, pass on, hand down, transfer

820 Willingness

ADJECTIVES 1 willing, agreeable, content, disposed, inclined, prone, ready, game, receptive, assenting, consenting **2 eager**, enthusiastic, keen, prompt, alacritous, zealous, overenthusiastic **3 amenable**, compliant, acquiescent, biddable, persuadable, pliable, pliant, tractable, manageable, obedient **4 helpful**, cooperative, collaborative, cordial, gracious, benevolent **5 voluntary**, unprompted, spontaneous, offered, unbidden, unforced, volunteering

NOUNS 6 willingness, readiness, gameness, consent **7 eagerness**, enthusiasm, keenness, promptness, alacrity, ardour, fervour, zeal, overeagerness **8 acquiescence**, amenability, compliance, pliancy, tractability, persuasability, docility **9 goodwill**, benevolence, graciousness, cordiality, helpfulness

VERBS 10 be willing, agree, assent, comply, acquiesce, consent, accept **11 cooperate**, collaborate, help, aid **12 volunteer**, offer

821 Wisdom

- *For in much wisdom is much grief: and he that increaseth knowledge increaseth sorrow.* Bible: Ecclesiastes.
- *No mention shall be made of coral, or of pearls: for the price of wisdom is above rubies.* Bible: Job.

NOUNS 1 wisdom, sagacity, sapience, reason, judgment, discretion, discernment, discrimination, perspicacity, penetration, perception, insight, intuition, understanding, comprehension, profundity, knowledge, erudition, learning, experience, enlightenment, objectivity, shrewdness, acumen, astuteness, tact, level-headedness, prudence, judiciousness, farsightedness, foresight, forethought, cunning **2 intelligence**, intellectualism, mind, understanding, quick-wittedness, cleverness, smartness, brightness, brilliance, aptitude, talent, genius, inspiration, brainwave

ADJECTIVES 3 wise, sagacious, sapient, thoughtful, thinking, reflecting, reasoning, rational, sensible, profound, deep, intellectual, highbrow, knowledgeable, erudite, learned, perspicacious, perceptive, oracular, level-headed, prudent, judicious, balanced, objective, impartial, just, fair-minded, broadminded, circumspect, unprejudiced, statesmanlike, diplomatic, discreet, tactful, politic **4 intelligent**, clever, smart, bright, brilliant, talented, gifted, able, skilful, quick-witted, sharp, alert, astute, shrewd, streetwise, canny, farsighted, clear-headed, calculating

VERBS 5 be wise, understand, grasp, fathom, discern, distinguish, discriminate, judge **6 be intelligent**, know

822 Wonder

NOUNS 1 wonder, awe, fascination, admiration, raptness, love, surprise, astonishment, astoundment, dumbfoundment, amazement, bafflement, bewilderment, puzzlement, stupefaction, uncertainty, consternation, shock **2 wonder-working**, miracle-working, magic, sorcery, spellbinding, thaumatology, teratology, feat, exploit, deed, transformation **3 object of wonder**, eye-opener, phenomenon, best-seller, miracle, portent, omen, sign, marvel, masterpiece, masterstroke, *chef-d'oeuvre*, drama, sensation, fantasy, Utopia, wonderland, fairyland

ADJECTIVES 4 wondering, astonished, astounded, amazed, awestruck, fascinated, admiring, impressed, surprised, inexpectant, marvelling, spellbound, rapt, dazzled, blinded, dumbfounded, flabbergasted, shocked, scandalized, thunderstruck, dazed, stupefied, bewildered, puzzled **5 wide-eyed**, round-eyed, popeyed, agog, openmouthed, agape, dumbstruck, inarticulate, speechless, breathless, wordless, silenced **6 wonderful**, marvellous, miraculous, astounding, aweful, amazing, beguiling, fantastic, imaginary, impossible, surprising, unexpected, improbable, unbelievable, incredible, inconceivable, unimaginable, indescribable, unutterable, unspeakable, ineffable, inexpressible, mind-boggling, mind-blowing, striking, overwhelming, awe-inspiring, breathtaking, impressive, admirable, exquisite, excellent, exceptional, extraordinary, unprecedented, unusual, remarkable, noteworthy, dramatic, sensational, shocking, exotic, outlandish, strange, odd, outré, weird, bizarre, peculiar, unaccountable, mysterious, enigmatic, puzzling, shattering, bewildering, thaumaturgic, phenomenal, stupendous

VERBS 7 wonder, marvel, admire, whistle, gasp, hero-worship, idolize, stare, goggle at, gawk, gape **8 be wonderful**, impress, spellbind, enchant, bewitch, dazzle, strike dumb, stun, daze, stupefy, awe, electrify, impress, petrify, dumbfound, confound, astound, astonish, amaze, flabbergast, surprise, baffle, bewilder, puzzle, startle, shock, stagger, frighten **9 wonder whether**, speculate, conjecture, ponder, meditate, muse, think, question

823 Work

NOUNS **1 work**, labour, toil, industry, assignment, spadework, donkeywork, legwork, sweat, housework, chores, travail, drudgery, slavery, grind, strain, treadmill, grindstone, corvee, compulsion, fatigue, duty, piecework, taskwork **2 task**, chore, job, operation, exercise, assignment, project, commission, deed, feat, trick, shift, stint, stretch, bout **3 job**, occupation, employment, profession, trade, métier, business, career, vocation, calling, mission **4 exertion**, effort, attempt, endeavour, struggle, strain, stress, tug, squeeze, pull, push, stretch, rub, scrub, heave, lift, throw, drive, force, pressure, energy, power, manpower, horsepower, ergonomics, muscle power, elbow grease, pains, assiduity, overwork, fray, ado, hassle **5 exercise**, practice, drill, training, preparation, warm-up, running, jogging, cycling, walking, swimming, rowing, gymnastics, weight-lifting, yoga, isometrics, eurhythmics, callisthenics, work-out, aerobics, athletics, games

VERBS **6 work**, labour, freelance, toil, drudge, fag, grind, slog, sweat, clean, scrub, rub, lift, heave, pull, haul, tug, push, shove, dig, plod, persevere, shift, slave, beaver away **7 work for**, serve, employ, task, tax **8 exert oneself**, strive, strain, struggle, try, attempt, endeavour, travail, persevere, slog at, battle **9 exercise**, practise, drill, train, prepare, warm up, keep fit, run, jog, cycle, walk

ADJECTIVES **10 working**, labouring, busy, industrious, employed, horny-handed, drudging, sweating, grinding, slogging, hard-working, plodding, persevering, tireless, energetic, active, painstaking, thorough, attentive, diligent, assiduous, exercising, practising **11 laborious**, strenuous, gruelling, punishing, unremitting, tiring, exhausting, backbreaking, crushing, killing, toilsome, troublesome, weary, painful, burdensome, heroic, Herculean, arduous, hard, heavy, uphill, difficult, hard-fought, hard-won, thorough, painstaking, laboured, elaborate

824 Worker

NOUNS **1 worker**, employee, hand, operative, volunteer, participator, freelance, housewife, toiler, drudge, hack, flunky, menial, factotum, handyman, wallah, servant, domestic, cook, chauffeur, gardener, charwoman, businessman, executive, breadwinner, teacher, scientist, artist, writer, performer, actor, actress, dancer, singer, musician, journalist, newscaster, presenter, secretary, seller, artisan, labourer, farmer, pieceworker, roadman, ganger, docker, stevedore, packer, porter **2 artisan**, artificer, master, technician, tradesman, journeyman, apprentice, learner, craftsman, potter, carpenter, joiner, woodworker, turner, sawyer, cooper, wheelwright, shipwright, builder, architect, mason, bricklayer, plasterer, thatcher, painter, decorator, metalworker, blacksmith, goldsmith, silversmith, gunsmith, locksmith, miner, collier, steelworker, foundryman, mechanic, machinist, fitter, engineer, plumber, welder, electrician, weaver, tailor, watchmaker, jeweller **3 agent**, operator, practitioner, perpetrator, minister, officer, functionary, instrument, tool, representative, delegate, official, spokesperson, mediator, go-between, deputy, proxy, substitute, executive, administrator, manager, industrialist, manufacturer, producer, wholesaler, middleman, merchant, dealer, broker **4 personnel**, employees, workers, staff, workforce, company, organization, team, gang, squad, crew, complement, cadre, band, cast, hands, payroll, labour **5 partner**, associate, co-worker

825 Worship

• *More things are wrought by prayer/ Than this world dreams of.* Alfred Lord Tennyson.

NOUNS 1 worship, honour, reverence, devotion, bhakti, dedication, veneration, adoration, adulation, esteem, dignification, glorification, exaltation, magnification, praise, extolment, celebration, thanksgiving, duty, obedience, homage, prostration, humility, piety, awe, propitiation, appeasement, confession, penitence, atonement, offering, oblation, sacrifice, muda, supplication, petition, praying, contemplation, meditation, asceticism, fasting, pilgrimage, hajj **2 idolatry**, iconolatry, superstition, cult, heathenism, paganism, pagano-Christianism, totemism, fetishism, phallicism, priestcraft, bibliolatry, ecclesiolatry, obi, allotheism, animism, anthropomorphism, zoolatry, theriolatry, ophiolatry, heliolatry, Sabaism, pyrolatry, dendrolatry, diabolism, demonism, Satanism, Mammonism, necrolatry **3 idol**, image, effigy, god, deity, joss, icon, fetish, symbol

VERBS 4 worship, honour, respect, revere, venerate, hallow, esteem, dignify, adulate, adore, glorify, exalt, magnify, laud, extol, praise, applaud, acclaim, celebrate, pray, meditate, contemplate, kneel, genuflect, obey, propitiate, appease, atone, sacrifice **5 idolatrize**, fetishize, totemize, heathenize, paganize, anthropomorphize, idolize, idealize, apotheosize, lionize, admire

ADJECTIVES 6 worshipful, reverential, venerational, adoring, praising, hero-worshipping, anthropolatrous, devoted, devotional, prostrate, humbled, supplicatory, penitent, prayerful, dutiful, meditative, contemplative **7 idolatrous**, iconolatrous, superstitious, cult, heathen, pagan, totemic, fetishistic, phallic, bibliolatrous, ecclesiolatrous, allotheistic, animistic, anthropomorphic, zoolatrous, theriolatrous, ophiolatrous, heliolatrous, Sabaic, pyrolatrous, dendrolatrous, diabolic, Satanic, mammonolatrous, necrolatrous **8 worshipped**, honoured, revered, venerated, blessed, esteemed, adored, glorified, extolled, praised, admired

826 Worth

ADJECTIVES 1 worthy, laudable, meritorious, deserving, admired, esteemed, respected, valued, admirable, estimable, creditable, approved, noble, exemplary, good, virtuous, preferable, better, superior, first-rate, capital, prime, quality, superfine, rare, vintage, classic, outstanding, superlative, top-flight, flawless, perfect, choice, select, handpicked, exquisite, recherche, chosen, selected, tested, exclusive, famous, great, notable, eminent, distinguished, glorious, dazzling, splendid, brilliant, magnificent, marvellous, sensational, terrific, wonderful, superb, grand, fantastic, fabulous, amazing, prodigious **2 best**, optimum, champion, winning, blue-ribbon, gold-medal, tiptop, first-class, first-rate, supreme, incomparable, unequalled, matchless, unparalleled, peerless, unsurpassed, perfect, record-breaking, chart-topping, crowning **3 valuable**, inestimable, priceless, costly, expensive, rich, irreplaceable, unique, rare, precious, prized, valued, treasured, gilt-edged **4 worthwhile**, profitable, useful, advantageous, beneficial, wholesome, healthy, salutary, sound, salubrious, refreshing, edifying, favourable, kind **5 not bad**, tolerable, adequate, sufficient, fair, satisfactory, passable, respectable, standard, nice, decent, unexceptionable, indifferent, middling, mediocre, ordinary, average

NOUNS 6 worth, praiseworthiness, merit, desert, admiration, esteem, respect, credit, value, pricelessness, costliness, rarity, excellence, greatness, goodness, virtue, quality, soundness, health, virtuosity, skill, eminence, superiority, flawlessness, perfection, quintessence, beneficence, nobility, brilliance **7 elite**, chosen few, prime, flower, cream, SAS, top people, meritocracy, aristocracy, gentry, nobility, jet set, plum

VERBS 8 be worthy, merit, deserve, qualify, pass muster, suffice, contend, vie, rival, equal, excel, surpass, transcend **9 do good**, benefit, improve, edify

827 Worthlessness

ADJECTIVES 1 worthless, valueless, unimportant, insignificant, paltry **2 inferior**, low-quality, low-grade, faulty, flawed, imperfect, defective, substandard, shoddy, punk, tawdry, trashy, rubbishy, cheap, second-class, second-rate, unsatisfactory, bad, incompetent, inefficient, unskilled, clumsy, bungled, botched, mangled, spoiled **3 bad**, nasty, obnoxious, objectionable, unpleasant, disagreeable, horrible, horrid, evil, base, gross, irredeemable, execrable, unspeakable, abominable, awful, horrific, horrendous, terrible, dreadful, gruesome, grim, onerous, tedious, distressing, vicious, villainous, wicked, heinous, depraved, sinful, dishonest **4 poor**, mean, wretched, miserable, sad, woeful, pitiful, grievous, lamentable, deplorable, contemptible, despicable, scruffy, shabby, grubby, nauseating, revolting, disgusting, hateful, coarse, vulgar, reprehensible, disgraceful, shameful, rotten, decaying, putrid, stinking, foul, corrupt, stale, mouldy, diseased **5 harmful**, hurtful, injurious, damaging, deleterious, detrimental, prejudicial, disadvantageous, destructive, wasting, pernicious, deadly, virulent, disastrous, calamitous, adverse, degenerative, noxious, malignant, infectious, poisonous, polluting, dangerous, sinister, ominous, dreadful, accursed, spiteful, vindictive, malicious, malevolent, mischief-making, cruel, bloodthirsty, violent, harsh, intolerant **6 damnable**, blasted, confounded, bothersome, execrable

NOUNS 7 worthlessness, unimportance, insignificance, uselessness **8 inferiority**, faultiness, flaw, defect, imperfection, shoddiness, tawdriness, trashiness, rubbish, cheapness, incompetence, inefficiency, clumsiness, bungle **9 badness**, nastiness, obnoxiousness, unpleasantness, horridness, evil, vileness, baseness, grossness, abomination, awfulness, horror, dreadfulness, grimness, distress, viciousness, villainy, wickedness, immorality, sinfulness, dishonesty, crime, wrongfulness **10 poverty**, meanness, wretchedness, misery, sadness, woe, melancholy, pitifulness, abjectness, contemptibleness, disreputability, sordidness, sleaziness, squalor, grubbiness, dirtiness, lowness, indecency, coarseness, obscenity, disgrace, rottenness, stink, corruption, taint, disorder, sickness, pestilence, contamination **11 harmfulness**, harm, hurt, injury, ill, damage, detriment, destruction, disaster, adversity, noxiousness, malignancy, poisonousness, pollution, danger, mischief, spitefulness, malice, malevolence, bitterness, suffering, anxiety, pain, cruelty, inhumanity, violence, intolerance, harassment, abuse, libel, slander

VERBS 12 be worthless, bungle, botch, spoil, ruin, hurt, injure, damage, impair, rot, pollute, contaminate, infect, corrupt, pervert, deprave, torment, plague, vex, harass, trouble, spite **13 ill-treat**, mishandle, misuse, burden, oppress, crush, harass, persecute, abuse, molest, wrong, distress, torment, violate, maul, strike, bruise, batter, spite, libel, slander, ruin

828 Wrong

NOUNS 1 unfairness, wrongness, injustice, inequity, discrimination, bias, unevenness, one-sidedness **2 incorrectness**, falseness, error, mistake, untruthfulness, inaccuracy, fallaciousness, erroneousness, unsoundness, invalidity **3 impropriety**, unseemliness, indecorousness **4 abnormality**, irregularity, oddness, queerness, aberrance **5 unrighteousness**, sinfulness, wickedness, badness **6 unlawfulness**, illegality, illegitimacy, illicitness, infraction, violation, delinquency **7 sense of wrong**, complaint, grouse, grievance, injury, injustice, tort **8 wrong-doing**, sin, vice, misdeed, abomination, crime, felony, misdemeanour, offence, transgression, trespass, infraction, infringement, injury, harm, hurt, abuse, error **9 dishonour**, disgrace, scandal, shame, crying shame, slur, stain

ADJECTIVES 10 wrong, unjust, biased, prejudiced, discriminatory, favouring, partial, partisan **11 incorrect**, inaccurate, imprecise, false, untrue, fallacious, unsound, invalid, erroneous, mistaken **12 improper**, incorrect, unsuitable, unfit, inappropriate, inapt, incongruous, indecorous, unseemly, unbecoming **13 abnormal**, irregular, odd, queer, aberrant, perverted **14 immoral**, corrupt, unprincipled, unethical, dishonest, dishonourable, disgraceful, shameful, scandalous, infamous **15 in the wrong**, guilty, blameworthy, culpable, sinful, bad, wicked, evil, vicious, abominable, unlawful, criminal, delinquent, transgressive, offensive, abusive, injurious **16 unforgivable**, unpardonable, unjustifiable, inexcusable, reprehensible **17 gone wrong**, awry, askew

VERBS 18 be wrong, blunder **19 wrong**, hurt, injure, offend, abuse, maltreat, oppress, malign **20 do wrong**, offend, trespass, transgress, infringe, violate **21 discriminate**, favour **22 sin**, err **23 go wrong**, break down

829 Wrong Time

NOUNS 1 wrong time, misdating, mistiming, untimeliness, lateness, tardiness, earliness, anticipation, pre-emption, prolepsis, anachronism, parachronism

VERBS 2 be untimely, arrive late **3 mistime**, antedate, anticipate, preempt, postdate

ADJECTIVES 4 mistimed, misdated, anachronistic **5 too early**, antedated, previous, precipitate, overhasty, prochronistic, pre-emptive **6 too late**, tardy, overdue, unpunctual, postdated, parachronistic

830 Yellowness

ADJECTIVES 1 yellow, creamy, beige, fallow, champagne, citron, chartreuse, primrose-yellow, citrine, gold, gilt, aureate, or, amber, honey-coloured, old-gold, mustard, buff **2 yellowish**, xanthous, luteous, fulvous, flavescent **3 yellow-haired**, fair-haired, flaxen-haired, golden-haired, tow-haired **4 yellow-faced**, sallow, jaundiced **5 cowardly**, craven

NOUNS 6 yellowness, towhead, jaundice, icterus **7 yellow pigment**, gamboge, chrome yellow, orpiment, Claude tint, massicot, weld, luteolin **8 yellow thing**, gold, topaz, amber, sulphur, brimstone, lemon, citron, banana, mustard, honey, butter, buttercup, primrose, yellowhammer, Yellow Pages

VERBS 9 make (*or* **become**) **yellow**, gild

831 Youth

• *Les enfants terribles.* / The embarrassing young. Paul Gavarni.

• *My salad days, / When I was green in judgment, cold in blood, / To say as I said then!* William Shakespeare.

NOUNS 1 youth, adolescence, puberty, teens, maidenhood, schooldays, pupilage, apprenticeship, wardship, salad days, immaturity, puerility, nonage **2 youthfulness**, juvenescence, youngness, childishness, maidenliness, vigour, freshness **3 immaturity**, inexperience, undevelopment, greenness, rawness, naivety, ingenuousness, awkwardness **4 young person**, youngster, youth, minor, adolescent, teenager, juvenile **5 child**, baby, infant, tot, mite

ADJECTIVES 6 young, juvenile, childlike, boyish, girlish, maidenly, virginal, innocent, underage, minor, preschool, junior, teenage, adolescent, pubescent, infantile, babyish, unfledged **7 immature**, inexperienced, undeveloped, green, raw, naive, ingenuous, awkward **8 maturing**, growing, budding, pullulating, burgeoning, developing, flowering, blooming

832 Zero

NOUNS 1 zero, nought, nothing, none, nil, love **2 nothing**, naught, aught, none **3 nothingness**, nullity, nonexistence, nonbeing **4 zero level**, nadir, lowest point, zero hour **5 nonentity**, anonymity
ADJECTIVES 6 zero, nil, no **7 null**, void, nonexistent, missing, lacking
VERBS 8 not exist, not occur, vanish **9 annihilate**, eradicate, nullify

INDEX